I0105052

FREE BLACKS and MULATTOS
in
SOUTH CAROLINA

1850 CENSUS

Abstracted by
Margaret Peckham Motes

CLEARFIELD

Other books co-authored by the author:

Laurens & Newberry Counties, S.C.: Saluda and Little River Settlements 1749-1775
Winner of the National Genealogical Society's 1995 Award for Excellence (Methods and Sources)

South Carolina Memorials: Abstracts of Land Titles - Vol. 1, 1774-1776

Copyright © 2000
by Margaret Peckham Motes
All Rights Reserved.
No part of this publication may be reproduced, stored in a
retrieval system, or transmitted in any form or by any means
without proper approval of the author and/or publisher.

Printed for
Clearfield Company, Inc. by
Genealogical Publishing Co., Inc.
Baltimore, Maryland
2000

Reprinted for
Clearfield Company, Inc. by
Genealogical Publishing Co., Inc.
Baltimore, Maryland
2002

International Standard Book Number: 0-8063-5026-1
Made in the United States of America

Contents

PREFACE

This book deals with free blacks and mulattos in the 1850 South Carolina Federal Census. It is the outgrowth of research on another book which will deal with those individuals who were listed in the 1850 South Carolina Federal Census and who were born outside of South Carolina. As I was abstracting data, I noticed an increasing number of free blacks and mulattos families appearing in the data. The majority of the free blacks and mulattos were born in South Carolina, but other places of birth appeared, and interest in this subject grew. In this book there are approximately 8,160 free black and mulatto names listed, who are between the ages of 1 month to 112 years.

Thirteen reels of microcopy were read, covering the 29 counties in the 1850 South Carolina Federal County Census. The abstracted data were put into a database. The information recorded includes: name, age, sex, occupation, color, place of birth, household and dwelling number, and county. Also noted were persons in the household of another family member; in the household of someone else; listed at hotels, e.g., servant, farm laborer; or in a household with a white head of household.

Occupations vary; the largest number were working as farmers, carpenters, laborers, planters, tailors, and shoemakers. Others were listed as apprentices, bakers, barbers, blacksmiths, boatmen, boot makers, brick masons, butchers, carriage makers, coopers, draymen, dressmakers, engineers, fishermen, hairdressers, laborers, laundresses, locksmiths, mariners, market women, mechanics, mill wrights, millers, paper hangers, painters, pilots, plowmen, porters, rafthands, saddlers, sawyers, servants, ship carpenters, shoemakers, stable attendants, stevedores, tailors, tinners, trimmers, wagon makers, waiters, washwomen, and wood factors.

Though the majority of the free blacks and mulattos were born in South Carolina, others were born in Africa, St. Domingo, Cuba, Virginia, Maryland, North Carolina, Georgia, Florida, and New York. While some places of birth were listed as Germany, Italy, and Ireland, this could be an error by the census taker and should be checked in later census records to confirm the place of birth.

Spelling of names is always difficult, and many variations appear for the same surnames. Every effort has been made to keep the spelling of first and last name as they appeared in the census record.

iv

MICROCOPY RECORDS:

1850 SOUTH CAROLINA CENSUS

M432-848	Abbeville and Anderson Counties
M432-849	Barnwell and Beauford Counties
M432-850	Charleston County
M432-851	Chester, Chesterfield, Colleton, and Darlington Counties
M432-852	Edgefield and Fairfield Counties
M432-853	Georgetown and Greenville Counties
M432-854	Horry, Kershaw, and Lancaster Counties
M432-855	Laurens and Lexington Counties
M432-856	Marion, Marlboro, and Newberry Counties
M432-857	Orangeburg and Pickens Counties
M432-858	Richland and Spartanburg Counties
M432-859	Sumter and Union Counties
M432-860	Williamsburg and York Counties

The Microcopy used was from American Genealogical Lending Library, Bountiful, Utah.

Abstract Format:

Last name, first name, age, sex, occupation {if indicated}, color, birthplace, dwelling #, family #, county. Notes if any apply.

Example:

ARTER, Simon, 16, M, Laborer, B, SC, 534, 534, RICH+. In HH of Sally Arter f 39 black born SC.

Abbreviations:

B   Black
M   Mulatto
*   by the surname in index lists whites with free black or mulatto in household.

County Codes :

ABB: Abbeville. Date of census: 20 July 1850 to 14 Dec. 1850.

AND: Anderson. Western Division. Date of census: 17 July 1850 to 12 Oct. 1850.

AND*:   Anderson. Eastern Division. Date of Census: 22 July to 19 Oct.1850.

BARN: Barnwell. Date of census: 16 July 1850 to 22 November 1950.

BEAU: Beaufort, St. Helena Parish: Date of census: 3 Oct. 1850 to 10 December 1950. (Note: last page out of order).

BEAU*:   Beaufort, Prince Williams Parish (Whites). Date of Census: 6 Sept. 16 December 1850.

BEAU#:   Beaufort, Prince Williams Parish (Free Black). Date of census: 6 Sept 1850 to 16 December 1850. (Pages 35-36.)

BEAU+:   Beaufort, Saint Lukes Parish. Date of census: 16 Sept.1850 to 16 November 1850.

BEAU-:   Beaufort, Saint Peters Parish. Date of census: 12 July 1850 to 12 September 1850.

CHAS: Charleston. City of Charleston, Ward 1, Parishes of St. Philips & St. Michael's. Date of census: 1 Aug. 1850 - 16 Aug. 1850

CHAS*:   Charleston. City of Charleston, Ward 2. The Parish of St. Philips & St. Michael's. Date of census: 20 Aug. 1850 to 18 Aug. 1850

CHAS+:   Charleston. City of Charleston, Ward 3,The Parish of St Philips & St. Michael's. Date of census: 19 Sept. to 10 Oct. 1850

CHAS-:   Charleston. City of Charleston, Parishes of St. Philips & St. Michael's, Ward 4. Date of census: 10 Oct. 1850 to 12 Nov. 1850.

CHAS%:   Charleston. Charleston Neck, Parish of St. Philips & St. Michael's. Date of census: 9 Nov. 1850 to 22 Dec. 1950.

CHAS#:   Charleston. The Parish of St. James Santee. Date of census: 23 July 1850 to 18 Aug. 1850.

CHAS!:   Charleston, St. Andrews Parish. Date of census: 26 Aug. 1850 to 18 Oct. 1850.

CHAS$:   Charleston, Christ Church Parish. Date of census: 1 Aug. 1850 to 30 Sept. 1850. CHAS & Charleston, Parish of St. Thomas and St. Dennis. Date of census: Nov. 1850 to 16 Nov. 1850.

CHAS^:   Charleston, Parish of St. Johns, Colleton. Date of census: 13 Aug. 1850 to 23 Oct. 1850.

CHAS~:	Charleston, St. Johns Berkley. Date of census: 2 Sept. 1850 to 12Oct. 1850.
CHAS2:	Charleston, St. Stephens Parish. Date of census: 21 Aug. 1850 to 19 Nov. 1850.
CHAS3:	Charleston, St. James Goosecreek. Date of census: 25 July 1850 to 26 Nov. 1850.
CHES:	Chester. Date of census: 22 July 1950 and 16 Nov. 1850.
CHFD:	Chesterfield. Date of Census: 30 July 1850 to 13 Jan. 1851.
COLL:	Colleton, St. Bartholomew's Parish. Date of census: 14 Aug. 1850 & 25 December 1850.
COLL*:	Colleton, St. George's Parish. Date of census: 28 Oct. 1850 to 16 Nov. 1850.
COLL+:	Colleton Co., St. Paul's Parish. Date of census: 21 Oct. 1850 to 24 Dec. 1850.
DARL:	Darlington. First Division. Date of census: 26 July 1850 to 5 Jan. 1851.
EDGE:	Edgefield. Date of census: 11 July 1850 to 19 Dec. 1850.
EDGE*:	Edgefield. Date of census: 23 Oct. to 19 Dec. 1850.
FAIR:	Fairfield. Date of census: 13 July 1850 and 23 Nov. 1850.
GEOR:	Georgetown. Date of census: 19 Aug. 1950 to 19 Aug. 1850. City of George Town.
GEOR*:	Georgetown, Prince George, Winyaw. Date of census: 20 Aug. 1850 to 22 Aug. 1850.
GEOR+:	Georgetown, Lower All Saints. Date of census: 23 Aug. 1850 to 23 Aug. 1850.
GREE:	Greenville. Date of census: 22 July 1850 and 13 Dec. 1850.
HORR:	Horry. Date of census: 24 July 1850 and 4 Nov. 1850.
KERS:	Kershaw. Date of census: 19 July 1850 and 16 Dec. 1850.
LANC:	Lancaster. Date of census: 11 Nov. 1850 to 16 Nov. 1850.
LAU:	Laurens. Date of census: 23 July 1850 to 13 Dec. 1850.
LEX:	Lexington. Date of census: 27 July 1850 to 14 Oct.1850.
MAR:	Marion. Date of census: 19 July 1850 to 26 Nov.1850.
MARL:	Marlboro. Date of census: 29 July 1850 and 15 Oct. 1850.
NEWB:	Newberry. Date of census: 18 July 1850 to 16 Nov. 1850.

ORNG:	Orangeburg. Between the River Road from Orangeburgh CH to Branchville and Four Hole Swamp. Date of census: 13 Dec. 1850 to 18 Jan. 1851.
ORNG*:	Orangeburg. Between Santee and Edisto North of Bellville Road. Census: taken 12 Nov. 1850 to 26 Dec. 1850.
ORAN+:	Orangeburg. Orangeburg District. Date of census: 29 July 1850 to 25 Dec. 1850.
PICK:	Pickens, Western Division. Date of census: 26 July 1850 to 12 Dec. 1850.
PICK+:	Pickens, Eastern Division. Date of census: 19 July 1850 to 12 Oct. 1850.
RICH:	Richland, Town of Columbia. Date of census: 3 Oct.1850 to 28 Oct. 1950. NOTE: Out of order in this census.
RICH+:	Richland. Date of census: 20 July 1850 to 1 Oct. 1850. Note: pages out of order.
SPART:	Spartanburg. Date of census: 15 July 1850 to 18 Dec. 1850.
SUMT:	Sumter. Date of census: 19 July 1850 to 22 Nov. 1850.
UNION:	Union . Date of census: 17 July 1850 to 23 Nov. 1850.
UNN+:	Union. Date of census: 29 Oct.1850 to 21 Nov. 1850.
WILL:	Williamsburg. Date of census: 22 July 1850 to 22 Nov. 1850.
YORK:	York. Date of census: 29 July 1850 to 22 Oct. 1850.
YORK*:	York. Date of census: 22 July 1850 to 10 Dec. 1850.

A

AARONS, JAMES, 25, M, Ploughman, M, SC, 218, 222, RICH+.

ABNEY, EDNEY, 33, F, (--), M, SC, 950, 950, EDGE. In HH of Hollery Abney f 50 born SC.

ABNEY, ELIZABETH, 19, F, (--), M, SC, 950, 950, EDGE. In HH of Hollery Abney f 50 born SC.

ABNEY, LUCIOUS, 7, M, (--), M, SC, 295, 295, EDGE. In HH of John Bledsoe m 53 born SC.

ADAMS, ELIZA, 12, F, (--), M, SC, 702, 702, LAU. In HH of Bill Jackson m 25 mulatto born SC.

ADAMS, GUSTAVIS, 4, M, (--), M, SC, 247, 232, CHAS-. In HH of Elizabeth Savage f 33 mulatto born SC.

ADDISON, ELIZABETH, 11, F, (--), B, SC, 508, 491, CHAS-. In HH of Martha Addison f 42 black born SC.

ADDISON, JOHN, 38, M, Shoemaker, B, SC, 508, 491, CHAS-. In HH of Martha Addison f 42 black born SC.

ADDISON, JOHN, 30, M, Sawyer, B, SC, 2093, 2100, EDGE. In HH of David Smith m 46 born SC.

ADDISON, LINDY, 4, F, (--), B, SC, 508, 491, CHAS-. In HH of Martha Addison f 42 black born SC.

ADDISON, MARTHA, 42, F, (--), B, SC, 508, 491, CHAS-.

ADDISON, PATSEY, 6, F, (--), B, SC, 508, 491, CHAS-. In HH of Martha Addison f 42 black born SC.

ADDISON, RICHARD, 17, M, Shoemaker, B, SC, 508, 491, CHAS-. In HH of Martha Addison f 42 black born SC.

ADDISON, WILLIAM, 14, M, (--), B, SC, 508, 491, CHAS-. In HH of Martha Addison f 42 black born SC.

AIKEN, A., 25, F, (--), M, SC, 25, 25, CHAS#. In HH of J. Aiken m 25 mulatto born SC.

AIKEN, CARTER, 41, M, Laborer, M, SC, 381, 379, CHAS%.

AIKEN, J., 75, F, (--), B, SC, 27, 27, CHAS#. In HH of Thos. Aiken m 80 black born SC.

AIKEN, J., 25, M, Farmer, M, SC, 25, 25, CHAS#.

AIKEN, PHILLIS, 47, F, (--), B, SC, 27, 27, CHAS#. In HH of Thos. Aiken m 80 black born SC.

AIKEN, THOS., 80, M, Farmer, B, SC, 27, 27, CHAS#.

AIMAR, ACHILLE, 11, M, (--), M, SC, 41, 37, CHAS$. In HH of Eveline Deban f 40 mulatto born SC.

AIMAR, BETARUS, 15, M, (--), M, SC, 41, 37, CHAS$. In HH of Eveline Deban f 40 mulatto born SC.

AIMAR, LAURA, 10, F, (--), M, SC, 41, 37, CHAS$. In HH of Eveline Deban f 40 mulatto born SC.

AIMAR, WM., 0, M, (--), M, SC, 41, 37, CHAS$. In HH of Eveline Deban f 40 mulatto born SC. Wm. Aimar age 5/12 yr.

ALFORD, JOSEPH, 28, F, Farmer, M, NC, 813, 817, AND.

ALLEN, ALLEN, 25, M, (--), M, SC, 448, 473, PICK. In HH of Polly Allen f 50 mulatto born SC.

ALLEN, ANN E., 34, F, (--), B, SC, 992, 992, ABB. In HH of Banister Allen m 59 black born SC.

ALLEN, BANISTER B., 2, M, (--), B, SC, 992, 992, ABB. In HH of Banister Allen m 59 black born SC.

ALLEN, BASIL B., 1, M, (--), B, SC, 992, 992, ABB. In HH of Banister Allen m 59 black born SC.

ALLEN, BETSY, 24, F, (--), M, SC, 448, 472, PICK. In HH of Polly Allen f 50 mulatto born SC.

ALLEN, ELIUS, 1, M, (--), M, SC, 1253, 1253, GREE. In HH of Willis Allen m 40 mulatto born SC.

ALLEN, JANE, 51, F, (--), M, SC, 557, 549, CHAS%.

ALLEN, JANE, 13, F, (--), M, SC, 1253, 1253, GREE. In HH of Willis Allen m 40 mulatto born SC.

ALLEN, JERRY, 8, M, (--), M, SC, 448, 473, PICK. In HH of Polly Allen f 50 mulatto born SC.

ALLEN, JERRY, 8, M, (--), M, SC, 448, 473, PICK. In HH of Allen Allen m 25 mulatto born SC.

ALLEN, JOHN, 5, M, (--), M, SC, 1253, 1253, GREE. In HH of Willis Allen m 40 mulatto born SC.

ALLEN, JOHN, 1, M, (--), M, SC, 448, 473, PICK. In HH of Polly Allen f 50 mulatto born SC.

ALLEN, JOHN, 1, M, (--), M, SC, 448, 473, PICK. In HH of Allen Allen m 25 mulatto born SC.

ALLEN, MARTHA, 18, F, (--), M, SC, 448, 473, PICK. In HH of Allen Allen m 25 mulatto born SC.

ALLEN, MARTHA, 18, F, (--), M, SC, 448, 473, PICK. In HH of Polly Allen f 50 mulatto born SC.

ALLEN, MARTHA E., 17, F, (--), B, SC, 992, 992, ABB. In HH of Banister Allen m 59 black born SC.

ALLEN, MARY, 14, F, (--), M, SC, 557, 549, CHAS%. In HH of Jane Allen f 51 mulatto born SC.

ALLEN, MARY, 30, F, (--), M, SC, 1253, 1253, GREE. In HH of Willis Allen m 40 mulatto born SC.

ALLEN, POLLY, 50, F, (--), M, SC, 448, 472, PICK.

ALLEN, WILLIAM, 6, M, (--), M, SC, 1253, 1253, GREE. In HH of Willis Allen m 40 mulatto born SC.

ALLEN, WILLIS, 40, M, Miller, M, SC, 1253, 1253, GREE.

ALLISON, CEASAR, 73, M, Laborer, B, SC, 571, 571, MARL.

ALLISON, JENNET, 48, F, (--), B, SC, 571, 571, MARL. In HH of Ceasar Allison m 73 black born SC.

ALLUMS, BENJAMIN, 94, M, (--), B, VA, 178, 178, GREE.

ALLUMS, EARLE, 17, M, (--), B, VA, 178, 178, GREE. In HH of Benjamin Allums m 94 black born VA.

ALLUMS, MARY, 60, F, (--), B, VA, 178, 178, GREE. In HH of Benjamin

Allums m 94 black born VA.

ALLUMS, MATHEW, 19, M, (--), B, VA, 178, 178, GREE. In HH of Benjamin Allums m 94 black born VA.

ALSTON, ANNA, 25, F, (--), M, SC, 106, 106, GEOR. In HH of Trial Poter m 57 mulatto born Siera Leone.

ALSTON, CATHERINE, 25, F, (--), M, SC, 556, 539, CHAS-.

ALSTON, CHLOE, 42, F, (--), M, SC, 63, 63, CHAS%. In HH of Samuel Alston m 40 mulatto born SC.

ALSTON, CHLOE, 12, F, (--), M, SC, 63, 63, CHAS%. In HH of Samuel Alston m 40 mulatto born SC.

ALSTON, CLARANCE, 8, M, (--), M, SC, 63, 63, CHAS%. In HH of Samuel Alston m 40 mulatto born SC.

ALSTON, DIANA, 38, F, (--), M, SC, 500, 483, CHAS-. In HH of Thomas Alston m 80 mulatto born VA.

ALSTON, GRACE, 26, F, (--), M, SC, 701, 659, CHAS+.

ALSTON, HANNAH, 28, F, (--), M, SC, 315, 289, CHAS*. In HH of Flora Commersal f 28 black born SC.

ALSTON, JAMES, 19, M, Carpenter, M, SC, 63, 63, CHAS%. In HH of Samuel Alston m 40 mulatto born SC.

ALSTON, JEMIMA, 10, F, (--), M, SC, 63, 63, CHAS%. In HH of Samuel Alston m 40 mulatto born SC.

ALSTON, JOHN, 16, M, Carpenter, M, SC, 63, 63, CHAS%. In HH of Samuel Alston m 40 mulatto born SC.

ALSTON, JOSEPH A., 21, M, (--), M, SC, 500, 483, CHAS-. In HH of Thomas Alston m 80 mulatto born VA.

ALSTON, JOSEPHINE, 2, F, (--), M, SC, 106, 106, GEOR. In HH of Trial Poter m 57 mulatto born Siera Leone.

ALSTON, JUNO, 6, M, (--), M, SC, 63, 63, CHAS%. In HH of Samuel Alston m 40 mulatto born SC.

ALSTON, MARY, 21, F, (--), M, SC, 63, 63, CHAS%. In HH of Samuel Alston m 40 mulatto born SC.

ALSTON, MARY ANN, 14, F, (--), M, SC, 63, 63, CHAS%. In HH of Samuel

Alston m 40 mulatto born SC.

ALSTON, NATHAN, 8, M, (--), M, SC, 500, 483, CHAS-. In HH of Thomas Alston m 80 mulatto born VA.

ALSTON, OLIVIA, 37, F, (--), M, SC, 500, 483, CHAS-. In HH of Thomas Alston m 80 mulatto born VA.

ALSTON, SAMUEL, 40, M, Bricklayer, M, SC, 63, 63, CHAS%.

ALSTON, STEPNEY, 6, F, (--), B, SC, 106, 106, GEOR. In HH of Trial Poter m 57 mulatto born Siera Leone.

ALSTON, THOMAS, 80, M, Drayman, M, VA, 500, 483, CHAS-.

ANCRUM, DIANA, 40, F, (--), B, SC, 154, 141, CHAS*.

ANDERS, BURTON, 14, M, (--), M, SC, 461, 461, BEAU-. In HH of John Anders m 48 born SC.

ANDERS, HESTER, 41, M, (--), M, SC, 461, 461, BEAU-. In HH of John Anders m 48 born SC.

ANDERS, MARY, 19, F, (--), M, SC, 458, 458, BEAU-. In HH of William Anders m 24 mulatto born SC.

ANDERS, MARY, 4, F, (--), M, SC, 461, 461, BEAU-. In HH of John Anders m 48 born SC.

ANDERS, MILTON, 7, M, (--), M, SC, 461, 461, BEAU-. In HH of John Anders m 48 born SC.

ANDERS, NATHAN, 11, M, (--), M, SC, 461, 461, BEAU-. In HH of John Anders m 48 born SC.

ANDERS, ROSE ANN, 15, F, (--), M, SC, 461, 461, BEAU-. In HH of John Anders m 48 born SC.

ANDERS, SARAH, 19, F, (--), M, SC, 461, 461, BEAU-. In HH of John Anders m 48 born SC.

ANDERS, WILLIAM, 24, M, Laborer, M, SC, 458, 458, BEAU-.

ANDERSON, ANDREW, 35, M, Carpenter, M, SC, 31, 30, CHAS&.

ANDERSON, ANDREW, 6, M, (--), M, SC, 31, 30, CHAS&. In HH of Andrew Anderson m 35 mulatto born SC.

ANDERSON, CECELIA, 30, F, (--),

M, SC, 31, 30, CHAS&. In HH of Andrew Anderson m 35 mulatto born SC.

ANDERSON, CECELIA, 10, F, (--), M, SC, 31, 30, CHAS&. In HH of Andrew Anderson m 35 mulatto born SC.

ANDERSON, JACOB, 1, M, (--), M, SC, 31, 30, CHAS&. In HH of Andrew Anderson m 35 mulatto born SC.

ANDERSON, JAMES S., 3, M, (--), M, SC, 2384, 2384, ABB. In HH of William W. Anderson m 36 white born SC.

ANDERSON, JIMMY, 8, M, (--), M, SC, 31, 30, CHAS&. In HH of Andrew Anderson m 35 mulatto born SC.

ANDERSON, JOSEPH, 4, M, (--), M, SC, 31, 30, CHAS&. In HH of Andrew Anderson m 35 mulatto born SC.

ANDERSON, JULIA, 12, F, (--), M, SC, 462, 420, CHAS+. In HH of Rebecca Bremar f 24 mulatto born SC.

ANDERSON, LOUISA, 30, F, (--), M, SC, 2384, 2384, ABB. In HH of William W. Anderson m 36 white born SC.

ANDERSON, MARY, 8, F, (--), M, SC, 462, 420, CHAS+. In HH of Rebecca Bremar f 24 mulatto born SC.

ANDERSON, NELSON, 30, M, (--), B, SC, 232, 232, CHAS%. In HH of Flora Scott f 37 mulatto born SC.

ANDERSON, PARITHA J., 12, F, (--), M, SC, 2384, 2384, ABB. In HH of William W. Anderson m 36 white born SC.

ANDERSON, ROBERT J., 10, F, (--), M, SC, 2384, 2384, ABB. In HH of William W. Anderson m 36 white born SC.

ANDERSON, TALLULAH, 1, F, (--), M, SC, 2384, 2384, ABB. In HH of William W. Anderson m 36 white born SC.

ANDERSON, THOMAS H., 8, M, (--), M, SC, 2384, 2384, ABB. In HH of William W. Anderson m 36 white born SC.

ANDERSON, WILLIAM W., 6, M, (--), M, SC, 2384, 2384, ABB. In HH of

3

William W. Anderson m 36 white born SC.

ANDREWS, AMELIA, 8, F, (--), M, SC, 399, 397, CHAS%. In HH of Emma Andrews f 37 mulatto born SC.

ANDREWS, ELIZA, 14, F, (--), M, SC, 399, 397, CHAS%. In HH of Emma Andrews f 37 mulatto born SC.

ANDREWS, EMMA, 38, F, (--), M, SC, 399, 397, CHAS%.

ANDREWS, JAMES, 35, M, Drayman, M, SC, 399, 397, CHAS%. In HH of Emma Andrews f 37 mulatto born SC.

ANDREWS, JOHN, 11, M, (--), M, SC, 399, 397, CHAS%. In HH of Emma Andrews f 37 mulatto born SC.

ANDREWS, MARY, 5, F, (--), M, SC, 1133, 1133, BARN. In HH of Sarah Andrews f 27 black born SC.

ANDREWS, SARAH, 27, M, Planter, B, SC, 1133, 1133, BARN.

ANDREWS, SARAH, 1, F, (--), M, SC, 1133, 1133, BARN. In HH of Sarah Andrews f 27 black born SC.

ANDREWS, WILLIAM, 30, M, (--), M, SC, 1133, 1133, BARN. In HH of Sarah Andrews f 27 black born SC.

ANDREWS, WILLIAM, 20, M, Planter, B, SC, 1133, 1133, BARN. In HH of Sarah Andrews f 27 black born SC.

ANTONIO, ADELINE, 40, F, (--), M, SC, 694, 652, CHAS+.

ANTONIO, AVELHIE, 40, M, Matras maker, M, St. Domingo, 514, 497, CHAS-.

ANTONIO, CORADO, 16, M, Tailor, M, SC, 514, 497, CHAS-. In HH of Avelhie Antonio m 40 mulatto born St. Domingo.

ANTONIO, EDWARD, 14, M, (--), M, SC, 430, 413, CHAS-. In HH of Francis Baneau m 36 mulatto born SC.

ANTONIO, ETINIERE, 38, F, (--), M, St. Domingo, 514, 497, CHAS-. In HH of Avelhie Antonio m 40 mulatto born St. Domingo.

ANTONIO, MARIA, 14, F, (--), M, SC, 514, 497, CHAS-. In HH of Avelhie

Antonio m 40 mulatto born St. Domingo.

ANTONIO, SOPHIA, 19, F, (--), M, SC, 514, 497, CHAS-. In HH of Avelhie Antonio m 40 mulatto born St. Domingo.

APPLETON, FANNY, 25, F, (--), M, SC, 129, 120, CHAS+. In HH of Hannah Dascher f 22 born Germany.

ARCHER, ABSOLOM, 24, M, Farmer, B, SC, 1117, 1117, CHES. In HH of John McElhanny m 75 born SC.

ARCHER, ALFRED, 22, M, (--), B, SC, 1114, 1114, CHES. In HH of William Archer m 25 black born SC.

ARCHER, AMY, 23, F, (--), B, SC, 1114, 1114, CHES. In HH of William Archer m 25 black born SC.

ARCHER, BIGAH, 50, M, Farmer, B, SC, 669, 669, CHES. In HH of Reuben Archer 54 m black born SC.

ARCHER, CATHE., 19, F, (--), B, SC, 1479, 1479, CHES. In HH of Nancy Archer 55 black born SC.

ARCHER, ELIZ., 17, F, (--), B, SC, 1479, 1479, CHES. In HH of Nancy Archer 55 black born SC.

ARCHER, ELIZA J., 2, F, (--), B, SC, 1196, 1196, CHES. In HH of Sucky Archer f 55 black born SC.

ARCHER, JAMES, 4, M, (--), M, SC, 1196, 1196, CHES. In HH of Sucky Archer f 55 black born SC.

ARCHER, JANE, 0, F, (--), B, SC, 1114, 1114, CHES. In HH of William Archer m 25 black born SC. Jane listed as 7/12 yr.

ARCHER, JAS., 23, M, Mechanic, B, SC, 669, 669, CHES. In HH of Reuben Archer 54 m black born SC.

ARCHER, JAS., 5, M, (--), B, SC, 669, 669, CHES. In HH of Reuben Archer 54 m black born SC.

ARCHER, JESSE, 36, M, Farmer, B, SC, 649, 649, CHES. In HH of Charles Valentine 35 m black born SC.

ARCHER, JOE, 16, M, (--), B, SC, 1479, 1479, CHES. In HH of Nancy Archer 55 black born SC.

ARCHER, JOHN, 25, M, Mechanic, B, SC, 669, 669, CHES. In HH of Reuben Archer 54 m black born SC.

ARCHER, JOHN, 10, M, (--), M, SC, 669, 669, CHES. In HH of Reuben Archer 54 m black born SC.

ARCHER, LEWIS, 5, M, (--), B, SC, 669, 669, CHES. In HH of Reuben Archer 54 m black born SC.

ARCHER, MAHALA, 27, F, (--), B, SC, 669, 669, CHES. In HH of Reuben Archer 54 m black born SC.

ARCHER, MARTHA, 21, F, (--), B, SC, 669, 669, CHES. In HH of Reuben Archer 54 m black born SC.

ARCHER, MARY, 18, F, (--), B, SC, 1196, 1196, CHES. In HH of Sucky Archer f 55 black born SC.

ARCHER, MARY, 15, F, (--), B, SC, 1479, 1479, CHES. In HH of Nancy Archer 55 black born SC.

ARCHER, N. A., 1, F, (--), B, SC, 669, 669, CHES. In HH of Reuben Archer 54 m black born SC.

ARCHER, NANCY, 55, F, (--), B, SC, 1479, 1479, CHES.

ARCHER, NELSON, 15, M, Farmer, B, SC, 364, 364, CHES. In HH of Silas Bradly m 41 born SC.

ARCHER, REUBEN, 54, M, Farmer, B, SC, 669, 669, CHES.

ARCHER, REUBEN, 38, M, Farmer, B, SC, 1097, 1097, CHES. In HH of Mary S. Neely 37 born SC.

ARCHER, REUBEN, 4, M, (--), B, SC, 669, 669, CHES. In HH of Reuben Archer 54 m black born SC.

ARCHER, S. E., 4, M, (--), B, SC, 669, 669, CHES. In HH of Reuben Archer 54 m black born SC.

ARCHER, S.J., 8, F, (--), B, SC, 669, 669, CHES. In HH of Reuben Archer 54 m black born SC.

ARCHER, SAML. C., 29, M, Farmer, B, SC, 1479, 1479, CHES. In HH of Nancy Archer 55 black born SC.

ARCHER, SAML., 16, M, Farmer, B, SC, 669, 669, CHES. In HH of Reuben Archer 54 m black born SC.

ARCHER, SARAH, 7, F, (--), B, SC, 669, 669, CHES. In HH of Reuben Archer 54 m black born SC.

ARCHER, SUCKY, 55, F, (--), B, SC, 1196, 1196, CHES.

ARCHER, SUSAN, 18, F, (--), B, SC, 1479, 1479, CHES. In HH of Nancy Archer 55 black born SC.

ARCHER, THOMAS, 13, M, (--), B, SC, 669, 669, CHES. In HH of Reuben Archer 54 m black born SC.

ARCHER, WILLIAM, 25, M, Farmer, B, SC, 1114, 1114, CHES.

ARCHER, WILLIAM, 10, M, (--), B, SC, 669, 669, CHES. In HH of Reuben Archer 54 m black born SC.

ARCHER, WM., 26, M, Farmer, B, SC, 1479, 1479, CHES. In HH of Nancy Archer 55 black born SC.

ARD, BEN, 67, M, Laborer, M, SC, 57, 57, WILL.

ARDIS, BENJAMIN, 60, M, Bapt. Scholar, B, SC, 1896, 1902, EDGE.

ARDIS, BENJAMIN, 5, M, (--), B, SC, 1896, 1902, EDGE. In HH of Benjamin Ardis m 60 black born SC.

ARDIS, HARRY, 4, M, (--), B, SC, 1896, 1902, EDGE. In HH of Benjamin Ardis m 60 black born SC.

ARDIS, MARTHA, 25, F, (--), B, SC, 1896, 1902, EDGE. In HH of Benjamin Ardis m 60 black born SC.

ARDIS, WILLIAM, 2, M, (--), B, SC, 1896, 1902, EDGE. In HH of Benjamin Ardis m 60 black born SC.

ARMAN, LOUISA, 70, F, (--), M, St. Domingo, 717, 675, CHAS+.

ARMS, MARY, 19, F, (--), M, SC, 36, 36, CHAS%. In HH of Maria Nelson f 21 mulatto born SC.

ARMSTRONG, SUSAN, 28, F, (--), M, SC, 218, 204, CHAS-.

ARNOLD, AMANDA, 12, F, (--), B, SC, 751, 751, UNION. In HH of Mary Arnold f 18 black born SC.

ARNOLD, HOLLY, 45, F, (--), M, SC, 753, 753, UNION.

ARNOLD, LOUIS, 8, M, (--), B, SC,

753, 753, UNION. In HH of Holly Arnold f 45 mulatto born SC.

ARNOLD, MARY, 18, F, (--), B, SC, 751, 751, UNION.

ARNOLD, SARAH, 14, F, (--), B, SC, 751, 751, UNION. In HH of Mary Arnold f 18 black born SC.

ARNOLD, THOMAS, 6, M, (--), B, SC, 753, 753, UNION. In HH of Holly Arnold f 45 mulatto born SC.

ARTER, ANN, 21, F, (--), B, SC, 534, 534, PICK+. In HH of Sally Arter f 39 black born SC.

ARTER, BETSEY, 52, M, (--), B, SC, 352, 352, PICK+.

ARTER, CAROLINE, 24, F, (--), M, SC, 660, 660, PICK+. In HH of Rachel Arter f 44 mulatto born SC.

ARTER, CLINTON, 13, M, (--), B, SC, 534, 534, PICK+. In HH of Sally Arter f 39 black born SC.

ARTER, DICK, 2, M, (--), B, SC, 534, 534, PICK+. In HH of Sally Arter f 39 black born SC.

ARTER, EDWARD, 1, M, (--), M, SC, 660, 660, PICK+. In HH of Rachel Arter f 44 mulatto born SC.

ARTER, GEORGE, 35, M, (--), B, SC, 665, 665, PICK+. In HH of Jack Arter m 37 mulatto born SC.

ARTER, GEORGE, 7, M, (--), B, SC, 534, 534, PICK+. In HH of Sally Arter f 39 black born SC.

ARTER, JACK, 37, M, Farmer, M, SC, 665, 665, PICK+.

ARTER, JACK, 5, M, (--), B, SC, 534, 534, PICK+. In HH of Sally Arter f 39 black born SC.

ARTER, JACKSON, 9, M, (--), M, SC, 660, 660, PICK+. In HH of Rachel Arter f 44 mulatto born SC.

ARTER, JAMES, 7, M, (--), M, SC, 660, 660, PICK+. In HH of Rachel Arter f 44 mulatto born SC.

ARTER, JESS, 15, M, Laborer, B, SC, 534, 534, PICK+. In HH of Sally Arter f 39 black born SC.

ARTER, JIM, 25, M, (--), B, SC, 665, 665, PICK+. In HH of Jack Arter m 37

mulatto born SC.

ARTER, JOHN, 10, M, (--), M, SC, 660, 660, PICK+. In HH of Rachel Arter f 44 mulatto born SC.

ARTER, JUDITH, 21, F, (--), B, SC, 665, 665, PICK+. In HH of Jack Arter m 37 mulatto born SC.

ARTER, LEROY, 21, M, (--), B, SC, 243, 243, YORK. In HH of Robert Brown m 44 born York Dist., SC. Leroy Arter born Chester Dist., SC.

ARTER, MAHALA, 15, F, (--), B, SC, 660, 660, PICK+. In HH of Rachel Arter f 44 mulatto born SC.

ARTER, MARIA, 3, F, (--), M, SC, 660, 660, PICK+. In HH of Rachel Arter f 44 mulatto born SC.

ARTER, MYRA, 4, F, (--), M, SC, 660, 660, PICK+. In HH of Rachel Arter f 44 mulatto born SC.

ARTER, NANCY, 8, F, (--), B, SC, 534, 534, PICK+. In HH of Sally Arter f 39 black born SC.

ARTER, PATHANA, 0, F, (--), M, SC, 660, 660, PICK+. In HH of Rachel Arter f 44 mulatto born SC. Pathana Arter age 8/12 yr.

ARTER, RACHEL, 44, M, (--), M, SC, 660, 660, PICK+.

ARTER, SARAH, 32, F, (--), M, SC, 665, 665, PICK+. In HH of Jack Arter m 37 mulatto born SC.

ARTER, SALLY, 39, F, (--), B, SC, 534, 534, PICK+.

ARTER, SARAH, 0, F, (--), B, SC, 534, 534, PICK+. In HH of Sally Arter f 39 black born SC. Sarah Arter age 2/12 yr.

ARTER, SARAH, 11, F, (--), B, SC, 534, 534, PICK+. In HH of Sally Arter f 39 black born SC.

ARTER, SARAH J., 5, F, (--), M, SC, 660, 660, PICK+. In HH of Rachel Arter f 44 mulatto born SC.

ARTER, SIMON, 16, M, Laborer, B, SC, 534, 534, PICK+. In HH of Sally Arter f 39 black born SC.

ARTER, TOM, 18, M, Laborer, B, SC, 534, 534, PICK+. In HH of Sally Arter f 39 black born SC.

ARTER, WASHINGTON, 12, M, (--), B, SC, 660, 660, PICK+. In HH of Rachel Arter f 44 mulatto born SC.

ARTER, WEST, 25, M, Laborer, B, SC, 524, 524, PICK+. In HH of Isaac Anderson, Jr. m 25 born SC.

ARTER, WM., 20, M, Laborer, B, SC, 660, 660, PICK+. In HH of Rachel Arter f 44 mulatto born SC.

ASHE, CLARA, 105, F, (--), B, Africa, 238, 238, CHAS%. In HH of John Simons m 37 mulatto born SC.

ASHE, PATTY, 100, F, (--), B, SC, 139, 127, CHAS*.

ASPINARD, ALBERT, 38, M, (--), M, SC, 247, 247, CHAS%. In HH of Mary Aspinard f 34 mulatto born SC.

ASPINARD, ALBERT, 13, M, (--), M, SC, 247, 247, CHAS%. In HH of Mary Aspinard f 34 mulatto born SC.

ASPINARD, ARTHUR, 6, M, (--), M, SC, 247, 247, CHAS%. In HH of Mary Aspinard f 34 mulatto born SC.

ASPINARD, LAWRENCE, 4, M, (--), M, SC, 247, 247, CHAS%. In HH of Mary Aspinard f 34 mulatto born SC.

ASPINARD, MARY, 34, F, (--), M, SC, 247, 247, CHAS%.

ASPINARD, NICHOLS, 12, M, (--), M, SC, 247, 247, CHAS%. In HH of Mary Aspinard f 34 mulatto born SC.

ASPINARD, SUSAN, 7, F, (--), M, SC, 247, 247, CHAS%. In HH of Mary Aspinard f 34 mulatto born SC.

AUBIN, ELIZA, 14, F, (--), M, SC, 503, 486, CHAS-. In HH of William Marshall m 29 mulatto born SC.

AUSELL, CLARA, 80, F, Servant, M, SC, 276, 253, CHAS. In HH of Robert Anderson m 52 born SC.

AZELE, ADELLE, 29, F, (--), M, SC, 565, 548, CHAS-.

AILEY, HARRIOTT, 15, F, (--), B, SC, 148, 136, CHAS*. In HH of Bedford Bailey m 70 black born SC.

B

BAILEY, BEDFORD, 70, M, Fisherman, B, SC, 136, 148, CHAS*

BAILEY, HARRIOTT, 15, F, (-), B, SC, 136, 148, CHAS*. In HH of Bedford Bailey m 70 black born SC.

BAILEY, HENRY, 6, M, (--), B, SC, 148, 136, CHAS*. In HH of Bedford Bailey m 70 black born SC.

BAILEY, ISAAC, 3, M, (--), B, SC, 148, 136, CHAS*. In HH of Bedford Bailey m 70 black born SC.

BAILEY, MARTHA, 25, F, (--), M, SC, 667, 625, CHAS+. In HH of Joseph Curtis m 56 born SC.

BAILEY, SILVA, 73, F, (--), B, SC, 148, 136, CHAS*. In HH of Bedford Bailey m 70 black born SC.

BAILEY, SILVERETTA, 9, F, (--), B, SC, 148, 136, CHAS*. In HH of Bedford Bailey m 70 black born SC.

BAILY, AMANDA, 12, F, (--), B, SC, 1003, 1003, ABB. In HH of Stepny Baily 73 m mulatto born SC.

BAILY, JULIA, 35, F, (--), B, SC, 1003, 1003, ABB. In HH of Stepny Baily 73 m mulatto born SC.

BAILY, MUGUSTER {?}, 15, M, (--), B, SC, 1003, 1003, ABB. In HH of Stepny Baily 73 m mulatto born SC.

BAILY, STEPHY, 75, M, Farmer, M, SC, 1003, 1003, ABB.

BAINBAGE, ALEXANDER, 22, M, Laborer, M, SC, 20, 20, CHAS~. In HH of Rebecca Bainbage f 48 mulatto born SC.

BAINBAGE, HARRIET, 15, F, (--), M, SC, 20, 20, CHAS~. In HH of Rebecca Bainbage f 48 mulatto born SC.

BAINBAGE, JANE, 33, F, (--), M, SC, 20, 20, CHAS~. In HH of Rebecca Bainbage f 48 mulatto born SC.

BAINBAGE, LAURA, 17, F, (--), M, SC, 20, 20, CHAS~. In HH of Rebecca Bainbage f 48 mulatto born SC.

BAINBAGE, RAMSONT, 12, M, (--), M, SC, 20, 20, CHAS~. In HH of Rebecca Bainbage f 48 mulatto born SC.

BAINBAGE, REBECCA, 48, F, (--), M, SC, 20, 20, CHAS~.

BAINBAGE, RICHARD, 0, M, (--), M, SC, 20, 20, CHAS~. In HH of Rebecca Bainbage f 48 mulatto born SC. Richard age 5/12 yr.

BAINBAGE, UNITY ANN, 25, F, (--), M, SC, 20, 20, CHAS~. In HH of Rebecca Bainbage f 48 mulatto born SC.

BAIRD, MARGARET, 79, F, (--), B, SC, 146, 136, CHAS-. In HH of Julia Barnet f 50 mulatto born SC.

BAKER, ELIZH., 8, F, (--), M, SC, 131, 131, KERS. In HH of Isaac Rodgers m 24 mulatto born SC.

BAKER, JOHN, 19, M, (--), B, SC, 101, 101, KERS. In HH of Wilson Baker m 39 black born NC.

BAKER, MARG, 17, F, (--), M, SC, 101, 101, KERS. In HH of Wilson Baker m 39 black born NC.

BAKER, MARY, 16, F, (--), B, SC, 101, 101, KERS. In HH of Wilson Baker m 39 black born NC.

BAKER, SARAH, 35, F, (--), B, SC, 101, 101, KERS. In HH of Wilson Baker m 39 black born NC.

BAKER, SUSAN, 36, F, (--), M, SC, 131, 131, KERS. In HH of Isaac Rodgers m 24 mulatto born SC.

BAKER, WILSON, 39, M, (--), B, NC, 101, 101, KERS.

BALL, CHARLOTTE, 59, F, (--), M, SC, 280, 280, CHAS%. In HH of Comming Ball m 21 mulatto born SC.

BALL, COMMING, 21, M, Ship carpenter, M, SC, 280, 280, CHAS%.

BALL, MARY, 7, F, (--), M, SC, 280, 280, CHAS%. In HH of Comming Ball Mulatto born SC.

BALL, MARY ANN, 85, F, (--), B, SC, 504, 462, CHAS+. In HH of Mary Ann Lee f 45 black born SC.

BALL, SARAH, 80, F, (--), M, SC, 280, 280, CHAS%. In HH of Comming Ball m 21 mulatto born SC.

BALLARD, LEVI, 37, M, (--), M, SC, 1392, 1392, CHES. In HH of Abner Triplet m 30 born SC.

BALLARD, SARAH, 26, F, (--), M, SC, 915, 895, CHAS-. In HH of Chloe Bowengen f 60 mulatto born SC.

BAMFIELD, LAWRENCE, 25, M, Shoemaker, M, SC, 58, 53, CHAS-.

BANEAU, FRANCIS, 36, M, Carpenter, M, SC, 430, 413, CHAS-.

BANEAU, FRANCIS, 4, M, (--), M, SC, 430, 413, CHAS-. In HH of Francis Baneau m 36 mulatto born SC.

BANEAU, JOSEPHINE, 33, F, (--), M, SC, 430, 413, CHAS-. In HH of Francis Baneau m 36 mulatto born SC.

BANEAU, MARY J., 76, F, (--), M, SC, 430, 413, CHAS-. In HH of Francis Baneau m 36 mulatto born SC.

BANFIELD, JOSEPH, 40, M, Wheelwright, M, SC, 602, 594, CHAS%.

BANOW, ANN, 41, F, (--), M, SC, 430, 413, CHAS-. In HH of Francis Baneau m 36 mulatto born SC.

BAREFIELD, CATHERINE, 0, F, (--), M, SC, 524, 533, RICH+. In HH of Harrington Barefield m 26 mulatto born SC. Catherine Barefield age 5/12.

BAREFIELD, ELEANOR, 45, F, (--), M, SC, 524, 533, RICH+. In HH of Harrington Barefield m 26 mulatto born SC.

BAREFIELD, HARRINGTON, 26, M, Laborer, M, SC, 524, 533, RICH+.

BAREFIELD, MARGARET, 25, F, (--), M, SC, 524, 533, RICH+. In HH of Harrington Barefield m 26 mulatto born SC.

BAREFIELD, WILLIAM P., 5, M, (--), M, SC, 524, 533, RICH+. In HH of Harrington Barefield m 26 mulatto born SC.

BARGET, J.P., 24, M, Saddler, B, SC, 1259, 1259, GREE. In HH of T. Kelly m 25 born SC.

BARNELL, CHARLOTTE, 5, F, (--), M, SC, 765, 723, CHAS+. In HH of Henry Barnell m 51 mulatto born SC.

BARNELL, HENRIETTA, 4, F, (--), M, SC, 765, 723, CHAS+. In HH of Henry Barnell m 51 mulatto born SC.

BARNELL, HENRY, 51, M, Carpenter, M, SC, 765, 723, CHAS+.

8

BARNELL, SARAH, 25, F, (--), M, SC, 765, 723, CHAS+. In HH of Henry Barnell m 51 mulatto born SC.

BARNER, CELIA, 5, F, (--), M, SC, 166, 156, CHAS-. In HH of Sarah Barner f 28 mulatto born SC.

BARNER, FRANCIS, 2, M, (--), M, SC, 166, 156, CHAS-. In HH of Sarah Barner f 28 mulatto born SC.

BARNER, JULIAS, 7, M, (--), M, SC, 166, 156, CHAS-. In HH of Sarah Barner f 28 mulatto born SC.

BARNER, JULIET M., 12, F, (--), M, SC, 166, 156, CHAS-. In HH of Sarah Barner f 28 mulatto born SC.

BARNER, MAGDALIN, 5, F, (--), M, SC, 166, 156, CHAS-. In HH of Sarah Barner f 28 mulatto born SC.

BARNER, SARAH, 28, F, (--), M, SC, 166, 156, CHAS-.

BARNER, THOMAS, 9, M, (--), M, SC, 166, 156, CHAS-. In HH of Sarah Barner f 28 mulatto born SC.

BARNES, ISAAC, 44, M, (--), B, SC, 242, 242, EDGE*.

BARNET, JULIA, 50, F, (--), M, SC, 146, 136, CHAS-.

BARNETT, ANN, 70, F, (--), M, SC, 284, 268, CHAS-. In HH of John Oliver m 50 mulatto born SC.

BARNETT, B., 12, F, (--), B, SC, 25, 25, CHAS#. In HH of J. Aiken m 25 mulatto born SC.

BARNETT, GEORGE, 19, M, (--), M, SC, 243, 243, KERS. In HH of Bolin Harris m 50 mulatto born SC.

BARNETT, J., 8, M, (--), B, SC, 25, 25, CHAS#. In HH of J. Aiken m 25 mulatto born SC.

BARNETT, JAMES, 12, M, (--), M, SC, 284, 268, CHAS-. In HH of John Oliver m 50 mulatto born SC.

BARNETT, ROSE, 9, F, (--), M, SC, 284, 268, CHAS-. In HH of John Oliver m 50 mulatto born SC.

BARNWELL, ANNA L., 5, F, (--), M, SC, 217, 203, CHAS-. In HH of Elizabeth Barnwell f 33 mulatto born SC.

BARNWELL, BENJAMIN, 42, M, Wheelwright, M, SC, 858, 835, CHAS%. In HH of Sarah Barnwell m 48 mulatto born SC.

BARNWELL, CYRUS, 67, M, (--), M, SC, 93, 85, CHAS+.

BARNWELL, EDWARD, 13, M, (--), M, SC, 858, 835, CHAS%. In HH of Sarah Barnwell m 48 mulatto born SC.

BARNWELL, EDWARD M., 70, M, (--), M, SC, 217, 203, CHAS-. In HH of Elizabeth Barnwell f 33 mulatto born SC.

BARNWELL, ELIZABETH, 33, F, (--), M, SC, 217, 203, CHAS-.

BARNWELL, JULIA, 1, F, (--), M, SC, 858, 835, CHAS%. In HH of Sarah Barnwell m 48 mulatto born SC.

BARNWELL, ROSETTA, 21, F, (--), M, SC, 858, 835, CHAS%. In HH of Sarah Barnwell m 48 mulatto born SC.

BARNWELL, SAMUEL, 10, M, (--), M, SC, 858, 835, CHAS%. In HH of Sarah Barnwell m 48 mulatto born SC.

BARNWELL, SARAH, 48, F, (--), M, SC, 858, 835, CHAS%.

BARNWELL, SARAH B., 30, F, (--), M, SC, 217, 203, CHAS-. In HH of Elizabeth Barnwell f 33 mulatto born SC.

BARNWELL, SILVA, 53, F, (--), M, SC, 93, 85, CHAS+. In HH of Cyrus Barnwell m 67 mulatto born SC.

BARNWELL, THOMAS, 2, M, (--), M, SC, 858, 835, CHAS%. In HH of Sarah Barnwell m 48 mulatto born SC.

BARNWELL, WILLIAM, 35, M, (--), M, SC, 80, 90, CHAS. In HH of Betty Wilson f 80 black born Africa.

BARON, EMELINE, 40, F, (--), M, SC, 432, 430, CHAS%.

BARON, SARAH A., 22, F, (--), M, SC, 432, 430, CHAS%. In HH of Emeline Baron f 40 mulatto born SC.

BARON, THOMAS, 17, M, Tailor, M, SC, 432, 430, CHAS%. In HH of Emeline Baron f 40 mulatto born SC.

BARRETT, TIMOTHY, 20, M, Laborer, M, SC, 1952, 1958, EDGE. In

HH of Sally Chaves f 55 black born SC.

BARRETT, ZEDAKIAH, 16, M, Laborer, M, SC, 1952, 1958, EDGE. In HH of Sally Chaves f 55 black born SC.

BARRON, ANN, 16, F, (--), B, SC, 378, 340, CHAS+. In HH of Phillis Barron f 44 mulatto born SC.

BARRON, ANNETTE, 10, F, (--), M, SC, 560, 552, CHAS%. In HH of Joseph Barron m 30 mulatto born SC.

BARRON, CORNELIA, 27, F, (--), M, SC, 152, 142, CHAS-. In HH of Julius Berney m 35 mulatto born SC.

BARRON, DANIEL, 4, M, (--), B, SC, 1150, 1129, CHAS%. In HH of Jacob Brown m 35 black born SC.

BARRON, EDWARD, 26, M, Porter, M, SC, 152, 142, CHAS-. In HH of Julius Berney m 35 mulatto born SC.

BARRON, ELIZABETH, 9, F, (--), B, SC, 1150, 1129, CHAS%. In HH of Jacob Brown m 35 black born SC.

BARRON, ESTHER, 40, F, (--), M, SC, 560, 552, CHAS%. In HH of Joseph Barron m 30 mulatto born SC.

BARRON, JACOB, 35, M, Laborer, B, SC, 1150, 1129, CHAS%.

BARRON, JAMES, 57, M, (--), M, SC, 560, 552, CHAS%. In HH of Joseph Barron m 30 mulatto born SC.

BARRON, JAMES, 12, M, (--), M, SC, 560, 552, CHAS%. In HH of Joseph Barron m 30 mulatto born SC.

BARRON, JOHN, 14, M, (--), M, SC, 560, 552, CHAS%. In HH of Joseph Barron m 30 mulatto born SC.

BARRON, JOSEPH, 30, M, (--), M, SC, 560, 552, CHAS%.

BARRON, JULIA, 16, F, (--), M, SC, 560, 552, CHAS%. In HH of Joseph Barron m 30 mulatto born SC.

BARRON, JULIA, 1, F, (--), B, SC, 1150, 1129, CHAS%. In HH of Jacob Brown m 35 black born SC.

BARRON, MARTHA, 15, F, (--), B, SC, 378, 340, CHAS+. In HH of Phillis Barron f 44 mulatto born SC.

BARRON, MARY, 30, F, (--), B, SC, 1150, 1129, CHAS%. In HH of Jacob Brown m 35 black born SC.

BARRON, PHILLIS, 44, F, (--), B, SC, 378, 340, CHAS+.

BARRON, RELIA, 11, F, (--), B, SC, 1150, 1129, CHAS%. In HH of Jacob Brown m 35 black born SC.

BARRON, RICHARD, 6, M, (--), B, SC, 1150, 1129, CHAS%. In HH of Jacob Brown m 35 black born SC.

BARRON, SARAH, 16, F, (--), M, SC, 560, 552, CHAS%. In HH of Joseph Barron m 30 mulatto born SC.

BARRON, SUSAN, 13, F, (--), B, SC, 1150, 1129, CHAS%. In HH of Jacob Brown m 35 black born SC.

BARRON, WILLIAM, 7, M, (--), M, SC, 152, 142, CHAS-. In HH of Julius Berney m 35 mulatto born SC.

BARROW, ELIJAH, 4, M, (--), M, SC, 541, 533, CHAS%. In HH with Paul Barrow m 8 {sic} mulatto born SC.

BARROW, PAUL, 8, M, (--), M, SC, 541, 533, CHAS%.

BARROW, REBECCA, 6, F, (--), M, SC, 541, 533, CHAS%. In HH with Paul Barrow m 8 {sic} mulatto born SC.

BARRS, ANN, 10, F, (--), M, SC, 37, 38, ORNG. In HH of Jno. J. Barrs m 38 mulatto born SC.

BARRS, HARIETT, 6, F, (--), M, SC, 37, 38, ORNG. In HH of Jno. J.Barrs m 38 mulatto born SC.

BARRS, JNO. J., 38, M, Planter, M, SC, 37, 38, ORNG.

BARRS, JOHN, 13, M, (--), M, SC, 37, 38, ORNG. In HH of Jno. J. Barrs m 38 mulatto born SC.

BARRS, KNOWLAND, 3, M, (--), M, SC, 37, 38, ORNG. In HH of Jno. J. Barrs m 38 mulatto born SC.

BARRS, MARY, 8, F, (--), M, SC, 37, 38, ORNG. In HH of Jno. J. Barrs m 38 mulatto born SC.

BARRS, RACHEL, 2, F, (--), M, SC, 37, 38, ORNG. In HH of Jno. J. Barrs m 38 mulatto born SC.

BARRS, SUEZER, 29, F, (--), M, SC, 37, 38, ORNG. In HH of Jno. J. Barrs m 38 mulatto born SC.

BARRS, SUSAN, 5, F, (--), M, SC, 37, 38, ORNG. In HH of Jno. J. Barrs m 38 mulatto born SC.

BARRS, WM., 7, M, (--), M, SC, 37, 38, ORNG. In HH of Jno. J. Barrs m 38 mulatto born SC.

BAS, CATHARINE, 2, F, (--), M, SC, 1042, 1042, DARL. In HH of John Bas m 30 mulatto born SC.

BAS, JNO., 4, M, (--), M, SC, 1042, 1042, DARL. In HH of John Bas m 30 mulatto born SC.

BAS, JOHN, 30, M, Mechanic, M, SC, 1042, 1042, DARL.

BAS, MARY, 7, F, (--), M, SC, 1042, 1042, DARL. In HH of John Bas m 30 mulatto born SC.

BAS, RACHEL, 20, F, (--), M, SC, 1042, 1042, DARL. In HH of John Bas m 30 mulatto born SC.

BASCOMB, ALEXANDER, 11, M, (--), M, SC, 101, 101, CHAS%. In HH of John Bascomb m 49 mulatto born SC.

BASCOMB, ASHLEY, 20, M, Tailor, M, SC, 101, 101, CHAS%. In HH of John Bascomb m 49 mulatto born SC.

BASCOMB, HENRY, 16, M, (--), M, SC, 101, 101, CHAS%. In HH of John Bascomb m 49 mulatto born SC.

BASCOMB, JOHN, 49, M, Tailor, M, SC, 101, 101, CHAS%.

BASCOMB, JOHN, 13, M, (--), M, SC, 101, 101, CHAS%. In HH of John Bascomb m 49 mulatto born SC.

BASCOMB, REBECCA, 9, F, (--), M, SC, 101, 101, CHAS%. In HH of John Bascomb m 49 mulatto born SC.

BASCOMB, SOPHIA, 46, F, (--), M, SC, 101, 101, CHAS%. In HH of John Bascomb m 49 mulatto born SC.

BASCOMB, WARLEY, 18, M, Carpenter, M, SC, 101, 101, CHAS%. In HH of John Bascomb m 49 mulatto born SC.

BASS, AMELIA, 13, F, (--), M, SC, 896, 896, KERS. In HH of Elyh Bass m 80 mulatto born SC.

BASS, CHARITY, 5, F, (--), B, SC, 482, 482, MARL. In HH of John Stancil

m 40 born NC.

BASS, CONSTANTIA, 6, F, (--), M, SC, 310, 286, CHAS+. In HH of L. Bass f 28 mulatto born SC.

BASS, ELIZA, 6, F, (--), B, SC, 482, 482, MARL. In HH of John Stancil m 40 born NC.

BASS, ELIZABETH, 18, F, (--), M, SC, 310, 286, CHAS+. In HH of L. Bass f 28 mulatto born SC.

BASS, ELYH., 80, M, Farmer, M, SC, 896, 896, KERS.

BASS, ELYH., 55, F, Farmer, M, SC, 896, 896, KERS. In HH of Elyh Bass m 80 mulatto born SC.

BASS, HUSRY, 14, M, (--), B, SC, 482, 482, MARL. In HH of John Stancil m 40 born NC.

BASS, JACOB, 12, M, (--), B, SC, 482, 482, MARL. In HH of John Stancil m 40 born NC.

BASS, JAS., 20, M, (--), M, SC, 896, 896, KERS. In HH of Elyh Bass m 80 mulatto born SC.

BASS, JOHN, 25, M, (--), M, SC, 896, 896, KERS. In HH of Elyh Bass m 80 mulatto born SC.

BASS, JOHN, 1, M, (--), B, SC, 482, 482, MARL. In HH of John Stancil m 40 born NC.

BASS, L., 50, F, (--), M, SC, 320, 320, LANC*. In HH of W. Bass m 50 black born SC.

BASS, L., 28, F, (--), M, SC, 310, 286, CHAS+.

BASS, LYDIA, 19, F, (--), B, SC, 482, 482, MARL. In HH of John Stancil m 40 born NC.

BASS, MARGARET, 61, F, (--), M, SC, 310, 286, CHAS+. In HH of L. Bass f 28 mulatto born SC.

BASS, MARY, 6, F, (--), B, SC, 482, 482, MARL. In HH of John Stancil m 40 born NC.

BASS, NANCY, 43, F, (--), M, SC, 482, 482, MARL. In HH of John Stancil m 40 born NC.

BASS, PERRY A., 9, M, (--), B, SC, 482, 482, MARL. In HH of John Stancil m 40 born NC.

BASS, PHILIP, 3, M, (--), B, SC, 482, 482, MARL. In HH of John Stancil m 40 born NC.

BASS, R., 15, M, (--), M, SC, 320, 320, LANC*. In HH of W. Bass m 50 black born SC.

BASS, RUBIN, 21, M, (--), M, SC, 896, 896, KERS. In HH of Elyh Bass m 80 mulatto born SC.

BASS, W., 50, M, Laborer, B, SC, 320, 320, LANC*.

BASS, W., 18, M, Laborer, M, SC, 320, 320, LANC*. In HH of W. Bass m 50 black born SC.

BASS, WILLIAM H., 4, M, (--), M, SC, 310, 286, CHAS+. In HH of L. Bass f 28 mulatto born SC.

BASS, WM., 16, M, (--), B, SC, 482, 482, MARL. In HH of John Stancil m 40 born NC.

BAXTER, ALEXANDER, 20, F, Millwright, M, SC, 531, 523, CHAS%. In HH of Susan Baxter f 39 mulatto born SC.

BAXTER, EDWARD, 14, M, (--), M, SC, 531, 523, CHAS%. In HH of Susan Baxter f 39 mulatto born SC.

BAXTER, JOHN, 12, M, (--), M, SC, 531, 523, CHAS%. In HH of Susan Baxter f 39 mulatto born SC.

BAXTER, SUSAN, 39, F, (--), M, SC, 531, 523, CHAS%.

BAXTER, SUSAN, 2, F, (--), M, SC, 531, 523, CHAS%. In HH of Susan Baxter f 39 mulatto born SC.

BEABOY, GEORETTE {?}, 3, F, (--), B, SC, 1103, 1103, BARN. In HH of George Beaboy m 30 black born SC.

BEABOY, GEORGE, 30, M, Raft hand, B, SC, 1103, 1103, BARN.

BEABOY, JACKY, 55, M, Raft hand, B, SC, 1102, 1102, BARN.

BEABOY, JAMES, 20, M, Raft hand, B, SC, 1102, 1102, BARN. In HH of Jacky Beaboy m 55 black born SC.

BEABOY, LAMIS, 30, M, Raft hand, M, SC, 1101, 1101, BARN. In HH of Eliza Alexander m 65 born SC.

BEABOY, NANCY, 40, F, (--), B, SC, 1102, 1102, BARN. In HH of Jacky Beaboy m 55 black born SC.

BEABOY, SARAH, 17, F, (--), M, SC, 1101, 1101, BARN. In HH of Eliza Alexander m 65 born SC.

BEABOY, STEPHEN, 19, M, Raft hand, B, SC, 1102, 1102, BARN. In HH of Jacky Beaboy m 55 black born SC.

BEABOY, TILDY, 20, F, Rafthand, B, SC, 1103, 1103, BARN. In HH of George Beaboy m 30 black born SC.

BEACH, RACHEL, 3, F, (--), M, SC, 37, 37, GEOR. In HH of Saml. Tunno m 26 mulatto born SC.

BEACH, SARAH, 25, F, (--), M, SC, 37, 37, GEOR. In HH of Saml. Tunno m 26 mulatto born SC.

BEACH, WM., 6, M, (--), M, SC, 37, 37, GEOR. In HH of Saml. Tunno m 26 mulatto born SC.

BEAK, HUGH, 30, M, Laborer, M, SC, 40, 40, GEOR*.

BEAN, JANE, 38, F, (--), B, SC, 343, 326, CHAS-.

BEAN, JOHN, 2, M, (--), B, SC, 343, 326, CHAS-. In HH of Jane Bean f 38 black born SC.

BEAN, JULIET, 4, F, (--), B, SC, 343, 326, CHAS-. In HH of Jane Bean f 38 black born SC.

BEAN, RALPH, 6, M, (--), B, SC, 343, 326, CHAS-. In HH of Jane Bean f 38 black born SC.

BEARD, ANNA, 31, F, (--), M, SC, 12, 12, CHAS~. Born: Marion Dist., SC.

BEARD, ELIAS, 8, M, (--), M, SC, 1594, 1594, BARN. In HH of Rachel Beard f 55 mulatto born SC.

BEARD, RACHEL, 55, F, None, M, SC, 1594, 1594, BARN.

BEAUBEAN, ELIZA, 4, F, (--), M, SC, 2253, 2253, GREE. In HH of Joe. C. Williams m 31 born SC.

BEAUBEAN, HENRY, 25, M, Tailor, M, SC, 2253, 2253, GREE. In HH of Joe. C. Williams m 31 born SC.

BEAUBEAN, ROSA, 25, F, (--), M, SC, 2253, 2253, GREE. In HH of Joe. C.

Williams m 31 born SC.

BEAUBEAN, SAMUEL, 0, M, (--), M, SC, 2253, 2253, GREE. In HH of Joe. C. Williams m 31 born SC. Samuel Beaubean 7/12 yr.

BEAUBIEN, GEORGE, 6, M, (--), B, SC, 174, 174, BEAU. In HH of Jane Beaubien f 30 black born SC.

BEAUBIEN, JANE, 30, F, Washer woman, B, SC, 174, 174, BEAU.

BEAUBIEN, MARY, 10, F, (--), B, SC, 174, 174, BEAU. In HH of Jane Beaubien f 30 black born SC.

BEAUBIEN, MATILDA, 8, F, (--), B, SC, 174, 174, BEAU. In HH of Jane Beaubien f 30 black born SC.

BEAUBIEN, WILLIAM, 2, M, (--), B, SC, 174, 174, BEAU. In HH of Jane Beaubien f 30 black born SC.

BEAUGARD, LUCY, 60, F, (--), M, SC, 236, 223, CHAS+. In HH of Peter Beaugard m 62 mulatto born SC.

BEAUGARD, PETER, 62, M, None, M, SC, 236, 223, CHAS+.

BECHARLES, 40, M, Laborer, M, SC, 711, 669, CHAS+.

BECAISE, CHARLES, 3, M, (--), M, SC, 711, 669, CHAS+. In HH of Charles Becaise m 40 mulatto born SC.

BECAISE, ELIZA, 0, F, (--), M, SC, 711, 669, CHAS+. In HH of Charles Becaise m 40 mulatto born SC. Eliza age 10/12yr.

BECAISE, EMILY, 2, F, (--), M, SC, 711, 669, CHAS+. In HH of Charles Becaise m 40 mulatto born SC.

BECAISE, MARY ANN, 30, F, (--), M, SC, 711, 669, CHAS+. In HH of Charles Becaise m 40 mulatto born SC.

BECKET, ALEXANDER, 11, M, (--), M, SC, 437, 437, BEAU-. In HH of John Becket m 65 mulatto born SC.

BECKET, ASHLEY, 17, M, Laborer, M, SC, 454, 454, BEAU-. In HH of William Becket m 26 mulatto born SC.

BECKET, CATHARINE A., 14, F,(--), M, SC, 454, 454, BEAU-. In HH of William Becket m 26 mulatto born SC.

BECKET, CHARLES, 9, M, (--), M,
SC, 454, 454, BEAU-. In HH of William Becket m 26 mulatto born SC.

BECKET, ELIZABETH, 19, F, (--), M, SC, 466, 466, BEAU-. In HH of Reubin Becket m 25 mulatto born SC.

BECKET, FRANCIS, 16, M, Laborer, M, SC, 437, 437, BEAU-. In HH of John Becket m 65 mulatto born SC.

BECKET, JOHN, 65, M, Farmer, M, SC, 437, 437, BEAU-.

BECKET, JOHN, 11, M, (--), M, SC, 454, 454, BEAU-. In HH of William Becket m 26 mulatto born SC.

BECKET, JOHN, 3, M, (--), M, SC, 439, 439, BEAU-. In HH of William Becket m 25 mulatto born SC.

BECKET, MARTHA, 24, F, (--), M, SC, 437, 437, BEAU-. In HH of John Becket m 65 mulatto born SC.

BECKET, MARY, 24, F, (--), M, SC, 439, 439, BEAU-. In HH of William Becket m 25 mulatto born SC.

BECKET, RACHAEL, 20, F, (--), M, SC, 454, 454, BEAU-. In HH of William Becket m 26 mulatto born SC.

BECKET, REUBIN, 24, M, Laborer, M, SC, 466, 466, BEAU-.

BECKET, SARAH, 15, F, (--), M, SC, 437, 437, BEAU-. In HH of John Becket m 65 mulatto born SC.

BECKET, TERRY, 8, M, (--), M, SC, 454, 454, BEAU-. In HH of William Becket m 26 mulatto born SC.

BECKET, WILLIAM, 26, M, Laborer, M, SC, 454, 454, BEAU-.

BECKET, WILLIAM, 25, M, Laborer, M, SC, 439, 439, BEAU-.

BECKET, WILLIAM, 1, M, (--), M, SC, 439, 439, BEAU-. In HH of William Becket m 25 mulatto born SC.

BEDFORD, 70, M, Fisherman, B, SC, 148, 136, CHAS*.

BEE, GEORGIANA, 0, F, (--), B, SC, 777, 757, CHAS-. In HH of Nero Horlbeck m 50 black born SC. Georgiana age 8/12 yr.

BEE, HENRY, 10, M, (--), B, SC, 777, 757, CHAS-. In HH of Nero Horlbeck m 50 black born SC.

BEE, MARY, 26, F, (--), B, SC, 777, 757, CHAS-. In HH of Nero Horlbeck m 50 black born SC.

BEEKMAN, HENRIETTA, 22, F, (--), M, SC, 876, 834, CHAS+. In HH of Paulina Beekman f 45 mulatto born SC.

BEEKMAN, PAULINA, 45, F, (--), M, SC, 876, 834, CHAS+.

BEEM, DANIEL, 17, M, Hireling, M, SC, 881, 881, ABB. In HH of Betsy Beem f 50 white born SC.

BEEM, DANIEL, 1, M, (--), M, SC, 881, 881, ABB. In HH of Betsy Beem f 50 white born SC.

BEEM, ELIZA, 25, F, (--), M, SC, 881, 881, ABB. In HH of Betsy Beem f 50 white born SC.

BEEM, MAHULDA, 4, F, (--), M, SC, 881, 881, ABB. In HH of Betsy Beem f 50 white born SC.

BELL, BENJAMIN, 24, M, Laborer, M, SC, 227, 227, CHAS3. In HH of Martha J. Bell f 60 mulatto born SC.

BELL, ELIZABETH, 21, F, (--), M, SC, 227, 227, CHAS3. In HH of Martha J. Bell f 60 mulatto born SC.

BELL, HENRY J., 27, M, Laborer, M, SC, 227, 227, CHAS3. In HH of Martha J. Bell f 60 mulatto born SC.

BELL, HOLLOW, 11, M, (--), M, SC, 1085, 1062, CHAS-. In HH of Sally Johnson f 60 mulatto born SC.

BELL, JAMES N., 29, M, Laborer, M, SC, 227, 227, CHAS3. In HH of Martha J. Bell f 60 mulatto born SC.

BELL, JEREMIAH, 22, M, Laborer, M, SC, 227, 227, CHAS3. In HH of Martha J. Bell f 60 mulatto born SC.

BELL, JOHN, 20, M, (--), M, SC, 346, 346, COLL*. In HH of James Fludd m 35 mulatto born SC.

BELL, JOHN W., 30, M, Laborer, M, SC, 227, 227, CHAS3. In HH of Martha J. Bell f 60 mulatto born SC.

BELL, MARTHA J., 60, F, (--), M, SC, 227, 227, CHAS3.

BELL, PERSEY, 56, F, (--), B, SC, 634, 626, CHAS%.

BELL, SARAH, 27, F, (--), M, SC, 1085, 1062, CHAS-. In HH of Sally Johnson f 60 mulatto born SC.

BEMAR, WILLIAM, 30, M, Painter, M, SC, 740, 720, CHAS-.

BEMMER, EDWARD, 14, M, (--), M, SC, 1174, 1174, CHES. In HH of D.W. Hardin m 41 born SC.

BEND, MARY, 46, F, (--), B, SC, 443, 426, CHAS-. In HH of Priscilla Diverer f 65 mulatto born SC.

BENDEBAUGH, A.B., 10, M, (--), M, SC, 215, 215, NEWB. In HH of Mary Shumpert f 60 born SC.

BENDEBAUGH, AMANDA, 12, F, (--), M, SC, 215, 215, NEWB. In HH of Mary Shumpert f 60 born SC.

BENDEBAUGH, HANNAH, 3, F, (--), M, SC, 215, 215, NEWB. In HH of Mary Shumpert f 60 born SC.

BENDEBAUGH, JANE, 8, F, (--), M, SC, 215, 215, NEWB. In HH of Mary Shumpert f 60 born SC.

BENDEBAUGH, JOEL, 6, M, (--), M, SC, 215, 215, NEWB. In HH of Mary Shumpert f 60 born SC.

BENDEBAUGH, JOSEPH, 25, M, Carpenter, M, SC, 215, 215, NEWB. In HH of Mary Shumpert f 60 born SC.

BENDEBAUGH, MARY, 1, F, (--), M, SC, 215, 215, NEWB. In HH of Mary Shumpert f 60 born SC.

BENDEBAUGH, RENA, 29, F, (--), M, SC, 215, 215, NEWB. In HH of Mary Shumpert f 60 born SC.

BENNETT, CATHERINE, 58, M, (--), B, SC, 376, 375, CHAS%.

BENNETT, ELLEN, 40, F, (--), M, SC, 371, 371, CHAS%.

BENNETT, JAMES, 37, M, Cooper, M, SC, 371, 371, CHAS%. In HH of Ellen Bennett f 40 mulatto born SC.

BENNETT, JAMES, 11, M, (--), M, SC, 378, 376, CHAS%. In HH of Peter Bennett m 30 mulatto born SC.

BENNETT, JOHN, 9, M, (--), M, SC, 378, 376, CHAS%. In HH of Peter Bennett m 30 mulatto born SC.

BENNETT, MARY, 12, F, (--), M, SC, 371, 371, CHAS%. In HH of Ellen

Bennett f 40 mulatto born SC.

BENNETT, PETER, 30, M, Porter, M, SC, 378, 376, CHAS%.

BENNETT, ROBERT, 55, M, (--), B, SC, 376, 375, CHAS%. In HH of Catherine Bennett f 58 black born SC.

BENNETT, SAMUEL, 28, M, Shoemaker, M, SC, 558, 541, CHAS-. In HH of Amelia Cornwall f 35 mulatto born SC.

BENNETT, SARAH, 28, F, (--), M, SC, 378, 376, CHAS%. In HH of Peter Bennett m 30 mulatto born SC.

BENNETT, THOMAS, 16, M, Cooper, M, SC, 371, 371, CHAS%. In HH of Ellen Bennett f 40 mulatto born SC.

BENNETT, THOMAS, 7, M, (--), M, SC, 378, 376, CHAS%. In HH of Peter Bennett m 30 mulatto born SC.

BENNETT, WILLIAM, 4, M, (--), M, SC, 378, 376, CHAS%. In HH of Peter Bennett m 30 mulatto born SC.

BENSETT, CATHERINE, 36, F, (--), M, SC, 114, 114, CHAS%. In HH of Mary Bensett f 42 mulatto born SC.

BENSETT, JAMES, 38, M, Drayman, M, SC, 114, 114, CHAS%. In HH of Mary Bensett f 42 mulatto born SC.

BENSETT, JAMES, 9, M, (--), M, SC, 114, 114, CHAS%. In HH of Mary Bensett f 42 mulatto born SC.

BENSETT, LOUISA, 12, F, (--), M, SC, 114, 114, CHAS%. In HH of Mary Bensett f 42 mulatto born SC.

BENSETT, MARY, 42, F, (--), M, SC, 114, 114, CHAS%.

BENSON, CELIA, 54, F, (--), M, SC, 339, 339, CHAS%. In HH of Samuel Mick m 28 black born SC.

BENSON, JULIUS, 8, M, (--), M, SC, 566, 549, CHAS-. In HH of Emmely Lafarge f 30 mulatto born Cuba.

BENTHAM, ANN, 30, F, (--), M, SC, 1066, 1043, CHAS-.

BENTHAM, CATHERINE, 6, F, (--), M, SC, 611, 603, CHAS%. In HH of William Bentham m 30 mulatto born SC.

BENTHAM, ELIZA, 24, F, (--), M, SC, 611, 603, CHAS%. In HH of William

Bentham m 30 mulatto born SC.

BENTHAM, GEORGE, 8, M, (--), M, SC, 611, 603, CHAS%. In HH of William Bentham m 30 mulatto born SC.

BENTHAM, WILLIAM, 30, M, Butcher, M, SC, 611, 603, CHAS%.

BENTON, CONRAD, 14, M, (--), M, Italy {sic}, 1131, 1110, CHAS%. In HH of Louisa Benton f 34 mulatto born Italy {sic}.

BENTON, EMMA, 1, F, (--), M, Italy {sic}, 1131, 1110, CHAS%. In HH of Louisa Benton f 34 mulatto born Italy {sic}.

BENTON, GEORGIANA, 11, F, (--), M, Italy {sic}, 1131, 1110, CHAS%. In HH of Louisa Benton f 34 mulatto born Italy {sic}.

BENTON, LOUISA, 34, F, (--), M, Italy {sic}, 1131, 1110, CHAS%.

BENTON, LOUISA, 9, F, (--), M, Italy {sic}, 1131, 1110, CHAS%. In HH of Louisa Benton f 34 mulatto born Italy {sic}.

BENTON, SUSAN, 3, F, (--), M, Italy {sic}, 1131, 1110, CHAS%. In HH of Louisa Benton f 34 mulatto born Italy {sic}.

BERNEY, JULIA, 9, F, (--), M, SC, 152, 142, CHAS-. In HH of Julius Berney m 35 mulatto born SC.

BERNEY, JULIUS, 35, M, Carpenter, M, SC, 152, 142, CHAS-.

BERNEY, ROSINA, 22, F, (--), M, SC, 365, 348, CHAS-. In HH of Mary McBride f 46 mulatto born SC.

BERNEY, SARAH, 35, F, (--), M, SC, 152, 142, CHAS-. In HH of Julius Berney m 35 mulatto born SC.

BERNEY, SARAH, 28, F, (--), M, SC, 455, 414, CHAS+. In HH of Narcissas Perchereau f 50 mulatto born St. Domingo.

BERNEY, WILLIAM, 8, M, (--), M, SC, 152, 142, CHAS%. In HH of Julius Berney m 35 mulatto born SC.

BERRY, ADELINE, 30, F, None, M, SC, 1597, 1597, BARN.

BERRY, AMANDA, 21, F, None, M,

SC, 1597, 1597, BARN. In HH of Adeline Berry f 30 mulatto born SC.

BERRY, AMELIA, 19, F, None, M, SC, 1597, 1597, BARN. In HH of Adeline Berry f 30 mulatto born SC.

BERRY, ANN, 6, F, (--), M, SC, 1597, 1597, BARN. In HH of Adeline Berry f 30 mulatto born SC.

BERRY, BENJ., 8, M, (--), M, SC, 1597, 1597, BARN. In HH of Adeline Berry f 30 mulatto born SC.

BERRY, BENJAMIN, 38, M, Fisherman, M, SC, 946, 926, CHAS-.

BERRY, DAVID, 34, M, None, M, SC, 1596, 1596, BARN. In HH of Isaac Berry m 36 mulatto born SC.

BERRY, DOZIER, 28, M, None, M, SC, 1597, 1597, BARN. In HH of Adeline Berry f 30 mulatto born SC.

BERRY, EDWARD, 10, M, (--), M, SC, 1597, 1597, BARN. In HH of Adeline Berry f 30 mulatto born SC.

BERRY, ELIZA, 1, F, (--), M, SC, 1597, 1597, BARN. In HH of Adeline Berry f 30 mulatto born SC.

BERRY, GEORGIANA, 18, F, None, M, SC, 1597, 1597, BARN. In HH of Adeline Berry f 30 mulatto born SC.

BERRY, ISAAC, 36, M, None, M, SC, 1596, 1596, BARN.

BERRY, JABEZ, 4, M, (--), M, SC, 1597, 1597, BARN. In HH of Adeline Berry f 30 mulatto born SC.

BERRY, JNO., 38, M, None, M, SC, 1595, 1595, BARN. In HH of Milly Berry f 60 mulatto born SC.

BERRY, JOHN, 15, M, (--), M, SC, 1597, 1597, BARN. In HH of Adeline Berry f 30 mulatto born SC.

BERRY, MARTHA, 10, F, (--), M, SC, 1597, 1597, BARN. In HH of Adeline Berry f 30 mulatto born SC.

BERRY, MARY, 35, F, (--), M, SC, 946, 926, CHAS-. In HH of Benjamin Berry m 38 mulatto born SC.

BERRY, MARY, 22, F, None, M, SC, 1596, 1596, BARN. In HH of Isaac Berry m 36 mulatto born SC.

BERRY, MILLY, 60, F, None, M, SC, 1595, 1595, BARN.

BERRY, TENET, 7, M, (--), M, SC, 1597, 1597, BARN. In HH of Adeline Berry f 30 mulatto born SC.

BERRY, THOMAS, 8, M, (--), M, SC, 1597, 1597, BARN. In HH of Adeline Berry f 30 mulatto born SC.

BERRY, WM., 40, M, None, M, SC, 1595, 1595, BARN. In HH of Milly Berry f 60 mulatto born SC.

BERY, ANN, 18, F, (--), M, SC, 1249, 1249, BARN. In HH of Daniel Bery m 60 mulatto born SC.

BERY, DANIEL, 60, M, Planter, M, SC, 1249, 1249, BARN.

BERY, PIGEON, 13, M, (--), M, SC, 1249, 1249, BARN. In HH of Daniel Bery m 60 mulatto born SC.

BERY, POLLY, 50, F, (--), M, SC, 1249, 1249, BARN. In HH of Daniel Bery m 60 mulatto born SC.

BEVEN, FRANK, 64, M, Sawyer, B, SC, 97, 109, CHAS.

BEVEN, MARY, 60, F, (--), B, SC, 97, 109, CHAS. In HH of Frank Beven m 64 black born SC.

BING, ALFRED, 10, M, (--), B, SC, 716, 716, COLL. In HH of Betsey Bing f 44 black born SC.

BING, ALLISON, 0, F, (--), M, SC, 482, 482,BEAU-. In HH of Charles W. Bing m 38 mulatto born SC. Allison Bing 6/12 yr.

BING, ANN, 21, F, (--), B, 8, 8,BEAU#. In HH of Hezekiah Bing m 28 black.

BING, BALAM, 12, M, (--), B, SC, 716, 716, COLL. In HH of Betsey Bing f 44 black born SC.

BING, BETSEY, 60, F, (--), M, SC, 291, 291, BEAU+. In HH of Francis Bing m 24 mulatto born SC.

BING, BETSY, 44, F, (--), B, SC, 716, 716, COLL.

BING, BRYANT, 4, M, (--), M, SC, 482, 482, BEAU-. In HH of Charles W. Bing m 38 mulatto born SC.

BING, CAROLINA, 43, F, (--), M, SC, 289, 289, BEAU+. In HH of Mathew Bing m 47 mulatto born SC.

BING, CAROLINE, 37, F, (--), M, SC, 810, 792, CHAS%. In HH of Robert Bing m 39 mulatto born SC.

BING, CAROLINE, 12, F, (--), B, 8, 8, BEAU#. In HH of Hezekiah Bing m 28 black.

BING, CAROLINE, 8, F, (--), M, SC, 383, 381, CHAS%. In HH of Gordon Bing m 56 mulatto born SC.

BING, CATHERINE, 6, F, (--), M, SC, 383, 381, CHAS%. In HH of Gordon Bing m 56 mulatto born SC.

BING, CHARLES W., 38, M, Laborer, M, SC, 482, 482, BEAU-.

BING, COLUMBUS, 1, M, (--), B, SC, 633, 633, BARN. In HH of Wm. Bing m 32 black born SC.

BING, ELIZABETH, 16, F, (--), M, SC, 289, 289, BEAU+. In HH of Mathew Bing m 47 mulatto born SC.

BING, FRANCIS, 41, M, Laborer, M, SC, 291, 291, BEAU+.

BING, FRANCES, 35, M, (--), M, SC, 633, 633, BARN. In HH of Wm. Bing m 32 black born SC.

BING, FREDERICK, 20, M, Tailor, M, SC, 383, 381, CHAS%. In HH of Gordon Bing m 56 mulatto born SC.

BING, GEORGIANA, 12, F, (--), M, SC, 383, 381, CHAS%. In HH of Gordon Bing m 56 mulatto born SC.

BING, GORDON, 56, M, Carter, M, SC, 383, 381, CHAS%.

BING, HAMPSTON, 3, M, (--), B, SC, 633, 633, BARN. In HH of Wm. Bing m 32 black born SC.

BING, HANNAH, 8, F, (--), B, SC, 716, 716, COLL. In HH of Betsey Bing f 44 black born SC.

BING, HARRIET, 25, F, (--), M, SC, 304, 304, BEAU+. In HH of Washington Bing m 26 mulatto born SC.

BING, HARRIET, 20, F, (--), B, SC, 293, 293, BEAU+. In HH of James Bing m 22 mulatto born SC.

BING, HENRY, 8, M, (--), M, SC, 482, 482, BEAU-. In HH of Charles W. Bing m 38 mulatto born SC.

BING, HEZEKIAH, 28, M, (--), B, 8,

8, BEAU#.

BING, IRVING, 14, M, (--), M, SC, 383, 381, CHAS%. In HH of Gordon Bing m 56 mulatto born SC.

BING, JAMES, 22, M, Laborer, M, SC, 293, 293, BEAU+.

BING, JAMES, 14, M, (--), B, SC, 716, 716, COLL. In HH of Betsey Bing f 44 black born SC.

BING, JAMES, 12, M, (--), B, SC, 716, 716, COLL. In HH of Betsey Bing f 44 black born SC.

BING, JANE, 1, F, (--), M, SC, 304, 304, BEAU+. In HH of Washington Bing m 26 mulatto born SC.

BING, JANE, 35, F, (--), M, SC, 482, 482, BEAU-. In HH of Charles W. Bing m 38 mulatto born SC.

BING, JANNET, 25, F, (--), B, SC, 715, 715, COLL. In HH of Saml. Bing m 39 black born SC.

BING, JAS., 44, M, None, B, SC, 1281, 1281, BARN.

BING, JOEL M., 0, F, (--), M, SC, 289, 289, BEAU+. In HH of Mathew Bing m 47 mulatto born SC. Joel M 3/12 yr.

BING, JOHAN, 4, M, (--), M, SC, 383, 381, CHAS%. In HH of Gordon Bing m 56 mulatto born SC.

BING, JOHN, 63, M, (--), B, 8, 8, BEAU#. In HH of Hezekiah Bing m 28 black.

BING, JOHN, 21, M, Tailor, M, SC, 810, 792, CHAS%. In HH of Robert Bing m 39 mulatto born SC.

BING, JOHN, 16, M, Tailor, M, SC, 383, 381, CHAS%. In HH of Gordon Bing m 56 mulatto born SC.

BING, JOHN, 10, M, (--), B, SC, 716, 716, COLL. In HH of Betsey Bing f 44 black born SC.

BING, JOHN, JR., 15, M, (--), B, 8, 8, BEAU#. In HH of Hezekiah Bing m 28 black.

BING, JULIA, 50, F, (--), M, SC, 383, 381, CHAS%. In HH of Gordon Bing m 56 mulatto born SC.

BING, JULIA, 16, F, (--), M, SC, 810, 792, CHAS%. In HH of Robert Bing m

39 mulatto born SC.

BING, JULIA, 2, F, (--), M, SC, 383, 381, CHAS%. In HH of Gordon Bing m 56 mulatto born SC.

BING, JULIUS, 15, M, Plowman, M, SC, 289, 289, BEAU+. In HH of Mathew Bing m 47 mulatto born SC.

BING, LAURA, 8, F, (--), M, SC, 289, 289, BEAU+. In HH of Mathew Bing m 47 mulatto born SC.

BING, LISBON, 10, M, (--), M, SC, 289, 289, BEAU+. In HH of Mathew Bing m 47 mulatto born SC.

BING, LOUISA, 8, F, (--), B, SC, 1023, 1000, CHAS%. In HH of Nelson Bing m 40 black born SC.

BING, LOUISA, 2, F, (--), B, SC, 1023, 1000, CHAS%. In HH of Nelson Bing m 40 black born SC.

BING, LOVEY ANN, 12, F, (--), M, SC, 482, 482, BEAU-. In HH of Charles W. Bing m 38 mulatto born SC.

BING, LUCY, 35, F, (--), B, SC, 716, 716, COLL. In HH of Betsey Bing f 44 black born SC.

BING, LUCY, 8, F, (--), B, SC, 716, 716, COLL. In HH of Betsey Bing f 44 black born SC.

BING, MARGARET, 11, F, (--), B, SC, 1023, 1000, CHAS%. In HH of Nelson Bing m 40 black born SC.

BING, MARIA ANN, 13, F, (--), M, SC, 810, 792, CHAS%. In HH of Robert Bing m 39 mulatto born SC.

BING, MARSHALL, 11, M, (--), B, SC, 633, 633, BARN. In HH of Wm. Bing m 32 black born SC.

BING, MARTHA, 20, F, (--), M, SC, 291, 291, BEAU+. In HH of Francis Bing m 24 mulatto born SC.

BING, MARTHA, 13, F, (--), M, SC, 633, 633, BARN. In HH of Wm. Bing m 32 black born SC.

BING, MARY, 21, F, (--), M, SC, 383, 381, CHAS%. In HH of Gordon Bing m 56 mulatto born SC.

BING, MARY, 20, F, (--), B, (-), 12, 12, BEAU#. In HH of Stephen Williamson m 28 black.

BING, MARY, 6, F, (--), M, SC, 289, 289, BEAU+. In HH of Mathew Bing m 47 mulatto born SC.

BING, MARY ANN, 6, F, (--), M, SC, 482, 482, BEAU-. In HH of Charles W. Bing m 38 mulatto born SC.

BING, MATHEW, 47, M, Farmer, M, SC, 289, 289, BEAU+.

BING, MAY, 7, F, (--), B, SC, 633, 633, BARN. In HH of Wm. Bing m 32 black born SC.

BING, NANCY, 16, F, (--), B, SC, 716, 716, COLL. In HH of Betsey Bing f 44 black born SC.

BING, NANCY, 6, F, (--), B, SC, 716, 716, COLL. In HH of Betsey Bing f 44 black born SC.

BING, NANCY, 5, F, (--), B, SC, 633, 633, BARN. In HH of Wm. Bing m 32 black born SC.

BING, NANCY, 2, F, (--), B, SC, 8, 8, BEAU#. In HH of Hezekiah Bing m 28 black.

BING, NATHANIEL, 9, M, (--), M, SC, 810, 792, CHAS%. In HH of Robert Bing m 39 mulatto born SC.

BING, NELSON, 40, M, Carpenter, B, SC, 1023, 1000, CHAS%.

BING, OLIVER, 10, M, (--), M, SC, 304, 304, BEAU+. In HH of Washington Bing m 26 mulatto born SC.

BING, OLIVER, 10, M, (--), M, SC, 482, 482, BEAU-. In HH of Charles W. Bing m 38 mulatto born SC.

BING, ROBERT, 39, M, Tailor, M, SC, 810, 792, CHAS%.

BING, ROBERT, 25, M, Carpenter, M, SC, 383, 381, CHAS%. In HH of Gordon Bing m 56 mulatto born SC.

BING, SAML., 39, M, Carpenter, B, SC, 715, 715, COLL.

BING, SAMUEL, 12, M, (--), B, SC, 715, 715, COLL. In HH of Saml. Bing m 39 black born SC.

BING, SARAH, 75, F, (--), M, SC, 275, 275, BEAU+. In HH of Wm. Harvy m 50 mulatto born SC.

BING, SAUL., 30, M, Carpenter, B, SC, 715, 715, COLL. In HH of Saml. Bing m 39 black born SC.

BING, SARAH, 10, F, (--), M, SC, 383, 381, CHAS%. In HH of Gordon Bing m 56 mulatto born SC.

BING, SELINA, 12, F, (--), M, SC, 289, 289, BEAU+. In HH of Mathew Bing m 47 mulatto born SC.

BING, SUE, 14, F, (--), B, SC, 716, 716, COLL. In HH of Betsey Bing f 44 black born SC.

BING, SUSAN, 8, F, (--), B, SC, 715, 715, COLL. In HH of Saml. Bing m 39 black born SC.

BING, TELITHA, 38, F, (--), B, SC, 1023, 1000, CHAS%. In HH of Nelson Bing m 40 black born SC.

BING, TURNER, 2, M, (--), M, SC, 482, 482, BEAU-. In HH of Charles W. Bing m 38 mulatto born SC.

BING, WASHINGTON, 26, M, Laborer, M, SC, 304, 304, BEAU+.

BING, WM., 32, M, Planter, B, SC, 633, 633, BARN.

BIRD, ADALINE, 7, F, (--), B, SC, 1167, 1167, NEWB. In HH of Martha Bird f 40 black born SC.

BIRD, AMOS, 38, M, Carpenter, B, SC, 699, 700, FAIR.

BIRD, ANTHONY, 30, M, (--), B, SC, 465, 465, FAIR. In HH of Mitchell L. Ourings {?} m 22 born SC.

BIRD, ARNEEL, 3, M, (--), M, SC, 702, 703, FAIR. In HH of James Bird m 35 mulatto born SC.

BIRD, AUSTIN., 2, M, (--), M, SC, 703, 704, FAIR. In HH of John Bird m 42 black born SC.

BIRD, BENJAMIN, 11, M, (--), B, SC, 1167, 1167, NEWB. In HH of Martha Bird f 40 black born SC.

BIRD, CAROLINE, 15, F, (--), B, SC, 1203, 1203, NEWB. In HH of Jestine Bird f 34 black born SC.

BIRD, CAROLINE, 8, F, (--), M, SC, 702, 703, FAIR. In HH of James Bird m 35 mulatto born SC.

BIRD, CHARITY, 0, F, (--), B, SC, 1203, 1203, NEWB. In HH of Jestine Bird f 34 black born SC. Charity 6/12 yr.

BIRD, CHARLOTTE, 7, F, (--), M, SC, 508, 508, FAIR. In HH of W.B. Peake m 35 born VA.

BIRD, DORCAS, 35, F, (--), B, SC, 699, 700, FAIR. In HH of Amos Bird m 38 black born SC.

BIRD, ELIZABETH, 18, F, (--), B, SC, 102, 102, FAIR. In HH of William F. Pearson m 66 born SC.

BIRD, EMELINE, 12, F, (--), B, SC, 703, 704, FAIR. In HH of John Bird m 42 black born SC.

BIRD, FANNY, 30, F, (--), B, SC, 703, 704, FAIR. In HH of John Bird m 42 black born SC.

BIRD, FANNY, 17, F, (--), B, SC, 699, 700, FAIR. In HH of Amos Bird m 38 black born SC.

BIRD, GEORGE, 12, M, (--), B, SC, 1203, 1203, NEWB. In HH of Jestine Bird f 34 black born SC.

BIRD, GEORGE, 11, M, (--), M, SC, 508, 508, FAIR. In HH of W.B. Peake m 35 born VA.

BIRD, HARRIET, 30, F, (--), M, SC, 702, 703, FAIR. In HH of James Bird m 35 mulatto born SC.

BIRD, HARRIET, 30, M, (--), M, SC, 508, 508, FAIR. In HH of W.B. Peake m 35 born VA.

BIRD, HARRIET, 18, F, (--), B, SC, 699, 700, FAIR. In HH of Amos Bird m 38 black born SC.

BIRD, ISRAEL, 9, M, (--), M, SC, 703, 704, FAIR. In HH of John Bird m 42 black born SC.

BIRD, JAMES, 35, M, (--), M, SC, 702, 703, FAIR.

BIRD, JANE, 3, F, (--), B, SC, 1167, 1167, NEWB. In HH of Martha Bird f 40 black born SC.

BIRD, JESSE, 15, M, (--), B, SC, 705, 706, FAIR. In HH of Nancy Frazier f 62 born SC.

BIRD, JESSE, 14, M, (--), B, SC, 1167, 1167, NEWB. In HH of Martha Bird f 40 black born SC.

BIRD, JESTINE, 34, F, (--), B, SC, 1203, 1203, NEWB.

BIRD, JOHN, 42, M, Carpenter, B, SC, 703, 704, FAIR.

BIRD, JOHN, 12, M, (--), B, SC, 699, 700, FAIR. In HH of Amos Bird m 38 black born SC.

BIRD, JULIUS, 6, M, (--), B, SC, 1203, 1203, NEWB. In HH of Jestine Bird f 34 black born SC.

BIRD, LEATHY, 40, F, (--), B, SC, 1165, 1165, NEWB.

BIRD, LILLA, 22, F, (--), B, SC, 699, 700, FAIR. In HH of Amos Bird m 38 black born SC.

BIRD, LOUISA, 10, F, (--), B, SC, 1203, 1203, NEWB. In HH of Jestine Bird f 34 black born SC.

BIRD, LOUISA, 1, F, (--), B, SC, 1167, 1167, NEWB. In HH of Martha Bird f 40 black born SC.

BIRD, LUCINDA, 0, F, (--), B, SC, 1167, 1167, NEWB. In HH of Martha Bird f 40 black born SC. Lucinda 3/12 yr.

BIRD, MARTHA, 40, F, (--), B, SC, 1167, 1167, NEWB.

BIRD, MARTHA, 10, F, (--), B, SC, 1167, 1167, NEWB. In HH of Martha Bird f 40 black born SC.

BIRD, MARY, 11, F, (--), B, SC, 1165, 1165, NEWB. In HH of Leathy Bird f 40 black born SC.

BIRD, MARY E., 4, F, (--), M, SC, 703, 704, FAIR. In HH of John Bird m 42 black born SC.

BIRD, ROSE, 80, F, (--), B, SC, 1174, 1174, NEWB. In HH of Andrew J. Hipp m 26 born SC.

BIRD, SARAH, 30, F, (--), B, SC, 699, 700, FAIR. In HH of Amos Bird m 38 black born SC.

BIRD, SARAH, 22, F, (--), M, SC, 699, 700, FAIR. In HH of Amos Bird m 38 black born SC.

BIRD, SARAH, 3, F, (--), M, SC, 702, 703, FAIR. In HH of James Bird m 35 mulatto born SC.

BIRD, SIMEON, 5, M, (--), B, SC, 1167, 1167, NEWB. In HH of Martha Bird f 40 black born SC.

BIRD, SPENSE, 30, M, Carpenter, M, SC, 619, 620, FAIR. In HH of R.D. Coleman m 28 born SC.

BIRD, TEXANNA, 3, F, (--), B, SC, 1203, 1203, NEWB. In HH of Jestine Bird f 34 black born SC.

BIRD, WESLEY, 11, M, (--), B, SC, 1203, 1203, NEWB. In HH of Jestine Bird f 34 black born SC.

BIRD, WILLIAM, 6, M, (--), M, SC, 703, 704, FAIR. In HH of John Bird m 42 black born SC.

BLACK, SARSEY, 12, F, (--), M, SC, 1351, 1351, NEWB. In HH of David Croomer m 60 born SC.

BLACKMON, GEORGE, 8, M, (--), M, SC, 580, 580, LANC*. In HH of W. Eastridge m 62 born SC.

BLAKE, EPHRAIM, 51, M, Laborer, B, SC, 428, 411, CHAS-.

BLAKE, JAMES, 6, M, (--), B, SC, 857, 834, CHAS%. In HH of Rebecca Wadkins f 39 black born SC.

BLAKE, PRINCE, 3, M, (--), B, SC, 857, 834, CHAS%. In HH of Rebecca Wadkins f 39 black born SC.

BLAKE, REBECCA, 18, F, (--), B, SC, 857, 834, CHAS%. In HH of Rebecca Wadkins f 39 black born SC.

BLAKE, SARAH, 26, F, (--), B, SC, 857, 834, CHAS%. In HH of Rebecca Wadkins f 39 black born SC.

BLAKE, SIMON, 35, M, (--), B, SC, 114, 106, CHAS+. In HH of Alfred P. Reignie m 40 born GA.

BLANCK, CELIA, 9, F, (--), B, SC, 158, 158, CHAS%. In HH of George Blanck m 38 black born SC.

BLANCK, ELIZABETH, 28, F, (--), M, SC, 649, 608, CHAS+. In HH of William Blanck m 30 mulatto born SC.

BLANCK, EMMA, 11, F, (--), B, SC, 158, 158, CHAS%. In HH of George Blanck m 38 black born SC.

BLANCK, GEORGE, 38, M, Drayman, B, SC, 158, 158, CHAS%.

BLANCK, JOSEPH, 14, M, (--), B, SC, 158, 158, CHAS%. In HH of George Blanck m 38 black born SC.

BLANCK, MARY, 34, F, (--), B, SC, 158, 158, CHAS%. In HH of George Blanck m 38 black born SC.

BLANCK, VICTORIA, 0, F, (--), M, SC, 649, 608, CHAS+. In HH of William Blanck m 30 mulatto born SC. Victoria Blanck age 8/12.

BLANCK, WILLIAM, 30, M, Porter, M, SC, 649, 608, CHAS+.

BLANCK, WILLIAM, 2, M, (--), M, SC, 649, 608, CHAS+. In HH of William Blanck m 30 mulatto born SC.

BLAND, FRANCES, 50, F, Mantua Maker, M, SC, 170, 170, CHAS%.

BLAND, JAMES M., 60, M, Carpenter, M, SC, 170, 170, CHAS%. In HH of Frances Bland f 50 mulatto born SC.

BLANKS, BENJAMIN, 12, M, (--), M, SC, 543, 535, CHAS%. In HH of Sarah Blanks f 30 mulatto born SC.

BLANKS, GEORGE, 6, M, (--), M, SC, 543, 535, CHAS%. In HH of Sarah Blanks f 30 mulatto born SC.

BLANKS, LOUISA, 8, F, (--), M, SC, 543, 535, CHAS%. In HH of Sarah Blanks f 30 mulatto born SC.

BLANKS, SARAH, 30, F, (--), M, SC, 543, 535, CHAS%.

BLANKS, SARAH, 3, F, (--), M, SC, 543, 535, CHAS%. In HH of Sarah Blanks f 30 mulatto born SC.

BLANTON, MARY, 6, F, (--), B, SC, 2189, 2189, SPART. In HH of Nancy Blanton f 40 born SC.

BLUE, DORA, 25, F, Washerwoman, B, SC, 176, 176, BEAU.

BOAG, ALICE, 18, F, (--), M, SC, 247, 232, CHAS-. In HH of Elizabeth Savage f 33 mulatto born SC.

BOBBETT, J., 20, M, Laborer, B, SC, 234, 234, LANC*. In HH of L. Bobbett f 35 mulatto born SC.

BOBBETT, J., 10, M, (--), B, SC, 234, 234, LANC*. In HH of L. Bobbett f 35 mulatto born SC.

BOBBETT, J., 8, M, (--), B, SC, 234, 234, LANC*. In HH of L. Bobbett f 35 mulatto born SC.

BOBBETT, L., 35, F, Laborer, M, SC, 234, 234, LANC*.

BOBBETT, M., 18, F, Wash woman, B, SC, 234, 234, LANC*. In HH of L. Bobbett f 35 mulatto born SC.

BOBBETT, S., 14, F, (--), B, SC, 234, 234, LANC*. In HH of L. Bobbett f 35 mulatto born SC.

BOG, ROSA, 15, F, (--), M, SC, 521, 521, EDGE*.

BOGIER, ANNA, 10, F, (--), B, SC, 493, 493, SUMT. In HH of Thos. Bogier m 60 black born SC.

BOGIER, LEONORAL, 2, F, (--), B, SC, 493, 493, SUMT. In HH of Thos. Bogier m 60 black born SC.

BOGIER, LUCY, 40, F, (--), B, SC, 493, 493, SUMT. In HH of Thos. Bogier m 60 black born SC.

BOGIER, MARY A., 12, F, (--), B, SC, 493, 493, SUMT. In HH of Thos. Bogier m 60 black born SC.

BOGIER, NANCY, 7, F, (--), B, SC, 493, 493, SUMT. In HH of Thos. Bogier m 60 black born SC.

BOGIER, RUFUS, 0, M, (--), B, SC, 493, 493, SUMT. In HH of Thos. Bogier m 60 black born SC. Rufus age 8/12.

BOGIER, THOS., 60, M, Planter, B, SC, 493, 493, SUMT.

BOGIER, THOS., 14, M, (--), B, SC, 493, 493, SUMT. In HH of Thos. Bogier m 60 black born SC.

BOGIER, WM., 7, M, (--), B, SC, 493, 493, SUMT. In HH of Thos. Bogier m 60 black born SC.

BOIL, ALLSTON, 13, M, (--), M, SC, 678, 687, RICH+. In HH of Mary Jones f 50 mulatto born SC.

BOIL, CUNNINGHAM, 18, M, Planter, M, SC, 678, 687, RICH+. In HH of Mary Jones f 50 mulatto born SC.

BOIL, EDWARD, 15, M, (--), M, SC, 678, 687, RICH+. In HH of Mary Jones f 50 mulatto born SC.

BOIL, EMILY, 26, F, (--), M, SC, 678, 687, RICH+. In HH of Mary Jones f 50 mulatto born SC.

BOIL, JANE, 24, F, (--), M, SC, 678,

687, RICH+. In HH of Mary Jones f 50 mulatto born SC.

BOIL, JOHN, 29, M, Planter, M, SC, 678, 687, RICH+. In HH of Mary Jones f 50 mulatto born SC.

BOIL, LOUISA, 16, F, (--), M, SC, 678, 687, RICH+. In HH of Mary Jones f 50 mulatto born SC.

BOIL, WILLIAM, 22, M, Planter, M, SC, 678, 687, RICH+. In HH of Mary Jones f 50 mulatto born SC.

BOLGART, JOHN, 50, M, Postboard maker, M, NC, 667, 647, CHAS-. In Boarding House.

BOLTON, AARON, 20, M, Laborer, M, SC, 270, 276, RICH+. In HH of Jesse Bolton m 60 mulatto born SC.

BOLTON, JESSE, 60, M, Planter, M, SC, 270, 276, RICH+.

BOLTON, JESSE, 28, M, Planter, M, SC, 278, 284, RICH+.

BOLTON, JOHN, 45, M, Farmer, B, SC, 2651, 2651, SPART.

BOLTON, WILLIAM, 12, M, (--), M, SC, 270, 276, RICH+. In HH of Jesse Bolton m 60 mulatto born SC.

BONDEAU, JAMES, 50, M, Stevedore, M, SC, 185, 174, CHAS+. In HH of Michael Herbert m 39 born France.

BONDEAU, NANCY, 50, F, (--), M, SC, 185, 174, CHAS+. In HH of Michael Herbert m 39 born France.

BONE, WM., 14, M, (--), M, SC, 597, 597, MARL. In HH of Nancy Campbell f 75 born Scotland.

BONFORD, MARY, 35, F, (--), M, SC, 1186, 1165, CHAS%. In HH of John Thorn m 40 black born SC.

BONNEAU, MARY ANN, 15, F, (--), M, SC, 172, 162, CHAS-. In HH of Matilda Bonneau f 17 mulatto born SC.

BONNEAU, MATILDA, 17, F, (--), M, SC, 172, 162, CHAS-.

BONNEAU, NANCY, 50, F, Shop keeper, B, SC, 61, 71, CHAS.

BONOT, ANTONIO, 5, M, (--), M, SC, 1052, 1030, CHAS%. In HH of John Bonot m 45 mulatto born SC.

BONOT, ELIZABETH, 12, F, (--), M, SC, 1052, 1030, CHAS%. In HH of John Bonot m 45 mulatto born SC.

BONOT, FRANCIS, 3, M, (--), M, SC, 1052, 1030, CHAS%. In HH of John Bonot m 45 mulatto born SC.

BONOT, JAMES, 16, M, Carpenter, M, SC, 1052, 1030, CHAS%. In HH of John Bonot m 45 mulatto born SC.

BONOT, JOHN, 45, M, Carpenter, M, SC, 1052, 1030, CHAS%.

BONOT, MARTHA, 7, F, (--), M, SC, 1052, 1030, CHAS%. In HH of John Bonot m 45 mulatto born SC.

BONOT, MARY, 10, F, (--), M, SC, 1052, 1030, CHAS%. In HH of John Bonot m 45 mulatto born SC.

BONOT, RAIFORD, 1, M, (--), M, SC, 1052, 1030, CHAS%. In HH of John Bonot m 45 mulatto born SC.

BONOT, SARAH, 40, F, (--), M, SC, 1052, 1030, CHAS%. In HH of John Bonot m 45 mulatto born SC.

BONOT, SARAH, 14, F, (--), M, SC, 1052, 1030, CHAS%. In HH of John Bonot m 45 mulatto born SC.

BORDEAUX, ANN, 25, f (--), F, SC, 861, 861, KERS.

BORDEAUX, CHAS., 8, M, (--), M, SC, 861, 861, KERS. In HH of Ann Bordeaux f 25 black born SC.

BORDEAUX, RACHEL, 3, F, (--), M, SC, 861, 861, KERS. In HH of Ann Bordeaux f 25 black born SC.

BORDEAUX, SUSAN, 7, F, (--), M, SC, 861, 861, KERS. In HH of Ann Bordeaux f 25 black born SC.

BORIN, BURRIS, 6, M, (--), M, SC, 143, 143, PICK+. In HH of Mary A. Borin f 32 mulatto born SC.

BORIN, JOHN, 4, M, (--), M, SC, 143, 143, PICK+. In HH of Mary A. Borin f 32 mulatto born SC.

BORIN, MARY A., 32, F, (--), M, SC, 143, 143, PICK+.

BORIN, MELINDA, 14, F, (--), B, SC, 143, 143, PICK+. In HH of Mary A. Borin f 32 mulatto born SC.

BORIN, SQUIRE, 2, M, (--), M, SC,

143, 143, PICK+. In HH of Mary A. Borin f 32 mulatto born SC.

BORIN, SUSAN, 11, F, (--), B, SC, 143, 143, PICK+. In HH of Mary A. Borin f 32 mulatto born SC.

BORIN, TOM, 8, M, (--), M, SC, 143, 143, PICK+. In HH of Mary A. Borin f 32 mulatto born SC.

BORSDEN, ELIZABTH, 15, F, (--), M, SC, 487, 470, CHAS-. In HH of Teresa LaPont f 60 mulatto born St. Domingo.

BORSDEN, JULIUS, 18, M, Laborer, M, SC, 487, 470, CHAS-. In HH of Teresa LaPont f 60 mulatto born St. Domingo.

BOSS, BENJAMINNE, 16, M, Shoemaker, M, SC, 337, 337, EDGE. In HH of Edney Boss f 35 mulatto born VA.

BOSS, CALVIN, 11, M, (--), M, SC, 337, 337, EDGE. In HH of Edney Boss f 35 mulatto born VA.

BOSS, EDNEY, 35, F, (--), M, VA, 337, 337, EDGE.

BOSS, ELIZABETH, 8, F, (--), M, SC, 337, 337, EDGE. In HH of Edney Boss f 35 mulatto born VA.

BOSS, ELVIN, 10, M, (--), M, SC, 337, 337, EDGE. In HH of Edney Boss f 35 mulatto born VA.

BOSS, HENRY, 12, M, (--), M, SC, 337, 337, EDGE. In HH of Edney Boss f 35 mulatto born VA.

BOSS, MARIAH, 2, F, (--), M, SC, 337, 337, EDGE. In HH of Edney Boss f 35 mulatto born VA.

BOSS, WILLIAM, 14, M, (--), M, SC, 337, 337, EDGE. In HH of Edney Boss f 35 mulatto born VA.

BOSTICK, DICEY, 14, F, (--), M, SC, 116, 119, RICH+. In HH of James Bostick m 21 mulatto born SC.

BOSTICK, JAMES, 21, M, Planter, M, SC, 116, 119, RICH+.

BOSTICK, JOEL, 19, M, Planter, M, SC, 116, 119, RICH+. In HH of James Bostick m 21 mulatto born SC.

BOSTICK, JOHN, 12, M, (--), M, SC,

116, 119, RICH+. In HH of James Bostick m 21 mulatto born SC.

BOSTICK, MARTHA, 16, F, (--), M, SC, 116, 119, RICH+. In HH of James Bostick m 21 mulatto born SC.

BOSTWICK, ELIZA, 15, F, (--), M, SC, 72, 73, RICH. In HH of Susan Bostwick f 50 mulatto born SC.

BOSTWICK, MARY, 19, F, (--), M, SC, 72, 73, RICH. In HH of Susan Bostwick f 50 mulatto born SC.

BOSTWICK, ROBERT, 22, M, None, M, SC, 72, 73, RICH. In HH of Susan Bostwick f 50 mulatto born SC.

BOSTWICK, SUSAN, 50, F, (--), M, SC, 72, 73, RICH.

BOUDO, LOUISA, 10, F, (--), M, SC, 185, 174, CHAS+. In HH of Michael Herbert m 39 born France.

BOUGH, CHARLOTTE, 11, M, (--), M, SC, 27, 26, CHAS&. In HH of Jacob Bough m 58 mulatto born SC. {sex listed as male}.

BOUGH, JACOB, 58, M, Carpenter, M, SC, 27, 26, CHAS&.

BOUGH, JACOB, 18, M, Carpenter, M, SC, 27, 26, CHAS&. In HH of Jacob Bough m 58 mulatto born SC.

BOUGH, JOHNATHAN, 14, M, (--), M, SC, 27, 26, CHAS&. In HH of Jacob Bough m 58 mulatto born SC.

BOUGH, ROBERT, 16, M, (--), M, SC, 27, 26, CHAS&. In HH of Jacob Bough m 58 mulatto born SC.

BOUGH, SARAH, 47, F, (--), M, SC, 27, 26, CHAS&. In HH of Jacob Bough m 58 mulatto born SC.

BOUGH, ZACHARIAH, 7, M, (--), M, SC, 27, 26, CHAS&. In HH of Jacob Bough m 58 mulatto born SC.

BOURDENAVE, HENRY, 13, M, Bootmaker, M, SC, 1009, 986, CHAS-. In HH of John Lewis m 40 mulatto born SC.

BOUTWELL, SARAH, 10, F, (--), M, SC, 1959, 1959, BARN. In HH of Elanson Boutwell m 60 born SC.

BOWE, AMMON, 27, M, Farmer, M, SC, 303, 303, ORNG*.

BOWE, ANN, 8, F, (--), M, SC, 303, 303, ORNG*. In HH of Ammon Bowe m 27 mulatto born SC.

BOWE, CAROLINE, 30, F, (--), M, SC, 303, 303, ORNG*. In HH of Ammon Bowe m 27 mulatto born SC.

BOWE, GEORGE, 10, M, (--), M, SC, 303, 303, ORNG*. In HH of Ammon Bowe m 27 mulatto born SC.

BOWE, JOHN, 3, M, (--), M, SC, 303, 303, ORNG*. In HH of Ammon Bowe m 27 mulatto born SC.

BOWE, MARY, 3, F, (--), M, SC, 303, 303, ORNG*. In HH of Ammon Bowe m 27 mulatto born SC.

BOWEN, FRANCIS, 10, F, (--), B, SC, 138, 138, KERS. In HH of John Bowen m 55 born SC.

BOWENGEN, CHLOE, 60, F, (--), M, SC, 915, 895, CHAS-.

BOWERS, EMILEY, 35, F, (--), M, SC, 98, 110, CHAS.

BOWERS, FRANKLIN, 14, M, Engineer, M, SC, 98, 110, CHAS. In HH of Emiley Bowers f 35 mulatto born SC.

BOWERS, PETER, 11, M, (--), M, SC, 98, 110, CHAS. In HH of Emiley Bowers f 35 mulatto born SC.

BOWERS, ROSA, 3, F, (--), M, SC, 98, 110, CHAS. In HH of Emiley Bowers f 35 mulatto born SC.

BOWSMAN, MARY, 50, F, (--), M, SC, 476, 476, BEAU-.

BOWZAR, HARRY, 36, M, Farmer, B, SC, 1510, 1510, CHES.

BOWZER, ANDY, 15, M, Farmer, B, SC, 1509, 1509, CHES. In HH of Judy Bowzer f 81 born SC.

BOWZER, ELIZA, 12, F, (--), B, SC, 1509, 1509, CHES. In HH of Judy Bowzer f 81 born SC.

BOWZER, ELIZABETH, 24, F, (--), B, SC, 1509, 1509, CHES. In HH of Judy Bowzer f 81 born SC.

BOWZER, HENRY, 10, M, (--), B, SC, 1509, 1509, CHES. In HH of Judy Bowzer f 81 born SC.

BOWZER, JOHN, 11, M, (--), B, SC, 1509, 1509, CHES. In HH of Judy

Bowzer f 81 born SC.

BOWZER, JOHN, 0, M, (--), B, SC, 1509, 1509, CHES. In HH of Judy Bowzer f 81 born SC. John 5/12 mo.

BOWZER, JUDY, 81, F, (--), B, GA, 1509, 1509, CHES.

BOWZER, JUDY, 2, F, (--), B, SC, 1509, 1509, CHES. In HH of Judy Bowzer f 81 born SC.

BOWZER, LUCINDA, 18, F, (--), B, SC, 1510, 1510, CHES. In HH of Harry Bowzar m 36 black born SC.

BOWZER, MALINDA, 25, F, (--), B, SC, 1509, 1509, CHES. In HH of Judy Bowzer f 81 born SC.

BOWZER, NATH., 41, M, Farmer, B, SC, 1509, 1509, CHES. In HH of Judy Bowzer f 81 born SC. John 5/12 mo.

BOWZER, NATHL., 8, M, (--), B, SC, 1509, 1509, CHES. In HH of Judy Bowzer f 81 born SC.

BOWZER, SAM, 5, M, (--), B, SC, 1509, 1509, CHES. In HH of Judy Bowzer f 81 born SC.

BOWZER, SARAH, 23, F, (--), B, SC, 1509, 1509, CHES. In HH of Judy Bowzer f 81 born SC. John 5/12 mo.

BOWZER, SARAH, 14, F, (--), B, SC, 1509, 1509, CHES. In HH of Judy Bowzer f 81 born SC.

BOYD, BARBARA E., 12, F, (--), B, SC, 223, 223, ABB. In HH of Jesse Boyd m 40 black born SC.

BOYD, {BLANK}, 1, M, (--), M, SC, 1414, 1414, BARN. In HH of Madison Boyd m 25 born SC.

BOYD, CAROLINE, 48, F, (--), B, SC, 1036, 1036, NEWB.

BOYD, CAROLINE, 4, F, (--), B, SC, 1006, 1006, NEWB. In HH of Rebecca Boyd f 25 black born SC.

BOYD, DRUCILLA, 23, F, (--), B, SC, 1111, 1111, NEWB.

BOYD, ELIZA, 16, F, (--), B, SC, 1036, 1036, NEWB. In HH of Caroline Boyd f 48 black born SC.

BOYD, FANNY, 60, F, (--), B, SC, 248, 248, CHAS%. In HH of Joseph Lacomb m 20 mulatto born SC.

24

BOYD, FANNY L., 4, F, (--), B, SC, 223, 223, ABB. In HH of Jesse Boyd m 40 black born SC.

BOYD, GEORGE, 2, M, (--), B, SC, 1111, 1111, NEWB. In HH of Drucilla Boyd f 23 black born SC.

BOYD, HARRIET, 5, F, (--), B, SC, 1036, 1036, NEWB. In HH of Caroline Boyd f 48 black born SC.

BOYD, HENRY, 38, M, (--), B, SC, 1018, 1018, NEWB.

BOYD, INDIANA, 1, F, (--), M, SC, 1414, 1414, BARN. In HH of Madison Boyd m 25 born SC.

BOYD, ISAAC, 12, M, (--), M, SC, 1414, 1414, BARN. In HH of Madison Boyd m 25 born SC.

BOYD, JAS., 3, M, (--), M, SC, 1414, 1414, BARN. In HH of Madison Boyd m 25 born SC.

BOYD, JESSE, 40, M, (--), B, SC, 223, 223, ABB.

BOYD, JOHN A., 7, M, (--), B, SC, 223, 223, ABB. In HH of Jesse Boyd m 40 black born SC.

BOYD, MARTHA A., 9, F, (--), B, SC, 223, 223, ABB. In HH of Jesse Boyd m 40 black born SC.

BOYD, MARY, 6, F, (--), B, SC, 1111, 1111, NEWB. In HH of Drucilla Boyd f 23 black born SC.

BOYD, REBECCA, 25, F, (--), B, SC, 1006, 1006, NEWB.

BOYD, ROSE, 14, F, (--), B, SC, 1036, 1036, NEWB. In HH of Caroline Boyd f 48 black born SC.

BOYD, SARAH, 32, F, (--), B, SC, 223, 223, ABB. In HH of Jesse Boyd m 40 black born SC.

BOYD, WILLIAM, 21, M, Farmer, B, SC, 1002, 1002, NEWB. In HH of Elizabeth Caldwell f 58 born SC.

BOYD, WILLIAM, 2, M, (--), B, SC, 1006, 1006, NEWB. In HH of Rebecca Boyd f 25 black born SC.

BRADBURY, MARY, 23, F, (--), M, SC, 258, 242, CHAS+. In HH of Rebecca Lawson f 25 mulatto born SC.

BRADY, PARMMILLA, 14, F, (--), B,

SC, 660, 660, CHFD.

BRAILSFORD, CORINA, 10, F, (--), M, SC, 393, 391, CHAS%. In HH of Maria Brailsford f 47 mulatto born SC.

BRAILSFORD, EDWARD, 75, M, Farmer, M, SC, 281, 281, BEAU+.

BRAILSFORD, EMMELINE, 22, F, (--), M, SC, 393, 391, CHAS%. In HH of Maria Brailsford f 47 mulatto born SC.

BRAILSFORD, JAMES, 18, M, Cooper, M, SC, 393, 391, CHAS%. In HH of Maria Brailsford f 47 mulatto born SC.

BRAILSFORD, JANE, 13, F, (--), M, SC, 393, 391, CHAS%. In HH of Maria Brailsford f 47 mulatto born SC.

BRAILSFORD, JOHN, 46, M, Carpenter, M, SC, 393, 391, CHAS%. In HH of Maria Brailsford f 47 mulatto born SC.

BRAILSFORD, LOUISA, 50, F, (--), B, SC, 281, 281, BEAU+. In HH of Edward Brailsford m 75 mulatto born SC.

BRAILSFORD, LOUISA, 16, F, (--), M, SC, 393, 391, CHAS%. In HH of Maria Brailsford f 47 mulatto born SC.

BRAILSFORD, MARGARET, 80, F, (--), B, (-), 13, 13, BEAU#.

BRAILSFORD, MARIA, 47, F, (--), M, SC, 393, 391, CHAS%.

BRANHAM, ABEL, 17, M, Planter, B, SC, 462, 470, RICH+. In HH of Simeon Branham m 65 black born SC.

BRANHAM, BENJAMIN, 8, M, (--), B, SC, 462, 470, RICH+. In HH of Simeon Branham m 65 black born SC.

BRANHAM, BINAH, 19, F, (--), B, SC, 462, 470, RICH+. In HH of Simeon Branham m 65 black born SC.

BRANHAM, CATHERINE, 22, F, (--), B, SC, 462, 470, RICH+. In HH of Simeon Branham m 65 black born SC.

BRANHAM, ELIZABETH, 24, F, (--), B, SC, 462, 470, RICH+. In HH of Simeon Branham m 65 black born SC.

BRANHAM, JOHN, 1, M, (--), B, SC, 462, 470, RICH+. In HH of Simeon Branham m 65 black born SC.

BRANHAM, MARY, 12, F, (--), B, SC, 462, 470, RICH+. In HH of Simeon Branham m 65 black born SC.

BRANHAM, PETER, 6, M, (--), B, SC, 462, 470, RICH+. In HH of Simeon Branham m 65 black born SC.

BRANHAM, SAMUEL, 2, M, (--), B, SC, 462, 470, RICH+. In HH of Simeon Branham m 65 black born SC.

BRANHAM, SARAH, 15, F, (--), B, SC, 462, 470, RICH+. In HH of Simeon Branham m 65 black born SC.

BRANHAM, SIMEON, 65, M, Planter, B, SC, 462, 470, RICH+.

BRANHAM, TABITHA, 4, F, (--), B, SC, 462, 470, RICH+. In HH of Simeon Branham m 65 black born SC.

BRANHAM, VILLEY, 45, F, (--), B, SC, 462, 470, RICH+. In HH of Simeon Branham m 65 black born SC.

BREEDLOVE, NATHAN, 16, M, (--), M, SC, 290, 296, RICH+. In HH of Sarah Jacobs f 50 black born SC.

BREMAR, REBECCA, 24, F, (--), M, SC, 462, 420, CHAS+.

BRENTFORD, WILLIAM, 45, M, Porter, M, SC, 138, 138, CHAS%. In HH of John Rich m 40 born SC.

BREWINGTON, JOHN, 60, M, Laborer, B, SC, 190, 190, CHAS3.

BREWINGTON, VICTORIA, 4, F, (--), M, SC, 190, 190, CHAS3. In HH of John Brewington m 60 black born SC.

BRIDGEWATER, CATHERINE, 98, F, (--), M, SC, 70, 70, CHAS%. In HH of John Clarke m 30 mulatto born SC.

BRIGG, AGGY, 30, F, (--), B, SC, 761, 761, NEWB. In HH of Eliza Volentine f 60 black born SC.

BRIGG, ELIZABETH, 35, F, (--), B, SC, 32, 32, NEWB.

BRIGG, PRISCILLA, 75, F, (--), B, SC, 760, 760, NEWB.

BRIGG, SAMSON, 15, M, Apprentice, M, SC, 9, 9, NEWB. In HH of J.M. Kraft m 40, bootmaker born Germany.

BRIGG, SARAH, 53, F, (--), B, SC, 21, 21, NEWB. In HH of Sol. P. Kinnard m 27, Jailor, born SC.

BRIGHT, CHARLOTTE, 40, F, (--), M, SC, 668, 626, CHAS+. In HH of Harriet Segan f 60 black born SC.

BRISBANE, FLORA, 52, F, (--), M, SC, 578, 536, CHAS+. In HH of Philip Cohen m 71 born SC.

BRITCH, HARRIET, 11, F, (--), B, SC, 27, 27, CHAS2. In HH of Harriet Palmer f 75 black born SC.

BRITCH, MARTHA, 9, F, (--), B, SC, 27, 27, CHAS2. In HH of Harriet Palmer f 75 black born SC.

BRITCH, MARY, 25, F, (--), B, SC, 27, 27, CHAS2. In HH of Harriet Palmer f 75 black born SC.

BRITCH, PETER, 12, M, (--), B, SC, 27, 27, CHAS2. In HH of Harriet Palmer f 75 black born SC.

BRITCH, SALLY, 13, F, (--), B, SC, 27, 27, CHAS2. In HH of Harriet Palmer f 75 black born SC.

BRODIE, ROBERT, 30, M, Tailor, M, SC, 57, 58, ORNG+. In HH of James Jones m 40 born England.

BRODIE, ROBERT, 12, M, (--), M, SC, 834, 815, CHAS%. In HH of Elizabeth Cambridge f 37 mulatto born SC.

BRODIE, THOMAS, 20, M, Tailor, M, SC, 805, 763, CHAS+. In HH of Rebecca Thomas f 55 mulatto born SC.

BRODIE, THOMAS, 9, M, (--), M, SC, 834, 815, CHAS%. In HH of Elizabeth Cambridge f 37 mulatto born SC.

BROGDEN, ELIZABETH, 26, F, (--), B, SC, 196, 196, SUMT. In HH of John Brogden m 52 born SC.

BROGDEN, INFANT, 0, M, (--), B, SC, 196, 196, SUMT. In HH of John Brogden m 52 born SC. Infant Brogden age 2/12.

BROGDEN, RUFUS, 6, M, (--), M, SC, 196, 196, SUMT. In HH of John Brogden m 52 born SC.

BROOKS, ANN, 7, F, (--), M, SC, 202, 203, MAR. In HH of Silas Brooks m 34 black born NC. Ann Brooks born Marion, SC.

BROOKS, MARY, 4, F, (--), M, SC,

202, 203, MAR. In HH of Silas Brooks m 34 black born NC. Mary Brooks born Marion, SC.

BROOKS, RACHAEL, 27, F, (--), M, SC, 202, 203, MAR. In HH of Silas Brooks m 34 black born NC. Rachel Brooks born Marion, SC.

BROOKS, SILAS, 34, M, Farmer, B, NC, 202, 203, MAR.

BROOKS, WILLIAM, 2, M, (--), M, SC, 202, 203, MAR. In HH of Silas Brooks m 34 black born NC. William Brooks born Marion, SC.

BROOMFIELD, REBA., 19, F, (--), B, SC, 260, 260, KERS. In HH of J.F. Sutherland m 35 born NY.

BROTHERS, ABRAHM, 10, M, (--), M, SC, 172, 172, COLL*. In HH of Charles Brothers m 50 mulatto born SC.

BROTHERS, ADELINE, 2, F, (--), M, SC, 172, 172, COLL*. In HH of Charles Brothers m 50 mulatto born SC.

BROTHERS, CALVIN, 15, M, Laborer, M, SC, 174, 174, COLL*. In HH of Jacob Brothers m 45 mulatto born SC.

BROTHERS, CALVIN, 5, M, (--), M, SC, 172, 172, COLL*. In HH of Charles Brothers m 50 mulatto born SC.

BROTHERS, CHARLES, 50, M, Farmer, M, SC, 172, 172, COLL*.

BROTHERS, CHRISTY, 3, F, (--), M, SC, 172, 172, COLL*. In HH of Charles Brothers m 50 mulatto born SC.

BROTHERS, DANIEL, 1 M, (--), M, SC, 172, 172, COLL*. In HH of Charles Brothers m 50 mulatto born SC.

BROTHERS, DAVID, 23, M, None, M, SC, 174, 174, COLL*. In HH of Jacob Brothers m 45 mulatto born SC.

BROTHERS, ELIZA., 28, F, (--), M, SC, 172, 172, COLL*. In HH of Charles Brothers m 50 mulatto born SC.

BROTHERS, EVE ANN, 12, F, (--), M, SC, 174, 174, COLL*. In HH of Jacob Brothers m 45 mulatto born SC.

BROTHERS, IRWIN, 4, M, (--), M, SC, 172, 172, COLL*. In HH of Charles Brothers m 50 mulatto born SC.

BROTHERS, JACOB, 45, M, Farmer, M, SC, 174, 174, COLL*.

BROTHERS, JNO., 21, M, (--), M, SC, 172, 172, COLL*. In HH of Charles Brothers m 50 mulatto born SC.

BROTHERS, LEWIS, 18, M, Laborer, M, SC, 174, 174, COLL*. In HH of Jacob Brothers m 45 mulatto born SC.

BROTHERS, LOUISA, 21, F, (--), M, SC, 174, 174, COLL*. In HH of Jacob Brothers m 45 mulatto born SC.

BROTHERS, MARY, 7, F, (--), M, SC, 172, 172, COLL*. In HH of Charles Brothers m 50 mulatto born SC.

BROTHERS, SARAH, 15, F, (--), M, SC, 172, 172, COLL*. In HH of Charles Brothers m 50 mulatto born SC.

BROTHERS, SARHA, 10, F, (--), M, SC, 174, 174, COLL*. In HH of Jacob Brothers m 45 mulatto born SC.

BROTHERS, TANCY, 44, F, (--), M, SC, 174, 174, COLL*. In HH of Jacob Brothers m 45 mulatto born SC.

BROWN, ANN, 47, F, (--), M, SC, 505, 488, CHAS-.

BROWN, ANN, 38, F, (--), B, SC, 616, 608, CHAS%.

BROWN, ANN, 27, F, (--), M, SC, 162, 152, CHAS-.

BROWN, CHANCY, 60, F, (--), B, SC, 610, 602, CHAS%.

BROWN, CHARLES, 80, M, Farmer, B, SC, 984, 984, NEWB.

BROWN, CYRUS, 30, M, Drayman, M, SC, 293, 270, CHAS+. In HH of Joseph Quash m 20 mulatto born SC.

BROWN, DEBORETTA, 9, F, (--), M, SC, 854, 854, SUMT. In HH of Wesley Sweat m 24 mulatto born SC.

BROWN, DINAH, 65, F, (--), B, SC, 984, 984, NEWB. In HH of Charles Brown m 80 born SC.

BROWN, DINAH, 24, F, (--), M, SC, 157, 144, CHAS*. In HH of Peter Brown m 55 mulatto born SC.

BROWN, E., 45, F, (--), B, SC, 984, 984, NEWB. In HH of Charles Brown m 80 born SC.

BROWN, EDWARD, 7, M, (--), B, Ireland {sic}, 77, 71, CHAS-. In HH of Sarah Brown f 35 black born Ireland {sic}.

BROWN, ELIZA, 5, F, (--), B, Ireland {sic}, 77, 71, CHAS-. In HH of Sarah Brown f 35 black born Ireland {sic}.

BROWN, ELLEN, 12, F, (--), M, SC, 505, 463, CHAS+. In HH of Rebecca W. Gross f 35 mulatto born SC.

BROWN, FRANCES, 15, F, (--), M, SC, 550, 542, CHAS%. In HH of Jane Brown f 60 mulatto born SC.

BROWN, HENRY, 19, M, Bricklayer, B, SC, 908, 908, KERS. In HH of Snely Brown f 40 black born SC.

BROWN, HENRY, 4, M, (--), B, SC, 610, 602, CHAS%. In HH of Chancy Brown f 60 black born SC.

BROWN, ISAAC, 70, M, Bricklayer, B, SC, 712, 712, COLL.

BROWN, JAMES, 11, M, (--), M, SC, 162, 152, CHAS-. In HH of Ann Brown f 27 mulatto born SC.

BROWN, JAMES, 2, M, (--), M, SC, 162, 152, CHAS-. In HH of Ann Brown f 27 mulatto born SC.

BROWN, JANE, 60, F, (--), M, SC, 550, 542, CHAS%.

BROWN, JANE E., 11, F, (--), M, SC, 421, 419, CHAS%. In HH of Malcom Brown m 58 mulatto born SC.

BROWN, JOSEPH, 12, M, (--), M, SC, 489, 472, CHAS-. In HH of James Wigfall m 52 black born SC.

BROWN, JOSEPHINE, 5, F, (--), M, SC, 492, 446, CHAS. In HH of Henry Rancken m 26 born Germany.

BROWN, JUDY, 7, F, (--), M, SC, 162, 152, CHAS-. In HH of Ann Brown f 27 mulatto born SC.

BROWN, KATY, 68, F, (--), B, SC, 712, 712, COLL. In HH of Isaac Brown m 70 black born SC.

BROWN, LAVINORA, 15, F, (--), M, SC, 854, 854, SUMT. In HH of Wesley Sweat m 24 mulatto born SC.

BROWN, LUCY, 9, F, (--), M, SC, 162, 152, CHAS-. In HH of Ann Brown f 27 mulatto born SC.

BROWN, MALCOM, 58, M, (--), M, SC, 421, 419, CHAS%.

BROWN, MALCOM, JR., 21, M, Wheelwright, M, SC, 421, 419, CHAS%. In HH of Malcom Brown m 58 mulatto born SC.

BROWN, MARGARET, 0, F, (--), M, SC, 492, 446, CHAS. In HH of Henry Rancken m 26 born Germany. Margaret Brown age 5/12 yr.

BROWN, MARTHA, 29, F, (--), M, SC, 492, 446, CHAS. In HH of Henry Rancken m 26 born Germany.

BROWN, MARTHA, 6, F, (--), B, SC, 610, 602, CHAS%. In HH of Chancy Brown f 60 black born SC.

BROWN, MARY, 54, M, (--), M, SC, 421, 419, CHAS%. In HH of Malcom Brown m 58 mulatto born SC.

BROWN, MORRIS, 16, M, (--), M, SC, 421, 419, CHAS%. In HH of Malcom Brown m 58 mulatto born SC.

BROWN, PETER, 55, M, Barber, M, SC, 157, 144, CHAS*.

BROWN, PETER, 29, M, (--), M, SC, 162, 152, CHAS-. In HH of Ann Brown f 27 mulatto born SC.

BROWN, PETER, 10, M, (--), M, SC, 489, 472, CHAS-. In HH of James Wigfall m 52 black born SC.

BROWN, PRINCE, 80, M, Painter, M, SC, 854, 834, CHAS-.

BROWN, REBECCA, 29, F, (--), B, SC, 863, 840, CHAS%. In HH of John Lewis m 38 black born SC.

BROWN, ROBERT, 10, F, (--), B, SC, 984, 984, NEWB. In HH of Charles Brown m 80 born SC.

BROWN, SARAH, 75, F, (--), M, SC, 854, 834, CHAS-. In HH of Prince Brown m 80 mulatto born SC.

BROWN, SARAH, 45, F, (--), M, SC, 157, 144, CHAS*. In HH of Peter Brown m 55 mulatto born SC.

BROWN, SARAH, 35, F, (--), B, Ireland {sic}, 77, 71, CHAS-.

BROWN, SARAH ANN, 13, F, (--), M, SC, 421, 419, CHAS%. In HH of

Malcom Brown m 58 mulatto born SC.

BROWN, SNELY, 40, F, (--), B, SC, 908, 908, KERS.

BROWN, STEPHEN, 21, M, Bricklayer, M, SC, 43, 44, ORNG. In HH of Mrs. R. Shular f 56 born SC.

BROWN, STRAPP, 45, M, (--), B, SC, 984, 984, NEWB. In HH of Charles Brown m 80 born SC.

BROWN, THOMAS, 16, M, (--), B, SC, 610, 602, CHAS%. In HH of Chancy Brown f 60 black born SC.

BROWN, THOMAS, 5, M, (--), M, SC, 162, 152, CHAS-. In HH of Ann Brown f 27 mulatto born SC.

BROWN, THOS., 15, M, (--), B, SC, 908, 908, KERS. In HH of Snely Brown f 40 black born SC.

BROWN, UNREDA, 16, F, (--), B, SC, 984, 984, NEWB. In HH of Charles Brown m 80 born SC.

BROWN, WILLIAM, 60, M, Gingercake Baker, B, SC, 1928, 1928, ABB.

BRUCE, ROBERT, 0, M, (--), M, SC, 2359, 2359, ABB. In HH of James Mars m 80 white born SC. Robert age ???

BRUCH, FRANCES, 12, F, (--), M, SC, 553, 536, CHAS-. In HH of Laura Bruch {sic} f 30 mulatto born SC.

BRUCH, GEORGE, 6, M, (--), M, SC, 553, 536, CHAS-. In HH of Laura Bruch {sic} f 30 mulatto born SC.

BRUCH, JULIA, 2, F, (--), M, SC, 553, 536, CHAS-. In HH of Laura Bruch {sic} f 30 mulatto born SC.

BRUCH, LAURA, 30, F, (--), M, SC, 553, 536, CHAS-.

BRYANT, MARY, 50, F, (--), B, SC, 571, 563, CHAS%.

BUCK, C., 8, F, (--), M, SC, 235, 235, LANC*. In HH of M. Buck f 35 mulatto born SC.

BUCK, J., 23, F, Washwoman, M, SC, 235, 235, LANC*. In HH of M. Buck f 35 mulatto born SC.

BUCK, JANE, 6, F, (--), M, SC, 235, 235, LANC*. In HH of M. Buck f 35 mulatto born SC.

BUCK, M., 35, F, Washwoman, M, SC, 235, 235, LANC*.

BUCK, W., 4, M, (--), M, SC, 235, 235, LANC*. In HH of M. Buck f 35 mulatto born SC.

BUCKNER, JOHN, 20, M, Ginmaker, M, SC, 1225, 1225, SUMT. In HH of Reubin Ellison m 29 mulatto born SC.

BUG, AFFEY, 50, F, (--), B, SC, 567, 567, EDGE*. In HH of Charles Bug m 57 black born SC.

BUG, ANNY, 26, F, (--), B, SC, 516, 516, LAU . In HH of Comb Bug m 45 black born SC.

BUG, CALEB, 14, M, (--), B, SC, 567, 567, EDGE*. In HH of Charles Bug m 57 black born SC.

BUG, CAROLINE, 46, F, (--), B, SC, 124, 124, EDGE*. In HH of Frances Bug m 67 black born SC.

BUG, CHARLES, 57, M, Laborer, B, SC, 567, 567, EDGE*.

BUG, CHARLES, 12, M, (--), B, SC, 124, 124, EDGE*. In HH of Frances Bug m 67 black born SC.

BUG, CLOA, 80, F, (--), B, SC, 516, 516, LAU. In HH of Comb Bug m 45 black born SC.

BUG, COMB, 45, M, (--), B, SC, 516, 516, LAU.

BUG, DANIEL, 17, M, (--), B, SC, 516, 516, LAU. In HH of Comb Bug m 45 black born SC.

BUG, DEMPSTAND, 34, M, (--), M, SC, 377, 377, EDGE*.

BUG, DRAYTON, 20, M, Laborer, B, SC, 462, 462, EDGE*. In HH of Sarah Bug f 21 black born SC.

BUG, ELIJAH, 8, M, (--), M, SC, 568, 568, EDGE*. In HH of Peggy Bug f 30 black born SC.

BUG, FRANCES, 67, M, (--), B, SC, 124, 124, EDGE*.

BUG, FRANKLIN, 16, M, (--), B, SC, 567, 567, EDGE*. In HH of Charles Bug m 57 black born SC.

BUG, HARRIET, 16, F, (--), B, SC, 516, 516, LAU. In HH of Comb Bug m 45 black born SC.

BUG, HASELTINE, 15, F, (--), M, SC, 568, 568, EDGE*. In HH of Peggy Bug f 30 black born SC.

BUG, JAIN, 5, F, (--), B, SC, 124, 124, EDGE*. In HH of Frances Bug m 67 black born SC.

BUG, LAWRENCE, 1 M, (--), M, SC, 377, 377, EDGE*. In HH of Dempstand Bug m 34 mulatto born SC.

BUG, MARTHA, 8, F, (--), B, SC, 124, 124, EDGE*. In HH of Frances Bug m 67 black born SC.

BUG, MARY, 30, F, (--), B, SC, 516, 516, LAU. In HH of Comb Bug m 45 black born SC.

BUG, MARY, 19, F, (--), B, SC, 567, 567, EDGE*. In HH of Charles Bug m 57 black born SC.

BUG, MARY, 8, F, (--), B, SC, 124, 124, EDGE*. In HH of Frances Bug m 67 black born SC.

BUG, NANCY, 43, F, (--), M, SC, 377, 377, EDGE*. In HH of Dempstand Bug m 34 mulatto born SC.

BUG, PEGGY, 30, F, (--), B, SC, 568, 568, EDGE*.

BUG, SALLIE, 10, F, (--), B, SC, 124, 124, EDGE*. In HH of Frances Bug m 67 black born SC.

BUG, SAMPSON, 2, M, (--), B, SC, 124, 124, EDGE*. In HH of Frances Bug m 67 black born SC.

BUG, SARAH, 22, F, (--), B, SC, 567, 567, EDGE*. In HH of Charles Bug m 57 black born SC.

BUG, SARAH, 21, F, (--), B, SC, 462, 462, EDGE*.

BUGG, ANGELINE, 17, F, (--), M, SC, 154, 158, RICH. HH out of order, follows 185/189. In HH of Julia Bugg f 42 mulatto born SC.

BUGG, ANNY, 7, F, (--), B, SC, 218, 218, ABB. In HH of Mathew Bugg m 27 born SC. Rebecca Bugg 3/12 yr.

BUGG, AUGUSTEN, 6, M, (--), B, SC, 2373, 2380, EDGE. In HH of Betsey Bugg f 26 black born SC.

BUGG, BETSEY, 26, F, (--), B, SC, 2373, 2380, EDGE.

BUGG, CLARISSA, 5, F, (--), B, SC, 2372, 2379, EDGE. In HH of Rebecca Bugg f 56 born SC.

BUGG, ELLEN, 6, F, (--), B, SC, 218, 218, ABB. In HH of Mathew Bugg m 27 born SC.

BUGG, FRANCES, 4, M, (--), B, SC, 2373, 2380, EDGE. In HH of Betsey Bugg f 26 black born SC.

BUGG, FRANKLIN, 16, M, Laborer, M, SC, 154, 158, RICH. HH out of order, follows 185/189. In HH of Julia Bugg f 42 mulatto born SC.

BUGG, HANNAH, 12, F, (--), B, SC, 2372, 2379, EDGE. In HH of Rebecca Bugg f 56 born SC.

BUGG, HENRY, 17, M, (--), B, SC, 2372, 2379, EDGE. In HH of Rebecca Bugg f 56 born SC.

BUGG, JAMES, 3, M, (--), B, SC, 218, 218, ABB. In HH of Mathew Bugg m 27 born SC.

BUGG, JOE, 1 M, (--), B, SC, 2372, 2379, EDGE. In HH of Rebecca Bugg f 56 born SC.

BUGG, JOHN, 8, M, (--), B, SC, 2374, 2381, EDGE. In HH of Nancy Bugg f 31 black born SC.

BUGG, JOSEPH, 8, M, (--), B, SC, 2372, 2379, EDGE. In HH of Rebecca Bugg f 56 born SC.

BUGG, JULIA, 42, F, (--), M, SC, 154, 158, RICH. HH out of order, follows 185/189.

BUGG, LAKE, 21, M, (--), B, SC, 2372, 2379, EDGE. In HH of Rebecca Bugg f 56 born SC.

BUGG, MARK, 27, M, (--), B, SC, 2348, 2355, EDGE. In HH of Charles W. Cochron m 58 born SC.

BUGG, MARTHA, 8, F, (--), M, SC, 2373, 2380, EDGE. In HH of Betsey Bugg f 26 black born SC.

BUGG, MARY, 20, F, (--), B, SC, 2372, 2379, EDGE. In HH of Rebecca Bugg f 56 born SC.

BUGG, MARYAN, 10, F, (--), M, SC, 2373, 2380, EDGE. In HH of Betsey Bugg f 26 black born SC.

BUGG, MATHEW, 27, M, (--), B, SC, 218, 218, ABB.

BUGG, MILLEY, 2, F, (--), B, SC, 2374, 2381, EDGE. In HH of Nancy Bugg f 31 black born SC.

BUGG, NANCY, 31, F, (--), B, SC, 2374, 2381, EDGE.

BUGG, PRISCILLA, 21, F, (--), B, SC, 218, 218, ABB. In HH of Mathew Bugg m 27 born SC.

BUGG, REBECCA, 56, F, (--), B, SC, 2372, 2379, EDGE.

BUGG, REBECCA, 4, F, (--), B, SC, 2374, 2381, EDGE. In HH of Nancy Bugg f 31 black born SC.

BUGG, REBECCA, 0, F, (--), B, SC, 218, 218, ABB. In HH of Mathew Bugg m 27 born SC. Rebecca Bugg 3/12 yr.

BUGG, RICHARD, 15, M, (--), B, SC, 2372, 2379, EDGE. In HH of Rebecca Bugg f 56 born SC.

BUGG, ROBERT, 10, M, (--), B, SC, 2372, 2379, EDGE. In HH of Rebecca Bugg f 56 born SC.

BUGG, ROBERT, 2, M, (--), B, SC, 2373, 2380, EDGE. In HH of Betsey Bugg f 26 black born SC.

BUGG, STERLING, 10, M, (--), B, SC, 2374, 2381, EDGE. In HH of Nancy Bugg f 31 black born SC.

BUGG, WILLIAM, 16, M, (--), B, SC, 2372, 2379, EDGE. In HH of Rebecca Bugg f 56 born SC.

BULKLEY, ELISA, 15, F, (--), M, SC, 15, 14, CHAS$. In HH of Henry Bulkley m 48 mulatto born SC.

BULKLEY, HENRY, 48, M, Carpenter, M, SC, 15, 14, CHAS$.

BULKLEY, JULIA, 8, F, (--), M, SC, 15, 14, CHAS$. In HH of Henry Bulkley m 48 mulatto born SC.

BULKLEY, LOUIS, 11, M, (--), M, SC, 15, 14, CHAS$. In HH of Henry Bulkley m 48 mulatto born SC.

BULKLEY, MARY, 34, F, (--), M, SC, 15, 14, CHAS$. In HH of Henry Bulkley m 48 mulatto born SC.

BULKLEY, MATILDA, 14, F, (--), M, SC, 15, 14, CHAS$. In HH of Henry Bulkley m 48 mulatto born SC.

BULKLEY, ROSELLA, 2, F, (--), M, SC, 15, 14, CHAS$. In HH of Henry Bulkley m 48 mulatto born SC.

BULKLEY, VINCENT, 13, M, (--), M, SC, 15, 14, CHAS$. In HH of Henry Bulkley m 48 mulatto born SC.

BULLARD, TERESA, 70, F, (--), M, SC, 344, 344, CHAS%.

BULLIN, ANN, 8, F, (--), M, SC, 105, 105, COLL+. In HH of Amelia Diver f 60 mulatto born SC.

BULLIN, BENJ., 10, M, (--), M, SC, 105, 105, COLL+. In HH of Amelia Diver f 60 mulatto born SC.

BULLIN, MIDDLETON, 12, M, (--), M, SC, 105, 105, COLL+. In HH of Amelia Diver f 60 mulatto born SC.

BUNCH, DEBORAH, 20, F, (--), M, SC, 129, 129, CHAS~. In HH of Mrs. Isabella Bunch f 52 born NC.

BUNCH, E. CAPIAS, 21, M, Farmer Laborer, M, SC, 130, 130, CHAS~.

BUNCH, ELIZA, 36, F, (--), M, SC, 956, 936, CHAS-.

BUNCH, GEORGIANA, 12, F, (--), M, SC, 956, 936, CHAS-. In HH of Eliza Bunch f 36 mulatto born SC.

BUNCH, JAMES, 6, M, (--), M, SC, 131, 131, CHAS~. In HH of Joshua Bunch m 25 mulatto born SC.

BUNCH, JAMES D., 5, M, (--), M, SC, 956, 936, CHAS-. In HH of Eliza Bunch f 36 mulatto born SC.

BUNCH, JOSHUA, 25, M, Farmer Laborer, M, SC, 131, 131, CHAS~.

BUNCH, JULIA MRS., 22, F, (--), M, SC, 131, 131, CHAS~. In HH of Joshua Bunch m 25 mulatto born SC.

BUNCH, LOUISA A., 8, F, (--), M, SC, 956, 936, CHAS-. In HH of Eliza Bunch f 36 mulatto born SC.

BUNCH, LYDIA, 1 F, (--), M, SC, 131, 131, CHAS~. In HH of Joshua Bunch m 25 mulatto born SC.

BUNCH, MARGARET, 17, F, (--), M, SC, 129, 129, CHAS~. In HH of Mrs. Isabella Bunch f 52 born NC.

BUNCH, MARTHA, 3, F, (--), M, SC, 131, 131, CHAS~. In HH of Joshua Bunch m 25 mulatto born SC.

BUNCH, MARY, 5, F, (--), M, SC, 131, 131, CHAS~. In HH of Joshua Bunch m 25 mulatto born SC.

BUNCH, NEBORA, MISS, 80, F, (--), M, NC, 129, 129, CHAS~. In HH of Mrs. Isabella Bunch f 52 born NC.

BUNCH, OLIVIA MRS., 27, F, (--), M, SC, 130, 130, CHAS~. In HH of E. Capias Bunch m 21 mulatto born SC.

BUNCH, PAUL, 10, M, (--), M, SC, 956, 936, CHAS-. In HH of Eliza Bunch f 36 mulatto born SC.

BURBAGE, JAMES, 60, M, Laborer, M, SC, 259, 259, CHAS3.

BURCKMEYER, ELLEN, 30, F, (--), M, SC, 391, 389, CHAS%. In HH of Isaac Burckmeyer m 50 mulatto born SC.

BURCKMEYER, EVE, 8, F, (--), M, SC, 391, 389, CHAS%. In HH of Isaac Burckmeyer m 50 mulatto born SC.

BURCKMEYER, ISAAC, 59, M, Butcher, M, SC, 391, 389, CHAS%.

BURCKMEYER, ISAAC, 10, M, (--), M, SC, 391, 389, CHAS%. In HH of Isaac Burckmeyer m 50 mulatto born SC.

BURCKMYER, ESTHER, 32, F, (--), M, SC, 542, 534, CHAS%.

BURCKMYER, ISAAC, 0, M, (--), M, SC, 542, 534, CHAS%. In HH of Esther Burckmyer f 32 mulatto born SC. Isaac age 6/12 yr.

BURCKMYER, JOHN, 23, M, (--), M, SC, 542, 534, CHAS%. In HH of Esther Burckmyer f 32 mulatto born SC.

BURCKMYER, LUCY, 5, F, (--), M, SC, 542, 534, CHAS%. In HH of Esther Burckmyer f 32 mulatto born SC.

BURCKMYER, SAMUEL, 60, M, Laborer, B, SC, 65, 59, CHAS-. In HH of Caroline Hillagas f 30 born SC.

BORDEAUX, ANN, 25, F, (--), B, SC, 861, 861, KERS.

BURDELL, CAROLINE, 39, F, (--), M, SC, 64, 64, CHAS%. In HH of R.

Burdell m 41 mulatto born SC.

BURDELL, CLAIBOURN, 16, M, (--), M, SC, 64, 64 CHAS%. In HH of R. Burdell m 41 mulatto born SC.

BURDELL, CLEMENTINA, 33, F, (--), M, SC, 64, 64 CHAS%. In HH of R. Burdell m 41 mulatto born SC.

BURDELL, JOHN, 37, M, Drayman, B, SC, 1126, 1105, CHAS%. In HH of Sarah Burdell f 34 black born SC.

BURDELL, R., 41, M, Carpenter, M, SC, 64, 64 CHAS%.

BURDELL, SARAH, 34, F, (--), B, SC, 1126, 1105, CHAS%.

BURDEN, CAROLINE, 30, F, (--), M, SC, 840, 840, PICK+. In HH of Jack Burden m 28 mulatto born SC.

BURDEN, CATHARINE, 3, F, (--), M, SC, 840, 840, PICK+. In HH of Jack Burden m 28 mulatto born SC.

BURDEN, EDLEY, 12, M, (--), M, SC, 861, 861, PICK+. In HH of Moses Burden m 50 mulatto born SC.

BURDEN, ELIZABETH, 1 F, (--), M, SC, 840, 840, PICK+. In HH of Jack Burden m 28 mulatto born SC.

BURDEN, HARRISON, 8, M, (--), M, SC, 861, 861, PICK+. In HH of Moses Burden m 50 mulatto born SC.

BURDEN, JACK, 28, M, Farmer, M, SC, 840, 840, PICK+.

BURDEN, JOHN, 10, M, (--), M, SC, 840, 840, PICK+. In HH of Jack Burden m 28 mulatto born SC.

BURDEN, JOHN A., 4, M, (--), M, SC, 861, 861, PICK+. In HH of Moses Burden m 50 mulatto born SC.

BURDEN, MOSES, 50, M, (--), M, SC, 861, 861, PICK+.

BURDEN, ?ONLY, 24, M, Farmer, M, SC, 840, 840, PICK+. In HH of Jack Burden m 28 mulatto born SC.

BURDEN, PERRY, 10, M, (--), M, SC, 861, 861, PICK+. In HH of Moses Burden m 50 mulatto born SC.

BURDEN, SUSAN, 45, F, (--), M, SC, 861, 861, PICK+. In HH of Moses Burden m 50 mulatto born SC.

BURDEN, WADE H., 7, M, (--), M, SC, 840, 840, PICK+. In HH of Jack Burden m 28 mulatto born SC.

BURDINE, MATILDA, 22, F, (--), M, SC, 1253, 1253, GREE. In HH of Willis Allen m 40 mulatto born SC.

BURDINE, SUSAN, 45, F, (--), M, SC, 1253, 1253, GREE. In HH of Willis Allen m 40 mulatto born SC.

BURGET, PETER, 62, M, Paper hanger, M, St. Eustatia, 181, 171, CHAS-.

BURIE, CECELIA, 12, F, (--), M, SC, 718, 698, CHAS-. In HH of Ellen Burie f 45 mulatto born SC.

BURIE, ELLEN, 45, F, (--), M, SC, 718, 698, CHAS-.

BURIE, HENRY, 25, M, Shoemaker, M, SC, 718, 698, CHAS-. In HH of Ellen Burie f 45 mulatto born SC.

BURIE, NUNAN, 30, F, (--), M, SC, 718, 698, CHAS-. In HH of Ellen Burie f 45 mulatto born SC.

BURIE, PALMIE, 18, F, (--), M, SC, 718, 698, CHAS-. In HH of Ellen Burie f 45 mulatto born SC.

BURIE, SILVANIE, 25, F, (--), M, SC, 718, 698, CHAS-. In HH of Ellen Burie f 45 mulatto born SC.

BURIE, URANIE, 14, F, (--), M, SC, 718, 698, CHAS-. In HH of Ellen Burie f 45 mulatto born SC.

BURIE, ZALINE, 64, F, (--), M, St. Domingo, 718, 698, CHAS-. In HH of Ellen Burie f 45 mulatto born SC.

BURKE, ANGELINE, 9, F, (--), M, SC, 720, 711, CHAS%. In HH of John Burke m 31 mulatto born SC.

BURKE, JAMES, 55, M, Carter, B, Barbadoes, 476, 434, CHAS+.

BURKE, JOHN, 31, M, Carpenter, M, SC, 720, 711, CHAS%.

BURKE, LOUISA, 12, F, (--), M, SC, 720, 711, CHAS%. In HH of John Burke m 31 mulatto born SC.

BURKE, MARY, 35, F, (--), B, SC, 476, 434, CHAS+. In HH of James Burke m 55 black born Barbadoes.

BURKE, MARY, 27, F, (--), M, SC,

720, 711, CHAS%. In HH of John Burke m 31 mulatto born SC.

BURKE, WILLIAM, 11, M, (--), B, SC, 476, 434, CHAS+. In HH of James Burke m 55 black born Barbadoes.

BURNESTER, ANNA, 20, F, (--), M, SC, 566, 549, CHAS-. In HH of Emmely Lafarge f 30 mulatto born Cuba.

BURNET, JOHN, 16, M, (--), B, SC, 470, 470, CHFD. In HH of Ralph Burnet m 45 mulatto born SC.

BURNET, MARGARET, 12, F, (--), B, SC, 470, 470, CHFD. In HH of Ralph Burnet m 45 mulatto born SC.

BURNET, NANCY, 40, F, (--), B, SC, 470, 470, CHFD. In HH of Ralph Burnet m 45 mulatto born SC.

BURNET, RALPH, 45, M, Blacksmith, M, SC, 470, 470, CHFD.

BURNET, REBECCA, 14, F, (--), B, SC, 470, 470, CHFD. In HH of Ralph Burnet m 45 mulatto born SC.

BURNET, SALLY, 0, F, (--), B, SC, 470, 470, CHFD. In HH of Ralph Burnet m 45 mulatto born SC. Sally Burnet age 2/12.

BURNET, SARAH A., 17, F, (--), B, SC, 470, 470, CHFD. In HH of Ralph Burnet m 45 mulatto born SC.

BURNET, WILSON, 10, M, (--), B, SC, 470, 470, CHFD. In HH of Ralph Burnet m 45 mulatto born SC.

BURNETT, ANGUISH, 21, M, Laborer, M, SC, 1365, 1371, MAR. In HH of Elizabeth Burnett f 60 mulatto born SC.

BURNETT, ELIZABETH, 60, F, (--), M, SC, 1365, 1371, MAR.

BURNETT, FLORA, 24, F, (--), M, SC, 1365, 1371, MAR. In HH of Elizabeth Burnett f 60 mulatto born SC.

BURNETT, JANE, 25, F, (--), M, SC, 1365, 1371, MAR. In HH of Elizabeth Burnett f 60 mulatto born SC.

BURNETT, LUCINDA, 12, F, (--), M, SC, 1365, 1371, MAR. In HH of Elizabeth Burnett f 60 mulatto born SC.

BURNETT, SAMUEL, 8, M, (--), M, SC, 1364, 1370, MAR. In HH of Edward

33

E. Garner m 52 born SC.

BURNS, EUGINA, 15, F, (--), M, SC, 145, 135, CHAS-. In HH of Mary Ann Burns f 30 mulatto born SC.

BURNS, MARY ANN, 30, F, (--), M, SC, 145, 135, CHAS-.

BURNS, PERRY, 9, M, (--), M, SC, 388, 388, GREE. In HH of Thomas Barnett m 70 born SC.

BURTON, ANNA, 6, F, (--), M, SC, 180, 180, CHAS%. In HH of Dorell LaMott f 56 mulatto born SC.

BURTON, MARY, 42, F, (--), M, SC, 180, 180, CHAS%. In HH of Dorell LaMott f 56 mulatto born SC.

BURTON, ROBELIA, 4, F, (--), M, SC, 180, 180, CHAS%. In HH of Dorell LaMott f 56 mulatto born SC.

BURTON, ROBERT, 2, M, (--), M, SC, 180, 180, CHAS%. In HH of Dorell LaMott f 56 mulatto born SC.

BURY, MOSES, 34, M, Porter, B, SC, 105, 105, CHAS%.

BUSBY, AMOS, 40, M, Laborer, M, SC, 279, 279, BEAU+.

BUSBY, ALBERT, 2, M, (--), M, SC, 19, 19, CHAS~. In HH of James Busby, m 50 mulatto born SC.

BUSBY, ANIER, 7, F, (--), M, SC, 19, 19, CHAS~. In HH of James Busby, m 50 mulatto born SC.

BUSBY, ANN, 4, F, (--), M, SC, 278, 278, BEAU+. In HH of Jessie Busby m 28 mulatto born SC.

BUSBY, ANNIE, 3, F, (--), M, SC, 279, 279, BEAU+. In HH of Amos Busby m 40 mulatto born SC.

BUSBY, BETSEY, 35, F, (--), M, SC, 278, 278, BEAU+. In HH of Jessie Busby m 28 mulatto born SC.

BUSBY, CATHARINE, 6, F, (--), B, SC, 281, 281, BEAU+. In HH of Edward Brailsford m 75 mulatto born SC.

BUSBY, CRETIA, 24, F, (--), B, SC, 277, 277, BEAU+. In HH of Jesse Busby m 31 mulatto born SC.

BUSBY, DELIA, 9, F, (--), B, SC, 277, 277, BEAU+. In HH of Jesse Busby m 31 mulatto born SC.

BUSBY, ELIZABETH, 1, F, (--), B, SC, 277, 277, BEAU+. In HH of Jesse Busby m 31 mulatto born SC.

BUSBY, FANNY, 20, F, (--), M, SC, 279, 279, BEAU+. In HH of Amos Busby m 40 mulatto born SC.

BUSBY, FANNY, 17, F, (--), B, SC, 280, 280, BEAU+. In HH of Isham Busby m 65 mulatto born SC.

BUSBY, HENRIETTA, 23, F, (--), M, SC, 19, 19, CHAS~. In HH of James Busby, m 50 mulatto born SC.

BUSBY, ISHAM, 65, M, (--), M, SC, 280, 280, BEAU+.

BUSBY, JAMES, 50, M, Laborer, M, SC, 19, 19, CHAS~.

BUSBY, JAMES, 4, M, (--), M, SC, 19, 19, CHAS~. In HH of James Busby, m 50 mulatto born SC.

BUSBY, JEREDIAH, 0, M, (--), M, SC, 278, 278, BEAU+. In HH of Jessie Busby m 28 mulatto born SC. Jerediah 6/12 mo.

BUSBY, JESSIE, 31, M, (--), M, SC, 277, 277, BEAU+.

BUSBY, JESSIE, 28, M, Farmer, M, SC, 278, 278, BEAU+.

BUSBY, LAWRENCE, 2, M, (--), M, SC, 278, 278, BEAU+. In HH of Jessie Busby m 28 mulatto born SC.

BUSBY, MARY, 60, F, (--), B, SC, 280, 280, BEAU+. In HH of Isham Busby m 65 mulatto born SC.

BUSBY, MARY, 2, F, (--), M, SC, 279, 279, BEAU+. In HH of Amos Busby m 40 mulatto born SC.

BUSBY, PATRICK, 0, M, (--), M, SC, 279, 279, BEAU+. In HH of Amos Busby m 40 mulatto born SC. Patrick 5/12 mo.

BUSBY, ULYSSES, 22, M, Laborer, B, SC, 280, 280, BEAU+. In HH of Isham Busby m 65 mulatto born SC.

BUSH, AUSTIN, 2, M, (--), M, SC, 1131, 1131, BARN. In HH of Wolloughby Bush m 65 black born SC.

BUSH, BILLY, 19, M, (--), B, SC, 1131, 1131, BARN. In HH of Wolloughby Bush m 65 black born SC.

BUSH, CLIPDOS {?}, 18, M, (--), M, SC, 1131, 1131, BARN. In HH of Wolloughby Bush m 65 black born SC.

BUSH, JOHN, 8, M, (--), M, SC, 1131, 1131, BARN. In HH of Wolloughby Bush m 65 black born SC.

BUSH, JOYCE, 4, M, (--), M, SC, 1131, 1131, BARN. In HH of Wolloughby Bush m 65 black born SC.

BUSH, ROBERT, 12, M, (--), B, SC, 1131, 1131, BARN. In HH of Wolloughby Bush m 65 black born SC.

BUSH, SAM, 6, M, (--), M, SC, 1131, 1131, BARN. In HH of Wolloughby Bush m 65 black born SC.

BUSH, SYLVIA, 27, F, (--), B, SC, 1131, 1131, BARN. In HH of Wolloughby Bush m 65 black born SC.

BUSH, WILLIAM P., 34, M, Overseer, M, GA, 324, 331, RICH+.

BUSH, WOLLOUGHBY, 65, M, Planter, B, SC, 1131, 1131, BARN.

BUTLER, MINUS, 46, M, (--), B, SC, 1015, 992, CHAS-. In HH of Rose Wilson f 45 black born SC.

BUZZARD, ANN C., 18, F, (--), M, SC, 389, 390, ORNG+. In HH of Joseph Buzzard m 64 mulatto born SC.

BUZZARD, ELLEN, 4, F, (--), M, SC, 389, 390, ORNG+. In HH of Joseph Buzzard m 64 mulatto born SC.

BUZZARD, ELWIN, 20, M, (--), M, SC, 389, 390, ORNG+. In HH of Joseph Buzzard m 64 mulatto born SC.

BUZZARD, FRANCES M., 13, F, (--), M, SC, 389, 390, ORNG+. In HH of Joseph Buzzard m 64 mulatto born SC.

BUZZARD, JOSEPH, 64, M, Farmer, M, SC, 389, 390, ORNG+.

BUZZARD, LOUISA A., 17, F, (--), M, SC, 389, 390, ORNG+. In HH of Joseph Buzzard m 64 mulatto born SC.

BUZZARD, MARY L., 15, F, (--), M, SC, 389, 390, ORNG+. In HH of Joseph Buzzard m 64 mulatto born SC.

BUZZARD, RACHEL, 8, F, (--), M, SC, 389, 390, ORNG+. In HH of Joseph Buzzard m 64 mulatto born SC.

BYING, BETSY, 40, F, Planter, M, SC, 1092, 1092, BARN.

BYING, EMMA, 5, F, (--), M, SC, 1092, 1092, BARN. In HH of Betsy Bying f 40 mulatto born SC.

BYING, JACK, 10, M, Planter, M, SC, 1092, 1092, BARN. In HH of Betsy Bying f 40 mulatto born SC.

BYING, MIKE, 20, M, Planter, M, SC, 1092, 1092, BARN. In HH of Betsy Bying f 40 mulatto born SC.

BYING, SALLY, 40, F, (--), M, SC, 1092, 1092, BARN. In HH of Betsy Bying f 40 mulatto born SC.

BYNG, ANGELIA, 10, F, (--), B, SC, 1089, 1089, BARN. In HH of James Byng m 35 black born SC.

BYNG, EMILY, 25, F, (--), B, SC, 1089, 1089, BARN. In HH of James Byng m 35 black born SC.

BYNG, FANNY, 4, F, (--), B, SC, 1089, 1089, BARN. In HH of James Byng m 35 black born SC.

BYNG, ISAAC, 40, M, (--), B, SC, 78, 78, BARN. In HH of Sally Dungee f 35 Black born SC.

BYNG, JAMES, 35, M, Planter, B, SC, 1089, 1089, BARN.

BYNG, JULIA, 6, F, (--), B, SC, 1089, 1089, BARN. In HH of James Byng m 35 black born SC.

BYNG, LUCIA, 20, F, (--), B, SC, 1089, 1089, BARN. In HH of James Byng m 35 black born SC.

BYRD, JIM, 0, M, (--), M, SC, 398, 398, UNN+. In HH of W.C. Lee m 34 born SC. Jim age 3/12.

BYRD, NANCY, 3, F, (--), M, SC, 398, 398, UNN+. In HH of W.C. Lee m 34 born SC.

BYRD, PEGGY, 24, F, (--), B, SC, 398, 398, UNN+. In HH of W.C. Lee m 34 born SC.

BYRD, SPENCER, 5, M, (--), M, SC, 398, 398, UNN+. In HH of W.C. Lee m 34 born SC.

C

CABUEL, LAURA, 22, F, (--), M, SC, 212, 198, CHAS-. In HH of Francis Smith m 20 mulatto born SC.

CABUNE, LEWIS, 25, M, Carpenter, M, SC, 154, 141, CHAS*. In HH of Diana Ancrum f 50 black born SC.

CABUNE, MARY, 25, F, (--), M, SC, 154, 141, CHAS*. In HH of Diana Ancrum f 50 black born SC.

CAIN, DANIEL, 38, M, Carpenter, B, SC, 1823, 1823, ABB.

CALDWELL, FRANCIS P., 1, F, (--), M, SC, 285, 285, SPART. In HH of Huey Caldwell m 80 born SC.

CALHOUN, DAVID, 65, M, Farmer, M, SC, 614, 618, AND.

CALHOUN, EVELINE, 26, F, (--), B, SC, 614, 618, AND. In HH of David Calhoun m 65 mulatto born SC.

CALHOUN, LOUISA, 23, F, (--), B, SC, 614, 618, AND. In HH of David Calhoun m 65 mulatto born SC.

CALHOUN, SOPHIA, 35, F, (--), M, SC, 343, 317, CHAS*.

CALLAHAM, ALFRED, 6, M, (--), B, SC, 1121, 1121, EDGE. IN HH of Lucy Callaham f 45 black born SC.

CALLAHAM, CORNELIUS, 8, M, (--), B, SC, 1126, 1126, EDGE. {Note: HH appears after 1122}. In HH of Patsey Callaham f 30 black born SC.

CALLAHAM, ELLICK, 12, M, (--), B, SC, 1121, 1121, EDGE. IN HH of Lucy Callaham f 45 black born SC.

CALLAHAM, LUCY, 45, F, (--), B, SC, 1121, 1121, EDGE.

CALLAHAM, MARCELLUS, 6, M, (--), B, SC, 1126, 1126, EDGE. {Note: appears after 1122} In HH of Patsey Callaham f 30 black born SC.

CALLAHAM, MILLY, 26, F, (--), B, SC, 1121, 1121, EDGE. IN HH of Lucy Callaham f 45 black born SC.

CALLAHAM, PATSEY, 30, F, (--), B, SC, 1126, 1126, EDGE. Note: appears after 1122}.

CALLAHAM, SQUIER, 4, M, (--), B, SC, 1121, 1121, EDGE. IN HH of Lucy Callaham f 45 black born SC.

CALLAHAM, STARLING, 1, M, (--), B, SC, 1126, 1126, EDGE. {Note: appears after 1122}. In HH of Patsey Callaham f 30 black born SC.

CALLAHAN, BOB, 32, M, Boatman, B, SC, 404, 404, CHFD.

CALLAHAN, MILLY, 21, F, (--), B, SC, 404, 404, CHFD. In HH of Bob Callahan m 32 black born SC.

CALLIHAM, AMANDA, 23, F, (--), B, SC, 1125, 1125, EDGE. {Note: Follows fam. 1127}. In HH of Nancy Calliham f 40 black born SC.

CALLIHAM, AMANDA, 8, F, (--), M, SC, 1692, 1692, EDGE. In HH of Pleasant Doolittle m 44 born SC.

CALLIHAM, AUGUSTA ANN, 6, F, (--), B, SC, 1125, 1125, EDGE. {Note: Follows fam. 1127} In HH of Nancy Calliham f 40 black born SC.

CALLIHAM, CAMILLA, 2, F, (--), B, SC, 1125, 1125, EDGE. {Note: Follows fam. 1127}. In HH of Nancy Calliham f 40 black born SC.

CALLIHAM, CYNTHA, 23, F, (--), B, SC, 1127, 1127, EDGE. In HH of Sarah Calliham f 50 black born VA.

CALLIHAM, FRANCES, 8, F, (--), B, SC, 1125, 1125, EDGE. {Note: Follows fam. 1127}. In HH of Nancy Calliham f 40 black born SC.

CALLIHAM, GEORGE, 5, M, (--), M, SC, 1692, 1692, EDGE. In HH of Pleasant Doolittle m 44 born SC.

CALLIHAM, GREEN, 32, M, (--), B, SC, 1125, 1125, EDGE. {Note: Follows fam. 1127}. In HH of Nancy Calliham f 40 black born SC.

CALLIHAM, GREEN A., 2, M, (--), B, SC, 1125, 1125, EDGE. {Note: Follows fam. 1127}. In HH of Nancy Calliham f 40 black born SC.

CALLIHAM, JAMES, 27, M, (--), B, SC, 1127, 1127, EDGE. In HH of Sarah Calliham f 50 black born VA.

CALLIHAM, JAMES, 11, M, (--), M, SC, 1692, 1692, EDGE. In HH of Pleasant Doolittle m 44 born SC.

CALLIHAM, JAMES, 4, M, (--), B,

SC, 1125, 1125, EDGE. {Note: Follows fam. 1127}. In HH of Nancy Calliham f 40 black born SC.

CALLIHAM, JAMES S., 2, M, (--), B, SC, 1127, 1127, EDGE. In HH of Sarah Calliham f 50 black born VA.

CALLIHAM, JOHN, 4, M, (--), B, SC, 1127, 1127, EDGE. In HH of Sarah Calliham f 50 black born VA.

CALLIHAM, LOUISA, 9, F, (--), M, SC, 1692, 1692, EDGE. In HH of Pleasant Doolittle m 44 born SC.

CALLIHAM, MARGARET, 1, F, (--), B, SC, 1127, 1127, EDGE. In HH of Sarah Calliham f 50 black born VA.

CALLIHAM, MATILDA, 18, F, (--), M, SC, 1692, 1692, EDGE. In HH of Pleasant Doolittle m 44 born SC.

CALLIHAM, NANCY, 40, F, (--), B, SC, 1125, 1125, EDGE.{Note: Follows fam. 1127}.

CALLIHAM, RICHARD, 12, M, (--), B, SC, 1127, 1127, EDGE. In HH of Sarah Calliham f 50 black born VA.

CALLIHAM, ROBERT, 38, M, (--), B, SC, 1125, 1125, EDGE. {Note: Follows fam. 1127}. In HH of Nancy Calliham f 40 black born SC.

CALLIHAM, SARAH, 50, F, (--), B, VA, 1127, 1127, EDGE.

CALLIHAM, SARAH, 17, F, (--), B, SC, 1125, 1125, EDGE. {Note: Follows fam. 1127}. In HH of Nancy Calliham f 40 black born SC.

CALLIHAM, SILLA, 32, F, (--), B, VA, 1125, 1125, EDGE. {Note: Follows fam. 1127}. In HH of Nancy Callifham f 40 black born SC.

CALVERT, ANN E., 39, F, (--), M, SC, 890, 870, CHAS-. In HH of Mary Prevost f 50 black born SC.

CALVERT, JOHN, 39, M, Drayman, M, SC, 890, 870, CHAS-. In HH of Mary Prevost f 50 black born SC.

CALVERT, JULIANA, 12, F, (--), M, SC, 890, 870, CHAS-. In HH of Mary Prevost f 50 black born SC.

CALVERT, LAURA, 9, F, (--), M, SC, 890, 870, CHAS-. In HH of Mary Prevost f 50 black born SC.

CALVERT, PETER, 15, M, Shoemaker, M, SC, 890, 870, CHAS-. In HH of Mary Prevost f 50 black born SC.

CALVIN, RUFUS, 18, M, Laborer, M, SC, 811, 811, Union. In HH of Garland Wing m 27 born SC.

CAMBLE, DAVID, 32, M, Carpenter, B, SC, 254, 254, Lanc*. In HH of John M. Craig m 40 born SC.

CAMBRIDGE, ELIZABETH, 37, F, (--), M, SC, 834, 815, CHAS%.

CAMBRIDGE, PETER, 35, M, Laborer, B, Ireland {sic}, 53, 48, CHAS-.

CAMBRIDGE, SOPHY, 30, F, (--), B, Ireland {sic}, 53, 48, CHAS-. In HH of Peter Cambridge m 35 black born Ireland {sic}.

CAMPBELL, ADELINE, 8, F, (--), M, SC, 501, 484, CHAS-. In HH of Frederick Campbell m 34 mulatto born SC.

CAMPBELL, FLORA, 38, F, (--), M, SC, 847, 825, CHAS%.

CAMPBELL, FRANCIS, 37, M, Laborer, M, SC, 106, 106, COLL. In HH of Ann C. Hoff 43 born SC.

CAMPBELL, FREDERICK, 34, M, Barber, M, SC, 501, 484, CHAS-.

CAMPBELL, HENRETTA, 12, F, (--), M, SC, 521, 514, CHAS%. In HH of Nancy Campbell f 29 mulatto born SC.

CAMPBELL, JANE, 40, F, (--), M, SC, 171, 161, CHAS+.

CAMPBELL, JOHN, 10, M, (--), M, SC, 847, 825, CHAS%. In HH of Flora Campbell f 38 mulatto born SC.

CAMPBELL, JULIA, 20, F, (--), M, SC, 501, 484, CHAS-. In HH of Frederick Campbell m 34 mulatto born SC.

CAMPBELL, JULIA, 2, F, (--), M, SC, 501, 484, CHAS-. In HH of Frederick Campbell m 34 mulatto born SC.

CAMPBELL, JULIET, 7, F, (--), M, SC, 847, 825, CHAS%. In HH of Flora Campbell f 38 mulatto born SC.

CAMPBELL, MARY, 36, M, (--), M,

SC, 618, 610, CHAS%.

CAMPBELL, MARY, 23, F, (--), M, SC, 950, 950, PICK+. In HH of Judith Campbell f 53 born SC.

CAMPBELL, NANCY, 29, M, (--), M, SC, 521, 514, CHAS%.

CAMPBELL, ROSALIE, 4, F, (--), M, SC, 501, 484, CHAS-. In HH of Frederick Campbell m 34 mulatto born SC.

CAMPBELL, THEADORA, 15, F,(--), M, SC, 618, 610, CHAS%. In HH of Mary Campbell f 36 mulatto born SC.

CAMPBELL, THOMAS, 4, M, (--), M, SC, 847, 825, CHAS%. In HH of Flora Campbell f 38 mulatto born SC.

CAMPBELL, WILLIAM, 3, M, (--), M, SC, 501, 484, CHAS-. In HH of Frederick Campbell m 34 mulatto born SC.

CAMPBELL, WILLIAM, 1, M, (--), M, SC, 618, 610, CHAS%. In HH of Mary Campbell f 36 mulatto born SC.

CANNADY, REBECCA, 17, F, (--), M, SC, 1, 1, COLL*. In HH of Lewis Westbury m 27 born SC.

CANNON, CANTY, 6, F, (--), B, SC, 661, 661, PICK+. In HH of Simon Cannon m 75 black born SC.

CANNON, MALYSA, 27, F, (--), B, SC, 661, 661, PICK+. In HH of Simon Cannon m 75 black born SC.

CANNON, PINCKNEY, 1, M, (--), B, SC, 661, 661, PICK+. In HH of Simon Cannon m 75 black born SC.

CANNON, SIMON, 75, M, Farmer, B, SC, 661, 661, PICK+.

CANNON, STEPHEN, 11, M, (--), M, SC, 661, 661, PICK+. In HH of Simon Cannon m 75 black born SC.

CANON, ELIZABETH, 17, F, (--), M, SC, 43, 43, CHAS2. In HH of Elisha Canon m 21 born SC.

CANTER, JULIET, 50, F, (--), M, SC, 179, 169, CHAS-.

CANTY, ELIZA, 7, F, (--), B, SC, 487, 487, SUMT. In HH of Martha Canty f 30 black born SC.

CANTY, MARTHA, 30, F, (--), B, SC, 487, 487, SUMT.

CANTY, MARY, 3, F, (--), B, SC, 487, 487, SUMT. In HH of Martha Canty f 30 black born SC.

CANTY, WM., 26, M, Laborer, M, SC, 212, 212, COLL. In HH of Henry Wackeman m 37 born SC.

CANTY, WM., 26, M, Laborer, M, SC, 212, 212, COLL.?

CAPERS, FRANK, 78, M, None, M, SC, 1126, 1104, CHAS%.

CAPERS, JOHN, 40, M, Butcher, M, SC, 135, 135, CHAS^. In HH of Catherine Conyers f 24 black born SC.

CARITY, CARITY, 18, F, (--), B, SC, 486, 486, SUMT. In HH of Elis Carity f 50 born SC.

CARITY, ELIS, 50, F, (--), B, SC, 486, 486, SUMT.

CARITY, GABRIEL, 5, M, (--), B, SC, 486, 486, SUMT. In HH of Elis Carity f 50 born SC.

CARITY, JARED, 12, M, (--), B, SC, 486, 486, SUMT. In HH of Elis Carity f 50 born SC.

CARITY, LEONIDAS, 12, M, (--), B, SC, 486, 486, SUMT. In HH of Elis Carity f 50 born SC.

CARITY, NELSON, 14, M, (--), B, SC, 486, 486, SUMT. In HH of Elis Carity f 50 born SC.

CARMAND, CHARLOTTE, 25, F,(--), M, SC, 877, 835, CHAS+. In HH of Frances Carmand m 29 mulatto born SC.

CARMAND, FRANCES, 29, M, Tinner, M, SC, 877, 835, CHAS+.

CARMAND, FRANCES, 5, M, (--), M, SC, 877, 835, CHAS+. In HH of Frances Carmand m 29 mulatto born SC.

CARMAND, WILSON, 2, M, (--), M, SC, 877, 835, CHAS+. In HH of Frances Carmand m 29 mulatto born SC.

CARMEL, JOHN, 2, M, (--), M, SC, 66, 66, GEOR. In HH of Sarah Gairin f 27 mulatto born SC.

CARR, CLARA, 54, F, (--), M, SC, 80, 90, CHAS. In HH of Betty Wilson f 80 black born Africa.

CARR, DIANA, 27, F, (--), M, SC, 80, 90, CHAS. In HH of Betty Wilson f 80 black born Africa.

CARR, EDWD., 0, M, (--), M, SC, 120, 120, KERS. In HH of Nora Carr f 21 mulatto born SC. Edwd. Carr 5/12 yr.

CARR, GLENN, 37, F, (--), M, SC, 428, 397, CHAS*.

CARR, HETTY, 4, F, (--), B, SC, 120, 120, KERS. In HH of Nora Carr f 21 mulatto born SC. M.E. Carr 8/12 yr.

CARR, M. E., 0, F, (--), M, SC, 120, 120, KERS. In HH of Nora Carr f 21 mulatto born SC. M.E. Carr 8/12 yr.

CARR, MARTHA, 23, F, (--), M, SC, 120, 120, KERS. In HH of Nora Carr f 21 mulatto born SC. M.E. Carr 8/12 yr.

CARR, NORA, 21, F, (--), M, SC, 120, 120, KERS.

CARR, SAMUEL, 87, M, (--), B, SC, 1059, 1059, ABB.

CARRLESS, CECELIA, 24, F, (--), M, SC, 53, 53, CHAS%.

CARRLESS, MARY, 16, F, (--), M, SC, 53, 53, CHAS%. In HH of Cecelia Carrless f 25 mulatto born SC.

CARRLESS, MATILDA, 57, F, (--), M, SC, 53, 53, CHAS%. In HH of Cecelia Carrless f 25 mulatto born SC.

CARSTEN, ANDREW, 11, M, (--), M, SC, 379, 377, CHAS%. In HH of Anna Carsten f 40 mulatto born SC.

CARSTEN, ANNA, 40, F, (--), M, SC, 379, 377, CHAS%.

CARSTEN, ELIZA, 42, F, (--), B, SC, 376, 375, CHAS%. In HH of Catherine Bennett f 58 black born SC.

CARSTEN, ELIZABETH, 14, F, (--), B, SC, 376, 375, CHAS%. In HH of Catherine Bennett f 58 black born SC.

CARSTEN, LOUISA, 33, F, (--), B, SC, 376, 375, CHAS%. In HH of Catherine Bennett f 58 black born SC.

CARSTEN, MARY, 12, F, (--), B, SC, 376, 375, CHAS%. In HH of Catherine Bennett f 58 black born SC.

CARSTEN, MARY ANN, 23, F, (--), M, SC, 142, 132, CHAS-. In HH of Joseph Maxwell m 70 mulatto born SC.

CARSTEN, SUSAN, 30, F, (--), M, SC, 379, 377, CHAS%. In HH of Anna Carsten f 40 mulatto born SC.

CART, DINAH, 40, F, (--), B, SC, 282, 282, CHAS%.

CART, FRANCES, 8, F, (--), M, SC, 282, 282, CHAS%. In HH of Dinah Cart f 40 black born SC.

CART, MARGARET, 6, F, (--), M, SC, 282, 282, CHAS%. In HH of Dinah Cart f 40 black born SC.

CART, SHAGER, 12, F, (--), B, SC, 282, 282, CHAS%. In HH of Dinah Cart f 40 black born SC.

CARTER, AARON, 21, M, Laborer, M, SC, 189, 189, SUMT. In HH of Mary Carter f 56 black born SC.

CARTER, AARON, 20, M, Laborer, M, SC, 359, 359, SUMT. In HH of Mary Carter f 50 born SC.

CARTER, ADALINE, 13, F, (--), B, SC, 189, 189, SUMT. In HH of Mary Carter f 56 black born SC.

CARTER, ADALINE, 12, F, (--), B, SC, 359, 359, SUMT. In HH of Mary Carter f 50 born SC.

CARTER, ALLEN, 14, M, (--), M, SC, 2133, 2133, BARN. In HH of Henry Carter m 40 born SC.

CARTER, AMELIA, 3, F, (--), M, SC, 155, 159, RICH. HH out of order. In HH of Ellen Carter f 28 mulatto born SC.

CARTER, CHARLTON, 1, M, (--), B, SC, 190, 190, SUMT. In HH of July Carter m 30 born SC.

CARTER, CLARENDER, 44, F, (--), M, SC, 380, 380, SUMT. In HH of Jas. Carter m 62 black born SC.

CARTER, COLUMBIA, 1, F, (--), M, SC, 155, 159, RICH. HH out of order. In HH of Ellen Carter f 28 mulatto born SC.

CARTER, ELLEN, 28, F, (--), M, SC, 155, 159, RICH. HH out of order.

CARTER, ERWIN, 5, M, (--), B, SC, 190, 190, SUMT. In HH of July Carter m 30 born SC.

CARTER, FRANCES, 80, F, (--), M, Unknown, 365, 365, SUMT.

CARTER, FRANCES, 12, F, (--), M,

SC, 365, 365, SUMT. In HH of Frances Carter f 80 born Unknown.

CARTER, HARRIET, 20, F, (--), B, SC, 361, 361, SUMT. In HH of Wesley Carter m 25 black born SC.

CARTER, HARRIET, 5, F, (--), B, SC, 380, 380, SUMT. In HH of Jas. Carter m 62 black born SC.

CARTER, HENRY, 10, M, (--), B, SC, 568, 551, CHAS-. In HH of Robert Morgan m 50 black born SC.

CARTER, HENRY, 3, M, (--), B, SC, 485, 485, SUMT. In HH of Jas. Carter m 32 black born SC.

CARTER, HETTY, 45, F, (--), B, SC, 475, 475, BEAU-. In HH of Samuel Carter m 50 black born SC.

CARTER, IRVIN, 6, M, (--), B, SC, 358, 358, SUMT. In HH of July Carter m 30 black born SC.

CARTER, ISHAM, 25, M, Planter, B, SC, 381, 381, SUMT.

CARTER, JACK, 35, M, Planter, M, SC, 2429, 2429, BARN.

CARTER, JANE, 33, F, (--), B, SC, 485, 485, SUMT. In HH of Jas. Carter m 32 black born SC.

CARTER, JANE, 17, F, (--), M, SC, 2133, 2133, BARN. In HH of Henry Carter m 40 born SC.

CARTER, JAS., 62, M, Planter, B, SC, 380, 380, SUMT.

CARTER, JAS., 32, M, Planter, B, SC, 485, 485, SUMT.

CARTER, JAS., 12, M, (--), B, SC, 485, 485, SUMT. In HH of Jas. Carter m 32 black born SC.

CARTER, JAS. H., 2, M, (--), B, SC, 361, 361, SUMT. In HH of Wesley Carter m 25 black born SC.

CARTER, JULIA, 14, F, (--), B, SC, 485, 485, SUMT. In HH of Jas. Carter m 32 black born SC.

CARTER, JULY, 30, M, Planter, B, SC, 358, 358, SUMT.?

CARTER, JULY, 30, M, (--), B, SC, 190, 190, SUMT.?

CARTER, JULY, 4, M, (--), B, SC, 358, 358, SUMT. In HH of July Carter m 30 black born SC.

CARTER, KENNEDY, 9, M, (--), B, SC, 485, 485, SUMT. In HH of Jas. Carter m 32 black born SC.

CARTER, LEONORA E., 1, F, (--), B, SC, 361, 361, SUMT. In HH of Wesley Carter m 25 black born SC.

CARTER, LEORWRAL?, 1, F, (--), B, SC, 485, 485, SUMT. In HH of Jas. Carter m 32 black born SC.

CARTER, LYBOY, 24, F, (--), B, SC, 358, 358, SUMT. In HH of July Carter m 30 black born SC.

CARTER, MARGT, 6, F, (--), B, SC, 380, 380, SUMT. In HH of Jas. Carter m 62 black born SC.

CARTER, MARIA, 11, M, (--), M, SC, 2074, 2078, EDGE. In HH of Thomas Ceaty m 30 born SC.

CARTER, MARY, 56, F, (--), B, SC, 189, 189, SUMT.

CARTER, MARY, 50, F, (--), B, SC, 359, 359, SUMT.

CARTER, MARY, 12, F, (--), M, SC, 1051, 1029, CHAS%. In HH of Sarah Carter f 38 mulatto born SC.

CARTER, MITCHELL, 12, M, (--), B, SC, 475, 475, BEAU-. In HH of Samuel Carter m 50 black born SC.

CARTER, PAUL, 11, M, (--), B, SC, 485, 485, SUMT. In HH of Jas. Carter m 32 black born SC.

CARTER, RICHARD, 19, M, Laborer, B, SC, 380, 380, SUMT. In HH of Jas. Carter m 62 black born SC.

CARTER, RUFUS, 8, M, (--), B, SC, 380, 380, SUMT. In HH of Jas. Carter m 62 black born SC.

CARTER, SAMUEL, 50, M, Mechanic, B, SC, 475, 475, BEAU-.

CARTER, SAMUEL, 10, M, (--), B, SC, 475, 475, BEAU-. In HH of Samuel Carter m 50 black born SC.

CARTER, SARAH, 38, F, (--), M, SC, 1051, 1029, CHAS%.

CARTER, SARAH A., 14, F, (--), B, SC, 380, 380, SUMT. In HH of Jas. Carter m 62 black born SC.

CARTER, SCIRTHA, 5, F, (--), B, SC, 485, 485, SUMT. In HH of Jas. Carter m 32 black born SC.

CARTER, SUSAN, 13, F, (--), B, SC, 380, 380, SUMT. In HH of Jas. Carter m 62 black born SC.

CARTER, SYLVY, 30, F, (--), B, SC, 190, 190, SUMT. In HH of July Carter m 30 born SC.

CARTER, THOS., 19, M, Laborer, B, SC, 187, 187, SUMT. In HH of Mary T. Tenant f 25 born SC.

CARTER, TOWNSEND, 9, M, (--), B, SC, 380, 380, SUMT. In HH of Jas. Carter m 62 black born SC.

CARTER, WASHINGTON, 17, M, Laborer, B, SC, 485, 485, SUMT. In HH of Jas. Carter m 32 black born SC.

CARTER, WASHINGTON, 10, M, (--), B, SC, 359, 359, SUMT. In HH of Mary Carter f 50 born SC.

CARTER, WESLEY, 25, M, Planter, B, SC, 361, 361, SUMT.

CARTER, WESLEY, 4, M, (--), B, SC, 190, 190, SUMT. In HH of July Carter m 30 born SC.

CARTER, WILLIAM H., 8, M, (--), M, SC, 155, 159, RICH. HH out of order, follows 185/189. In HH of Ellen Carter f 28 mulatto born SC.

CARTER, WISLEY, 8, M, (--), B, SC, 358, 358, SUMT. In HH of July Carter m 30 black born SC.

CARTER, WM., 21, M, Laborer, B, SC, 380, 380, SUMT. In HH of Jas. Carter m 62 black born SC.

CARTER, WM., 8, M, (--), B, SC, 190, 190, SUMT. In HH of July Carter m 30 born SC.

CARTERS, DAVID, 40, M, Servant, B, SC, 397, 381, CHAS-. In HH of Edward Cassady m 30 born Ireland {sic}.

CASKIN, GRENWELLE, 30, M, Drayman, M, SC, 812, 770, CHAS+. In HH of Isabella Caskin f 22 mulatto born SC.

CASKIN, ISABELLA, 22, F, (--), M, SC, 812, 770, CHAS+.

CASKIN, JOHN, 12, M, (--), M, SC, 812, 770, CHAS+. In HH of Isabella Caskin f 22 mulatto born SC.

CASKIN, NANCY, 58, F, (--), M, SC, 812, 770, CHAS+. In HH of Isabella Caskin f 22 mulatto born SC.

CASTINO, ALFRED, 6, M, (--), M, SC, 430, 413, CHAS-. In HH of Francis Baneau m 36 mulatto born SC.

CASTINO, EUGENE, 10, M, (--), M, SC, 430, 413, CHAS-. In HH of Francis Baneau m 36 mulatto born SC.

CASTINO, JOHN, 42, M, Cigar maker, M, SC, 430, 413, CHAS-. In HH of Francis Baneau m 36 mulatto born SC.

CASTINO, LEONORA, 4, F, (--), M, SC, 430, 413, CHAS-. In HH of Francis Baneau m 36 mulatto born SC.

CASTINO, MARY, 37, F, (--), M, SC, 430, 413, CHAS-. In HH of Francis Baneau m 36 mulatto born SC.

CASTINO, THEODORE, 12, M, (--), M, SC, 430, 413, CHAS-. In HH of Francis Baneau m 36 mulatto born SC.

CATTEL, MARY C., 30, F, (--), M, SC, 389, 362, CHAS*. In HH of Robert Cattel m 35 mulatto born SC.

CATTEL, ROBERT, 35, M, Drayman, M, SC, 389, 362, CHAS*.

CATTERTON, SUSAN, 10, F, (--), M, SC, 105, 105, COLL+. In HH of Amelia Diver f 60 mulatto born SC.

CHAGOL, JOHN, 29, M, (--), M, St. Domingo, 61, 55, CHAS+. In HH of Margaret Fancy f 65 mulatto born SC.

CHAMBERS, ANN, 24, F, (--), M, SC, 1160, 1139, CHAS%. In HH of Christiana Chambers f 23 mulatto born SC.

CHAMBERS, CHRISTIANA, 23, F, (--), M, SC, 1160, 1139, CHAS%.

CHAMBERS, ELLEN, 6, F, (--), M, SC, 1160, 1139, CHAS%. In HH of Christiana Chambers f 23 mulatto born SC.

CHAPMAN, BLUFORD, 7, M, (--), M, SC, 2092, 2099, EDGE. In HH of James Chapman m 40 mulatto born SC.

CHAPMAN, ELLISY, 90, F, (--), M, SC, 166, 166, CHAS%. In HH of Isaac

Perry m 30 black born SC.

CHAPMAN, JAMES, 40, M, Miller, M, SC, 2092, 2099, EDGE.

CHAPMAN, MARY ANN, 27, F, (--), M, SC, 2092, 2099, EDGE. In HH of James Chapman m 40 mulatto born SC.

CHAPMAN, SARAH JANE, 3, F, (--), M, SC, 139, 127, CHAS*. In HH of Patty Ashe f 100 black born SC.

CHAPMAN, SUSAN, 1, F, (--), M, SC, 2092, 2099, EDGE. In HH of James Chapman m 40 mulatto born SC.

CHAPMAN, THOS., 3, M, (--), M, SC, 2092, 2099, EDGE. In HH of James Chapman m 40 mulatto born SC.

CHAPMAN, VENUS, 30, F, (--), B, SC, 139, 127, CHAS*. In HH of Patty Ashe f 100 black born SC.

CHARLES, CECELIA, 32, F, (--), M, GA, 448, 431, CHAS-.

CHARONS, {BLANK}, 1, F, (--), M, SC, 1090, 1090, BARN. In HH of Len Charons m 40 mulatto born SC.

CHARONS, ELIZA, 14, F, (--), M, SC, 1090, 1090, BARN. In HH of Len Charons m 40 mulatto born SC.

CHARONS, FRANCES, 18, F, (--), M, SC, 1090, 1090, BARN. In HH of Len Charons m 40 mulatto born SC.

CHARONS, JOHN, 15, M, (--), M, SC, 1090, 1090, BARN. In HH of Len Charons m 40 mulatto born SC.

CHARONS, LEN, 40, M, Planter, M, SC, 1090, 1090, BARN.

CHARONS, LEN, 8, M, (--), M, SC, 1090, 1090, BARN. In HH of Len Charons m 40 mulatto born SC.

CHARONS, NANCY, 25, F, (--), M, SC, 1090, 1090, BARN. In HH of Len Charons m 40 mulatto born SC.

CHATTERS, BETSEY, 38, F, (--), M, SC, 22, 20, CHAS-. In HH of Owen Chatters m 40 mulatto born SC.

CHATTERS, HENRY, 4, M, (--), M, SC, 22, 20, CHAS-. In HH of Owen Chatters m 40 mulatto born SC.

CHATTERS, OWEN, 40, M, Drayman, M, SC, 22, 20, CHAS-.

CHATTERS, OWEN, 33, M, Servant, M, SC, 53, 63, CHAS. In HH of Henry Gourdin m 45 born SC.

CHATTERS, OWEN, 30, M, Laborer, B, SC, 330, 304, CHAS*. In HH of Mary Legard f 21 mulatto born SC.

CHATTERS, SARAH, 9, F, (--), M, SC, 22, 20, CHAS-. In HH of Owen Chatters m 40 mulatto born SC.

CHAVAS, ALBERT, 16, M, Laborer, M, SC, 664, 664, SUMT. In HH of Thos. Chavas m 46 black born SC.

CHAVAS, CALDWELL, 10, M, (--), M, SC, 664, 664, SUMT. In HH of Thos. Chavas m 46 black born SC.

CHAVAS, CAROLINE, 48, F, (--), B, SC, 665, 665, SUMT.

CHAVAS, ELIJAH, 6, M, (--), M, SC, 664, 664, SUMT. In HH of Thos. Chavas m 46 black born SC.?

CHAVAS, ELISHA, 6, M, (--), M, SC, 664, 664, SUMT. In HH of Thos. Chavas m 46 black born SC.?

CHAVAS, ELIZA, 8, F, (--), M, SC, 663, 663, SUMT. In HH of Wm. Chavas m 50 black born SC.

CHAVAS, ERVIN, 10, M, (--), M, SC, 663, 663, SUMT. In HH of Wm. Chavas m 50 black born SC.

CHAVAS, FRANKLIN, 0, M, (--), M, SC, 664, 664, SUMT. In HH of Thos. Chavas m 46 black born SC. Franklin age 2/12 yr.

CHAVAS, HARRIET, 8, F, (--), M, SC, 664, 664, SUMT. In HH of Thos. Chavas m 46 black born SC.

CHAVAS, JARED, 4, M, (--), M, SC, 664, 664, SUMT. In HH of Thos. Chavas m 46 black born SC.

CHAVAS, MAHALEY, 18, F, (--), M, SC, 664, 664, SUMT. In HH of Thos. Chavas m 46 black born SC.

CHAVAS, MARANDA, 21, F, (--), M, SC, 663, 663, SUMT. In HH of Wm. Chavas m 50 black born SC.

CHAVAS, MARY, 14, F, (--), M, SC, 664, 664, SUMT. In HH of Thos. Chavas m 46 black born SC.

CHAVAS, NELSON, 12, M, (--), M,

SC, 664, 664, SUMT. In HH of Thos. Chavas m 46 black born SC.

CHAVAS, THOS., 46, M, Planter, B, SC, 664, 664, SUMT.

CHAVAS, WM., 50, M, Planter, B, SC, 663, 663, SUMT.

CHAVAS, WM. O., 13, M, Laborer, M, SC, 665, 665, SUMT. In HH of Caroline Chavas f 48 black born SC.

CHAVAS, WORKEY, 5, M, (--), M, SC, 663, 663, SUMT. In HH of Wm. Chavas m 50 black born SC.

CHAVERS, ALFRED, 11, M, (--), M, SC, 346, 353, RICH+. In HH of Lorenzo Chavers m 38 mulatto born SC.

CHAVERS, ELIZABETH, 28, F, (--), M, SC, 346, 353, RICH+. In HH of Lorenzo Chavers m 38 mulatto born SC.

CHAVERS, ELIZABETH, 16, F, (--), M, SC, 611, 620, RICH+. In HH of John Chavers m 25 mulatto born SC.

CHAVERS, EPHRAIM, 30, M, Carpenter, M, SC, 721, 730, RICH+. In HH of Mary Chavers f 60 mulatto born SC.

CHAVERS, HOLLEY, 3, F, (--), M, SC, 333, 340, RICH+. In HH of John S. Chavers m 31 mulatto born SC.

CHAVERS, JESSIE, 5, F, (--), M, SC, 346, 353, RICH+. In HH of Lorenzo Chavers m 38 mulatto born SC.

CHAVERS, JOHN, 25, M, Laborer, M, SC, 611, 620, RICH+.

CHAVERS, JOHN, 5, M, (--), M, SC, 333, 340, RICH+. In HH of John S. Chavers m 31 mulatto born SC.

CHAVERS, JOHN L., 31, M, Planter, M, SC, 333, 340, RICH+.

CHAVERS, LORENZO, 38, M, Planter, M, SC, 346, 353, RICH+.

CHAVERS, LORENZO, 9, M, (--), M, SC, 346, 353, RICH+. In HH of Lorenzo Chavers m 38 mulatto born SC.

CHAVERS, MARCUS, 1, M, (--), M, SC, 333, 340, RICH+. In HH of John S. Chavers m 31 mulatto born SC.

CHAVERS, MARTHA, 35, F, (--), M, SC, 721, 730, RICH+. In HH of Mary Chavers f 60 mulatto born SC.

CHAVERS, MARY, 60, F, (--), M, SC, 721, 730, RICH+.

CHAVERS, MARY, 7, F, (--), M, SC, 346, 353, RICH+. In HH of Lorenzo Chavers m 38 mulatto born SC.

CHAVERS, NANCY, 65, F, (--), M, SC, 2095, 2102, EDGE.

CHAVERS, RANSOME, 8, M, (--), M, SC, 333, 340, RICH+. In HH of John S. Chavers m 31 mulatto born SC.

CHAVERS, SARAH, 3, F, (--), M, SC, 346, 353, RICH+. In HH of Lorenzo Chavers m 38 mulatto born SC.

CHAVERS, SOPHIA, 50, F, (--), M, SC, 351, 358, RICH+.

CHAVERS, SUSAN, 28, F, (--), M, SC, 333, 340, RICH+. In HH of John S. Chavers m 31 mulatto born SC.

CHAVERS, SUSAN, 6, F, (--), M, SC, 333, 340, RICH+. In HH of John S. Chavers m 31 mulatto born SC.

CHAVERS, WILLIAM, 10, M, (--), M, SC, 333, 340, RICH+. In HH of John S. Chavers m 31 mulatto born SC.

CHAVES, SALLY, 55, F, (--), B, SC, 1952, 1958, EDGE.

CHAVIS, CALVIN, 22, M, None, M, SC, 1161, 1161, LEX.

CHAVIS, JAMES, 35, M, Laborer, M, SC, 488, 488, BEAU-.

CHAVIS, JAMES, 1, M, (--), M, SC, 488, 488, BEAU-. In HH of James Chavis m 35 mulatto born SC.

CHAVIS, ROBT., 66, M, Laborer, B, NC, 673, 673, MARL.

CHAVIS, SUSAN, 25, F, (--), M, SC, 488, 488, BEAU-. In HH of James Chavis m 35 mulatto born SC.

CHAVOUS, DAVID, 28, M, Planter, M, SC, 1134, 1134, BARN.

CHAVOUS, GEORGE, 65, M, (--), M, SC, 1134, 1134, BARN. In HH of David Chavous m 28 mulatto born SC.

CHAVOUS, ZED, 65, M, Planter, M, SC, 1135, 1135, BARN.

CHAVUS, ANN E., 4, F, (--), M, SC, 1950, 1956, EDGE. In HH of Brrry {sic} Chavis m 35 mulatto born SC.

43

CHAVUS, BRRRY {sic}, 35, M, Laborer, M, SC, 1950, 1956, EDGE.

CHAVUS, CASPER, 25, M, Farmer, M, SC, 1808, 1814, EDGE.

CHAVUS, DOLPHN, 5, M, (--), M, SC, 1810, 1814, EDGE. In HH of Frederick Chavus m 62 mulatto born SC.

CHAVUS, ELIZ., 14, F, (--), M, SC, 1810, 1814, EDGE. In HH of Frederick Chavus m 62 mulatto born SC.

CHAVUS, ELIZABETH, 27, F, (--), M, SC, 1810, 1814, EDGE. In HH of Frederick Chavus m 62 mulatto born SC.

CHAVUS, FREDERICK, 62, M, Farmer, M, SC, 1810, 1814, EDGE.

CHAVUS, GIDEON, 52, M, Laborer, B, SC, 1819, 1825, EDGE. In HH of A.J. Dow m 45 born Ireland {sic}.

CHAVUS, JERNAIA, 32, F, (--), M, SC, 1810, 1814, EDGE. In HH of Frederick Chavus m 62 mulatto born SC.

CHAVUS, LEWIS, 30, M, Laborer, M, SC, 1810, 1814, EDGE. In HH of Frederick Chavus m 62 mulatto born SC.

CHAVUS, MARTHA, 35, F, (--), M, SC, 1950, 1956, EDGE. In HH of Brrry {sic} Chavis m 35 mulatto born SC.

CHAVUS, MARY, 25, F, (--), M, SC, 1808, 1814, EDGE. In HH of Casper Chuvas m 25 mulatto born SC.

CHAVUS, MILLIDGE, 13, M, (--), M, SC, 1810, 1814, EDGE. In HH of Frederick Chavus m 62 mulatto born SC.

CHAVUS, NANCY, 21, F, (--), M, SC, 1810, 1814, EDGE. In HH of Frederick Chavus m 62 mulatto born SC.

CHAVUS, PICKINS, 16, M, (--), M, SC, 1810, 1814, EDGE. In HH of Frederick Chavus m 62 mulatto born SC.

CHAVUS, SARAH, 7, F, (--), M, SC, 1810, 1814, EDGE. In HH of Frederick Chavus m 62 mulatto born SC.

CHAVUS, WM., 27, M, Laborer, M, SC, 1810, 1814, EDGE. In HH of Frederick Chavus m 62 mulatto born SC.

CHENEY, WM. H., 28, M, Carpenter, M, SC, 837, 818, CHAS%.

CHENUSA?, MAT, 25, M, (--), B, SC, 2074, 2078, EDGE. In HH of Thomas Ceaty m 30 born SC.

CHESNUT, ANN, 7, F, (--), M, SC, 906, 906, KERS. In HH of Susan Chesnut f 28 mulatto born SC.

CHESNUT, EDWD., 0, M, (--), M, SC, 906, 906, KERS. In HH of Susan Chesnut f 28 mulatto born SC. Edwd. Chesnut 8/12 yr.

CHESNUT, JOSEPH, 3, M, (--), M, SC, 906, 906, KERS. In HH of Susan Chesnut f 28 mulatto born SC.

CHESNUT, PHEBE, 54, F, (--), B, SC, 164, 164, CHES. In HH of J.B. Wylie m 45 born SC.

CHESNUT, SUSAN, 28, F, (--), M, SC, 906, 906, KERS.

CHESTNUT, CALVIN, 5, M, (--), B, SC, 165, 165, CHES. In HH of D.C. McWilliams m 31 born SC.

CHESTNUT, ELI, 10, M, (--), B, SC, 212, 212, CHES. In HH of E.A. McCaw m 29 born SC.

CHESTNUT, HARRIET, 34, F, (--), B, SC, 165, 165, CHES. In HH of D.C. McWilliams m 31 born SC.

CHESTNUT, JOHN, 14, M, (--), B, SC, 207, 207, CHES. In HH of W.T. Bigham m 28 born SC.

CHESTNUT, OSMOND, 1, M, (--), B, SC, 165, 165, CHES. In HH of D.C. McWilliams m 31 born SC.

CHESTNUT, RICHARD, 8, M, (--), B, SC, 165, 165, CHES. In HH of D.C. McWilliams m 31 born SC.

CHEVES, ELIZABETH, 27, F, (--), M, SC, 553, 536, CHAS-. In HH of Laura Bruch {sic} f 30 mulatto born SC.

CHICHISTER, ELLEN, 35, F, (--), M, SC, 435, 432, CHAS%.

CHICHISTER, FRANCES, 14, F, (--), M, SC, 435, 432, CHAS%. In HH of Ellen Chichister f 35 mulatto born SC.

CHICHISTER, JOHN, 32, M, Millwright, M, SC, 435, 432, CHAS%. In HH of Ellen Chichister f 35 mulatto born SC.

CHICHISTER, JULIANA, 9, F, (--), M, SC, 435, 432, CHAS%. In HH of Ellen Chichister f 35 mulatto born SC.

CHICHISTER, JULIET, 12, F, (--), M, SC, 435, 432, CHAS%. In HH of Ellen Chichister f 35 mulatto born SC.

CHICHISTER, THEADOR, 6, M, (--), M, SC, 435, 432, CHAS%. In HH of Ellen Chichister f 35 mulatto born SC.

CHISOLM, ANDREW, 30, M, Planter, M, SC, 1132, 1132, BARN.

CHISOLM, BETSY, 30, F, (--), M, SC, 1132, 1132, BARN. In HH of Andrew Chisolm m 30 mulatto born SC.

CHISOLM, EDMUND, 14, M, (--), M, SC, 787, 745, CHAS+. In HH of William Chisolm m 16 mulatto born SC.

CHISOLM, ELIZABETH, 35, F, (--), M, SC, 787, 745, CHAS+. In HH of William Chisolm m 16 mulatto born SC.

CHISOLM, FRANCES, 55, F, (--), M, SC, 1132, 1132, BARN. In HH of Andrew Chisolm m 30 mulatto born SC.

CHISOLM, HANNAH, 7, F, (--), M, SC, 56, 55, CHAS*. In HH of Sarah Chisolm f 25 mulatto born SC.

CHISOLM, JINNY, 60, F, (--), B, SC, 1132, 1132, BARN. In HH of Andrew Chisolm m 30 mulatto born SC.

CHISOLM, MARY, 3, F, (--), M, SC, 1132, 1132, BARN. In HH of Andrew Chisolm m 30 mulatto born SC.

CHISOLM, MORTIMORE, 12, M, (--), M, SC, 787, 745, CHAS+. In HH of William Chisolm m 16 mulatto born SC.

CHISOLM, SARAH, 24, F, (--), M, SC, 56, 55, CHAS*.

CHISOLM, SARAH, 9, F, (--), M, SC, 1132, 1132, BARN. In HH of Andrew Chisolm m 30 mulatto born SC.

CHISOLM, THADDEUS, 9, M, (--), M, SC, 787, 745, CHAS+. In HH of William Chisolm m 16 mulatto born SC.

CHISOLM, . WILLIAM, 16, M, Bootmaker, M, SC, 787, 745, CHAS+.

CHISOLM, WILLIAM, 1, M, (--), M, SC, 56, 55, CHAS*. In HH of Sarah Chisolm f 25 mulatto born SC.

CHISOLM, WM., 6, M, (--), M, SC, 1132, 1132, BARN. In HH of Andrew Chisolm m 30 mulatto born SC.

CHISTMAS, A., 45, M, Miller, M, SC, 870, 870, CHES.

CHISTMAS, GEORGE, 0, M, (--), B, SC, 870, 870, CHES. In HH of A. Chistmas m 45 Mulatto born SC. George Chistmas 3/12 yr.

CHISTMAS, JOHN, 14, M, (--), B, SC, 870, 870, CHES. In HH of A. Chistmas m 45 Mulatto born SC.

CHISTMAS, MARY, 12, F, (--), B, SC, 870, 870, CHES. In HH of A. Chistmas m 45 Mulatto born SC.

CHISTMAS, T., 35, F, (--), B, SC, 870, 870, CHES. In HH of A. Chistmas m 45 Mulatto born SC.

CHISTMAS, WILLIAM, 8, M, (--), B, SC, 870, 870, CHES. In HH of A. Chistmas m 45 Mulatto born SC.

CHOATE, GEORGIANA, 19, F, (--), M, FL, 215, 201, CHAS-. In HH of Laura Purse f 21 mulatto born SC.

CHOING, AMANDA, 12, F, (--), M, SC, 1124, 1102, CHAS%. In HH of Louisa Johnson f 53 mulatto born SC.

CHOING, JANE, 2, F, (--), M, SC, 1124, 1102, CHAS%. In HH of Louisa Johnson f 53 mulatto born SC.

CHOING, LONORA, 8, F, (--), M, SC, 1124, 1102, CHAS%. In HH of Louisa Johnson f 53 mulatto born SC.

CHOING, SUSAN, 29, F, (--), M, SC, 1124, 1102, CHAS%. In HH of Louisa Johnson f 53 mulatto born SC.

CHOING, THOMAS, 30, M, Tailor, M, SC, 1124, 1102, CHAS%. In HH of Louisa Johnson f 53 mulatto born SC.

CHOING, USEBIA, 6, F, (--), M, SC, 1124, 1102, CHAS%. In HH of Louisa Johnson f 53 mulatto born SC.

CHOW, CATHERANE, 4, F, (--), M, SC, 1227, 1206, CHAS%. In HH of Thomas D. Condy m 52 born SC.

CHOW, CORNELIA, 18, F, (--), M, SC, 1227, 1206, CHAS%. In HH of Thomas D. Condy m 52 born SC.

CHOW, THEODORE P., 2, M, (--), M, SC, 1227, 1206, CHAS%. In HH of Thomas D. Condy m 52 born SC.

CHOW, THEOPHILUS, 5, M, (--), M, SC, 1227, 1206, CHAS%. In HH of

Thomas D. Condy m 52 born SC.

CHOW, VENIS, 6, F, (--), M, SC, 1227, 1206, CHAS%. In HH of Thomas D. Condy m 52 born SC.

CHRISTIE, ELVIRA, 49, F, (--), B, SC, 197, 197, NEWB.

CHRISTIE, ELVIRA, 6, F, (--), B, SC, 197, 197, NEWB. In HH of Elvira Christie f 49 black born SC.

CLAGGETT, EDMUND, 2, M, (--), M, GA, 448, 431, CHAS-. In HH of Cecelia Charles f 32 mulatto born GA.

CLAGGETT, EMMING, 10, F, (--), M, GA, 448, 431, CHAS-. In HH of Cecelia Charles f 32 mulatto born GA.

CLAGGETT, MARY, 4, F, (--), M, GA, 448, 431, CHAS-. In HH of Cecelia Charles f 32 mulatto born GA.

CLAGGETT, WILLIAM, 8, M, (--), M, GA, 448, 431, CHAS-. In HH of Cecelia Charles f 32 mulatto born GA.

CLANCEY, CAROLINE, 40, F, Pastry cook, M, Cuba, 204, 187, CHAS*.

CLARK, AARON, 56, M, Laborer, M, SC, 221, 221, MARL.

CLARK, AARON, 30, M, Laborer, M, SC, 342, 342, MARL.

CLARK, ADALINE, 15, F, (--), M, SC, 221, 221, MARL. In HH of Aaron Clark m 56 mulatto born SC.

CLARK, ALEXANDER, 7, M, (--), M, SC, 19, 19, CHAS~. In HH of James Busby, m 50 mulatto born SC.

CLARK, ANN, 23, F, (--), M, SC, 221, 221, MARL. In HH of Aaron Clark m 56 mulatto born SC.

CLARK, ANNA, 15, F, (--), M, SC, 70, 62, CHAS+. In HH of Charles Clark m 60 born NY.

CLARK, ARCHD., 1, M, (--), M, SC, 221, 221, MARL. In HH of Aaron Clark m 56 mulatto born SC.

CLARK, ASA, 5, M, (--), M, SC, 342, 342, MARL. IN HH of Aaron Clark m 30 mulatto born SC.

CLARK, ELIZABETH, 18, F, (--), M, SC, 70, 62, CHAS+. In HH of Charles Clark m 60 born NY.

CLARK, ELIZABETH, 6, F, (--), M, SC, 885, 885, MARL. In HH of Reuben Clark m 46 mulatto born SC.

CLARK, ELLISON, 8, M, (--), M, SC, 221, 221, MARL. In HH of Aaron Clark m 56 mulatto born SC.

CLARK, EVANDER, 4, M, (--), B, SC, 200, 200, MARL. IN HH of Reddin Clark m 29 black born NC.

CLARK, HANNAH, 60, M, (--), M, SC, 343, 343, MARL.

CLARK, HANNAH, 7, F, (--), M, SC, 343, 343, MARL. In HH of Hannah Clark f 60 mulatto born SC.

CLARK, HENRY, 27, M, Tinner, M, SC, 70, 62, CHAS+. In HH of Charles Clark m 60 born NY.

CLARK, HUGH, 20, M, (--), M, SC, 343, 343, MARL. In HH of Hannah Clark f 60 mulatto born SC.

CLARK, ISAAC, 35, M, Farmer, M, SC, 1306, 1311, MAR.

CLARK, JAMES, 13, M, (--), M, SC, 221, 221, MARL. In HH of Aaron Clark m 56 mulatto born SC.

CLARK, JENNEY, 86, F, None, M, SC, 885, 885, MARL. In HH of Reuben Clark m 46 mulatto born SC. Age of Jenny Clark {smeared}, possibly 86.

CLARK, JOHN, 25, M, Tinner, M, SC, 70, 62, CHAS+. In HH of Charles Clark m 60 born NY.

CLARK, JOHN, 8, M, (--), M, SC, 1123, 1128, MAR. In HH of Mary Clark f 60 mulatto born SC.

CLARK, JOHN, 1, M, (--), M, SC, 342, 342, MARL. IN HH of Aaron Clark m 30 mulatto born SC.

CLARK, JOHNSON, 25, M, Laborer, M, SC, 221, 221, MARL. In HH of Aaron Clark m 56 mulatto born SC.

CLARK, JOSEPH, 15, M, (--), M, SC, 1306, 1311, MAR. In HH of Isaac Clark m 35 mulatto born SC.

CLARK, JOSEPH, 3, M, (--), M, SC, 342, 342, MARL. IN HH of Aaron Clark m 30 mulatto born SC.

CLARK, MARGARET, 2, F, (--), B, SC, 200, 200, MARL. IN HH of Reddin

Clark m 29 black born NC.

CLARK, MARY, 60, F, (--), M, SC, 1123, 1128, MAR.

CLARK, MARY, 35, F, (--), M, SC, 885, 885, MARL. In HH of Reuben Clark m 46 mulatto born SC.

CLARK, MARY, 8, F, (--), M, SC, 885, 885, MARL. In HH of Reuben Clark m 46 mulatto born SC.

CLARK, MASTIN, 4, M, (--), M, SC, 221, 221, MARL. In HH of Aaron Clark m 56 mulatto born SC.

CLARK, MINTA, 30, F, (--), M, SC, 342, 342, MARL. IN HH of Aaron Clark m 30 mulatto born SC.

CLARK, NANCY, 24, F, (--), B, NC, 200, 200, MARL. In HH of Riddin Clark m 29 B, born in NC.

CLARK, NANCY, 17, F, (--), M, SC, 343, 343, MARL. In HH of Hannah Clark f 60 mulatto born SC.

CLARK, NANCY, 14, F, (--), M, SC, 885, 885, MARL. In HH of Reuben Clark m 46 mulatto born SC.

CLARK, NIRGE ?, 11, M, (--), M, SC, 343, 343, MARL. In HH of Hannah Clark f 60 mulatto born SC.

CLARK, POLLY, 28, F, (--), M, SC, 221, 221, MARL. In HH of Aaron Clark m 56 mulatto born SC.

CLARK, REUBEN, 46, M, Laborer, M, SC, 885, 885, MARL.

CLARK, RHODA, 2, F, (--), M, SC, 885, 885, MARL. In HH of Reuben Clark m 46 mulatto born SC.

CLARK, RIDDIN, 29, M, Laborer, B, NC, 200, 200, MARL.

CLARK, ROBT., 17, M, (--), M, NC, 852, 852, HORR. In HH of Tho. Sessions m 43 born SC.

CLARK, SARAH, 40, F, (--), M, SC, 1123, 1128, MAR. In HH of Mary Clark f 60 mulatto born SC.

CLARK, WASHINGTON, 12, M, (--), M, SC, 42, 42, GEOR*. In HH of John Booth m 45 born SC.

CLARK, ZEYLPHA, 40, F, (--), M, SC, 221, 221, MARL. In HH of Aaron Clark m 56 mulatto born SC.

CLARKE, CATHERINE, 3, F, (--), M, SC, 70, 70, CHAS%. In HH of John Clarke m 30 mulatto born SC.

CLARKE, JOHN, 30, M, Porter, M, SC, 70, 70, CHAS%.

CLARKE, MARY, 32, F, (--), M, SC, 70, 70, CHAS%. In HH of John Clarke m 30 mulatto born SC.

CLATOR, HESTER, 30, F, (--), M, SC, 97, 98, MAR. In HH of Avant Williams m 60 born SC. Hester Clator born Marion, SC.

CLATOR, JANE, 1, F, (--), M, SC, 97, 98, MAR. In HH of Avant Williams m 60 born SC. Jane Clator born Marion, SC.

CLAYTON, ADAM, 84, M, None, M, SC, 504, 454, CHAS.

CLAYTON, ELIZABETH, 20, F, (--), M, SC, 504, 454, CHAS. In HH of Adam Clayton m 84 mulatto born SC.

CLAYTON, JOHN, 22, M, Fisherman, M, SC, 504, 454, CHAS. In HH of Adam Clayton m 84 mulatto born SC.

CLAYTON, MARY, 15, F, (--), M, SC, 504, 454, CHAS. In HH of Adam Clayton m 84 mulatto born SC.

CLEMENS, JNO., 20, M, Laborer, M, SC, 289, 289, CHAS3. In HH of Ann Haggard f 36 born SC.

CLEVELAND, ALONZO, 4, M, (--), M, SC, 708, 688, CHAS-. In HH of Martha Cleveland f 29 mulatto born SC.

CLEVELAND, AMELIA, 12, M, (--), B, SC, 1040, 1017, CHAS-. In HH of Paul Cleveland m 48 black born SC.

CLEVELAND, ARTHUR, 16, M, (--), M, SC, 358, 358, CHAS%. In HH of Eliza Cleveland f 35 mulatto born SC.

CLEVELAND, CATHERINE, 55, F, (--), B, SC, 366, 366, CHAS%.

CLEVELAND, CHARLOTTE, 45, F, (--), B, SC, 1040, 1017, CHAS-. In HH of Paul Cleveland m 48 black born SC.

CLEVELAND, CHRISTIANA, 50, F, (--), M, SC, 264, 232, CHAS. In HH of James Ogier m 70 mulatto born SC.

CLEVELAND, CUFF, 2, M, (--), B, SC, 40, 40, CHAS2. In HH of James

Cleveland m 51 black born SC.

CLEVELAND, DIANA, 19, F, (--), B, SC, 1040, 1017, CHAS-. In HH of Paul Cleveland m 48 black born SC.

CLEVELAND, EDWARD, 12, M, (--), M, SC, 405, 378, CHAS*. In HH of Rebecca Cleveland f 28 mulatto born SC.

CLEVELAND, ELIZA, 35, F, (--), M, SC, 358, 358, CHAS%.

CLEVELAND, HARRIET, 2, F, (--), M, SC, 708, 688, CHAS-. In HH of Martha Cleveland f 29 mulatto born SC.

CLEVELAND, HENRY, 22, M, Carpenter, M, SC, 264, 232, CHAS. In HH of James Ogier m 70 mulatto born SC.

CLEVELAND, ISAAC, 35, M, Carpenter, M, SC, 405, 378, CHAS*. In HH of Rebecca Cleveland f 28 mulatto born SC.

CLEVELAND, JACK, 40, M, (--), M, SC, 260, 260, KERS. In HH of J.F. Sutherland m 35 born NY.

CLEVELAND, JACK, 35, M, Brick maker, B, SC, 129, 129, KERS.

CLEVELAND, JACK, 7, M, (--), B, SC, 40, 40, CHAS2. In HH of James Cleveland m 51 black born SC.

CLEVELAND, JAMES, 51, M, Farmer, B, SC, 40, 40, CHAS2.

CLEVELAND, JAMES, 8, M, (--), B, SC, 40, 40, CHAS2. In HH of James Cleveland m 51 black born SC.

CLEVELAND, JOE, 16, M, (--), B, SC, 40, 40, CHAS2. In HH of James Cleveland m 51 black born SC.

CLEVELAND, JOHN, 60, M, Fisherman, M, SC, 264, 232, CHAS. In HH of James Ogier m 70 mulatto born SC.

CLEVELAND, JOHN, 16, M, Cooper, B, SC, 1040, 1017, CHAS-. In HH of Paul Cleveland m 48 black born SC.

CLEVELAND, JOHN, 9, M, (--), M, SC, 358, 358, CHAS%. In HH of Eliza Cleveland f 35 mulatto born SC.

CLEVELAND, JULIET, 6, F, (--), M, SC, 708, 688, CHAS-. In HH of Martha

Cleveland f 29 mulatto born SC.

CLEVELAND, KATE, 95, F, (--), B, Africa, 40, 40, CHAS2. In HH of James Cleveland m 51 black born SC.

CLEVELAND, KATE, 3, F, (--), B, SC, 40, 40, CHAS2. In HH of James Cleveland m 51 black born SC.

CLEVELAND, L.C., 36, F, (--), M, SC, 129, 129, KERS. In HH of Jack Cleveland m 35 mulatto born SC.

CLEVELAND, MARTHA, 29, F, (--), M, SC, 708, 688, CHAS-.

CLEVELAND, MARTHA, 17, F, (--), B, SC, 40, 40, CHAS2. In HH of James Cleveland m 51 black born SC.

CLEVELAND, MARY, 14, F, (--), M, SC, 358, 358, CHAS%. In HH of Eliza Cleveland f 35 mulatto born SC.

CLEVELAND, PAUL, 48, M, (--), B, SC, 1040, 1017, CHAS-.

CLEVELAND, REBECCA, 28, F, (--), M, SC, 405, 378, CHAS*.

CLEVELAND, SAM, 3, M, (--), B, SC, 40, 40, CHAS2. In HH of James Cleveland m 51 black born SC.

CLEVELAND, SUSAN, 36, F, (--), B, SC, 40, 40, CHAS2. In HH of James Cleveland m 51 black born SC.

CLEVELAND, SUSAN, 14, F, (--), B, SC, 40, 40, CHAS2. In HH of James Cleveland m 51 black born SC.

CLEVELAND, WILLIAM, 6, M, (--), B, SC, 40, 40, CHAS2. In HH of James Cleveland m 51 black born SC.

CLIFT, MENDRUS, 39, M, Ostler, B, SC, 676, 634, CHAS+. In HH of F. Devinier m 30 mulatto born SC.

CLINE, BENJAMIN, 7, M, (--), B, SC, 645, 645, CHFD. In HH of John Cline m 54 black born SC.

CLINE, CATHERINE, 10, F, (--), M, SC, 332, 339, RICH+. page out of order.

CLINE, CYNTHIA A., 5, F, (--), M, SC, 130, 133, RICH+. In HH of Robert Cline m 27 mulatto born SC.

CLINE, FRANCES, 0, F, (--), M, SC, 332, 339, RICH+. page out of order. Francis Cline 4/12 yr.

CLINE, JANE, 2, F, (--), M, SC, 332, 339, RICH+. page out of order.

CLINE, JOHN, 59, M, Laborer, M, SC, 131, 134, RICH+.

CLINE, JOHN, 54, M, Farmer, B, SC, 645, 645, CHFD.

CLINE, JOHN, 11, M, (--), B, SC, 645, 645, CHFD. In HH of John Cline m 54 black born SC.

CLINE, JOHN J., 12, M, (--), M, SC, 332, 339, RICH+. page out of order.

CLINE, LEANA, 10, F, (--), B, SC, 402, 402, CHFD. In HH of Jerry Farbs m 35 mulatto born SC.

CLINE, LEANA, 9, F, (--), B, SC, 645, 645, CHFD. In HH of John Cline m 54 black born SC.

CLINE, MARTHA, 4, F, (--), M, SC, . 332, 339, RICH+. page out of order.

CLINE, MARTHA, 3, F, (--), M, SC, 130, 133, RICH+. In HH of Robert Cline m 27 mulatto born SC.

CLINE, MARY, 7, F, (--), M, SC, 130, 133, RICH+. In HH of Robert Cline m 27 mulatto born SC.

CLINE, POLLY, 20, F, (--), B, SC, 645, 645, CHFD. In HH of John Cline m 54 black born SC.

CLINE, ROBERT, 27, M, Planter, M, SC, 130, 133, RICH+.

CLINE, SALLY, 18, F, (--), B, SC, 645, 645, CHFD. In HH of John Cline m 54 black born SC.

CLINE, SARAH, 33, F, (--), M, SC, 130, 133, RICH+. In HH of Robert Cline m 27 mulatto born SC.

CLINE, SARAH, 7, F, (--), M, SC, 332, 339, RICH+. page out of order.

CLINE, TIM, 13, M, (--), B, SC, 645, 645, CHFD. In HH of John Cline m 54 black born SC.

CLOUD, HANNAH, 80, F, (--), B, Unknown, 82, 82, CHES. In HH of Wm. M. Hemphill m 63 born SC.

COATES, CAROLINE, 7, F, (--), M, SC, 311, 311, EDGE*. In HH of Harriet Coates f 37 mulatto born SC.

COATES, HARRIET, 37, F, (--), M, SC, 311, 311, EDGE*.

COATES, HARRIET, 4, F, (--), M, SC, 311, 311, EDGE*. In HH of Harriet Coates f 37 mulatto born SC.

COATES, NANCY, 2, F, (--), M, SC, 311, 311, EDGE*. In HH of Harriet Coates f 37 mulatto born SC.

COATES, SAVANNAH, 0, F, (--), M, SC, 311, 311, EDGE*. In HH of Harriet Coates f 37 mulatto born SC. Savannah Coates 3/12 yr.

COATS, ANTHONY, 70, M, Farmer, B, VA, 584, 585, AND*.

COBB, JINNY, 60, F, (--), M, SC, 307, 307, EDGE.

COBLE, G.B., 15, M, Laborer, B, SC, 445, 445, NEWB. In HH of Nancy Coble f 44 black born SC.

COBLE, H.C., 13, M, (--), B, SC, 445, 445, NEWB. In HH of Nancy Coble f 44 black born SC.

COBLE, J.Y., 20, M, Laborer, B, SC, 445, 445, NEWB. In HH of Nancy Coble f 44 black born SC.

COBLE, MARY ANN, 9, F, (--), B, SC, 445, 445, NEWB. In HH of Nancy Coble f 44 black born SC.

COBLE, NANCY, 44, F, (--), B, SC, 445, 445, NEWB.

COBLER, YOUNG, 21, M, Farmer, B, SC, 1254, 1254, NEWB. In HH of Abraham Moore m 55 born SC.

COCHRAN, ARTHUR, 16, M, Carpenter, M, SC, 792, 775, CHAS%. In HH of Thomas Cochran m 49 mulatto born SC.

COCHRAN, CHLOE, 65, F, (--), B, SC, 460, 418, CHAS+. In HH of Susan Williams f 60 black born SC.

COCHRAN, ELIZA, 47, F, (--), M, SC, 269, 237, CHAS. In HH of Conrad Roge m 56 born Bermuda.

COCHRAN, ELIZABETH, 46, F, (--), M, SC, 792, 775, CHAS%. In HH of Thomas Cochran m 49 mulatto born SC.

COCHRAN, STEPHEN, 46, M, Carpenter, M, SC, 8, 8, CHAS. In HH of Caroline Y. Trotto f 40 born SC.

COCHRAN, THOMAS, 49, M,

Carpenter, M, SC, 792, 775, CHAS%.

COCHRAN, VIRGINIA, 13, F, (--), M, SC, 792, 775, CHAS%. In HH of Thomas Cochran m 49 mulatto born SC.

COCKRAN MITCHEL, 0, M, (--), B, ?, 5, 5, BEAU#. In HH of James Cockran m 27 black. Mitchel Cockran 6/12 yr.

COCKRAN, AMELIA, 23, F, (--), B, ?, 5, 5, BEAU#. In HH of James Cockran m 27 black.

COCKRAN, ANDREW, 21, M, (--), B, ?, 5, 5, BEAU#. In HH of James Cockran m 27 black. Mitchel Cockran 6/12 yr.

COCKRAN, ANN, 20, F, (--), B, ?, 6, 6, BEAU#. In HH of Charles Cockran m 26 black.

COCKRAN, CHARLES, 26, M, (--), B, ?, 6, 6, BEAU#.

COCKRAN, JAMES, 27, M, (--), B, ?, 5, 5, BEAU#.

COCKRAN, JOHN, 23, M, (--), B, ?, 6, 6, BEAU#. In HH of Charles Cockran m 26 black.

COCKRAN, JOSHUA, 3, M, (--), B, ?, 5, 5, BEAU#. In HH of James Cockran m 27 black.

COCKRAN, MARGARET, 57, F, (--), B, ?, 6, 6, BEAU#. In HH of Charles Cockran m 26 black.

COCKRAN, MARGARET, 1, F, (--), B, ?, 6, 6, BEAU#. In HH of Charles Cockran m 26 black.

COCKRAN, THOMAS, 20, M, (--), B, ?, 4, 4, BEAU#. In HH of Charles Jackson m 34 black.

COGDELL, SARAH, 30, F, (--), M, SC, 15, 18, CHAS.

COHEN, ADALINE, 10, F, (--), M, SC, 438, 438, BEAU-. In HH of Sheldon Cohen m 38 mulatto born SC.

COHEN, ALLISON, 14, F, (--), M, SC, 438, 438, BEAU-. In HH of Sheldon Cohen m 38 mulatto born SC.

COHEN, ARTHUR P., 22, M, Laborer, M, SC, 451, 451, BEAU-.

COHEN, BARTLEY, 40, M, Laborer, M, SC, 480, 480, BEAU-.

COHEN, ELIAS, 21, M, Laborer, M,

SC, 438, 438, BEAU-. In HH of Sheldon Cohen m 38 mulatto born SC.

COHEN, ELIZA, 6, F, (--), M, SC, 480, 480, BEAU-. In HH of Bartley Cohen m 40 mulatto born SC.

COHEN, ELIZABETH, 40, F, (--), M, SC, 480, 480, BEAU-. In HH of Bartley Cohen m 40 mulatto born SC.

COHEN, JOHN, 16, M, Laborer, M, SC, 438, 438, BEAU-. In HH of Sheldon Cohen m 38 mulatto born SC.

COHEN, LAURA, 5, F, (--), M, SC, 438, 438, BEAU-. In HH of Sheldon Cohen m 38 mulatto born SC.

COHEN, LAVINA, 7, F, (--), M, SC, 438, 438, BEAU-. In HH of Sheldon Cohen m 38 mulatto born SC.

COHEN, LEVINIA, 45, F, (--), M, SC, 438, 438, BEAU-. In HH of Sheldon Cohen m 38 mulatto born SC.

COHEN, LEWIS, 12, M, (--), M, SC, 480, 480, BEAU-. In HH of Bartley Cohen m 40 mulatto born SC.

COHEN, MARTIN, 12, M, (--), M, SC, 438, 438, BEAU-. In HH of Sheldon Cohen m 38 mulatto born SC.

COHEN, MARY, 10, F, (--), M, SC, 480, 480, BEAU-. In HH of Bartley Cohen m 40 mulatto born SC.

COHEN, PEARSON, 8, M, (--), M, SC, 438, 438, BEAU-. In HH of Sheldon Cohen m 38 mulatto born SC.

COHEN, SAMUEL, 4, M, (--), M, SC, 451, 451, BEAU-. In HH of Arthur P. Cohen m 22 mulatto born SC.

COHEN, SHELDON, 38, M, Farmer, M, SC, 438, 438, BEAU-.

COHEN, SHELDON, 18, M, Laborer, M, SC, 438, 438, BEAU-. In HH of Sheldon Cohen m 38 mulatto born SC.

COHEN, TAMER, 35, F, (--), M, SC, 451, 451, BEAU-. In HH of Arthur P. Cohen m 22 mulatto born SC.

COLB, LINNY, 56, F, (--), M, SC, 87, 87, LAU. IN HH of Thomas Colb m 55 mulatto born SC.

COLB, THOMAS, 55, M, Farmer, M, SC, 87, 87, LAU.

COLE, AMANDA, 11, F, (--), B, SC,

214, 214, ABB. In HH of Mary Cannon 45 born SC.

COLE, ANNET, 40, F, (--), M, SC, 206, 192, CHAS-. In HH of Philip Benjamin m 69 born Nevis {sic}.

COLE, CHARLES, 3, M, (--), M, SC, 206, 192, CHAS-. In HH of Philip Benjamin m 69 born Nevis {sic}.

COLE, CHARLOTTE, 16, F, (--), M, SC, 206, 192, CHAS-. In HH of Philip Benjamin m 69 born Nevis {sic}.

COLE, DANIEL, 15, M, Hireling, B, SC, 214, 214, ABB. In HH of Mary Cannon 45 born SC.

COLE, EDWD., 2, M, (--), B, SC, 886, 886, KERS. In HH of Nancy Cole f 30 black born SC.

COLE, JOHN, 3, M, (--), B, SC, 214, 214, ABB. In HH of Mary Cannon 45 born SC.

COLE, MARY, 7, F, (--), B, SC, 886, 886, KERS. In HH of Nancy Cole f 30 black born SC.

COLE, MITCHAL, 8, M, (--), B, SC, 214, 214, ABB. In HH of Mary Cannon 45 born SC.

COLE, MILES, 5, M, (--), B, SC, 214, 214, ABB. In HH of Mary Cannon 45 born SC.

COLE, NANCY, 30, F, (--), B, SC, 886, 886, KERS.

COLE, NANCY, 22, F, (--), B, SC, 118, 118, KERS. In HH of Harriet Hammond f 20 black born SC.

COLE, SUSAN, 1, F, (--), M, SC, 206, 192, CHAS-. In HH of Philip Benjamin m 69 born Nevis {sic}.

COLE, WILLIAM, 29, M, (--), B, SC, 135, 135, CHAS^. In HH of Catherine Conyers f 24 black born SC.

COLE, WINNY, 13, F, (--), B, SC, 214, 214, ABB. In HH of Mary Cannon 45 born SC.

COLEMAN, CATO, 7, M, Farmer, B, SC, 179, 179, ABB.

COLEMAN, DAVID, 45, M, (--), M, SC, 1111, 1111, BARN.

COLEMAN, JOHN, 26, M, Raft hand, M, SC, 1110, 1110, BARN.

COLEMAN, JUDY, 56, F, (--), B, SC, 179, 179, ABB. In HH of Cato Coleman m black age 7 {sic} born SC.

COLEMAN, KITTY, 25, F, Raft hand, M, SC, 1110, 1110, BARN. In HH of John Coleman m 26 mulatto born SC.

COLEMAN, SUCKEY, 50, F, (--), M, SC, 1111, 1111, BARN. In HH of David Coleman m 45 mulatto born SC.

COLLINS, ANN, 14, F, (--), M, SC, 70, 70, GEOR*. In HH of R.M. Collins m 51 mulatto born SC.

COLLINS, CHARLOTTE, 45, F, (--), M, SC, 29, 28, CHAS&.

COLLINS, ELIZABETH, 50, F, (--), M, SC, 70, 70, GEOR*. In HH of R.M. Collins m 51 mulatto born SC.

COLLINS, ESTHER, 12, F, (--), M, SC, 70, 70, GEOR*. In HH of R.M. Collins m 51 mulatto born SC.

COLLINS, LUCRETIA, 50, F, (--), B, SC, 25, 25, RICH.

COLLINS, MARTHA, 33, F, (--), M, SC, 29, 28, CHAS&. In HH of Charlotte Collins f 45 mulatto born SC.

COLLINS, NELLY, 56, F, (--), M, SC, 30, 29, CHAS&.

COLLINS, R.M., 51, M, Farmer, M, SC, 70, 70, GEOR*.

COLLINS, ROBT., 17, M, (--), M, SC, 70, 70, GEOR*. In HH of R.M. Collins m 51 mulatto born SC.

COLLINS, SANDFORD, 44, M, Farmer, B, SC, 622, 623, FAIR.

COLMON, BABY, 0, M, (--), M, SC, 2226, 2226, GREE. In HH of Samuel Colmon m 36 mulatto born SC. Baby 3/12 yr.

COLMON, FLEMING, 9, M, (--), M, SC, 2226, 2226, GREE. In HH of Samuel Colmon m 36 mulatto born SC.

COLMON, FRANCES, 35, F, (--), M, SC, 2226, 2226, GREE. In HH of Samuel Colmon m 36 mulatto born SC.

COLMON, HARRIET, 7, F, (--), M, SC, 2226, 2226, GREE. In HH of Samuel Colmon m 36 mulatto born SC.

COLMON, JOHN, 5, M, (--), M, SC, 2226, 2226, GREE. In HH of Samuel

Colmon m 36 mulatto born SC.

COLMON, REBECCA, 11, F, (--), M, SC, 2226, 2226, GREE. In HH of Samuel Colmon m 36 mulatto born SC.

COLMON, SAMUEL, 36, M, Laborer, M, SC, 2226, 2226, GREE.

COLMON, WILLSON, 13, M, (--), M, SC, 2226, 2226, GREE. In HH of Samuel Colmon m 36 mulatto born SC.

COLVIN, CORNELIUS, 3, M, (--), M, SC, 1925, 1931, EDGE. In HH of Mary Colvin f 32 mulatto born SC.

COLVIN, MARY, 32, F, (--), M, SC, 1925, 1931, EDGE.

COLVIN, MILLEDGE, 5, M, (--), M, SC, 1925, 1931, EDGE. In HH of Mary Colvin f 32 mulatto born SC.

COLWELL, JOHN, 5, M, (--), M, SC, 63, 63, PICK+. In HH of David Rusell m 56 born SC.

COMEER, THOS., 23, M, Mechanic, M, SC, 907, 907, KERS. In HH of A. Pinson m 20 black born SC.

COMMERSAL, CAROLINE, 11, F, (--), M, SC, 315, 289, CHAS*. In HH of Flora Commersal f 28 black born SC.

COMMERSAL, EMMA, 22, F, (--), B, SC, 315, 289, CHAS*. In HH of Flora Commersal f 28 black born SC.

COMMERSAL, EMMELINE, 0, F, (--), M, SC, 315, 289, CHAS*. In HH of Flora Commersal f 28 black born SC. Emmeline age 9/12 yr.

COMMERSAL, FLORA, 28, F, (--), B, SC, 315, 289, CHAS*.

COMMERSAL, HENRY, 11, M, (--), B, SC, 315, 289, CHAS*. In HH of Flora Commersal f 28 black born SC.

COMMERSAL, JOHN, 13, M, (--), B, SC, 315, 289, CHAS*. In HH of Flora Commersal f 28 black born SC.

COMMERSAL, LIMERICK, 2, M, (--), B, SC, 315, 289, CHAS*. In HH of Flora Commersal f 28 black born SC.

COMMERSAL, LOUISA, 2, F, (--), M, SC, 315, 289, CHAS*. In HH of Flora Commersal f 28 black born SC.

COMMERSAL, MARGARET ANN, 10, F, (--), M, SC, 315, 289, CHAS*. In HH of Flora Commersal f 28 black born SC.

COMMERSAL, SAMUEL, 7, M, (--), M, SC, 315, 289, CHAS*. In HH of Flora Commersal f 28 black born SC.

CONNER, ISAAC, 10, M, (--), M, SC, 228, 228, CHAS3. In HH of John Conner m 44 mulatto born SC.

CONNER, JOHN, 44, M, (--), M, SC, 228, 228, CHAS3.

CONNER, MARY ANN, 6, F, (--), M, SC, 228, 228, CHAS3. In HH of John Conner m 44 mulatto born SC.

CONNER, SUSANAH, 38, F, (--), M, SC, 228, 228, CHAS3. In HH of John Conner m 44 mulatto born SC.

CONSTANCE, AMELIA, 10, F, (--), M, SC, 1192, 1171, CHAS%. In HH of Mary Constance f 32 mulatto born SC.

CONSTANCE, LOUISA, 13, F, (--), M, SC, 1192, 1171, CHAS%. In HH of Mary Constance f 32 mulatto born SC.

CONSTANCE, MARY, 32, F, (--), M, SC, 1192, 1171, CHAS%.

CONSTANCE, SOPHIA, 15, F, (--), M, SC, 1192, 1171, CHAS%. In HH of Mary Constance f 32 mulatto born SC.

CONWAY, ADEL, 7, F, (--), M, SC, 559, 525, CHAS*. In HH of James Conway m 36 mulatto born SC.

CONWAY, ANNA, 14, F, (--), M, SC, 559, 525, CHAS*. In HH of James Conway m 36 mulatto born SC.

CONWAY, CHRISTOPHER, 9, M, (--), M, SC, 559, 525, CHAS*. In HH of James Conway m 36 mulatto born SC.

CONWAY, GEORGIANA, 28, F, (--), M, SC, 559, 525, CHAS*. In HH of James Conway m 36 mulatto born SC.

CONWAY, HARRIET, 52, F, (--), B, SC, 102, 102, KERS.

CONWAY, J.L., 11, M, (--), B, SC, 102, 102, KERS. In HH of Harriet Conway f 52 black born SC.

CONWAY, JAMES, 36, M, Bricklayer, M, SC, 559, 525, CHAS*.

CONWAY, JAMES, 12, M, (--), M, SC, 559, 525, CHAS*. In HH of James Conway m 36 mulatto born SC.

CONWAY, THOS., 24, M, Mechanic, M, SC, 907, 907, KERS. In HH of A. Pinson m 20 black born SC.

CONWELL, GEORGE, 31, M, Laborer, M, SC, 503, 454, CHAS.

CONWELL, SAMUEL, 55, M, Carpenter, M, SC, 503, 454, CHAS. In HH of George Conwell m 31 mulatto born SC.

CONYERS, CATHERINE, 24, F, (--), B, SC, 135, 135, CHAS^.

CONYERS, MARY, 4, F, (--), B, SC, 135, 135, CHAS^. In HH of Catherine Conyers f 24 black born SC.

CONYERS, SARAH, 1, F, (--), B, SC, 135, 135, CHAS^. In HH of Catherine Conyers f 24 black born SC.

COOK, FERGUSON, 15, M, Carpenter, M, SC, 1080, 1057, CHAS-. In HH of Emeline Ferguson f 30 mulatto born SC.

COOK, FERRIBA, 40, F, (--), M, SC, 1527, 1533, MAR.

COOK, MINDAY, 65, M, Bricklayer, B, SC, 881, 881, KERS.

COOK, OLIVER, 11, M, (--), M, SC, 1080, 1057, CHAS-. In HH of Emeline Ferguson f 30 mulatto born SC.

COOK, TENAH, 36, F, (--), B, SC, 881, 881, KERS. In HH of Minday Cook m 65 black born SC.

COOKSON, JOSEPHINE, 47, F, (--), M, SC, 207, 193, CHAS-. In HH of Sarah Motte f 30 mulatto born SC.

COOLER, BALERN, 0, M, (--), B, ?, 15, 15, BEAU#. In HH of Kitty Newton f 35 Mulatto. Balern Cooler age 8/12 yr.

COOLER, BARNWELL, 3, M, (--), B, ?, 15, 15, BEAU#. In HH of Kitty Newton f 35 Mulatto.

COOLER, FRANCIS, 25, F, (--), B, ?, 15, 15, BEAU#. In HH of Kitty Newton f 35 Mulatto.

COOPER, ANGELINE, 48, F, (--), B, SC, 1076, 1098, CHAS%.

COOPER, FRANCIS, 6, F, (--), M, SC, 652, 611, CHAS+. In HH of Susan Cooper f 40 mulatto born SC.

COOPER, HENRY, 11, M, (--), B, SC, 1076, 1098, CHAS%. In HH of Angeline Cooper f 48 black born SC.

COOPER, JOHN, 41, M, Carter, B, SC, 1076, 1098, CHAS%. In HH of Angeline Cooper f 48 black born SC.

COOPER, JOHN, 8, M, (--), B, SC, 1076, 1098, CHAS%. In HH of Angeline Cooper f 48 black born SC.

COOPER, JOHN, 2, M, (--), M, SC, 652, 611, CHAS+. In HH of Susan Cooper f 40 mulatto born SC.

COOPER, MARY, 14, F, (--), B, SC, 1076, 1098, CHAS%. In HH of Angeline Cooper f 48 black born SC.

COOPER, PHILIP, 19, M, Blacksmith, B, SC, 1076, 1098, CHAS%. In HH of Angeline Cooper f 48 black born SC.

COOPER, SUSAN, 40, F, (--), M, SC, 652, 611, CHAS+.

COOPER, SUSAN, 8, F, (--), M, SC, 652, 611, CHAS+. In HH of Susan Cooper f 40 mulatto born SC.

COOPER, WILLIAM, 4, M, (--), M, SC, 652, 611, CHAS+. In HH of Susan Cooper f 40 mulatto born SC.

COPLAS, PERIN, 27, M, Mechanic, M, SC, 907, 907, KERS. In HH of A. Pinson m 20 black born SC.

CORCORAN, JOHN, 37, M, Laborer, B, SC, 484, 442, CHAS+. In HH of H. Heimseth m 26 born Germany.

CORNWELL, AMELIA, 35, F, (--), M, SC, 558, 541, CHAS-.

CORNWELL, CATHERINE, 32, F, (--), M, SC, 115, 115, CHAS%.

CORNWELL, REBECCA, 9, F, (--), M, SC, 115, 115, CHAS%. In HH of Catherine Cornwell f 32 mulatto born SC.

CORWAIN, MARY, 100, F, (--), B, West Indies, 554, 520, CHAS*. In HH of Sarah Finlay f 16 mulatto born SC.

COTTIDE, FRANCIS, 9, M, (--), B, SC, 66, 66, GEOR. In HH of Sarah Gairin f 27 mulatto born SC.

COTTIDE, JUDY, 8, F, (--), B, SC, 66, 66, GEOR. In HH of Sarah Gairin f 27 mulatto born SC.

COTTON, ANN, 28, F, (--), B, SC, 245,

230, CHAS-.

COTTON, CHARLOTTE, 9, F, (--), M, SC, 698, 656, CHAS+. In HH of Elizabeth Cotton f 28 mulatto born SC.

COTTON, EDWARDINA, 2, F, (--), M, SC, 698, 656, CHAS+. In HH of Elizabeth Cotton f 28 mulatto born SC.

COTTON, ELIZABETH, 28, F, (--), M, SC, 698, 656, CHAS+.

COTTON, ELIZABETH, 5, F, (--), M, SC, 698, 656, CHAS+. In HH of Elizabeth Cotton f 28 mulatto born SC.

COTTON, MARY, 11, F, (--), M, SC, 698, 656, CHAS+. In HH of Elizabeth Cotton f 28 mulatto born SC.

COUNTS, PHEBE, 95, F, (--), B, SC, 612, 612, NEWB.

COX, ALFRED, 4, M, (--), M, SC, 208, 208, HORR. In HH of Robt. Anderson m 65 born SC.

COX, CHARLOTT, 8, F, (--), M, SC, 208, 208, HORR. In HH of Robt. Anderson m 65 born SC.

COX, COLMAN, 1, M, (--), M, SC, 208, 208, HORR. In HH of Robt. Anderson m 65 born SC.

COX, DANIEL, 50, M, Butcher, B, SC, 582, 574, CHAS%.

COX, DANL., 50, M, Butcher, B, SC, 36, 32, CHAS$. In HH of J.F. Pease m 29 born ME.

COX, ELLEN, 14, F, (--), B, SC, 582, 574, CHAS%. In HH of Daniel Cox m 50 black born SC.

COX, FLORA, 32, F, (--), B, SC, 582, 574, CHAS%. In HH of Daniel Cox m 50 black born SC.

COX, GRIFFEN, 10, M, (--), M, SC, 208, 208, HORR. In HH of Robt. Anderson m 65 born SC.

COX, JENNEY, 40, F, (--), M, SC, 208, 208, HORR. In HH of Robt. Anderson m 65 born SC.

COX, JULIET, 75, F, (--), B, SC, 832, 790, CHAS+. In HH of George Creighton m 50 black born SC.

COX, NELLEY, 17, F, (--), M, SC, 208, 208, HORR. In HH of Robt. Anderson m 65 born SC.

COX, SARAH B., 20, F, (--), M, Germany{sic}, 346, 329, CHAS-.

COX, SUSAN, 30, F, (--), M, Germany{sic}, 346, 329, CHAS-. In HH of Sarah B. Cox f 20 mulatto born Germany {sic}.

CRAFTS, LYDIA, 6, F, (--), M, SC, 865, 845, CHAS-. In HH of William Deas m 35 mulatto born SC.

CRANNAY, EDWD., 32, M, Blacksmith, B, SC, 126, 126, KERS. In HH of Manson House m 33 black born SC.

CRANNAY, EDWD., 6, M, (--), B, SC, 126, 126, KERS. In HH of Manson House m 33 black born SC.

CRANNAY, JOE, 25, M, Apprentice, B, SC, 126, 126, KERS. In HH of Manson House m 33 black born SC. Saml. House 4/12 yr.

CRAWFORD, CELISLE, 30, F, (--), M, Cuba, 242, 227, CHAS-.

CRAWFORD, CUTA, 3, F, (--), M, SC, 242, 227, CHAS-. In HH of Celisle Crawford f 30 mulatto born Cuba.

CRAWFORD, JOHN, 2, M, (--), M, SC, 242, 227, CHAS-. In HH of Celisle Crawford f 30 mulatto born Cuba.

CRAWFORD, MAC, 85, M, Farmer, B, VA, 403, 403, CHES. In HH of Ralph McFadden m 39 born SC.

CRAWFORD, SUGARDO, 10, F, (--), M, SC, 242, 227, CHAS-. In HH of Celisle Crawford f 30 mulatto born Cuba.

CREIGHTON, ANNE, 31, F, (--), B, SC, 1082, 1104, CHAS%.

CREIGHTON, GEORGE, 50, M, Barber, B, SC, 832, 790, CHAS+.

CREIGHTON, JOHN, 9, M, (--), B, SC, 1082, 1104, CHAS%. In HH of Anne Creighton f 31 black born SC.

CREIGHTON, THOMAS, 55, M, (--), B, SC, 556, 556, Union. In Hotel.

CRIPPS, JOHN, 50, M, Svila Water Maker, M, SC, 297, 274, CHAS. In HH of John A. Gylis m 36 born SC.

CROFT, FERDEMAND, 1, M, (--), M, SC, 2254, 2254, GREE. In HH of

Margarit Walker f 42 mulatto born SC.

CROFT, PERMILIA, 22, F, (--), M, SC, 2254, 2254, GREE. In HH of Margarit Walker f 42 mulatto born SC.

CROFT, WILLIAM, 25, M, Blacksmith, M, SC, 2254, 2254, GREE. In HH of Margarit Walker f 42 mulatto born SC.

CROKER, 36, M, Farmer, M, SC, 11, 11, CHAS#. In HH of Mrs. McDowall f 78 born SC.

CROKER, E.J., 26, F, (--), M, SC, 11, 11, CHAS#. In HH of Mrs. McDowall f 78 born SC.

CROKER, EDWARD, 3, M, (--), M, SC, 11, 11, CHAS#. In HH of Mrs. McDowall f 78 born SC.

CROKER, ELLINOR, 5, F, (--), M, SC, 11, 11, CHAS#. In HH of Mrs. McDowall f 78 born SC.

CROKER, JAMES, 6, M, (--), M, SC, 11, 11, CHAS#. In HH of Mrs. McDowall f 78 born SC.

CROKER, WILLIAM, 2, M, (--), M, SC, 11, 11, CHAS#. In HH of Mrs. McDowall f 78 born SC.

CROOKER, EMILY, 9, F, (--), M, SC, 434, 431, CHAS%. In HH of Caroline Dingle f 40 mulatto born SC.

CROOKER, JAMES, 7, M, (--), M, SC, 434, 431, CHAS%. In HH of Caroline Dingle f 40 mulatto born SC.

CROOKER, JOHN, 28, M, Porter, M, SC, 434, 431, CHAS%. In HH of Caroline Dingle f 40 mulatto born SC.

CROOKER, MARTHA, 30, F, (--), M, SC, 434, 431, CHAS%. In HH of Caroline Dingle f 40 mulatto born SC.

CROSBY, JOHN, 12, M, (--), M, SC, 631, 623, CHAS%. In HH of Mary Crosby f 54 mulatto born SC.

CROSBY, MARGARET, 17, F, (--), M, SC, 109, 109, COLL. In HH of Wm. Goopy m 27 white born SC.

CROSBY, MARY, 54, F, (--), M, SC, 631, 623, CHAS%.

CROSBY, MARY, 51, F, (--), M, SC, 42, 42, GEOR*. In HH of John Booth m 45 born SC.

CROSBY, SARAH, 18, F, (--), M, SC, 42, 42, GEOR*. In HH of John Booth m 45 born SC.

CROSBY, WILLIAM, 20, M, Laborer, M, SC, 631, 623, CHAS%. In HH of Mary Crosby f 54 mulatto born SC.

CROSS, JAMES, 50, M, Stevedore, B, SC, 144, 132, CHAS*. In HH of Rose Roper f 50 black born SC.

CROUCH, MARY, 43, F, (--), B, SC, 146, 136, CHAS-. In HH of Julia Barnet f 50 mulatto born SC.

CUEL, ALLEN, 9, M, (--), M, SC, 213, 213, COLL. In HH of Wm. B. Cuel m 29 mulatto born SC.

CUEL, ELIZABETH, 30, F, (--), M, SC, 213, 213, COLL. In HH of Wm. B. Cuel m 29 mulatto born SC.

CUEL, FRANCIS, 11, M, (--), M, SC, 213, 213, COLL. In HH of Wm. B. Cuel m 29 mulatto born SC.

CUEL, HENDERSON, 7, M, (--), M, SC, 213, 213, COLL. In HH of Wm. B. Cuel m 29 mulatto born SC.

CUEL, HENRY, 15, M, (--), M, SC, 213, 213, COLL. In HH of Wm. B. Cuel m 29 mulatto born SC.

CUEL, JAMES, 3, M, (--), M, SC, 213, 213, COLL. In HH of Wm. B. Cuel m 29 mulatto born SC. Levinia sex m {sic}.

CUEL, JOHN, 13, M, (--), M, SC, 213, 213, COLL. In HH of Wm. B. Cuel m 29 mulatto born SC.

CUEL, LEVINIA, 5, M, (--), M, SC, 213, 213, COLL. In HH of Wm. B. Cuel m 29 mulatto born SC. Levinia sex m{sic}.

CUEL, WM. B., 29, M, Laborer, M, SC, 213, 213, COLL.

CUFF, ANN, 33, F, (--), M, SC, 137, 137, CHAS2. In HH of Zachariah Cuff m 28 black born SC.

CUFF, C., 13, M, (--), B, SC, 140, 140, CHAS2. In HH of John Thurston m 21 born SC.

CUFF, ELIEZA, 10, F, (--), M, SC, 137, 137, CHAS2. In HH of Zachariah Cuff m 28 black born SC.

CUFF, FRANCES, 14, F, (--), M, SC, 137, 137, CHAS2. In HH of Zachariah Cuff m 28 black born SC.

CUFF, ZACHARIAH, 28, M, Bricklayer, B, SC, 137, 137, CHAS2.

CUMBEE, E., 8, M, (--), M, SC, 34, 34, CHAS#. In HH of Elias Cumbee m 35 mulatto born SC.

CUMBEE, ELIAS, 35, M, Farmer, M, SC, 34, 34, CHAS#.

CUMBEE, GEORGIANA, 2, F, (--), M, SC, 34, 34, CHAS#. In HH of Elias Cumbee m 35 mulatto born SC.

CUMBEE, J., 12, F, (--), M, SC, 35, 35, CHAS#. In HH of Robert Cumbee m 30 mulatto born SC.

CUMBEE, J., 10, M, (--), M, SC, 34, 34, CHAS#. In HH of Elias Cumbee m 35 mulatto born SC.

CUMBEE, JO., 7, M, (--), M, SC, 34, 34, CHAS#. In HH of Elias Cumbee m 35 mulatto born SC.

CUMBEE, P., 11, M, (--), M, SC, 34, 34, CHAS#. In HH of Elias Cumbee m 35 mulatto born SC.

CUMBEE, ROBERT, 30, M, (--), M, SC, 35, 35, CHAS#.

CUMBEE, S., 13, M, (--), M, SC, 34, 34, CHAS#. In HH of Elias Cumbee m 35 mulatto born SC.

CUNNINGHAM, CAROLINE, 14, F, (--), B, SC, 899, 899, CHFD. In HH of Jane Cunningham 27 black born SC.

CUNNINGHAM, ABRAM, 12, M, (--), B, SC, 899, 899, CHFD. In HH of Jane Cunningham 27 black born SC.

CUNNINGHAM, JANE, 27, F, (--), B, SC, 899, 899, CHFD.

CUNNINGHAM, LEWIS, 11, M, (--), B, SC, 899, 899, CHFD. In HH of Jane Cunningham 27 black born SC.

CUNNINGHAM, SAMUEL, 10, M, (--), B, SC, 899, 899, CHFD. In HH of Jane Cunningham 27 black born SC.

CURTIS, MARY, 45, F, (--), M, SC, 1598, 1598, BARN.

CURTIS, NANCY, 40, F, (--), M, SC, 1598, 1598, BARN. In HH of Mary Curtis f 45 mulatto born SC.

D

DACOSTA, HENRY, 10, M, (--), M, Ireland {sic}, 56, 51, CHAS-. In HH of W.P. DaCosta m 40 mulatto born Ireland {sic}.

DACOSTA, JAMES, 17, M, Shoemaker, M, Ireland {sic}, 56, 51, CHAS-. In HH of W.P. DaCosta m 40 mulatto born Ireland {sic}.

DACOSTA, JOSEPH, 8, M, (--), M, Ireland {sic}, 56, 51, CHAS-. In HH of W.P. DaCosta m 40 mulatto born Ireland {sic}.

DACOSTA, LOUISA R., 35, F, (--), M, Ireland {sic}, 56, 51, CHAS-. In HH of W.P. DaCosta m 40 mulatto born Ireland {sic}.

DACOSTA, LOUISA V., 6, F, (--), M, Ireland {sic}, 56, 51, CHAS-. In HH of W.P. DaCosta m 40 mulatto born Ireland {sic}.

DACOSTA, THOMAS, 14, M, (--), M, Ireland {sic}, 56, 51, CHAS-. In HH of W.P. DaCosta m 40 mulatto born Ireland {sic}.

DACOSTA, W.P., 40, M, Cotton Ginmaker, M, Ireland {sic}, 56, 51, CHAS-.

DACOSTA, WILLIAM, 12, M, (--), M, Ireland {sic}, 56, 51, CHAS-. In HH of W.P. DaCosta m 40 mulatto born Ireland {sic}.

DAILEY, JAMES, 60, M, Carpenter, M, SC, 81, 81, COLL*.

DAIMER, ELIZABETH, 5, F, (--), B, SC, 288, 288, BEAU+. In HH of James Daimer m 58 black born SC.

DAIMER, ELLA, 4, F, (--), M, SC, 288, 288, BEAU+. In HH of James Daimer m 58 black born SC.

DAIMER, HENRY, 3, M, (--), M, SC, 288, 288, BEAU+. In HH of James Daimer m 58 black born SC.

DAIMER, JAMES, 58, M, Farmer, B, SC, 288, 288, BEAU+.

DAIMER, JAMES, 7, M, (--), B, SC, 288, 288, BEAU+. In HH of James Daimer m 58 black born SC.

DAIMER, JOHN, 3, M, (--), M, SC, 288, 288, BEAU+. In HH of James Daimer m 58 black born SC.

DAIMER, MARY, 37, F, (--), M, SC, 288, 288, BEAU+. In HH of James Daimer m 58 black born SC.

DAIMER, MARY JANE, 15, F, (--), B, SC, 288, 288, BEAU+. In HH of James Daimer m 58 black born SC.

DAIMER, MINTY, 15, F, (--), B, SC, 288, 288, BEAU+. In HH of James Daimer m 58 black born SC.

DAIMER, RITTA, 1, F, (--), M, SC, 288, 288, BEAU+. In HH of James Daimer m 58 black born SC.

DANGERFIELD, CAROLINE, 2, F, (--), M, SC, 26, 26, CHAS~. In HH of John R. Dangerfield m 58 born SC.

DANGERFIELD, ELIZA, 7, F, (--), M, SC, 26, 26, CHAS~. In HH of John R. Dangerfield m 58 born SC.

DANGERFIELD, HANNAH, 5, F, (--), M, SC, 26, 26, CHAS~. In HH of John R. Dangerfield m 58 born SC.

DANGERFIELD, HENRIETTA, 27, F, (--), M, SC, 26, 26, CHAS~. In HH of John R. Dangerfield m 58 born SC.

DANGERFIELD, WILLIAM, 3, M, (--), M, SC, 26, 26, CHAS~. In HH of John R. Dangerfield m 58 born SC.

DART, ANTOINETTA, 12, F, (--), B, SC, 382, 380, CHAS%. In HH of William Dart m 46 black born SC.

DART, EMMA, 16, F, (--), B, SC, 382, 380, CHAS%. In HH of William Dart m 46 black born SC.

DART, SARAH, 70, F, (--), B, SC, 480, 438, CHAS+.

DART, SUSAN, 40, F, (--), B, SC, 382, 380, CHAS%. In HH of William Dart m 46 black born SC.

DART, WILLIAM, 46, M, (--), B, SC, 382, 380, CHAS%.

DAVEAUX, ISABELLA, 28, F, (--), M, SC, 106, 99, CHAS-.

DAVID, MARIA, 40, F, (--), M, SC, 329, 304, CHAS. In HH of Daniel Furth m 40 born Germany.

DAVIDSON, GEORGE, 21, M, Laborer, M, SC, 190, 190, COLL.

DAVIDSON, ISAAC, 17, M, Laborer, M, SC, 190, 190, COLL. In HH of George Davidson m 21 mulatto born SC.

DAVIS, ABSOLUM, 52, M, Carpenter, M, SC, 54, 54, GEOR.

DAVIS, C., 8, F, (--), M, SC, 37, 37, CHAS#. In HH of Frederick Davis m 34 mulatto born SC.

DAVIS, CAROLINE, 17, F, (--), M, SC, 216, 202, CHAS-. In HH of Eliza Davis f 35 born mulatto born SC.

DAVIS, E., 5, F, (--), M, SC, 37, 37, CHAS#. In HH of Frederick Davis m 34 mulatto born SC.

DAVIS, EDWAN, 22, M, (--), B, SC, 797, 797, SUMT. In HH of John Davis m 25 black born SC.

DAVIS, ELIZA, 40, F, (--), M, SC, 40, 40, GEOR. In HH of Rachel Davis f 70 mulatto born SC.

DAVIS, ELIZA, 35, F, (--), M, SC, 216, 202, CHAS-.

DAVIS, ELIZA M., 14, F, (--), M, SC, 54, 54, GEOR. In HH of Absolum Davis m 52 mulatto born SC.

DAVIS, ELIZABETH, 55, F, (--), M, SC, 54, 54, GEOR. In HH of Absolum Davis m 52 mulatto born SC.

DAVIS, ELIZABETH, 30, F, (--), M, SC, 74, 74, CHAS3. In HH of Ranson Joyner m 21 born SC.

DAVIS, ELLEN, 30, F, (--), M, SC, 368, 368, CHAS%.

DAVIS, ELMIRA, 2, F, (--), M, SC, 13, 11, CHAS-. In HH of Frances Davis f 40 mulatto born SC.

DAVIS, EMMA, 10, F, (--), M, SC, 368, 368, CHAS%. In HH of Ellen Davis f 30 mulatto born SC.

DAVIS, FRANCES, 40, F, (--), M, SC, 13, 11, CHAS-.

DAVIS, FRANCIS, 5, F, (--), M, SC, 13, 11, CHAS-. In HH of Frances Davis f 40 mulatto born SC.

DAVIS, FRANCIS, 3, M, (--), M, SC, 343, 343, CHAS%. In HH of Jane Davis f 40 mulatto born SC.

DAVIS, FREDERICK, 34, M, Farmer, M, SC, 37, 37, CHAS#.

DAVIS, H., 3, M, (--), M, SC, 37, 37, CHAS#. In HH of Frederick Davis m 34 mulatto born SC.

DAVIS, HENRY, 8, M, (--), M, SC, 13, 11, CHAS-. In HH of Frances Davis f 40 mulatto born SC.

DAVIS, ISABELLA, 16, F, (--), M, SC, 13, 11, CHAS-. In HH of Frances Davis f 40 mulatto born SC.

DAVIS, J., 9, M, (--), M, SC, 37, 37, CHAS#. In HH of Frederick Davis m 34 mulatto born SC.

DAVIS, JANE, 40, F, (--), M, SC, 343, 343, CHAS%.

DAVIS, JOHN, 35, M, Carpenter, M, SC, 135, 135, CHAS^. In HH of Catherine Conyers f 24 black born SC.

DAVIS, JOHN, 29, M, Glazier, M, SC, 368, 368, CHAS%. In HH of Ellen Davis f 30 mulatto born SC.

DAVIS, JOHN, 25, M, Carpenter, B, SC, 797, 797, SUMT.

DAVIS, JOHN J., 3, M, (--), M, SC, 74, 74, CHAS3. In HH of Ranson Joyner m 21 born SC.

DAVIS, JULIA, 14, F, (--), M, SC, 343, 343, CHAS%. In HH of Jane Davis f 40 mulatto born SC.

DAVIS, JULIANA, 6, F, (--), M, SC, 396, 380, CHAS-. In HH of William Davis m 30 mulatto born SC.

DAVIS, KEMPTON, 26, M, Engineer, M, SC, 193, 176, CHAS. In HH of Elizabeth Henson f 60 mulatto born SC.

DAVIS, LAWRENCE, 9, M, (--), B, SC, 343, 343, CHAS%. In HH of Jane Davis f 40 mulatto born SC.

DAVIS, M., 35, F, (--), M, SC, 37, 37, CHAS#. In HH of Frederick Davis m 34 mulatto born SC.

DAVIS, M., 0, F, (--), M, SC, 37, 37, CHAS#. In HH of Frederick Davis m 34 mulatto born SC. M. Davis age 1/12 yr.

DAVIS, MARGARET, 25, F, (--), M,

SC, 396, 380, CHAS-. In HH of William Davis m 30 mulatto born SC.

DAVIS, MARTHA, 14, F, (--), M, SC, 74, 74, CHAS3. In HH of Ranson Joyner m 21 born SC.

DAVIS, MARY, 2, F, (--), M, SC, 13, 11, CHAS-. In HH of Frances Davis f 40 mulatto born SC.

DAVIS, OLIVER, 9, M, (--), M, SC, 74, 74, CHAS3. In HH of Ranson Joyner m 21 born SC.

DAVIS, RACHEL, 70, F, (--), M, SC, 40, 40, GEOR.

DAVIS, RACHAEL, 1, F, (--), M, SC, 13, 11, CHAS-. In HH of Frances Davis f 40 mulatto born SC.

DAVIS, ROSALINE, 14, F, (--), M, SC, 13, 11, CHAS-. In HH of Frances Davis f 40 mulatto born SC.

DAVIS, SEPTIMER, 7, F, (--), M, SC, 343, 343, CHAS%. In HH of Jane Davis f 40 mulatto born SC.

DAVIS, SUSAN, 7, F, (--), M, SC, 54, 54, GEOR. In HH of Absolum Davis m 52 mulatto born SC.

DAVIS, THOMAS, 7, M, (--), M, SC, 368, 368, CHAS%. In HH of Ellen Davis f 30 mulatto born SC.

DAVIS, THOMAS, 4, M, (--), M, SC, 74, 74, CHAS3. In HH of Ranson Joyner m 21 born SC.

DAVIS, THOMAS, 4, M, (--), M, SC, 396, 380, CHAS-. In HH of William Davis m 30 mulatto born SC.

DAVIS, WILLIAM, 90, M, Drummer to Gen., B, SC, 146, 146, CHAS~. Occupation: Drummer to Genl. Marion. In HH of Francis Edy m 36 black born SC.

DAVIS, WILLIAM, 30, M, (--), M, SC, 396, 380, CHAS-.

DAVIS, WILLIAM, 11, M, (--), M, SC, 74, 74, CHAS3. In HH of Ranson Joyner m 21 born SC.

DAVISON, CHESTLEY, 12, M, (--), B, SC, 699, 700, AND*. In HH of Solloman Davison m 80 black born VA.

DAVISON, JANE, 45, F, (--), B, SC, 699, 700, AND*. In HH of Solloman

Davison m 80 black born VA.

DAVISON, SAMINDA, 9, F, (--), B, SC, 699, 700, AND*. In HH of Solloman Davison m 80 black born VA.

DAVISON, SAMUEL, 5, M, (--), B, SC, 699, 700, AND*. In HH of Solloman Davison m 80 black born VA.

DAVISON, SARAH, 8, F, (--), B, SC, 699, 700, AND*. In HH of Solloman Davison m 80 black born VA.

DAVISON, SOLLOMAN, 80, M, Farmer, B, VA, 699, 700, AND*.

DAVISON, TAYLOR, 2, M, (--), B, SC, 699, 700, AND*. In HH of Solloman Davison m 80 black born VA.

DAVISON, WRIGHT, 14, M, (--), B, SC, 699, 700, AND*. In HH of Solloman Davison m 80 black born VA.

DAWDLE, HANNAH, 35, F, (--), B, SC, 172, 173, AND*. In HH of Morris Dawdle m 72 black born SC.

DAWDLE, HARRIET, 12, F, (--), B, SC, 172, 173, AND*. In HH of Morris Dawdle m 72 black born SC.

DAWDLE, MORRIS, 72, M, Farmer, B, SC, 172, 173, AND*.

DAWDLE, WILLIAM, 10, M, (--), B, SC, 172, 173, AND*. In HH of Morris Dawdle m 72 black born SC.

DAWKINS, HENRY, 40, M, Carpenter, B, SC, 1397, 1397, NEWB. In HH of Thomas Deriker m 46 black born SC.

DAYS, CATHERINE, 3, F, (--), M, SC, 206, 206, CHAS%. In HH of Eliza W. Days f 45 mulatto born SC.

DAYS, ELIAS, 6, M, (--), M, SC, 206, 206, CHAS%. In HH of Eliza W. Days f 45 mulatto born SC.

DAYS, ELIZA, 1, F, (--), M, SC, 206, 206, CHAS%. In HH of Eliza W. Days f 45 mulatto born SC.

DAYS, ELIZA W., 45, F, (--), M, SC, 206, 206, CHAS%.

DAYS, JAMES, 11, M, (--), M, SC, 206, 206, CHAS%. In HH of Eliza W. Days f 45 mulatto born SC.

DAYS, JOHN, 13, M, (--), M, SC, 206, 206, CHAS%. In HH of Eliza W. Days f

45 mulatto born SC.

DAYS, MARION, 5, M, (--), M, SC, 206, 206, CHAS%. In HH of Eliza W. Days f 45 mulatto born SC.

DAYS, WILLIAM, 50, M, (--), M, SC, 206, 206, CHAS%. In HH of Eliza W. Days f 45 mulatto born SC.

DAYS, WILLIAM, 14, M, (--), M, SC, 206, 206, CHAS%. In HH of Eliza W. Days f 45 mulatto born SC.

DEAL, CAROLINE, 24, F, (--), B, SC, 405, 405, LAU . In HH of George Deal m 60 black born SC.

DEAL, ELIZABETH, 50, F, (--), B, SC, 405, 405, LAU . In HH of George Deal m 60 black born SC.

DEAL, GEORGE, 60, M, (--), B, SC, 405, 405, LAU .

DEAL, JAMES, 14, M, (--), M, SC, 405, 405, LAU . In HH of George Deal m 60 black born SC.

DEAS, ANN, 37, F, (--), M, SC, 185, 169, CHAS*.

DEAS, CHARLES, 18, M, Blacksmith, M, SC, 102, 102, CHAS%. In HH of Jane Deas f 60 mulatto born SC.

DEAS, ELIZA, 35, F, (--), M, SC, 235, 235, CHAS%. In HH of Robert Deas m 40 mulatto born SC.

DEAS, FREDERICK, 15, M, (--), M, SC, 102, 102, CHAS%. In HH of Jane Deas f 60 mulatto born SC.

DEAS, JANE, 60, F, (--), M, SC, 102, 102, CHAS%.

DEAS, JENNETTE, 8, F, (--), M, SC, 235, 235, CHAS%. In HH of Robert Deas m 40 mulatto born SC.

DEAS, JOHN, 5, M, (--), M, SC, 235, 235, CHAS%. In HH of Robert Deas m 40 mulatto born SC.

DEAS, LOUISA, 32, F, (--), M, SC, 102, 102, CHAS%. In HH of Jane Deas f 60 mulatto born SC.

DEAS, MARTHA, 28, F, (--), M, SC, 102, 102, CHAS%. In HH of Jane Deas f 60 mulatto born SC.

DEAS, ROBERT, 40, M, Butcher, M, SC, 235, 235, CHAS%.

DEAS, SARAH J., 24, F, (--), M, SC, 102, 102, CHAS%. In HH of Jane Deas f 60 mulatto born SC.

DEAS, WILLIAM, 35, M, Trimmer, M, SC, 865, 845, CHAS-.

DEAS, THOMAS, 24, M, (--), M, SC, 757, 757, YORK. In HH of Nancy Watson f 60 mulatto born SC.

DEBAN, EVELINE, 40, F, (--), M, SC, 41, 37, CHAS$.

DEBBLE, ANDREW, 25, M, Tailor, M, SC, 100, 100, KERS.

DEBBLE, ELLEN, 21, F, (--), M, SC, 100, 100, KERS. In HH of Andrew Dibble m 25 mulatto born SC.

DEBBLE, JOHN, 2, M, (--), M, SC, 100, 100, KERS. In HH of Andrew Dibble m 25 mulatto born SC.

DEBBLE, M.L., 4, F, (--), M, SC, 100, 100, KERS. In HH of Andrew Dibble m 25 mulatto born SC.

DEEN, ALFRED, 1, M, (--), M, SC, 1803, 1809, EDGE. In HH of Elbuson Deen m 24 mulatto born SC.

DEEN, BARBARY, 25, F, (--), M, SC, 1803, 1809, EDGE. In HH of Elbuson Deen m 24 mulatto born SC.

DEEN, BENJ., 7, M, (--), M, SC, 1808, 1812, EDGE. In HH of John Deen m 55 mulatto born SC.

DEEN, ELBUSON, 24, M, Laborer, M, SC, 1803, 1809, EDGE.

DEEN, EVELINE, 18, F, (--), M, SC, 1808, 1812, EDGE. In HH of John Deen m 55 mulatto born SC.

DEEN, FRANK, 5, M, (--), M, SC, 1808, 1812, EDGE. In HH of John Deen m 55 mulatto born SC.

DEEN, HEINSFORD, 26, M, Laborer, M, SC, 1804, 1810, EDGE.

DEEN, HENRY, 12, M, (--), M, SC, 1808, 1812, EDGE. In HH of John Deen m 55 mulatto born SC.

DEEN, INBUS, 1, M, (--), M, SC, 1808, 1812, EDGE. In HH of John Deen m 55 mulatto born SC.

DEEN, JACKSON, 16, M, Laborer, M, SC, 1808, 1812, EDGE. In HH of John Deen m 55 mulatto born SC.

DEEN, JACKSON, 3, M, (--), M, SC, 1803, 1809, EDGE. In HH of Elbuson Deen m 24 mulatto born SC.

DEEN, JAMES, 21, M, Laborer, M, SC, 1808, 1812, EDGE. In HH of John Deen m 55 mulatto born SC.

DEEN, JOHN, 55, M, Laborer, M, SC, 1808, 1812, EDGE.

DEEN, JOHN, 8, M, (--), M, SC, 1808, 1812, EDGE. In HH of John Deen m 55 mulatto born SC.

DEEN, KEZZIAH, 5, F, (--), M, SC, 1803, 1809, EDGE. In HH of Elbuson Deen m 24 mulatto born SC.

DEEN, PATSY, 50, F, (--), M, SC, 1808, 1812, EDGE. In HH of John Deen m 55 mulatto born SC.

DEEN, POLLY, 25, F, (--), M, SC, 1808, 1812, EDGE. In HH of John Deen m 55 mulatto born SC.

DEEN, URIAH, 10, M, (--), M, SC, 1808, 1812, EDGE. In HH of John Deen m 55 mulatto born SC.

DEES, JAMES, 3, M, (--), M, SC, 755, 755, MARL. In HH of Minty Dees f 30 mulatto born SC.

DEES, LUCY, 7, F, (--), M, SC, 754, 754, MARL. In HH of David Smith m 60 born SC.

DEES, MINTY, 30, F, (--), M, SC, 755, 755, MARL.

DEES, POLLY, 5, F, (--), M, SC, 755, 755, MARL. In HH of Minty Dees f 30 mulatto born SC.

DELANCEY, MARY, 28, F, (--), B, SC, 188, 172, CHAS*.

DELANCEY, NANCY, 2, F, (--), B, SC, 188, 172, CHAS*. In HH of Mary DeLancey f 28 black born SC.

DELARGE, DAVID, 12, M, (--), M, SC, 1593, 1593, BARN. In HH of Jon DeLarge m 40 mulatto born SC.

DELARGE, JOHN, 7, M, (--), M, SC, 1593, 1593, BARN. In HH of Jon DeLarge m 40 mulatto born SC.

DELARGE, JON, 40, M, (--), M, SC, 1593, 1593, BARN.

DELARGE, JULIA, 37, F, (--), M, SC, 1593, 1593, BARN. In HH of Jon

DeLarge m 40 mulatto born SC.

DELARGE, MARY, 40, F, (--), M, SC, 699, 657, CHAS+.

DELARGE, OCTAVIA, 5, F, (--), M, SC, 1593, 1593, BARN. In HH of Jon DeLarge m 40 mulatto born SC.

DELARGE, ROBERT, 8, M, (--), M, SC, 1593, 1593, BARN. In HH of Jon DeLarge m 40 mulatto born SC.

DELEON, EMMA, 34, F, (--), M, SC, 161, 165, RICH.

DELEON, HENRY, 17, M, Blacksmith, M, SC, 161, 165, RICH. In HH of Emma DeLeon f 34 mulatto born SC.

DELEON, JAMES, 13, M, (--), M, SC, 161, 165, RICH. In HH of Emma DeLeon f 34 mulatto born SC.

DELEON, MARIA, 15, F, (--), M, SC, 161, 165, RICH. In HH of Emma DeLeon f 34 mulatto born SC.

DELONA, THOS., 55, M, Laborer, M, SC, 1222, 1222, SUMT. In HH of Sarah McDuffie f 55 born SC.

DEMERRY, DANIEL, 25, M, (--), M, SC, 69, 69, MARL. In HH of Alexr. Miller m 50 born SC.   .

DEMONY, DANIEL, 40, M, (--), M, SC, 40, 40, HORR. In HH of G.W. Warde m 43 born ME.

DEMPS, JOHN, 12, M, (--), M, SC, 667, 667, MARL. In HH of Lydia Hantz f 48 mulatto born SC.

DEMPS, PETER, 54, M, Ferryman, B, SC, 672, 672, MARL.

DEMPSEY, ADAM W., 5, M, (--), M, SC, 157, 157, CHAS3. In HH of L.W. Dempsey m 30 mulatto born SC.

DEMPSEY, DANIEL, 50, M, Mechanic, M, SC, 334, 334, CHAS3.

DEMPSEY, DANIEL, 3, M, (--), M, SC, 334, 334, CHAS3. In HH of Daniel Dempsey m 50 mulatto born SC.

DEMPSEY, ELIZA E., 2, F, (--), M, SC, 157, 157, CHAS3. In HH of L.W. Dempsey m 30 mulatto born SC.

DEMPSEY, ELIZABETH, 45, F, (--), M, SC, 334, 334, CHAS3. In HH of Daniel Dempsey m 50 mulatto born SC.

DEMPSEY, L.W., 30, M, Laborer, M, SC, 157, 157, CHAS3.

DEMPSEY, RACHAEL, 28, F, (--), M, SC, 157, 157, CHAS3. In HH of L.W. Dempsey m 30 mulatto born SC.

DEMPSEY, RACHEL, 25, F, (--), M, SC, 334, 334, CHAS3. In HH of Daniel Dempsey m 50 mulatto born SC.

DEMPSY, ALPHA, 60, F, (--), M, SC, 303, 303, ORAN*. In HH of Ammon Bowe m 27 mulatto born SC.

DEMPSY, HOWARD, 25, M, Laborer, M, SC, 618, 619, ORNG+. In HH of George L. Smith m 35 born SC.

DEMPSY, MATHEW, 36, M, Wheelwright, M, SC, 314, 314, ORNG*. In HH of Richard Dempsy m 40 mulatto born SC.

DEMPSY, RICHARD, 40, M, Farmer, M, SC, 314, 314, ORNG*.

DEMUERE, EULICES, 0, M, (--), M, SC, 228, 228, COLL. In HH of Mathew Demuere m 59 mulatto born SC. Eulices age 3/12 yr.

DEMUERE, HENRIETTA, 5, F, (--), M, SC, 228, 228, COLL. In HH of Mathew Demuere m 59 mulatto born SC.

DEMUERE, MARGARET A., 35, F, (--), M, SC, 228, 228, COLL. In HH of Mathew Demuere m 59 mulatto born SC.

DEMUERE, MARTHA, 14, F, (--), M, SC, 228, 228, COLL. In HH of Mathew Demuere m 59 mulatto born SC.

DEMUERE, MARY E., 7, F, (--), M, SC, 228, 228, COLL. In HH of Mathew Demuere m 59 mulatto born SC.

DEMUERE, MASSEY J., 4, M, (--), M, SC, 228, 228, COLL. In HH of Mathew Demuere m 59 mulatto born SC.

DEMUERE, MATHEW, 59, M, Farmer, M, SC, 228, 228, COLL.

DEMUERE, MILEY, 13, F, (--), M, SC, 228, 228, COLL. In HH of Mathew Demuere m 59 mulatto born SC.

DEMUERE, RACHIEL, 2, F, (--), M, SC, 228, 228, COLL. In HH of Mathew Demuere m 59 mulatto born SC.

DEMUERE, WM. H., 9, M, (--), M, SC, 228, 228, COLL. In HH of Mathew

Demuere m 59 mulatto born SC.

DENNIS, AGNES, 42, M, (--), B, SC, 621, 621, CHES. In HH of David Dennis m 50, Black born SC.

DENNIS, AXEY, 12, F, (--), M, SC, 377, 377, EDGE*. In HH of Dempstand Bug m 34 mulatto born SC.

DENNIS, BITSEY, 12, F, (--), B, SC, 621, 621, CHES. In HH of David Dennis m 50, Black born SC.

DENNIS, DAVID, 50, M, Farmer, B, SC, 621, 621, CHES.

DENNIS, DAVID, 10, M, (--), B, SC, 621, 621, CHES. In HH of David Dennis m 50, Black born SC.

DENNIS, ELIZA, 10, F, (--), B, SC, 401, 401, EDGE*.

DENNIS, ELIZA, 9, F, (--), B, SC, 621, 621, CHES. In HH of David Dennis m 50, Black born SC.

DENNIS, ELLICK, 16, M, (--), B, SC, 377, 377, EDGE*. In HH of Dempstand Bug m 34 mulatto born SC.

DENNIS, JAMES, 1, M, (--), M, SC, 621, 621, CHES. In HH of David Dennis m 50, Black born SC.

DENNIS, MARY E., 14, F, (--), B, SC, 621, 621, CHES. In HH of David Dennis m 50, Black born SC.

DENNIS, MILLEGE, 3, M, (--), B, SC, 377, 377, EDGE*. In HH of Dempstand Bug m 34 mulatto born SC.

DENNIS, PETER, 26, M, (--), B, SC, 621, 621, CHES. In HH of David Dennis m 50, Black born SC.

DENNIS, POLLY, 18, F, (--), B, SC, 621, 621, CHES. In HH of David Dennis m 50, Black born SC.

DENNIS, SAMPSON, 1, M, (--), B, SC, 401, 401, EDGE*. In HH of Eliza Dennis f 10 black born SC. age 10 {sic}

DENNIS, SARAH, 6, F, (--), B, SC, 377, 377, EDGE*. In HH of Dempstand Bug m 34 mulatto born SC.

DENNIS, WADE, 14, M, (--), B, SC, 377, 377, EDGE*. In HH of Dempstand Bug m 34 mulatto born SC.

DENSMOOR, WILLIAM, 70, M, Laborer, M, SC, 479, 479, BEAU-.

DEREEF, ABIGAL, 7, M, (--), M, SC, 681, 673, CHAS%. In HH of Joseph Dereef m 45 mulatto born SC.

DEREEF, CAROLINE, 22, F, (--), M, SC, 805, 763, CHAS+. In HH of Rebecca Thomas f 55 mulatto born SC.

DEREEF, CAROLINE, 14, F, (--), M, SC, 348, 348, CHAS%. In HH of R.E. Dereef m 52 mulatto born SC.

DEREEF, CHARLOTTE, 3, F, (--), M, SC, 681, 673, CHAS%. In HH of Joseph Dereef m 45 mulatto born SC.

DEREEF, EDWARD, 24, M, Wood Factor, M, SC, 805, 763, CHAS+. In HH of Rebecca Thomas f 55 mulatto born SC.

DEREEF, ELIZABETH, 14, F, (--), M, SC, 681, 673, CHAS%. In HH of Joseph Dereef m 45 mulatto born SC.

DEREEF, GARDNER, 1, M, (--), M, SC, 805, 763, CHAS+. In HH of Rebecca Thomas f 55 mulatto born SC.

DEREEF, HARRIET, 10, F, (--), M, SC, 348, 348, CHAS%. In HH of R.E. Dereef m 52 mulatto born SC.

DEREEF, ISABELLA, 52, F, (--), M, SC, 348, 348, CHAS%. In HH of R.E. Dereef m 52 mulatto born SC.

DEREEF, ISABELLA, 16, F, (--), M, SC, 348, 348, CHAS%. In HH of R.E. Dereef m 52 mulatto born SC.

DEREEF, JOSEPH, 45, M, Wood Factor, M, SC, 681, 673, CHAS%.

DEREEF, JOSEPH, 20, M, (--), M, SC, 348, 348, CHAS%. In HH of R.E. Dereef m 52 mulatto born SC.

DEREEF, JUSTINA, 5, F, (--), M, SC, 681, 673, CHAS%. In HH of Joseph Dereef m 45 mulatto born SC.

DEREEF, MARY, 45, F, (--), M, SC, 681, 673, CHAS%. In HH of Joseph Dereef m 45 mulatto born SC.

DEREEF, R., 2, M, (--), M, SC, 805, 763, CHAS+. In HH of Rebecca Thomas f 55 mulatto born SC.

DEREEF, R.E., 52, M, Wood factor, M, SC, 348, 348, CHAS%.

DEREEF, RICHARD, 2, M, (--), M, SC, 681, 673, CHAS%. In HH of Joseph

Dereef m 45 mulatto born SC.

DERIKER, THOMAS, 46, M, Farmer, B, SC, 1397, 1397, NEWB.

DESESSELINE, ANSEL, 59, M, Laborer, B, SC, 582, 564, CHAS-. In HH of Susan Grain f 39 black born SC.

DESESSELINE, LOUISA, 30, F, (--), B, SC, 582, 564, CHAS-. In HH of Susan Grain f 39 black born SC.

DESETTRE, ADELLA, 35, F, (--), M, SC, 717, 675, CHAS+. In HH of Louisa Arman f 70 mulatto born St. Domingo.

DESETTRE, ANN, 13, F, (--), M, SC, 717, 675, CHAS+. In HH of Louisa Arman f 70 mulatto born St. Domingo.

DESETTRE, CAROLINE, 5, F, (--), M, SC, 717, 675, CHAS+. In HH of Louisa Arman f 70 mulatto born St. Domingo.

DESETTRE, GEORGE, 9, M, (--), M, SC, 717, 675, CHAS+. In HH of Louisa Arman f 70 mulatto born St. Domingo.

DESETTRE, JOHN, 14, M, (--), M, SC, 717, 675, CHAS+. In HH of Louisa Arman f 70 mulatto born St. Domingo.

DESETTRE, SARAH, 11, F, (--), M, SC, 717, 675, CHAS+. In HH of Louisa Arman f 70 mulatto born St. Domingo.

DESOMIR {?}, EDWARD, 9, M, (--), M, SC, 1601, 1601, BARN. In HH of Sarah Desomire{?} f 45 mulatto born SC.

DESOMIR{?}, SARAH, 45, F, None, M, SC, 1601, 1601, BARN.

DESOMIR{?}, WILLIAM, 13, M, (--), M, SC, 1601, 1601, BARN. In HH of Sarah Desomire {?} f 45 mulatto born SC.

DESPRATT, ADAM, 10, M, (--), M, SC, 815, 773, CHAS+. In HH of Carolina Despratt m 54 mulatto born SC.

DESPRATT, CAROLINA, 54, M, Drayman, M, SC, 815, 773, CHAS+.?

DESPRATT, JOHN, 14, M, (--), M, SC, 815, 773, CHAS+. In HH of Carolina Despratt m 54 mulatto born SC.

DESPRATT, LEWIS, 44, M, Drayman, M, SC, 815, 773, CHAS+. In HH of Carolina Despratt m 54 mulatto born SC.

DESPRATT, MARY JANE, 21, F, (--), M, SC, 815, 773, CHAS+. In HH of Carolina Despratt m 54 mulatto born SC.

DESPRATT, SYNTHIA, 40, F, (--), M, SC, 815, 773, CHAS+. In HH of Carolina Despratt m 54 mulatto born SC.

DESVERNIEZ, ISABELLA, 28, F, (--), M, SC, 30, 26, CHAS$.

DESVERNIEZ, JOHN, 3, M, (--), M, SC, 30, 26, CHAS$. In HH of Isabella Desverniez f 28 mulatto born SC.

DEVANER, JOHN, 30, M, Laborer, B, SC, 233, 233, CHAS%. In HH of Bridy McKenzie m 50 black born SC.

DEVINE, ALEXANDER, 20, M, Blacksmith, M, SC, 487, 470, CHAS-. In HH of Teresa LaPont f 60 mulatto born St.Domingo.

DEVINE, EDWARD, 25, M, Barber, M, SC, 487, 470, CHAS-. In HH of Teresa LaPont f 60 mulatto born St.Domingo.

DEVINE, JOHN, 33, M, Confectioner, M, SC, 487, 470, CHAS-. In HH of Teresa LaPont f 60 mulatto born St.Domingo.

DEVINE, JOHN, 2, M, (--), M, SC, 487, 470, CHAS-. In HH of Teresa LaPont f 60 mulatto born St.Domingo.

DEVINEAU, EDWARD, 5, M, (--), M, SC, 588, 580, CHAS%. In HH of Peter Devineau m 60 mulatto born SC.

DEVINEAU, PETER, 60, M, Drayman, M, SC, 588, 580, CHAS%.

DEVINEAU, SARAH, 50, F, (--), M, SC, 588, 580, CHAS%. In HH of Peter Devineau m 60 mulatto born SC.

DEVINIER, CLARA, 10, F, (--), M, SC, 676, 634, CHAS+. In HH of F. Devinier m 30 mulatto born SC.

DEVINIER, F., 30, M, Stable keeper, M, SC, 676, 634, CHAS+.

DEVINIER, FRANCIS, 8, M, (--), M, SC, 676, 634, CHAS+. In HH of F. Devinier m 30 mulatto born SC.

DEVINIER, ROSWELL, 5, M, (--), M, SC, 676, 634, CHAS+. In HH of F. Devinier m 30 mulatto born SC.

DEVINIER, SOPHIA, 28, M, (--), M,

SC, 676, 634, CHAS+. In HH of F. Devinier m 30 mulatto born SC.

DEVINIER, THOMAS, 3, M, (--), M, SC, 676, 634, CHAS+. In HH of F. Devinier m 30 mulatto born SC.

DEVINIER, WALTER, 1, M, (--), M, SC, 676, 634, CHAS+. In HH of F. Devinier m 30 mulatto born SC.

DEWEES, CONSTANTIA, 5, F, (--), M, SC, 584, 576, CHAS%. In HH of Wm. C. Dewees m 30 mulatto born SC.

DEWEES, EDWARD, 8, M, (--), M, SC, 584, 576, CHAS%. In HH of Wm. C. Dewees m 30 mulatto born SC.

DEWEES, ELIZA, 30, F, (--), M, SC, 584, 576, CHAS%. In HH of Wm. C. Dewees m 30 mulatto born SC.

DEWEES, FRANCIS, 3, M, (--), M, SC, 584, 576, CHAS%. In HH of Wm. C. Dewees m 30 mulatto born SC.

DEWEES, WM. C., 30, M, Wheelwright, M, SC, 584, 576, CHAS%.

DEWITT, JULIA, 15, F, (--), M, SC, 941, 921, CHAS-. In HH of Joshua Mishaw m 27 mulatto born SC.

DICKENSON, STEPHEN, 35, M, Cooper, M, SC, 492, 446, CHAS. In HH of Henry Rancken m 26 born Germany.

DICKEY, CARY, 60, M, (--), M, NC, 1028, 1028, YORK. In HH of Cary Moleham f 50 mulatto born SC.

DICKIN, EMMA, 9, F, (--), M, Germany {sic}, 349, 332, CHAS-. In HH of Louisa Dickin f 37 mulatto born Germany {sic}.

DICKIN, HENRY, 31, M, Laborer, M, Germany {sic}, 349, 332, CHAS-. In HH of Louisa Dickin f 37 mulatto born Germany {sic}.

DICKIN, JOHN, 11, M, (--), M, Germany {sic}, 349, 332, CHAS-. In HH of Louisa Dickin f 37 mulatto born Germany {sic}.

DICKIN, JULIET, 4, F, (--), M, Germany {sic}, 349, 332, CHAS-. In HH of Louisa Dickin f 37 mulatto born Germany {sic}.

DICKIN, LOUISA, 37, F, (--), M,

Germany {sic}, 349, 332, CHAS-.

DICKIN, LOUISA, 6, F, (--), M, Germany {sic}, 349, 332, CHAS-. In HH of Louisa Dickin f 37 mulatto born Germany {sic}.

DICKIN, PHILIP, 2, M, (--), M, Germany {sic}, 349, 332, CHAS-. In HH of Louisa Dickin f 37 mulatto born Germany {sic}.

DICKIN, THOMAS, 14, M, (--), M, Germany {sic}, 349, 332, CHAS-. In HH of Louisa Dickin f 37 mulatto born Germany {sic}.

DIEDERICK, LOUISA, 12, F, (--), M, SC, 834, 815, CHAS%. In HH of Elizabeth Cambridge f 37 mulatto born SC.

DIGGERS, ELIZABETH, 76, F, (--), M, SC, 1231, 1236, MAR.

DIGGERS, NELLY, 25, F, (--), M, SC, 376, 376, MARL. In HH of John Pearson m 54 born SC.

DILMAN, J., 40, M, (--), M, SC, 2457, 2457, BARN. In HH of A. Dunbar m 29 born SC.

DIME, JOHN, 1, M, (--), M, SC, 80, 80, GEOR. In HH of Elizabeth Wale f 35 mulatto born SC.

DIME, LOUISA, 3, F, (--), M, SC, 80, 80, GEOR. In HH of Elizabeth Wale f 35 mulatto born SC.

DIME, M.G., 24, F, (--), M, SC, 80, 80, GEOR. In HH of Elizabeth Wale f 35 mulatto born SC.

DIMERY EADY, 2, F, (--), M, SC, 835, 835, MARL. In HH of Uriah Dimery m 45 mulatto born SC.

DIMERY, ANN, 30, F, (--), M, SC, 835, 835, MARL. In HH of Uriah Dimery m 45 mulatto born SC.

DIMERY, DANIEL, 7, M, (--), M, SC, 835, 835, MARL. In HH of Uriah Dimery m 45 mulatto born SC.

DIMERY, ELIZABETH, 2, F, (--), B, SC, 580, 580, MARL. In HH of Mary Jackson f 54 mulatto born SC.

DIMERY, LUCY, 5, F, (--), M, SC, 835, 835, MARL. In HH of Uriah Dimery m 45 mulatto born SC.

DIMERY, MILLY, 11, F, (--), M, SC, 835, 835, MARL. In HH of Uriah Dimery m 45 mulatto born SC.

DIMERY, NOAH, 9, M, (--), M, SC, 835, 835, MARL. In HH of Uriah Dimery m 45 mulatto born SC.

DIMERY, URIAH, 45, M, Farmer, M, SC, 835, 835, MARL.

DINGLE, CAROLINE, 40, F, (--), M, SC, 434, 431, CHAS%.

DINGLE, JNO., 21, M, Laborer, M, SC, 183, 183, SUMT. In HH of Moses Dingle m 52 mulatto born SC.

DINGLE, JOHN, 14, M, (--), M, SC, 183, 183, SUMT. In HH of Moses Dingle m 52 mulatto born SC.

DINGLE, LEONORA, 7, F, (--), M, SC, 183, 183, SUMT. In HH of Moses Dingle m 52 mulatto born SC.

DINGLE, MARY, 2, F, (--), M, SC, 183, 183, SUMT. In HH of Moses Dingle m 52 mulatto born SC.

DINGLE, MILLY, 36, F, (--), M, SC, 183, 183, SUMT. In HH of Moses Dingle m 52 mulatto born SC.

DINGLE, MOSES, 52, M, Planter, M, SC, 183, 183, SUMT.

DINGLE, MOSES, 37, M, Drayman, M, SC, 434, 431, CHAS%. In HH of Caroline Dingle f 40 mulatto born SC.

DINGLE, MOSES, 18, M, Laborer, M, SC, 183, 183, SUMT. In HH of Moses Dingle m 52 mulatto born SC.

DINGLE, RUFUS, 20, M, Laborer, M, SC, 183, 183, SUMT. In HH of Moses Dingle m 52 mulatto born SC.

DINGLE, SARAH, 12, F, (--), M, SC, 183, 183, SUMT. In HH of Moses Dingle m 52 mulatto born SC.

DINGLE, WM., 11, M, (--), M, SC, 183, 183, SUMT. In HH of Moses Dingle m 52 mulatto born SC.

DIVER, AMELIA, 60, F, (--), M, SC, 105, 105, COLL+.

DIVER, ELIZABETH, 16, F, (--), M, SC, 105, 105, COLL+. In HH of Amelia Diver f 60 mulatto born SC.

DIVER, GEORGE, 15, M, (--), M, SC, 105, 105, COLL+. In HH of Amelia

Diver f 60 mulatto born SC.

DIVER, JOHN, 23, M, (--), M, SC, 105, 105, COLL+. In HH of Amelia Diver f 60 mulatto born SC.

DIVER, SARAH, 18, F, (--), M, SC, 105, 105, COLL+. In HH of Amelia Diver f 60 mulatto born SC.

DIVER, SUSAN, 20, F, (--), M, SC, 105, 105, COLL+. In HH of Amelia Diver f 60 mulatto born SC.

DIVERER, PETER, 68, M, Painter, B, SC, 443, 426, CHAS-. In HH of Priscilla Diverer f 65 mulatto born SC.

DIVERER, PRISCILLA, 65, F, (--), M, SC, 443, 426, CHAS-.

DIVOR, ADAM, 5, M, (--), M, SC, 108, 108, COLL+. In HH of Wm. Divor m 27 mulatto born SC.

DIVOR, CHRISTOPHER, 8, M, (--), M, SC, 108, 108, COLL+. In HH of Wm. Divor m 27 mulatto born SC.

DIVOR, HARRIET, 35, F, (--), M, SC, 108, 108, COLL+. In HH of Wm. Divor m 27 mulatto born SC.

DIVOR, SARAH A., 9, F, (--), M, SC, 108, 108, COLL+. In HH of Wm. Divor m 27 mulatto born SC.

DIVOR, WM., 27, M, Raftman, M, SC, 108, 108, COLL+.

DOBIN, ANTHONY, 55, M, Farmer, B, SC, 86, 86, GEOR*.

DOBIN, LISBY, 19, F, (--), M, SC, 87, 87, GEOR*. In HH of Wm. Dobin m 23 mulatto born SC.

DOBIN, MARY, 56, F, (--), M, SC, 86, 86, GEOR*. In HH of Anthony Dobin m 55 black born SC.

DOBIN, SAML., 25, M, Carpenter, M, SC, 86, 86, GEOR*. In HH of Anthony Dobin m 55 black born SC.

DOBIN, WM., 23, M, Carpenter, M, SC, 87, 87, GEOR*.

DOE, BETSEY, 38, F, Planter, M, SC, 1859, 1859, BARN.

DOE, CATHERINE, 4, F, (--), M, SC, 2221, 2221, BARN. In HH of Esther Doe f 25 mulatto born SC.

DOE, CORNELIA, 4, F, (--), M, SC,

2219, 2219, BARN. In HH of July Doe f 38 mulatto born SC.

DOE, CULLER, 8, M, (--), M, SC, 2219, 2219, BARN. In HH of July Doe f 38 mulatto born SC.

DOE, EDWARD, 21, M, Planter, M, SC, 2222, 2222, BARN.

DOE, ESTHER, 25, F, Planter, M, SC, 2221, 2221, BARN.

DOE, HEDDY, 2, M, (--), M, SC, 2222, 2222, BARN. In HH of Edward Doe m 21 mulatto born SC.

DOE, HESTER, 16, F, (--), M, SC, 1859, 1859, BARN. IN HH of Betsey Doe f 38 mulatto born SC.

DOE, HESTER, 12, M, (--), M, SC, 2220, 2220, BARN. In HH of Louisa Doe f 29 mulatto born SC.

DOE, JNO., 15, M, (--), M, SC, 1600, 1600, BARN. In HH of Sarah Doe f 23 mulatto born SC.

DOE, JOHN, 16, M, (--), M, SC, 2219, 2219, BARN. In HH of July Doe f 38 mulatto born SC.

DOE, JOS., 1, M, (--), M, SC, 2222, 2222, BARN. In HH of Edward Doe m 21 mulatto born SC.

DOE, JUDY, 38, F, Planter, M, SC, 2219, 2219, BARN.

DOE, JULIA, 27, F, (--), M, SC, 2222, 2222, BARN. In HH of Edward Doe m 21 mulatto born SC.

DOE, JULIA, 14, F, (--), M, SC, 2219, 2219, BARN. In HH of July Doe f 38 mulatto born SC.

DOE, LAURENCE, 18, M, (--), M, SC, 1859, 1859, BARN. IN HH of Betsey Doe f 38 mulatto born SC.

DOE, LIZZY, 5, F, (--), M, SC, 1859, 1859, BARN. IN HH of Betsey Doe f 38 mulatto born SC.

DOE, LOUISA, 29, F, Planter, M, SC, 2220, 2220, BARN.

DOE, MARY, 10, F, (--), M, SC, 1859, 1859, BARN. IN HH of Betsey Doe f 38 mulatto born SC.

DOE, MARY, 6, F, (--), M, SC, 2219, 2219, BARN. In HH of July Doe f 38 mulatto born SC.

DOE, NED, 20, M, (--), M, SC, 1859, 1859, BARN. IN HH of Betsey Doe f 38 mulatto born SC.

DOE, REBECCA, 20, F, (--), M, SC, 1600, 1600, BARN. In HH of Sarah Doe f 23 mulatto born SC.

DOE, REBECCA, 18, F, (--), M, SC, 2219, 2219, BARN. In HH of July Doe f 38 mulatto born SC.

DOE, SAML., 8, M, (--), M, SC, 2223, 2223, BARN. In HH of Thrallessa Doe m 30 mulatto born SC.

DOE, SARAH, 23, F, (--), M, SC, 1600, 1600, BARN.

DOE, SARAH, 20, F, (--), M, SC, 2219, 2219, BARN. In HH of July Doe f 38 mulatto born SC.

DOE, SERVILLITY, 12, M, (--), M, SC, 2219, 2219, BARN. In HH of July Doe f 38 mulatto born SC.

DOE, THRALLESSA, 30, M, Planter, M, SC, 2223, 2223, BARN.

DOE, WARREN, 2, M, (--), M, SC, 2223, 2223, BARN. In HH of Thrallessa Doe m 30 mulatto born SC.

DOE, WESLEY, 15, M, (--), M, SC, 1859, 1859, BARN. IN HH of Betsey Doe f 38 mulatto born SC.

DOE, WILSON, 9, M, (--), M, SC, 2219, 2219, BARN. In HH of July Doe f 38 mulatto born SC.

DOE, WM., 6, M, (--), M, SC, 2222, 2222, BARN. In HH of Edward Doe m 21 mulatto born SC.

DOE, WM., 2, M, (--), M, SC, 2219, 2219, BARN. In HH of July Doe f 38 mulatto born SC.

DONALDSON, CHARLOTTE, 6, F, (--), B, SC, 1585, 1585, ABB . In HH of Benjamin Cockran m 31 white born SC.

DONALSON, AMANDA E., 8, F, (--), B, SC, 830, 830, CHFD. In HH of Lucy Donalson f 24 black born SC.

DONALSON, BETSEY A., 0, F, (--), B, SC, 836, 836, CHFD. In HH of Dinah Donalson f 45 mulatto born SC. Betsey A. Donalson 3/12 yr.

DONALSON, BETSY A., 0, F, (--), B, SC, 922, 922, ABB . In HH of Harriet

Donalson 20 black born SC. Betsy A. age 2/12 yr.

DONALSON, CHARLOTTE, 9, F,(--), B, SC, 836, 836, CHFD. In HH of Dinah Donalson f 45 mulatto born SC.

DONALSON, DERRY, 1, M, (--), B, SC, 830, 830, CHFD. In HH of Lucy Donalson f 24 black born SC.

DONALSON, DERRY, 0, M, (--), B, SC, 836, 836, CHFD. In HH of Dinah Donalson f 45 mulatto born SC. Derry Donalson 1/12 yr.

DONALSON, DINAH, 45, F, (--), M, SC, 836, 836, CHFD.

DONALSON, HANNAH, 8, F, (--), M, SC, 2335, 2335, ABB . In HH of Bowe Dayl m 25 white born SC.

DONALSON, HANNAH, 6, F, (--), B, SC, 830, 830, CHFD. In HH of Lucy Donalson f 24 black born SC.

DONALSON, HARRIET, 20, F, (--), B, SC, 836, 836, CHFD. In HH of Dinah Donalson f 45 mulatto born SC.

DONALSON, HARRIET, 20, F, (--), B, SC, 922, 922, ABB .

DONALSON, JACOB, 33, M, Blacksmith, B, SC, 579, 579, CHFD.

DONALSON, JANE, 2, F, (--), B, SC, 836, 836, CHFD. In HH of Dinah Donalson f 45 mulatto born SC.

DONALSON, LAURA, 11, F, (--), B, SC, 836, 836, CHFD. In HH of Dinah Donalson f 45 mulatto born SC.

DONALSON, LOUISA, 10, F, (--), B, SC, 836, 836, CHFD. In HH of Dinah Donalson f 45 mulatto born SC.

DONALSON, LUCY, 24, F, (--), B, SC, 830, 830, CHFD.

DONALSON, RANSOM, 4, M, (--), B, SC, 830, 830, CHFD. In HH of Lucy Donalson f 24 black born SC.

DONALSON, REBECCA, 4, F, (--), B, SC, 836, 836, CHFD. In HH of Dinah Donalson f 45 mulatto born SC. Derry Donalson 1/12 yr.

DONALSON, ROBERT, 50, M, Hireling, B, SC, 862, 862, ABB .

DONALSON, ROBERT, 7, M, (--), B, SC, 836, 836, CHFD. In HH of Dinah

Donalson f 45 mulatto born SC.

DONALSON, SAMUEL, 14, M, (--), B, SC, 922, 922, ABB . In HH of Harriet Donalson 20 black born SC.

DONALSON, SARAH, 15, F, (--), M, SC, 836, 836, CHFD. In HH of Dinah Donalson f 45 mulatto born SC.

DONALSON, SUCKEY, 20, F, (--), B, SC, 830, 830, CHFD. In HH of Lucy Donalson f 24 black born SC.

DONALSON, THOMAS P., 1, M, (--), B, SC, 836, 836, CHFD. In HH of Dinah Donalson f 45 mulatto born SC. yr.

DONALSON, WILLIS, 1, M, (--), B, SC, 830, 830, CHFD. In HH of Lucy Donalson f 24 black born SC.

DORMAN, CATHERINE, 30, F, (--), M, SC, 245, 246, MAR . Catherine Dorman born Marion, SC.

DORMAN, CHARLES, 4, M, (--), M, SC, 245, 246, MAR . In HH of Catherine Dorman 30 f mulatto born Marion, SC. Charles Dorman born Marion, SC.

DORMAN, JOHN, 60, M, (--), M, SC, 245, 246, MAR . In HH of Catherine Dorman 30 f mulatto born Marion, SC. John Dorman born Marion, SC.

DORMAN, SARAH, 10, F, (--), M, SC, 245, 246, MAR . In HH of Catherine Dorman 30 f mulatto born Marion, SC. Sarah Dorman born Marion, SC.

DORMAN, SUSAN, 0, F, (--), M, SC, 245, 246, MAR . In HH of Catherine Dorman 30 f mulatto born Marion, SC. Susan Dorman born Marion, SC, 1/12 yr.

DORRILL, W.L., 6, M, (--), M, SC, 148, 127, CHAS$. In HH of Ann Dorrill f 60 born SC.

DOUGLAS, ELIZABETH, 41, F, (--), M, SC, 53, 53, CHAS*.

DOUGLAS, ELIZABETH, 24, F, (--), M, SC, 26, 26, RICH.

DOUGLAS, GEORGE, 22, M, Barber, M, SC, 820, 803, CHAS%.

DOUGLAS, HANNAH, 50, F, (--), M, SC, 820, 803, CHAS%. In HH of George Douglas m 22 mulatto born SC.

DOUGLAS, ISAAC, 16, M, Laborer, B, SC, 339, 322, CHAS-. In HH of

Margaret Douglas f 59 black born SC.

DOUGLAS, ISADORA, 2, F, (--), M, SC, 26, 26, RICH.

DOUGLAS, JIM, 4, M, (--), M, SC, 26, 26, RICH.

DOUGLAS, LYDIA, 47, F, (--), B, SC, 339, 322, CHAS-. In HH of Margaret Douglas f 59 black born SC.

DOUGLAS, M., 25, F, (--), M, SC, 729, 730, ORNG+. In HH of R. Stone m 38 born SC.

DOUGLAS, MARGARET, 59, F, (--), B, SC, 339, 322, CHAS-.

DOUGLAS, THOMAS, 0, M, (--), M, SC, 729, 730, ORNG+. In HH of R. Stone m 38 born SC. Thomas Douglas age 3/12 yr.

DOUGLAS, WILLIAM, 1, M, (--), M, SC, 26, 26, RICH.

DOUGLASS, GEORGE, 13, M, (--), M, SC, 415, 413, CHAS%. In HH of Harriet Douglass f 41 mulatto born SC.

DOUGLASS, HARRIET, 41, F, (--), M, SC, 415, 413, CHAS%.

DOUGLASS, MARIA, 18, F, (--), M, SC, 415, 413, CHAS%. In HH of Harriet Douglass f 41 mulatto born SC.

DOWNELL, ABBY, 30, F, (--), M, SC, 622, 580, CHAS+. In HH of Isabella Grant f 25 mulatto born SC.

DOWNELL, JAMES D., 37, M, (--), B, SC, 622, 580, CHAS+. In HH of Isabella Grant f 25 mulatto born SC.

DRAYTON, ABBEY, 40, F, (--), M, SC, 982, 961, CHAS-. In HH of Z.R. Jessup m 46 born CT.

DRAYTON, DIANA, 40, F, (--), B, SC, 317, 292, CHAS.

DRAYTON, DIANA, 28, F, (--), B, NY, 475, 433, CHAS+. In HH of Sarah Drayton m 45 black born NY.

DRAYTON, FRANCIS, 25, M, Butcher, B, SC, 649, 641, CHAS%. In HH of Sarah Drayton f 60 black born SC.

DRAYTON, HARRIET, 28, F, (--), B, SC, 857, 834, CHAS%. In HH of Rebecca Wadkins f 39 black born SC.

DRAYTON, HARRIOT, 10, F, (--), M, NY, 475, 433, CHAS+. In HH of Sarah Drayton m 45 black born NY.

DRAYTON, JANE, 7, F, (--), M, SC, 629, 621, CHAS%. In HH of Louisa Drayton f 35 mulatto born SC.

DRAYTON, LOUISA, 35, F, (--), M, SC, 629, 621, CHAS%.

DRAYTON, LOUISA, 20, F, (--), B, SC, 649, 641, CHAS%. In HH of Sarah Drayton f 60 black born SC.

DRAYTON, LUCY, 60, F, (--), B, Ireland {sic}, 407, 405, CHAS%.

DRAYTON, MICHAEL, 23, M, Drayman, B, SC, 649, 641, CHAS%. In HH of Sarah Drayton f 60 black born SC.

DRAYTON, PATIENCE, 11, F, (--), M, NY, 475, 433, CHAS+. In HH of Sarah Drayton m 45 black born NY.

DRAYTON, SARAH, 60, F, (--), B, SC, 649, 641, CHAS%.

DRAYTON, SARAH, 45, F, (--), B, NY, 475, 433, CHAS+.

DRAYTON, THOS., 24, M, (--), M, SC, 323, 323, DARL. In HH of Jno. K. Meigs m 31 born SC.

DREGAN, STEPHEN, 53, M, Shoemaker, B, SC, 221, 221, UNION.

DRENNAN, MELU, 92, M, (--), M, SC, 1205, 1205, YORK. In HH of Sarah Lockheist? f 55 born SC.

DRUMMOND, SUSAN, 22, F, (--), M, SC, 548, 514, CHAS*. In HH of David Johnson m 50 born SC.

DRUMOND, HENRIETTA, 7, F, (--), M, SC, 953, 930, CHAS%. In HH of Rebecca Drumond f 26 mulatto born SC.

DRUMOND, REBECCA, 26, F, (--), M, SC, 953, 930, CHAS%.

DRUMOND, SUSAN, 8, F, (--), M, SC, 953, 930, CHAS%. In HH of Rebecca Drumond f 26 mulatto born SC.

DUBOSE, MAY, 38, M, Drayman, B, SC, 863, 840, CHAS%. In HH of John Lewis m 38 black born SC.

DUCKETT, CHARLES, 70, M, (--), B, SC, 1132, 1132, LAU . In HH of Thom Duckett m 75 black born SC.

DUCKETT, NANCE, 70, F, (--), B, SC, 1132, 1132, LAU . In HH of Thom Duckett m 75 black born SC.

DUCKETT, THOM, 75, M, (--), B, SC, 1132, 1132, LAU .

DUKE, RODAH, 75, F, (--), B, SC, 664, 664, PICK+.

DUN, ELLEN, 25, F, (--), M, SC, 107, 107, COLL+.

DUN, HARRIET, 11, F, (--), M, SC, 107, 107, COLL+. In HH of Ellen Dun 25 mulatto born SC.

DUN, JOHN, 9, M, (--), M, SC, 107, 107, COLL+. In HH of Ellen Dun 25 mulatto born SC.

DUN, LOUISA, 12, F, (--), M, SC, 107, 107, COLL+. In HH of Ellen Dun 25 mulatto born SC.

DUNGEE, BENY, 8, M, (--), B, SC, 78, 78, BARN. In HH of Sally Dungee f 35 Black born SC.

DUNGEE, CANDLYS, 14, F, (--), B, SC, 78, 78, BARN. In HH of Sally Dungee f 35 Black born SC.

DUNGEE, DANA, 9, M, (--), B, SC, 78, 78, BARN. In HH of Sally Dungee f 35 Black born SC.

DUNGEE, EVELINE, 20, F, (--), B, SC, 78, 78, BARN. In HH of Sally Dungee f 35 Black born SC.

DUNGEE, NANE {?}, 12, F, (--), B, SC, 78, 78, BARN. In HH of Sally Dungee f 35 Black born SC.

DUNGEE, SALLY, 35, F, None, B, SC, 78, 78, BARN.

DUNGEE, THOS., 4, M, (--), B, SC, 78, 78, BARN. In HH of Sally Dungee f 35 Black born SC.

DUNKIN, ELZA, 21, F, (--), M, SC, 520, 520, HORR. In HH of Deliah McCliduff, f 65 born SC.

DUPRAT, ANN, 64, F, (--), B, SC, 408, 381, CHAS*.

DUPRAT, ELIZABETH, 37, F, (--), M, SC, 408, 381, CHAS*. In HH of Ann Duprat f 60 black born SC.

DUPRAT, MARY, 25, F, (--), M, SC, 408, 381, CHAS*. In HH of Ann Duprat f 60 black born SC.

DURR, ANDREW, 66, M, Miller, M, SC, 1024, 1001, CHAS%.

DURR, CAROLINE, 18, F, (--), M, SC, 1024, 1001, CHAS%. In HH of Andrew Durr m 66 mulatto born SC.

DURR, ELIZABETH, 22, F, (--), M, SC, 1024, 1001, CHAS%. In HH of Andrew Durr m 66 mulatto born SC.

DURR, MARY, 60, F, (--), M, SC, 1024, 1001, CHAS%. In HH of Andrew Durr m 66 mulatto born SC.

DURR, MARY, 26, F, (--), M, SC, 1024, 1001, CHAS%. In HH of Andrew Durr m 66 mulatto born SC.

DUTCH, REBECCA, 2, F, (--), M, SC, 774, 774, MARL. In HH of James Sweat {?} m 30 born SC.

DUTCH, TEMPE, 25, F, (--), M, SC, 774, 774, MARL. In HH of James Sweat {?} m 30 born SC.

DYE, BENJAMIN, 30, M, Carpenter, M, SC, 135, 135, CHAS^. In HH of Catherine Conyers f 24 black born SC.

E

EADY, DANIEL P., 27, M, Laborer, M, SC, 42, 42, CHAS2. In HH of J. Eady m 73 mulatto born SC.

EADY, J.C., 73, M, Farmer, M, SC, 42, 42, CHAS2.

EADY, JAMES J., 24, M, Laborer, M, SC, 42, 42, CHAS2. In HH of J. Eady m 73 mulatto born SC.

EADY, ROBERT B., 23, M, Laborer, M, SC, 42, 42, CHAS2. In HH of J. Eady m 73 mulatto born SC.

EARLE, BETTY, 65, F, (--), B, SC, 110, 110, GREE. In HH of Henry Earle m 80 black born SC.

EARLE, HENRY, 80, M, Laborer, B, SC, 110, 110, GREE.

EARLE, JAMES, 65, M, Laborer, B, SC, 110, 110, GREE. In HH of Henry Earle m 80 black born SC.

EARLE, LISTER, 35, M, Laborer, B,

SC, 110, 110, GREE. In HH of Henry Earle m 80 black born SC.

EARLE, MATTY, 65, M, Laborer, B, SC, 110, 110, GREE. In HH of Henry Earle m 80 black born SC.

EARLE, MILLY, 65, F, (--), B, SC, 110, 110, GREE. In HH of Henry Earle m 80 black born SC.

ECHARD, ELIZABETH , 0, F, (--), M, SC, 348, 348, CHAS%. In HH of R.E. Dereef m 52 mulatto born SC. Elizabeth Echard age 9/12 yr.

ECHARD, ISABELLA, 2, F, (--), M, SC, 348, 348, CHAS%. In HH of R.E. Dereef m 52 mulatto born SC.

ECHARD, JOANA, 28, F, (--), M, SC, 348, 348, CHAS%. In HH of R.E. Dereef m 52 mulatto born SC.

ECHARD, JOANA, 0, F, (--), M, SC, 348, 348, CHAS%. In HH of R.E. Dereef m 52 mulatto born SC. Joana Echard age 9/12 yr.

ECHARD, JOSAPHINE , 4, F, (--), M, SC, 348, 348, CHAS%. In HH of R.E. Dereef m 52 mulatto born SC.

ECHARD, M.G., 28, M, Wheelwright, M, SC, 348, 348, CHAS%. In HH of R.E. Dereef m 52 mulatto born SC.

EDWARDS, ALEXANDER , 8, M, (--), M, SC, 970, 947, CHAS%. In HH of Anna Norsett f 25 mulatto born SC.

EDWARDS, ASA, 20, F, (--), B, SC, 309, 315, RICH+. In HH of Raphael Edwards m 27 black born SC.

EDWARDS, ELIZA, 18, F, (--), M, SC, 619, 611, CHAS%. In HH of Benjamin Johnson m 48 mulatto born SC.

EDWARDS, ELIZABETH, 9, F, (--), M, SC, 970, 947, CHAS%. In HH of Anna Norsett f 25 mulatto born SC.

EDWARDS, FLORA, 54, F, (--), M, SC, 619, 611, CHAS%. In HH of Benjamin Johnson m 48 mulatto born SC.

EDWARDS, HARRIET, 38, F, (--), B, SC, 672, 664, CHAS%.

EDWARDS, HARRIET, 16, F, (--), M, SC, 619, 611, CHAS%. In HH of Benjamin Johnson m 48 mulatto born

SC.

EDWARDS, HENRY, 12, M, (--), M, SC, 970, 947, CHAS%. In HH of Anna Norsett f 25 mulatto born SC.

EDWARDS, JAMES, 26, M, Carpenter, M, SC, 516, 509, CHAS%.

EDWARDS, JAMES, 4, M, (--), M, SC, 970, 947, CHAS%. In HH of Anna Norsett f 25 mulatto born SC.

EDWARDS, JOHN, 35, M, Bricklayer, M, SC, 970, 947, CHAS%. In HH of Anna Norsett f 25 mulatto born SC.

EDWARDS, JOSEPHINE, 28, F, (--), M, SC, 970, 947, CHAS%. In HH of Anna Norsett f 25 mulatto born SC.

EDWARDS, MARY C., 7, F, (--), M, SC, 970, 947, CHAS%. In HH of Anna Norsett f 25 mulatto born SC.

EDWARDS, PAUL, 2, M, (--), M, SC, 970, 947, CHAS%. In HH of Anna Norsett f 25 mulatto born SC.

EDWARDS, RAPHAEL, 27, M, Planter, B, SC, 309, 315, RICH+.

EDWARDS, ROBERT, 5, M, (--), M, SC, 970, 947, CHAS%. In HH of Anna Norsett f 25 mulatto born SC.

EDWARDS, ROSE, 10, F, (--), B, SC, 309, 315, RICH+. In HH of Raphael Edwards m 27 black born SC.

EDWARDS, SALENA, 16, F, (--), B, SC, 672, 664, CHAS%. In HH of Harriet Edwards f 38 black born SC.

EDWARDS, SAMUEL, 6, M, (--), B, SC, 672, 664, CHAS%. In HH of Harriet Edwards f 38 black born SC.

EDWARDS, SARAH, 21, F, (--), M, SC, 516, 509, CHAS%. In HH of James Edwards m 26 mulatto born SC.

EDWARDS, TRIM, 3, M, (--), B, SC, 672, 664, CHAS%. In HH of Harriet Edwards f 38 black born SC.

EDWARDS, WILLIAM, 22, M, Carpenter, M, SC, 619, 611, CHAS%. In HH of Benjamin Johnson m 48 mulatto born SC.

EDY, AGNES, 34, F, (--), B, SC, 145, 145, CHAS~. In HH of Alfred Edy m 34 black born SC.

EDY, ALFRED, 34, M, (--), B, SC,

145, 145, CHAS~.

EDY, ANN JANE, 14, F, (--), M, SC, 262, 262, GEOR*. In HH of John Williams m 85 mulatto born SC.

EDY, CATHARINE, 48, F, (--), B, SC, 148, 148, CHAS~.

EDY, CATHARINE, 11, F, (--), B, SC, 145, 145, CHAS~. In HH of Alfred Edy m 34 black born SC.

EDY, DANIEL, 23, M, Laborer, B, SC, 149, 149, CHAS~. In HH of Anna Edy f 80 black born SC.

EDY, EDWARD, 9, M, (--), M, SC, 150, 150, CHAS~. In HH of Joshua Weaver m 41 mulatto born SC.

EDY, EZEKIEL, 7, M, (--), B, SC, 149, 149, CHAS~. In HH of Anna Edy f 80 black born SC.

EDY, FRANCES, 45, F, (--), B, SC, 144, 144, CHAS~.

EDY, FRANCIS, 36, M, Laborer, B, SC, 146, 146, CHAS~.

EDY, GABRIEL, 25, M, Laborer, B, SC, 144, 144, CHAS~. In HH of Frances Edy f 45 black born SC.

EDY, HENRY, 18, M, (--), B, SC, 144, 144, CHAS~. In HH of Frances Edy f 45 black born SC.

EDY, HENRY, 9, M, (--), B, SC, 149, 149, CHAS~. In HH of Anna Edy f 80 black born SC.

EDY, JACOB, 8, M, (--), M, SC, 150, 150, CHAS~. In HH of Joshua Weaver m 41 mulatto born SC.

EDY, JAMES, 20, M, (--), B, SC, 144, 144, CHAS~. In HH of Frances Edy f 45 black born SC.

EDY, JEREMIAH, 35, M, Farmer, B, SC, 148, 148, CHAS~. In HH of Catharine Edy f 48 black born SC.

EDY, JOHN, 56, M, Carpenter, B, SC, 78, 78, GEOR*.

EDY, JOSEPH, 50, M, Laborer, B, SC, 149, 149, CHAS~. In HH of Anna Edy f 80 black born SC.

EDY, LOUISA, 21, F, (--), B, SC, 144, 144, CHAS~. In HH of Frances Edy f 45 black born SC.

EDY, MARTHA, 26, F, (--), B, SC, 144, 144, CHAS~. In HH of Frances Edy f 45 black born SC.

EDY, MARY, 13, F, (--), B, SC, 147, 147, CHAS~.

EDY, RACHEL, 26, F, (--), B, SC, 146, 146, CHAS~. In HH of Francis Edy m 36 black born SC.

EDY, RACHEL C., 5, F, (--), B, SC, 149, 149, CHAS~. In HH of Anna Edy f 80 black born SC.

EDY, RANSOM, 32, M, Laborer, B, SC, 148, 148, CHAS~. In HH of Catharine Edy f 48 black born SC.

EDY, ROBERT, 38, M, Laborer, B, SC, 147, 147, CHAS~. In HH of Mary Edy f 13 black born SC.

EDY, SUSAN, 27, F, (--), B, SC, 146, 146, CHAS~. In HH of Francis Edy m 36 black born SC.

EDY, WILLIAM, 41, M, Laborer, B, SC, 149, 149, CHAS~. In HH of Anna Edy f 80 black born SC.

ELFE, AGATHE, 0, F, (--), M, SC, 210, 188, CHAS. In HH of Robert Elfe m 27 mulatto born SC. Agathe Elfe age 8/12 yr.

ELFE, ARAMANTH, 28, F, (--), M, SC, 210, 188, CHAS. In HH of Robert Elfe m 27 mulatto born SC.

ELFE, CORNELIA, 11, F, (--), M, SC, 247, 232, CHAS-. In HH of Elizabeth Savage f 33 mulatto born SC.

ELFE, MARIA, 39, F, (--), M, SC, 237, 237, CHAS%.

ELFE, ROBERT, 27, M, Hair dresser, M, SC, 210, 188, CHAS.

ELFE, SAMUEL, 22, M, Carpenter, M, SC, 237, 237, CHAS%. In HH of Martha Elfe f 39 mulatto born SC.

ELFE, TOM, 70, M, (--), B, SC, 482, 440, CHAS+. In HH of Ned. Lloyd m 30 black born SC.

ELFE, WILLIAM, 7, M, (--), M, SC, 247, 232, CHAS-. In HH of Elizabeth Savage f 33 mulatto born SC.

ELLIOT, BENJAMIN, 42, M, Drayman, M, SC, 843, 801, CHAS+.

ELLIOT, EMELINE, 30, F, (--), M,

SC, 307, 283, CHAS+.

ELLIOT, JOHN, 10, M, (--), M, SC, 843, 801, CHAS+. In HH of Benjamin Elliot m 42 mulatto born SC.

ELLIOT, JULIA, 20, F, (--), M, SC, 843, 801, CHAS+. In HH of Benjamin Elliot m 42 mulatto born SC.

ELLIOT, MARY, 37, F, (--), M, SC, 843, 801, CHAS+. In HH of Benjamin Elliot m 42 mulatto born SC.

ELLIOT, ROBERT, 16, M, (--), M, SC, 843, 801, CHAS+. In HH of Benjamin Elliot m 42 mulatto born SC.

ELLIOTT, ANNETT, 57, F, (--), M, SC, 107, 119, CHAS.

ELLIOTT, EMELY, 32, M, (--), M, SC-, 244, 246, AND.

ELLIOTT, JANE, 45, F, (--), M, SC, 425, 423, CHAS%. In HH of Lizzy Elliott f 60 mulatto born SC.

ELLIOTT, LIZZY, 60, F, (--), M, SC, 425, 423, CHAS%.

ELLIS, ELIZABETH, 72, F, (--), B, SC, 166, 166, FAIR.

ELLIS, JAMES, 25, M, (--), B, SC, 166, 166, FAIR. In HH of Elizabeth Ellis f 72 black born SC.

ELLISON, ELIZA A. , 3, F, (--), M, SC, 1224, 1224, SUMT. In HH of Wm. Ellison m 29 mulatto born SC.

ELLISON, HARRIET M., 1, F, (--), M, SC, 1224, 1224, SUMT. In HH of Wm. Ellison m 29 mulatto born SC.

ELLISON, HENRY, 33, M, Ginmaker, M, SC, 1224, 1224, SUMT. In HH of Wm. Ellison m 29 mulatto born SC.

ELLISON, MARY E., 26, F, (--), M, SC, 1224, 1224, SUMT. In HH of Wm. Ellison m 29 mulatto born SC.

ELLISON, MARY T., 23, F, (--), M, SC, 1224, 1224, SUMT. In HH of Wm. Ellison m 29 mulatto born SC.

ELLISON, MATILDA J., 3, F, (--), M, SC, 1224, 1224, SUMT. In HH of Wm. Ellison m 29 mulatto born SC.

ELLISON, REUBIN, 29, M, (--), M, SC, 1225, 1225, SUMT.

ELLISON, WM., 31, M, Ginmaker, M, SC, 1224, 1224, SUMT. In HH of Wm. Ellison m 29 mulatto born SC.

ELLISON, WM., 29, M, Ginmaker, M, SC, 1224, 1224, SUMT.

ELLISON, WM. J., 5, M, (--), M, SC, 1224, 1224, SUMT. In HH of Wm. Ellison m 29 mulatto born SC.

EMMERLY, DIANA, 6, F, (--), B, SC, 155, 142, CHAS*. In HH of William Emmerly m 30 black born SC.

EMMERLY, HENRY, 8, M, (--), B, SC, 155, 142, CHAS*. In HH of William Emmerly m 30 black born SC.

EMMERLY, JOSEPHINE , 14, F, (--), B, SC, 155, 142, CHAS*. In HH of William Emmerly m 30 black born SC.

EMMERLY, MARY, 25, F, (--), B, SC, 155, 142, CHAS*. In HH of William Emmerly m 30 black born SC.

EMMERLY, WILLIAM, 30, M, Barber, B, SC, 155, 142, CHAS*.

EMMERLY, WILLIAM, 10, M, (--), B, SC, 155, 142, CHAS*. In HH of William Emmerly m 30 black born SC.

ENGLES, REBECCA, 75, F, (--), M, SC, 119, 119, GEOR. In HH of D.J. Wilson m 46 mulatto born SC.

ESLES, PATIENCE, 65, F, (--), B, SC, 1220, 1220, CHES. In HH of Randal Esles 75 m, black born NC. {name could be Estes}

ESLES, RANDAL, 75, M, None, B, NC, 1220, 1220, CHES.

EUBANKS, NANCE, 12, F, (--), M, SC, 702, 702, LAU. In HH of Bill Jackson m 25 mulatto born SC.

EVANS, BERKOP WILES, 2, M, (--), M, SC, 598, 598, YORK. In HH of Elesinga W. Smith m 49 born York Dist., SC.

EVANS, CARROL, 12, M, (--), B, SC, 59, 59, CHAS%. In HH of Friday Evans m 53 black born SC.

EVANS, FRIDAY, 53, M, Carpenter, B, SC, 59, 59, CHAS%.

EVANS, HAZARD, 35, M, Laborer in WH, M, SC, 2066, 2069, EDGE.

EVANS, JANE, 52, F, (--), B, SC, 59, 59, CHAS%. In HH of Friday Evans m

53 black born SC.

EVANS, MARTHA, 55, F, (--), M, SC,630,622, CHAS%. In HH of John Hilson m 40 born Germany.

EVANS, MARY ANN, 24, F, (--), B, SC, 59, 59, CHAS%. In HH of Friday Evans m 53 black born SC.

EVANS, MORGIANA, 19, F, (--), B, SC, 59, 59, CHAS%. In HH of Friday Evans m 53 black born SC.

EVANS, THOMAS, 26, M, Shoemaker, B, SC, 59, 59, CHAS%. In HH of Friday Evans m 53 black born SC.

EVANS, THOMASSINA, 14, F, (--), B, SC, 59, 59, CHAS%. In HH of Friday Evans m 53 black born SC.

EVANS, WILLIAM, 16, M, (--), B, SC, 59, 59, CHAS%. In HH of Friday Evans m 53 black born SC.

EVENS, KASEAH, 35, F, (--), W, TN, 2, 2, ABB. In HH of James Evans m 32, Farmer, born SC.

EWBANKS, PERRIN, 22, M, Laborer, M, SC, 596, 596, UNION. In HH of Jane Bond f 30 born SC. {Eubanks?}.

EWBANKS, SAL, 14, F, (--), M, SC, 596, 596, UNION. In HH of Jane Bond f 30 born SC.{Eubanks?}.

F

FABER, ELIZABETH, 18, F, (--), M, SC, 192, 180, CHAS-. In HH of John Faber m 21 mulatto born SC.

FABER, JOHN, 21, M, Upholsterer, M, SC, 192, 180, CHAS-.

FALBO, ELLEN, 16, F, (--), M, SC, 391, 364, CHAS*. In HH of Elizabeth Kohno f 60 born SC.

FALBO, EMMA, 39, F, (--), M, SC, 391, 364, CHAS*. In HH of Elizabeth Kohno f 60 born SC.

FALBO, JACOB, 45, M, (--), M, SC, 391, 364, CHAS*. In HH of Elizabeth Kohno f 60 born SC.

FALBO, MARTHA, 10, F, (--), M, SC,

391, 364, CHAS*. In HH of Elizabeth Kohno f 60 born SC.

FANCY, MARGARET, 65, F, Fruiterer, M, St. Domingo, 61, 55, CHAS+.

FARBS, JANE, 37, F, (--), B, SC, 402, 402, CHFD. In HH of Jerry Farbs m 35 mulatto born SC.

FARBS, JERRY, 35, M, Farmer, M, SC, 402, 402, CHFD.

FARR, ALBY, 65, F, (--), B, SC, 97, 97, UNN+. In HH of Balen Farr m 70 black born SC.

FARR, BALEN, 70, M, (--), B, SC, 97, 97, UNN+.

FARR, {BLANK}, 8, M, (--), B, SC, 97, 97, UNN+. In HH of Balen Farr m 70 black born SC.

FARR, {BLANK}, 6, M, (--), B, SC, 97, 97, UNN+. In HH of Balen Farr m 70 black born SC.

FARR, {BLANK}, 4, M, (--), B, SC, 97, 97, UNN+. In HH of Balen Farr m 70 black born SC.

FARR, {BLANK}, 1, F, (--), B, SC, 97, 97, UNN+. In HH of Balen Farr m 70 black born SC.

FARR, FRANCIS, 50, F, (--), M, SC, 762, 762, NEWB.

FARR, MARTHA, 25, F, (--), B, SC, 97, 97, UNN+. In HH of Balen Farr m 70 black born SC.

FARR, TENAR, 60, F, (--), M, SC, 701, 659, CHAS+. In HH of Grace Alston f 26 mulatto born SC.

FAUST, CAROLINE, 47, F, (--), M, SC, 826, 784, CHAS+.

FAUST, MARY ANN, 17, F, (--), M, SC, 826, 784, CHAS+. In HH of Caroline Faust f 47 mulatto born SC.

FELDER, JOSEPH, 5, M, (--), M, SC, 699, 657, CHAS+. In HH of Mary DeLarge f 40 mulatto born SC.

FELDER, MARGARET, 21, F, (--), M, SC, 699, 657, CHAS+. In HH of Mary DeLarge f 40 mulatto born SC.

FELDER, MARTHA G., 7, F, (--), M, SC, 699, 657, CHAS+. In HH of Mary DeLarge f 40 mulatto born SC.

FELDER, MARY, 1, F, (--), M, SC, 699, 657, CHAS+. In HH of Mary DeLarge f 40 mulatto born SC.

FELL, MARY, 53, F, (--), B, SC, 342, 316, CHAS*. In HH of Robert Fell m 55 black born SC.

FELL, ROBERT, 55, M, Tailor, B, SC, 342, 316, CHAS*.

FELLOWS, WILLIAM, 35, M, Drayman, B, SC, 1015, 992, CHAS%. In HH of Eliza Fludd f 35 born SC.

FENWICK, EASTON, 4, M, (--), B, SC, 384, 367, CHAS-. In HH of John Fenwick m 30 black born SC.

FENWICK, EMMA, 20, F, (--), B, SC, 384, 367, CHAS-. In HH of John Fenwick m 30 black born SC.

FENWICK, GEORGE, 2, M, (--), B, SC, 384, 367, CHAS-. In HH of John Fenwick m 30 black born SC.

FENWICK, JOHN, 30, M, Laborer, B, SC, 384, 367, CHAS-.

FERGUSON, EMELINE, 30, F, (--), M, SC, 1080, 1057, CHAS-.

FERGUSON, EMELINE, 8, F, (--), M, SC, 1080, 1057, CHAS-. In HH of Emeline Ferguson f 30 mulatto born SC.

FERGUSON, JAMES, 18, M, Drayman, B, SC, 336, 310, CHAS. In HH of Jerry Ferguson m 50 mulatto born SC.

FERGUSON, JANE, 24, F, (--), M, SC, 336, 310, CHAS. In HH of Jerry Ferguson m 50 mulatto born SC.

FERGUSON, JERRY, 50, M, Drayman, M, SC, 336, 310, CHAS.

FERGUSON, JOSHUA, 38, M, Tailor, B, SC, 887, 864, CHAS%. In HH of Nancy Godfrey f 35 black born SC.

FERGUSON, JULIA, 11, F, (--), M, SC, 1080, 1057, CHAS-. In HH of Emeline Ferguson f 30 mulatto born SC.

FERGUSON, MARGARET, 34, F,(--), M, SC, 1080, 1057, CHAS-. In HH of Emeline Ferguson f 30 mulatto born SC.

FERRELL, CHARLES L., 20, M, Carpenter, M, SC, 59, 53, CHAS+. In HH of John F. Tenett m 65 born Germany.

FERRELL, FINNEY, 10, F, (--), M, SC, 934, 914, CHAS-. In HH of John Barre m 59 born France.

FERRELL, FRANCES, 12, F, (--), M, SC, 934, 914, CHAS-. In HH of John Barre m 59 born France.

FERRELL, GEORGE, 75, M, Farmer, M, SC, 105, 105, COLL.

FERRELL, HENRY, 6, M, (--), M, SC, 473, 476, MAR. In HH of James Ferrell m 64 born Marion, SC. Henry born Marion, SC.

FERRELL, JOHN, 14, M, (--), M, SC, 934, 914, CHAS-. In HH of John Barre m 59 born France.

FERRELL, JULIUS, 6, M, (--), M, SC, 934, 914, CHAS-. In HH of John Barre m 59 born France.

FERRELL, MADELINE, 4, F, (--), M, SC, 934, 914, CHAS-. In HH of John Barre m 59 born France.

FERRELL, TIENENE, 8, F, (--), M, SC, 934, 914, CHAS-. In HH of John Barre m 59 born France.

FERRELL, VIRGINIA, 33, F, (--), M, SC, 934, 914, CHAS-. In HH of John Barre m 59 born France.

FERRISTON, BRISTOE, 80, M, Laborer, B, VA, 653, 653, UNION.

FIELD, DANIEL, 35, M, Tailor, B, SC, 23, 23, NEWB. In HH of J. Wilson m 33, Hotel keeper, born SC.

FIELDS, ALEXANDER, 28, M, Laborer, B, SC, 714, 714, COLL.

FIELDS, ANN, 22, F, (--), B, SC, 714, 714, COLL. In HH of Alexander Fields m 28 black born SC.

FIELDS, ANN, 8, F, (--), B, SC, 714, 714, COLL. In HH of Alexander Fields m 28 black born SC.

FIELDS, BENJAMIN, 6, M, (--), M, SC, 555, 521, CHAS*. In HH of Hannah Fields f 22 mulatto born SC.

FIELDS, CHARLES, 10, M, (--), M, SC, 502, 485, CHAS-. In HH of Martha Young f 40 mulatto born SC.

FIELDS, HANNAH, 22, F, (--), M, SC, 555, 521, CHAS*.

FIELDS, JOHN, 4, M, (--), M, SC, 502,

485, CHAS-. In HH of Martha Young f 40 mulatto born SC.

FIELDS, MARY, 60, F, (--), B, SC, 714, 714, COLL. In HH of Alexander Fields m 28 black born SC.

FIELDS, MARY, 10, F, (--), B, SC, 714, 714, COLL. In HH of Alexander Fields m 28 black born SC.

FIELDS, NANCY, 45, F, (--), B, SC, 713, 713, COLL.

FIELDS, PRINCE, 45, M, Tailor, B, SC, 714, 714, COLL. In HH of Alexander Fields m 28 black born SC.

FIELDS, ROSEBELLA, 8, F, (--), M, SC, 502, 485, CHAS-. In HH of Martha Young f 40 mulatto born SC.

FIELDS, WILLIAM, 33, M, Carpenter, B, SC, 713, 713, COLL. In HH of Nancy Fields 45 black born SC.

FINLAY, ELIZABETH, 39, F, (--), M, SC, 370, 370, CHAS%.

FINLAY, JAMES, 20, M, Carpenter, M, SC, 370, 370, CHAS%. In HH of Elizabeth Finlay f 39 mulatto born SC.

FINLAY, JULIET, 14, F, (--), M, SC, 370, 370, CHAS%. In HH of Elizabeth Finlay f 39 mulatto born SC.

FINLAY, SARAH, 16, F, (--), M, SC, 554, 520, CHAS*.

FINNICK, ANN, 27, F, (--), M, SC, 161, 151, CHAS-. In HH of Frances Hatcher f 28 mulatto born SC.

FINNICK, JAMES, 3, M, (--), M, SC, 161, 151, CHAS-. In HH of Frances Hatcher f 28 mulatto born SC.

FINNICK, JULIA, 7, F, (--), M, SC, 161, 151, CHAS-. In HH of Frances Hatcher f 28 mulatto born SC.

FINNICK, MARY, 5, F, (--), M, SC, 161, 151, CHAS-. In HH of Frances Hatcher f 28 mulatto born SC.

FINNICK, ROBERT, 10, M, (--), M, SC, 161, 151, CHAS-. In HH of Frances Hatcher f 28 mulatto born SC.

FISK, JAMES, 19, M, Bricklayer, M, SC, 27, 27, CHAS2. In HH of Harriet Palmer f 75 black born SC.

FLAGG, DIANA, 87, F, (--), B, SC, 21, 21, CHAS%. In HH of Tenah Griffin f 40 black born SC.

FLAGG, DIANA, 10, F, (--), B, SC, 21, 21, CHAS%. In HH of Tenah Griffin f 40 black born SC.

FLAGG, ISAAC, 2, M, (--), B, SC, 21, 21, CHAS%. In HH of Tenah Griffin f 40 black born SC.

FLAGG, JACOB, 4, M, (--), B, SC, 21, 21, CHAS%. In HH of Tenah Griffin f 40 black born SC.

FLAGG, SYLVILA, 48, F, (--), M, SC, 756, 714, CHAS+. In HH of Wm. C. Bruse m 44 born NY {could be Breese}

FLAGG, WASHINGTON, 37, M, Drayman, B, SC, 21, 21, CHAS%. In HH of Tenah Griffin f 40 black born SC.

FLAGG, WILLIAM, 8, M, (--), B, SC, 21, 21, CHAS%. In HH of Tenah Griffin f 40 black born SC.

FLAHARATY, EDWARD, 33, 0, Laborer, M, Ireland {sic}, 1197, 1176, CHAS%. In Boarding House.

FLEETIN, ANNA, 5, F, (--), M, SC, 2238, 2238, BARN. In HH of Sarah Fleetin f 35 born SC.

FLEETIN, GEORGE, 8, M, (--), M, SC, 2238, 2238, BARN. In HH of Sarah Fleetin f 35 born SC.

FLEMING, EMMA, 12, F, (--), M, SC, 690, 648, CHAS+. In HH of John Fleming m 36 mulatto born SC.

FLEMING, JANE, 30, F, (--), M, SC, 690, 648, CHAS+. In HH of John Fleming m 36 mulatto born SC.

FLEMING, JOHN, 36, M, Carpenter, M, SC, 690, 648, CHAS+.

FLIN, AMANDA, 0, F, (--), M, SC, 587, 587, CHFD. In HH of Samuel Flin m 48 mulatto born SC. Amanda Flin 8/12 yr.

FLIN, BETSY, 33, F, (--), M, SC, 587, 587, CHFD. In HH of Samuel Flin m 48 mulatto born SC.

FLIN, GEORGE, 2, M, (--), M, SC, 587, 587, CHFD. In HH of Samuel Flin m 48 mulatto born SC.

FLIN, JARVIS, 4, M, (--), M, SC, 587, 587, CHFD. In HH of Samuel Flin m 48 mulatto born SC.

FLIN, PETER, 6, M, (--), M, SC, 587, 587, CHFD. In HH of Samuel Flin m 48 mulatto born SC.

FLIN, SAMUEL, 48, M, Blacksmith, M, SC, 587, 587, CHFD.

FLOOD, MARY ANN, 30, F, (--), M, SC, 114, 114, COLL+. In HH of Doyly Flood m 45 white born SC.

FLORY, ANN, 65, F, (--), M, SC, 694, 652, CHAS+. In HH of Adeline Antonio f 40 mulatto born SC.

FLORY, MARY, 50, F, (--), M, SC, 353, 353, CHAS%. In HH of Sarah Hemetry f 56 mulatto born SC.

FLOYD, ABERNETHA, 38, F, (--), M, SC, 774, 732, CHAS+.

FLOYD, ALBERT, 25, M, Planter, B, SC, 1121, 1121, BARN.

FLOYD, {BLANK}, 1, F, (--), B, SC, 1120, 1120, BARN. In HH of Henry Floyd m 44 black born SC. Child age 3/12 yr., not named.

FLOYD, HENRY, 44, M, Planter, B, SC, 1120, 1120, BARN.

FLOYD, JOHN, 7, M, (--), M, SC, 774, 732, CHAS+. In HH of Abernetha Floyd f 38 mulatto born SC.

FLOYD, MARY, 16, F, (--), M, SC, 774, 732, CHAS+. In HH of Abernetha Floyd f 38 mulatto born SC.

FLOYD, PATSY, 14, F, (--), B, SC, 1120, 1120, BARN. In HH of Henry Floyd m 44 black born SC.

FLOYD, SALLY, 18, F, (--), B, SC, 1121, 1121, BARN. In HH of Albert Floyd m 25 black born SC.

FLOYD, TEMER {?}, 35, F, (--), B, SC, 1120, 1120, BARN. In HH of Henry Floyd m 44 black born SC.

FLUDD, ELIZTH., 3, F, (--), M, SC, 336, 336, COLL*. In HH of James Fludd m 27 mulatto born SC.

FLUDD, JAMES, 35, M, (--), M, SC, 346, 346, COLL*.

FLUDD, JAMES, 27, M, Laborer, M, SC, 336, 336, COLL*.

FLUDD, JNCO, 19, M, Laborer, M, SC, 338, 338, COLL*. In HH of Robt. J. Limehouse, Jr. m 24 white, born SC.

FLUDD, MARIA, 21, F, (--), M, SC, 346, 346, COLL*. In HH of James Fludd m 35 mulatto born SC.

FLUDD, SARAH, 22, F, (--), M, SC, 336, 336, COLL*. In HH of James Fludd m 27 mulatto born SC.

FLUSH, DOILSY, 15, M, (--), M, SC, 184, 184, COLL. In HH of Eleanor Thornly f 32 mulatto born SC.

FOLLIN, ELIZABETH, 27, F, (--), M, Germany {sic}, 347, 330, CHAS-. In HH of Sarah Wilson f 54 mulatto born Germany {sic}.

FOLLIN, JOE, 13, M, (--), M, SC, 482, 440, CHAS+. In HH of Ned. Lloyd m 30 black born SC.

FOON, E., 50, F, (--), B, SC, 699, 699, NEWB.

FORD, CAROLINE, 22, F, (--), B, SC, 813, 771, CHAS+. In HH of Jane Ramsay f 38 black born SC.

FORD, EDWARD, 5, M, (--), M, SC, 597, 589, CHAS%. In HH of William Ford m 35 mulatto born SC.

FORD, FRED, 5, M, (--), M, SC, 271, 271, GEOR*. In HH of Ladson Ford m 42 mulatto born SC.

FORD, JAMES, 53, M, (--), B, SC, 99, 99, CHAS%. In HH of Susan Ford f 50 black born SC.

FORD, JAMES, 25, M, Bricklayer, B, SC, 813, 771, CHAS+. In HH of Jane Ramsay f 38 black born SC.

FORD, JAMES, 19, M, Laborer, B, SC, 813, 771, CHAS+. In HH of Jane Ramsay f 38 black born SC.

FORD, JANE, 33, F, (--), M, SC, 597, 589, CHAS%. In HH of William Ford m 35 mulatto born SC.

FORD, JOHN, 9, M, (--), M, SC, 597, 589, CHAS%. In HH of William Ford m 35 mulatto born SC.

FORD, LADSON, 42, M, Carpenter, M, SC, 271, 271, GEOR*.

FORD, LISBY, 35, F, (--), M, SC, 271, 271, GEOR*. In HH of Ladson Ford m 42 mulatto born SC.

FORD, MARGARET, 18, F, (--), B, SC, 813, 771, CHAS+. In HH of Jane

Ramsay f 38 black born SC.

FORD, MARGARET, 4, F, (--), M, SC, 597, 589, CHAS%. In HH of William Ford m 35 mulatto born SC.

FORD, MARY, 39, F, (--), M, VA, 2261, 2261, GREE. In HH of Sarah Ford f 64 mulatto born VA.

FORD, NANCY, 3, F, (--), M, SC, 271, 271, GEOR*. In HH of Ladson Ford m 42 mulatto born SC.

FORD, PEGGY, 48, F, (--), B, SC, 813, 771, CHAS+. In HH of Jane Ramsay f 38 black born SC.

FORD, SARAH, 64, F, (--), M, VA, 2261, 2261, GREE.

FORD, SARAH, 7, F, (--), M, SC, 271, 271, GEOR*. In HH of Ladson Ford m 42 mulatto born SC.

FORD, STEPHEN, 7, M, (--), M, SC, 597, 589, CHAS%. In HH of William Ford m 35 mulatto born SC.

FORD, SUSAN, 50, F, (--), B, SC, 99, 99, CHAS%.

FORD, THO, 2, M, (--), M, SC, 271, 271, GEOR*. In HH of Ladson Ford m 42 mulatto born SC.

FORD, WILLIAM, 35, M, Millwright, M, SC, 597, 589, CHAS%.

FORD, WILLIAM, 17, M, Bricklayer, B, SC, 813, 771, CHAS+. In HH of Jane Ramsay f 38 black born SC.

FORD, WILLIAM, 0, M, (--), M, SC, 597, 589, CHAS%. In HH of William Ford m 35 mulatto born SC. William age 7/12 yr.

FORDHAM, HANNAH, 30, F, (--), B, SC, 825, 783, CHAS+. In HH of Geo. A. Locke m 33 born MA.

FORREST, AMANDA, 15, F, (--), M, SC, 424, 422, CHAS%. In HH of R. Forrest m 29 mulatto born SC.

FORREST, ANN, 18, F, (--), M, SC, 424, 422, CHAS%. In HH of R. Forrest m 29 mulatto born SC.

FORREST, FRANCES, 25, F, (--), M, SC, 424, 422, CHAS%. In HH of R. Forrest m 29 mulatto born SC.

FORREST, JAMES, 22, M, Shoemaker, M, SC, 424, 422, CHAS%.

In HH of R. Forrest m 29 mulatto born SC.

FORREST, JOHN J., 12, M, (--), M, SC, 424, 422, CHAS%. In HH of R. Forrest m 29 mulatto born SC.

FORREST, R., 29, M, Shoemaker, M, SC, 424, 422, CHAS%.

FOSE, ELIZABETH, 26, F, (--), M, SC, 283, 267, CHAS-. In HH of Sarah Fose f 69 mulatto born SC.

FOSE, JAMES, 13, M, (--), M, SC, 283, 267, CHAS-. In HH of Sarah Fose f 69 mulatto born SC.

FOSE, SARAH, 69, F, (--), M, SC, 283, 267, CHAS-.

FOSE, THEODORE, 11, M, (--), M, SC, 283, 267, CHAS-. In HH of Sarah Fose f 69 mulatto born SC.

FOSTER, BIDDY, 70, F, (--), B, VA, 1152, 1152, UNION. In HH of Pompey Foster m 80 black born VA.

FOSTER, CAROLINE, 3, F, (--), M, SC, 706, 706, Edge. In HH of Marhsal Thompson m 51 born SC.

FOSTER, EDNEY, 22, F, (--), B, SC, 706, 706, Edge. In HH of Marhsal Thompson m 51 born SC.

FOSTER, ELINEZER, 1, M, (--), B, SC, 706, 706, Edge. In HH of Marhsal Thompson m 51 born SC.

FOSTER, JANE E., 22, F, (--), M, SC, 47, 47, CHAS%. In HH of Sarah A. Foster f 50 mulatto born SC.

FOSTER, POMPEY, 80, M, (--), B, VA, 1152, 1152, UNION.

FOSTER, SARAH, 19, F, (--), M, SC, 155, 159, RICH. {Note HH out of order, follows 185/189}. In HH of Ellen Carter f 28 mulatto born SC.

FOSTER, SARAH A., 50, F, (--), M, SC, 47, 47, CHAS%.

FOSTER, THOMAS P., 19, M, Blacksmith, M, SC, 47, 47, CHAS%. In HH of Sarah A. Foster f 50 mulatto born SC.

FOWLER, C., 37, M, Carpenter, M, SC, 40, 39, CHAS&.

FOWLER, ELIZABETH, 19, F, (--), M, SC, 26, 25, CHAS&. In HH of

Stanhope Fowler m 55 mulatto born SC.

FOWLER, HARRIET, 40, F, (--), M, SC, 98, 98, CHAS%.

FOWLER, JACOB, 13, M, (--), M, SC, 26, 25, CHAS&. In HH of Stanhope Fowler m 55 mulatto born SC.

FOWLER, JEPEN, 34, M, Drayman, M, SC, 374, 374, CHAS%. In HH of Sarah Fowler f 38 mulatto born SC.

FOWLER, JESSE, 11, M, (--), M, SC, 1273, 1273, YORK. In HH of William G. Lackey m 46 born UNION Dist., SC.

FOWLER, JOHN, 34, M, Tailor, M, SC, 98, 98, CHAS%. In HH of Harriet Fowler f 40 mulatto born SC.

FOWLER, JOHN, 11, M, (--), M, SC, 26, 25, CHAS&. In HH of Stanhope Fowler m 55 mulatto born SC.

FOWLER, LEONORA, 10, F, (--), M, SC, 374, 374, CHAS%. In HH of Sarah Fowler f 38 mulatto born SC.

FOWLER, MARIA, 3, F, (--), M, SC, 26, 25, CHAS&. In HH of Stanhope Fowler m 55 mulatto born SC.

FOWLER, MARIE, 26, F, (--), M, SC, 26, 25, CHAS&. In HH of Stanhope Fowler m 55 mulatto born SC.

FOWLER, MARTHA, 24, F, (--), M, SC, 26, 25, CHAS&. In HH of Stanhope Fowler m 55 mulatto born SC.

FOWLER, MARY J., 17, F, (--), M, SC, 98, 98, CHAS%. In HH of Harriet Fowler f 40 mulatto born SC.

FOWLER, MICHAEL, 21, M, Carpenter, M, SC, 26, 25, CHAS&. In HH of Stanhope Fowler m 55 mulatto born SC.

FOWLER, RICHARD, 13, M, (--), M, SC, 374, 374, CHAS%. In HH of Sarah Fowler f 38 mulatto born SC.

FOWLER, ROBINSON, 3, M, (--), M, SC, 26, 25, CHAS&. In HH of Stanhope Fowler m 55 mulatto born SC.

FOWLER, SARAH, 38, F, (--), M, SC, 374, 374, CHAS%.

FOWLER, SARAH, 8, F, (--), M, SC, 26, 25, CHAS&. In HH of Stanhope Fowler m 55 mulatto born SC.

FOWLER, STANHOPE, 55, M, Millwright, M, SC, 26, 25, CHAS&.

FRANCES, HANNAH, 50, F, (--), B, SC, 286, 265, CHAS+.

FRANCES, HENRY, 39, M, Carpenter, M, SC, 157, 157, CHAS%.

FRANCES, JAMES, 16, M, (--), M, SC, 157, 157, CHAS%. In HH of Henry Frances m 39 mulatto born SC.

FRANCES, JOHN, 40, M, Hair dresser, M, SC, 808, 788, CHAS-.

FRANCES, MARY, 35, F, (--), M, SC, 157, 157, CHAS%. In HH of Henry Frances m 39 mulatto born SC.

FRANCIS, EDWARD, 37, M, Rigger, B, SC, 814, 772, CHAS+.

FRANCIS, EDWARD, 10, M, (--), M, SC, 591, 583, CHAS%. In HH of John Francis m 41 mulatto born SC.

FRANCIS, ELIZABETH, 2, F, (--), M, SC, 483, 483, BEAU-. In HH of Frank Francis m 30 mulatto born SC.

FRANCIS, FRANCIS, 30, F, (--), M, SC, 591, 583, CHAS%. In HH of John Francis m 41 mulatto born SC.

FRANCIS, FRANK, 30, M, Laborer, M, SC, 483, 483, BEAU-.

FRANCIS, HISTER, 22, F, (--), M, SC, 483, 483, BEAU-. In HH of Frank Francis m 30 mulatto born SC.

FRANCIS, ISAAC, 12, M, (--), M, SC, 814, 772, CHAS+. In HH of Edward Francis m 37 black born SC.

FRANCIS, ISAAC, 1, M, (--), M, SC, 591, 583, CHAS%. In HH of John Francis m 41 mulatto born SC.

FRANCIS, JAMES, 43, M, Barber, M, SC, 626, 644, RICH.

FRANCIS, JOHN, 41, M, Laborer, M, SC, 591, 583, CHAS%.

FRANCIS, JOHN, 20, M, Rigger, B, SC, 814, 772, CHAS+. In HH of Edward Francis m 37 black born SC.

FRANCIS, JOHN, 8, M, (--), M, SC, 591, 583, CHAS%. In HH of John Francis m 41 mulatto born SC.

FRANCIS, JOHN, 4, M, (--), M, SC, 483, 483, BEAU-. In HH of Frank Francis m 30 mulatto born SC.

FRANCIS, MARGARET, 14, F, (--), M, SC, 814, 772, CHAS+. In HH of Edward Francis m 37 black born SC.

FRANCIS, MARGARET, 7, F, (--), M, SC, 591, 583, CHAS%. In HH of John Francis m 41 mulatto born SC.

FRANCIS, RACHAEL, 0, F, (--), M, SC, 483, 483, BEAU-. In HH of Frank Francis m 30 mulatto born SC. Rachel 2/12 yr.

FRANCIS, WILLIAM, 19, M, Locksmith, M, SC, 318, 302, CHAS-. In HH of C.Y. Richardson m 35 born England.

FRASER, AMELIA, 12, F, (--), M, SC, 557, 540, CHAS-. In HH of Susan Marshall f 28 mulatto born SC.

FRASER, DIANA, 0, F, (--), B, SC, 259, 233, CHAS*. In HH of Julia Anna Johnson f 27 black born SC. Diana Fraser age 5/12 yr.

FRASER, DIANAH, 0, F, (--), M, SC, 441, 408, CHAS*. In HH of Phoebe Mathews f 22 black born SC.

FRASER, GEORGIANA, 30, F, (--), M, SC, 557, 540, CHAS-. In HH of Susan Marshall f 28 mulatto born SC.

FRASER, JASPER, 8, M, (--), M, SC, 557, 540, CHAS-. In HH of Susan Marshall f 28 mulatto born SC.

FRASER, NINA, 18, F, (--), M, SC, 557, 540, CHAS-. In HH of Susan Marshall f 28 mulatto born SC.

FRASER, PHOEBE, 23, F, (--), B, SC, 259, 233, CHAS*. In HH of Julia Anna Johnson f 27 black born SC.

FRASIER, ANNE, 4, F, (--), B, SC, 329, 329, CHAS%. In HH of Emma Frasier f 35 black born SC.

FRASIER, CATHERINE, 10, F, (--), B, SC, 329, 329, CHAS%. In HH of Emma Frasier f 35 black born SC.

FRASIER, EMMA, 35, F, (--), B, SC, 329, 329, CHAS%.

FRASIER, JOB, 3, M, (--), B, SC, 329, 329, CHAS%. In HH of Emma Frasier f 35 black born SC.

FRASIER, THOMAS, 9, M, (--), B, SC, 329, 329, CHAS%. In HH of Emma

Frasier f 35 black born SC.

FRAZER, CATHERINE, 11, F, (--), M, SC, 134, 134, CHAS%. In HH of Sarah Frazer f 40 mulatto born SC.

FRAZER, CHARLOTTE, 16, F, (--), M, SC, 134, 134, CHAS%. In HH of Sarah Frazer f 40 mulatto born SC.

FRAZER, FRANCIS, 25, F, (--), M, SC, 664, 622, CHAS+. In HH of Robert Elfe m 50 born SC.

FRAZER, HENRY, 4, M, (--), M, SC, 664, 622, CHAS+. In HH of Robert Elfe m 50 born SC.

FRAZER, JAMES, 13, M, (--), M, SC, 134, 134, CHAS%. In HH of Sarah Frazer f 40 mulatto born SC.

FRAZER, JOHN, 50, M, Tailor, M, SC, 220, 206, CHAS-.

FRAZER, LIZZY, 20, F, (--), M, SC, 134, 134, CHAS%. In HH of Sarah Frazer f 40 mulatto born SC.

FRAZER, ROZANNAH, 18, F, (--), M, SC, 134, 134, CHAS%. In HH of Sarah Frazer f 40 mulatto born SC.

FRAZER, SARAH, 40, F, (--), M, SC, 134, 134, CHAS%.

FRAZIER, FRANCIS, 14, M, (--), B, SC, 1025, 1002, CHAS%. In HH of Nathaniel Frazier m 40 black born SC.

FRAZIER, ISAAC, 19, M, (--), B, SC, 1025, 1002, CHAS%. In HH of Nathaniel Frazier m 40 black born SC.

FRAZIER, JANE, 40, F, (--), B, SC, 1025, 1002, CHAS%. In HH of Nathaniel Frazier m 40 black born SC.

FRAZIER, MARY, 13, F, (--), B, SC, 1025, 1002, CHAS%. In HH of Nathaniel Frazier m 40 black born SC.

FRAZIER, NATHANIEL, 40, M, Wheelwright, B, SC, 1025, 1002, CHAS%.

FRAZIER, ROBERT, 12, M, (--), B, SC, 1025, 1002, CHAS%. In HH of Nathaniel Frazier m 40 black born SC.

FREEMAN, B., 27, F, (--), B, SC, 127, 127, CHAS2. In HH of Jacob Freeman m 78 mulatto born SC.

FREEMAN, CAROLINE, 10, F, (--), M, SC, 2335, 2335, ABB. In HH of

Bowe Dayl m 25 white born SC.

FREEMAN, CATHARINE, 8, F, (--), M, SC, 2335, 2335, ABB. In HH of Bowe Dayl m 25 white born SC.

FREEMAN, E., 6, F, (--), B, SC, 127, 127, CHAS2. In HH of Jacob Freeman m 78 mulatto born SC.

FREEMAN, EMELY, 29, F, (--), M, SC, 2335, 2335, ABB. In HH of Bowe Dayl m 25 white born SC.

FREEMAN, G., 10, M, (--), B, SC, 127, 127, CHAS2. In HH of Jacob Freeman m 78 mulatto born SC.

FREEMAN, GRACY, 35, F, (--), M, SC, 627, 619, CHAS%. In HH of John Freeman m 38 mulatto born SC.

FREEMAN, JACOB, 35, M, Farmer, M, SC, 127, 127, CHAS2.

FREEMAN, JOHN, 38, M, Carpenter, M, SC, 627, 619, CHAS%.

FREEMAN, M., 12, F, (--), B, SC, 127, 127, CHAS2. In HH of Jacob Freeman m 78 mulatto born SC.

FREEMAN, S., 32, M, Farmer, B, SC, 127, 127, CHAS2. In HH of Jacob Freeman m 78 mulatto born SC.

FREEMAN, S., 25, F, (--), B, SC, 127, 127, CHAS2. In HH of Jacob Freeman m 78 mulatto born SC.

FREEMAN, S., 4, F, (--), B, SC, 127, 127, CHAS2. In HH of Jacob Freeman m 78 mulatto born SC.

FREEMAN, S., 2, F, (--), B, SC, 127, 127, CHAS2. In HH of Jacob Freeman m 78 mulatto born SC.

FREEMAN, SYLVIA, 35, F, Servant, B, SC, 526, 492, CHAS*. In HH of C.B. Northrop m 37 born SC.

FREEMAN, T., 35, M, Farmer, B, SC, 127, 127, CHAS2. In HH of Jacob Freeman m 78 mulatto born SC.

FREEMAN, T., 8, M, (--), B, SC, 127, 127, CHAS2. In HH of Jacob Freeman m 78 mulatto born SC.

FREZEVANT, DIANA, 60, F, (--), M, SC, 284, 258, CHAS*.

FRIDAY, PRIMUS, 40, M, (--), B, SC, 299, 299, CHAS%.

FROST, ANNA, 2, F, (--), M, Germany {sic}, 531, 546, RICH. In HH of Henry Frost m 26 mulatto born Germany {sic}.

FROST, CAROLINE, 14, F, (--), M, SC, 319, 325, RICH+. In HH of Charles Frost m 44 mulatto born SC.

FROST, CELELIA, 44, F, (--), M, SC, 319, 325, RICH+. In HH of Charles Frost m 44 mulatto born SC.

FROST, CHARLES, 44, M, Planter, M, SC, 319, 325, RICH+.

FROST, DANIEL, 42, M, Laborer, M, SC, 182, 185, RICH+.

FROST, DANIEL, 2, M, (--), M, SC, 319, 325, RICH+. In HH of Charles Frost m 44 mulatto born SC.

FROST, ELIZA, 4, F, (--), M, SC, 319, 325, RICH+. In HH of Charles Frost m 44 mulatto born SC.

FROST, HENRY, 26, M, Shoemaker, M, Germany {sic}, 531, 546, RICH.

FROST, HENRY, 10, M, (--), M, SC, 319, 325, RICH+. In HH of Charles Frost m 44 mulatto born SC.

FROST, HENRY, 3, M, (--), M, Germany {sic}, 531, 546, RICH. In HH of Henry Frost m 26 mulatto born Germany {sic}.

FROST, JAMES, 0, M, (--), M, SC, 182, 185, RICH+. In HH of Daniel Frost m 42 mulatto born SC. James Frost age 6/12 yr.

FROST, JANE, 8, F, (--), M, SC, 319, 325, RICH+. In HH of Charles Frost m 44 mulatto born SC.

FROST, LYDIA, 25, F, (--), M, Germany {sic}, 531, 546, RICH. In HH of Henry Frost m 26 mulatto born Germany {sic}.

FROST, MARTHA, 6, F, (--), M, SC, 319, 325, RICH+. In HH of Charles Frost m 44 mulatto born SC.

FROST, MARY, 16, F, (--), M, SC, 319, 325, RICH+. In HH of Charles Frost m 44 mulatto born SC.

FROST, MARY A., 26, F, (--), M, SC, 182, 185, RICH+. In HH of Daniel Frost m 42 mulatto born SC.

FROST, MARY A., 4, F, (--), M, SC,

182, 185, RICH+. In HH of Daniel Frost m 42 mulatto born SC.

FROST, SARAH, 18, F, (--), M, SC, 319, 325, RICH+. In HH of Charles Frost m 44 mulatto born SC.

FROSTERN, CLARINDA, 4, F, (--), B, SC, 375, 348, CHAS*. In HH of Henry R. Frost m 54 born SC.

FROSTERN, SARAH, 25, F, (--), B, SC, 375, 348, CHAS*. In HH of Henry R. Frost m 54 born SC.

FULLER, ALONGZA, 3, M, (--), M, SC, 244, 229, CHAS-. In HH of Mary Ann Fuller f 25 mulatto born SC.

FULLER, ISAIH, 10, M, (--), M, SC, 244, 229, CHAS-. In HH of Mary Ann Fuller f 25 mulatto born SC.

FULLER, JANE, 76, F, (--), B, SC, 227, 202, CHAS*.

FULLER, JUSTINE, 6, M, (--), M, SC, 244, 229, CHAS-. In HH of Mary Ann Fuller f 25 mulatto born SC.

FULLER, MARY ANN, 25, F, (--), M, SC, 244, 229, CHAS-.

FULLERWIDER {?}, SARAH, 60, F, (--), M, VA, 1136, 1136, YORK. In HH of James Dunn m 58 born NC.

FURTH, DANIEL, 3, M, (--), M, SC, 329, 304, CHAS. In HH of Daniel Furth m 40 born Germany.

G

GADSDEN, ANN, 17, F, (--), M, SC, 587, 579, CHAS%. In HH of Rebecca Gadsden f 70 mulatto born SC.

GADSDEN, HECTOR, 35, M, Farmer, ?, B, SC, 84, 84, CHAS!.

GADSDEN, HENRY, 40, M, Drayman, M, SC, 546, 505, CHAS+. In HH of Mary James f 38 mulatto born SC.

GADSDEN, JOSEPH, 64, M, (--), B, VA, 553, 545, CHAS%.

GADSDEN, JULIA, 6, F, (--), B, SC, 623, 615, CHAS%. In HH of Martha Gadsden f 30 black born SC.

GADSDEN, MARTHA, 30, F, (--), B, SC, 623, 615, CHAS%.

GADSDEN, MARY, 18, F, (--), M, SC, 587, 579, CHAS%. In HH of Rebecca Gadsden f 70 mulatto born SC.

GADSDEN, REBECCA, 70, F, (--), M, SC, 587, 579, CHAS%.

GADSDEN, REBECCA, 15, F, (--), M, SC, 587, 579, CHAS%. In HH of Rebecca Gadsden f 70 mulatto born SC.

GADSDEN, REUBEN, 30, M, Farmer, B, SC, 86, 86, CHAS!.

GADSDEN, ROBERT, 23, M, (--), M, SC, 587, 579, CHAS%. In HH of Rebecca Gadsden f 70 mulatto born SC.

GADSDEN, WILLIAM, 40, M, Farmer, B, SC, 85, 85, CHAS!.

GAILLARD, AMELIA, 28, F, (--), M, SC, 257, 241, CHAS+.

GAILLARD, CHARLES, 38, M, Tailor, M, SC, 830, 788, CHAS+. In HH of J.B. Mathews m 47 black born SC.

GAILLARD, EMMA, 1, F, (--), M, SC, 830, 788, CHAS+. In HH of J.B. Mathews m 47 black born SC.

GAILLARD, FORRET, 40, F, (--), M, SC, 830, 788, CHAS+. In HH of J.B. Mathews m 47 black born SC.

GAILLARD, JANE, 75, F, (--), B, SC, 87, 87, CHAS!.

GAILLARD, LAVINIA, 3, F, (--), M, SC, 830, 788, CHAS+. In HH of J.B. Mathews m 47 black born SC.

GAILLARD, PATSY, 6, F, (--), M, SC, 830, 788, CHAS+. In HH of J.B. Mathews m 47 black born SC.

GAILLARD, REBECCA, 40, F, (--), B, SC, 598, 579, CHAS-.

GAILLARD, SUSAN, 8, F, (--), M, SC, 830, 788, CHAS+. In HH of J.B. Mathews m 47 black born SC.

GAILLARD, WILLIAM, 40, M, Carpenter, M, SC, 143, 133, CHAS-.

GAILLIARD, ELIZABETH, 45, F, (--), B, SC, 198, 198, CHAS%.

GAINS, EDY, 70, F, (--), M, SC, 662, 662, SUMT. In HH of Thos. Gibbs m 72 mulatto born SC.

GAIRIN, ANN, 24, F, (--), M, SC, 66, 66, GEOR. In HH of Sarah Gairin f 27 mulatto born SC.

GAIRIN, CRETIA, 50, F, (--), M, SC, 66, 66, GEOR. In HH of Sarah Gairin f 27 mulatto born SC.

GAIRIN, ELIZA A., 9, F, (--), M, SC, 66, 66, GEOR. In HH of Sarah Gairin f 27 mulatto born SC.

GAIRIN, ELIZABETH, 5, F, (--), M, SC, 66, 66, GEOR. In HH of Sarah Gairin f 27 mulatto born SC.

GAIRIN, JAMES, 7, M, (--), M, SC, 66, 66, GEOR. In HH of Sarah Gairin f 27 mulatto born SC.

GAIRIN, MARY, 30, F, (--), M, SC, 66, 66, GEOR. In HH of Sarah Gairin f 27 mulatto born SC.

GAIRIN, NESBIT, 11, M, (--), M, SC, 66, 66, GEOR. In HH of Sarah Gairin f 27 mulatto born SC.

GAIRIN, PETER, 25, M, Laborer, M, SC, 66, 66, GEOR. In HH of Sarah Gairin f 27 mulatto born SC.

GAIRIN, SARAH, 27, F, (--), M, SC, 66, 66, GEOR.

GAIRIN, WASHINGTON W., 9, M, (--), M, SC, 66, 66, GEOR. In HH of Sarah Gairin f 27 mulatto born SC.

GALLAMER, JACOB, 70, M, (--), B, SC, 1542, 1542, York, SC.

GALPHIN, BRYANT, 17, M, (--), M, SC, 634, 634, BARN. In HH of Geo. Galphin m 45 mulatto born SC.

GALPHIN, GEO., 45, M, (--), M, SC, 634, 634, BARN.

GALPHIN, LOUISA, 13, F, (--), M, SC, 634, 634, BARN. In HH of Geo. Galphin m 45 mulatto born SC.

GALPHIN, MARTHA, 6, F, (--), M, SC, 634, 634, BARN. In HH of Geo. Galphin m 45 mulatto born SC.

GALPHIN, MATILDA, 45, F, (--), M, SC, 634, 634, BARN. In HH of Geo. Galphin m 45 mulatto born SC.

GALPHIN, MILLULS 15, M, (--), M, SC, 634, 634, BARN. In HH of Geo. Galphin m 45 mulatto born SC.

GALPHIN, SALLY, 18, F, (--), M, SC,

634, 634, BARN. In HH of Geo. Galphin m 45 mulatto born SC.

GALPHIN, WM., 11, F, (--), M, SC, 634, 634, BARN. In HH of Geo. Galphin m 45 mulatto born SC.

GARDEN, ANNE, 38, F, (--), M, SC, 221, 221, CHAS%.

GARDENER, REBECCA, 35, F, (--), M, SC, 1081, 1058, CHAS-.

GARDNER, ALEXANDER, 8, M, (--), M, SC, 499, 492, CHAS%. In HH of Elias Gardner m 35 mulatto born SC.

GARDNER, AMELIA, 13, F, (--), B, SC, 810, 768, CHAS+.

GARDNER, ANN L., 9, F, (--), M, SC, 499, 492, CHAS%. In HH of Elias Gardner m 35 mulatto born SC.

GARDNER, CLAUDIA, 35, F, (--), M, SC, 499, 492, CHAS%. In HH of Elias Gardner m 35 mulatto born SC.

GARDNER, ELIAS, 35, M, Butcher, M, SC, 499, 492, CHAS%.

GARDNER, ELOISE, 12, F, (--),. M, SC, 416, 414, CHAS%. In HH of M. Gardner f 29 mulatto born SC.

GARDNER, HENRY, 10, M, (--), M, SC, 307, 283, CHAS+. In HH of Emeline Elliot f 30 mulatto born SC.

GARDNER, JOHN J., 7, M, (--), M, SC, 416, 414, CHAS%. In HH of M. Gardner f 29 mulatto born SC.

GARDNER, JOSEPH, 28, M, Tailor, M, SC, 416, 414, CHAS%. In HH of M. Gardner f 29 mulatto born SC.

GARDNER, JOSEPH, 13, M, (--), M, SC, 307, 283, CHAS+. In HH of Emeline Elliot f 30 mulatto born SC.

GARDNER, M., 29, F, (--), M, SC, 416, 414, CHAS%.

GARDNER, MARY, 41, F, (--), B, SC, 487, 487, SUMT. In HH of Martha Canty f 30 black born SC.

GARDNER, MARY, 35, F, (--), M, SC, 306, 282, CHAS+.

GARDNER, MARY, 9, F, (--), M, SC, 416, 414, CHAS%. In HH of M. Gardner f 29 mulatto born SC.

GARDNER, MOSES, 36, M, Laborer,

B, SC, 182, 171, CHAS-.

GARDNER, SUSAN, 49, F, (--), M, SC, 144, 134, CHAS-.

GARDNER, THOMAS, 7, M, (--), M, SC, 99, 99, CHAS%. In HH of Susan Ford f 50 black born SC.

GARDNER, WILLIAM, 30, M, Drayman, M, SC, 99, 99, CHAS%. In HH of Susan Ford f 50 black born SC.

GARDNER, WILLIAM, 10, M, (--), M, SC, 99, 99, CHAS%. In HH of Susan Ford f 50 black born SC.

GARNER, HENRY, 10, M, (--), M, SC, 453, 453, BEAU-. In HH of Knot Garner m 45 mulatto born SC.

GARNER, JOANNAH, 7, F, (--), M, SC, 453, 453, BEAU-. In HH of Knot Garner m 45 mulatto born SC.

GARNER, KNOT, 45, M, Laborer, M, SC, 453, 453, BEAU-.

GARNER, REBECCA, 1, F, (--), M, SC, 453, 453, BEAU-. In HH of Knot Garner m 45 mulatto born SC.

GARNER, ROSELLA, 3, F, (--), M, SC, 453, 453, BEAU-. In HH of Knot Garner m 45 mulatto born SC.

GARNER, RUTHA, 32, F, (--), M, SC, 453, 453, BEAU-. In HH of Knot Garner m 45 mulatto born SC.

GARNER, TERRY, 5, M, (--), M, SC, 453, 453, BEAU-. In HH of Knot Garner m 45 mulatto born SC.

GARRET, ADAM, 32, M, Locksmith, B, SC, 318, 302, CHAS-. In HH of C.Y. Richardson m 35 born England.

GARRET, SYLVIA, 40, F, Seamstress, B, SC, 12, 15, CHAS.

GARRETT, ELIZABETH, 39, F, (--), B, SC, 722, 713, CHAS%.

GARRETT, HENRY, 10, M, (--), B, SC, 722, 713, CHAS%. In HH of Elizabeth Garrett f 39 black born SC.

GARRETT, JESSE, 12, F, (--), B, SC, 12, 15, CHAS. In HH of Sylvia Garret, 40 f, black born SC.

GARRETT, LUCY ANN, 12, F, (--), B, SC, 722, 713, CHAS%. In HH of Elizabeth Garrett f 39 black born SC.

GARRETT, LUSHER, 3, M, (--), B, SC, 12, 15, CHAS. In HH of Sylvia Garret, 40 f, black born SC.

GARRETT, PHILLIP, 50, M, Laborer, M, SC, 671, 671, UNION. In HH of Nancy Corry f 58 born SC.

GARRETT, SAMUEL, 32, M, Drayman, B, SC, 722, 713, CHAS%. In HH of Elizabeth Garrett f 39 black born SC.

GARTMAN, ANNA, 10, F, (--), M, SC, 669, 669, LEX. In HH of Lazarus Gartman m 35 mulatto born SC.

GARTMAN, AUMNAS, 8, F, (--), M, SC, 669, 669, LEX. In HH of Lazarus Gartman m 35 mulatto born SC.

GARTMAN, CATHARINE P., 12, F, (--), M, SC, 736, 736, LEX. In HH of Timothy Gartman m 44 mulatto born SC.

GARTMAN, LAZARUS, 35, M, Carpenter, M, SC, 669, 669, LEX.

GARTMAN, MARCILLA, 8, F, (--), M, SC, 736, 736, LEX. In HH of Timothy Gartman m 44 mulatto born SC.

GARTMAN, MARTHA, 25, F, (--), M, SC, 669, 669, LEX. In HH of Lazarus Gartman m 35 mulatto born SC.

GARTMAN, PICKENS, 6, M, (--), M, SC, 669, 669, LEX. In HH of Lazarus Gartman m 35 mulatto born SC.

GARTMAN, PIERCE, 4, M, (--), M, SC, 669, 669, LEX. In HH of Lazarus Gartman m 35 mulatto born SC.

GARTMAN, SOLOMON, 5, M, (--), M, SC, 736, 736, LEX. In HH of Timothy Gartman m 44 mulatto born SC.

GARTMAN, TIMOTHY, 44, M, (--), M, SC, 736, 736, LEX.

GARTMAN, WILLIAM P. 13, M, (--), M, SC, 736, 736, LEX. In HH of Timothy Gartman m 44 mulatto born SC.

GARTMAN, (Blank), 0, M, (--), M, SC, 669, 669, LEX. In HH of Lazarus Gartman m 35 mulatto born SC. Blank Gartman age 8/12 yr.

GAYLE, RICHD., 55, M, Planter, M, VA, 1205, 1205, SUMT.

GEAROT, E.A., 60, M, Carpenter, M, SC, 10, 10, CHAS~.

GENTRY, SAMUEL, 0, M, (--), B, SC, 2679, 2679, SPART. In HH of Sarah Gentry f 37 born SC.

GEO, J.H., 22, M, Laborer, B, SC, 732, 732, LANC*. In HH of D.M. Usery m 50 born SC.

GEORGE, ANNA, 7, F, (--), M, SC, 103, 103, KERS. In HH of Caroline George f 28 mulatto born SC.

GEORGE, AUGUSTIN, 12, M, (--), M, SC, 104, 104, KERS. In HH of Mary J. George f 33 born SC.

GEORGE, C., 9, F, (--), M, SC, 104, 104, KERS. In HH of Mary J. George f 33 born SC.

GEORGE, CAROLINE, 28, F, (--), M, SC, 103, 103, KERS.

GEORGE, E., 8, M, (--), M, SC, 104, 104, KERS. In HH of Mary J. George f 33 born SC.

GEORGE, EDWIN, 0, M, (--), M, SC, 103, 103, KERS. In HH of Caroline George f 28 mulatto born SC. Edwin George 4/12 yr.

GEORGE, ELYH., 10, F, (--), B, SC, 894, 894, KERS. In HH of Sarah George f 27 black born SC.

GEORGE, HARRIETT, 11, F, (--), M, SC, 104, 104, KERS. In HH of Mary J. George f 33 born SC.

GEORGE, JAS., 2, M, (--), M, SC, 103, 103, KERS. In HH of Caroline George f 28 mulatto born SC.

GEORGE, LEWIS, 15, M, (--), M, SC, 33, 33, KERS. In boarding house.

GEORGE, MARY, 4, F, (--), B, SC, 894, 894, KERS. In HH of Sarah George f 27 black born SC.

GEORGE, MARY J., 33, F, (--), M, SC, 104, 104, KERS.

GEORGE, MGT., 4, F, (--), B, SC, 142, 142, KERS. In HH of Fred Bowen born SC.

GEORGE, ROBT., 30, M, (--), B, SC, 142, 142, KERS. In HH of Fred Bowen m 48 born SC.

GEORGE, SAML., 10, M, (--), M, SC, 142, 142, KERS. In HH of Fred Bowen m 48 born SC.

GEORGE, SARAH, 27, F, (--), B, SC, 894, 894, KERS.

GEORGE, WM., 0, M, (--), B, SC, 142, 142, KERS. In HH of Fred Bowen m 48 born SC. Wm. George 3/12 yr.

GERMAN, LIZZEY, 30, F, (--), M, SC, 1796, 1802, Edge.

GERMAN, LUKE, 12, M, (--), M, SC, 1796, 1802, Edge. In HH of Lizzey German f 30 mulatto born SC.

GERMAN, WM., 8, M, (--), M, SC, 1796, 1802, Edge. In HH of Lizzey German f 30 mulatto born SC.

GIBBES, HANNAH, 40, F, (--), M, SC, 530, 489, CHAS+. In HH of F.R. Shackelford m 50 born SC.

GIBBES, MARY, 35, F, (--), M, SC, 229, 215, CHAS-.

GIBBS, EDY, 1, M, (--), M, SC, 661, 661, SUMT. In HH of Jas. Gibbs m 52 black born SC.

GIBBS, ELIS, 20, F, (--), M, SC, 661, 661, SUMT. In HH of Jas. Gibbs m 52 black born SC.

GIBBS, FREDERICK, 4, M, (--), M, SC, 661, 661, SUMT. In HH of Jas. Gibbs m 52 black born SC.

GIBBS, JAS., 52, M, Planter, B, SC, 661, 661, SUMT.

GIBBS, JOHN, 12, M, (--), M, SC, 661, 661, SUMT. In HH of Jas. Gibbs m 52 black born SC.

GIBBS, JOSIAH, 8, M, (--), M, SC, 661, 661, SUMT. In HH of Jas. Gibbs m 52 black born SC.

GIBBS, JULIA, 10, F, (--), M, SC, 661, 661, SUMT. In HH of Jas. Gibbs m 52 black born SC.

GIBBS, M., 7, F, (--), M, SC, 566, 566, LANC*. In HH of Mrs. E. Gibbs f 44 born SC.

GIBBS, MARY, 16, F, (--), M, SC, 661, 661, SUMT. In HH of Jas. Gibbs m 52 black born SC.

GIBBS, THOS., 72, M, Planter, M, SC, 662, 662, SUMT.

GIBBS, THOS, 14, M, (--), M, SC, 661, 661, SUMT. In HH of Jas. Gibbs m 52 black born SC.

GIBSON, DAVID, 30, M, (--), M, SC, 702, 702, LAU. In HH of Bill Jackson m 25 mulatto born SC.

GIBSON, GEORGE, 25, M, Farmer, M, SC, 712, 712, LAU.

GIBSON, JOHN, 5, M, (--), M, SC, 712, 712, LAU. In HH of George Gibson m 25 mulatto born SC.

GIBSON, JOSEPH, 19, M, Laborer, B, SC, 1177, 1177, UNION. In HH of William F. Reynolds m 60 born NC.

GIBSON, POLLY, 35, F, (--), M, SC, 781, 781, UNION. In HH of Robert Thompson m 83 born VA.

GIBSON, REBECCA, 34, F, (--), M, SC, 740, 728, CHAS%.

GIBSON, SALLY, 26, F, (--), M, SC, 712, 712, LAU. In HH of George Gibson m 25 mulatto born SC.

GIBSON, TIMOTHY, 31, M, Drayman, M, SC, 740, 728, CHAS%. In HH of Rebecca Gibson f 34 mulatto born SC.

GILBURG, CATHERINE, 80, F, (--), M, SC, 207, 193, CHAS-. In HH of Sarah Motte f 30 mulatto born SC.

GILES, ANNETT, 9, F, (--), M, SC, 417, 415, CHAS%. In HH of Lavina Requan f 31 mulatto born SC.

GILES, CAROLINE, 12, F, (--), M, SC, 417, 415, CHAS%. In HH of Lavina Requan f 31 mulatto born SC.

GILES, EMILY, 34, F, (--), M, SC, 417, 415, CHAS%. In HH of Lavina Requan f 31 mulatto born SC.

GILES, LAWRENCE, 31, M, Drayman, M, SC, 417, 415, CHAS%. In HH of Lavina Requan f 31 mulatto born SC.

GILES, THOMAS, 14, M, (--), M, SC, 417, 415, CHAS%. In HH of Lavina Requan f 31 mulatto born SC.

GILL, BENJAMIN, 24, M, Manager, B, SC, 990, 990, ABB.

GILL, SARAH A., 19, F, (--), B, SC, 990, 990, ABB. In HH of Benjamin Gill m 24 born SC.

GILLIARD, AMELIA, 30, F, (--), M, SC, 520, 503, CHAS-.

GILLIARD, HESTER, 5, F, (--), M, SC, 520, 503, CHAS-. In HH of Amelia Gilliard f 30 mulatto born SC.

GILMORE, FANNY, 20, F, (--), B, VA, 2317, 2317, GREE. In HH of Thomas Payne m 72 born NC.

GILSBURY, JOSIAH, 45, M, (--), M, SC, 35, 35, CHAS*. In HH of Ann P. Smith f 65 born SC.

GIST, EMMA, 24, F, (--), B, SC, 111, 111, CHAS%. In HH of Juba Gist f 50 black born SC.

GIST, JAMES, 20, M, (--), B, SC, 111, 111, CHAS%. In HH of Juba Gist f 50 black born SC.

GIST, JUBA, 50, F, (--), B, SC, 111, 111, CHAS%.

GLENCAMP, BECKY, 38, F, (--), B, SC, 11, 11, CHAS2. In HH of Isaac Glencamp m 51 mulatto born SC.

GLENCAMP, EMMA, 39, F, (--), M, SC, 17, 17, CHAS2. In HH of Henry Glencamp m 41 mulatto born SC.

GLENCAMP, HENRY, 41, M, Blacksmith, M, SC, 17, 17, CHAS2.

GLENCAMP, ISAAC, 51, M, Farmer, M, SC, 11, 11, CHAS2.

GLENCAMP, MARTHA, 14, F, (--), M, SC, 17, 17, CHAS2. In HH of Henry Glencamp m 41 mulatto born SC.

GLOSTER, BROOKS, 3, M, (--), B, SC, 1108, 1108, NEWB. In HH of Jesse Gloster m 73 black born SC.

GLOSTER, CORNELIUS, 11, M, (--), B, SC, 1108, 1108, NEWB. In HH of Jesse Gloster m 73 black born SC.

GLOSTER, DOUGLAS, 2, M, (--), B, SC, 1108, 1108, NEWB. In HH of Jesse Gloster m 73 black born SC.

GLOSTER, EDNEY, 24, F, (--), B, SC, 1108, 1108, NEWB. In HH of Jesse Gloster m 73 black born SC.

GLOSTER, EDNEY J., 3, F, (--), B, SC, 1108, 1108, NEWB. In HH of Jesse

Gloster m 73 black born SC.

GLOSTER, EMILY, 30, F, (--), B, SC, 1108, 1108, NEWB. In HH of Jesse Gloster m 73 black born SC.

GLOSTER, ISAAH, 1, M, (--), B, SC, 1108, 1108, NEWB. In HH of Jesse Gloster m 73 black born SC.

GLOSTER, JANE, 9, F, (--), B, SC, 1108, 1108, NEWB. In HH of Jesse Gloster m 73 black born SC.

GLOSTER, JESSE, 73, M, Farmer, B, SC, 1108, 1108, NEWB.

GLOSTER, JOHN, 4, M, (--), B, SC, 1108, 1108, NEWB. In HH of Jesse Gloster m 73 black born SC.

GLOSTER, JOHNSON, 16, M, Farmer, B, SC, 1108, 1108, NEWB. In HH of Jesse Gloster m 73 black born SC.

GLOSTER, MARINDA, 8, F, (--), B, SC, 1108, 1108, NEWB. In HH of Jesse Gloster m 73 black born SC.

GLOSTER, MARY, 14, F, (--), B, SC, 1108, 1108, NEWB. In HH of Jesse Gloster m 73 black born SC.

GLOSTER, NANCY, 6, F, (--), B, SC, 1108, 1108, NEWB. In HH of Jesse Gloster m 73 black born SC.

GLOSTER, OCTAVIA, 5, F, (--), B, SC, 1108, 1108, NEWB. In HH of Jesse Gloster m 73 black born SC.

GLOSTER, SARAH, 40, F, (--), B, SC, 1108, 1108, NEWB. In HH of Jesse Gloster m 73 black born SC.

GLOSTER, STEPHEN, 1, M, (--), B, SC, 1108, 1108, NEWB. In HH of Jesse Gloster m 73 black born SC.

GLOSTER, THOMAS, 19, M, Farmer, B, SC, 1108, 1108, NEWB. In HH of Jesse Gloster m 73 black born SC.

GLOSTER, WM., 6, M, (--), B, SC, 1108, 1108, NEWB. In HH of Jesse Gloster m 73 black born SC.

GLOVER, ANN, 23, F, (--), M, SC, 865, 845, CHAS-. In HH of William Deas m 35 mulatto born SC.

GLOVER, BENJAMIN, 15, M, (--), M, SC, 625, 617, CHAS%. In HH of William Glover m 38 mulatto born SC.

GLOVER, CATHARINE, 40, F, (--),

M, SC, 625, 617, CHAS%. In HH of William Glover m 38 mulatto born SC.

GLOVER, EDWARD, 10, M, (--), M, SC, 167, 157, CHAS-. In HH of Maria L. Wall f 28 mulatto born SC.

GLOVER, ELIZABETH, 18, F, (--), M, SC, 363, 325, CHAS+. In HH of Henry Triscott m 55 born SC.

GLOVER, ELIZABETH, 4, F, (--), M, SC, 211, 189, CHAS. In HH of George Glover m 26 mulatto born SC.

GLOVER, GEORGANA, 3, F, (--), M, SC, 625, 617, CHAS%. In HH of William Glover m 38 mulatto born SC.

GLOVER, GEORGE, 26, M, Sadler, M, SC, 211, 189, CHAS.

GLOVER, GEORGE, 14, M, (--), B, SC, 181, 181, ABB. In HH of Isabella Glover f 45 black born SC.

GLOVER, HENRETTA, 34, F, (--), B, SC, 598, 579, CHAS-. In HH of Rebecca Gaillard f 40 black born SC.

GLOVER, ISABELLA, 45, F, (--), B, SC, 181, 181, ABB.

GLOVER, JACOB, 4, M, (--), M, SC, 167, 157, CHAS-. In HH of Maria L. Wall f 28 mulatto born SC.

GLOVER, JAMES, 17, M, (--), M, SC, 363, 325, CHAS+. In HH of Henry Triscott m 55 born SC.

GLOVER, JAMES, 11, M, (--), B, SC, 598, 579, CHAS-. In HH of Rebecca Gaillard f 40 black born SC.

GLOVER, JOHN, 10, M, (--), M, SC, 181, 181, ABB. In HH of Isabella Glover f 45 black born SC.

GLOVER, JOSEPH, 23, M, Carpenter, M, SC, 363, 325, CHAS+. In HH of Henry Triscott m 55 born SC.

GLOVER, JULIA, 8, F, (--), M, SC, 167, 157, CHAS-. In HH of Maria L. Wall f 28 mulatto born SC.

GLOVER, JULIA, 8, F, (--), M, SC, 625, 617, CHAS%. In HH of William Glover m 38 mulatto born SC.

GLOVER, LUCY, 9, F, (--), B, SC, 598, 579, CHAS-. In HH of Rebecca Gaillard f 40 black born SC.

GLOVER, MARY, 24, F, (--), M, SC,

211, 189, CHAS. In HH of George Glover m 26 mulatto born SC.

GLOVER, MICHAEL, 6, M, (--), M, SC, 167, 157, CHAS-. In HH of Maria L. Wall f 28 mulatto born SC.

GLOVER, REBECCA, 16, F, (--), B, SC, 181, 181, ABB. In HH of Isabella Glover f 45 black born SC.

GLOVER, RICHARD, 27, M, Carpenter, M, SC, 344, 327, CHAS-. In HH of Louisa Smith f 78 mulatto born SC.

GLOVER, SAMUEL H., 42, M, Barber, M, SC, 252, 257, RICH.

GLOVER, SOPHIA, 26, F, (--), M, SC, 160, 164, RICH.

GLOVER, THEOPHILAS, 1, M, (--), M, SC, 167, 157, CHAS-. In HH of Maria L. Wall f 28 mulatto born SC.

GLOVER, WILLIAM, 38, M, (--), M, SC, 625, 617, CHAS%.

GLOVER, WILLIAM, 11, M, (--), M, SC, 625, 617, CHAS%. In HH of William Glover m 38 mulatto born SC.

GODBOLD, JAMES, 17, M, (--), M, SC, 1128, 1133, MAR. In HH of John M. Godbold m 49 born SC.

GODFREY, FRANCES, 5, F, (--), B, SC, 887, 864, CHAS%. In HH of Nancy Godfrey f 35 black born SC.

GODFREY, GEORGE, 5, M, (--), B, SC, 887, 864, CHAS%. In HH of Nancy Godfrey f 35 black born SC.

GODFREY, JOHN, 7, M, (--), B, SC, 887, 864, CHAS%. In HH of Nancy Godfrey f 35 black born SC.

GODFREY, MARGARET, 2, F, (--), B, SC, 887, 864, CHAS%. In HH of Nancy Godfrey f 35 black born SC.

GODFREY, NANCY, 35, F, (--), B, SC, 887, 864, CHAS%.

GOFF, ABIGAIL, 23, F, (--), M, SC, 256, 241, CHAS+.

GOFF, CLAIMDER, 45, F, (--), B, SC, 289, 289, CHAS%.

GOFF, HENRY, 5, M, (--), M, SC, 256, 241, CHAS+. In HH of Abigail Goff f 23 mulatto born SC.

GOFF, MARY, 50, F, (--), B, SC, 290, 290, CHAS%. In HH of Jane Lloyd f 38 black born SC.

GOFF, WILLIAM, 11, M, (--), B, SC, 289, 289, CHAS%. In HH of Climder Goff f 45 black born SC.

GOINGS, EMMA, 2, F, (--), M, SC, 520, 503, CHAS-. In HH of Amelia Gilliard f 30 mulatto born SC.

GOINGS, JOHN, 6, M, (--), M, SC, 520, 503, CHAS-. In HH of Amelia Gilliard f 30 mulatto born SC.

GOINGS, THOMAS, 4, M, (--), M, SC, 520, 503, CHAS-. In HH of Amelia Gilliard f 30 mulatto born SC.

GOINS, DRUCILLA, 1, F, (--), M, SC, 851, 851, SUMT. In HH of Thos. Goins m 28 mulatto born SC.

GOINS, ELIS, 24, F, (--), M, SC, 851, 851, SUMT. In HH of Thos. Goins m 28 mulatto born SC.

GOINS, HENRY, 14, M, (--), M, SC, 853, 853, SUMT. In HH of Louisa Goins f 45 mulatto born SC.

GOINS, HENRY, 3, M, (--), M, SC, 850, 850, SUMT. In HH of John Goins m 28 mulatto born SC.

GOINS, JAS., 30, M, Planter, M, SC, 849, 849, SUMT.

GOINS, JAS. M., 3, M, (--), M, SC, 849, 849, SUMT. In HH of Jas. Goins m 30 born SC.

GOINS, JOHN, 28, M, Planter, M, SC, 850, 850, SUMT.

GOINS, JUDSON, 4, M, (--), M, SC, 850, 850, SUMT. In HH of John Goins m 28 mulatto born SC.

GOINS, LIDIA, 1, F, (--), M, SC, 850, 850, SUMT. In HH of John Goins m 28 mulatto born SC.

GOINS, LOUISA, 45, F, (--), M, SC, 853, 853, SUMT.

GOINS, MADRY, 23, M, Laborer, M, SC, 853, 853, SUMT. In HH of Louisa Goins f 45 mulatto born SC.

GOINS, MARIAH, 5, F, (--), M, SC, 851, 851, SUMT. In HH of Thos. Goins m 28 mulatto born SC.

GOINS, MARTHA, 22, F, (--), M, SC,

849, 849, SUMT. In HH of Jas. Goins m 30 born SC.

GOINS, THOS., 28, M, Planter, M, SC, 851, 851, SUMT.

GOINS, WADE, 26, M, Planter, M, SC, 852, 852, SUMT.

GOINS, WASHINGTON, 13, M, (--), M, SC, 853, 853, SUMT. In HH of Louisa Goins f 45 mulatto born SC.

GOINS, WM., 3, M, (--), M, SC, 851, 851, SUMT. In HH of Thos. Goins m 28 mulatto born SC.

GOLDIN, ROSE, 1, F, (--), M, SC, 1146, 1146, PICK+. In HH of Mary Goldin f 55 born SC.

GONZALUS, BASELLIO, 6, M, (--), M, SC, 835, 793, CHAS+. In HH of B. Gonzalus m 55 born Spain.

GONZALUS, EDWARD, 15, M, (--), M, SC, 835, 793, CHAS+. In HH of B. Gonzalus m 55 born Spain.

GONZALUS, HANNAH, 40, F, (--), M, SC, 835, 793, CHAS+. In HH of B. Gonzalus m 55 born Spain.

GONZALUS, ISABELL, 3, F, (--), M, SC, 835, 793, CHAS+. In HH of B. Gonzalus m 55 born Spain.

GONZALUS, JANE, 12, F, (--), M, SC, 835, 793, CHAS+. In HH of B. Gonzalus m 55 born Spain.

GONZALUS, JOSEPH, 14, M, (--), M, SC, 835, 793, CHAS+. In HH of B. Gonzalus m 55 born Spain.

GONZALUS, JULIA, 4, F, (--), M, SC, 835, 793, CHAS+. In HH of B. Gonzalus m 55 born Spain.

GONZALUS, MARIA, 8, F, (--), M, SC, 835, 793, CHAS+. In HH of B. Gonzalus m 55 born Spain.

GOOD, ELLEN, 30, F, (--), M, SC, 313, 289, CHAS+.

GOOD, GEORGE, 14, M, (--), M, SC, 313, 289, CHAS+. In HH of Ellen Good f 30 mulatto born SC.

GOOD, PERCY, 5, M, (--), M, SC, 313, 289, CHAS+. In HH of Ellen Good f 30 mulatto born SC.

GOOD, SIDNEY, 9, M, (--), M, SC, 313, 289, CHAS+. In HH of Ellen Good

f 30 mulatto born SC.

GOODMAN, SUSANNA, 28, F, (--), M, SC, 1408, 1408, NEWB.

GOODWYN, ALEXINA, 8, F, (--), M, SC, 71, 72, RICH. In HH of Isabella Goodwyn f 25 mulatto born SC.

GOODWYN, CATHERINE, 6, F, (--), M, SC, 71, 72, RICH. In HH of Isabella Goodwyn f 25 mulatto born SC.

GOODWYN, ISABELLA, 25, F, (--), M, SC, 71, 72, RICH.

GOODWYN, JAMES, 2, M, (--), M, SC, 71, 72, RICH. In HH of Isabella Goodwyn f 25 mulatto born SC.

GOODWYN, MARION, 5, F, (--), M, SC, 71, 72, RICH. In HH of Isabella Goodwyn f 25 mulatto born SC.

GOOPEY, AMELIA, 13, F, (--), B, SC, 109, 109, COLL. In HH of Wm. Goopy m 27 white born SC.

GOOPEY, BELLA, 24, F, (--), B, SC, 109, 109, COLL. In HH of Wm. Goopy m 27 white born SC.

GOOPEY, BETSEY, 35, F, (--), B, SC, 109, 109, COLL. In HH of Wm. Goopy m 27 white born SC.

GOOPEY, BILLEY, 10, M, (--), B, SC, 109, 109, COLL. In HH of Wm. Goopy m 27 white born SC.

GOOPEY, BOB, 5, M, (--), B, SC, 109, 109, COLL. In HH of Wm. Goopy m 27 white born SC.

GOOPEY, JOSEPH, 26, M, (--), B, SC, 109, 109, COLL. In HH of Wm. Goopy m 27 white born SC.

GOOPEY, MOLLEY, 8, F, (--), B, SC, 109, 109, COLL. In HH of Wm. Goopy m 27 white born SC.

GOOPEY, NANCY, 15, F, (--), B, SC, 109, 109, COLL. In HH of Wm. Goopy m 27 white born SC.

GOOPEY, SUSAN, 13, F, (--), B, SC, 109, 109, COLL. In HH of Wm. Goopy m 27 white born SC.

GOOPEY, TATE, 50, M, (--), B, SC, 109, 109, COLL. In HH of Wm. Goopy m 27 white born SC.

GORCIAN, FANNY, 18, F, (--), M, Ireland, 12, 12, CHAS+. In HH of

Caroline Douglas f 30 born GA.

GORDEN, E.W., 32, M, Planter, M, SC, 155, 145, CHAS-. In HH of Ann Mitchell f 60 mulatto born SC.

GORDEN, HANNAH, 9, F, (--), M, SC, 155, 145, CHAS-. In HH of Ann Mitchell f 60 mulatto born SC.

GORDEN, HENRETTA, 30, F, (--), M, SC, 155, 145, CHAS-. In HH of Ann Mitchell f 60 mulatto born SC.

GORDEN, JULIA, 19, F, (--), M, SC, 155, 145, CHAS-. In HH of Ann Mitchell f 60 mulatto born SC.

GORDEN, MARGARET E. 7, F, (--), M, SC, 155, 145, CHAS-. In HH of Ann Mitchell f 60 mulatto born SC.

GORDON, ALEXANDER, 4, M, (--), M, SC, 188, 188, COLL. In HH of Zachariah Gordon m 34 born SC.

GORDON, ANNA, 13, F, (--), M, SC, 455, 455, BEAU-. In HH of Benjamin Gordon m 36 mulatto born SC.

GORDON, ANNIE, 34, F, (--), B, SC, 456, 456, BEAU-. IN HH of Archer Gordon m 36 black born SC.

GORDON, ARCHER, 36, M, Mechanic, B, SC, 456, 456, BEAU-.

GORDON, ARCHER, 6, M, (--), M, SC, 455, 455, BEAU-. In HH of Benjamin Gordon m 36 mulatto born SC.

GORDON, ARCHIBAND H., 7, M, (--), B, SC, 191, 191, COLL. In HH of James Jones m 25 mulatto born SC.

GORDON, BENJAMIN, 36, M, Laborer, M, SC, 455, 455, BEAU-.

GORDON, BENJAMIN, 4, M, (--), M, SC, 455, 455, BEAU-. In HH of Benjamin Gordon m 36 mulatto born SC.

GORDON, CATHERINE, 7, F, (--), M, SC, 188, 188, COLL. In HH of Zachariah Gordon m 34 born SC.

GORDON, CATY, 30, F, (--), M, SC, 455, 455, BEAU-. In HH of Benjamin Gordon m 36 mulatto born SC.

GORDON, CHARITY, 34, F, (--), B, SC, 191, 191, COLL. In HH of James Jones m 25 mulatto born SC.

GORDON, CHARLES, 21, M, (--), M, SC, 305, 305, BEAU+. In HH of David Gordon m 45 mulatto born SC.

GORDON, DAVID, 45, M, Laborer, M, SC, 305, 305, BEAU+.

GORDON, DAVID, 5, M, (--), M, SC, 305, 305, BEAU+. In HH of David Gordon m 45 mulatto born SC.

GORDON, DAVID O., 1, M, (--), M, SC, 188, 188, COLL. In HH of Zachariah Gordon m 34 born SC.

GORDON, ELIAS, 3, M, (--), M, SC, 305, 305, BEAU+. In HH of David Gordon m 45 mulatto born SC.

GORDON, ELIAS D., 7, M, (--), B, SC, 191, 191, COLL. In HH of James Jones m 25 mulatto born SC.

GORDON, ELIZA, 45, F, (--), M, SC, 305, 305, BEAU+. In HH of David Gordon m 45 mulatto born SC.

GORDON, ELIZABETH, 48, F, (--), M, SC, 431, 431, BEAU-. In HH of William Gordon m 50 mulatto born SC.

GORDON, ELLEN, 8, F, (--), M, SC, 455, 455, BEAU-. In HH of Benjamin Gordon m 36 mulatto born SC.

GORDON, EUGENIA, 5, F, (--), M, SC, 431, 431, BEAU-. In HH of William Gordon m 50 mulatto born SC.

GORDON, HENSUS, 9, M, (--), M, SC, 431, 431, BEAU-. In HH of William Gordon m 50 mulatto born SC.

GORDON, ISAAC, 14, M, (--), M, SC, 305, 305, BEAU+. In HH of David Gordon m 45 mulatto born SC.

GORDON, ISAAC, 1, M, (--), M, SC, 455, 455, BEAU-. In HH of Benjamin Gordon m 36 mulatto born SC.

GORDON, JAMES, 15, M, (--), M, SC, 682, 674, CHAS%. In HH of John Gordon m 24 mulatto born SC.

GORDON, JAMES, 7, M, (--), B, SC, 456, 456, BEAU-. IN HH of Archer Gordon m 36 black born SC.

GORDON, JOHN, 24, M, Butcher, M, SC, 682, 674, CHAS%.

GORDON, JOHN, 16, M, Laborer, M, SC, 431, 431, BEAU-. In HH of William Gordon m 50 mulatto born SC.

GORDON, JOSEPH, 17, M, (--), M, SC, 682, 674, CHAS%. In HH of John Gordon m 24 mulatto born SC.

GORDON, JOSHUA, 20, M, Laborer, M, SC, 305, 305, BEAU+. In HH of David Gordon m 45 mulatto born SC.

GORDON, JULIA, 18, F, (--), M, SC, 600, 592, CHAS%. In HH of Robert Gordon m 23 mulatto born SC.

GORDON, JULIA, 11, F, (--), M, SC, 431, 431, BEAU-. In HH of William Gordon m 50 mulatto born SC.

GORDON, JULIA, 1, F, (--), M, SC, 600, 592, CHAS%. In HH of Robert Gordon m 23 mulatto born SC.

GORDON, LAFAYETTE, 22, M, Laborer, M, SC, 431, 431, BEAU-. In HH of William Gordon m 50 mulatto born SC.

GORDON, LOOTIE, 20, F, (--), M, SC, 431, 431, BEAU-. In HH of William Gordon m 50 mulatto born SC.

GORDON, MARIA, 2, F, (--), M, SC, 431, 431, BEAU-. In HH of William Gordon m 50 mulatto born SC.

GORDON, MITCHEL, 13, M, (--), M, SC, 431, 431, BEAU-. In HH of William Gordon m 50 mulatto born SC.

GORDON, MORGAN, 1, F, (--), M, SC, 431, 431, BEAU-. In HH of William Gordon m 50 mulatto born SC.

GORDON, NARRISSA, 7, F, (--), M, SC, 431, 431, BEAU-. In HH of William Gordon m 50 mulatto born SC.

GORDON, NEHEMIAH, 5, M, (--), B, SC, 191, 191, COLL. In HH of James Jones m 25 mulatto born SC.

GORDON, RACHAEL, 70, F, (--), B, SC, 80, 90, CHAS. In HH of Betty Wilson f 80 black born Africa.

GORDON, ROBERT, 23, M, Shoemaker, M, SC, 600, 592, CHAS%.

GORDON, SARAH, 20, F, (--), M, SC, 682, 674, CHAS%. In HH of John Gordon m 24 mulatto born SC.

GORDON, SARAH, 14, F, (--), M, SC, 455, 455, BEAU-. In HH of Benjamin Gordon m 36 mulatto born SC.

GORDON, SARAH, 8, F, (--), M, SC,

305, 305, BEAU+. In HH of David Gordon m 45 mulatto born SC.

GORDON, SELINA, 6, F, (--), M, SC, 305, 305, BEAU+. In HH of David Gordon m 45 mulatto born SC.

GORDON, SIDNEY, 3, M, (--), M, SC, 431, 431, BEAU-. In HH of William Gordon m 50 mulatto born SC.

GORDON, TEMPY, 15, M, Laborer, M, SC, 431, 431, BEAU-. In HH of William Gordon m 50 mulatto born SC.

GORDON, THERESA, 13, F, (--), M, SC, 682, 674, CHAS%. In HH of John Gordon m 24 mulatto born SC.

GORDON, WADE, 17, M, Laborer, M, SC, 431, 431, BEAU-. In HH of William Gordon m 50 mulatto born SC.

GORDON, WILLIAM, 50, M, Planter/mechanic, M, SC, 431, 431, BEAU-.

GORDON, WILLIAM, 14, M, (--), M, SC, 305, 305, BEAU+. In HH of David Gordon m 45 mulatto born SC.

GORMAN, JANE, 25, F, (--), M, Ireland, 312, 318, RICH. In HH of James Cathcart m 55 born Ireland.

GOUGH, EDWARD, 15, M, Shoemaker, M, SC, 875, 833, CHAS+.

GOWEN, HESTER, 6, F, (--), M, SC, 257, 241, CHAS+. In HH of Amelia Gaillard f 28 mulatto born SC.

GRAHAM, BECKER, 12, F, (--), M, SC, 111, 106, CHAS*. In Boarding House.

GRAHAM, IRVAN, 2, M, (--), M, SC, 111, 106, CHAS*. In Boarding House.

GRAHAM, JANE, 17, F, (--), M, SC, 111, 106, CHAS*. In Boarding House.

GRAHAM, MARTHA, 35, F, (--), M, SC, 821, 821, SUMT. In HH of Aaron Abrahams m 46 born Poland.

GRAHAM, NANCY, 18, F, (--), M, SC, 111, 106, CHAS*. In Boarding House.

GRAHAM, SALLY, 40, F, (--), M, SC, 111, 106, CHAS*. In Boarding House.

GRAHAM, SAM, 3, M, (--), M, SC, 111, 106, CHAS*. In Boarding House.

GRAHAM, SARAH, 10, F, (--), M, SC,

111, 106, CHAS*. In Boarding House.

GRAHAM, TELEY, 15, F, (--), M, SC, 111, 106, CHAS*. In Boarding House.

GRAIN, SUSAN, 39, F, (--), B, SC, 582, 564, CHAS-.

GRANT, ANN, 29, F, (--), M, SC, 614, 606, CHAS%. In HH of James Grant m 30 mulatto born SC.

GRANT, ANN, 0, F, (--), M, SC, 614, 606, CHAS%. In HH of James Grant m 30 mulatto born SC. Ann Grant age 1/12 yr.

GRANT, CATHERINE, 35, F, (--), M, SC, 579, 571, CHAS%.

GRANT, ISAAC, 6, M, (--), M, SC, 579, 571, CHAS%. In HH of Catherine Grant f 35 mulatto born SC.

GRANT, ISABELLA, 25, F, (--), M, SC, 622, 580, CHAS+.

GRANT, JAMES, 30, M, Butcher, M, SC, 614, 606, CHAS%.

GRANT, JAMES, 11, M, (--), M, SC, 614, 606, CHAS%. In HH of James Grant m 30 mulatto born SC.

GRANT, JAMES, 10, M, (--), B, SC, 942, 922, CHAS-. In HH of Josephine Sasportas f 30 black born SC.

GRANT, JAMES, 1, M, (--), M, SC, 622, 580, CHAS+. In HH of Isabella Grant f 25 mulatto born SC.

GRANT, JESSE, 3, M, (--), M, SC, 614, 606, CHAS%. In HH of James Grant m 30 mulatto born SC.

GRANT, JOSEPH, 7, M, (--), M, SC, 614, 606, CHAS%. In HH of James Grant m 30 mulatto born SC.

GRANT, PETER, 6, M, (--), M, SC, 614, 606, CHAS%. In HH of James Grant m 30 mulatto born SC.

GRANT, SUSAN, 15, F, (--), B, SC, 174, 164, CHAS-. In HH of Maria Hasell f 30 black born SC.

GRANT, THOMAS, 30, M, Carpenter, M, SC, 622, 580, CHAS+. In HH of Isabella Grant f 25 mulatto born SC.

GRANT, WASHINGTON, 9, M, (--), M, SC, 614, 606, CHAS%. In HH of James Grant m 30 mulatto born SC.

GRANT, WILLIAM, 12, M, (--), M, SC, 614, 606, CHAS%. In HH of James Grant m 30 mulatto born SC.

GRANTHAM, ELIZH., 32, F, (--), M, SC, 125, 125, KERS. In HH of Susan Scott f, 60 mulatto born SC.

GRANTHAM, JOHN, 12, M, (--), M, SC, 125, 125, KERS. In HH of Susan Scott f, 60 mulatto born SC.

GRANTZ, JOHN, 21, M, Laborer, M, SC, 763, 763, MARL. In HH of Edward D. Smith m 25 born SC.

GRAY, ANN, 8, F, (--), M, SC, 506, 489, CHAS-. In HH of Jane Gray f 30 mulatto born SC.

GRAY, JAMES, 2, M, (--), M, SC, 506, 489, CHAS-. In HH of Jane Gray f 30 mulatto born SC.

GRAY, JANE, 30, F, (--), M, SC, 506, 489, CHAS-.

GRAY, LOUISA, 4, F, (--), M, SC, 506, 489, CHAS-. In HH of Jane Gray f 30 mulatto born SC.

GRAY, MARTHA, 6, F, (--), M, SC, 506, 489, CHAS-. In HH of Jane Gray f 30 mulatto born SC.

GREARSON, TONEY, 65, M, Cooper, B, SC, 86, 96, CHAS.

GREEN, ADRIAN, 7, M, (--), B, SC, 1071, 1071, ABB. In HH of Anthony Green m 50 black born SC.

GREEN, ALICE, 6, F, (--), M, SC, 400, 364, CHAS. In HH of Mary Green f 28 mulatto born SC. {twin}.

GREEN, ALICIA, 6, F, (--), M, SC, 400, 364, CHAS. In HH of Mary Green f 28 mulatto born SC. {twin}.

GREEN, ANN, 14, F, (--), M, SC, 400, 364, CHAS. In HH of Mary Green f 28 mulatto born SC.

GREEN, ANTHONY, 50, M, Carpenter, B, SC, 1071, 1071, ABB.

GREEN, ANTHONY, 14, M, (--), B, SC, 1071, 1071, ABB. In HH of Anthony Green m 50 black born SC.

GREEN, AUGUSTUS, 2, M, (--), M, SC, 400, 364, CHAS. In HH of Mary Green f 28 mulatto born SC.

GREEN, BENJAMIN, 10, M, (--), B,

SC, 1071, 1071, ABB. In HH of Anthony Green m 50 black born SC.

GREEN, DAPHNEY, 3, F, (--), B, SC, 63, 63, GEOR. In HH of Lucy Green f 30 black born SC.

GREEN, DRAYTON, 25, M, Overseer, B, SC, 603, 603, CHFD.

GREEN, ELIZABETH, 13, F, (--), B, SC, 1071, 1071, ABB. In HH of Anthony Green m 50 black born SC.

GREEN, ELLIS, 5, F, (--), B, SC, 63, 63, GEOR. In HH of Lucy Green f 30 black born SC.

GREEN, FRANCES, 8, F, (--), M, SC, 400, 364, CHAS. In HH of Mary Green f 28 mulatto born SC.

GREEN, HANNAH, 70, F, (--), M, SC, 215, 215, NEWB. In HH of Mary Shumpert f 60 born SC.

GREEN, HULDA, 15, F, (--), B, SC, 1071, 1071, ABB. In HH of Anthony Green m 50 black born SC.

GREEN, JACOB, 29, M, Stable Attendant, M, SC, 400, 364, CHAS. In HH of Mary Green f 28 mulatto born SC.

GREEN, JACOB, 29, M, (--), M, SC, 293, 270, CHAS+. In HH of Joseph Quash m 20 mulatto born SC.

GREEN, JACOB, 20, M, Stable Attendant, M, SC, 400, 364, CHAS. In HH of Mary Green f 28 mulatto born SC.

GREEN, JOHN W., 21, M, Farmer, B, SC, 1071, 1071, ABB. In HH of Anthony Green m 50 black born SC.

GREEN, LUCY, 30, F, (--), B, SC, 63, 63, GEOR.

GREEN, MARY, 70, F, (--), B, SC, 549, 508, CHAS+.

GREEN, MARY, 28, M, Stable keeper, M, SC, 400, 364, CHAS.

GREEN, MINDER, 1, M, (--), B, SC, 63, 63, GEOR. In HH of Lucy Green f 30 black born SC.

GREEN, NANCY, 13, F, (--), B, SC, 1071, 1071, ABB. In HH of Anthony Green m 50 black born SC.

GREEN, RACHEL, 40, F, (--), B, SC, 1071, 1071, ABB. In HH of Anthony Green m 50 black born SC.

GREEN, SARAH, 18, F, (--), B, SC, 1071, 1071, ABB. In HH of Anthony Green m 50 black born SC.

GREEN, SARAH, 10, F, (--), M, SC, 400, 364, CHAS. In HH of Mary Green f 28 mulatto born SC.

GREEN, SUSAN, 21, F, (--), M, SC, 293, 270, CHAS+. In HH of Joseph Quash m 20 mulatto born SC.

GREEN, THOMAS W., 17, M, Farmer, B, SC, 1071, 1071, ABB. In HH of Anthony Green m 50 black born SC.

GREEN, WILLIAM, 24, M, Fisherman, B, SC, 52, 52, CHAS*.

GREEN, WM., 7, M, (--), B, SC, 63, 63, GEOR. In HH of Lucy Green f 30 black born SC.

GREER, DANIEL, 24, M, Carpenter, B, SC, 1104, 1104, NEWB.

GREER, DANIEL, 3, M, (--), B, SC, 1120, 1120, NEWB. In HH of George Greer m 30 black born SC.

GREER, DELENA, 50, F, (--), M, SC, 506, 472, CHAS*. In HH of Mary Greer f 16 mulatto born St. Augustine.

GREER, DELILIA, 27, F, (--), B, SC, 1120, 1120, NEWB. In HH of George Greer m 30 black born SC.

GREER, E., 20, F, (--), B, SC, 1120, 1120, NEWB. In HH of George Greer m 30 black born SC.

GREER, GEORGE, 30, M, (--), B, SC, 1120, 1120, NEWB.

GREER, GEORGIANA, 1, F, (--), B, SC, 1120, 1120, NEWB. In HH of George Greer m 30 black born SC.

GREER, J.C., 5, M, (--), B, SC, 1104, 1104, NEWB. In HH of Daniel Greer m 24 black born SC.

GREER, JAMES, 2, M, (--), B, SC, 1120, 1120, NEWB. In HH of George Greer m 30 black born SC.

GREER, MARIA, 22, F, (--), B, SC, 1104, 1104, NEWB. In HH of Daniel Greer m 24 black born SC.

GREER, MARY, 16, F, (--), M, St. Augustine, 506, 472, CHAS*.

GREGG, ANGELINE, 2, F, (--), M, SC, 835, 816, CHAS%. In HH of Ann

Gregg f 40 mulatto born SC.

GREGG, ANN, 40, F, (--), M, SC, 835, 816, CHAS%.

GREGG, JOHN, 6, M, (--), M, SC, 835, 816, CHAS%. In HH of Ann Gregg f 40 mulatto born SC.

GREGG, JOSEPH, 8, M, (--), M, SC, 835, 816, CHAS%. In HH of Ann Gregg f 40 mulatto born SC.

GREGG, JULIANA, 65, F, (--), M, SC, 314, 314, CHAS%.

GREGG, REBECCA, 10, F, (--), M, SC, 835, 816, CHAS%. In HH of Ann Gregg f 40 mulatto born SC.

GREGG, WILLIAM, 4, M, (--), M, SC, 835, 816, CHAS%. In HH of Ann Gregg f 40 mulatto born SC.

GREGORY, ABERDEEN, 49, M, (--), B, SC, 183, 183, CHAS%. In HH of Titus Gregory m 73 black born SC.

GREGORY, AMELIA, 1, F, (--), M, SC, 570, 562, CHAS%. In HH of Isabella Gregory f 38 black born SC.

GREGORY, ARTHUR, 37, M, (--), B, SC, 183, 183, CHAS%. In HH of Titus Gregory m 73 black born SC.

GREGORY, GEORGE, 7, M, (--), M, SC, 570, 562, CHAS%. In HH of Isabella Gregory f 38 black born SC.

GREGORY, ISABELLA, 38, F, (--), B, SC, 570, 562, CHAS%.

GREGORY, TITUS, 73, M, Cooper, B, SC, 183, 183, CHAS%.

GRIER, DAVID, 22, M, Hireling, B, SC, 1633, 1633, ABB.

GRIFFIN, EMANUEL, 20, M, Planter, M, SC, 334, 341, +. In HH of George Griffin m 56 mulatto born SC.

GRIFFIN, EML., 25, M, (--), M, SC, 142, 142, KERS. In HH of Fred Bowen m 48 born SC. Wm. George 3/12 yr.

GRIFFIN, GEORGE, 56, M, Planter, M, SC, 334, 341, +.

GRIFFIN, GEORGE, 11, M, (--), M, SC, 334, 341, +. In HH of George Griffin m 56 mulatto born SC.

GRIFFIN, GIBBES, 25, M, Planter, M, SC, 334, 341, +. In HH of George

Griffin m 56 mulatto born SC.

GRIFFIN, HALY, 45, F, (--), M, NC, 776, 776, MARL. In HH of George Lowery m 52 mulatto born NC.

GRIFFIN, HARRIET, 22, F, (--), M, SC, 334, 341, +. In HH of George Griffin m 56 mulatto born SC.

GRIFFIN, JAMES, 11, M, (--), M, SC, 334, 341, +. In HH of George Griffin m 56 mulatto born SC.

GRIFFIN, LEAH, 50, F, (--), M, SC, 312, 318, RICH+. In HH of Alexander Bailey m 55 born SC.

GRIFFIN, PATSEY, 48, F, (--), M, SC, 334, 341, RICH+. In HH of George Griffin m 56 mulatto born SC.

GRIFFIN, PATSEY, 22, F, (--), M, SC, 342, 349, RICH+.

GRIFFIN, PURLINE, 1, F, (--), M, NC, 776, 776, MARL. In HH of George Lowery m 52 mulatto born NC.

GRIFFIN, REBECCA, 16, F, (--), M, SC, 312, 318, RICH+. In HH of Alexander Bailey m 55 born SC.

GRIFFIN, SOPHIA, 17, F, (--), M, SC, 334, 341, RICH+. In HH of George Griffin m 56 mulatto born SC.

GRIFFIN, TENAH, 40, F, (--), B, SC, 21, 21, CHAS%.

GRIFFIN, VIRGINIA, 7, F, (--), M, SC, 334, 341, RICH+. In HH of George Griffin m 56 mulatto born SC.

GRIFFIN, WESLEY, 9, M, (--), M, SC, 334, 341, RICH+. In HH of George Griffin m 56 mulatto born SC.

GRIFFIN, WM., 50, M, Farmer, B, SC, 102, 102, LANC*.

GRIMES, WILLIAM, 24, M, Laborer, M, SC, 322, 322, UNION. In HH of Thomas Cofield m 43 born SC.

GRIPOP ?, ELIZABETH, 25, F, (--), M, SC, 1011, 1015, AND. In HH of Rebecca Gripop ? f 50 mulatto born SC.

GRIPOP ?, JOHN, 16, M, (--), M, SC, 1011, 1015, AND. In HH of Rebecca Gripop ? f 50 mulatto born SC.

GRIPOP ?, NANCY J. 3, F, (--), M, SC, 1011, 1015, AND. In HH of Rebecca Gripop ? f 50 mulatto born SC.

GRIPOP ?, REBECCA, 50, F, (--), M, SC, 1011, 1015, AND.

GRIPOP ?, WILLIAM, 0, M, (--), M, SC, 1011, 1015, AND. In HH of Rebecca Gripop ? f 50 mulatto born SC. William age 2/12 yr.

GROOMS, AGNES, 55, F, (--), B, SC, 244, 249, RICH+. In HH of Thomas Grooms m 50 black born SC.

GROOMS, ALEXDR., 18, M, Laborer, M, SC, 377, 377, SUMT. In HH of Mary Grooms f 50 mulatto born SC.

GROOMS, ANDREW, 21, M, Laborer, M, SC, 228, 228, CHAS3. In HH of John Conner m 44 mulatto born SC.

GROOMS, CATHARINE, 8, F, (--), M, SC, 377, 377, SUMT. In HH of Mary Grooms f 50 mulatto born SC.

GROOMS, DAVID, 35, M, Planter, B, SC, 263, 268, RICH+.

GROOMS, ELIZA, 7, F, (--), B, SC, 263, 268, RICH+. In HH of David Grooms m 35 black born SC.

GROOMS, JAMES, 14, M, (--), B, SC, 263, 268, RICH+. In HH of David Grooms m 35 black born SC.

GROOMS, MARY, 40, F, (--), M, SC, 377, 377, SUMT.

GROOMS, MARY, 1, F, (--), M, SC, 377, 377, SUMT. In HH of Mary Grooms f 50 mulatto born SC.

GROOMS, NANCY, 32, F, (--), B, SC, 263, 268, RICH+. In HH of David Grooms m 35 black born SC.

GROOMS, PATSEY, 1, F, (--), B, SC, 263, 268, RICH+. In HH of David Grooms m 35 black born SC.

GROOMS, RUFUS, 19, M, Planter, B, SC, 244, 249, RICH+. In HH of Thomas Grooms m 50 black born SC.

GROOMS, SARAH, 9, F, (--), B, SC, 263, 268, RICH+. In HH of David Grooms m 35 black born SC.

GROOMS, THOMAS, 50, M, Planter, B, SC, 244, 249, RICH+.

GROOMS, THOMAS, 12, M, (--), B, SC, 244, 249, RICH+. In HH of Thomas Grooms m 50 black born SC.

GROOMS, WINNEY, 11, F, (--), B, SC, 263, 268, RICH+. In HH of David Grooms m 35 black born SC.

GROSS, REBECCA W., 35, F, (--), M, SC, 505, 463, CHAS+.

GUIGNARAD, GREEN, 66, M, Carpenter, M, SC, 170, 174, RICH.

GUIGNARAD, MARY, 56, F, (--), M, SC, 170, 174, RICH. In HH of Green Guignard m 66 mulatto born SC.

GUINARD, ADAM, 12, M, (--), B, SC, 82, 82, FAIR. In HH of Martha Guinard f 41 black born SC.

GUINARD, CAROLINE, 16, F, (--), B, SC, 82, 82, FAIR. In HH of Martha Guinard f 41 black born SC.

GUINARD, EDWARD, 5, M, (--), B, SC, 82, 82, FAIR. In HH of Martha Guinard f 41 black born SC.

GUINARD, JEFFERSON, 18, M, (--), B, SC, 82, 82, FAIR. In HH of Martha Guinard f 41 black born SC.

GUINARD, MARTHA, 41, F, (--), B, SC, 82, 82, FAIR.

GUINARD, MARTHA, 2, F, (--), B, SC, 82, 82, FAIR. In HH of Martha Guinard f 41 black born SC.

GUINARD, REASON, 9, M, (--), B, SC, 82, 82, FAIR. In HH of Martha Guinard f 41 black born SC.

GUINARD, SARAH, 14, F, (--), B, SC, 82, 82, FAIR. In HH of Martha Guinard f 41 black born SC.

GUINN, DANIEL, 6, M, (--), M, SC, 815, 815, MARL. In HH of Wm. Guinn m 52 born NC.

GUNTER, ALEX, 2, M, (--), M, SC, 601, 601, MARL. In HH of Polly Gunter f 35 mulatto born SC.

GUNTER, ANN, 10, F, (--), M, SC, 601, 601, MARL. In HH of Polly Gunter f 35 mulatto born SC.

GUNTER, HUGH, 14, M, (--), M, SC, 601, 601, MARL. In HH of Polly Gunter f 35 mulatto born SC.

GUNTER, JANE, 8, F, (--), M, SC, 601, 601, MARL. In HH of Polly Gunter f 35 mulatto born SC.

GUNTER, JOHN, 12, M, (--), M, SC, 601, 601, MARL. In HH of Polly Gunter f 35 mulatto born SC.

GUNTER, MARY, 5, F, (--), M, SC, 601, 601, MARL. In HH of Polly Gunter f 35 mulatto born SC.

GUNTER, POLLY, 35, F, (--), M, SC, 601, 601, MARL.

GUTHREY, MARY THEUS, 30, F, (--), M, SC, 446, 405, CHAS+.

GWIN, ALFRED, 1, M, (--), B, SC, 830, 830, CHES. In HH of Eliza Gwin f 26 black born in SC.

GWIN, ELIZA, 26, F, (--), B, SC, 830, 830, CHES.

GWIN, EMELINE, 25, F, (--), M, SC, 1006, 1010, AND. In HH of John Gwinn m 22 mulatto born SC.

GWIN, HARRIS, 5, M, (--), M, SC, 1005, 1009, AND. In HH of Leonard Gwin m 75 mulatto born VA.

GWIN, JEFFERSON, 38, M, (--), M, SC, 1005, 1009, AND. In HH of Leonard Gwin m 75 mulatto born VA.

GWIN, JOHN, 22, M, Farmer, M, SC, 1006, 1010, AND.

GWIN, KEZIAH, 26, F, (--), M, SC, 1005, 1009, AND. In HH of Leonard Gwin m 75 mulatto born VA.

GWIN, LEONARD, 75, M, Farmer, M, VA, 1005, 1009, AND.

GWIN, MARY, 6, F, (--), B, SC, 830, 830, CHES. In HH of Eliza Gwin f 26 black born in SC.

GWIN, MARY, 1, F, (--), M, SC, 1005, 1009, AND. In HH of Leonard Gwin m 75 mulatto born VA.

GWIN, MITCHEL, 23, M, (--), M, SC, 1005, 1009, AND. In HH of Leonard Gwin m 75 mulatto born VA.

GWIN, POLLY, 35, F, (--), M, SC, 1005, 1009, AND. In HH of Leonard Gwin m 75 mulatto born VA.

GWIN, SIDNEY, 19, M, Farmer, M, SC, 1005, 1009, AND. In HH of Leonard Gwin m 75 mulatto born VA.

GWIN, THOMAS, 4, M, (--), B, SC, 830, 830, CHES. In HH of Eliza Gwin f 26 black born in SC.

GWIN, WILLIAM, 4, M, (--), M, SC, 1006, 1010, AND. In HH of John Gwinn m 22 mulatto born SC.

GWIN, WILLIAM, 3, M, (--), M, SC, 1005, 1009, AND. In HH of Leonard Gwin m 75 mulatto born VA.

GYLES, JANE, 2, F, (--), M, SC, 915, 895, CHAS-. In HH of Chloe Bowengen f 60 mulatto born SC.

GYLES, JOANA, 17, F, (--), M, SC, 915, 895, CHAS-. In HH of Chloe Bowengen f 60 mulatto born SC.

GYLES, LOUISA, 4, F, (--), M, SC, 915, 895, CHAS-. In HH of Chloe Bowengen f 60 mulatto born SC.

H

HAGOOD, S.T., 8, M, (--), M, SC, 185, 187, AND. In HH of William Drennar m 50 white born SC.

HAIG, HARRIET, 39, F, (--), B, SC, 582, 564, CHAS-. In HH of Susan Grain f 39 black born SC.

HAIG, JEMMIMA, 16, F, (--), B, SC, 582, 564, CHAS-. In HH of Susan Grain f 39 black born SC.

HAIG, JOHN, 12, M, (--), B, SC, 582, 564, CHAS-. In HH of Susan Grain f 39 black born SC.

HAITHCOCK, ISAAC, 50, M, Planter, B, SC, 1414, 1414, Sumter, SC.

HALE, AMELIA, 17, F, (--), M, SC, 164, 168, RICH. In HH of Rosa Rawls f 35 mulatto born SC.

HALE, ANN, 35, F, (--), M, SC, 515, 518, MAR. Ann Hale born Marion, SC.

HALE, ARRINGTON, 90, F, (--), M, SC, 905, 885, CHAS-.

HALE, FRANCIS, 42, M, Stevedore, B, SC, 342, 325, CHAS-. In HH of Mary Williams f 38 mulatto born SC.

HALE, JEMMIMA, 48, F, (--), B, SC, 342, 325, CHAS-. In HH of Mary Williams f 38 mulatto born SC.

HALE, JOHN, 3, M, (--), M, SC, 515, 518, MAR. In HH of Ann Hale f 35 mulatto born Marion, SC. John born Marion, SC.

HALE, ROBERT, 11, M, (--), M, SC, 164, 168, RICH. In HH of Rosa Rawls f 35 mulatto born SC.

HALE, SARAH, 3, F, (--), M, SC, 515, 518, MAR. In HH of Ann Hale f 35 mulatto born Marion, SC. Sarah born Marion, SC.

HALE, THOMAS, 54, M, Tailor, M, SC, 905, 885, CHAS-. In HH of Arrington Hale f 90 mulatto born SC.

HALE, WILLIAM, 33, M, Laborer, M, SC, 164, 168, RICH. In HH of Rosa Rawls f 35 mulatto born SC.

HALE, WILLIAM H., 1, M, (--), M, SC, 164, 168, RICH. In HH of Rosa Rawls f 35 mulatto born SC.

HALL, C., 30, F, (--), M, SC, 492, 475, CHAS-.

HALL, DAVID, 36, M, (--), B, SC, 476, 476, KERS. In HH of Laban Fergerson m 43 born SC.

HALL, DAVID, 10, M, (--), M, SC, 492, 475, CHAS-. In HH of C. Hall f 30 mulatto born SC.

HALL, EPHRAIM, 12, M, (--), M, SC, 492, 475, CHAS-. In HH of C. Hall f 30 mulatto born SC.

HALL, JOSEPH, 10, M, (--), B, SC, 623, 623, NEWB. In HH of James Morris m 26 born SC.

HALL, MARY, 8, F, (--), M, SC, 492, 475, CHAS-. In HH of C. Hall f 30 mulatto born SC.

HALLOWAY, CHARLES, 9, M, (--), M, SC, 944, 924, CHAS-. In HH of Mary Holloway f 47 mulatto born SC.

HALLOWAY, CLARA, 24, F, (--), B, SC, 544, 544, PICK+.

HALLOWAY, DANIEL, 15, M, (--), M, SC, 944, 924, CHAS-. In HH of Mary Holloway f 47 mulatto born SC.

HALLOWAY, DICK, 4, M, (--), B, SC, 544, 544, PICK+. In HH of Clara Halloway f 24 black born SC.

HALLOWAY, MARY, 47, F, (--), M, SC, 944, 924, CHAS-.

HALLOWAY, RICHARD, 17, M, Cooper, M, SC, 944, 924, CHAS-. In HH of Mary Holloway f 47 mulatto born SC.

HALLOWAY, SARAH A., 12, F, (--), M, SC, 944, 924, CHAS-. In HH of Mary Holloway f 47 mulatto born SC.

HALLOWAY, WILLIAM, 6, M, (--), M, SC, 944, 924, CHAS-. In HH of Mary Holloway f 47 mulatto born SC.

HALLOWAY, ZACK, 5, M, (--), B, SC, 544, 544, PICK+. In HH of Clara Halloway f 24 black born SC.

HALSTEAD, EDWARD, 24, M, (--), B, SC, 52, 52, CHAS^. In HH of John Amiel m 54 born England.

HAM, BETSEY, 43, F, (--), M, SC, 115, 107, CHAS-. In HH of Diana Ham f 50 mulatto born SC.

HAM, DIANA, 50, F, (--), M, SC, 115, 107, CHAS-.

HAM, ELIZA, 5, F, (--), M, SC, 115, 107, CHAS-. In HH of Diana Ham f 50 mulatto born SC.

HAM, EMMA, 18, F, (--), M, SC, 115, 107, CHAS-. In HH of Diana Ham f 50 mulatto born SC.

HAMELTON, HILLIARD, 19, M, Farmer, M, SC, 1003, 1003, CHES. In HH of Jesse Hamelton 44 m mulatto born SC.

HAMELTON, JESSE, 44, M, Farmer, M, SC, 1003, 1003, CHES.

HAMELTON, JESSE, 17, M, Farmer, M, SC, 1003, 1003, CHES. In HH of Jesse Hamelton 44 m mulatto born SC.

HAMELTON, M ANYE, 14, M, (--), M, SC, 1003, 1003, CHES. In HH of Jesse Hamelton 44 m mulatto born SC.

HAMELTON, M., 11, F, (--), M, SC, 1003, 1003, CHES. In HH of Jesse Hamelton 44 m mulatto born SC.

HAMELTON, THOMAS, 8, M, (--), M, SC, 1003, 1003, CHES. In HH of Jesse Hamelton 44 m mulatto born SC.

HAMILTON, ALLEN, 20, M, Farmer, M, SC, 215, 215, CHES.

HAMILTON, S.A., 18, F, (--), B, SC, 215, 215, CHES. In HH of Allen Hamilton m age 20 born SC.

HAMLIN, ALICE, 20, F, (--), M, VA, 402, 400, CHAS%. In HH of William Hamlin m 39 mulatto born VA.

HAMLIN, ANN, 10, F, (--), M, VA, 402, 400, CHAS%. In HH of William Hamlin m 39 mulatto born VA.

HAMLIN, BAZEL, 1, M, (--), M, VA, 402, 400, CHAS%. In HH of William Hamlin m 39 mulatto born VA.

HAMLIN, FURMAN, 12, M, (--), M, VA, 402, 400, CHAS%. In HH of William Hamlin m 39 mulatto born VA.

HAMLIN, JULIA, 7, F, (--), M, VA, 402, 400, CHAS%. In HH of William Hamlin m 39 mulatto born VA.

HAMLIN, NANCY, 34, F, (--), M, VA, 402, 400, CHAS%. In HH of William Hamlin m 39 mulatto born VA.

HAMLIN, THOMAS, 16, M, (--), M, VA, 402, 400, CHAS%. In HH of William Hamlin m 39 mulatto born VA.

HAMLIN, WILLIAM, 39, M, Carpenter, M, VA, 402, 400, CHAS%.

HAMLIN, ZACHARIAH, 4, M, (--), M, VA, 402, 400, CHAS%. In HH of William Hamlin m 39 mulatto born VA.

HAMMOND, ANNA, 12, F, (--), M, SC, 1008, 1008, DARL. In HH of David Hammond m 50 mulatto born SC.

HAMMOND, BETSY, 16, F, (--), M, SC, 1008, 1008, DARL. In HH of David Hammond m 50 mulatto born SC.

HAMMOND, CALVIN, 13, M, (--), M, SC, 1008, 1008, DARL. In HH of David Hammond m 50 mulatto born SC.

HAMMOND, CATEY, 18, F, (--), M, SC, 1008, 1008, DARL. In HH of David Hammond m 50 mulatto born SC.

HAMMOND, DAVID, 50, M, Farmer, M, SC, 1008, 1008, DARL.

HAMMOND, DAVID, 10, M, (--), M, SC, 1008, 1008, DARL. In HH of David Hammond m 50 mulatto born SC.

HAMMOND, HARRIET, 20, F, (--), B, SC, 118, 118, KERS.

HAMMOND, HENRY, 19, M, (--), M, SC, 1008, 1008, DARL. In HH of David Hammond m 50 mulatto born SC.

HAMMOND, SUSAN, 55, F, (--), M, SC, 1008, 1008, DARL. In HH of David Hammond m 50 mulatto born SC.

HAMMOND, WM., 10, M, (--), B, SC, 116, 116, KERS. In HH of Maria Johnson f 52 black born SC.

HAMPTON, BENJAMIN, 19, M, Tailor, M, SC, 396, 379, CHAS-. In HH of Daphney Hampton f 60 mulatto born SC.

HAMPTON, DAPHNEY, 60, F, (--), M, SC, 396, 379, CHAS-.

HAMPTON, EDWARD, 5, M, (--), M, SC, 284, 258, CHAS*. In HH of Diana Frezevant f 60 mulatto born SC.

HAMPTON, ELLEN, 22, F, (--), M, SC, 396, 379, CHAS-. In HH of Daphney Hampton f 60 mulatto born SC.

HAMPTON, ELLEN, 22, F, (--), M, SC, 578, 570, CHAS%.

HAMPTON, GEORGE, 15, M, Shoemaker, M, SC, 396, 379, CHAS-. In HH of Daphney Hampton f 60 mulatto born SC.

HAMPTON, HARRIOT, 3, F, (--), M, SC, 284, 258, CHAS*. In HH of Diana Frezevant f 60 mulatto born SC.

HAMPTON, HENRIETTA, 4, F, (--), M, SC, 284, 258, CHAS*. In HH of Diana Frezevant f 60 mulatto born SC.

HAMPTON, JAMES, 6, M, (--), M, SC, 284, 258, CHAS*. In HH of Diana Frezevant f 60 mulatto born SC.

HAMPTON, MARGARET, 25, F, (--), M, SC, 396, 379, CHAS-. In HH of Daphney Hampton f 60 mulatto born SC.

HAMPTON, ROBERT, 40, M, Tailor, M, SC, 284, 258, CHAS*. In HH of Diana Frezevant f 60 mulatto born SC.

HAMPTON, SOPHIA, 38, F, (--), M, SC, 284, 258, CHAS*. In HH of Diana Frezevant f 60 mulatto born SC.

HANKS, BENDOL, 2, M, (--), M, SC, 855, 855, SUMT. In HH of Wm. Hanks m 27 mulatto born SC.

HANKS, SARAH, 24, F, (--), M, SC, 855, 855, SUMT. In HH of Wm. Hanks m 27 mulatto born SC.

HANKS, WM., 27, M, Carpenter, M, SC, 855, 855, SUMT.

HANSCOME, BESS, 60, F, (--), B, SC, 249, 223, CHAS*.

HANTZ, ANN M., 8, F, (--), M, SC, 667, 667, MARL. In HH of Lydia Hantz f 48 mulatto born SC.

HANTZ, CATHARINE, 16, F, (--), M, SC, 667, 667, MARL. In HH of Lydia Hantz f 48 mulatto born SC.

HANTZ, EFFY JANE, 21, F, (--), M, SC, 667, 667, MARL. In HH of Lydia Hantz f 48 mulatto born SC.

HANTZ, JOHN E., 11, M, (--), M, SC, 667, 667, MARL. In HH of Lydia Hantz f 48 mulatto born SC.

HANTZ, LYDIA, 48, F, (--), M, SC, 667, 667, MARL.

HANTZ, MARTHA A., 24, F, (--), M, SC, 667, 667, MARL. In HH of Lydia Hantz f 48 mulatto born SC.

HARDEN, LUCRETIA, 89, F, (--), B, SC, 108, 101, CHAS-.

HARDWICK, ELZTH., 3, F, (--), M, SC, 333, 333, HORR. In HH of John Ounercy m 70 mulatto born SC.

HARDY, AGNES, 28, F, (--), B, SC, 1247, 1247, UNION. In HH of Hannah Hardy f 65 black born SC.

HARDY, CLARISSA, 8, F, (--), B, SC, 1247, 1247, UNION. In HH of Hannah Hardy f 65 black born SC.

HARDY, FRANKLIN, 13, M, (--), B, SC, 580, 580, UNION. In HH of Jane Hardy f 32 black born SC.

HARDY, HANNAH, 65, F, (--), M, SC, 1247, 1247, UNION.

HARDY, HENRY, 18, M, Blacksmith, B, SC, 580, 580, UNION. In HH of Jane Hardy f 32 black born SC.

HARDY, ISAAC, 75, M, None, B, MD, 1242, 1242, UNION.

HARDY, JANE, 70, F, (--), B, VA, 1242, 1242, UNION. In HH of Isaac Hardy m 75 black born MD.

HARDY, JANE, 32, F, (--), B, SC, 580, 580, UNION.

HARDY, JOHN, 35, M, Laborer, B, SC, 580, 580, UNION. In HH of Jane Hardy f 32 black born SC.

HARDY, LOUISA, 7, F, (--), B, SC, 1247, 1247, UNION. In HH of Hannah Hardy f 65 black born SC.

HARDY, MARY ANN, 20, F, (--), B, SC, 1247, 1247, UNION. In HH of Hannah Hardy f 65 black born SC.

HARDY, PEGGY, 30, F, (--), B, SC, 1247, 1247, UNION. In HH of Hannah Hardy f 65 black born SC.

HARDY, SOPHRONIA, 9, F, (--), B, SC, 1247, 1247, UNION. In HH of Hannah Hardy f 65 black born SC.

HARDY, SUSAN, 8, F, (--), B, SC, 1247, 1247, UNION. In HH of Hannah Hardy f 65 black born SC.

HARIMAN, DUNCAN, 14, M, (--), M, SC, 636, 636, Will. In HH of Enoch A. Hariman m 52 mulatto born SC.

HARIMAN, ENOCH A., 52, M, Farmer, M, SC, 636, 636, Will.

HARIMAN, JANE, 32, F, (--), M, SC, 636, 636, Will. In HH of Enoch A. Hariman m 52 mulatto born SC.

HARIMAN, OBEDENCE, 11, F, (--), M, SC, 636, 636, Will. In HH of Enoch A. Hariman m 52 mulatto born SC.

HARIMAN, SHOECRAFT, 13, M, (--), M, SC, 636, 636, Will. In HH of Enoch A. Hariman m 52 mulatto born SC.

HARIMAN, THOMAS, 12, M, (--), M, SC, 636, 636, Will. In HH of Enoch A. Hariman m 52 mulatto born SC.

HARIMAN, WILLIAM, 7, M, (--), M, SC, 636, 636, Will. In HH of Enoch A. Hariman m 52 mulatto born SC.

HARKSTON, ANN, 14, F, (--), B, SC, 290, 290, CHAS%. In HH of Jane Lloyd f 38 black born SC.

HARKSTON, EDWARD, 18, M, (--), B, SC, 290, 290, CHAS%. In HH of Jane Lloyd f 38 black born SC.

HARKSTON, JOSEPH, 10, M, (--), B, SC, 290, 290, CHAS%. In HH of Jane Lloyd f 38 black born SC.

HARKSTON, RACHAEL, 16, F, (--), B, SC, 290, 290, CHAS%. In HH of Jane Lloyd f 38 black born SC.

HARKSTON, SYLVIA, 70, F, (--), B,

SC, 290, 290, CHAS%. In HH of Jane Lloyd f 38 black born SC.

HARLISTON, LYDIA, 25, F, (--), M, SC, 109, 102, CHAS-. In HH of John Fink m 60 born Germany.

HARMON, ANN, 9, F, (--), M, SC, 261, 262, MAR. In HH of Thomas L. Harmon m 34 mulatto born Marion, SC. Born Marion, SC.

HARMON, ARCHIBALD, 40, M, Planter, M, SC, 245, 245, CHAS3.

HARMON, CELIA, 39, F, (--), M, SC, 245, 245, CHAS3. In HH of Archibald Harmon m 40 mulatto born SC.

HARMON, DANL. T., 2, M, (--), M, SC, 245, 245, CHAS3. In HH of Archibald Harmon m 40 mulatto born SC.

HARMON, ELIJAH, 6, M, (--), M, SC, 261, 262, MAR. In HH of Thomas L. Harmon m 34 mulatto born Marion, SC. Born Marion, SC.

HARMON, ELISHA, 4, M, (--), M, SC, 261, 262, MAR,. In HH of Thomas L. Harmon m 34 mulatto born Marion, SC. Elisha born Marion, SC.

HARMON, ELIZABETH, 14, F, (--), M, SC, 245, 245, CHAS3. In HH of Archibald Harmon m 40 mulatto born SC.

HARMON, HORRACE, 20, M, None,, M, SC, 261, 262, MAR,. In HH of Thomas L. Harmon m 34 mulatto born Marion, SC. Horrace born Marion, SC.

HARMON, JEREMIAH, 10, M, (--), M, SC, 245, 245, CHAS3. In HH of Archibald Harmon m 40 mulatto born SC.

HARMON, JNO., 16, M, (--), M, SC, 245, 245, CHAS3. In HH of Archibald Harmon m 40 mulatto born SC.

HARMON, MARTHA., 40, F, (--), M, SC, 261, 262, MAR,. In HH of Thomas L. Harmon m 34 mulatto born Marion, SC. Martha born Marion, SC.

HARMON, SEMORE, 6, M, (--), M, SC, 245, 245, CHAS3. In HH of Archibald Harmon m 40 mulatto born SC.

HARMON, THOMAS, 4, M, (--), M, SC, 245, 245, CHAS3. In HH of Archibald Harmon m 40 mulatto born SC.

HARMON, THOMAS L., 34, M, Ferryman, M, SC, 261, 262, MAR,. Thomas L. Harmon born Marion, SC.

HARPER, ANNA, 4, F, (--), M, SC, 665, 623, CHAS+. In HH of Jack Harper m 60 mulatto born SC.

HARPER, ANTHONY, 11, M, (--), B, SC, 1171, 1171, ABB,. In HH of Cely Harper f 30 black born SC.

HARPER, CELY, 30, F, (--), B, SC, 1171, 1171, ABB,.

HARPER, CHARLES, 4, M, (--), M, SC, 163, 167, RICH. In HH of James Harper m 38 mulatto born SC.

HARPER, CLARISSA, 10, F, (--), M, SC, 163, 167, RICH. In HH of James Harper m 38 mulatto born SC.

HARPER, ELIZABETH, 7, F, (--), B, SC, 1171, 1171, ABB,. In HH of Cely Harper f 30 black born SC.

HARPER, GEORGE, 14, M, (--), M, SC, 163, 167, RICH. In HH of James Harper m 38 mulatto born SC.

HARPER, JACK, 60, M, Wood Factor, M, SC, 665, 623, CHAS+.

HARPER, JAMES, 38, M, Carpenter, M, SC, 163, 167, RICH.

HARPER, JARUSHA, 1, F, (--), B, SC, 1171, 1171, ABB,. In HH of Cely Harper f 30 black born SC.

HARPER, JOHN, 4, M, (--), B, SC, 1171, 1171, ABB,. In HH of Cely Harper f 30 black born SC.

HARPER, JOSEPH, 1, M, (--), M, SC, 163, 167, RICH. In HH of James Harper m 38 mulatto born SC.

HARPER, LYDIA, 53, F, (--), M, SC, 665, 623, CHAS+. In HH of Jack Harper m 60 mulatto born SC.

HARPER, MARGARET, 40, F, (--), M, SC, 163, 167, RICH. In HH of James Harper m 38 mulatto born SC.

HARPER, MARGARET, 8, F, (--), M, SC, 163, 167, RICH. In HH of James Harper m 38 mulatto born SC.

HARPER, MARTHA, 9, F, (--), B, SC, 1171, 1171, ABB,. In HH of Cely Harper f 30 black born SC.

HARPER, MARY, 3, F, (--), M, SC, 163, 167, RICH. In HH of James Harper m 38 mulatto born SC.

HARPER, NATHANIEL, 13, M, (--), M, SC, 665, 623, CHAS+. In HH of Jack Harper m 60 mulatto born SC.

HARPER, PRISCILLA, 27, F, (--), M, SC, 665, 623, CHAS+. In HH of Jack Harper m 60 mulatto born SC.

HARPER, ROSE, 18, F, (--), M, SC, 665, 623, CHAS+. In HH of Jack Harper m 60 mulatto born SC.

HARPER, SARAH, 12, F, (--), M, SC, 665, 623, CHAS+. In HH of Jack Harper m 60 mulatto born SC.

HARPER, SOPHIA, 15, F, (--), M, SC, 665, 623, CHAS+. In HH of Jack Harper m 60 mulatto born SC.

HARPNEY, ANTONIO, 18, M, Shoemaker, M, SC, 554, 520, CHAS*. In HH of Sarah Finlay f 16 mulatto born SC.

HARRIS, BETSEY, 45, F, (--), M, SC, 243, 243, KERS. In HH of Bolin Harris m 50 mulatto born SC.

HARRIS, BOLIN, 50, M, (--), M, SC, 243, 243, KERS.

HARRIS, CAROLINE, 2, F, (--), B, SC, 864, 865, FAIR. In HH of George Harris m 34 black born SC.

HARRIS, CATHERINE, 19, F, (--), M, SC, 344, 318, CHAS*. In HH of Mary Gesiness f 55 born SC.

HARRIS, CATHERINE, 1, F, (--), M, SC, 237, 242, RICH+. In HH of John Harris m 40 mulatto born SC.

HARRIS, EDWARD, 22, M, Laborer, M, SC, 317, 323, RICH+. In HH of Isaac Snead m 38 born SC.

HARRIS, ELIZA, 36, F, (--), M, SC, 43, 44, RICH.

HARRIS, ELIZABETH, 60, F, (--), M, SC, 40, 41, RICH. In HH of Robland Harris m 55 mulatto born SC.

HARRIS, EMMA, 17, F, (--), M, SC, 317, 323, RICH+. In HH of Isaac Snead m 38 born SC.

HARRIS, EUGENE, 16, F, (--), M, SC, 344, 318, CHAS*. In HH of Mary Gesiness f 55 born SC.

HARRIS, FRANCIS, 13, F, (--), M, SC, 243, 243, KERS. In HH of Bolin Harris m 50 mulatto born SC.

HARRIS, GEORGE, 34, M, Planter, B, SC, 864, 865, FAIR.

HARRIS, HOLLAND, 16, M, (--), M, SC, 243, 243, KERS. In HH of Bolin Harris m 50 mulatto born SC.

HARRIS, ISHAM, 50, M, Laborer, M, SC, 208, 212, RICH+.

HARRIS, JAMES H., 2, M, (--), M, SC, 223, 227, RICH+. In HH of Susan Harris f 22 mulatto born SC.

HARRIS, JANE, 30, F, (--), M, SC, 226, 230, RICH+. In HH of Moses Harris m 40 mulatto born SC.

HARRIS, JOHN, 40, M, Planter, M, SC, 237, 242, RICH+.

HARRIS, JOHN, 1, M, (--), M, SC, 226, 230, RICH+. In HH of Moses Harris m 40 mulatto born SC.

HARRIS, JOHN A., 2, M, (--), M, SC, 237, 242, RICH+. In HH of John Harris m 40 mulatto born SC.

HARRIS, LEONORA M., 6, F, (--), M, SC, 226, 230, RICH+. In HH of Moses Harris m 40 mulatto born SC.

HARRIS, LYDIA, 21, F, (--), M, SC, 237, 242, RICH+. In HH of John Harris m 40 mulatto born SC.

HARRIS, MAHALEY, 86, F, (--), M, SC, 42, 43, RICH. In HH of Priscilla Harris f 36 mulatto born SC.

HARRIS, MARGARET, 50, F, (--), M, SC, 234, 234, GEOR*. In HH of Vandal Harris m 46 mulatto born SC.

HARRIS, MARTHA, 38, F, (--), M, SC, 42, 43, RICH. In HH of Priscilla Harris f 36 mulatto born SC.

HARRIS, MARY, 26, F, (--), M, SC, 243, 243, KERS. In HH of Bolin Harris m 50 mulatto born SC.

HARRIS, MOSES, 40, M, Planter, M, SC, 226, 230, RICH+.

HARRIS, MOSES, 2, M, (--), M, SC, 226, 230, RICH+. In HH of Moses Harris m 40 mulatto born SC.

HARRIS, POLLY, 40, F, (--), M, SC, 239, 244, RICH+. In HH of Stark Harris m 50 mulatto born SC.

HARRIS, PRISCILLA, 50, F, (--), M, SC, 208, 212, RICH+. In HH of Isham Harris m 50 mulatto born SC.

HARRIS, PRISCILLA, 36, F, (--), M, SC, 42, 43, RICH.

HARRIS, ROLAND, 55, M, Laborer, M, SC, 40, 41, RICH.

HARRIS, SARAH, 30, F, (--), B, SC, 864, 865, FAIR. In HH of George Harris m 34 black born SC.

HARRIS, STARK, 50, M, Planter, M, SC, 239, 244, RICH+.

HARRIS, SUSAN, 22, F, (--), M, SC, 223, 227, RICH+.

HARRIS, VANDAL, 46, M, Farmer, M, SC, 234, 234, GEOR*.

HARRIS, WILLIAM J., 4, M, (--), M, SC, 226, 230, RICH+. In HH of Moses Harris m 40 mulatto born SC.

HARRISON, AMANDA, 5, F, (--), M, SC, 581, 581, MARL. In HH of Betty Hathcock f 60 mulatto born SC.

HARRISON, ANN, 51, F, (--), M, SC, 354, 337, CHAS-. In HH of James Harrison m 50 mulatto born SC.

HARRISON, BENJAMIN, 19, M, (--), M, SC, 238, 238, COLL. In HH of Mary Harrison f 47 white, born SC.

HARRISON, CHARLES, 9, M, (--), M, SC, 238, 238, COLL. In HH of Mary Harrison f 47 white, born SC.

HARRISON, FERRIBY, 80, F, (--), B, VA, 925, 926, FAIR. In HH of George Harrison m 110 black born FL, notes Free from merit.

HARRISON, FRANCIS, 17, M, (--), M, SC, 238, 238, COLL. In HH of Mary Harrison f 47 white, born SC.

HARRISON, GEORGE, 110, M, Free from merit, B, FL, 925, 926, FAIR.

HARRISON, JAMES, 50, M, Shoemaker, M, SC, 354, 337, CHAS-.

HARRISON, JAMES, 25, M, Farmer, M, SC, 238, 238, COLL. In HH of Mary Harrison f 47 white, born SC.

HARRISON, JAMES, 21, M, Tailor, M, SC, 220, 206, CHAS-. In HH of John Frazer m 50 mulatto born SC.

HARRISON, JOHN L., 26, M, Farmer, M, SC, 238, 238, COLL. In HH of Mary Harrison f 47 white, born SC.

HARRISON, JOSIAH, 6, M, (--), M, SC, 238, 238, COLL. In HH of Mary Harrison f 47 white, born SC.

HARRISON, JULIA A., 30, F, (--), M, SC, 581, 581, MARL. In HH of Betty Hathcock f 60 mulatto born SC.

HARRISON, THOMAS, 18, M, Tailor, M, SC, 220, 206, CHAS-. In HH of John Frazer m 50 mulatto born SC.

HARVY, GEORGE ANNA, 16, F, (--), M, SC, 275, 275, BEAU+. In HH of Wm. Harvy m 50 mulatto born SC.

HARVY, RACHEL, 55, F, (--), M, SC, 275, 275, BEAU+. In HH of Wm. Harvy m 50 mulatto born SC.

HARVY, WM., 50, M, Laborer, M, SC, 275, 275, BEAU+.

HASELL, CHARLES, 50, M, Blacksmith, B, SC, 55, 55, CHAS%.

HASELL, DIANA, 10, F, (--), B, SC, 55, 55, CHAS%. In HH of Charles Hasell m 50 black born SC.

HASELL, ELLEN, 16, F, (--), B, SC, 55, 55, CHAS%. In HH of Charles Hasell m 50 black born SC.

HASELL, LAVINA, 12, F, (--), B, SC, 55, 55, CHAS%. In HH of Charles Hasell m 50 black born SC.

HASELL, MARIA, 30, F, (--), B, SC, 174, 164, CHAS-.

HASELL, PATTEY, 42, F, (--), B, SC, 55, 55, CHAS%. In HH of Charles Hasell m 50 black born SC.

HASELL, SARAH, 14, F, (--), B, SC, 55, 55, CHAS%. In HH of Charles Hasell m 50 black born SC.

HASSETT, JANE, 11, F, (--), M, SC, 282, 266, CHAS-. In HH of Peter Hassett m 38 mulatto born SC.

HASSETT, JOHN, 18, M, Painter, M,

SC, 282, 266, CHAS-. In HH of Peter Hassett m 38 mulatto born SC.

HASSETT, LOUISA, 14, F, (--), M, SC, 282, 266, CHAS-. In HH of Peter Hassett m 38 mulatto born SC.

HASSETT, MARY, 16, F, (--), M, SC, 282, 266, CHAS-. In HH of Peter Hassett m 38 mulatto born SC.

HASSETT, PETER, 38, M, Painter, M, SC, 282, 266, CHAS-.

HATCHELL, WILLIAM, 35, M, Farmer, M, SC, 604, 607, MAR, William Hatchell born Marion, SC.

HATCHER, FRANCES, 28, F, (--), M, SC, 161, 151, CHAS-.

HATCHER, JAMES W., 12, M, (--), M, SC, 161, 151, CHAS-. In HH of Frances Hatcher f 28 mulatto born SC.

HATHCOCK, BETTY, 60, F, (--), M, SC, 581, 581, MARL.

HATHCOCK, JOHN, 21, M, Laborer, M, SC, 1368, 1374, MAR,.

HAYDEN, BELLA, 70, F, (--), B, SC, 178, 168, CHAS-.

HAZARD, ANGELINE, 50, F, (--), M, SC, 1070, 1092, CHAS%.

HAZARD, CATHERINE, 10, F, (--), M, SC, 773, 756, CHAS%. In HH of William Hazard m 70 mulatto born SC.

HAZARD, ELSEY, 28, F, (--), M, SC, 773, 756, CHAS%. In HH of William Hazard m 70 mulatto born SC.

HAZARD, EMILY, 20, F, (--), M, SC, 1070, 1092, CHAS%. In HH of Angline Hazard f 50 mulatto born SC.

HAZARD, JANE, 14, F, (--), M, SC, 1070, 1092, CHAS%. In HH of Angline Hazard f 50 mulatto born SC.

HAZARD, JOHN, 46, M, Carpenter, M, SC, 1070, 1092, CHAS%. In HH of Angline Hazard f 50 mulatto born SC.

HAZARD, JOSEPH, 4, M, (--), M, SC, 773, 756, CHAS%. In HH of William Hazard m 70 mulatto born SC.

HAZARD, LOUISA, 6, F, (--), M, SC, 773, 756, CHAS%. In HH of William Hazard m 70 mulatto born SC.

HAZARD, MARY, 68, F, (--), M, SC,

773, 756, CHAS%. In HH of William Hazard m 70 mulatto born SC.

HAZARD, MARY, 30, F, (--), B, SC, 897, 874, CHAS%. In HH of Timothy Hazard m 40 black born SC.

HAZARD, RACHAEL, 8, F, (--), M, SC, 773, 756, CHAS%. In HH of William Hazard m 70 mulatto born SC.

HAZARD, TIMOTHY, 40, M, Shoemaker, B, SC, 897, 874, CHAS%.

HAZARD, WILLIAM, 70, M, Laborer, M, SC, 773, 756, CHAS%.

HAZARD, WILLIAM, 30, M, Carpenter, M, SC, 773, 756, CHAS%. In HH of William Hazard m 70 mulatto born SC.

HAZEL, ALMIRA, 17, F, (--), M, SC, 1213, 1213, BARN. In HH of Giden Hazel m 26 mulatto born SC.

HAZEL, ASA, 13, M, (--), M, SC, 1213, 1213, BARN. In HH of Giden Hazel m 26 mulatto born SC.

HAZEL, EDWARD, 8, M, (--), B, SC, 1221, 1221, BARN. In HH of Jack Hazel m 39 black born SC.

HAZEL, EMELINE, 14, F, (--), B, SC, 1221, 1221, BARN. In HH of Jack Hazel m 39 black born SC.

HAZEL, GIDEN, 26, M, Planter, M, SC, 1213, 1213, BARN.

HAZEL, JACK, 39, M, Planter, B, SC, 1221, 1221, BARN.

HAZEL, JAS., 10, M, (--), B, SC, 1221, 1221, BARN. In HH of Jack Hazel m 39 black born SC.

HAZEL, JOSEPH, 7, M, (--), B, SC, 1221, 1221, BARN. In HH of Jack Hazel m 39 black born SC.

HAZEL, MARY, 30, F, (--), B, SC, 1221, 1221, BARN. In HH of Jack Hazel m 39 black born SC. Mary age listed as 3 but appears to be missing a digit.

HAZEL, PIPIN, 21, M, (--), B, SC, 1213, 1213, BARN. In HH of Giden Hazel m 26 mulatto born SC.

HAZEL, RICHARD, 15, M, (--), B, SC, 1221, 1221, BARN. In HH of Jack Hazel m 39 black born SC.

HAZELE, BETTY, 6, F, (--), M, SC,

1309, 1309, BARN. In HH of David Hazele m 35 mulatto born SC.

HAZELE, BOB, 10, M, (--), M, SC, 1309, 1309, BARN. In HH of David Hazele m 35 mulatto born SC.

HAZELE, DAVID, 35, M, Planter, M, SC, 1309, 1309, BARN.

HAZELE, JNO., 25, M, (--), M, SC, 1310, 1310, BARN.

HAZELE, NELLY, 16, F, (--), M, SC, 1310, 1310, BARN. In HH of Jno. Hazle m 25 mulatto born SC.

HAZELE, RACHEL, 25, F, (--), M, SC, 1309, 1309, BARN. In HH of David Hazele m 35 mulatto born SC.

HAZZARD, ESTHER, 28, F, (--), B, SC, 612, 593, CHAS-.

HAZZARD, JOHN, 26, M, Carpenter, B, SC, 612, 593, CHAS-. In HH of Esther Hazzard f 28 black born SC.

HAZZARD, PHILLIS, 7, F, (--), B, SC, 612, 593, CHAS-. In HH of Esther Hazzard f 28 black born SC.

HEATHCOX, M., 40, M, Carpenter, B, SC, 177, 177, KERS. In HH of Joseph Murphy m 59 born SC.

HEDLEY, EUGINE, 27, F, (--), M, SC, 365, 348, CHAS-. In HH of Mary McBride f 46 mulatto born SC.

HEDLEY, THERESE, 24, F, (--), M, SC, 365, 348, CHAS-. In HH of Mary McBride f 46 mulatto born SC.

HEEPBURN, HARRIET, 49, F, (--), M, SC, 70, 70, CHAS%. In HH of John Clarke m 30 mulatto born SC.

HELLER, MOSES, 80, M, Farmer, B, VA, 1387, 1387, NEWB.

HEMETRY, SARAH, 56, F, (--), M, SC, 353, 353, CHAS%.

HENDERSON, JOHN, 3, M, (--), B, SC, 471, 471, GREE. In HH of N.H. Dill m 32 born SC.

HENDERSON, LOUISA, 25, F, (--), M, SC, 676, 634, CHAS+. In HH of F. Devinier m 30 mulatto born SC.

HENDRICKS, ELIZA, 14, F, (--), M, SC, 931, 911, CHAS-. In HH of Henry Hendricks m 47 mulatto born Scotland {sic}.

HENDRICKS, HENRY, 47, M, (--), M, Scotland{sic}, 931, 911, CHAS-.

HENDRICKS, MARIA, 45, F, (--), M, Scotland{sic}, 931, 911, CHAS-. In HH of Henry Hendricks m 47 mulatto born Scotland {sic}.

HENDRICKS, MARY, 17, F, (--), M, Scotland{sic}, 931, 911, CHAS-. In HH of Henry Hendricks m 47 mulatto born Scotland {sic}.

HENRY, BETSEY, 40, F, (--), M, SC, 797, 755, CHAS+.

HENRY, BILLY, 9, M, (--), B, SC, 797, 755, CHAS+. In HH of Betsey Henry f 49 mulatto born SC.

HENRY, JAMES, 38, M, Laborer, M, SC, 797, 755, CHAS+. In HH of Betsey Henry f 49 mulatto born SC.

HENRY, PHOEBE, 32, F, (--), B, SC, 797, 755, CHAS+. In HH of Betsey Henry f 49 mulatto born SC.

HENRY, SUSAN, 10, F, (--), B, SC, 797, 755, CHAS+. In HH of Betsey Henry f 49 mulatto born SC.

HENRY, THOMAS, 16, M, Shoemaker, M, SC, 149, 137, CHAS*.

HENSON, ELIZABETH, 60, F, (--), M, SC, 193, 176, CHAS.

HENSON, EUGENIA JONES, 3, F, (--), M, SC, 282, 282, BEAU+. In HH of Henry Henson m 22 mulatto born SC.

HENSON, HENRY, 22, M, Laborer, M, SC, 282, 282, BEAU+.

HENSON, JAMES, 22, M, Laborer, M, SC, 300, 300, BEAU+.

HENSON, MANER, 4, M, (--), M, SC, 300, 300, BEAU+. In HH of James Henson m 22 mulatto born SC.

HENSON, MARTHA, 20, F, (--), M, SC, 300, 300, BEAU+. In HH of James Henson m 22 mulatto born SC.

HENSON, MARY, 20, F, (--), M, SC, 282, 282, BEAU+. In HH of Henry Henson m 22 mulatto born SC.

HENSON, SUSAN, 65, F, (--), M, SC, 193, 176, CHAS. In HH of Elizabeth Henson f 60 mulatto born SC.

HEPBURN, MARY, 37, F, (--), B, SC, 65, 65, CHAS%. In HH of Mary McKee

f 46 black born SC.

HERIN, MARGARET, 64, F, (--), M, SC, 599, 599, EDGE*.

HERIN, PATEN, 38, M, (--), M, SC, 599, 599, EDGE*. In HH of Margaret Herin f 64 born SC.

HERON, JULIA E., 25, F, (--), B, SC, 363, 363, CHAS%. In HH of Cornelius Heron m 41 born SC.

HEWSTON, CORNELUS, 25, M, Blacksmith, M, SC, 193, 176, CHAS. In HH of Elizabeth Henson f 60 mulatto born SC.

HEYWARD, NANCY, 30, F, (--), B, SC, 774, 754, CHAS-. In HH of Samuel Read m 28 black born SC.

HICKS, ELLEN, 50, F, (--), M, SC, 298, 298, CHAS%.

HICKS, SARAH, 30, F, (--), M, SC, 547, 513, CHAS*.

HILL, CHARLES, 15, M, (--), M, SC, 891, 871, CHAS-. In HH of Grace Lee f 62 mulatto born SC.

HILL, EMMA, 10, F, (--), M, SC, 891, 871, CHAS-. In HH of Grace Lee f 62 mulatto born SC.

HILL, JOHN, 38, M, Laborer, M, SC, 201, 201, CHAS%.

HILL, NANCY, 32, F, (--), M, SC, 891, 871, CHAS-. In HH of Grace Lee f 62 mulatto born SC.

HILLIGAS, JANE, 23, F, (--), M, SC, 175, 161, CHAS*. In HH of Caroline LeBate f 39 mulatto born SC.

HILLIGNS, CAROLINE, 4, F, (--), M, SC, 449, 432, CHAS-. In HH of Celest Hilligns f 26 mulatto born SC.

HILLIGNS, CELEST, 26, F, (--), M, SC, 449, 432, CHAS-.

HILLIGNS, EUGENA, 1, F, (--), M, SC, 449, 432, CHAS-. In HH of Celest Hilligns f 26 mulatto born SC.

HILLIGNS, EVELINA, 5, F, (--), M, SC, 449, 432, CHAS-. In HH of Celest Hilligns f 26 mulatto born SC.

HILLIGNS, JULIA, 7, F, (--), M, SC, 449, 432, CHAS-. In HH of Celest Hilligns f 26 mulatto born SC.

HILLIGNS, ROBERT, 12, M, (--), M, SC, 449, 432, CHAS-. In HH of Celest Hilligns f 26 mulatto born SC.

HILTON, MARY, 80, F, (--), B, VA, 566, 583, RICH.

HINES, J.A., 5, M, (--), M, SC, 308, 308, CHES. In HH of William Chistmas m 36 born SC.

HINES, M.L., 5, F, (--), M, SC, 308, 308, CHES. In HH of William Chistmas m 36 born SC.

HODGES, DORCAS, 21, F, (--), B, SC, 883, 883, KERS. In HH of Ely Hodges m 31 mulatto born SC.

HODGES, ELY, 31, M, (--), B, SC, 883, 883, KERS.

HOFF, ANN, 31, F, (--), M, SC, 436, 433, CHAS%. In HH of John Hoff m 30 mulatto born SC.

HOFF, ELIZA, 37, F, (--), M, SC, 193, 193, CHAS%. In HH of Charles Legare m 50 black born SC.

HOFF, ELIZABETH, 6, F, (--), M, SC, 436, 433, CHAS%. In HH of John Hoff m 30 mulatto born SC.

HOFF, HARRIET, 4, F, (--), M, SC, 436, 433, CHAS%. In HH of John Hoff m 30 mulatto born SC.

HOFF, JAMES, 28, M, Millwright, M, SC, 436, 433, CHAS%. In HH of John Hoff m 30 mulatto born SC.

HOFF, JOHN, 39, M, Tailor, M, SC, 436, 433, CHAS%.

HOFF, JOHN, 15, M, (--), M, SC, 193, 193, CHAS%. In HH of Charles Legare m 50 black born SC.

HOFF, JULIA, 8, F, (--), M, SC, 436, 433, CHAS%. In HH of John Hoff m 30 mulatto born SC.

HOFF, ROMES, 2, M, (--), M, SC, 436, 433, CHAS%. In HH of John Hoff m 30 mulatto born SC.

HOFFMAN, JOSEPH, 8, M, (--), M, SC, 1023, 1000, CHAS-. In HH of Catherine Lewis f 50 mulatto born SC.

HOFFMAN, LOUISA, 11, F, (--), M, SC, 1023, 1000, CHAS-. In HH of Catherine Lewis f 50 mulatto born SC.

HOFFMAN, ROSA, 29, F, (--), M, SC,

1023, 1000, CHAS-. In HH of Catherine Lewis f 50 mulatto born SC.

HOGG, JAMES, 23, M, (--), M, SC, 284, 285, AND*. In HH of James Banister m 36 white born SC.

HOGG, JANE C., 8, F, (--), M, SC, 287, 288, AND*. In HH of John Hogg m 54 mulatto born SC.

HOGG, JOHN, 54, M, (--), M, SC, 287, 288, AND*.

HOGG, MARTHA J., 13, F, (--), M, SC, 287, 288, AND*. In HH of John Hogg m 54 mulatto born SC.

HOGG, MARY ANN, 15, F, (--), M, SC, 287, 288, AND*. In HH of John Hogg m 54 mulatto born SC.

HOGG, THOMPSON, 11, M, (--), M, SC, 287, 288, AND*. In HH of John Hogg m 54 mulatto born SC.

HOLAND, ABIGAIL, 29, F, (--), M, SC, 72, 72, GEOR. In HH of James Holand m 37 mulatto born SC.

HOLAND, JAMES, 37, M, Tailor, M, SC, 72, 72, GEOR.

HOLAND, MARY, 5, F, (--), M, SC, 72, James Holand m 37 mulatto born SC.

HOLAND, ROSA, 4, F, (--), M, SC, 72, 72, GEOR. In HH of James Holand m 37 mulatto born SC.

HOLAND, WM., 2, M, (--), M, SC, 72, 72, GEOR. In HH of James Holand m 37 mulatto born SC.

HOLCOMBE, MELISSA, 12, F, (--), M, SC, 446, 446, UNION. In HH of Mary Holcombe f 40 born SC.

HOLDMAN, HENRY, 21, M, Shoemaker, M, SC-, 506, 506, AND. In HH of J.T. Horn m 26 white born NC.

HOLLAND, SARAH, 30, F, Fruiterer, M, SC, 401, 365, CHAS.

HOLLENSBY, MARY, 24, F, (--), M, SC, 147, 135, CHAS*. In HH of Rebecca Naylor f 35 black born SC.

HOLLENSBY, MARY E., 8, F, (--), M, SC, 147, 135, CHAS*. In HH of Rebecca Naylor f 35 black born SC.

HOLLINGSWORTH, VILETT, 90, F, (--), B, VA, 291, 291, EDGE. Name Hollingsworth in {brackets}.

HOLLOWAY, CAROLINE, 8, F, (--), M, SC, 970, 950, CHAS-. In HH of Katey Halloway f 24 mulatto born SC.

HOLLOWAY, CHARLES, 2, M, (--), M, SC, 357, 340, CHAS-. In HH of Elizabeth Holloway f 30 mulatto born SC.

HOLLOWAY, EDWIN, 6, M, (--), M, SC, 131, 122, CHAS-. In HH of Richard Holloway m 45 mulatto born SC.

HOLLOWAY, ELIZA, 37, F, (--), M, SC, 131, 122, CHAS-. In HH of Richard Holloway m 45 mulatto born SC.

HOLLOWAY, ELIZABETH, 30, F, (--), M, SC, 357, 340, CHAS-.

HOLLOWAY, ISAAC, 15, M, Carter, M, SC, 357, 340, CHAS-. In HH of Elizabeth Holloway f 30 mulatto born SC.

HOLLOWAY, JOHN, 14, M, (--), M, SC, 131, 122, CHAS-. In HH of Richard Holloway m 45 mulatto born SC.

HOLLOWAY, KATEY, 24, F, (--), M, SC, 970, 950, CHAS-.

HOLLOWAY, MARY, 13, F, (--), M, SC, 131, 122, CHAS-. In HH of Richard Holloway m 45 mulatto born SC.

HOLLOWAY, RICHARD, 45, M, Carpenter, M, SC, 131, 122, CHAS-.

HOLLOWAY, RICHARD, 40, M, Carpenter, M, SC, 357, 340, CHAS-. In HH of Elizabeth Holloway f 30 mulatto born SC.

HOLLOWAY, SAMUEL, 6, M, (--), M, SC, 357, 340, CHAS-. In HH of Elizabeth Holloway f 30 mulatto born SC.

HOLLOWAY, WILLIAM T. , 24, M, Tailor, M, SC, 970, 950, CHAS-. In HH of Katey Halloway f 24 mulatto born SC.

HOLLY, CELEIA, 1, F, (--), B, SC, 787, 787, PICK+. In HH of Lucind Holly f 27 mulatto born NC.

HOLLY, CHARLES, 21, M, (--), M, SC, 40, 40, ORNG*. In HH of Sarah Holly f 45 mulatto born SC.

HOLLY, EMELINE, 30, F, (--), M, SC, 114, 114, PICK+. In HH of Ezekiel Holly m 39 black born SC.

HOLLY, EZEKIEL, 39, M, Currier, B, SC, 114, 114, PICK+.

HOLLY, JANE, 50, F, (--), M, SC, 40, 40, ORNG*. In HH of Sarah Holly f 45 mulatto born SC.

HOLLY, LUCIND, 27, F, (--), B, NC, 787, 787, PICK+.

HOLLY, LYDIA, 51, F, (--), M, SC, 786, 786, PICK+.

HOLLY, MARGARET, 43, F, (--), M, SC, 40, 40, ORNG*. In HH of Sarah Holly f 45 mulatto born SC.

HOLLY, NANCY, 2, F, (--), B, SC, 787, 787, PICK+. In HH of Lucind Holly f 27 mulatto born NC.

HOLLY, SARAH, 45, F, (--), M, SC, 40, 40, ORNG*.

HOLMES, ALEX, 70, M, Farmer, M, SC, 256, 256, GEOR*.

HOLMES, EDWARD, 9, M, (--), M, SC, 156, 143, CHAS*. In HH of Elizabeth Holmes f 40 mulatto born SC.

HOLMES, EDWIN, 34, M, Carpenter, M, SC, 46, 46, CHAS%.

HOLMES, ELIZA, 15, F, (--), M, SC, 213, 213, GEOR*. In HH of Rebec Holmes f 35 mulatto born SC.

HOLMES, ELIZABETH, 40, F, (--), M, SC, 156, 143, CHAS*.

HOLMES, ELLEN, 40, F, (--), M, SC, 122, 113, CHAS-. In HH of Thomas Holmes m 38 mulatto born SC.

HOLMES, ELLEN, 14, F, (--), M, SC, 136, 136, CHAS%. In HH of Lucy Williams f 40 mulatto born SC.

HOLMES, EMELINE, 19, F, (--), B, SC, 283, 283, CHAS%.

HOLMES, GEORGE, 35, M, Fisherman, M, SC, 82, 80, CHAS*. In HH of Ann Axton f 69 born SC.

HOLMES, JAMES, 13, M, (--), M, SC, 213, 213, GEOR*. In HH of Rebec Holmes f 35 mulatto born SC.

HOLMES, JANE, 12, F, (--), M, SC, 156, 143, CHAS*. In HH of Elizabeth Holmes f 40 mulatto born SC.

HOLMES, JERRY, 24, M, Fisherman, M, SC, 547, 506, CHAS+.

HOLMES, JULIA, 22, F, (--), M, SC, 130, 122, CHAS*. In HH of William Holmes m 28 mulatto born SC.

HOLMES, LUCINDA, 13, F, (--), M, SC, 46, 46, CHAS%. In HH of Edwin Holmes m 34 mulatto born SC.

HOLMES, MARIA, 29, F, (--), M, SC, 46, 46, CHAS%. In HH of Edwin Holmes m 34 mulatto born SC.

HOLMES, MARIAH, 70, F, (--), M, SC, 145, 145, GEOR*. In HH of Martha Williams f 37 mulatto born SC.

HOLMES, MARIAH, 0, F, (--), M, SC, 213, 213, GEOR*. In HH of Rebec Holmes f 35 mulatto born SC. Mariah Holmes 8/12 yr.

HOLMES, MARY, 17, F, (--), M, SC, 344, 344, CHAS%. In HH of Teres Bullard f 70 mulatto born SC.

HOLMES, NATHANIEL, 30, M, Carpenter, M, SC, 136, 136, GEOR.

HOLMES, REBEC, 35, F, (--), M, SC, 213, 213, GEOR*.

HOLMES, REBECCA, 70, F, (--), M, SC, 256, 256, GEOR*. In HH of Alex Holmes m 70 mulatto born SC.

HOLMES, REBECCA, 4, F, (--), M, SC, 213, 213, GEOR*. In HH of Rebec Holmes f 35 mulatto born SC.

HOLMES, RENETTA, 29, F, (--), M, SC, 136, 136, CHAS%. In HH of Lucy Williams f 40 mulatto born SC.

HOLMES, RICHARD, 55, M, Carpenter, M, SC, 562, 578, RICH.

HOLMES, RICHARD, 34, M, (--), M, SC, 136, 136, GEOR. In HH of Nathaniel Holmes m 30 mulatto born SC.

HOLMES, ROSE, 30, F, Seamstress, M, SC, 262, 230, CHAS.

HOLMES, SARAH, 60, F, (--), B, SC, 562, 578, RICH. In HH of Richard Holmes m 55 mulatto born SC.

HOLMES, SARAH, 24, F, (--), M, SC, 136, 136, GEOR. In HH of Nathaniel Holmes m 30 mulatto born SC.

HOLMES, SARAH ANN, 49, F, (--), M, SC, 110, 102, CHAS-.

HOLMES, TENAH, 30, F, (--), B, SC,

857, 834, CHAS%. In HH of Rebecca Wadkins f 39 black born SC.

HOLMES, THEODORE, 11, M, (--), M, SC, 46, 46, CHAS%. In HH of Edwin Holmes m 34 mulatto born SC.

HOLMES, THOMAS, 38, M, Sexton St. Pete, M, SC, 122, 113, CHAS-. Occupation: Sexton St. Peters Church.

HOLMES, WILLIAM, 28, M, Tailor, M, SC, 130, 122, CHAS*.

HOLTON, ELIZA, 30, F, (--), M, SC, 197, 185, CHAS-. In HH of Mary Holton f 60 mulatto born SC.

HOLTON, MARY, 60, F, (--), M, SC, 197, 185, CHAS-.

HOOD, GEORGE, 20, M, Farmer, M, SC, 186, 186, COLL.

HOOD, MARY, 18, F, (--), M, SC, 186, 186, COLL. In HH of George Hood m 20 born SC.

HOOPER, MARTHA, 14, F, (--), M, SC, 398, 405,? Rick+. In HH of Rozetta Weston f 40 mulatto born SC.

HOOPER, SALLY, 10, F, (--), M, SC, 398, 405, ?Rick+. In HH of Rozetta Weston f 40 mulatto born SC.

HOPKINS, CYNTHIA, 50, F, (--), B, SC, 169, 169, CHAS%.

HORLBLECK, NERO, 50, M, Carpenter, B, SC, 777, 757, CHAS-.

HORRY, A.L., 19, M, Tailor, M, SC, 265, 250, CHAS-.

HOUSE, FRANCIS, 2, M, (--), B, SC, 126, 126, KERS. In HH of Manson House m 33 black born SC.

HOUSE, FRANCIS, 1, F, (--), B, SC, 130, 130, KERS. In HH of Joseph House m 30 black born SC.

HOUSE, JOSEPH, 30, M, (--), B, SC, 130, 130, KERS.

HOUSE, MANSON, 33, M, Carpenter, B, SC, 126, 126, KERS.

HOUSE, SAML., 0, M, (--), B, SC, 126, 126, KERS. In HH of Manson House m 33 black born SC. Saml. House 4/12 yr.

HOUSE, SARAH, 30, F, (--), B, SC, 126, 126, KERS. In HH of Manson House m 33 black born SC.

HOUSE, SARAH, 17, F, (--), B, SC, 130, 130, KERS. In HH of Joseph House m 30 black born SC.

HOUSE, WARREN, 35, M, (--), B, SC, 456, 456, SUMT.

HOUSE, WM., 13, M, (--), B, SC, 126, 126, KERS. In HH of Manson House m 33 black born SC.

HOUSTON, CRIPTON J., 12, M, (--), M, SC, 141, 141, CHAS%. In HH of Robert Houston m 40 mulatto born SC.

HOUSTON, DANCIN, 12, M, (--), M, SC, 177, 177, BEAU. In HH of Sarah Houston f 52 mulatto born SC.

HOUSTON, JAMES, 46, M, Tailor, M, SC, 529, 529, FAIR. In HH of Grandy Parker m 36 born NC.

HOUSTON, JOHN, 14, M, (--), M, SC, 177, 177, BEAU. In HH of Sarah Houston f 52 mulatto born SC.

HOUSTON, ROBERT, 40, M, Tailor, M, SC, 141, 141, CHAS%.

HOUSTON, ROBERT, 14, M, (--), M, SC, 141, 141, CHAS%. In HH of Robert Houston m 40 mulatto born SC.

HOUSTON, SARAH, 52, F, Pastry Cook, M, SC, 177, 177, BEAU.

HOUSTON, SARAH, 36, F, (--), M, SC, 141, 141, CHAS%. In HH of Robert Houston m 40 mulatto born SC.

HOUSTON, SARAH, 11, F, (--), M, SC, 141, 141, CHAS%. In HH of Robert Houston m 40 mulatto born SC.

HOWARD, ABBEY, 65, F, (--), M, SC, 287, 264, CHAS. In HH of M.T. Geredeau f 37 born SC.

HOWARD, ABBY, 60, F, (--), B, SC, 149, 137, CHAS*. In HH of Thomas Henry m 16 mulatto born SC.

HOWARD, ANJELINE, 18, F, (--), M, SC, 1162, 1141, CHAS%. In HH of Harriet Shira f 50 born SC.

HOWARD, ANN, 6, F, (--), B, SC, 287, 264, CHAS. In HH of M.T. Geredeau f 37 born SC.

HOWARD, BOB, 65, M, (--), B, SC, 219, 219, ABB .

HOWARD, CECELIA, 3, F, (--), M, SC, 459, 417, CHAS+. In HH of Robert

Howard m 45 mulatto born SC.

HOWARD, FRANCIS, 10, M, (--), M, SC, 149, 137, CHAS*. In HH of Thomas Henry m 16 mulatto born SC.

HOWARD, HARRIET, 30, F, (--), M, SC, 459, 417, CHAS+. In HH of Robert Howard m 45 mulatto born SC.

HOWARD, JANE, 13, F, (--), M, SC, 459, 417, CHAS+. In HH of Robert Howard m 45 mulatto born SC.

HOWARD, JOHN, 0, M, (--), M, SC, 459, 417, CHAS+. In HH of Robert Howard m 45 mulatto born SC. John Howard age 9/12 yr.

HOWARD, JOSEPH, 10, M, (--), M, SC, 459, 417, CHAS+. In HH of Robert Howard m 45 mulatto born SC.

HOWARD, PHILIS, 26, F, (--), B, SC, 287, 264, CHAS. In HH of M.T. Geredeau f 37 born SC.

HOWARD, ROBERT, 45, M, Wood Factor, M, SC, 459, 417, CHAS+.

HOWARD, ROBERT, 5, M, (--), M, SC, 459, 417, CHAS+. In HH of Robert Howard m 45 mulatto born SC.

HOWARD, THOMAS, 4, M, (--), M, SC, 287, 264, CHAS. In HH of M.T. Geredeau f 37 born SC.

HOWARD, WILLIAM, 14, M, Ship joiner, M, SC, 149, 137, CHAS*. In HH of Thomas Henry m 16 mulatto born SC.

HOWARD, ROBERT, 24, M, Engineer, M, SC, 193, 176, CHAS. In HH of Elizabeth Henson f 60 mulatto born SC.

HOWERTON, GRACY, 25, M, (--), B, NC, 675, 675, YORK. In HH of Reuben Swann m 38 born TN.

HUCKSON, EMMELINE, 38, F, (--), M, SC, 848, 826, CHAS%. In HH of Isaac Huckson m 40 mulatto born SC.

HUCKSON, ISAAC, 40, M, Drayman, M, SC, 848, 826, CHAS%.

HUCKSON, JAMES, 14, M, (--), M, SC, 848, 826, CHAS%. In HH of Isaac Huckson m 40 mulatto born SC.

HUCKSON, LOUISA, 12, F, (--), M, SC, 848, 826, CHAS%. In HH of Isaac Huckson m 40 mulatto born SC.

HUGER, BENJAMIN T., 55, M, Tailor, M, SC, 973, 953, CHAS-.

HUGER, HARRIET, 50, F, (--), M, SC, 973, 953, CHAS-. In HH of Benjamin T. Huger m 55 mulatto born SC.

HUGER, STOCKTON, 7, M, (--), M, SC, 973, 953, CHAS-. In HH of Benjamin T. Huger m 55 mulatto born SC.

HUNT, DAVID, 56, M, Raftman, M, SC, 280, 280, ORNG*.

HUNT, G., 64, M, Laborer, M, SC, 721, 721, LANC*.

HUNT, GREEN, 7, M, (--), M, SC, 1470, 1470, CHES. In HH of Jane Hunt 31 mulatto born SC.

HUNT, HUGH, 0, M, (--), M, SC, 1470, 1470, CHES. In HH of Jane Hunt 31 mulatto born SC. Hugh listed as 3/12 mo.

HUNT, JAMES, 9, M, (--), M, SC, 1470, 1470, CHES. In HH of Jane Hunt 31 mulatto born SC.

HUNT, JANE, 31, F, (--), M, SC, 1470, 1470, CHES.

HUNT, RICHD. G., 30, M, Farmer, M, SC, 537, 537, DARL.

HUNT, S., 80, F, (--), M, SC, 721, 721, LANC*. In HH of G. Hunt m 64 mulatto born SC.

HUNT, TOBIAS, 11, M, (--), M, SC, 1661, 1667, MAR . In HH of William C. Miller m 50 born SC.

HUNT, WILLIS, 4, M, (--), M, SC, 1470, 1470, CHES. In HH of Jane Hunt 31 mulatto born SC.

HUNTER, ALLEN, 14, M, (--), M, SC, 671, 671, LAU . In HH of Dublin Hunter m 65 mulatto born SC.

HUNTER, CAROLINE, 6, F, (--), B, SC, 882, 882, KERS. In HH of Patsey Hunter f 30 mulatto born SC.

HUNTER, DUBLIN, 65, M, Mechanic, M, SC, 671, 671, LAU .

HUNTER, ELIZA, 7, F, (--), M, SC, 389, 387, CHAS%. In HH of John Hunter m 39 black born SC.

HUNTER, ELIZA., 11, F, (--), B, SC, 882, 882, KERS. In HH of Patsey Hunter f 30 mulatto born SC.

HUNTER, JAS., 21, M, (--), M, SC, 164, 164, KERS. In HH of B.W. Chambers m 28 born SC.

HUNTER, JOHN, 39, M, Painter, B, SC, 389, 387, CHAS%.

HUNTER, LAURA, 1, F, (--), M, SC, 861, 861, KERS. In HH of Ann Burdeaux f 25 black born SC.

HUNTER, LOUISA, 20, F, (--), M, SC, 861, 861, KERS. In HH of Ann Burdeaux f 25 black born SC.

HUNTER, PATSEY, 30, F, (--), B, SC, 882, 882, KERS.

HUNTER, PETER, 21, M, Mechanic, B, SC, 907, 907, KERS. In HH of A. Pinson m 20 black born SC.

HUNTER, REBECCA, 30, F, (--), M, SC, 389, 387, CHAS%. In HH of John Hunter m 39 black born SC.

HUNTER, SALLY, 60, F, (--), M, SC, 671, 671, LAU . In HH of Dublin Hunter m 65 mulatto born SC.

HUNTER, THOMAS, 9, M, (--), M, SC, 389, 387, CHAS%. In HH of John Hunter m 39 black born SC.

HUNTLEY, ROBT., 13, M, (--), M, SC, 453, 453, MARL. In HH of John Webster m 50 born SC.

HUSTICE, HILLIARD, 8, M, (--), M, SC, 317, 323, RICH+. In HH of Isaac Snead m 38 born SC.

HUTCHINSON, ANN, 20, F, (--), B, SC, 345, 345, CHAS%. In HH of Ellen Hutchinson f 40 black born SC.

HUTCHINSON, ELLEN, 40, F, (--), B, SC, 345, 345, CHAS%.

HUTCHINSON, JAMES, 1, M, (--), B, SC, 345, 345, CHAS%. In HH of Ellen Hutchinson f 40 black born SC.

HUTCHINSON, MARY, 45, F, (--), B, SC, 500, 458, CHAS+.

HUTSON, CATHARINE, 14, F, (--), M, SC, 414, 412, CHAS%. In HH of Timothy Hutson m 40 mulatto born SC.

HUTSON, JAMES D., 9, M, (--), M, SC, 414, 412, CHAS%. In HH of Timothy Hutson m 40 mulatto born SC.

HUTSON, MARY, 37, F, (--), M, SC, 414, 412, CHAS%. In HH of Timothy Hutson m 40 mulatto born SC.

HUTSON, MARY, 11, F, (--), M, SC, 414, 412, CHAS%. In HH of Timothy Hutson m 40 mulatto born SC.

HUTSON, SAMUEL, 2, M, (--), M, SC, 247, 232, CHAS-. In HH of Elizabeth Savage f 33 mulatto born SC.

HUTSON, TIMOTHY, 40, M, Painter, M, SC, 414, 412, CHAS%.

HUTTO, JAMES, 47, M, Farmer, M, SC, 105, 106, ORNG+.

I

INGLES, CLARA A., 2, F, (--), M, SC, 172, 176, RICH. In HH of Harriet Ingles f 18 mulatto born SC.

INGLES, ELLEN, 27, F, (--), M, SC, 557, 540, CHAS-. In HH of Susan Marshall f 28 mulatto born SC.

INGLES, HARRIET, 18, F, (--), M, SC, 172, 176, RICH.

INGLES, WILLIAM, 30, M, Hairdresser, M, SC, 106, 98, CHAS+.

IRVIN, MARY, 50, F, (--), M, SC, 77, 78, RICH.

IVERS, SOPHIA, 80, F, (--), M, SC, 147, 137, CHAS-. In HH of H.G. Stromer f 50 mulatto born SC.

IZARD, JOHN, 23, M, Carpenter, M, SC, 11, 12, CHAS. In HH of Nancy Izard f 40 mulatto born Charleston, SC.

IZARD, NANCY, 40, F, Laundress, M, SC, 11, 12, CHAS.

J

JACKSEN, CAMILLA, 4, F, (--), B, SC, 494, 494, SUMT. In HH of Jas. Jacksen m 25 black born SC.

JACKSEN, ELIZA, 30, F, (--), B, SC,

494, 494, SUMT. In HH of Jas. Jacksen m 25 black born SC.

JACKSEN, JAS., 25, M, Planter, B, SC, 494, 494, SUMT.

JACKSEN, JOSEPH, 3, M, (--), B, SC, 494, 494, SUMT. In HH of Jas. Jacksen m 25 black born SC.

JACKSEN, JULIA, 6, F, (--), B, SC, 494, 494, SUMT. In HH of Jas. Jacksen m 25 black born SC.

JACKSEN, MORGAN, 10, M, (--), B, SC, 494, 494, SUMT. In HH of Jas. Jacksen m 25 black born SC.

JACKSEN, SARAH, 0, F, (--), B, SC, 494, 494, SUMT. In HH of Jas. Jacksen m 25 black born SC. Sarah age 2/12 yr.

JACKSON, ADALINE, 25, F, (--), B, SC, 19, 19, NEWB. In HH of C.M. Jones m 27 born SC.

JACKSON, AGNES, 33, F, (--), B, 4, 4, BEAU#. In HH of Charles Jackson m 34 black.

JACKSON, ALEXANDER, 4, M, (--), B, SC, 518, 511, CHAS%. In HH of Rosella Jackson f 26 black born SC.

JACKSON, BILL, 25, M, Mechanic, M, SC, 702, 702, LAU.

JACKSON, CAROLINE, 34, F, (--), M, SC, 308, 308, BEAU+. In HH of Richard Jackson m 35 mulatto born SC.

JACKSON, CHARLES, 34, M, (--), B, 4, 4, BEAU#.

JACKSON, CLARA, 45, F, (--), B, SC, 189, 189, MARL. In HH of Thos. Jackson m 65 black born SC.

JACKSON, DAVID, 21, M, Laborer, B, SC, 452, 452, MARL. In HH of Ann McDaniel f 56 born SC.

JACKSON, DAVID, 6, M, (--), B, SC, 518, 511, CHAS%. In HH of Rosella Jackson f 26 black born SC.

JACKSON, EDWARD, 9, M, (--), M, SC, 136, 136, CHAS~. In HH of Moses Jackson m 42 mulatto born SC.

JACKSON, ELI, 30, M, Laborer, M, SC, 62, 62, MARL. In HH of William Bristow m 44, Tavern Keeper born SC.

JACKSON, ELIZA, 14, F, (--), B, (-) 10, 10, BEAU#. In HH of Peter Jackson m 62 black.

JACKSON, ELIZABETH, 11, F, (--), B, SC, 518, 511, CHAS%. In HH of Rosella Jackson f 26 black born SC.

JACKSON, ELIZABETH, 7, F, (--), M, SC, 136, 136, CHAS~. In HH of Moses Jackson m 42 mulatto born SC.

JACKSON, ELLICK, 4, M, (--), M, SC, 2059, 2065, EDGE. In HH of Matilda Jackson f 35 mulatto born SC.

JACKSON, ELY, 7, M, (--), M, SC, 2059, 2065, EDGE. In HH of Matilda Jackson f 35 mulatto born SC.

JACKSON, EMILY, 62, F, (--), B, (-) 11, 11, BEAU#.

JACKSON, EMMELINE, 30, F, (--), M, SC, 564, 547, CHAS-. In HH of James F. Gray m 35 born SC.

JACKSON, ESTHER, 46, F, (--), M, SC, 1205, 1205, UNION.

JACKSON, FRANCIS, 60, F, (--), B, SC, 52, 52, NEWB. In HH of Reuben H. Sigman m 29 born NC.

JACKSON, FRANCIS, 17, F, (--), B, SC, 70, 70, NEWB. In HH of Nancy Jackson f 35 black born SC.

JACKSON, H., 16, M, Hotel Servant, M, SC, 524, 524, CHES. In HH of G.F. Kennedy m 39 Hotel Keeper.

JACKSON, HARRIET, 21, F, (--), B, SC, 24, 24, RICH.

JACKSON, HARRY, 18, M, Apprentice, B, SC, 710, 710, COLL. In HH of Wm. Jackson m 65 black born SC.

JACKSON, HENRY, 1, M, (--), M, SC, 1205, 1205, UNION. In HH of Esther Jackson f 46 mulatto born SC.

JACKSON, HEZEKIAH, 9, M, (--), M, SC, 1205, 1205, UNION. In HH of Esther Jackson f 46 mulatto born SC.

JACKSON, ISABELLA, 1, F, (--), B, SC, 518, 511, CHAS%. In HH of Rosella Jackson f 26 black born SC.

JACKSON, JAMES, 14, M, (--), M, SC, 136, 136, CHAS~. In HH of Moses Jackson m 42 mulatto born SC.

JACKSON, JAMES, 12, M, (--), M, SC, 308, 308, BEAU+. In HH of Richard

Jackson m 35 mulatto born SC.

JACKSON, JOHN, 6, M, (--), M, SC, 308, 308, BEAU+. In HH of Richard Jackson m 35 mulatto born SC.

JACKSON, JOSIAH, 25, M, (--), B, (-) 7, 7, BEAU#.

JACKSON, KERELY, 31, F, (--), M, SC, 2098, 2105, EDGE. In HH of Elizabeth Clarke f 56 born SC.

JACKSON, LOUISA, 20, F, (--), B, SC, 52, 52, NEWB. In HH of Reuben H. Sigman m 29 born NC.

JACKSON, MARGARET, 1, F, (--), B, (-) 4, 4, BEAU#. In HH of Charles Jackson m 34 black.

JACKSON, MARGARET ANNA, 2, F, (--), M, SC, 136, 136, CHAS~. In HH of Moses Jackson m 42 mulatto born SC.

JACKSON, MARGARET MRS., 43, F, (--), M, SC, 136, 136, CHAS~. In HH of Moses Jackson m 42 mulatto born SC.

JACKSON, MARIA, 22, F, (--), B, SC, 580, 580, MARL. In HH of Mary Jackson f 54 mulatto born SC.

JACKSON, MARIA, 4, F, (--), B, SC, 19, 19, NEWB. In HH of C.M. Jones m 27 born SC.

JACKSON, MARIA, 1, F, (--), M, SC, 308, 308, BEAU+. In HH of Richard Jackson m 35 mulatto born SC.

JACKSON, MARTHA, 48, F, (--), B, (-) 11, 11, BEAU#. In HH of Emily Jackson f 62 black.

JACKSON, MARTHA, 12, F, (--), M, SC, 1205, 1205, UNION. In HH of Esther Jackson f 46 mulatto born SC.

JACKSON, MARTHA, 4, F, (--), M, SC, 308, 308, BEAU+. In HH of Richard Jackson m 35 mulatto born SC.

JACKSON, MARY, 54, F, (--), M, SC, 580, 580, MARL.

JACKSON, MARY, 25, F, (--), M, SC, 62, 62, MARL. In HH of William Bristow m 44, Tavern Keeper born SC..

JACKSON, MARY, 8, F, (--), M, SC, 308, 308, BEAU+. In HH of Richard Jackson m 35 mulatto born SC.

JACKSON, MARY, 5, F, (--), B, (-) 4, 4, BEAU#. In HH of Charles Jackson m

34 black.

JACKSON, MARY, 2, F, (--), M, SC, 702, 702, LAU. IN HH of Bill Jackson m 25 mulatto born SC.

JACKSON, MATILDA, 35, F, (--), M, SC, 2059, 2065, EDGE.

JACKSON, MOLSEY, 23, F, (--), B, (-) 7, 7, BEAU#. In HH of Josiah Jackson m 25 black.

JACKSON, MOS, 10, M, (--), M, SC, 2059, 2065, EDGE. In HH of Matilda Jackson f 35 mulatto born SC.

JACKSON, MOSES, 42, M, Farmer, M, SC, 136, 136, CHAS~.

JACKSON, NANCY, 60, F, (--), B, SC, 710, 710, COLL. In HH of Wm. Jackson m 65 black born SC.

JACKSON, NANCY, 35, F, (--), B, SC, 70, 70, NEWB.

JACKSON, PETER, 62, M, (--), B, (-) 10, 10, BEAU#.

JACKSON, PETER, 3, M, (--), B, (-) 4, 4, BEAU#. In HH of Charles Jackson m 34 black.

JACKSON, POLLY A., 25, F, (--), M, SC, 68, 70, PICK. In HH of Patrick Kelly m 80 born SC.

JACKSON, PRINGLE, 17, M, (--), M, SC, 136, 136, CHAS~. In HH of Moses Jackson m 42 mulatto born SC.

JACKSON, REBECCA, 10, F, (--), B, SC, 518, 511, CHAS%. In HH of Rosella Jackson f 26 black born SC.

JACKSON, RICHARD, 35, M, Laborer, M, SC, 308, 308, BEAU+.

JACKSON, ROSELLA, 26, F, (--), B, SC, 518, 511, CHAS%.

JACKSON, SARAH, 44, F, (--), B, (-) 10, 10, BEAU#. In HH of Peter Jackson m 62 black.

JACKSON, SARAH, 20, F, (--), M, SC, 52, 52, NEWB. In HH of Reuben H. Sigman m 29 born NC.

JACKSON, SARAH, 7, F, (--), B, (-) 4, 4, BEAU#. In HH of Charles Jackson m 34 black.

JACKSON, SARAH, 2, F, (--), M, SC, 19, 19, NEWB. In HH of C.M. Jones m

27 born SC.

JACKSON, SOLOMIN, 5, M, (--), M, SC, 136, 136, CHAS~. In HH of Moses Jackson m 42 mulatto born SC.

JACKSON, SUSAN, 56, F, (--), B, (-) 9, 9, BEAU#. In HH of Daniel Walker m 35 mulatto.

JACKSON, SUSAN, 18, F, (--), M, SC, 702, 702, LAU. IN HH of Bill Jackson m 25 mulatto born SC.

JACKSON, THOMAS, 12, M, (--), B, (-) 10, 10, BEAU#. In HH of Peter Jackson m 62 black.

JACKSON, THOMAS, 0, M, (--), M, SC, 19, 19, NEWB. In HH of C.M. Jones m 27 born SC. Thomas Jackson 8/12 yr.

JACKSON, THOS., 65, M, Laborer, B, SC, 189, 189, MARL.

JACKSON, THOS., 12, M, (--), B, SC, 189, 189, MARL. In HH of Thos. Jackson m 65 black born SC.

JACKSON, TOM, 21, M, Carpenter, B, SC, 710, 710, COLL. In HH of Wm. Jackson m 65 black born SC.

JACKSON, WILLIAM, 12, M, (--), M, SC, 136, 136, CHAS~. In HH of Moses Jackson m 42 mulatto born SC.

JACKSON, WM., 65, M, Carpenter, B, SC, 710, 710, COLL.

JACOBS, A., 13, F, (--), B, SC, 231, 231, LANC*. In HH of B. Jacobs m 60 black born SC.

JACOBS, A., 8, F, (--), M, SC, 231, 231, LANC*. In HH of B. Jacobs m 60 black born SC.

JACOBS, ABRAM, 17, M, Farmer, M, SC, 1036, 1036, CHES. In HH of Henry Lee m 38 born SC.

JACOBS, ANDREW, 25, M, Planter, M, SC, 245, 250, RICH+.

JACOBS, B., 60, M, Farmer, B, SC, 231, 231, LANC*.

JACOBS, BENJAMIN, 6, M, (--), M, SC, 288, 294, RICH+. In HH of Lavitia Jacobs f 35 mulatto born SC.

JACOBS, C., 10, F, (--), B, SC, 231, 231, LANC*. In HH of B. Jacobs m 60 black born SC.

JACOBS, C., 2, F, (--), M, SC, 233, 233, LANC*. In HH of Peter Jacobs m 45 black born SC.

JACOBS, C., 0, F, (--), M, SC, 233, 233, LANC*. In HH of Peter Jacobs m 45 black born SC. C. Jacobs 4/12 yr.

JACOBS, CALVY, 28, M, Planter, M, SC, 261, 266, RICH+.

JACOBS, CHARITY, 2, F, (--), M, SC, 245, 250, RICH+. In HH of Andrew Jacobs m 35 mulatto born SC.

JACOBS, CHARLES, 17, M, Waiter, M, SC, 553, 553, CHES. In HH of Mary Gill f 44 born SC.

JACOBS, DIANAH, 25, F, (--), M, SC, 580, 572, CHAS%.

JACOBS, ELIAS, 35, M, Laborer, M, SC, 227, 231, RICH+.

JACOBS, ELIZA, 7, F, (--), M, SC, 162, 165, RICH+. In HH of Mack Jacobs m 38 mulatto born SC.

JACOBS, ELIZA, 2, F, (--), M, SC, 288, 294, RICH+. In HH of Lavitia Jacobs f 35 mulatto born SC.

JACOBS, ELIZABETH, 38, F, (--), M, SC, 282, 288, RICH+. In HH of John Jacobs m 32 mulatto born SC.

JACOBS, ELIZABETH, 7, F, (--), M, SC, 282, 288, RICH+. In HH of John Jacobs m 32 mulatto born SC.

JACOBS, EMMA, 2, F, (--), B, SC, 575, 575, CHES. In HH of W.M. McDonald m 39 born SC.

JACOBS, ESTHER, 1, F, (--), M, SC, 245, 250, RICH+. In HH of Andrew Jacobs m 35 mulatto born SC.

JACOBS, FRANCES, 25, F, (--), M, SC, 245, 250, RICH+. In HH of Andrew Jacobs m 35 mulatto born SC.

JACOBS, FRANK, 30, M, Carpenter, B, SC, 231, 231, LANC*. In HH of B. Jacobs m 60 black born SC.

JACOBS, GEORGE, 4, M, (--), M, SC, 580, 572, CHAS%. In HH of Dianah Jacobs f 25 mulatto born SC.

JACOBS, GREEN, 4, M, (--), M, SC, 288, 294, RICH+. In HH of Lavitia Jacobs f 35 mulatto born SC.

JACOBS, H., 8, M, (--), M, SC, 233,

233, LANC*. In HH of Peter Jacobs m 45 black born SC.

JACOBS, HARRIET, 23, F, (--), M, SC, 800, 800, MARL. In HH of Nathan Jacobs m 27 mulatto born NC.

JACOBS, HENRY, 35, M, Carriage Maker, M, SC, 502, 502, FAIR.

JACOBS, ISAAIAH, 22, M, Butcher, M, Germany {sic}, 1179, 1158, CHAS%. In HH of Susan Jacobs f 40 mulatto born Germany {sic}.

JACOBS, ISREAL, 12, M, (--), M, Germany {sic}, 1179, 1158, CHAS%. In HH of Susan Jacobs f 40 mulatto born Germany {sic}.

JACOBS, J., 10, M, (--), M, SC, 233, 233, LANC*. In HH of Peter Jacobs m 45 black born SC.

JACOBS, JAMES, 27, M, (--), M, SC, 31, 31, YORK. In HH of James Burnet m 48 born England. James Jacobs born Chester Dist., SC.

JACOBS, JAMES, 9, M, (--), M, SC, 693, 712, RICH. In HH of Martha Jacobs f 30 mulatto born SC.

JACOBS, JANE, 22, F, (--), M, SC, 502, 502, FAIR. In HH of Henry Jacobs m 35 mulatto born SC.

JACOBS, JANE, 7, F, (--), M, SC, 245, 250, RICH+. In HH of Andrew Jacobs m 35 mulatto born SC.

JACOBS, JANE, 3, F, (--), M, SC, 261, 266, RICH+. In HH of Calby Jacobs m 28 mulatto born SC.

JACOBS, JOHN, 32, M, Planter, M, SC, 282, 288, RICH+.

JACOBS, JOHN, 5, M, (--), M, SC, 245, 250, RICH+. In HH of Andrew Jacobs m 35 mulatto born SC.

JACOBS, JOHN, 4, M, (--), M, SC, 37, 38, RICH. In HH of Sarah Jacobs f 25 black born SC.

JACOBS, JOHN, 3, M, (--), M, SC, 162, 165, RICH+. In HH of Mack Jacobs m 38 mulatto born SC.

JACOBS, KIT, 9, M, (--), M, SC, 282, 288, RICH+. In HH of John Jacobs m 32 mulatto born SC.

JACOBS, L., 35, F, (--), M, SC, 233,

233, LANC*. In HH of Peter Jacobs m 45 black born SC.

JACOBS, LAVITIA, 35, F, (--), M, SC, 288, 294, RICH+.

JACOBS, LEWIS S., 7, M, (--), M, SC, 693, 712, RICH. In HH of Martha Jacobs f 30 mulatto born SC.

JACOBS, M., 56, F, (--), B, SC, 231, 231, LANC*. In HH of B. Jacobs m 60 black born SC.

JACOBS, M., 20, F, Laborer, B, SC, 231, 231, LANC*. In HH of B. Jacobs m 60 black born SC.

JACOBS, M., 15, F, (--), B, SC, 231, 231, LANC*. In HH of B. Jacobs m 60 black born SC.

JACOBS, MACK, 38, M, None, M, SC, 162, 165, RICH+.

JACOBS, MAHALA, 24, F, (--), B, SC, 575, 575, CHES. In HH of W.M. McDonald m 39 born SC.

JACOBS, MAHALEY, 9, F, (--), M, SC, 245, 250, RICH+. In HH of Andrew Jacobs m 35 mulatto born SC.

JACOBS, MAITENON, 2, M, (--), M, SC, 261, 266, RICH+. In HH of Calby Jacobs m 28 mulatto born SC.

JACOBS, MARGARET, 35, F, (--), B, SC, 454, 411, CHAS. In HH of Susan Williams f 35 black born SC.

JACOBS, MARIA, 35, F, (--), M, SC, 502, 502, FAIR. In HH of Henry Jacobs m 35 mulatto born SC.

JACOBS, MARTHA, 39, F, (--), M, SC, 693, 712, RICH.

JACOBS, MARTHA, 1, F, (--), M, SC, 288, 294, RICH+. In HH of Lavitia Jacobs f 35 mulatto born SC.

JACOBS, MARY, 25, F, (--), M, SC, 261, 266, RICH+. In HH of Calby Jacobs m 28 mulatto born SC.

JACOBS, MARY, 5, F, (--), M, SC, 580, 572, CHAS%. In HH of Dianah Jacobs f 25 mulatto born SC.

JACOBS, MARY, 3, F, (--), M, SC, 245, 250, RICH+. In HH of Andrew Jacobs m 35 mulatto born SC.

JACOBS, MATTHEW, 5, M, (--), M, SC, 261, 266, RICH+. In HH of Calby

Jacobs m 28 mulatto born SC.

JACOBS, MINERA, 18, F, (--), M, Germany {sic}, 1179, 1158, CHAS%. In HH of Susan Jacobs f 40 mulatto born Germany {sic}.

JACOBS, NANCY, 10, F, (--), M, SC, 288, 294, RICH+. In HH of Lavitia Jacobs f 35 mulatto born SC.

JACOBS, NANCY, 5, F, (--), M, SC, 162, 165, RICH+. In HH of Mack Jacobs m 38 mulatto born SC.

JACOBS, NATHAN, 27, M, Laborer, M, NC, 800, 800, MARL.

JACOBS, PETER, 45, M, Coach maker, B, SC, 233, 233, LANC*.

JACOBS, REBECCA, 3, F, (--), M, SC, 288, 294, RICH+. In HH of Lavitia Jacobs f 35 mulatto born SC.

JACOBS, REBECCA, 1, F, (--), M, SC, 580, 572, CHAS%. In HH of Dianah Jacobs f 25 mulatto born SC.

JACOBS, S., 24, F, (--), M, SC, 103, 103, LANC*. In HH of C. McDow m 25 black born SC.

JACOBS, S., 10, F, (--), B, SC, 231, 231, LANC*. In HH of B. Jacobs m 60 black born SC.

JACOBS, S., 6, M, (--), M, SC, 233, 233, LANC*. In HH of Peter Jacobs m 45 black born SC.

JACOBS, SARAH, 50, M, (--), B, SC, 290, 296, RICH+.

JACOBS, SARAH, 30, F, (--), M, SC, 162, 165, RICH+. In HH of Mack Jacobs m 38 mulatto born SC.

JACOBS, SARAH, 25, F, (--), M, SC, 37, 38, RICH.

JACOBS, SARAH, 8, F, (--), M, SC, 53, 53, CHAS*. In HH of Elizabeth Douglas f 41 mulatto born SC.

JACOBS, SARAH, 5, F, (--), M, SC, 693, 712, RICH. In HH of Martha Jacobs f 30 mulatto born SC.

JACOBS, SUSAN, 40, F, (--), M, Germany {sic}, 1179, 1158, CHAS%.

JACOBS, SUSAN, 21, F, (--), B, SC, 454, 411, CHAS. In HH of Susan Williams f 35 black born SC.

JACOBS, T., 28, F, Laborer, B, SC, 231, 231, LANC*. In HH of B. Jacobs m 60 black born SC.

JACOBS, THOMAS, 10, M, (--), M, SC, 37, 38, RICH. In HH of Sarah Jacobs f 25 black born SC.

JACOBS, WILLIAM, 14, M, (--), M, SC, 275, 281, RICH+. In HH of William Pote m 35 mulatto born SC.

JACOBS, WILLIAM H., 8, M, (--), M, SC, 37, 38, RICH. In HH of Sarah Jacobs f 25 black born SC.

JAMES, DANIEL, 38, M, Carpenter, M, SC, 660, 652, CHAS%.

JAMES, ELIZABETH, 29, F, (--), M, SC, 115, 115, CHAS%. In HH of Catherine Cornwell f 32 mulatto born SC.

JAMES, JOSEPH, 3, M, (--), M, SC, 660, 652, CHAS%. In HH of Daniel James m 38 mulatto born SC.

JAMES, MARY, 38, F, (--), M, SC, 546, 505, CHAS+.

JAMES, MARY JANE, 7, F, (--), M, SC, 115, 115, CHAS%. In HH of Catherine Cornwell f 32 mulatto born SC.

JAMES, RACHAEL, 25, F, (--), M, SC, 660, 652, CHAS%. In HH of Daniel James m 38 mulatto born SC.

JAMES, SIMON, 5, M, (--), M, SC, 660, 652, CHAS%. In HH of Daniel James m 38 mulatto born SC.

JEFFERSON, ELEANOR, 41, F, (--), B, SC, 209, 195, CHAS-.

JEFFERSON, ELIAS, 5, M, (--), B, SC, 209, 195, CHAS-. In HH of Eleanor Jefferson f 41 black born SC.

JEFFERSON, IRVINA, 10, F, (--), B, SC, 209, 195, CHAS-. In HH of Eleanor Jefferson f 41 black born SC.

JEFFERSON, MARY, 40, F, (--), M, SC, 58, 58, CHAS2. In HH of Thomas Jefferson m 43 black born SC.

JEFFERSON, THOMAS, 43, M, Blacksmith, B, SC, 58, 58, CHAS2.

JENKINS, CHARLES, 22, M, Laborer, M, SC, 295, 295, BEAU+.

JENKINS, ELSY, 23, F, (--), M, SC,

299, 299, BEAU+. In HH of Thomas Jenkins m 27 mulatto born SC.

JENKINS, G.H. LEE, 7, M, (--), M, SC, 487, 453, CHAS*. In HH of Margaret Jenkins f 35 mulatto born SC.

JENKINS, HAMPTON, 3, M, (--), M, SC, 299, 299, BEAU+. In HH of Thomas Jenkins m 27 mulatto born SC.

JENKINS, HANNAH, 9, F, (--), M, SC, 487, 453, CHAS*. In HH of Margaret Jenkins f 35 mulatto born SC.

JENKINS, JAMES, 25, M, Laborer, M, SC, 294, 294, BEAU+.

JENKINS, JIM, 7, F, (--), M, SC, 299, 299, BEAU+. In HH of Thomas Jenkins m 27 mulatto born SC.

JENKINS, LOUISA, 21, F, (--), M, SC, 294, 294, BEAU+. In HH of James Jenkins m 25 mulatto born SC.

JENKINS, MARGARET, 35, F, (--), M, SC, 487, 453, CHAS*.

JENKINS, MARGARET, 0, F, (--), M, SC, 299, 299, BEAU+. In HH of Thomas Jenkins m 27 mulatto born SC. Margaret 6/12 yr.

JENKINS, MOLEY, 20, F, (--), M, SC, 295, 295, BEAU+. In HH of Charles Jenkins m 22 mulatto born SC.

JENKINS, MYNIRVA, 1, F, (--), M, SC, 295, 295, BEAU+. In HH of Charles Jenkins m 22 mulatto born SC.

JENKINS, PEMPA, 27, F, (--), M, SC, 1809, 1815, EDGE. In HH of Wm. Jenkins m 30 born SC.

JENKINS, SAMUEL, 45, M, Cabinetmaker, B, SC, 206, 210, RICH.

JENKINS, SARAH, 2, F, (--), M, SC, 294, 294, BEAU+. In HH of James Jenkins m 25 mulatto born SC.

JENKINS, THIRSA, 4, F, (--), M, SC, 294, 294, BEAU+. In HH of James Jenkins m 25 mulatto born SC.

JENKINS, THOMAS, 27, M, Farmer, M, SC, 299, 299, BEAU+.

JENKINS, TIMOTHY, 1, M, (--), M, SC, 294, 294, BEAU+. In HH of James Jenkins m 25 mulatto born SC.

JENKINS, VIRGINIA, 7, F, (--), M, SC, 487, 453, CHAS*. In HH of

Margaret Jenkins f 35 mulatto born SC.

JENNINGS, AMELIA, 8, F, (--), M, SC, 433, 430, CHAS%. In HH of Martha Jennings f 28 mulatto born SC.

JENNINGS, ELLEN, 24, F, Market woman, B, SC, 145, 133, CHAS*.

JENNINGS, EPSEY, 53, F, (--), M, SC, 568, 585, RICH.

JENNINGS, MARTHA, 28, F, (--), M, SC, 433, 430, CHAS%.

JENNINGS, PAUL, 2, M, (--), B, SC, 145, 133, CHAS*. In HH of Ellen Jennings f 25 black born SC.

JENNINGS, SARAH ANN, 3, F, (--), B, SC, 145, 133, CHAS*. In HH of Ellen Jennings f 25 black born SC.

JENNINS, JOHN, 7, M, (--), M, SC, 147, 135, CHAS*. In HH of Rebecca Naylor f 35 black born SC.

JENNINS, PHOEBE SCOTT, 20, F, (--), B, SC, 145, 133, CHAS*. In HH of Ellen Jennings f 25 black born SC.

JEST, CHARLES, 35, M, (--), M, SC, 558, 550, CHAS%.

JEST, JAMES, 3, M, (--), M, SC, 558, 550, CHAS%. In HH of Charles Jest m 35 mulatto born SC.

JEST, MARY, 29, F, (--), M, SC, 558, 550, CHAS%. In HH of Charles Jest m 35 mulatto born SC.

JEST, SIMON, 12, M, (--), M, SC, 558, 550, CHAS%. In HH of Charles Jest m 35 mulatto born SC.

JOHNSON, ALEXANDER, 29, M, Tailor, B, SC, 440, 408, CHAS*. In HH of Juliana Johnson f 27 black born SC.

JOHNSON, ALEXANDER, 24, M, Tailor, B, SC, 259, 233, CHAS*. In HH of Julia Anna Johnson f 27 black born SC.

JOHNSON, ALEXANDER, 14, M, (--), B, SC, 61, 61, CHAS%. In HH of Mary Ann Johnson f 40 black born SC.

JOHNSON, ALICE, 12, F, (--), B, (-) 11, 11, BEAU#. In HH of Emily Jackson f 62 black.

JOHNSON, AMELIA, 20, F, (--), B, SC, 52, 52, CHAS%. In HH of Rebecca Johnson f 53 black born SC.

JOHNSON, ANDERSON, 3, M, (--), B, SC, 130, 130, KERS. In HH of Joseph House m 30 black born SC.

JOHNSON, ANN, 22, F, (--), M, SC, 1081, 1103, CHAS%. In HH of Kitty Simons f 50 mulatto born SC.

JOHNSON, BENJAMIN, 48, M, Butcher, M, SC, 619, 611, CHAS%.

JOHNSON, CAROLINE, 58, F, (--), B, SC, 155, 155, CHAS%.

JOHNSON, CAROLINE, 28, F, (--), M, SC, 1085, 1062, CHAS-. In HH of Sally Johnson f 60 mulatto born SC.

JOHNSON, CAROLINE, 13, F, (--), B, SC, 52, 52, CHAS%. In HH of Rebecca Johnson f 53 black born SC.

JOHNSON, CATHERINE, 49, F, (--), B, SC, 104, 104, CHAS^.

JOHNSON, CATHERINE, 18, F, (--), M, SC, 406, 379, CHAS*.

JOHNSON, CHARLES, 1, M, (--), M, SC, 900, 877, CHAS%. In HH of Harriet Johnson f 30 mulatto born SC.

JOHNSON, CORNELIUS, 72, M, Laborer, B, SC, 183, 186, RICH+.

JOHNSON, DANIEL, 55, M, Tailor, B, SC, 635, 635, SUMT.

JOHNSON, DANIEL, 28, M, Butcher, M, SC, 1124, 1102, CHAS%. In HH of Louisa Johnson f 53 mulatto born SC.

JOHNSON, DILITHY, 17, F, (--), M, SC, 737, 737, KERS. In HH of Jack Johnson m 50 mulatto born SC.

JOHNSON, ELIZA, 40, F, (--), M, Scotland {sic}, 930, 910, CHAS-.

JOHNSON, ELIZABETH, 46, F, (--), B, SC, 184, 184, CHAS%. In HH of John W. Mitchel m 20 black born SC.

JOHNSON, ELIZH., 2, F, (--), M, SC, 737, 737, KERS. In HH of Jack Johnson m 50 mulatto born SC.

JOHNSON, ELLEN, 44, F, (--), M, SC, 737, 737, KERS. In HH of Jack Johnson m 50 mulatto born SC.

JOHNSON, EMMA, 20, F, (--), B, SC, 61, 61, CHAS%. In HH of Mary Ann Johnson f 40 black born SC.

JOHNSON, EMMA, 1, F, (--), B, SC, 259, 233, CHAS*. In HH of Julia Anna Johnson f 27 black born SC.

JOHNSON, EMMA, 0, F, (--), B, SC, 440, 408, CHAS*. In HH of Juliana Johnson f 27 black born SC. Emma Johnson age 7/12 yr.

JOHNSON, EMMELINE, 20, F, (--), B, SC, 155, 155, CHAS%. In HH of Caroline Johnson f 58 black born SC.

JOHNSON, EMMELINE, 9, F, (--), B, SC, 384, 382, CHAS%. In HH of Nathaniel Johnson m 35 black born SC.

JOHNSON, EPSY, 26, F, (--), M, SC, 1223, 1223, SUMT. In HH of Hale Johnson m 34 mulatto born SC.

JOHNSON, GEORGE, 2, M, (--), B, SC, 440, 408, CHAS*. In HH of Juliana Johnson f 27 black born SC.

JOHNSON, GEORGE, 2, M, (--), B, SC, 259, 233, CHAS*. In HH of Julia Anna Johnson f 27 black born SC.

JOHNSON, HAGAR, 85, F, (--), B, SC, 186, 186, CHAS%.

JOHNSON, HALE, 34, M, Cabinet maker, M, SC, 1223, 1223, SUMT.

JOHNSON, HARRIET, 30, F, (--), M, SC, 900, 877, CHAS%.

JOHNSON, HENRY, 6, M, (--), M, SC, 900, 877, CHAS%. In HH of Harriet Johnson f 30 mulatto born SC.

JOHNSON, HENRY, 2, M, (--), M, SC, 307, 283, CHAS+. In HH of Emeline Elliot f 30 mulatto born SC.

JOHNSON, IMOGENE, 12, F, (--), B, SC, 61, 61, CHAS%. In HH of Mary Ann Johnson f 40 black born SC.

JOHNSON, ISAAC, 13, M, (--), B, SC, 186, 186, CHAS%. In HH of Hagar Johnson f 85 black born SC.

JOHNSON, ISAAC, 0, M, (--), M, SC, 307, 283, CHAS+. In HH of Emeline Elliot f 30 mulatto born SC. Issac Johnson age 10/12yr. {twin to Rebecca}.

JOHNSON, ISABELLA, 36, F, (--), B, SC, 186, 186, CHAS%. In HH of Hagar Johnson f 85 black born SC.

JOHNSON, JACK, 50, M, Farmer, M, SC, 737, 737, KERS.

JOHNSON, JAMES, 35, M, (--), M,

SC, 380, 378, CHAS%.

JOHNSON, JAMES T., 18, M, Tailor, B, SC, 52, 52, CHAS%. In HH of Rebecca Johnson f 53 black born SC.

JOHNSON, JAS., 47, M, (--), B, SC, 117, 117, KERS. In HH of Jas. Freeman m 22 born SC.

JOHNSON, JESTUS, 5, M, (--), B, SC, 130, 130, KERS. In HH of Joseph House m 30 black born SC.

JOHNSON, JOHN, 48, M, Carpenter, B, SC, 52, 52, CHAS%. In HH of Rebecca Johnson f 53 black born SC.

JOHNSON, JOHN, 38, M, Carpenter, B, SC, 61, 61, CHAS%. In HH of Mary Ann Johnson f 40 black born SC.

JOHNSON, JOHN, 35, M, Bricklayer, B, SC, 1081, 1058, CHAS-. In HH of Rebecca Gardener f 35 mulatto born SC.

JOHNSON, JOHN, 8, M, (--), M, SC, 794, 798, MAR. In HH of Henry B. Cook m 33 born SC. John Johnson born Marion, SC.

JOHNSON, JOHN, 7, M, (--), B, SC, 901, 878, CHAS%. In HH of Mary Johnson f 25 black born SC.

JOHNSON, JOHN, 6, M, (--), M, SC, 836, 836, SUMT. In HH of Roxy Johnson f 25 black born SC.

JOHNSON, JOHN T., 5, M, (--), M, Scotland {sic}, 930, 910, CHAS-. In HH of Eliza Johnson f 40 mulatto born Scotland {sic}.

JOHNSON, JOSEPH, 1, M, (--), M, SC, 381, 343, CHAS+. In HH of Martha Johnson f 29 mulatto born SC.

JOHNSON, JOSEPHINE, 16, F, (--), B, SC, 61, 61, CHAS%. In HH of Mary Ann Johnson f 40 black born SC.

JOHNSON, JOSEPHINE, 13, F, (--), M, SC, 900, 877, CHAS%. In HH of Harriet Johnson f 30 mulatto born SC.

JOHNSON, JULIA, 30, F, (--), M, SC, 380, 378, CHAS%. In HH of James Johnson m 35 mulatto born SC.

JOHNSON, JULIA ANNE, 27, F, (--), B, SC, 259, 233, CHAS*.

JOHNSON, JULIANA, 40, F, (--), B, SC, 186, 186, CHAS%. In HH of Hagar Johnson f 85 black born SC.

JOHNSON, JULIANA, 27, F, (--), B, SC, 440, 408, CHAS*.

JOHNSON, LEWIS, 9, M, (--), M, SC, 381, 343, CHAS+. In HH of Martha Johnson f 29 mulatto born SC.

JOHNSON, LOUISA, 8, F, (--), M, Scotland {sic}, 930, 910, CHAS-. In HH of Eliza Johnson f 40 mulatto born Scotland {sic}.

JOHNSON, LOUSA, 53, F, (--), M, SC, 1124, 1102, CHAS%.

JOHNSON, MARGARET, 10, F, (--), M, (-) 7, 7, BEAU#. In HH of Josiah Jackson m 25 black.

JOHNSON, MARIA, 10, F, (--), M, SC, 900, 877, CHAS%. In HH of Harriet Johnson f 30 mulatto born SC.

JOHNSON, MARIE, 52, F, (--), B, SC, 116, 116, KERS.

JOHNSON, MARTHA, 29, F, (--), M, SC, 381, 343, CHAS+.

JOHNSON, MARTHA, 14, F, (--), B, (-) 6, 6, BEAU#. In HH of Charles Cockran m 26 black.

JOHNSON, MARTHA, 8, F, (--), M, SC, 836, 836, SUMT. In HH of Roxy Johnson f 25 black born SC.

JOHNSON, MARTHA, 4, F, (--), B, SC, 130, 130, KERS. In HH of Joseph House m 30 black born SC.

JOHNSON, MARY, 25, F, (--), B, SC, 901, 878, CHAS%.

JOHNSON, MARY ANN, 40, F, (--), B, SC, 61, 61, CHAS%.

JOHNSON, NATHANIEL, 35, M, Butcher, B, SC, 384, 382, CHAS%.

JOHNSON, PHOEBE, 26, F, (--), M, SC, 703, 661, CHAS+. In HH of W. Johnson m 28 mulatto born SC.

JOHNSON, PRISCILLA, 22, F, (--), B, SC, 155, 155, CHAS%. In HH of Caroline Johnson f 58 black born SC.

JOHNSON, REBECCA, 53, F, (--), B, SC, 52, 52, CHAS%.

JOHNSON, REBECCA, 17, F, (--), B, SC, 155, 155, CHAS%. In HH of Caroline Johnson f 58 black born SC.

JOHNSON, REBECCA, 0, F, (--), M, SC, 307, 283, CHAS+. In HH of Emeline Elliot f 30 mulatto born SC. Rebecca Johnson age 10/12 yr., {twin to Isaac}.

JOHNSON, ROBERT, 6, M, (--), B, SC, 259, 233, CHAS*. In HH of Julia Anna Johnson f 27 black born SC.

JOHNSON, ROBERT, 5, M, (--), B, SC, 440, 408, CHAS*. In HH of Juliana Johnson f 27 black born SC.

JOHNSON, ROXY, 25, F, (--), B, SC, 836, 836, SUMT.

JOHNSON, SALLY, 60, F, (--), M, SC, 1085, 1062, CHAS-.

JOHNSON, SAMUEL, 11, M, (--), M, Scotland {sic}, 930, 910, CHAS-. In HH of Eliza Johnson f 40 mulatto born Scotland {sic}.

JOHNSON, SAMUEL H., 22, M, (--), B, SC, 366, 366, YORK. In HH of Barbara Hargate f 50 born NC.

JOHNSON, SARAH, 4, F, (--), B, SC, 259, 233, CHAS*. In HH of Julia Anna Johnson f 27 black born SC.

JOHNSON, SARAH, 4, F, (--), B, SC, 901, 878, CHAS%. In HH of Mary Johnson f 25 black born SC.

JOHNSON, SARAH, 3, F, (--), B, SC, 440, 408, CHAS*. In HH of Juliana Johnson f 27 black born SC.

JOHNSON, SARAH ANN, 32, F, (--), B, SC, 384, 382, CHAS%. In HH of Nathaniel Johnson m 35 black born SC.

JOHNSON, SIMON, 11, M, (--), B, SC, 52, 52, CHAS%. In HH of Rebecca Johnson f 53 black born SC.

JOHNSON, SUSAN, 28, F, (--), M, SC, 307, 283, CHAS+. In HH of Emeline Elliot f 30 mulatto born SC.

JOHNSON, SUSAN, 7, F, (--), M, SC, 900, 877, CHAS%. In HH of Harriet Johnson f 30 mulatto born SC.

JOHNSON, THOMAS, 6, M, (--), B, SC, 384, 382, CHAS%. In HH of Nathaniel Johnson m 35 black born SC.

JOHNSON, W., 28, M, Shoemaker, M, SC, 703, 661, CHAS+.

JOHNSON, WILLIAM, 57, M, (--), B, SC, 155, 155, CHAS%. In HH of Caroline Johnson f 58 black born SC.

JOHNSON, WILLIAM, 18, M, (--), M, Scotland {sic}, 930, 910, CHAS-. In HH of Eliza Johnson f 40 mulatto born Scotland {sic}.

JOHNSON, WILLIAM P., 11, M, (--), M, SC, 380, 378, CHAS%. In HH of James Johnson m 35 mulatto born SC.

JOHNSON, WM., 5, M, (--), M, SC, 737, 737, KERS. In HH of Jack Johnson m 50 mulatto born SC.

JOHNSTON, AUGUSTUS, 22, M, Blacksmith, M, SC, 1127, 1106, CHAS%. In HH of Emma Johnston f 51 mulatto born SC.

JOHNSTON, CAMILLA, 3, F, (--), M, SC, 542, 508, CHAS*. In HH of James Johnston m 50 mulatto born SC.

JOHNSTON, CAROLINE, 13, F, (--), M, SC, 542, 508, CHAS*. In HH of James Johnston m 50 mulatto born SC.

JOHNSTON, CHARLES, 31, M, Tailor, B, SC, 431, 414, CHAS-. In HH of James D. Johnston m 40 black born SC.

JOHNSTON, DANIEL, 18, M, Carpenter, M, SC, 1127, 1106, CHAS%. In HH of Emma Johnston f 51 mulatto born SC.

JOHNSTON, DELIA, 37, F, (--), B, SC, 431, 414, CHAS-. In HH of James D. Johnston m 40 black born SC.

JOHNSTON, DELIA, 14, F, (--), M, SC, 542, 508, CHAS*. In HH of James Johnston m 50 mulatto born SC.

JOHNSTON, DIEDERICK, 20, M, Millwright, M, SC, 1127, 1106, CHAS%. In HH of Emma Johnston f 51 mulatto born SC.

JOHNSTON, ELEANOR, 8, F, (--), M, SC, 428, 397, CHAS*. In HH of Glenn Carr f 37 mulatto born SC.

JOHNSTON, ELIZA J., 33, F, (--), M, SC, 542, 508, CHAS*. In HH of James Johnston m 50 mulatto born SC.

JOHNSTON, EMMA, 51, F, (--), M, SC, 1127, 1106, CHAS%.

JOHNSTON, GEORGE, 32, M, (--),

M, SC, 186, 186, COLL. In HH of George Hood m 20 born SC.

JOHNSTON, HUMPHUETTA, 30, F, (--), B, SC, 431, 414, CHAS-. In HH of James D. Johnston m 40 black born SC.

JOHNSTON, JAMES, 50, M, Tailor, M, SC, 542, 508, CHAS*.

JOHNSTON, JAMES D., 40, M, Tailor, B, SC, 431, 414, CHAS-.

JOHNSTON, JOHN, 70, M, Farmer, M, SC, 186, 186, COLL. In HH of George Hood m 20 born SC.

JOHNSTON, JOHN, 14, M, (--), M, SC, 1127, 1106, CHAS%. In HH of Emma Johnston f 51 mulatto born SC.

JOHNSTON, JOHN D., 1, M, (--), B, SC, 431, 414, CHAS-. In HH of James D. Johnston m 40 black born SC.

JOHNSTON, JOSEPHINE, 12, F, (--), M, SC, 428, 397, CHAS*. In HH of Glenn Carr f 37 mulatto born SC.

JOHNSTON, MARIA, 38, F, (--), M, SC, 174, 160, CHAS*. In HH of Mary Ann McCale f 28 mulatto born SC.

JOHNSTON, SARAH, 0, F, (--), M, SC, 542, 508, CHAS*. In HH of James Johnston m 50 mulatto born SC. Sarah Johnston age 10/12 yr.

JOHNSTON, SUSANNAH, 70, M, (--), B, SC, 157, 157, GEOR*. In HH of Benj. Lewis m 50 black born SC.

JONES, ABBEY, 56, F, (--), M, SC, 326, 300, CHAS*.

JONES, ABRAHAM, 30, M, Carpenter, M, SC, 228, 203, CHAS*.

JONES, ADAM, 49, M, Laborer, M, SC, 499, 457, CHAS+. In HH of Francis Scott m 38 mulatto born SC.

JONES, ADELA, 30, F, (--), B, SC, 182, 182, CHAS%. In HH of Nancy Stenet f 50 mulatto born SC.

JONES, AGATHA, 10, F, (--), M, SC, 326, 300, CHAS*. In HH of Abbey Jones f 56 mulatto born SC.

JONES, ALBERT, 9, M, (--), M, SC, 303, 303, BEAU+. In HH of Cornelius Jones m 27 mulatto born SC.

ES, ALFRED, 25, M, Caster, M, SC, 333, 307, CHAS. In HH of Margaret Fitzgerald f 18 born SC.

JONES, ALFRED, 10, M, (--), M, SC, 445, 445, BEAU-. In HH of James Jones m 52 mulatto born SC.

JONES, ALLISON, 2, M, (--), M, SC, 303, 303, BEAU+. In HH of Cornelius Jones m 27 mulatto born SC.

JONES, AMANDA, 4, F, (--), B, SC, 450, 450, BEAU-. In HH of Sylvester Jones m 33 black born SC.

JONES, ANDREW, 20, M, Laborer, B, SC, 430, 430, BEAU-. In HH of Daniel Jones m 62 black born SC.

JONES, ANN, 4, F, (--), M, SC, 290, 290, BEAU+. In HH of Thomas Jones m 25 mulatto born SC.

JONES, ANNE, 22, F, (--), M, SC, 602, 594, CHAS%. In HH of Joseph Banfield m 40 mulatto born SC.

JONES, ANTONIO, 16, M, (--), B, SC, 547, 506, CHAS+. In HH of Jerry Holmes m 24 mulatto born SC.

JONES, BARNEY, 1, M, (--), B, SC, 302, 302, BEAU+. In HH of Daniel Jones m 40 black born SC.

JONES, BARTLETT, 30, M, Planter, M, SC, 1202, 1202, BARN.

JONES, BERRY, 26, M, Planter, M, SC, 1203, 1203, BARN.

JONES, CAROLINE, 30, F, (--), M, SC, 390, 388, CHAS%.

JONES, CAROLINE, 25, F, (--), B, SC, 430, 430, BEAU-. In HH of Daniel Jones m 62 black born SC.

JONES, CAROLINE, 11, M, (--), B, SC, 999, 976, CHAS%. In HH of George Jones m 38 black born SC.

JONES, CAROLINE, 1, F, (--), B, SC, 464, 464, BEAU-. In HH of William H. Jones m 32 black born SC.

JONES, CATHARIN, 24, F, (--), M, SC, 283, 283, BEAU+. In HH of James Jones m 27 mulatto born SC.

JONES, CATHARINE, 34, F, (--), M, SC, 569, 561, CHAS%. In HH of Richard Jones m 38 mulatto born SC.

JONES, CATHARINE, 6, F, (--), M, SC, 569, 561, CHAS%. In HH of Richard Jones m 38 mulatto born SC.

119

JONES, CELINA, 4, F, (--), M, SC, 445, 445, BEAU-. In HH of James Jones m 52 mulatto born SC.

JONES, CHARITY, 55, F, (--), M, SC, 306, 306, BEAU+. In HH of Richard Jones m 53 mulatto born SC.

JONES, CHARLES, 13, M, (--), B, SC, 354, 337, CHAS-. In HH of James Harrison m 50 mulatto born SC.

JONES, CORNELIUS, 35, M, Laborer, M, SC, 303, 303, BEAU+.

JONES, CUPID, 18, F, (--), B, SC, 406, 379, CHAS*. In HH of Catherine Johnson f 18 mulatto born SC.

JONES, DANIEL, 62, M, Farmer/mechanic, B, SC, 430, 430, BEAU-.

JONES, DANIEL, 40, M, Laborer, B, SC, 302, 302, BEAU+.

JONES, DINAH, 34, F, (--), B, SC, 999, 976, CHAS%. In HH of George Jones m 38 black born SC.

JONES, DINAH, 7, F, (--), B, SC, 999, 976, CHAS%. In HH of George Jones m 38 black born SC.

JONES, ELIZA, 45, F, (--), M, SC, 445, 445, BEAU-. In HH of James Jones m 52 mulatto born SC.

JONES, ELIZA, 25, F, (--), B, SC, 464, 464, BEAU-. In HH of William H. Jones m 32 black born SC.

JONES, ELIZA, 1, F, (--), B, SC, 450, 450, BEAU-. In HH of Sylvester Jones m 33 black born SC.

JONES, ELIZABETH, 60, F, (--), M, SC, 467, 467, BEAU-.

JONES, ELLEN, 51, F, (--), M, SC, 904, 884, CHAS-.

JONES, EMILY, 30, F, (--), M, SC, 1202, 1202, BARN. In HH of Bartlett Jones m 30 mulatto born SC.

JONES, F., 12, M, (--), M, SC, 273, 273, BEAU+. In HH of Charles Scott m 27 mulatto born SC.

JONES, FERMAN, 4, M, (--), M, SC, 303, 303, BEAU+. In HH of Cornelius Jones m 27 mulatto born SC.

JONES, FRANCIS, 7, M, (--), B, SC, 302, 302, BEAU+. In HH of Daniel

Jones m 40 black born SC.

JONES, FREDERICK, 6, M, (--), B, SC, 302, 302, BEAU+. In HH of Daniel Jones m 40 black born SC.

JONES, FREDERICK, 5, M, (--), B, SC, 464, 464, BEAU-. In HH of William H. Jones m 32 black born SC.

JONES, GEORGE, 38, M, Farmer, B, SC, 999, 976, CHAS%.

JONES, GEORGE, 5, M, (--), M, SC, 290, 290, BEAU+. In HH of Thomas Jones m 25 mulatto born SC.

JONES, HABERSHAM, 18, M, Laborer, B, SC, 189, 189, COLL. In HH of Nehemiah Jones m 60 black born SC.

JONES, HAMPTON, 35, M, Mechanic, M, SC, 444, 444, BEAU-.

JONES, HANSEL, 19, M, (--), M, SC, 1412, 1412, BARN. In HH of Jas. Jones m 50 mulatto born SC.

JONES, HARDEE, 4, M, (--), B, SC, 302, 302, BEAU+. In HH of Daniel Jones m 40 black born SC.

JONES, HELEN, 45, F, (--), M, SC, 1413, 1413, BARN. In HH of Isaac Jones m 60 mulatto born SC.

JONES, HENRY, 12, M, (--), B, SC, 430, 430, BEAU-. In HH of Daniel Jones m 62 black born SC.

JONES, HENRY, 2, M, (--), M, SC, 569, 561, CHAS%. In HH of Richard Jones m 38 mulatto born SC.

JONES, IRVIN, 11, M, (--), M, SC, 303, 303, BEAU+. In HH of Cornelius Jones m 27 mulatto born SC.

JONES, ISAAC, 60, M, Mechanic, M, SC, 1413, 1413, BARN.

JONES, ISAAC, 35, M, (--), M, SC, 182, 182, CHAS%. In HH of Nancy Stenet f 50 mulatto born SC.

JONES, ISAAC, 18, M, (--), M, SC, 1412, 1412, BARN. In HH of Jas. Jones m 50 mulatto born SC.

JONES, ISAAC, 1, M, (--), M, SC, 1412, 1412, BARN. In HH of Jas. Jones m 50 mulatto born SC. Isaac Jones ate 8/12 yr.

JONES, JACK, 54, M, Fisherman, M, SC, 326, 300, CHAS*. In HH of Abbey

Jones f 56 mulatto born SC.

JONES, JAMES, 52, M, Laborer, M, SC, 445, 445, BEAU-.

JONES, JAMES, 30, M, Fisherman, M, SC, 907, 887, CHAS-. In HH of Ann Latham f 43 mulatto born SC.

JONES, JAMES, 27, M, Laborer, M, SC, 283, 283, BEAU+.

JONES, JAMES, 25, M, Farmer, M, SC, 191, 191, COLL.

JONES, JAMES, 25, M, (--), M, SC, 182, 182, CHAS%. In HH of Nancy Stenet f 50 mulatto born SC.

JONES, JAMES, 9, M, (--), M, SC, 390, 388, CHAS%. In HH of Caroline Jones f 30 mulatto born SC.

JONES, JAMES M., 3, M, (--), B, SC, 464, 464, BEAU-. In HH of William H. Jones m 32 black born SC.

JONES, JANE, 27, F, (--), M, SC, 303, 303, BEAU+. In HH of Cornelius Jones m 27 mulatto born SC.

JONES, JANE, 11, F, (--), M, SC, 298, 298, BEAU+. In HH of William Jones m 60 mulatto born SC.

JONES, JAS., 50, M, Mechanic, M, SC, 1412, 1412, BARN.

JONES, JENNETT, 15, F, (--), M, SC, 303, 303, BEAU+. In HH of Cornelius Jones m 27 mulatto born SC.

JONES, JENNY, 15, F, (--), M, SC, 326, 300, CHAS*. In HH of Abbey Jones f 56 mulatto born SC.

JONES, JEREMIAH, 25, M, (--), B, SC, 486, 486, BEAU-. In HH of Sarah Jones f 38 mulatto born SC.

JONES, JOHN, 12, M, (--), M, SC, 182, 182, CHAS%. In HH of Nancy Stenet f 50 mulatto born SC.

JONES, JOSHUA, 30, M, Wheelwright, M, SC, 182, 182, CHAS%. In HH of Nancy Stenet f 50 mulatto born SC.

JONES, JULIA, 5, F, (--), M, SC, 1202, 1202, BARN. In HH of Bartlett Jones m 30 mulatto born SC.

JONES, KIRTUS, 12, M, (--), M, SC, 445, 445, BEAU-. In HH of James Jones m 52 mulatto born SC.

JONES, LUTHER, 8, M, (--), M, SC, 445, 445, BEAU-. In HH of James Jones m 52 mulatto born SC.

JONES, LYDIA, 10, F, (--), M, SC, 189, 189, COLL. In HH of Nehemiah Jones m 60 black born SC.

JONES, MAHALA, 19, F, (--), M, SC, 445, 445, BEAU-. In HH of James Jones m 52 mulatto born SC.

JONES, MARGARET, 22, F, (--), M, SC, 863, 821, CHAS+. In HH of E. Pringle f 51 born SC.

JONES, MARGARET, 13, F, (--), M, SC, 303, 303, BEAU+. In HH of Cornelius Jones m 27 mulatto born SC.

JONES, MARGARET, 4, F, (--), B, SC, 465, 465, BEAU-. In HH of Sarah Jones f 28 black born SC.

JONES, MARIAH, 60, F, (--), B, SC, 430, 430, BEAU-. In HH of Daniel Jones m 62 black born SC.

JONES, MARTHA, 33, F, (--), M, SC, 863, 821, CHAS+. In HH of E. Pringle f 51 born SC.

JONES, MARY, 50, F, (--), M, SC, 678, 687, RICH+.

JONES, MARY, 25, F, (--), M, SC, 1412, 1412, BARN. In HH of Jas. Jones m 50 mulatto born SC.

JONES, MARY, 16, F, (--), M, SC, 486, 486, BEAU-. In HH of Sarah Jones f 38 mulatto born SC.

JONES, MARY, 12, F, (--), B, SC, 999, 976, CHAS%. In HH of George Jones m 38 black born SC.

JONES, MARY, 4, F, (--), M, SC, 569, 561, CHAS%. In HH of Richard Jones m 38 mulatto born SC.

JONES, MARY, 2, F, (--), M, SC, 445, 445, BEAU-. In HH of James Jones m 52 mulatto born SC.

JONES, MARY ANN, 25, F, (--), B, SC, 182, 182, CHAS%. In HH of Nancy Stenet f 50 mulatto born SC.

JONES, MARY ANN, 19, F, (--), M, SC, 297, 297, BEAU+. In HH of Wistley Jones m 26 mulatto born SC.

JONES, MARY ANN, 15, F, (--), B, SC, 430, 430, BEAU-. In HH of Daniel

Jones m 62 black born SC.

JONES, MARY JANE, 9, F, (--), M, SC, 182, 182, CHAS%. In HH of Nancy Stenet f 50 mulatto born SC.

JONES, MATHEW, 21, M, Laborer, B, SC, 189, 189, COLL. In HH of Nehemiah Jones m 60 black born SC.

JONES, MATILDA, 25, F, (--), M, SC, 1810, 1816, EDGE. In HH of Wm. Thomas m 30 born SC.

JONES, MICHAEL, 7, M, (--), M, SC, 326, 300, CHAS*. In HH of Abbey Jones f 56 mulatto born SC.

JONES, MISINIAH, 8, F, (--), B, SC, 302, 302, BEAU+. In HH of Daniel Jones m 40 black born SC.

JONES, MOSES, 10, M, (--), M, SC, 486, 486, BEAU-. In HH of Sarah Jones f 38 mulatto born SC.

JONES, NANCY, 18, F, (--), M, SC, 1413, 1413, BARN. In HH of Isaac Jones m 60 mulatto born SC.

JONES, NANCY, 5, F, (--), M, SC, 499, 457, CHAS+. In HH of Francis Scott m 38 mulatto born SC.

JONES, NAOMI, 19, F, (--), M, SC, 306, 306, BEAU+. In HH of Richard Jones m 53 mulatto born SC.

JONES, NARCISSA, 11, F, (--), M, SC, 1202, 1202, BARN. In HH of Bartlett Jones m 30 mulatto born SC.

JONES, NEHEMIAH, 66, M, Carpenter, B, SC, 189, 189, COLL.

JONES, OPHELIA, 14, F, (--), M, SC, 1413, 1413, BARN. In HH of Isaac Jones m 60 mulatto born SC.

JONES, PATRICK, 21, M, Laborer, M, SC, 306, 306, BEAU+. In HH of Richard Jones m 53 mulatto born SC.

JONES, PAUL, 48, M, Farmer, M, SC, 904, 884, CHAS-. In HH of Ellen Jones f 51 mulatto born SC.

JONES, PAUL, 11, M, (--), M, SC, 326, 300, CHAS*. In HH of Abbey Jones f 56 mulatto born SC.

JONES, PHOEBE, 40, F, (--), B, SC, 436, 388, CHAS.

JONES, RACHAEL, 22, F, (--), B, SC, 182, 182, CHAS%. In HH of Nancy

Stenet f 50 mulatto born SC.

JONES, RACHEL, 30, F, (--), M, SC, 298, 298, BEAU+. In HH of William Jones m 60 mulatto born SC.

JONES, REBECCA, 35, F, (--), M, SC, 302, 302, BEAU+. In HH of Daniel Jones m 40 black born SC.

JONES, REDDIN, 14, M, (--), M, SC, 445, 445, BEAU-. In HH of James Jones m 52 mulatto born SC.

JONES, RICHARD, 62, M, Laborer, M, SC, 468, 468, BEAU-.

JONES, RICHARD, 53, M, (--), M, SC, 306, 306, BEAU+.

JONES, RICHARD, 38, M, Drayman, M, SC, 569, 561, CHAS%.

JONES, RICHARD, 9, M, (--), M, SC, 569, 561, CHAS%. In HH of Richard Jones m 38 mulatto born SC.

JONES, RICHARD, 3, M, (--), M, SC, 499, 457, CHAS+. In HH of Francis Scott m 38 mulatto born SC.

JONES, SAMMY, 11, M, (--), M, SC, 499, 457, CHAS+. In HH of Francis Scott m 38 mulatto born SC.

JONES, SARAH, 60, F, (--), M, SC, 333, 307, CHAS. In HH of Margaret Fitzgerald f 18 born SC.

JONES, SARAH, 38, F, (--), B, SC, 547, 506, CHAS+. In HH of Jerry Holmes m 24 mulatto born SC.

JONES, SARAH, 38, F, (--), M, SC, 486, 486, BEAU-.

JONES, SARAH, 28, F, (--), B, SC, 465, 465, BEAU-.

JONES, SARAH, 25, F, (--), M, SC, 450, 450, BEAU-. In HH of Sylvester Jones m 33 black born SC.

JONES, SARAH, 20, F, (--), M, SC, 395, 368, CHAS*. In HH of Andrew Turnbull m 35 born SC.

JONES, SARAH, 1, F, (--), M, SC, 290, 290, BEAU+. In HH of Thomas Jones m 25 mulatto born SC.

JONES, SARAH, 1, F, (--), M, SC, 1202, 1202, BARN. In HH of Bartlett Jones m 30 mulatto born SC. Sarah Jones age 6/12 yr.

JONES, SARAH ANN, 10, F, (--), M, SC, 333, 307, CHAS. In HH of Margaret Fitzgerald f 18 born SC.

JONES, SARARIAH, 28, F, (--), M, SC, 1412, 1412, BARN. In HH of Jas. Jones m 50 mulatto born SC.

JONES, SCIPIO, 9, M, (--), B, SC, 999, 976, CHAS%. In HH of George Jones m 38 black born SC.

JONES, SEABORN, 22, M, Mechanic, B, SC, 430, 430, BEAU-. In HH of Daniel Jones m 62 black born SC.

JONES, SHARLOT, 41, F, (--), B, SC, 87, 87, LAU. In HH of Thomas Colb m 55 mulatto born SC.

JONES, SILAS, 6, M, (--), M, SC, 445, 445, BEAU-. In HH of James Jones m 52 mulatto born SC.

JONES, SUSAN, 20, F, (--), M, SC, 290, 290, BEAU+. In HH of Thomas Jones m 25 mulatto born SC.

JONES, SYLVESTER, 33, M, Brick mason, B, SC, 450, 450, BEAU-.

JONES, TERRY, 18, M, Laborer, M, SC, 445, 445, BEAU-. In HH of James Jones m 52 mulatto born SC.

JONES, THADEUS, 2, M, (--), B, SC, 465, 465, BEAU-. In HH of Sarah Jones f 28 black born SC.

JONES, THOMAS, 25, M, Laborer, M, SC, 290, 290, BEAU+.

JONES, THOMAS, 24, M, Laborer, M, SC, 907, 887, CHAS-. In HH of Ann Latham f 43 mulatto born SC.

JONES, THOMAS, 22, M, Laborer, M, SC, 326, 300, CHAS*. In HH of Abbey Jones f 56 mulatto born SC.

JONES, THOMAS, 8, M, (--), M, SC, 569, 561, CHAS%. In HH of Richard Jones m 38 mulatto born SC.

JONES, THURSEY, 7, F, (--), B, SC, 464, 464, BEAU-. In HH of William H. Jones m 32 black born SC.

JONES, ULYSSES, 23, M, Laborer, M, SC, 306, 306, BEAU+. In HH of Richard Jones m 53 mulatto born SC.

JONES, VENUS, 89, F, (--), B, SC, 406, 379, CHAS*. In HH of Catherine Johnson f 18 mulatto born SC.

JONES, VERITY, 17, F, (--), M, SC, 1413, 1413, BARN. In HH of Isaac Jones m 60 mulatto born SC.

JONES, WESLEY, 21, M, (--), B, SC, 302, 302, BEAU+. In HH of Daniel Jones m 40 black born SC.

JONES, WILEY, 35, M, Drayman, B, SC, 2061, 2067, EDGE. In HH of Isaac Mitchell m 60 black born SC.

JONES, WILLIAM, 60, M, Carpenter, M, SC, 298, 298, BEAU+.

JONES, WILLIAM, 8, M, (--), M, SC, 1202, 1202, BARN. In HH of Bartlett Jones m 30 mulatto born SC.

JONES, WILLIAM H., 32, M, Mechanic, B, SC, 464, 464, BEAU-.

JONES, WILLIAM T., 28, M, Shoemaker, M, SC, 390, 388, CHAS%. In HH of Caroline Jones f 30 mulatto born SC.

JONES, WILLIS, 13, M, (--), B, SC, 302, 302, BEAU+. In HH of Daniel Jones m 40 black born SC.

JONES, WINBORN, 17, M, Laborer, B, SC, 430, 430, BEAU-. In HH of Daniel Jones m 62 black born SC.

JONES, WISTLEY, 26, M, Farmer, M, SC, 297, 297, BEAU+.

JONES, WM., 30, M, Tailor, M, SC, 71, 71, GEOR*. In HH of Francis Morce {? or Moru} m 30 mulatto born SC.

JOSEPH, EMMELINE, 24, F, (--), M, SC, 566, 549, CHAS-. In HH of Emmely Lafarge f 30 mulatto born Cuba.

K

KEATH, FANNY, 50, F, (--), B, SC, 248, 248, CHAS%. In HH of Joseph Lacomb m 20 mulatto born SC.

KEATH, ZEPHYR, 9, F, (--), B, SC, 248, 248, CHAS%. In HH of Joseph Lacomb m 20 mulatto born SC.

KELLAR, JACOL, 65, M, Farmer, B, Africa, 173, 173, ABB.

KELLECKER, ANN, 14, F, (--), M, SC, 430, 413, CHAS-. In HH of Francis Baneau m 36 mulatto born SC.

KELLON, DAVID S., 62, M, (--), B, SC, 615, 615, GREE.

KELLY, BERRY, 35, M, Rafthand, M, SC, 1225, 1225, BARN.

KELLY, CELIA, 8, F, (--), M, SC, 1225, 1225, BARN. In HH of Berry Kelly m 35 mulatto born SC.

KELLY, CLARA, 7, M, (--), M, SC, 2024, 2031, EDGE. In HH of Elizabeth Kelly f 25 mulatto born SC.

KELLY, ELIZA, 23, F, (--), M, SC, 2066, 2069, EDGE. In HH of Hazard Evans m 35 mulatto born SC.

KELLY, ELIZABETH, 25, F, (--), M, SC, 2024, 2031, EDGE.

KELLY, ELIZABETH, 24, F, (--), M, SC, 2066, 2069, EDGE. In HH of Hazard Evans m 35 mulatto born SC.

KELLY, EUGENIA, 6, F, (--), M, SC, 1225, 1225, BARN. In HH of Berry Kelly m 35 mulatto born SC.

KELLY, JOHN, 75, M, Rafthand, M, SC, 1226, 1226, BARN.

KELLY, JULIA, 28, F, (--), M, SC, 1225, 1225, BARN. In HH of Berry Kelly m 35 mulatto born SC.

KELLY, KESIAH, 60, F, (--), M, SC, 1226, 1226, BARN. In HH of John Kelly m 75 mulatto born SC.

KELLY, LUCINDA, 25, F, (--), B, SC, 2066, 2069, EDGE. In HH of Hazard Evans m 35 mulatto born SC.

KELLY, NANCY, 10, F, (--), M, SC, 1225, 1225, BARN. In HH of Berry Kelly m 35 mulatto born SC.

KENLOCK, MARIA, 16, F, (--), M, SC, 1026, 1003, CHAS-. In HH of Richard Kenlock m 54 mulatto born SC.

KENLOCK, RICHARD, 54, M, Wheelwright, M, SC, 1026, 1003, CHAS-.

KENLOCK, RICHMOND, 14, M, (--), M, SC, 1026, 1003, CHAS-. In HH of Richard Kenlock m 54 mulatto born SC.

KENLOCK, SOPHIA, 51, F, (--), M, SC, 1026, 1003, CHAS-. In HH of Richard Kenlock m 54 mulatto born SC.

KENNEDY, ALEXANDER, 14, M, (--), M, SC, 1537, 1537, YORK. In HH of Reuben Kennedy m 42 mulatto born SC.

KENNEDY, ELIZABETH, 9, F, (--), M, SC, 1537, 1537, YORK. In HH of Reuben Kennedy m 42 mulatto born SC.

KENNEDY, HESTER, 7, F, (--), M, SC, 1537, 1537, YORK. In HH of Reuben Kennedy m 42 mulatto born SC.

KENNEDY, MARY, 35, F, (--), M, SC, 1537, 1537, YORK. In HH of Reuben Kennedy m 42 mulatto born SC.

KENNEDY, NANCY, 11, F, (--), M, SC, 1537, 1537, YORK. In HH of Reuben Kennedy m 42 mulatto born SC.

KENNEDY, REUBEN, 42, M, (--), M, SC, 1537, 1537, YORK.

KENNEDY, THOMAS, 4, M, (--), M, SC, 1537, 1537, YORK. In HH of Reuben Kennedy m 42 mulatto born SC.

KERSEY, ELIS, 47, M, (--), M, SC, 325, 325, SUMT. In HH of Charles L.O. Steen m 44 born SC.

KING, EUGENA, 4, F, (--), M, SC, 365, 348, CHAS-. In HH of Mary McBride f 46 mulatto born SC.

KING, VELERIA, 2, F, (--), M, SC, 365, 348, CHAS-. In HH of Mary McBride f 46 mulatto born SC.

KINLOCK, BENJAMIN, 50, M, Millwright, M, SC, 502, 485, CHAS-. In HH of Martha Young f 40 mulatto born SC.

KINLOCK, EMMELINE, 39, F, (--), M, SC, 502, 485, CHAS-. In HH of Martha Young f 40 mulatto born SC.

KINLOCK, JANET, 4, F, (--), M, SC, 502, 485, CHAS-. In HH of Martha Young f 40 mulatto born SC.

KINLOCK, SOPHIA, 6, F, (--), M, SC, 502, 485, CHAS-. In HH of Martha Young f 40 mulatto born SC.

KNIGHT, ANGEL, 16, F, (--), M, SC, 460, 460, BEAU-.

KNIGHT, ELIZABETH, 8, F, (--), M, SC, 459, 459, BEAU-. In HH of Melvina Knight f 45 born SC.

KNIGHT, FRANK, 9, M, (--), M, SC,

459, 459, BEAU-. In HH of Melvina Knight f 45 born SC.

KNIGHT, ROBINSON, 18, M, Laborer, M, SC, 459, 459, BEAU-. In HH of Melvina Knight f 45 born SC.

KNIGHT, SARAH, 4, F, (--), M, SC, 459, 459, BEAU-. In HH of Melvina Knight f 45 born SC.

KNIGHT, STEPHEN, 1, M, (--), M, SC, 460, 460, BEAU-. In HH of Angel Knight f 16 mulatto born SC.

KNIGHT, THOMAS, 16, M, Laborer, M, SC, 459, 459, BEAU-. In HH of Melvina Knight f 45 born SC.

KNIGHT, WILLIAM, 7, M, (--), M, SC, 459, 459, BEAU-. In HH of Melvina Knight f 45 born SC.

KNIGHTS, ROSELINE, 14, F, (--), M, SC, 941, 921, CHAS-. In HH of Joshua Mishaw m 27 mulatto born SC.

KOOLER, NANCY, 18, F, (--), B, SC, 776, 756, CHAS-. In HH of Josephine Watkins f 21 black born SC.

KOOLER, ROSA, 30, F, (--), B, SC, 138, 128, CHAS-. In HH of Kate Veitch f 60 black born SC.

KOOLER, WILLIAM, 28, M, Bricklayer, B, SC, 138, 128, CHAS-. In HH of Kate Veitch f 60 black born SC.

KUTCHESON, JAMES, 29, M, Laborer, M, SC, 80, 80, GEOR. In HH of Elizabeth Wale f 35 mulatto born SC.

L

LABATE, JAMES, 16, M, Blacksmith, M, SC, 2254, 2254, GREE. In HH of Margarit Walker f 42 mulatto born SC.

LABATE, MARY, 56, F, (--), M, SC, 172, 162, CHAS-. In HH of Matilda Bonneau f 17 mulatto born SC.

LABUTAT, FRANCOIS, 60, F, (--), M, St. Domingo, 1035, 1012, CHAS-. In HH of Isidore Labutat m 69 born France.

LABUTAT, HENRY, 17, M, Carpenter, M, SC, 45, 45, CHAS%. In HH of Mary

Labutat f 57 mulatto born SC.

LABUTAT, MARY, 57, F, (--), M, St. Domingo, 45, 45, CHAS%.

LACOMB, ELIZABETH, 40, F, (--), M, SC, 248, 248, CHAS%. In HH of Joseph Lacomb m 20 mulatto born SC.

LACOMB, JOSEPH, 20, M, Tailor, M, SC, 248, 248, CHAS%.

LACOMB, LAVINA, 19, F, (--), M, SC, 248, 248, CHAS%. In HH of Joseph Lacomb m 20 mulatto born SC.

LACOMPTE, ANTONIO, 60, M, None, M, St. Domingo, 398, 396, CHAS%. In HH of Felicity LaCompte f 58 mulatto born St. Domingo.

LACOMPTE, ELOISE, 28, F, (--), M, St. Domingo, 398, 396, CHAS%. In HH of Felicity LaCompte f 58 mulatto born St. Domingo.

LACOMPTE, FELICITY, 58, F, (--), M, St. Domingo, 398, 396, CHAS%.

LACOMPTE, JULIUS, 20, M, Cigar maker, M, SC, 398, 396, CHAS%. In HH of Felicity LaCompte f 58 mulatto born St. Domingo.

LACOMPTE, MADELINE, 14, F, (--), M, SC, 398, 396, CHAS%. In HH of Felicity LaCompte f 58 mulatto born St. Domingo.

LAFAR, CAROLINE, 50, M, (--), M, SC, 187, 171, CHAS*. Caroline Lafar listed as male.

LAFARGE, EMMELY, 30, F, (--), M, Cuba, 566, 549, CHAS-.

LAFAYETTE, CHARLES, 1, M, (--), M, SC, 372, 334, CHAS+. In HH of Susan Philips f 30 mulatto born SC.

LAFAYETTE, HARRIOT, 70, F, (--), M, SC, 372, 334, CHAS+. In HH of Susan Philips f 30 mulatto born SC.

LAFAYETTE, JOSHUA, 8, M, (--), M, SC, 372, 334, CHAS+. In HH of Susan Philips f 30 mulatto born SC.

LAFAYETTE, MARTHA, 28, F, (--), M, SC, 372, 334, CHAS+. In HH of Susan Philips f 30 mulatto born SC.

LAFAYETTE, WILLIAM, 3, M, (--), M, SC, 372, 334, CHAS+. In HH of Susan Philips f 30 mulatto born SC.

LAKE, DIANA, 33, F, (--), M, SC, 60, 60, CHAS%.

LAKE, PETER, 30, M, Laborer, M, SC, 60, 60, CHAS%. In HH of Diana Lake f 33 mulatto born SC.

LAMOTT, DORELL, 56, F, (--), M, SC, 180, 180, CHAS%.

LANCE, JOHN, 24, M, Mariner, M, SC, 193, 176, CHAS. In HH of Elizabeth Henson f 60 mulatto born SC.

LANDER, JAMES, 31, M, (--), B, SC, 105, 105, CHAS%. In HH of Moses Bury m 34 black born SC.

LANEY, ABRAM, 19, M, Laborer, B, SC, 1113, 1113, UNION. In HH of Eleazer Parker m 42 born SC.

LANEY, AMANDA, 6, F, (--), B, SC, 653, 653, UNION. In HH of Bristoe Ferriston m 80 black born VA.

LANEY, BETSEY, 40, F, (--), B, SC, 653, 653, UNION. In HH of Bristoe Ferriston m 80 black born VA.

LANEY, BRISTOE, 7, M, (--), B, SC, 653, 653, UNION. In HH of Bristoe Ferriston m 80 black born VA.

LANEY, CYNTHIA, 9, F, (--), B, SC, 653, 653, UNION. In HH of Bristoe Ferriston m 80 black born VA.

LANEY, GRAFTON, 17, M, Laborer, B, SC, 1113, 1113, UNION. In HH of Eleazer Parker m 42 born SC.

LANEY, HENRY, 12, M, (--), B, SC, 653, 653, UNION. In HH of Bristoe Ferriston m 80 black born VA.

LANEY, LAWSON, 1, M, (--), B, SC, 653, 653, UNION. In HH of Bristoe Ferriston m 80 black born VA.

LANGLOIS, MARIA, 80, F, (--), B, West Indies, 554, 520, CHAS*. In HH of Sarah Finlay f 16 mulatto born SC.

LAPONT, TERESA, 60, F, (--), M, St. Domingo., 487, 470, CHAS-.

LATHAM, ANN, 43, F, (--), M, SC, 907, 887, CHAS-.

LAWRENCE, ABRAHAM, 26, M, Carpenter, B, SC, 121, 112, CHAS-. In HH of Ben Lawrence m 55 black born SC.

LAWRENCE, ALBERT, 11, M, (--),

B, SC, 643, 624, CHAS-. In HH of Mary Lawrence f 36 black born SC.

LAWRENCE, ANN, 6, F, (--), B, SC, 121, 112, CHAS-. In HH of Ben Lawrence m 55 black born SC.

LAWRENCE, BEN, 55, M, Carpenter, B, SC, 121, 112, CHAS-.

LAWRENCE, CLAUDIA, 30, F, (--), M, SC, 397, 361, CHAS.

LAWRENCE, DIANA, 22, F, (--), M, SC, 51, 51, CHAS%.

LAWRENCE, EDWARD, 35, M, Carpenter, B, SC, 392, 390, CHAS%.

LAWRENCE, ELIZABETH, 18, F, (--), B, SC, 121, 112, CHAS-. In HH of Ben Lawrence m 55 black born SC.

LAWRENCE, ISADORA, 5, F, (--), M, SC, 397, 361, CHAS. In HH of Claudia Lawrence f 30 mulatto born SC.

LAWRENCE, JAMES, 10, M, (--), B, SC, 392, 390, CHAS%. In HH of Edward Lawrence m 35 black born SC.

LAWRENCE, JANE, 26, F, (--), B, SC, 121, 112, CHAS-. In HH of Ben Lawrence m 55 black born SC.

LAWRENCE, JOSEPHINE, 6, F, (--), M, SC, 397, 361, CHAS. In HH of Claudia Lawrence f 30 mulatto born SC.

LAWRENCE, LAURA, 7, F, (--), B, SC, 643, 624, CHAS-. In HH of Mary Lawrence f 36 black born SC.

LAWRENCE, LOUISA, 57, F, (--), B, SC, 50, 50, CHAS%.

LAWRENCE, LOUISA, 30, F, (--), B, SC, 392, 390, CHAS%. In HH of Edward Lawrence m 35 black born SC.

LAWRENCE, LYDIA, 18, F, (--), B, SC, 643, 624, CHAS-. In HH of Mary Lawrence f 36 black born SC.

LAWRENCE, MARY, 36, F, (--), B, SC, 643, 624, CHAS-.

LAWRENCE, MARY, 20, F, (--), B, SC, 121, 112, CHAS-. In HH of Ben Lawrence m 55 black born SC.

LAWRENCE, MARY, 1, F, (--), B, SC, 643, 624, CHAS-. In HH of Mary Lawrence f 36 black born SC.

LAWRENCE, MARY J., 9, F, (--), B,

SC, 643, 624, CHAS-. In HH of Mary Lawrence f 36 black born SC.

LAWRENCE, RICHARD, 3, M, (--), B, SC, 643, 624, CHAS-. In HH of Mary Lawrence f 36 black born SC.

LAWRENCE, SARAH, 48, F, (--), B, SC, 121, 112, CHAS-. In HH of Ben Lawrence m 55 black born SC.

LAWRENCE, SARAH, 27, F, (--), B, SC, 121, 112, CHAS-. In HH of Ben Lawrence m 55 black born SC.

LAWRENCE, WILLIAM, 30, M, Barber, B, SC, 293, 270, CHAS+. In HH of Joseph Quash m 20 mulatto born SC.

LAWRENCE, WILLIAM, 8, M, (--), B, SC, 392, 390, CHAS%. In HH of Edward Lawrence m 35 black born SC.

LAWSON, REBECCA, 25, F, (--), M, SC, 258, 242, CHAS+.

LAWTON, CUDY, 20, F, (--), M, SC, 318, 318, CHFD. In HH of Thomas Frith m 22 born SC.

LAZARUS, HARRIOT, 40, F, (--), M, SC, 376, 338, CHAS+. In HH of John Bonner m 63 born PA.

LEBATE, CAROLINE, 39, F, (--), M, SC, 175, 161, CHAS*.

LEBATE, CLARA, 3, F, (--), M, SC, 175, 161, CHAS*. In HH of Caroline LeBate f 39 mulatto born SC.

LEBATE, FREDERICK, 13, M, (--), M, SC, 175, 161, CHAS*. In HH of Caroline LeBate f 39 mulatto born SC.

LEBATE, GEORGE, 23, M, Porter, M, SC, 175, 161, CHAS*. In HH of Caroline LeBate f 39 mulatto born SC.

LEBATE, LAWRENCE, 10, M, (--), M, SC, 175, 161, CHAS*. In HH of Caroline LeBate f 39 mulatto born SC. {a twin}.

LEBATE, LEOPOLD, 9, M, (--), M, SC, 175, 161, CHAS*. In HH of Caroline LeBate f 39 mulatto born SC.

LEBATE, WILLIAM, 10, M, (--), M, SC, 175, 161, CHAS*. In HH of Caroline LeBate f 39 mulatto born SC. {a twin}.

LEBUFF, ETIENESSE, 58, F, (--), M, St. Domingo, 603, 561, CHAS+. In HH

of Francis LeBuff m 60 mulatto born St. Domingo.

LEBUFF, FRANCIS, 60, M, Mattress maker, M, St. Domingo, 603, 561, CHAS+.

LECHAIN, FRANCIS, 60, F, (--), M, St. Domingo, 139, 129, CHAS-. In HH of Hugh Stoop m 60 born Ireland.

LECOMPLE, SERAPHINE, 60, F, (--), M, St. Domingo, 542, 501, CHAS+.

LECOMPT, MARIA, 16, F, (--), B, SC, 806, 764, CHAS+. In HH of Susan LeCompt f 51 black born SC.

LECOMPT, MARY, 8, F, (--), B, SC, 806, 764, CHAS+. In HH of Susan LeCompt f 51 black born SC.

LECOMPT, ROSE, 90, F, (--), B, SC, 806, 764, CHAS+. In HH of Susan LeCompt f 51 black born SC.

LECOMPT, SUSAN, 51, F, (--), B, St. Domingo, 806, 764, CHAS+.

LEE, ALLEN, 17, M, Shoemaker, M, SC, 173, 177, RICH. In HH of Henry Lee m 50 mulatto born SC.

LEE, ANN, 55, F, (--), M, SC, 926, 926, ABB. In HH of Sam Lee 50 m mulatto born SC.

LEE, ANN, 29, F, (--), M, SC, 563, 555, CHAS%. In HH of Florence Lee m 29 mulatto born SC.

LEE, ANN, 28, F, (--), M, SC, 375, 374, CHAS%. In HH of Sarah Lee f 31 mulatto born SC.

LEE, ARTHUR, 13, M, (--), M, SC, 238, 216, CHAS. In HH of Edward Lee m 45 mulatto born SC.

LEE, ARTHUR, 3, M, (--), M, SC, 563, 555, CHAS%. In HH of Florence Lee m 29 mulatto born SC.

LEE, BELLA, 10, F, (--), M, SC, 926, 926, ABB. In HH of Sam Lee 50 m mulatto born SC.

LEE, BETSEY, 27, F, (--), M, SC, 891, 871, CHAS-. In HH of Grace Lee f 62 mulatto born SC.

LEE, BETSY, 23, F, (--), M, SC, 926, 926, ABB. In HH of Sam Lee 50 m mulatto born SC.

LEE, CAROLINA, 8, F, (--), M, SC,

173, 177, RICH. In HH of Henry Lee m 50 mulatto born SC.

LEE, CHARLOTTE, 7, F, (--), M, SC, 238, 216, CHAS. In HH of Edward Lee m 45 mulatto born SC.

LEE, DIANAH, 16, F, (--), M, SC, 228, 228, CHAS%. In HH of Elsy Lee f 60 black born SC.

LEE, EDWARD, 45, M, Hairdresser, M, SC, 238, 216, CHAS.

LEE, EDWARD, 19, M, Hairdresser, M, SC, 238, 216, CHAS. In HH of Edward Lee m 45 mulatto born SC.

LEE, ELIZA, 52, F, (--), M, SC, 173, 177, RICH. In HH of Henry Lee m 50 mulatto born SC.

LEE, ELIZA, 12, F, (--), M, SC, 926, 926, ABB. In HH of Sam Lee 50 m mulatto born SC.

LEE, ELIZA JANE, 14, F, (--), M, SC, 238, 216, CHAS. In HH of Edward Lee m 45 mulatto born SC.

LEE, ELIZABETH, 18, F, (--), M, SC, 179, 169, CHAS-. In HH of Juliet Canter f 50 mulatto born SC.

LEE, ELSY, 60, F, (--), B, SC, 228, 228, CHAS%.

LEE, EMILY, 11, F, (--), M, SC, 238, 216, CHAS. In HH of Edward Lee m 45 mulatto born SC.

LEE, FILIMAN, 1, M, (--), M, SC, 926, 926, ABB. In HH of Sam Lee 50 m mulatto born SC.

LEE, FLORENCE, 29, M, (--), M, SC, 563, 555, CHAS%.

LEE, FRANCES, 5, M, (--), M, SC, 563, 555, CHAS%. In HH of Florence Lee m 29 mulatto born SC.

LEE, GRACE, 62, F, (--), M, SC, 891, 871, CHAS-.

LEE, HENRY, 50, M, Carpenter, M, SC, 173, 177, RICH.

LEE, JAMES, 7, M, (--), M, SC, 563, 555, CHAS%. In HH of Florence Lee m 29 mulatto born SC.

LEE, JOHN, 58, M, Hotel keeper, M, SC, 251, 229, CHAS.

LEE, JOHN, 18, M, (--), B, SC, 228,

228, CHAS%. In HH of Elsy Lee f 60 black born SC.

LEE, JOHN, 14, M, (--), M, SC, 173, 177, RICH. In HH of Henry Lee m 50 mulatto born SC.

LEE, JOHN, 5, M, (--), M, SC, 926, 926, ABB. In HH of Sam Lee 50 m mulatto born SC.

LEE, JOHN, 2, M, (--), M, SC, 563, 555, CHAS%. In HH of Florence Lee m 29 mulatto born SC.

LEE, JOSEPH, 8, M, (--), M, SC, 179, 169, CHAS-. In HH of Juliet Canter f 50 mulatto born SC.

LEE, JULIA, 5, F, (--), M, SC, 563, 555, CHAS%. In HH of Florence Lee m 29 mulatto born SC.

LEE, MARTHA, 10, F, (--), M, SC, 173, 177, RICH. In HH of Henry Lee m 50 mulatto born SC.

LEE, MARTHA, 5, F, (--), M, SC, 1123, 1101, CHAS%. In HH of Emma McCall f 30 mulatto born SC.

LEE, MARTHA, 5, F, (--), M, SC, 238, 216, CHAS. In HH of Edward Lee m 45 mulatto born SC.

LEE, MARY, 23, F, (--), M, SC, 926, 926, ABB. In HH of Sam Lee 50 m mulatto born SC.

LEE, MARY ANN, 45, F, (--), B, SC, 504, 462, CHAS+.

LEE, MARY E., 1, F, (--), M, SC, 926, 926, ABB. In HH of Sam Lee 50 m mulatto born SC.

LEE, SAM, 50, M, (--), M, SC, 926, 926, ABB.

LEE, SAMUEL, 8, M, (--), M, SC, 926, 926, ABB. In HH of Sam Lee 50 m mulatto born SC.

LEE, SARAH, 31, F, (--), M, SC, 375, 374, CHAS%.

LEE, SARAH, 14, F, (--), M, SC, 926, 926, ABB. In HH of Sam Lee 50 m mulatto born SC.

LEE, SUSAN, 17, F, (--), M, SC, 891, 871, CHAS-. In HH of Grace Lee f 62 mulatto born SC.

LEE, SUSAN, 9, F, (--), M, SC, 238, 216, CHAS. In HH of Edward Lee m 45 mulatto born SC.

LEE, WILLIAM, 0, M, (--), M, SC, 563, 555, CHAS%. In HH of Florence Lee m 29 mulatto born SC. William Lee age 9/12 yr.

LEGARD, LAVINA, 51, F, (--), M, NY, 473, 431, CHAS+. In HH of Susan Legard f 18 mulatto born NY.

LEGARD, SUSAN, 18, F, (--), M, NY, 473, 431, CHAS+.

LEGARE, BENJ., 40, M, Planter, B, SC, 812, 812, SUMT. In HH of Nathan Legare m 37 black born SC.

LEGARE, CHARLES, 40, M, Carpenter, B, SC, 193, 193, CHAS%.

LEGARE, EMILINE, 1, F, (--), B, SC, 812, 812, SUMT. In HH of Nathan Legare m 37 black born SC.

LEGARE, HENRIETTA, 25, F, (--), B, SC, 812, 812, SUMT. In HH of Nathan Legare m 37 black born SC.

LEGARE, JACOB, 40, M, Painter, M, SC, 330, 304, CHAS*. In HH of Mary Legard f 21 mulatto born SC.

LEGARE, JULIA ANN, 25, F, (--), B, SC, 504, 462, CHAS+. In HH of Mary Ann Lee f 45 black born SC.

LEGARE, MARTHA, 52, F, (--), B, SC, 193, 193, CHAS%. In HH of Charles Legare m 50 black born SC.

LEGARE, MARY, 70, F, (--), B, SC, 812, 812, SUMT. In HH of Nathan Legare m 37 black born SC.

LEGARE, MARY, 30, F, (--), M, SC, 772, 752, CHAS-.

LEGARE, MARY, 21, F, (--), M, SC, 330, 304, CHAS*.

LEGARE, NATHAN, 37, M, Carpenter, B, SC, 812, 812, SUMT.

LEGARE, NATHAN, 4, M, (--), B, SC, 812, 812, SUMT. In HH of Nathan Legare m 37 black born SC.

LEGARE, PETER, 50, M, (--), M, SC, 293, 270, CHAS+. In HH of Joseph Quash m 20 mulatto born SC.

LEGARE, PRISCILLA, 3, F, (--), B, SC, 812, 812, SUMT. In HH of Nathan Legare m 37 black born SC.

LEGARE, SARAH, 15, F, (--), B, SC, 608, 600, CHAS%.

LEGRAND, CHARLOTTE, 4, F, (--), B, SC, 778, 758, CHAS-. In HH of Nancy LeGrand f 32 black born SC.

LEGRAND, DIANA, 0, F, (--), B, SC, 778, 758, CHAS-. In HH of Nancy LeGrand f 32 black born SC. Diana LeGrand age 8/12 yr.

LEGRAND, JOHN, 38, M, (--), B, SC, 778, 758, CHAS-. In HH of Nancy LeGrand f 32 black born SC.

LEGRAND, JOHN, 12, M, (--), B, SC, 778, 758, CHAS-. In HH of Nancy LeGrand f 32 black born SC.

LEGRAND, NANCY, 32, F, (--), B, SC, 778, 758, CHAS-.

LEGRAND, NANCY, 6, F, (--), B, SC, 778, 758, CHAS-. In HH of Nancy LeGrand f 32 black born SC.

LEMACKS, ANDREW, 3, M, (--), B, SC, 652, 652, COLL. In HH of Elizabeth Lemacks 30 black born SC.

LEMACKS, ANNE, 1, F, (--), B, SC, 652, 652, COLL. In HH of Elizabeth Lemacks 30 black born SC.

LEMACKS, DANIEL, 5, M, (--), B, SC, 652, 652, COLL. In HH of Elizabeth Lemacks 30 black born SC.

LEMACKS, ELIZABETH, 30, F, (--), B, SC, 652, 652, COLL.

LEO, MARGARET, 40, F, (--), M, SC, 155, 145, CHAS-. In HH of Ann Mitchell f 60 mulatto born SC.

LEONARD, HARRIOT, 30, F, (--), M, SC, 229, 204, CHAS*. In HH of Harriot Nelme f 56 black born SC.

LEWIS, ANNA, 28, F, (--), M, SC, 36, 33, CHAS-.

LEWIS, ANNE, 8, F, (--), M, SC, 171, 171, COLL*. In HH of Barbara Lewis f 32 mulatto born SC.

LEWIS, BARBARA, 32, F, (--), M, SC, 171, 171, COLL*.

LEWIS, BENJ., 55, M, Farmer, B, SC, 157, 157, GEOR*.

LEWIS, CATHERINE, 50, F, (--), M, SC, 1023, 1000, CHAS-.

LEWIS, ELIZA, 30, F, (--), M, SC,

1023, 1000, CHAS-. In HH of Catherine Lewis f 50 mulatto born SC.

LEWIS, ELIZA, 21, F, (--), M, SC, 1067, 1044, CHAS-. In HH of Sarah Lewis f 25 mulatto born SC.

LEWIS, EVAN, 11, M, (--), M, SC, 171, 171, COLL*. In HH of Barbara Lewis f 32 mulatto born SC.

LEWIS, FATHER, 3, M, (--), M, SC, 171, 171, COLL*. In HH of Barbara Lewis f 32 mulatto born SC.

LEWIS, HARRIET, 14, F, (--), M, SC, 17, 17, CHAS2. In HH of Henry Glencamp m 41 mulatto born SC.

LEWIS, JACOB, 15, M, (--), M, SC, 171, 171, COLL*. In HH of Barbara Lewis f 32 mulatto born SC.

LEWIS, JAMES, 33, M, Tailor, B, SC, 387, 370, CHAS-.

LEWIS, JANE, 75, F, (--), M, St. Domingo, 223, 209, CHAS-.

LEWIS, JANE, 19, F, (--), B, SC, 387, 370, CHAS-. In HH of James Lewis m 33 black born SC.

LEWIS, JOHN, 40, M, Bootmaker, M, SC, 1009, 986, CHAS-.

LEWIS, JOHN, 38, M, Shoemaker, B, SC, 863, 840, CHAS%.

LEWIS, JOHN C., 30, M, Bricklayer, B, SC, 64, 55, CHAS$. In HH of John M. Fairell m 30 born SC.

LEWIS, JULIET, 13, F, (--), B, SC, 875, 855, CHAS-. In HH of Peter Lewis m 38 black born SC.

LEWIS, LEMILLU {?}, 1, F, (--), B, SC, 171, 171, COLL*. In HH of Barbara Lewis f 32 mulatto born SC.

LEWIS, LETETIA, 28, F, (--), M, SC, 1067, 1044, CHAS-. In HH of Sarah Lewis f 25 mulatto born SC.

LEWIS, LUCINDA, 12, F, (--), B, SC, 387, 370, CHAS-. In HH of James Lewis m 33 black born SC.

LEWIS, MARY, 10, F, (--), M, SC, 428, 397, CHAS*. In HH of Glenn Carr f 37 mulatto born SC.

LEWIS, MARY ANN, 32, F, (--), B, SC, 875, 855, CHAS-. In HH of Peter Lewis m 38 black born SC.

LEWIS, NANCY, 45, F, (--), M, SC, 17, 17, CHAS2. In HH of Henry Glencamp m 41 mulatto born SC.

LEWIS, PEDRO, 69, M, (--), M, St. Domingo, 223, 209, CHAS-. In HH of Jane Lewis f 75 mulatto born St. Domingo.

LEWIS, PETER, 38, M, Tailor, B, SC, 875, 855, CHAS-.

LEWIS, PETER, 30, M, Painter, B, SC, 500, 458, CHAS+. In HH of Mary Hutchinson f 45 black born SC.

LEWIS, PETER, 16, M, Shoemaker, B, SC, 387, 370, CHAS-. In HH of James Lewis m 33 black born SC.

LEWIS, PHILLIS, 60, F, (--), B, SC, 157, 157, GEOR*. In HH of Benj. Lewis m 50 black born SC.

LEWIS, PHOEBE, 38, F, (--), M, SC, 305, 281, CHAS+.

LEWIS, REUBEN, 36, M, Carpenter, B, SC, 131, 131, NEWB. In HH of Samuel Caldwell m 40 born SC.

LEWIS, ROSE, 26, F, (--), M, SC, 247, 232, CHAS+. In HH of Rebecca Swinton f 40 black born SC.

LEWIS, SARAH, 25, F, (--), M, SC, 693, 651, CHAS+. In HH of William Hislop m 43 born MD.

LEWIS, SARAH, 25, F, (--), M, SC, 1067, 1044, CHAS-.

LEWIS, SARAH, 10, F, (--), M, SC, 17, 17, CHAS2. In HH of Henry Glencamp m 41 mulatto born SC.

LEWIS, SUSANAH, 35, F, (--), B, SC, 387, 370, CHAS-. In HH of James Lewis m 33 black born SC.

LEWIS, THEODORE, 9, M, (--), B, SC, 875, 855, CHAS-. In HH of Peter Lewis m 38 black born SC.

LEWIS, THOMPSON, 14, M, (--), M, SC, 171, 171, COLL*. In HH of Barbara Lewis f 32 mulatto born SC.

LEWIS, WILLIAM, 8, M, (--), M, SC, 17, 17, CHAS2. In HH of Henry Glencamp m 41 mulatto born SC.

LILLE, J., 16, M, Laborer, M, SC, 598, 598, LANC*. In HH of J. Shehaw m 40 born SC.

LILLE, J., 12, M, (--), M, SC, 598, 598, LANC*. In HH of J. Shehaw m 40 born SC.

LINCOLN, SARAH, 25, F, (--), M, SC, 215, 201, CHAS-. In HH of Laura Purse f 21 mulatto born SC.

LINDSAY, ANDREW, 0, M, (--), M, SC, 25, 25, COLL*. In HH of Richard Hill m 49 born SC. Andrew age 6/12 yr.

LINDSAY, ANN, 25, F, (--), M, SC, 25, 25, COLL*. In HH of Richard Hill m 49 born SC.

LINDSAY, MARCH, 3, M, (--), M, SC, 25, 25, COLL*. In HH of Richard Hill m 49 born SC.

LISINTON, ISABELEA, 27, F, (--), M, SC, 339, 339, GEOR*. In HH of Susanna Nights f 60 mulatto born SC.

LISMORE, POLLY, 28, F, (--), B, SC, 353, 353, PICK+.

LISTON, CATHERINE, 12, F, (--), M, SC, 936, 916, CHAS-. In HH of Rose Liston f 37 mulatto born SC.

LISTON, JAMES, 14, M, (--), M, SC, 936, 916, CHAS-. In HH of Rose Liston f 37 mulatto born SC.

LISTON, ROSE, 37, F, (--), M, SC, 936, 916, CHAS-.

LISTON, WILLIAM, 9, M, (--), M, SC, 936, 916, CHAS-. In HH of Rose Liston f 37 mulatto born SC.

LIVINGSTON, KATE, 95, F, (--), B, SC, 1938, 1938, ABB.

LLOYD, BEUAH, 40, F, (--), B, SC, 482, 440, CHAS+. In HH of Ned. Lloyd m 30 black born SC.

LLOYD, JANE, 38, F, (--), B, SC, 290, 290, CHAS%.

LLOYD, NED., 30, M, Laborer, B, SC, 482, 440, CHAS+.

LOCKELIER, ANN, 22, F, (--), M, SC, 51, 51, CHAS2. In HH of John Lockelier m 30 mulatto born SC.

LOCKELIER, BENJAMIN, 1, M, (--), M, SC, 51, 51, CHAS2. In HH of John Lockelier m 30 mulatto born SC.

LOCKELIER, GABRIELLA, 2, F, (--), M, SC, 52, 52, CHAS2. In HH of Stephen Lockelier m 28 mulatto born SC.

LOCKELIER, JOHN, 30, M, Blacksmith, M, SC, 51, 51, CHAS2.

LOCKELIER, MARGARET, 1, F, (--), M, SC, 52, 52, CHAS2. In HH of Stephen Lockelier m 28 mulatto born SC.

LOCKELIER, MARY MRS., 19, F, (--), M, SC, 52, 52, CHAS2. In HH of Stephen Lockelier m 28 mulatto born SC.

LOCKELIER, STEPHEN, 28, M, Laborer, M, SC, 52, 52, CHAS2.

LOCKLAYER, CATHERINE, 18, F, (--), M, SC, 1583, 1589, MAR. In HH of John Locklayer m 45 mulatto born SC.

LOCKLAYER, ELIAS, 7, M, (--), M, SC, 1583, 1589, MAR. In HH of John Locklayer m 45 mulatto born SC.

LOCKLAYER, HANNAH, 40, F, (--), M, SC, 1583, 1589, MAR. In HH of John Locklayer m 45 mulatto born SC.

LOCKLAYER, JAMES, 12, M, (--), M, SC, 1583, 1589, MAR. In HH of John Locklayer m 45 mulatto born SC.

LOCKLAYER, JANE, 15, F, (--), M, SC, 1583, 1589, MAR. In HH of John Locklayer m 45 mulatto born SC.

LOCKLAYER, JOHN, 45, M, Laborer, M, SC, 1583, 1589, MAR.

LOCKLAYER, JOHN, 10, M, (--), M, SC, 1583, 1589, MAR. In HH of John Locklayer m 45 mulatto born SC.

LOCKLAYER, MARY, 20, F, (--), M, SC, 1583, 1589, MAR. In HH of John Locklayer m 45 mulatto born SC.

LOCKLAYER, ORPAH, 1, F, (--), M, SC, 1583, 1589, MAR. In HH of John Locklayer m 45 mulatto born SC.

LOCKLAYER, SAMUEL, 3, M, (--), M, SC, 1583, 1589, MAR. In HH of John Locklayer m 45 mulatto born SC.

LOCKLAYER, SUSAN, 5, F, (--), M, SC, 1583, 1589, MAR. In HH of John Locklayer m 45 mulatto born SC.

LOCKLEAR, ALIX, 20, M, Laborer, M, NC, 228, 228, MARL. In HH of George Locklear m 54 M born NC.

LOCKLEAR, ARCHD., 13, M, (--), M,

NC, 298, 298, MARL. In HH of Lauchlin Locklear m 40 Mulatto born NC.

LOCKLEAR, DAVID, 30, M, Farmer, M, SC, 21, 21, CHAS~.

LOCKLEAR, DUNCAN, 11, M, (--), M, NC, 298, 298, MARL. In HH of Lauchlin Locklear m 40 Mulatto born NC.

LOCKLEAR, ELIGAH, 2, M, (--), M, NC, 298, 298, MARL. In HH of Lauchlin Locklear m 40 Mulatto born NC.

LOCKLEAR, ELISHA, 5, M, (--), M, NC, 298, 298, MARL. In HH of Lauchlin Locklear m 40 Mulatto born NC.

LOCKLEAR, ELIZABETH, 40, F, (--), M, NC, 298, 298, MARL. In HH of Lauchlin Locklear m 40 Mulatto born NC.

LOCKLEAR, ELIZABETH, 23, F, (--), M, NC, 228, 228, MARL. In HH of George Locklear m 54 M born NC.

LOCKLEAR, ELIZTH., 20, M, (--), M, SC, 314, 314, COLL*. In HH of Charles Rose m 21 white born SC.

LOCKLEAR, GEORGE, 53, M, Laborer, M, NC, 228, 228, MARL.

LOCKLEAR, GEORGE M., 3, M, (--), M, SC, 21, 21, CHAS~. In HH of David Locklear m 30 mulatto born SC.

LOCKLEAR, JANE, MRS., 27, F, (--), M, SC, 21, 21, CHAS~. In HH of David Locklear m 30 mulatto born SC.

LOCKLEAR, JOHN, 14, F, (--), M, NC, 228, 228, MARL. In HH of George Locklear m 54 M born NC.

LOCKLEAR, JOHN J., 9, M, (--), M, SC, 21, 21, CHAS~. In HH of David Locklear m 30 mulatto born SC.

LOCKLEAR, LAUCHLIN, 40, M, Laborer, M, NC, 298, 298, MARL.

LOCKLEAR, MARGARET, 16, F, (--), M, NC, 228, 228, MARL. In HH of George Locklear m 54 M born NC.

LOCKLEAR, MARY, 15, F, (--), M, NC, 298, 298, MARL. In HH of Lauchlin Locklear m 40 Mulatto born NC.

LOCKLEAR, SHEPHERD, 26, M, Laborer, M, NC, 775, 775, MARL. In HH of John Cope m 43 born SC.

LOCKLEAR, WILLIAM J., 7, M, (--), M, SC, 21, 21, CHAS~. In HH of David Locklear m 30 mulatto born SC.

LOCKRIDGE, LINDA, 10, F, (--), B, SC, 522, 522, FAIR. In HH of Charles Laughlin m 58 born Ireland.

LOCKWOOD, BETSEY, 38, F, (--), B, SC, 250, 235, CHAS+.

LOCKWOOD, PATTY, 98, F, (--), B, SC, 139, 127, CHAS*. In HH of Patty Ashe f 100 black born SC.

LOCUS, JAMES, 10, M, (--), B, SC, 164, 164, CHAS%. In HH of Joseph Scott m 39 black born SC.

LOCUS, MATILDA, 12, F, (--), B, SC, 164, 164, CHAS%. In HH of Joseph Scott m 39 black born SC.

LOCUS, SARAH, 5, F, (--), B, SC, 164, 164, CHAS%. In HH of Joseph Scott m 39 black born SC.

LOCUS, WILLIAM, 13, M, (--), B, SC, 164, 164, CHAS%. In HH of Joseph Scott m 39 black born SC.

LOGIER, CAROLINE, 1, F, (--), M, SC, 77, 77, CHAS%. In HH of Martha Logier f 33 mulatto born SC.

LOGIER, JOSEPHINE, 3, F, (--), M, SC, 77, 77, CHAS%. In HH of Martha Logier f 33 mulatto born SC.

LOGIER, MARTHA, 33, F, (--), M, SC, 77, 77, CHAS%.

LOGIER, MARY J., 10, F, (--), M, SC, 77, 77, CHAS%. In HH of Martha Logier f 33 mulatto born SC.

LOGIER, SARAH, 5, F, (--), M, SC, 77, 77, CHAS%. In HH of Martha Logier f 33 mulatto born SC.

LOGIER, SIRE, 7, M, (--), M, SC, 77, 77, CHAS%. In HH of Martha Logier f 33 mulatto born SC.

LONG, CATHERINE ANN, 5, F, (--), M, SC, 257, 235, CHAS. In HH of William Stevens m 58 mulatto born SC.

LONG, F.H., 33, M, Shoemaker, M, SC, 276, 260, CHAS-.

LONG, FLORIN H., 28, M, Bookmaker, M, SC, 257, 235, CHAS. In HH of William Stevens m 58 mulatto born SC.

LONG, JOHN, 3, M, (--), M, SC, 276, 260, CHAS-. In HH of F.H. Long m 33 mulatto born SC.

LONG, LYDIA, 0, F, (--), M, SC, 257, 235, CHAS. In HH of William Stevens m 58 mulatto born SC. Lydia Long age 5/12 yr.

LONG, MARTHA, 23, F, (--), M, SC, 257, 235, CHAS. In HH of William Stevens m 58 mulatto born SC.

LONG, MARTHA S., 25, F, (--), M, SC, 276, 260, CHAS-. In HH of F.H. Long m 33 mulatto born SC.

LONG, PRISORA {?}, 75, F, (--), B, SC, 276, 276, NEWB. In HH of Jacob Long m 47 born SC.

LONG, WM. HENRY, 4, M, (--), M, SC, 257, 235, CHAS. In HH of William Stevens m 58 mulatto born SC.

LORD, ANGELINE, 9, F, (--), M, SC, 840, 821, CHAS%. In HH of Isabella Simons f 50 mulatto born SC.

LORD, ELLA, 14, F, (--), M, SC, 840, 821, CHAS%. In HH of Isabella Simons f 50 mulatto born SC.

LORD, JAMES, 12, M, (--), M, SC, 840, 821, CHAS%. In HH of Isabella Simons f 50 mulatto born SC.

LORD, ROBERT, 45, M, Carpenter, M, SC, 840, 821, CHAS%. In HH of Isabella Simons f 50 mulatto born SC.

LORD, SUSAN, 17, F, (--), M, SC, 840, 821, CHAS%. In HH of Isabella Simons f 50 mulatto born SC.

LORD, THOMAS, 6, M, (--), M, SC, 840, 821, CHAS%. In HH of Isabella Simons f 50 mulatto born SC.

LOTT, ANNA, 40, F, (--), B, SC, 36, 37, RICH.

LOTT, CROESA, 60, M, (--), M, VA, 463, 477, RICH. In HH of Clarissa Taylor m 70 mulatto born SC.

LOTT, HENRY, 23, M, Laborer, B, SC, 36, 37, RICH. In HH of Anna Lott f 40 black born SC.

LOVELAND, ARTHER, 20, M, Laborer, B, SC, 269, 269, GREE. In HH of Nancy Loveland f 40 black born SC.

LOVELAND, CALVIN, 12, M, (--), B, SC, 269, 269, GREE. In HH of Nancy Loveland f 40 black born SC.

LOVELAND, CAROLINE, 1, F, (--), B, SC, 269, 269, GREE. In HH of Nancy Loveland f 40 black born SC.

LOVELAND, ELIZA, 18, F, (--), B, SC, 269, 269, GREE. In HH of Nancy Loveland f 40 black born SC.

LOVELAND, GEORGE, 6, M, (--), B, SC, 269, 269, GREE. In HH of Nancy Loveland f 40 black born SC.

LOVELAND, JACK, 8, M, (--), B, SC, 269, 269, GREE. In HH of Nancy Loveland f 40 black born SC.

LOVELAND, JOHN, 2, M, (--), B, SC, 269, 269, GREE. In HH of Nancy Loveland f 40 black born SC.

LOVELAND, KING, 15, M, (--), B, SC, 269, 269, GREE. In HH of Nancy Loveland f 40 black born SC.

LOVELAND, MARY, 16, F, (--), B, SC, 269, 269, GREE. In HH of Nancy Loveland f 40 black born SC.

LOVELAND, NANCY, 40, F, (--), B, SC, 269, 269, GREE.

LOVELAND, SALLY, 12, F, (--), B, SC, 269, 269, GREE. In HH of Nancy Loveland f 40 black born SC.

LOVELAND, SAMUEL, 7, M, (--), B, SC, 269, 269, GREE. In HH of Nancy Loveland f 40 black born SC.

LOVELAND, SOLOMON, 22, M, Laborer, B, SC, 269, 269, GREE. In HH of Nancy Loveland f 40 black born SC.

LOVELY, ISAAC, 10, M, (--), M, SC, 297, 274, CHAS. In HH of John A. Gylis m 36 born SC.

LOVELY, JOHN, 35, M, Stevedore, M, SC, 297, 274, CHAS. In HH of John A. Gylis m 36 born SC.

LOW, MARION, 8, M, (--), B, SC, 2009, 2009, SPART. In HH of Muer Low f 40 born SC.

LOWNDIS, AMELIA, 19, F, (--), B, SC, 597, 578, CHAS-. In HH of Jane

Lowndis f 40 black born SC.

LOWNDIS, CAROLINE, 27, F, (--), B, SC, 597, 578, CHAS-. In HH of Jane Lowndis f 40 black born SC.

LOWNDIS, CORINA, 7, F, (--), B, SC, 597, 578, CHAS-. In HH of Jane Lowndis f 40 black born SC.

LOWNDIS, JANE, 40, F, (--), B, SC, 597, 578, CHAS-.

LOWNDIS, TERESA, 27, F, (--), B, SC, 597, 578, CHAS-. In HH of Jane Lowndis f 40 black born SC.

LOWREY, ALLEN, 14, M, (--), M, NC, 776, 776, MARL. In HH of George Lowery m 52 Mulatto born NC.

LOWREY, ALLISON, 6, M, (--), M, NC, 776, 776, MARL. In HH of George Lowery m 52 Mulatto born NC.

LOWREY, ANDREW, 20, M, Laborer, M, NC, 776, 776, MARL. In HH of George Lowery m 52 Mulatto born NC.

LOWREY, GEORGE, 52, M, Laborer, M, NC, 776, 776, MARL.

LOWREY, GERMAIN, 12, M, (--), M, NC, 776, 776, MARL. In HH of George Lowery m 52 Mulatto born NC.

LOWREY, PRISCILLA, 50, F, (--), M, NC, 776, 776, MARL. In HH of George Lowery m 52 Mulatto born NC.

LOWREY, WESLEY, 15, M, Laborer, M, NC, 776, 776, MARL. In HH of George Lowery m 52 Mulatto born NC.

LOWRY, THOS., 48, M, Planter, M, SC, 1303, 1303, SUMT.

LOYD, ELIZABETH, 15, F, (--), M, SC, 2109, 2109, LAU. In HH of Sally Loyd f 50 born SC.

LOYD, WILLIAM, 13, M, (--), M, SC, 2109, 2109, LAU. In HH of Sally Loyd f 50 born SC.

LUCAS, GEORGE, 45, M, Millwright, M, SC, 519, 512, CHAS%.

LUCAS, JEREMIAH, 45, M, Coachman, M, SC, 11, 11, CHAS%. In HH of Charles R. Brewster m 42 born ME.

LUCAS, LYDIA, 28, F, (--), M, SC, 519, 512, CHAS%. In HH of George Lucas m 45 mulatto born SC.

LYONS, ANN, 20, F, (--), M, SC, 367, 367, CHAS%.

LYONS, HARRIET, 1, F, (--), M, SC, 367, 367, CHAS%. In HH of Ann Lyons f 20 mulatto born SC.

LYONS, JAMES, 6, M, (--), M, SC, 367, 367, CHAS%. In HH of Ann Lyons f 20 mulatto born SC.

LYONS, THOMAS, 0, M, (--), M, SC, 367, 367, CHAS%. In HH of Ann Lyons f 20 mulatto born SC. Thomas Lyon age 2/12 yr.

M

MACAPPIN, ARIANNA, 12, F, (--), B, SC, 854, 854, ABB. In HH of Milly Macappin 33 born SC.

MACAPPIN, CAROLINE, 4, F, (--), B, SC, 854, 854, ABB. In HH of Milly Macappin 33 born SC.

MACAPPIN, EDNA, 10, F, (--), B, SC, 854, 854, ABB. In HH of Milly Macappin 33 born SC.

MACAPPIN, EMEZURA, 0, F, (--), B, SC, 854, 854, ABB. In HH of Milly Macappin 33 born SC. Emezure Macappin age 5/12 yr.

MACAPPIN, ISAAC, 18, M, Hireling, B, SC, 854, 854, ABB. In HH of Milly Macappin 33 born SC.

MACAPPIN, JOHN, 7, M, (--), B, SC, 854, 854, ABB. In HH of Milly Macappin 33 born SC.

MACAPPIN, MILLY, 33, F, (--), B, SC, 854, 854, ABB.

MAFSON, CAMILLA, 7, F, (--), M, SC, 236, 221, CHAS-. In HH of Pierre J. Mafsow m 49 mulatto born St. Domingo.

MAFSON, CECELIA, 12, F, (--), M, SC, 236, 221, CHAS-. In HH of Pierre J. Mafsow m 49 mulatto born St. Domingo.

MAFSON, ELODIA, 47, F, (--), M, St. Domingo, 236, 221, CHAS-. In HH of Pierre J. Mafson m 49 mulatto born St. Domingo.

MAFSON, JULIET, 20, F, (--), M, SC, 236, 221, CHAS-. In HH of Pierre J. Mafson m 49 mulatto born St. Domingo.

MAFSON, PEDRO, 16, M, Shoemaker, M, SC, 236, 221, CHAS-. In HH of Pierre J. Mafson m 49 mulatto born St. Domingo.

MAFSON, PIERRE J., 49, M, Laborer, M, St. Domingo, 236, 221, CHAS-.

MAIN, FRANCIS, 42, M, Carpenter, M, SC, 117, 117, CHAS%.

MAIN, JAMES, 11, M, (--), M, SC, 117, 117, CHAS%. In HH of Francis Main m 42 mulatto born SC.

MAIN, JULIA, 39, F, (--), M, SC, 117, 117, CHAS%. In HH of Francis Main m 42 mulatto born SC.

MAIN, PAUL, 13, M, (--), M, SC, 117, 117, CHAS%. In HH of Francis Main m 42 mulatto born SC.

MAIRS, GEORGIANA, 1, F, (--), M, SC, 675, 633, CHAS+. In HH of Clainda Simons f 35 black born SC.

MAIRS, MARGARET, 28, F, (--), M, SC, 215, 201, CHAS-. In HH of Laura Purse f 21 mulatto born SC.

MAIRS, SAMUEL, 40, M, Laborer, B, SC, 675, 633, CHAS+. In HH of Clainda Simons f 35 black born SC.

MALLAN, MARY, 56, F, (--), M, St. Domingo, 127, 118, CHAS-. In HH of Thomas W. Malone m 43 born England.

MALLARD, JANE, 34, F, (--), M, SC, 708, 666, CHAS+.

MALLARD, MARY, 28, F, (--), M, SC, 708, 666, CHAS+. In HH of Jane Mallard f 34 mulatto born SC.

MARRION, AMANDA, 9, F, (--), B, SC, 211, 211, ABB. In HH of William Marrion m 33 black born SC.

MARRION, DAVID, 19, M, (--), B, SC, 217, 217, ABB. In HH of John Marrion m 62 black born SC.

MARRION, JAMES, 16, M, (--), B, SC, 217, 217, ABB. In HH of John Marrion m 62 black born SC.

MARRION, JOHN, 62, M, (--), B, SC, 217, 217, ABB.

MARRION, JOHN, 23, M, (--), B, SC, 217, 217, ABB. In HH of John Marrion m 62 black born SC.

MARRION, JOHN, 7, M, (--), B, SC, 211, 211, ABB. In HH of William Marrion m 33 black born SC.

MARRION, JOSEPH, 8, M, (--), B, SC, 217, 217, ABB. In HH of John Marrion m 62 black born SC.

MARRION, JOSEPHINE, 5, F, (--), B, SC, 211, 211, ABB. In HH of William Marrion m 33 black born SC.

MARRION, LEVINIA, 32, F, (--), B, SC, 211, 211, ABB. In HH of William Marrion m 33 black born SC.

MARRION, MARY J., 0, F, (--), B, SC, 211, 211, ABB. In HH of William Marrion m 33 black born SC. Mary J is 1/12 yr.

MARRION, PRISCILLA, 62, F, (--), B, SC, 217, 217, ABB. In HH of John Marrion m 62 black born SC.

MARRION, SARAH, 11, F, (--), B, SC, 211, 211, ABB. In HH of William Marrion m 33 black born SC.

MARRION, SUSAN, 11, F, (--), B, SC, 217, 217, ABB. In HH of John Marrion m 62 black born SC.

MARRION, WILLIAM, 33, M, Farmer, B, SC, 211, 211, ABB.

MARRION, WILLIAM B., 2, M, (--), B, SC, 211, 211, ABB. In HH of William Marrion m 33 black born SC.

MARSH, ABIGAIL, 6, F, (--), M, SC, 171, 175, RICH. In HH of Catherine Marsh f 25 mulatto born SC.

MARSH, CATHERINE, 25, F, (--), M, SC, 171, 175, RICH.

MARSH, JAMES, 2, M, (--), M, SC, 171, 175, RICH. In HH of Catherine Marsh f 25 mulatto born SC.

MARSH, JOSEPH, 4, M, (--), M, SC, 171, 175, RICH. In HH of Catherine Marsh f 25 mulatto born SC.

MARSHAL, FREDERICK, 13, M, Boot maker, M, SC, 1009, 986, CHAS-. In HH of John Lewis m 40 mulatto born SC.

MARSHAL, JOSEPH, 3, M, (--), M, SC, 805, 763, CHAS+. In HH of

Rebecca Thomas f 55 mulatto born SC.

MARSHAL, MARY, 18, F, (--), M, SC, 430, 389, CHAS+. In HH of Saml. Marshal m 39 mulatto born SC.

MARSHAL, SAML., 30, M, Tailor, M, SC, 430, 389, CHAS+.

MARSHAL, THOMAS, 11, M, (--), M, SC, 805, 763, CHAS+. In HH of Rebecca Thomas f 55 mulatto born SC.

MARSHALL, ADOLPHUS, 8, M, (--), M, SC, 1004, 1008, AND. In HH of The Strother f 69 black born SC.

MARSHALL, MARGARET, 20, F, (--), M, SC, 503, 486, CHAS-. In HH of William Marshall m 29 mulatto born SC.

MARSHALL, SUSAN, 28, F, (--), M, SC, 557, 540, CHAS-.

MARSHALL, WILLIAM, 29, M, Barber, M, SC, 503, 486, CHAS-.

MARTIN, ALBERT, 15, M, (--), B, SC, 67, 67, COLL. In HH of John H. Martin m 48 black born SC.

MARTIN, AUGUSTUS, 2, M, (--), B, SC, 68, 68, COLL. In HH of John H. Martin m 27 black born SC.

MARTIN, CAROLINE, 30, F, (--), M, SC, 309, 309, BEAU+.

MARTIN, ELIZABETH, 30, F, (--), M, SC, 442, 400, CHAS.

MARTIN, ELIZABETH, 21, F, (--), M, SC, 67, 67, COLL. In HH of John H. Martin m 48 black born SC.

MARTIN, ELIZABETH, 18, F, (--), M, SC, 217, 195, CHAS. In HH of Robt. Kain m 43 born England.

MARTIN, EMMA, 20, F, (--), B, SC, 612, 605, CHAS%. In HH of Sarah Martin f 50 black born SC.

MARTIN, GEORGE, 70, M, (--), B, SC, 612, 605, CHAS%. In HH of Sarah Martin f 50 black born SC.

MARTIN, JOHN H., 48, M, Tailor, B, SC, 67, 67, COLL.

MARTIN, JOHN H., 27, M, Baker, B, SC, 68, 68, COLL.

MARTIN, JOSEPH, 4, M, (--), B, SC, 68, 68, COLL. In HH of John H. Martin m 27 black born SC.

MARTIN, MARIA, 25, F, (--), B, SC, 68, 68, COLL. In HH of John H. Martin m 27 black born SC.

MARTIN, MARY, 26, F, (--), M, SC, 217, 195, CHAS. In HH of Robt. Kain m 43 born England.

MARTIN, PETER, 21, M, (--), B, SC, 612, 605, CHAS%. In HH of Sarah Martin f 50 black born SC.

MARTIN, SARAH, 50, F, (--), B, SC, 612, 605, CHAS%.

MARTIN, SARAH, 6, F, (--), B, SC, 67, 67, COLL. In HH of John H. Martin m 48 black born SC.

MARTIN, TIMOTHY, 30, M, Laborer, B, SC, 69, 69, MARL. In HH of Alexr. Miller m 50 born SC..

MARTIN, TUCKER, 5, M, (--), B, SC, 2007, 2007, SPART. In HH of John Martin m 67 born SC.

MASHON, CHARLOTTE, 17, F, (--), M, SC, 903, 880, CHAS%. In HH of Rebecca Mashon f 60 mulatto born SC.

MASHON, ELIZABETH, 20, F, (--), M, SC, 903, 880, CHAS%. In HH of Rebecca Mashon f 60 mulatto born SC.

MASHON, REBECCA, 60, F, (--), M, SC, 903, 880, CHAS%.

MASON, ELIZA, 9, F, (--), M, SC, 622, 614, CHAS%. In HH of George Mason m 40 mulatto born SC.

MASON, FRANCES, 12, F, (--), M, SC, 622, 614, CHAS%. In HH of George Mason m 40 mulatto born SC.

MASON, GEORGE, 40, M, Drayman, M, SC, 622, 614, CHAS%.

MASON, GEORGE, 7, M, (--), M, SC, 622, 614, CHAS%. In HH of George Mason m 40 mulatto born SC.

MASON, ISADORA, 2, F, (--), M, SC, 622, 614, CHAS%. In HH of George Mason m 40 mulatto born SC.

MASON, JANE, 41, F, (--), M, SC, 622, 614, CHAS%. In HH of George Mason m 40 mulatto born SC.

MASON, PAULINE, 6, F, (--), M, SC, 622, 614, CHAS%. In HH of George Mason m 40 mulatto born SC.

MASTON, ABRAM, 37, M, (--), B, (-),

14, 14, BEAU#.

MATHEWS, ANN, 35, F, (--), B, SC, 1140, 1119, CHAS%.

MATHEWS, ANNA, 45, F, (--), M, SC, 830, 788, CHAS+. In HH of J.B. Mathews m 47 black born SC.

MATHEWS, CAROLINE, 15, F, (--), M, SC, 41, 41, CHAS%. In HH of Edward Mathews m 43 mulatto born SC.

MATHEWS, CELIA, 8, F, (--), B, SC, 811, 769, CHAS+. In HH of Sarah Mathews f 29 black born SC.

MATHEWS, CHARLOTTE, 89, F, (--), M, SC, 545, 511, CHAS*. In HH of Louisa Mathews f 20 mulatto born SC.

MATHEWS, EDWARD, 43, M, Carpenter, M, SC, 41, 41, CHAS%.

MATHEWS, EDWARD, 30, M, (--), B, SC, 811, 769, CHAS+. In HH of Sarah Mathews f 29 black born SC.

MATHEWS, ELEANORA, 19, F, (--), M, SC, 545, 511, CHAS*. In HH of Louisa Mathews f 20 mulatto born SC.

MATHEWS, EMELINE, 39, F, (--), M, SC, 41, 41, CHAS%. In HH of Edward Mathews m 43 mulatto born SC.

MATHEWS, EMMA, 20, F, (--), B, SC, 571, 563, CHAS%. In HH of Mary Bryant f 50 black born SC.

MATHEWS, HARRIET, 25, F, (--), M, SC, 330, 304, CHAS*. In HH of Mary Legard f 21 mulatto born SC.

MATHEWS, HENRY, 26, M, Livery Stable, M, SC, 545, 511, CHAS*. Occupation: Livery Stable Keeper. In HH of Louisa Mathews f 20 mulatto born SC.

MATHEWS, J.B., 47, M, Tailor, B, SC, 830, 788, CHAS+.

MATHEWS, JAMES, 17, M, Tailor, M, SC, 41, 41, CHAS%. In HH of Edward Mathews m 43 mulatto born SC.

MATHEWS, LOUISA, 20, F, (--), M, SC, 545, 511, CHAS*.

MATHEWS, LUCRETIA, 5, M, (--), B, SC, 811, 769, CHAS+. In HH of Sarah Mathews f 29 black born SC.

MATHEWS, LYDIA, 14, F, (--), B, SC, 811, 769, CHAS+. In HH of Sarah Mathews f 29 black born SC.

MATHEWS, MALCOLM, 9, M, (--), M, SC, 545, 511, CHAS*. In HH of Louisa Mathews f 20 mulatto born SC.

MATHEWS, MARY, 50, F, (--), B, SC, 1132, 1111, CHAS%. In HH of James Fetyan m 35 born Germany.

MATHEWS, MARY, 40, F, (--), B, SC, 571, 563, CHAS%. In HH of Mary Bryant f 50 black born SC.

MATHEWS, MARY, 18, F, (--), M, SC, 830, 788, CHAS+. In HH of J.B. Mathews m 47 black born SC.

MATHEWS, MARY, 15, F, (--), M, SC, 545, 511, CHAS*. In HH of Louisa Mathews f 20 mulatto born SC.

MATHEWS, OGILVIE, 4, M, (--), M, SC, 545, 511, CHAS*. In HH of Louisa Mathews f 20 mulatto born SC.

MATHEWS, PETER, 43, M, Carpenter, B, SC, 571, 563, CHAS%. In HH of Mary Bryant f 50 black born SC.

MATHEWS, PHOEBE, 22, F, (--), B, SC, 441, 408, CHAS*.

MATHEWS, SARAH, 29, F, (--), B, SC, 811, 769, CHAS+.

MATHEWS, THOMAS, 10, M, (--), B, SC, 811, 769, CHAS+. In HH of Sarah Mathews f 29 black born SC.

MATHEWS, WILLIAM, 2, M, (--), M, SC, 330, 304, CHAS*. In HH of Mary Legard f 21 mulatto born SC.

MATTHEWS, MARIA, 12, F, (--), B, SC, 170, 170, CHAS%. In HH of Frances Bland f 50 mulatto born SC.

MAXWELL, ANN, 12, F, (--), M, SC, 1040, 1018, CHAS%. In HH of Stephen Maxwell m 50 mulatto born SC.

MAXWELL, ELLEN R., 9, F, (--), M, SC, 6, 6, CHAS%. In HH of Thomas W. Maxwell m 49 mulatto born SC.

MAXWELL, GEORGE, 7, M, (--), M, SC, 673, 631, CHAS+. In HH of Mary Maxwell f 40 black born SC.

MAXWELL, HARRIET, 10, F, (--), B, SC, 1080, 1102, CHAS%. In HH of Martha Maxwell f 47 black born SC.

MAXWELL, HENRY, 13, F, (--), M, SC, 1040, 1018, CHAS%. In HH of

Stephen Maxwell m 50 mulatto born SC.

MAXWELL, HENRY, 8, M, (--), B, SC, 1080, 1102, CHAS%. In HH of Martha Maxwell f 47 black born SC.

MAXWELL, ISAAC, 2, M, (--), B, SC, 1080, 1102, CHAS%. In HH of Martha Maxwell f 47 black born SC.

MAXWELL, JACOB, 29, M, (--), M, SC, 673, 631, CHAS+. In HH of Mary Maxwell f 40 black born SC.

MAXWELL, JAMES, 40, M, Carpenter, M, Germany {sic}, 348, 331, CHAS-.

MAXWELL, JAMES, 19, M, Tailor, M, Germany {sic}, 348, 331, CHAS-. In HH of James Maxwell m 40 mulatto born Germany {sic}.

MAXWELL, JAMES T., 16, M, Tailor, M, SC, 6, 6, CHAS%. In HH of Thomas W. Maxwell m 49 mulatto born SC.

MAXWELL, JANE, 24, F, (--), M, SC, 551, 510, CHAS+. In HH of Selena Ward f 28 mulatto born SC.

MAXWELL, JOHN, 13, M, (--), M, SC, 6, 6, CHAS%. In HH of Thomas W. Maxwell m 49 mulatto born SC.

MAXWELL, JOHN, 6, M, (--), B, SC, 1080, 1102, CHAS%. In HH of Martha Maxwell f 47 black born SC.

MAXWELL, JOSEPH, 70, M, Fisherman, M, SC, 142, 132, CHAS-.

MAXWELL, LEAH, 16, F, (--), M, Germany {sic}, 348, 331, CHAS-. In HH of James Maxwell m 40 mulatto born Germany {sic}.

MAXWELL, LOUIS, 4, M, (--), B, SC, 1080, 1102, CHAS%. In HH of Martha Maxwell f 47 black born SC.

MAXWELL, LOUISA, 19, F, (--), M, SC, 673, 631, CHAS+. In HH of Mary Maxwell f 40 black born SC.

MAXWELL, MARIA, 18, F, (--), M, SC, 6, 6, CHAS%. In HH of Thomas W. Maxwell m 49 mulatto born SC.

MAXWELL, MARTHA, 47, F, (--), B, SC, 1080, 1102, CHAS%.

MAXWELL, MARTHA, 15, F, (--), M, SC, 1040, 1018, CHAS%. In HH of Stephen Maxwell m 50 mulatto born SC.

MAXWELL, MARY, 40, F, (--), B, SC, 673, 631, CHAS+.

MAXWELL, MARY, 24, F, (--), M, SC, 1040, 1018, CHAS%. In HH of Stephen Maxwell m 50 mulatto born SC.

MAXWELL, MARY, 12, F, (--), B, SC, 1080, 1102, CHAS%. In HH of Martha Maxwell f 47 black born SC.

MAXWELL, MARY JANE, 47, F, (--), M, SC, 6, 6, CHAS%. In HH of Thomas W. Maxwell m 49 mulatto born SC.

MAXWELL, PETER, 6, M, (--), M, SC, 6, 6, CHAS%. In HH of Thomas W. Maxwell m 49 mulatto born SC.

MAXWELL, REBECCA, 50, F, (--), M, Germany {sic}, 348, 331, CHAS-. In HH of James Maxwell m 40 mulatto born Germany {sic}.

MAXWELL, ROBERT J., 14, M, (--), M, SC, 673, 631, CHAS+. In HH of Mary Maxwell f 40 black born SC.

MAXWELL, SAMUEL, 9, M, (--), M, SC, 673, 631, CHAS+. In HH of Mary Maxwell f 40 black born SC.

MAXWELL, SARAH, 14, F, (--), B, SC, 1080, 1102, CHAS%. In HH of Martha Maxwell f 47 black born SC.

MAXWELL, STEPHEN, 50, M, (--), M, SC, 1040, 1018, CHAS%.

MAXWELL, STEPHEN, 28, M, Blacksmith, M, SC, 551, 510, CHAS+. In HH of Selena Ward f 28 mulatto born SC.

MAXWELL, STEPHEN, 25, M, Laborer, B, SC, 675, 633, CHAS+. In HH of Clainda Simons f 35 black born SC.

MAXWELL, THOMAS, 17, M, Carpenter, M, Germany {sic}, 348, 331, CHAS-. In HH of James Maxwell m 40 mulatto born Germany {sic}.

MAXWELL, THOMAS W., 49, M, Tailor, M, SC, 6, 6, CHAS%.

MAXWELL, THURSON, 23, F, (--), M, SC, 1040, 1018, CHAS%. In HH of Stephen Maxwell m 50 mulatto born SC.

MAXWELL, THURSTON, 56, F, (--), M, SC, 1040, 1018, CHAS%. In HH of Stephen Maxwell m 50 mulatto born SC.

MAXWELL, TOBIAS, 45, M, Carpenter, B, SC, 1080, 1102, CHAS%. In HH of Martha Maxwell f 47 black born SC.

MAYRANT, EDWARD, 7, M, (--), M, SC, 516, 499, CHAS-. In HH of Maria Mayrant f 40 mulatto born SC.

MAYRANT, EDWARD, 6, M, (--), M, SC, 810, 768, CHAS+. In HH of Amelia Gardner f 13 black born SC.

MAYRANT, ELOISE, 1, F, (--), M, SC, 516, 499, CHAS-. In HH of Maria Mayrant f 40 mulatto born SC.

MAYRANT, JAMES, 19, M, (--), M, SC, 810, 768, CHAS+. In HH of Amelia Gardner f 13 black born SC.

MAYRANT, JAMES, 10, M, (--), M, SC, 516, 499, CHAS-. In HH of Maria Mayrant f 40 mulatto born SC.

MAYRANT, JOHN, 45, M, (--), B, SC, 87, 87, CHAS!.

MAYRANT, JOSEPHINE, 5, F, (--), M, SC, 516, 499, CHAS-. In HH of Maria Mayrant f 40 mulatto born SC.

MAYRANT, JULIANA, 16, F, (--), M, SC, 516, 499, CHAS-. In HH of Maria Mayrant f 40 mulatto born SC.

MAYRANT, LOUISA, 8, F, (--), M, SC, 810, 768, CHAS+. In HH of Amelia Gardner f 13 black born SC.

MAYRANT, LYDIA, 28, F, (--), M, SC, 810, 768, CHAS+. In HH of Amelia Gardner f 13 black born SC.

MAYRANT, MARGARET, 4, F, (--), M, SC, 454, 411, CHAS. In HH of Susan Williams f 35 black born SC.

MAYRANT, MARIA, 40, F, (--), M, SC, 516, 499, CHAS-.

MAYRANT, MARIA, 40, F, (--), M, SC, 454, 411, CHAS. In HH of Susan Williams f 35 black born SC.

MAYRANT, SARAH, 12, F, (--), M, SC, 810, 768, CHAS+. In HH of Amelia Gardner f 13 black born SC.

MAYRANT, SOPHIA, 13, F, (--), M, SC, 516, 499, CHAS-. In HH of Maria Mayrant f 40 mulatto born SC.

MAYS, PEGGY, 65, F, (--), B, SC, 393, 357, CHAS.

MAZYCK, PETER, 19, M, Barber, B, SC, 156, 143, CHAS*. In HH of Elizabeth Holmes f 40 mulatto born SC.

MCBETH, JULIA, 18, F, (--), B, SC, 33, 33, CHAS%. In HH of Maria Robertson f 40 black born SC.

MCBETH, SARAH, 14, F, (--), B, SC, 33, 33, CHAS%. In HH of Maria Robertson f 40 black born SC.

MCBRIDE, MARY, 46, F, (--), M, SC, 365, 348, CHAS-.

MCCALE, MARY ANN, 28, F, (--), M, SC, 174, 160, CHAS*.

MCCALL, EMMA, 30, F, (--), M, SC, 1123, 1101, CHAS%.

MCCALL, EMMA, 8, F, (--), M, SC, 1123, 1101, CHAS%. In HH of Emma McCall f 30 mulatto born SC.

MCCALL, MARIA, 11, F, (--), M, SC, 1123, 1101, CHAS%. In HH of Emma McCall f 30 mulatto born SC.

MCCALL, MARIA ANN, 19, F, (--), M, SC, 243, 228, CHAS-. In HH of Elizabeth McLindsay f 30 mulatto born SC.

MCCANNA, DINAH, 80, F, (--), M, SC, 499, 457, CHAS+. In HH of Francis Scott m 38 mulatto born SC.

MCCAPIN, SAMUEL, 17, M, Hireling, B, SC, 989, 989, ABB.

MCCARTY, SARAH, 2, F, (--), M, SC, 265, 265, BEAU+. In HH of John McCarty m 45 born Ireland.

MCCARTY, SARAH DANUR, 20, F, (--), B, SC, 265, 265, BEAU+. In HH of John McCarty m 45 born Ireland.

MCCARVER, AMELIA J., 6, F, (--), M, SC, 171, 171, YORK*. In HH of Sarah Wright f 30 mulatto born York Dist., SC.

MCCARVER, HARVEY, 4, M, (--), M, SC, 171, 171, YORK*. In HH of Sarah Wright f 30 mulatto born York Dist., SC.

MCCARVER, MOSES, 19, M, (--), M, SC, 171, 171, YORK*. In HH of Sarah Wright f 30 mulatto born York Dist., SC.

MCCAULEY, EMMA, 27, F, (--), M, SC, 915, 895, CHAS-. In HH of Chloe

Bowengen f 60 mulatto born SC.

MCCAULEY, JAMES, 9, M, (--), M, SC, 915, 895, CHAS-. In HH of Chloe Bowengen f 60 mulatto born SC.

MCCAULEY, JOHN, 5, M, (--), M, SC, 915, 895, CHAS-. In HH of Chloe Bowengen f 60 mulatto born SC.

MCCHIRKIN, FRANKY, 32, M, (--), B, SC, 245, 245, YORK.

MCCLANE, DIANA, 50, F, (--), M, SC, 129, 120, CHAS+. In HH of Hannah Dascher f 22 born Germany.

MCCLURY, DOLLY, 70, F, (--), B, VA, 1010, 1010, ABB. In HH of Jim McClury m 60 black born VA.

MCCOPPIN, ISAAC, 60, M, Wagoner, B, SC, 995, 995, ABB.

MCCOPPIN, JERUSHA, 16, F, (--), B, SC, 995, 995, ABB. In HH of Isaac McCoppin m 60 black born SC.

MCCOPPIN, JOHN, 23, M, Hireling, B, SC, 1020, 1020, ABB.

MCCOPPIN, NANCY, 50, F, (--), B, SC, 995, 995, ABB. In HH of Isaac McCoppin m 60 black born SC.

MCCOY, MARY MRS., 16, F, (--), M, SC, 49, 49, CHAS2. In HH of John McCoy m 22 born SC.

MCDANIEL, CEASAR, 100, M, None, B, SC, 580, 580, MARL. In HH of Mary Jackson f 54 mulatto born SC.

MCDANIEL, MARTHA, 84, F, (--), B, SC, 580, 580, MARL. In HH of Mary Jackson f 54 mulatto born SC.

MCDOLE, ANN, 5, F, (--), M, SC, 1230, 1235, MAR. In HH of Easter McDole f 41 mulatto born SC.

MCDOLE, EASTER, 41, F, (--), M, SC, 1230, 1235, MAR.

MCDOLE, EASTER, 14, F, (--), M, SC, 1230, 1235, MAR. In HH of Easter McDole f 41 mulatto born SC.

MCDOLE, ELI, 9, M, (--), M, SC, 1230, 1235, MAR. In HH of Easter McDole f 41 mulatto born SC.

MCDOLE, ELIZA, 10, F, (--), M, SC, 1230, 1235, MAR. In HH of Easter McDole f 41 mulatto born SC.

MCDOLE, ELIZABETH, 18, F, (--), M, SC, 1230, 1235, MAR. In HH of Easter McDole f 41 mulatto born SC.

MCDOLE, JANE, 12, F, (--), M, SC, 1230, 1235, MAR. In HH of Easter McDole f 41 mulatto born SC.

MCDOLE, MARY, 7, F, (--), M, SC, 1230, 1235, MAR. In HH of Easter McDole f 41 mulatto born SC.

MCDOLE, SAMUEL, 16, M, (--), M, SC, 1230, 1235, MAR. In HH of Easter McDole f 41 mulatto born SC.

MCDOLE, WILLIAM, 20, M, (--), M, SC, 1230, 1235, MAR. In HH of Easter McDole f 41 mulatto born SC.

MCDONALD, REBECCA, 27, F, (--), M, SC, 48, 48, GEOR.

MCDOW, B., 2, M, (--), B, SC, 101, 101, LANC*. In HH of Jane McDow f 54 mulatto born SC.

MCDOW, C., 25, M, Farmer, B, SC, 103, 103, LANC*.

MCDOW, C., 9, M, (--), B, SC, 101, 101, LANC*. In HH of Jane McDow f 54 mulatto born SC.

MCDOW, F., 3, F, (--), B, SC, 34, 34, LANC. In HH of Minerva McDow f 22 black born SC.

MCDOW, J., 27, F, (--), B, SC, 103, 103, LANC*. In HH of C. McDow m 25 black born SC.

MCDOW, J., 12, F, (--), B, SC, 101, 101, LANC*. In HH of Jane McDow f 54 mulatto born SC.

MCDOW, JANE, 54, F, Farmer, M, SC, 101, 101, LANC*.

MCDOW, JAS., 5, M, (--), B, SC, 34, 34, LANC. In HH of Minerva McDow f 22 black born SC.

MCDOW, M., 16, F, (--), M, SC, 101, 101, LANC*. In HH of Jane McDow f 54 mulatto born SC.

MCDOW, M.J., 1, F, (--), B, SC, 34, 34, LANC. In HH of Minerva McDow f 22 black born SC.

MCDOW, MINERVA, 22, F, (--), B, SC, 34, 34, LANC.

MCDOW, W., 15, M, (--), B, SC, 101, 101, LANC*. In HH of Jane McDow f

54 mulatto born SC.

MCDOWELL, HARRIET, 30, F, (--), B, SC, 136, 136, CHAS%. In HH of Lucy Williams f 40 mulatto born SC.

MCDOWELL, JOHN, 1, M, (--), B, SC, 136, 136, CHAS%. In HH of Lucy Williams f 40 mulatto born SC.

MCDOWELL, MARIA, 3, F, (--), B, SC, 136, 136, CHAS%. In HH of Lucy Williams f 40 mulatto born SC.

MCGEE, HENRY, 18, M, Laborer, M, SC, 509, 509, MARL. In HH of Moses Quick m 33 born SC.

MCGILERAY, MARY C., 3, F, (--), M, SC, 344, 318, CHAS*. In HH of Mary Gesiness f 55 born SC.

MCGILRAY, JANE, 30, F, (--), M, SC, 118, 118, CHAS%. In HH of John McGilray m 37 mulatto born SC.

MCGILRAY, JOHN, 37, M, Carpenter, M, SC, 118, 118, CHAS%.

MCGILRAY, WILLIAM C., 14, M, (--), M, SC, 118, 118, CHAS%. In HH of John McGilray m 37 mulatto born SC.

MCGILROY, THOMAS, 40, M, Fisherman, B, SC, 66, 60, CHAS-. In HH of R.W. Seymour m 45 born SC.

MCGILVRAY, JOSEPH, 40, M, (--), B, SC, 375, 337, CHAS+.

MCGOMERY, LAVINCA, 30, F, (--), B, SC, 26, 26, CHAS2.

MCGREER, ALFRED, 30, M, Hireling, M, SC, 2252, 2252, ABB. In HH of Thomas J. Roberts m 37 white born SC.

MCGUFFIE, CAROLINE, 10, F, (--), M, SC, 146, 136, CHAS-. In HH of Julia Barnet f 50 mulatto born SC.

MCGUFFIE, JAMES, 36, M, Carpenter, B, SC, 146, 136, CHAS-. In HH of Julia Barnet f 50 mulatto born SC.

MCGUFFIE, JAMES EDWD., 16, M, Carpenter, B, SC, 146, 136, CHAS-. In HH of Julia Barnet f 50 mulatto born SC.

MCGUFFIE, MARGARET, 13, F, (--), M, SC, 146, 136, CHAS-. In HH of Julia Barnet f 50 mulatto born SC.

MCGUFFIE, MARY ANN, 15, F, (--), M, SC, 146, 136, CHAS-. In HH of Julia

Barnet f 50 mulatto born SC.

MCGUFFIE, ROSA, 30, F, (--), B, SC, 146, 136, CHAS-. In HH of Julia Barnet f 50 mulatto born SC.

MCGUFFY, EDWARD, 40, M, Carpenter, B, SC, 32, 32, CHAS%.

MCGUFFY, JOANA, 9, F, (--), B, SC, 32, 32, CHAS%. In HH of Edward McGuffy m 40 black born SC.

MCGUFFY, LEWIS, 12, M, (--), B, SC, 32, 32, CHAS%. In HH of Edward McGuffy m 40 black born SC.

MCGUFFY, MARGARET, 30, F, (--), B, SC, 32, 32, CHAS%. In HH of Edward McGuffy m 40 black born SC.

MCGUFFY, MARY E., 14, F, (--), B, SC, 32, 32, CHAS%. In HH of Edward McGuffy m 40 black born SC.

MCHENRY, MARTHA S., 16, F, (--), M, SC, 189, 189, ABB. In HH of Samuel Abny m 52 born SC.

MCKEE, BENJAMIN, 25, M, (--), B, SC, 302, 302, CHAS%. In HH of James Williamson m 25 mulatto born SC.

MCKEE, JAMES T., 43, M, (--), B, SC, 65, 65, CHAS%. In HH of Mary McKee f 46 black born SC.

MCKEE, LEWIS, 14, M, (--), B, SC, 65, 65, CHAS%. In HH of Mary McKee f 46 black born SC.

MCKEE, MARTHA, 20, F, (--), B, SC, 65, 65, CHAS%. In HH of Mary McKee f 46 black born SC.

MCKEE, MARY, 46, F, (--), B, SC, 65, 65, CHAS%.

MCKENNY, NANCY, 18, F, (--), M, GA, 107, 107, ABB. In HH of Francis Wideman m 35 born SC.

MCKENNY, ORRY, 12, F, (--), M, GA, 107, 107, ABB. In HH of Francis Wideman m 35 born SC.

MCKENSIE, ANTHONY, 40, M, Wheelwright, B, SC, 330, 330, CHAS%.

MCKENZIE, BRIDY, 50, M, Barber, B, SC, 233, 233, CHAS%.

MCKILDUFF, HENRY, 7, M, (--), M, SC, 520, 520, HORR. In HH of Deliah McCliduff, f 65 born SC.

MCKINCH, T., 27, M, Tailor, M, SC, 782, 782, CHES. In HH of Daniel Canoll m 30 Tailor born SC.

MCKINLAY, ALBERT, 9, M, (--), M, SC, 498, 481, CHAS-. In HH of Martha McKinlay f 60 mulatto born SC.

MCKINLAY, ARCHIBALD, 6, M, (--), M, SC, 504, 487, CHAS-. In HH of William McKinlay m 25 mulatto born SC.

MCKINLAY, DIANA, 30, F, (--), M, SC, 504, 487, CHAS-. In HH of William McKinlay m 25 mulatto born SC.

MCKINLAY, ELIZABETH, 25, F, (--), M, SC, 498, 481, CHAS-. In HH of Martha McKinlay f 60 mulatto born SC.

MCKINLAY, ELVIRA, 8, F, (--), M, SC, 504, 487, CHAS-. In HH of William McKinlay m 25 mulatto born SC.

MCKINLAY, EMMA, 1, F, (--), M, SC, 498, 481, CHAS-. In HH of Martha McKinlay f 60 mulatto born SC.

MCKINLAY, FRANCIS, 4, M, (--), M, SC, 504, 487, CHAS-. In HH of William McKinlay m 25 mulatto born SC.

MCKINLAY, GEORGE T., 10, M, (--), M, SC, 504, 487, CHAS-. In HH of William McKinlay m 25 mulatto born SC.

MCKINLAY, JANE, 7, F, (--), M, SC, 498, 481, CHAS-. In HH of Martha McKinlay f 60 mulatto born SC.

MCKINLAY, JOHN, 2, M, (--), M, SC, 504, 487, CHAS-. In HH of William McKinlay m 25 mulatto born SC.

MCKINLAY, MARTHA, 60, F, (--), M, SC, 498, 481, CHAS-.

MCKINLAY, MARY, 14, F, (--), M, SC, 504, 487, CHAS-. In HH of William McKinlay m 25 mulatto born SC.

MCKINLAY, SUSAN, 5, F, (--), M, SC, 498, 481, CHAS-. In HH of Martha McKinlay f 60 mulatto born SC.

MCKINLAY, THOMAS, 27, M, Tailor, M, SC, 498, 481, CHAS-. In HH of Martha McKinlay f 60 mulatto born SC.

MCKINLAY, WILLIAM, 25, M, Tailor, M, SC, 504, 487, CHAS-.

MCKINLAY, WILLIAM J., 12, M, (--), M, SC, 504, 487, CHAS-. In HH of William McKinlay m 25 mulatto born SC.

MCKINLEY, ARCHIBALD, 30, M, Tailor, M, SC, 285, 285, BEAU+.

MCKINLEY, ARCHIBALD, 25, M, Tailor, M, SC, 491, 491, BEAU-.

MCKINLEY, ARCHIBALD, 4, M, (--), M, SC, 285, 285, BEAU+. In HH of Archibald McKinley m 30 mulatto born SC.

MCKINLEY, J. MORRISON, 0, M, (--), M, SC, 285, 285, BEAU+. In HH of Archibald McKinley m 30 mulatto born SC. J. Morrison McKinley 6/12 yr.

MCKINLEY, JOHN, 14, M, (--), M, SC, 491, 491, BEAU-. IN HH of Archibald McKinley m 25 mulatto born SC.

MCKINLEY, MARY, 6, F, (--), M, SC, 285, 285, BEAU+. In HH of Archibald McKinley m 30 mulatto born SC.

MCKINLEY, SARAH, 26, F, (--), M, SC, 285, 285, BEAU+. In HH of Archibald McKinley m 30 mulatto born SC.

MCKINLEY, VALERIA, 2, F, (--), M, SC, 285, 285, BEAU+. In HH of Archibald McKinley m 30 mulatto born SC.

MCKINNY, JOHN H., 14, M, (--), M, SC, 502, 502, CHFD. In HH of Sarah Reed f 61 mulatto born SC.

MCKINNY, VINCENT, 29, M, Hireling, M, SC, 914, 914, ABB.

MCKNIGHT, DAPHNEY, 18, F, (--), M, SC, 99, 99, CHAS%. In HH of Susan Ford f 50 black born SC.

MCKNIGHT, EDWARD, 15, M, (--), M, SC, 99, 99, CHAS%. In HH of Susan Ford f 50 black born SC.

MCKNIGHT, FLORA, 46, F, (--), B, SC, 99, 99, CHAS%. In HH of Susan Ford f 50 black born SC.

MCKNIGHT, FORTUNE, 12, F, (--), M, SC, 99, 99, CHAS%. In HH of Susan Ford f 50 black born SC.

MCKNIGHT, MILTON, 42, M, (--),

M, SC, 99, 99, CHAS%. In HH of Susan Ford f 50 black born SC.

MCKNIGHT, SARAH, 8, F, (--), M, SC, 99, 99, CHAS%. In HH of Susan Ford f 50 black born SC.

MCLEAN, ALONZO, 0, M, (--), M, SC, 543, 509, CHAS*. In HH of Stephen McLean m 50 mulatto born SC. Alonzo McLean age 7/12 yr.

MCLEAN, CATHERINE, 36, F, (--), M, SC, 543, 509, CHAS*. In HH of Stephen McLean m 50 mulatto born SC.

MCLEAN, JULIA, 3, F, (--), M, SC, 543, 509, CHAS*. In HH of Stephen McLean m 50 mulatto born SC.

MCLEAN, MARGARET, 12, F, (--), M, SC, 543, 509, CHAS*. In HH of Stephen McLean m 50 mulatto born SC.

MCLEAN, MARIA, 5, F, (--), M, SC, 543, 509, CHAS*. In HH of Stephen McLean m 50 mulatto born SC.

MCLEAN, STEPHEN, 50, M, Carpenter, M, SC, 543, 509, CHAS*.

MCLEHANY, GEORGIANA, 1, F, (--), B, SC, 39, 40, ORNG+. In HH of Daniel Kitterell m 44 born SC.

MCLEHANY, HENRITTA, 3, F, (--), B, SC, 39, 40, ORNG+. In HH of Daniel Kitterell m 44 born SC.

MCLEHANY, J., 60, M, Farmer, M, SC, 967, 968, ORNG+.

MCLEHANY, JACOB, 17, M, (?), B, SC, 39, 40, ORNG+. In HH of Daniel Kitterell m 44 born SC.

MCLEHANY, JANE, 30, F, (--), B, SC, 39, 40, ORNG+. In HH of Daniel Kitterell m 44 born SC.

MCLEHANY, JOHN, 5, M, (--), B, SC, 39, 40, ORNG+. In HH of Daniel Kitterell m 44 born SC.

MCLINDSAY, ELIZABETH, 30, F, (--), M, SC, 243, 228, CHAS-.

MCLURKIN, ANNA, 16, F, (--), B, SC, 640, 640, CHES. In HH of Len McLurkin 23 m Black born SC.

MCLURKIN, ARING, 50, F, (--), B, SC, 640, 640, CHES. In HH of Len McLurkin 23 m Black born SC.

MCLURKIN, BETSEY, 28, F, (--), B,

SC, 640, 640, CHES. In HH of Len McLurkin 23 m Black born SC.

MCLURKIN, EMELINE, 12, F, (--), B, SC, 640, 640, CHES. In HH of Len McLurkin 23 m Black born SC.

MCLURKIN, J.J., 10, M, (--), B, SC, 640, 640, CHES. In HH of Len McLurkin 23 m Black born SC.

MCLURKIN, JAMES, 22, M, Farmer, B, SC, 640, 640, CHES. In HH of Len McLurkin 23 m Black born SC.

MCLURKIN, JANE, 3, F, (--), B, SC, 640, 640, CHES. In HH of Len McLurkin 23 m Black born SC.

MCLURKIN, LEN, 23, M, Farmer, B, SC, 640, 640, CHES.

MCLURKIN, M.P., 7, F, (--), B, SC, 640, 640, CHES. In HH of Len McLurkin 23 m Black born SC.

MCLURKIN, MARGARET, 14, F, (--), B, SC, 640, 640, CHES. In HH of Len McLurkin 23 m Black born SC.

MCLURKIN, T.L., 1, M, (--), B, SC, 640, 640, CHES. In HH of Len McLurkin 23 m Black born SC.

MCMANUS, A., 4, M, (--), M, SC, 531, 531, LANC*. In HH of Green McManus m 35 mulatto born SC.

MCMANUS, C., 7, M, (--), M, SC, 531, 531, LANC*. In HH of Green McManus m 35 mulatto born SC.

MCMANUS, C.M., 10, F, (--), M, SC, 531, 531, LANC*. In HH of Green McManus m 35 mulatto born SC.

MCMANUS, D.M., 30, F, (--), M, SC, 531, 531, LANC*. In HH of Green McManus m 35 mulatto born SC.

MCMANUS, GREEN, 35, M, Miller, M, SC, 531, 531, LANC*.

MCMANUS, H., 0, M, (--), M, SC, 531, 531, LANC*. In HH of Green McManus m 35 mulatto born SC. H. McManus 6/12 yr.

MCMANUS, S., 8, F, (--), M, SC, 531, 531, LANC*. In HH of Green McManus m 35 mulatto born SC.

MCNEEL, SARAH, 33, F, (--), M, SC, 214, 200, CHAS-.

MCNEILL, ELIZA S., 40, F, (--), M,

SC, 237, 212, CHAS*. In HH of John Lee McNeill m 50 mulatto born SC.

MCNEILL, GEORGE, 19, M, Engineer, M, SC, 237, 212, CHAS*. In HH of John Lee McNeill m 50 mulatto born SC.

MCNEILL, HENRIETTA, 79, F, (--), M, SC, 73, 71, CHAS*.

MCNEILL, JOHN LEE, 50, M, Confectioner, M, SC, 237, 212, CHAS*.

MCNEILL, JOSEPHINE, 12, F, (--), M, SC, 237, 212, CHAS*. In HH of John Lee McNeill m 50 mulatto born SC.

MCNEILL, JULIUS, 20, M, Engineer, M, SC, 237, 212, CHAS*. In HH of John Lee McNeill m 50 mulatto born SC.

MCNEILL, RICHARD ALEXDR., 6, M, (--), M, SC, 237, 212, CHAS*. In HH of John Lee McNeill m 50 mulatto born SC.

MCNEILL, ROSAMOND, 17, F, (--), M, SC, 237, 212, CHAS*. In HH of John Lee McNeill m 50 mulatto born SC.

MCNEILL, SARAH ANN, 22, F, (--), M, SC, 237, 212, CHAS*. In HH of John Lee McNeill m 50 mulatto born SC.

MCNEILL, WM. ALONZO, 8, M, (--), M, SC, 237, 212, CHAS*. In HH of John Lee McNeill m 50 mulatto born SC.

MCNELLAGE, CAROLINE, 13, F, (--), M, SC, 36, 33, CHAS-. In HH of Anna Lewis f 28 mulatto born SC.

MCNELLAGE, ELIZA, 30, F, (--), M, SC, 36, 33, CHAS-. In HH of Anna Lewis f 28 mulatto born SC.

MCNELLAGE, JAMES, 9, M, (--), M, SC, 36, 33, CHAS-. In HH of Anna Lewis f 28 mulatto born SC.

MCNINCH, JUDO, 43, F, (--), B, VA, 245, 245, CHES.

MCWICKER, EMILY, 0, F, (--), M, SC, 639, 631, CHAS%. In HH of Louisa McWicker f 25 mulatto born SC. Emily McWicker age 4/12 yr.

MCWICKER, JULIA, 4, F, (--), M, SC, 639, 631, CHAS%. In HH of Louisa McWicker f 25 mulatto born SC.

MCWICKER, LOUISA, 25, F, (--), M, SC, 639, 631, CHAS%.

MCWICKER, MARTHA, 9, F, (--), M, SC, 639, 631, CHAS%. In HH of Louisa McWicker f 25 mulatto born SC.

MCWICKER, MARY, 6, F, (--), M, SC, 639, 631, CHAS%. In HH of Louisa McWicker f 25 mulatto born SC.

MCWICKER, THOMAS, 10, M, (--), M, SC, 639, 631, CHAS%. In HH of Louisa McWicker f 25 mulatto born SC.

MCWICKER, WILLIAM, 2, M, (--), M, SC, 639, 631, CHAS%. In HH of Louisa McWicker f 25 mulatto born SC.

MEANS, GABRIEL, 18, M, Laborer, M, SC, 87, 87, COLL+. In HH of Elijah Patrick m 35 mulatto born SC. Charles sex f {sic}.

MERCHANT, ADOLPHUS, 1, M, (--), M, SC, 301, 301, CHAS%. In HH of Benjamin Merchant m 20 mulatto born SC.

MERCHANT, BENJAMIN, 20, M, (--), M, SC, 301, 301, CHAS%.

MERRELL, AMELIA, 6, F, (--), M, SC, 721, 712, CHAS%. In HH of Sarah Merrell f 36 mulatto born SC.

MERRELL, ANN, 27, F, (--), M, SC, 467, 425, CHAS+. In HH of Charlotte Williams f 62 mulatto born SC.

MERRELL, JOSHUA, 32, M, Carpenter, M, SC, 721, 712, CHAS%. In HH of Sarah Merrell f 36 mulatto born SC.

MERRELL, LESLIE, 5, M, (--), M, SC, 467, 425, CHAS+. In HH of Charlotte Williams f 62 mulatto born SC.

MERRELL, SARAH, 36, F, (--), M, SC, 721, 712, CHAS%.

MICHAELS, ISABELLA, 27, F, (--), M, SC, 80, 90, CHAS. In HH of Betty Wilson f 80 black born Africa.

MICHAELS, JOHN, 11, M, (--), M, SC, 80, 90, CHAS. In HH of Betty Wilson f 80 black born Africa.

MICHEL, ELLEN, 82, F, (--), B, SC, 335, 334, CHAS%. In HH of Julia Michel f 20 black born SC.

MICHEL, JULIA, 20, F, (--), B, SC, 335, 334, CHAS%.

MICHEL, WILLIAM, 1, M, (--), B,

SC, 335, 334, CHAS%. In HH of Julia Michel f 20 black born SC.

MICHOUN, GIRL, 1, F, (--), M, SC, 667, 667, UNION. In HH of Monroe Michoun m 24 mulatto born SC.

MICHOUN, MONROE, 24, M, (--), M, SC, 667, 667, UNION.

MICHOUN, NANCY, 24, F, (--), M, SC, 667, 667, UNION. In HH of Monroe Michoun m 24 mulatto born SC.

MICK, HARRIET, 25, F, (--), M, SC, 339, 339, CHAS%. In HH of Samuel Mick m 28 black born SC.

MICK, JANE, 2, F, (--), M, SC, 339, 339, CHAS%. In HH of Samuel Mick m 28 black born SC.

MICK, MARY, 1, F, (--), M, SC, 339, 339, CHAS%. In HH of Samuel Mick m 28 black born SC.

MICK, SAMUEL, 28, M, Tailor, B, SC, 339, 339, CHAS%.

MICKEY, EDWARD, 32, M, Tailor, M, SC, 270, 272, AND. In HH of Elam Sharp m 29 white born SC.

MICKEY, FANNY, 6, F, (--), B, SC, 270, 272, AND. In HH of Elam Sharp m 29 white born SC.

MIDDLETON, ?, 12, M, (--), M, SC, 11, 11, CHAS#. In HH of Mrs. McDowall f 78 born SC.

MIDDLETON, CLEMINTINE, 2, F, (--), M, SC, 340, 323, CHAS-. In HH of Harry Middleton m 30 mulatto born SC.

MIDDLETON, DANIEL, 6, M, (--), B, SC, 166, 166, CHAS%. In HH of Isaac Perry m 30 black born SC.

MIDDLETON, EUDORA, 5, F, (--), M, SC, 340, 323, CHAS-. In HH of Harry Middleton m 30 mulatto born SC.

MIDDLETON, GEORGE, 15, M, (--), M, SC, 340, 323, CHAS-. In HH of Harry Middleton m 30 mulatto born SC.

MIDDLETON, HARRY, 30, M, (--), M, SC, 340, 323, CHAS-.

MIDDLETON, JOANA, 10, F, (--), M, SC, 340, 323, CHAS-. In HH of Harry Middleton m 30 mulatto born SC.

MIDDLETON, JOHN, 18, M, (--), B, SC, 166, 166, CHAS%. In HH of Isaac

Perry m 30 black born SC.

MIDDLETON, JULIA, 17, F, (--), M, SC, 340, 323, CHAS-. In HH of Harry Middleton m 30 mulatto born SC.

MIDDLETON, LINDA, 12, F, (--), M, SC, 340, 323, CHAS-. In HH of Harry Middleton m 30 mulatto born SC.

MIDDLETON, LOUIS, 8, M, (--), M, SC, 340, 323, CHAS-. In HH of Harry Middleton m 30 mulatto born SC.

MIDDLETON, RACHAEL, 4, F, (--), B, SC, 166, 166, CHAS%. In HH of Isaac Perry m 30 black born SC.

MIDDLETON, ROSETTA, 27, F, (--), M, SC, 340, 323, CHAS-. In HH of Harry Middleton m 30 mulatto born SC.

MIDDLETON, SYLVA, 40, F, (--), B, SC, 165, 165, CHAS%. In HH of John B. Otten m 29 born Germany.

MIKELL, CHARLES, 30, M, Stevedore, M, SC, 298, 275, CHAS+. In HH of Henry Davis m 28 born Germany.

MILES, ANNA, 12, F, (--), B, SC, 407, 380, CHAS*. In HH of Lucretia Miles f 35 black born SC.

MILES, JOSEPH, 12, M, (--), M, SC, 353, 353, CHAS%. In HH of Sarah Hemetry f 56 mulatto born SC.

MILES, LILOY, 50, F, (--), M, SC, 353, 353, CHAS%. In HH of Sarah Hemetry f 56 mulatto born SC.

MILES, LUCRETIA, 35, F, (--), B, SC, 407, 380, CHAS*.

MILES, MARGARET, 10, F, (--), M, SC, 353, 353, CHAS%. In HH of Sarah Hemetry f 56 mulatto born SC.

MILES, MARY, 65, F, (--), M, SC, 284, 268, CHAS-. In HH of John Oliver m 50 mulatto born SC.

MILES, MARY, 16, F, (--), M, SC, 941, 921, CHAS-. In HH of Joshua Mishaw m 27 mulatto born SC.

MILES, SUSAN, 5, F, (--), M, SC, 353, 353, CHAS%. In HH of Sarah Hemetry f 56 mulatto born SC.

MILLER, A., 40, M, Ginmaker, M, SC, 1225, 1225, SUMT. In HH of Reubin Ellison m 29 mulatto born SC.

MILLER, ANNA, 10, F, (--), M, SC,

439, 436, CHAS%. In HH of Eliza Miller f 30 mulatto born SC.

MILLER, CAROLINE, 30, F, (--), M, SC, 233, 238, RICH+.

MILLER, DAVID, 23, M, Planter, M, SC, 308, 314, RICH+. In HH of Elizabeth Miller f 73 mulatto born SC.

MILLER, DENNIS, 24, M, (--), M, SC, 453, 453, FAIR. In HH of H.J. Lyles m 33 born SC.

MILLER, ELIZA, 48, F, (--), M, SC, 592, 574, CHAS-.

MILLER, ELIZA, 30, F, (--), M, SC, 439, 436, CHAS%.

MILLER, ELIZABETH, 73, F, (--), M, SC, 308, 314, RICH+.

MILLER, ELIZABETH, 56, F, (--), B, SC, 811, 794, CHAS%.

MILLER, ELIZABETH, 35, F, (--), B, SC, 701, 702, FAIR. In HH of Isaac Miller m 70 black born SC.

MILLER, ELIZABETH, 22, F, (--), B, SC, 269, 275, RICH+. In HH of Jonas Miller Sr. m 35 black born SC.

MILLER, EMMA R., 5, F, (--), M, SC, 308, 314, RICH+. In HH of Elizabeth Miller f 73 mulatto born SC.

MILLER, GABRILLA, 22, F, (--), M, SC, 592, 574, CHAS-. In HH of Eliza Miller f 48 mulatto born SC.

MILLER, GEORGIANA, 11, F, (--), M, SC, 1085, 1062, CHAS-. In HH of Sally Johnson f 60 mulatto born SC.

MILLER, ISAAC, 70, M, (--), B, SC, 701, 702, FAIR.

MILLER, ISAAC, 18, M, (--), B, SC, 701, 702, FAIR. In HH of Isaac Miller m 70 black born SC.

MILLER, JAMES, 5, M, (--), M, SC, 439, 436, CHAS%. In HH of Eliza Miller f 30 mulatto born SC.

MILLER, JANE, 31, F, (--), B, SC, 811, 794, CHAS%. In HH of Elizabeth Miller f 56 black born SC.

MILLER, JANE, 19, F, (--), M, SC, 592, 574, CHAS-. In HH of Eliza Miller f 48 mulatto born SC.

MILLER, JEPE, 7, M, (--), M, SC,

233, 238, RICH+. In HH of Caroline Miller f 30 mulatto born SC.

MILLER, JOHN, 10, M, (--), M, SC, 112, 112, COLL+. In HH of Thos. Miller m 38 mulatto born SC.

MILLER, JOHN, 2, M, (--), M, SC, 308, 314, RICH+. In HH of Elizabeth Miller f 73 mulatto born SC.

MILLER, JOHN, 2, M, (--), M, SC, 233, 238, RICH+. In HH of Caroline Miller f 30 mulatto born SC.

MILLER, JONAS, 10, M, (--), M, SC, 233, 238, RICH+. In HH of Caroline Miller f 30 mulatto born SC.

MILLER, JONAS SR., 25, M, Planter, B, SC, 269, 275, RICH+.

MILLER, JOSEPHINE, 12, F, (--), M, SC, 112, 112, COLL+. In HH of Thos. Miller m 38 mulatto born SC.

MILLER, KELLY, 20, M, (--), B, SC, 701, 702, FAIR. In HH of Isaac Miller m 70 black born SC.

MILLER, LOUISA, 6, F, (--), B, SC, 210, 214, RICH+. In HH of John R.F. Tilghman m 50 born SC.

MILLER, LOUISA, 4, F, (--), M, SC, 233, 238, RICH+. In HH of Caroline Miller f 30 mulatto born SC.

MILLER, MARGARET, 27, F, (--), B, SC, 507, 522, RICH.

MILLER, MARGARET, 0, F, (--), M, SC, 308, 314, RICH+. In HH of Elizabeth Miller f 73 mulatto born SC. Margert age 5/12 yr.

MILLER, MARTHA, 32, F, (--), M, SC, 308, 314, RICH+. In HH of Elisabeth Miller f 73 mulatto born SC.

MILLER, MARY, 28, F, (--), M, SC, 112, 112, COLL+. In HH of Thos. Miller m 38 mulatto born SC.

MILLER, MARY, 19, M, (--), B, SC, 701, 702, FAIR. In HH of Isaac Miller m 70 black born SC. Mary sex m {sic}.

MILLER, MARY, 7, F, (--), M, SC, 439, 436, CHAS%. In HH of Eliza Miller f 30 mulatto born SC.

MILLER, MARY A., 4, F, (--), M, SC, 112, 112, COLL+. In HH of Thos. Miller m 38 mulatto born SC.

MILLER, MILLY, 66, F, (--), B, SC, 701, 702, FAIR. In HH of Isaac Miller m 70 black born SC.

MILLER, REBECCA, 42, F, (--), B, SC, 701, 702, FAIR. In HH of Isaac Miller m 70 black born SC.

MILLER, ROBERT, 50, M, Fisherman, B, SC, 62, 72, CHAS.

MILLER, THOMAS, 28, M, (--), B, SC, 701, 702, FAIR. In HH of Isaac Miller m 70 black born SC.

MILLER, THOMAS, 16, M, Shoemaker, M, SC, 592, 574, CHAS-. In HH of Eliza Miller f 48 mulatto born SC.

MILLER, THOS., 38, M, Farmer, M, SC, 112, 112, COLL+.

MILLER, TOM, 25, M, Laborer, B, SC, 424, 424, FAIR. In HH of Isaac K. James m 26 born SC.

MILLIE, GRATIA, 2, F, (--), B, SC, 599, 591, CHAS%. In HH of William Millie m 26 black born SC.

MILLIE, REBECCA, 28, F, (--), B, SC, 599, 591, CHAS%. In HH of William Millie m 26 black born SC.

MILLIE, WILLIAM, 26, M, (--), B, SC, 599, 591, CHAS%.

MINES, SOPHIA, 65, F, (--), M, SC, 156, 143, CHAS*. In HH of Elizabeth Holmes f 40 mulatto born SC.

MINNY, AFRED, 2, M, (--), M, SC, 274, 274, BEAU+. In HH of John Minny m 40 black born SC.

MINNY, AGNES, 5, F, (--), M, SC, 274, 274, BEAU+. In HH of John Minny m 40 black born SC.

MINNY, AMANDA, 7, F, (--), M, SC, 274, 274, BEAU+. In HH of John Minny m 40 black born SC.

MINNY, ANNIE, 16, F, (--), M, SC, 274, 274, BEAU+. In HH of John Minny m 40 black born SC.

MINNY, ISABELLA, 30, F, (--), M, SC, 274, 274, BEAU+. In HH of John Minny m 40 black born SC.

MINNY, JOHN, 40, M, Farmer, B, SC, 274, 274, BEAU+.

MINNY, JOHN, 10, M, (--), M, SC, 274, 274, BEAU+. In HH of John Minny

m 40 black born SC.

MIOTT, ANN, 39, F, (--), M, SC, 59, 53, CHAS-. In HH of Sarah Weston f 50 mulatto born SC.

MIOTT, HENRY, 2, M, (--), M, SC, 59, 53, CHAS-. In HH of Sarah Weston f 50 mulatto born SC.

MIOTT, WILLIAM, 16, M, Tailor, M, SC, 59, 53, CHAS-. In HH of Sarah Weston f 50 mulatto born SC.

MISHAN, DINAH, 25, F, (--), M, SC, 157, 144, CHAS*. In HH of Peter Brown m 55 mulatto born SC.

MISHAN, THOMAS, 30, M, Tailor, M, SC, 157, 144, CHAS*. In HH of Peter Brown m 55 mulatto born SC.

MISHAW, ABIGAIL,? 25, F, (--), M, SC, 1084, 1061, CHAS-. In HH of Joshua Mishau m 27 mulatto born SC.

MISHAW, ABIGAIL, ?25, F, (--), M, SC, 941, 921, CHAS-. In HH of Joshua Mishaw m 27 mulatto born SC.

MISHAW, CAROLINE, 28, F, (--), M, SC, 162, 166, RICH. In HH of William Mishaw m 35 mulatto born SC.

MISHAW, CORDELIA, 65, F, (--), M, SC, 174, 160, CHAS*. In HH of Mary Ann McCale f 28 mulatto born SC.

MISHAW, DANIEL, 13, M, (--), M, SC, 6, 6, CHAS+. In HH of John Mishaw m 53 mulatto born SC.

MISHAW, DINAH, 22, F, (--), M, SC, 174, 160, CHAS*. In HH of Mary Ann McCale f 28 mulatto born SC.

MISHAW, EDWARD, 4, M, (--), M, SC, 941, 921, CHAS-. In HH of Joshua Mishaw m 27 mulatto born SC.

MISHAW, EDWARD L., 2, M, (--), M, SC, 1084, 1061, CHAS-. In HH of Joshua Mishau m 27 mulatto born SC.

MISHAW, ELIZA, 53, F, (--), M, SC, 6, 6, CHAS+. In HH of John Mishaw m 53 mulatto born SC.

MISHAW, ELLEN G., 1, F, (--), M, SC, 174, 160, CHAS*. In HH of Mary Ann McCale f 28 mulatto born SC.

MISHAW, EMMA, 3, F, (--), M, SC, 162, 166, RICH. In HH of William Mishaw m 35 mulatto born SC.

MISHAW, FRANCIS, 70, M, (--), M, SC, 174, 160, CHAS*. In HH of Mary Ann McCale f 28 mulatto born SC.

MISHAW, GEORGIANNA, 5, F, (--), M, SC, 162, 166, RICH. In HH of William Mishaw m 35 mulatto born SC.

MISHAW, JOHN, 53, M, Shoemaker, M, SC, 6, 6, CHAS+.

MISHAW, JOHN, 15, M, Millwright, M, SC, 6, 6, CHAS+. In HH of John Mishaw m 53 mulatto born SC.

MISHAW, JOSHUA, 27, M, Carpenter, M, SC, 1084, 1061, CHAS-.

MISHAW, JOSUA, 27, M, Carpenter, M, SC, 941, 921, CHAS-.

MISHAW, JULIA, 8, F, (--), M, SC, 6, 6, CHAS+. In HH of John Mishaw m 53 mulatto born SC.

MISHAW, JULIAN, 1, M, (--), M, SC, 162, 166, RICH. In HH of William Mishaw m 35 mulatto born SC.

MISHAW, LEWIS, 0, M, (--), M, SC, 1084, 1061, CHAS-. In HH of Joshua Mishau m 27 mulatto born SC. Lewis Lishaw age 8/12 yr.

MISHAW, LOUIS, 2, M, (--), M, SC, 941, 921, CHAS-. In HH of Joshua Mishaw m 27 mulatto born SC.

MISHAW, MARY, 1, F, (--), M, SC, 941, 921, CHAS-. In HH of Joshua Mishaw m 27 mulatto born SC.

MISHAW, ROSE, 18, F, (--), M, SC, 6, 6, CHAS+. In HH of John Mishaw m 53 mulatto born SC.

MISHAW, THOMAS, 11, M, (--), M, SC, 6, 6, CHAS+. In HH of John Mishaw m 53 mulatto born SC.

MISHAW, WILLIAM, 35, M, Shoemaker, M, SC, 162, 166, RICH.

MISHAW, WILLIAM, 8, M, (--), M, SC, 941, 921, CHAS-. In HH of Joshua Mishaw m 27 mulatto born SC.

MISHAW, WILLIAM H., 6, M, (--), M, SC, 174, 160, CHAS*. In HH of Mary Ann McCale f 28 mulatto born SC.

MISHAW, WILLIAM L., 4, M, (--), M, SC, 1084, 1061, CHAS-. In HH of Joshua Mishau m 27 mulatto born SC.

MITCHAEL, BEAUFORT, 6, M, (--), B, SC, 1359, 1359, LAU. In HH of Anderson Medcok {?} m 24 born SC.

MITCHEL, ANN, 16, F, (--), M, SC, 234, 234, GEOR*. In HH of Vandal Harris m 46 mulatto born SC.

MITCHEL, JOHN W., 20, M, Carpenter, B, SC, 184, 184, CHAS%.

MITCHEL, MILTON, 13, M, (--), B, SC, 1938, 1938, ABB. In HH of Kate Livingston 95 b black born SC.

MITCHEL, NANCY, 35, F, (--), B, SC, 342, 342, CHAS%.

MITCHELL, A., 50, F, (--), M, SC, 143, 143, KERS.

MITCHELL, AGNES, 21, F, (--), M, SC, 300, 300, CHAS%. In HH of Ann Mitchell f 50 mulatto born SC.

MITCHELL, AMELIA, 50, F, (--), B, SC, 659, 651, CHAS%. In HH of Simeon Mitchell m 55 black born SC.

MITCHELL, AMELIA, 27, F, (--), M, SC, 355, 338, CHAS-.

MITCHELL, ANN, 60, F, (--), M, SC, 155, 145, CHAS-.

MITCHELL, ANN, 60, F, (--), M, SC, 525, 525, FAIR. In HH of Joseph W. Purcell m 38 mulatto born SC.

MITCHELL, ANN, 50, F, (--), M, SC, 300, 300, CHAS%.

MITCHELL, ANN, 20, F, (--), M, SC, 2104, 2108, EDGE. In HH of Polly Smith f 49 black born SC.

MITCHELL, BARWELL, 11, M, (--), M, SC, 143, 143, KERS. In HH of A. Mitchell f 50 mulatto born SC.

MITCHELL, CAROLINE, 20, F, (--), M, SC, 360, 343, CHAS-. In HH of Jane Mitchell f 70 mulatto born SC.

MITCHELL, CAROLINE, 17, F, (--), B, SC, 1876, 1876, ABB. In HH of Harrington Mitchell m 23 black born SC.

MITCHELL, CHARLES, 24, M, Laborer, M, VA, 299, 276, CHAS+.

MITCHELL, CHARLES, 1, M, (--), M, SC, 299, 276, CHAS+. In HH of Charles Mitchell m 24 mulatto born VA.

MITCHELL, ELISA, 7, F, (--), B, SC, 613, 613, EDGE. In HH of Nancy

Mitchell f 55 black born SC.

MITCHELL, ELIZA, 38, F, (--), B, SC, 2099, 2106, EDGE. In HH of Polly Mitchell f 85 black born SC.

MITCHELL, ELLEN, 55, F, (--), M, SC, 2061, 2067, EDGE. In HH of Isaac Mitchell m 60 black born SC.

MITCHELL, HARRINGTON, 23, M, Hireling, B, SC, 1876, 1876, ABB.

MITCHELL, HARRINGTON, 8, M, (--), B, SC, 2099, 2106, EDGE. In HH of Polly Mitchell f 85 black born SC.

MITCHELL, ISAAC, 60, M, Laborer, B, SC, 2061, 2067, EDGE.

MITCHELL, JAMES, 25, M, Hireling, B, SC, 1875, 1875, ABB.

MITCHELL, JANE, 70, F, (--), M, SC, 360, 343, CHAS-.

MITCHELL, JANE, 3, F, (--), M, SC, 143, 143, KERS. In HH of A. Mitchell f 50 mulatto born SC.

MITCHELL, JAS., 24, M, (--), M, SC, 748, 748, KERS.

MITCHELL, JAS., 1, M, (--), M, SC, 143, 143, KERS. In HH of A. Mitchell f 50 mulatto born SC.

MITCHELL, JASPER, 14, M, (--), M, SC, 300, 300, CHAS%. In HH of Ann Mitchell f 50 mulatto born SC.

MITCHELL, JEFFERSON, 12, M, (--), B, SC, 613, 613, EDGE. In HH of Nancy Mitchell f 55 black born SC.

MITCHELL, JEFFERSON, 5, M, (--), B, SC, 614, 614, EDGE. In HH of Mary Mitchell 25 black born SC.

MITCHELL, JOHN, 23, M, Carpenter, B, SC, 1802, 1802, ABB.

MITCHELL, JOHN, 8, M, (--), B, SC, 659, 651, CHAS%. In HH of Simeon Mitchell m 55 black born SC.

MITCHELL, JOHN, 1, M, (--), M, SC, 2099, 2106, EDGE. In HH of Polly Mitchell f 85 black born SC.

MITCHELL, JOHN, 1, M, (--), B, SC, 614, 614, EDGE. In HH of Mary Mitchell 25 black born SC.

MITCHELL, LEWIS, 27, M, (--), M, SC, 360, 343, CHAS-. In HH of Jane

MITCHELL, LORIANE, 16, F, (--), B, SC, 1876, 1876, ABB. In HH of Harrington Mitchell m 23 black born SC.

MITCHELL, LOUVINIA, 14, F, (--), B, SC, 2099, 2106, EDGE. In HH of Polly Mitchell f 85 black born SC.

MITCHELL, LUCINDA, 16, F, (--), B, SC, 1876, 1876, ABB. In HH of Harrington Mitchell m 23 black born SC.

MITCHELL, M., 23, F, (--), M, SC, 143, 143, KERS. In HH of A. Mitchell f 50 mulatto born SC.

MITCHELL, MARTHA, 28, F, (--), M, SC, 360, 343, CHAS-. In HH of Jane Mitchell f 70 mulatto born SC.

MITCHELL, MARTHA, 10, F, (--), M, SC, 299, 276, CHAS+. In HH of Charles Mitchell m 24 mulatto born VA.

MITCHELL, MARY, 25, F, (--), B, SC, 614, 614, EDGE.

MITCHELL, MARY, 24, F, (--), M, SC, 85, 77, CHAS+. In HH of Anthony Robbins m 60 born Portugal.

MITCHELL, MARY, 22, F, (--), M, SC, 299, 276, CHAS+. In HH of Charles Mitchell m 24 mulatto born VA.

MITCHELL, MARY ANN, 20, F, (--), B, SC, 250, 235, CHAS+. In HH of Betsey Lockwood f 38 black born SC.

MITCHELL, MARY ANN, 3, F, (--), M, SC, 299, 276, CHAS+. In HH of Charles Mitchell m 24 mulatto born VA.

MITCHELL, MARY J., 0, F, (--), M, SC, 2104, 2108, EDGE. In HH of Polly Smith .f 49 black born SC. Mary J. age 8/12 yr.

MITCHELL, MINONA, 8, F, (--), M, SC, 360, 343, CHAS-. In HH of Jane Mitchell f 70 mulatto born SC.

MITCHELL, NANCY, 55, F, (--), B, SC, 613, 613, EDGE.

MITCHELL, PAULINA, 16, F, (--), M, SC, 360, 343, CHAS-. In HH of Jane Mitchell f 70 mulatto born SC.

MITCHELL, POLLY, 85, F, (--), B, SC, 2099, 2106, EDGE.

MITCHELL, ROBERT, 10, M, (--), M, SC, 300, 300, CHAS%. In HH of

Ann Mitchell f 50 mulatto born SC.
MITCHELL, ROSA, 2, F, (--), B, SC, 614, 614, EDGE. In HH of Mary Mitchell 25 black born SC.
MITCHELL, SIMEON, 55, M, (--), B, SC, 659, 651, CHAS%.
MITCHELL, SUSAN, 1, F, (--), B, SC, 1876, 1876, ABB. In HH of Harrington Mitchell m 23 black born SC.
MITCHELL, THEODORE, 12, M, (--), M, SC, 360, 343, CHAS-. In HH of Jane Mitchell f 70 mulatto born SC.
MITCHELL, THEOPHILUS, 11, M, (--), B, SC, 2099, 2106, EDGE. In HH of Polly Mitchell f 85 black born SC.
MITCHELL, THOS., 14, M, (--), M, SC, 143, 143, KERS. In HH of A. Mitchell f 50 mulatto born SC.
MITCHELL, TOM, 6, M, (--), M, SC, 2099, 2106, EDGE. In HH of Polly Mitchell f 85 black born SC.
MITCHELL, WILLIAM, 30, M, Millwright, M, SC, 155, 145, CHAS-. In HH of Ann Mitchell f 60 mulatto born SC.
MITCHUM, ANN, 76, F, (--), M, SC, 55, 55, CHAS3. In HH of Stephen Mitchum m 74 mulatto born SC.
MITCHUM, CATHERINE, 30, F, (--), M, SC, 380, 380, COLL. In HH of Jenkins Mitchum m 30 mulatto born SC.
MITCHUM, CATHERINE, 1, F, (--), M, SC, 380, 380, COLL. In HH of Jenkins Mitchum m 30 mulatto born SC.
MITCHUM, HENRY, 6, M, (--), M, SC, 380, 380, COLL. In HH of Jenkins Mitchum m 30 mulatto born SC.
MITCHUM, JENKINS, 30, M, Laborer, M, SC, 380, 380, COLL.
MITCHUM, LAURA, 2, F, (--), M, SC, 380, 380, COLL. In HH of Jenkins Mitchum m 30 mulatto born SC.
MITCHUM, MILES, 32, M, Laborer, M, SC, 376, 376, COLL.
MITCHUM, PHILIP, 7, M, (--), M, SC, 376, 376, COLL. In HH of Miles Mitchum m 32 mulatto born SC.
MITCHUM, PINCKNEY, 9, M, (--), M, SC, 376, 376, COLL. In HH of Miles

Mitchum m 32 mulatto born SC.
MITCHUM, SARAH, 4, F, (--), M, SC, 380, 380, COLL. In HH of Jenkins Mitchum m 30 mulatto born SC.
MITCHUM, SARAH, 1, F, (--), M, SC, 376, 376, COLL. In HH of Miles Mitchum m 32 mulatto born SC.
MITCHUM, STEPHEN, 74, M, Planter, M, SC, 55, 55, CHAS3.
MITCHUM, VALENTINE, 8, M, (--), M, SC, 380, 380, COLL. In HH of Jenkins Mitchum m 30 mulatto born SC.
MITCHUM, VIOLET, 30, F, (--), M, SC, 376, 376, COLL. In HH of Miles Mitchum m 32 mulatto born SC.
MITCHUM, WILLIAM, 36, M, Laborer, M, SC, 285, 285, CHAS3. In HH of Sookey Bunch f 50 born SC.
MOLEHAM, CARY, 50, M, (--), M, SC, 1028, 1028, YORK.
MOLEHAM, LANCASTER, 12, M, (--), M, SC, 1028, 1028, YORK. In HH of Cary Moleham f 50 mulatto born SC.
MOLEHAM, SARAH, 15, F, (--), M, SC, 1028, 1028, YORK. In HH of Cary Moleham f 50 mulatto born SC.
MONIES, JANE, 45, F, (--), M, SC, 124, 115, CHAS-. In HH of Joseph P. McCall m 58 born SC.
MONROE, BERRY, 36, M, Hireling, M, SC, 1360, 1360, SPART.
MONROE, ELIZA, 30, F, (--), M, SC, 1360, 1360, SPART. In HH of Berry Monroe m 36 mulatto born SC.
MONROE, GORAM, 3, M, (--), M, SC, 1360, 1360, SPART. In HH of Berry Monroe m 36 mulatto born SC.
MONTAGUE, CHARLOTTE, 37, F, (--), M, SC, 869, 849, CHAS-.
MONTAGUE, JULIA, 10, F, (--), M, SC, 869, 849, CHAS-. In HH of Charlotte Montague f 37 mulatto born SC.
MONTAGUE, LOUISA, 17, F, (--), M, SC, 869, 849, CHAS-. In HH of Charlotte Montague f 37 mulatto born SC.
MONTAGUE, MARY ANN, 13, F, (--), M, SC, 869, 849, CHAS-. In HH of

Charlotte Montague f 37 mulatto born SC.

MONTANG, FELIX J., 64, M, Tailor, M, SC, 115, 116, RICH.

MONTANG, SARAH J., 53, F, (--), M, SC, 115, 116, RICH. In HH of Felix J. Montang m 64 mulatto born SC.

MONTANGUE, ANTONIO, 0, M, (--), M, SC, 32, 33, RICH. In HH of Grace Montangue f 23 mulatto born SC. Antonio Montangue age 7/12 yr.

MONTANGUE, GRACE, 23, F, (--), M, SC, 32, 33, RICH.

MONTANGUE, SARAH, 4, F, (--), M, SC, 32, 33, RICH. In HH of Grace Montangue f 23 mulatto born SC.

MONTGOMERY, BURGESS, 12, M, (--), B, SC, 486, 486, SUMT. In HH of Elis Carity f 50 born SC.

MONTGOMERY, CANTY, 1, M, (--), B, SC, 486, 486, SUMT. In HH of Elis Carity f 50 born SC.

MONTGOMERY, DANIEL, 40, M, Carpenter, B, SC, 490, 490, SUMT. In HH of Ellen Montgomery f 25 black born SC.

MONTGOMERY, DANIEL, 6, M, (--), B, SC, 486, 486, SUMT. In HH of Elis Carity f 50 born SC.

MONTGOMERY, DOLLY, 3, F, (--), B, SC, 491, 491, SUMT. In HH of Mary Montgomery f 48 black born SC.

MONTGOMERY, ELI, 3, M, (--), B, SC, 486, 486, SUMT. In HH of Elis Carity f 50 born SC.

MONTGOMERY, ELIZABETH, 27, F, (--), B, SC, 486, 486, SUMT. In HH of Elis Carity f 50 born SC.

MONTGOMERY, ELLEN, 25, F, (--), B, SC, 489, 489, SUMT.

MONTGOMERY, FRASER, 26, M, Planter, B, SC, 492, 492, SUMT.

MONTGOMERY, JAMES, 11, M, (--), M, SC, 919, 899, CHAS-. In HH of Phillis Montgomery f 30 mulatto born SC.

MONTGOMERY, JANE, 9, F, (--), M, SC, 919, 899, CHAS-. In HH of Phillis Montgomery f 30 mulatto born SC.

MONTGOMERY, JAS, 14, M, (--), B, SC, 486, 486, SUMT. In HH of Elis Carity f 50 born SC.

MONTGOMERY, JEFFERSON, 14, M, (--), B, SC, 489, 489, SUMT. In HH of Ellen Montgomery f 25 black born SC.

MONTGOMERY, JULIET, 13, F, (--), M, SC, 919, 899, CHAS-. In HH of Phillis Montgomery f 30 mulatto born SC.

MONTGOMERY, MARY, 48, F, (--), B, SC, 491, 491, SUMT.

MONTGOMERY, MOLISON, 16, F, (--), B, SC, 491, 491, SUMT. In HH of Mary Montgomery f 48 black born SC.

MONTGOMERY, PARIS, 7, M, (--), B, SC, 486, 486, SUMT. In HH of Elis Carity f 50 born SC.

MONTGOMERY, PHILLIS, 30, F, (--), M, SC, 919, 899, CHAS-.

MONTGOMERY, ROBT., 16, M, Laborer, B, SC, 489, 489, SUMT. In HH of Ellen Montgomery f 25 black born SC.

MONTGOMERY, RUFUS, 5, M, (--), B, SC, 486, 486, SUMT. In HH of Elis Carity f 50 born SC.

MONTGOMERY, SARAH, 26, F, (--), B, SC, 492, 492, SUMT. In HH of Fraser Montgomery m 26 black born SC.

MONTGOMERY, SARAH, 7, F, (--), M, SC, 919, 899, CHAS-. In HH of Phillis Montgomery f 30 mulatto born SC.

MONTGOMERY, SARAH A., 0, F, (--), B, SC, 492, 492, SUMT. In HH of Fraser Montgomery m 26 black born SC. Sarah A. age 1/12 yr.

MONTGOMERY, TENES, 13, F, (--), B, SC, 491, 491, SUMT. In HH of Mary Montgomery f 48 black born SC.

MONTGOMERY, THOMAS, 5, M, (--), M, SC, 919, 899, CHAS-. In HH of Phillis Montgomery f 30 mulatto born SC.

MONTGOMERY, WESLEY, 10, M, (--), B, SC, 491, 491, SUMT. In HH of Mary Montgomery f 48 black born SC.

MONTGOMERY, WM., 12, M, (--), B, SC, 489, 489, SUMT. In HH of Ellen Montgomery f 25 black born SC.

MOODIE, BETSEY, 50, F, (--), M, SC, 201, 188, CHAS-.

MOORE, CATHARINE, 54, F, (--), M, SC, 366, 366, SUMT.

MOORE, ELIZA, 27, F, (--), M, SC, 419, 417, CHAS%.

MOORE, MARY J., 8, F, (--), M, SC, 419, 417, CHAS%. In HH of Eliza Moore f 27 mulatto born SC.

MOORE, SUSAN, 50, F, (--), M, SC, 604, 604, EDGE*.

MOORE, WILLIAM, 6, M, (--), M, SC, 419, 417, CHAS%. In HH of Eliza Moore f 27 mulatto born SC.

MORCE {?}, FRANCIS, 30, M, Tailor, M, SC, 71, 71, GEOR*.

MORE, FREDERICK, 14, M, (--), M, SC, 54, 54, CHAS2. In HH of John More m 28 mulatto born SC.

MORE, HARRIET, 6, F, (--), M, SC, 54, 54, CHAS2. In HH of John More m 28 mulatto born SC.

MORE, HENRY J., 13, M, (--), M, SC, 55, 55, CHAS2. In HH of Mrs. Elizabeth Linson f 68 born SC.

MORE, JANE, 20, F, (--), M, SC, 54, 54, CHAS2. In HH of John More m 28 mulatto born SC.

MORE, JOHN, 37, M, Farmer, M, SC, 38, 38, CHAS#.

MORE, JOHN, 28, M, Laborer, M, SC, 54, 54, CHAS2.

MORE, MARGE, 36, F, (--), B, SC, 38, 38, CHAS#. In HH of John More m 37 mulatto born SC.

MORE, SAM, 60, M, Farmer, M, SC, 53, 53, CHAS2.

MORE, SAM, 32, M, Laborer, M, SC, 53, 53, CHAS2. In HH of Sam More m 60 mulatto born SC.

MORE, SARAH ANN, 10, F, (--), M, SC, 55, 55, CHAS2. In HH of Mrs. Elizabeth Linson f 68 born SC.

MORE, STEPHEN, 8, M, (--), M, SC, 54, 54, CHAS2. In HH of John More m 28 mulatto born SC.

MORE, STEPHEN M., 7, M, (--), M, SC, 55, 55, CHAS2. In HH of Mrs. Elizabeth Linson f 68 born SC.

MORE, SUSAN, 30, F, (--), M, SC, 55, 55, CHAS2. In HH of Mrs. Elizabeth Linson f 68 born SC.

MORGAN, ADOLPHUS, 22, M, (--), M, SC, 833, 833, NEWB.

MORGAN, ANN, 3, F, (--), B, SC, 1045, 1045, UNION. In HH of William Brown m 45 born SC.

MORGAN, DENNIS, 21, M, Laborer, B, SC, 1045, 1045, UNION. In HH of William Brown m 45 born SC.

MORGAN, DIANA, 50, F, (--), B, SC, 568, 551, CHAS-. In HH of Robert Morgan m 50 black born SC.

MORGAN, DINAH, 6, F, (--), B, SC, 1045, 1045, UNION. In HH of William Brown m 45 born SC.

MORGAN, FRANCES, 7, F, (--), B, SC, 1045, 1045, UNION. In HH of William Brown m 45 born SC.

MORGAN, JORDAN, 21, M, (--), M, SC, 834, 834, NEWB.

MORGAN, REBECCA, 30, F, (--), B, SC, 1045, 1045, UNION. In HH of William Brown m 45 born SC.

MORGAN, ROBERT, 50, M, Bricklayer, B, SC, 568, 551, CHAS-.

MORRIS, ALECK, 38, M, Drayman, B, SC, 864, 841, CHAS%. In HH of Sarah Morris f 40 black born SC.

MORRIS, ANN ELIZA, 17, F, (--), M, SC, 354, 337, CHAS-. In HH of James Harrison m 50 mulatto born SC.

MORRIS, BINER, 50, F, (--), B, SC, 641, 633, CHAS%.

MORRIS, CHARLES, 8, M, (--), B, SC, 864, 841, CHAS%. In HH of Sarah Morris f 40 black born SC.

MORRIS, DIANA, 21, F, (--), M, SC, 354, 337, CHAS-. In HH of James Harrison m 50 mulatto born SC.

MORRIS, ELIZABETH, 15, F, (--), B, SC, 641, 633, CHAS%. In HH of Morris Biner f 50 black born SC.

MORRIS, ELLY, 16, F, (--), B, SC, 641, 633, CHAS%. In HH of Morris Biner f 50 black born SC.

MORRIS, JAMES, 12, M, (--), B, SC, 864, 841, CHAS%. In HH of Sarah Morris f 40 black born SC.

MORRIS, JOHN, 24, M, Blacksmith, B, SC, 641, 633, CHAS%. In HH of Morris Biner f 50 black born SC.

MORRIS, SARAH, 40, F, (--), B, SC, 864, 841, CHAS%.

MORRIS, SUSAN, 23, F, (--), B, SC, 990, 990, ABB. In HH of Benjamin Gill m 24 born SC.

MORRIS, SUSAN, 14, F, (--), B, SC, 864, 841, CHAS%. In HH of Sarah Morris f 40 black born SC.

MORRIS, TONY, 12, M, (--), B, SC, 641, 633, CHAS%. In HH of Morris Biner f 50 black born SC.

MORRISON, JAMES, 40, M, Carpenter, M, SC, 284, 284, BEAU+.

MORRISON, JAMES, 17, M, Apprentice, M, SC, 284, 284, BEAU+. In HH of James Morrison m 40 mulatto born SC.

MORRISON, REBECCA, 35, F, (--), B, SC, 208, 282, CHAS*.

MORRISON, REGINE, 4, F, (--), M, SC, 208, 282, CHAS*. In HH of Rebecca Morrison f 35 black born SC.

MORRISON, SARAH, 40, F, (--), M, SC, 284, 284, BEAU+. In HH of James Morrison m 40 mulatto born SC.

MORRISON, WILLIAM, 13, M, Wheelwright, B, SC, 208, 282, CHAS*. In HH of Rebecca Morrison f 35 black born SC.

MORTIMORE, DANIEL, 24, M, Fisherman, B, SC, 369, 331, CHAS+.

MORTIMORE, ELLEN, 21, F, (--), B, SC, 369, 331, CHAS+. In HH of Daniel Mortimore m 24 black born SC.

MORTIMORE, GRACE, 3, F, (--), B, SC, 369, 331, CHAS+. In HH of Daniel Mortimore m 24 black born SC.

MORTIMORE, SARAH, 2, F, (--), B, SC, 369, 331, CHAS+. In HH of Daniel Mortimore m 24 black born SC.

MORTIMORE, WILLIAM, 4, M, (--), B, SC, 369, 331, CHAS+. In HH of Daniel Mortimore m 24 black born SC.

MOTT, AMELIA, 22, F, (--), M, SC, 626, 618, CHAS%. In HH of Jacob Mott m 30 mulatto born SC.

MOTT, FANNY, 45, F, (--), M, SC, 236, 236, CHAS%. In HH of Joseph Mott m 50 mulatto born SC.

MOTT, JACOB, 30, M, Tailor, M, SC, 626, 618, CHAS%.

MOTT, JOSEPH, 50, M, Drummer, M, SC, 236, 236, CHAS%.

MOTT, JOSEPH, 1, M, (--), M, SC, 626, 618, CHAS%. In HH of Jacob Mott m 30 mulatto born SC.

MOTTE, LOUISA, 1, F, (--), M, SC, 207, 193, CHAS-. In HH of Sarah Motte f 30 mulatto born SC.

MOTTE, SARAH, 30, F, (--), M, SC, 207, 193, CHAS-.

MOULTREE, BENJAMIN, 12, M, (--), M, SC, 974, 954, CHAS-. In HH of Roxana Moultree f 60 mulatto born SC.

MOULTREE, CATHERINE, 17, F, (--), M, SC, 974, 954, CHAS-. In HH of Roxana Moultree f 60 mulatto born SC.

MOULTREE, CLAUS, 28, M, Laborer, B, SC, 177, 167, CHAS-.

MOULTREE, ELLEN, 38, F, (--), B, SC, 50, 50, CHAS%. In HH of Louisa Lawrence f 57 black born SC.

MOULTREE, JULIA, 15, F, (--), M, SC, 974, 954, CHAS-. In HH of Roxana Moultree f 60 mulatto born SC.

MOULTREE, ROBERT, 20, M, (--), M, SC, 974, 954, CHAS-. In HH of Roxana Moultree f 60 mulatto born SC.

MOULTREE, ROXANA, 60, F, (--), M, SC, 974, 954, CHAS-.

MOULTREE, WILLIAM, 23, M, Barber, M, SC, 974, 954, CHAS-. In HH of Roxana Moultree f 60 mulatto born SC.

MOULTRIE, ARTHUR, 6, M, (--), M, SC, 945, 925, CHAS-. In HH of Justina White f 36 mulatto born SC.

MOULTRIE, ELLA, 4, F, (--), M, SC, 945, 925, CHAS-. In HH of Justina

White f 36 mulatto born SC.

MOULTRIE, ELOISA, 8, F, (--), M, SC, 945, 925, CHAS-. In HH of Justina White f 36 mulatto born SC.

MOULTRIE, JOSEPH, 12, M, (--), B, SC, 693, 685, CHAS%. In HH of Susan Moultrie f 42 black born SC.

MOULTRIE, JULIET, 2, F, (--), M, SC, 945, 925, CHAS-. In HH of Justina White f 36 mulatto born SC.

MOULTRIE, LIZZY, 15, F, (--), B, SC, 693, 685, CHAS%. In HH of Susan Moultrie f 42 black born SC.

MOULTRIE, MARIA, 7, F, (--), B, SC, 693, 685, CHAS%. In HH of Susan Moultrie f 42 black born SC.

MOULTRIE, MARY, 15, F, (--), M, SC, 945, 925, CHAS-. In HH of Justina White f 36 mulatto born SC.

MOULTRIE, RICHARD, 38, M, Drayman, B, SC, 693, 685, CHAS%. In HH of Susan Moultrie f 42 black born SC.

MOULTRIE, ROBERT, 27, M, Barber, M, New Providence, 361, 323, CHAS+.

MOULTRIE, SUSAN, 42, F, (--), B, SC, 693, 685, CHAS%.

MOULTRIE, SUSAN, 10, F, (--), B, SC, 693, 685, CHAS%. In HH of Susan Moultrie f 42 black born SC.

MOULTRIEL, DAFREY, 45, F, (--), B, SC, 550, 542, CHAS%. In HH of Jane Brown f 60 mulatto born SC.

MOURAY, EDWARD, 6, M, (--), M, SC, 1080, 1057, CHAS-. In HH of Emeline Ferguson f 30 mulatto born SC.

MOWER, WILSON P., 33, M, Farmer, M, SC, 1155, 1155, LEX.

MUCKINFOSS, WILLIAM, 35, M, Farmer, M, SC, 20, 20, COLL*.

MUCKINFUSS, GEO., 20, M, (--), M, SC, 292, 292, COLL*. In HH of James Hutsen m 27 born SC.

MULKY, SARAH S., 1, F, (--), M, SC, 1170, 1171, AND*. In HH of Charity Mulky f 35 white born SC.

MUMS, AGNES, 31, F, (--), M, SC, 404, 402, CHAS%. In HH of Dianah Mums f 64 mulatto born SC.

MUMS, CINDA, 12, F, (--), M, SC, 404, 402, CHAS%. In HH of Dianah Mums f 64 mulatto born SC.

MUMS, DIANAH, 64, F, (--), M, SC, 404, 402, CHAS%.

MUMS, HENRY, 9, M, (--), M, SC, 404, 402, CHAS%. In HH of Dianah Mums f 64 mulatto born SC.

MUMS, JOHN P., 30, M, Painter, M, SC, 404, 402, CHAS%. In HH of Dianah Mums f 64 mulatto born SC.

MUNEL, DELIA, 33, F, (--), M, SC, 135, 135, GEOR.

MUNEL, HENRY, 6, M, (--), M, SC, 135, 135, GEOR. In HH of Delia Munel f 33 mulatto born SC.

MUNEL, JAMES, 7, M, (--), M, SC, 135, 135, GEOR. In HH of Delia Munel f 33 mulatto born SC.

MUNEL, JOHN F., 13, M, (--), M, SC, 135, 135, GEOR. In HH of Delia Munel f 33 mulatto born SC.

MUNEL, JULIAN, 11, M, (--), M, SC, 135, 135, GEOR. In HH of Delia Munel f 33 mulatto born SC.

MUNEL, SUSAN, 10, F, (--), M, SC, 135, 135, GEOR. In HH of Delia Munel f 33 mulatto born SC.

MUNEL, THEODORE, 1, M, (--), M, SC, 135, 135, GEOR. In HH of Delia Munel f 33 mulatto born SC.

MURLEY, HAMLET, 35, M, Drayman, M, SC, 741, 699, CHAS+.

MUSHINGTON, ELLEN, 7, F, (--), M, SC, 200, 188, CHAS-. In HH of Mary Mushington f 30 mulatto born SC.

MUSHINGTON, JOHN, 13, M, (--), M, SC, 200, 188, CHAS-. In HH of Mary Mushington f 30 mulatto born SC.

MUSHINGTON, MARY, 30, F, (--), M, SC, 200, 188, CHAS-.

MUSTAPHA, ABBEY, 38, F, (--), M, SC, 379, 341, CHAS+. In HH of Thomas Mustapha m 44 mulatto born SC.

MUSTAPHA, BECK, 37, F, (--), B, SC, 29, 29, CHAS2. In HH of Crawford Mustapha m 37 black born SC.

MUSTAPHA, CRAWFORD, 37, M, Laborer, B, SC, 29, 29, CHAS2.

MUSTAPHA, DAVID, 6, M, (--), B, SC, 29, 29, CHAS2. In HH of Crawford Mustapha m 37 black born SC.

MUSTAPHA, ELIZABETH, 15, F, (--), B, SC, 29, 29, CHAS2. In HH of Crawford Mustapha m 37 black born SC.

MUSTAPHA, ELIZABETH, 5, F, (--), M, SC, 379, 341, CHAS+. In HH of Thomas Mustapha m 44 mulatto born SC.

MUSTAPHA, LAURA, 1, F, (--), B, SC, 29, 29, CHAS2. In HH of Crawford Mustapha m 37 black born SC.

MUSTAPHA, MARIA, 7, F, (--), B, SC, 29, 29, CHAS2. In HH of Crawford Mustapha m 37 black born SC.

MUSTAPHA, MARY, 3, F, (--), M, SC, 379, 341, CHAS+. In HH of Thomas Mustapha m 44 mulatto born SC.

MUSTAPHA, PHEOBE, 7, F, (--), M, SC, 379, 341, CHAS+. In HH of Thomas Mustapha m 44 mulatto born SC.

MUSTAPHA, THOMAS, 44, M, Bricklayer, M, SC, 379, 341, CHAS+.

MUSTAPHA, WILLIAM, 9, M, (--), B, SC, 29, 29, CHAS2. In HH of Crawford Mustapha m 37 black born SC.

MYERS, ALICE, 2, F, (--), M, SC, 751, 709, CHAS+. In HH of Gersham Myers m 25 mulatto born SC.

MYERS, ELLEN, 5, F, (--), M, SC, 22, 21, CHAS&. In HH of John G. Myers m 26 born Barvaria.

MYERS, GERSHAM, 25, M, Porter, M, SC, 751, 709, CHAS+.

MYERS, HENRY, 4, M, (--), M, SC, 751, 709, CHAS+. In HH of Gersham Myers m 25 mulatto born SC.

MYERS, JANET, 33, F, (--), M, SC, 22, 21, CHAS&. In HH of John G. Myers m 26 born Barvaria.

MYERS, JOHN, 3, M, (--), M, SC, 22, 21, CHAS&. In HH of John G. Myers m 26 born Barvaria.

MYERS, MARY, 22, F, (--), M, SC, 751, 709, CHAS+. In HH of Gersham Myers m 25 mulatto born SC.

N

NAT, 50, M, Hostler, B, SC, 52, 52, CHAS#. In HH of Mr. J. Council m 36 born SC.

NATHAN, ELIZABETH, 45, F, (--), M, SC, 289, 295, RICH+.

NATHAN, ELIZABETH, 20, F, (--), M, SC, 289, 295, RICH+. In HH of Elisabeth Nathan f 45 mulatto born SC.

NATHAN, JANE, 5, F, (--), M, SC, 289, 295, RICH+. In HH of Elizabeth Nathan f 45 mulatto born SC, {page out of order}.

NAYLOR, ELLINOR, 4, F, (--), M, SC, 147, 135, CHAS*. In HH of Rebecca Naylor f 35 black born SC.

NAYLOR, HANNAH, 20, F, (--), B, SC, 147, 135, CHAS*. In HH of Rebecca Naylor f 35 black born SC.

NAYLOR, REBECCA, 35, F, (--), B, SC, 147, 135, CHAS*.

NAYLOR, REBECCA, 2, F, (--), M, SC, 147, 135, CHAS*. In HH of Rebecca Naylor f 35 black born SC.

NEAL, JAMES, 3, M, (--), B, SC, 204, 204, LANC*. In HH of M. Neal m 34 born SC.

NEAL, ROSE, 40, F, (--), B, SC, 204, 204, LANC*. In HH of M. Neal m 34 born SC.

NEIGHBOUR, ANDREW, 35, M, Wheelwright, M, SC, 807, 790, CHAS%.

NEIGHBOUR, ANNE, 14, F, (--), M, SC, 807, 790, CHAS%. In HH of Andrew Neighbour m 36 mulatto born SC.

NEIGHBOUR, JAMES, 10, M, (--), M, SC, 807, 790, CHAS%. In HH of Andrew Neighbour m 36 mulatto born SC.

NEIGHBOUR, JOHN, 7, M, (--), M, SC, 807, 790, CHAS%. In HH of Andrew Neighbour m 36 mulatto born

SC.

NEIGHBOUR, MODESTINE, 30, F, (--), M, SC, 807, 790, CHAS%. In HH of Andrew Neighbour m 36 mulatto born SC.

NELL, ALANLIN, 10, M, (--), B, SC, 108, 101, CHAS-. In HH of Lucretia Harden f 89 black born SC.

NELL, ANGELINE, 26, F, (--), M, SC, 108, 101, CHAS-. In HH of Lucretia Harden f 89 black born SC.

NELL, CAROLINE, 5, F, (--), M, SC, 108, 101, CHAS-. In HH of Lucretia Harden f 89 black born SC.

NELL, ISAAC, 35, M, (--), B, SC, 810, 768, CHAS+. In HH of Amelia Gardner f 13 black born SC.

NELL, THOMAS, 1, M, (--), M, SC, 108, 101, CHAS-. In HH of Lucretia Harden f 89 black born SC.

NELME, HARRIOT, 56, F, (--), B, SC, 229, 204, CHAS*.

NELSON, BONET, 50, F, (--), M, SC, 503, 454, CHAS. In HH of George Conwell m 31 mulatto born SC.

NELSON, CHARLOTTE, 46, F, (--), M, SC, 577, 569, CHAS%. In HH of John Nelson m 48 mulatto born SC.

NELSON, CHARLOTTE, 9, F, (--), M, SC, 577, 569, CHAS%. In HH of John Nelson m 48 mulatto born SC.

NELSON, ELIZABETH, 35, F, (--), M, SC, 69, 69, CHAS%. In HH of Patsey Nelson f 40 mulatto born SC.

NELSON, FREDERICK, 14, M, (--), M, SC, 69, 69, CHAS%. In HH of Patsey Nelson f 40 mulatto born SC.

NELSON, HANNAH, 48, F, (--), B, SC, 997, 974, CHAS%. In HH of Martin Nelson m 50 black born SC.

NELSON, HARRIETT, 30, F, (--), M, SC, 96, 88, CHAS+. In HH of Peter Nelson m 37 mulatto born SC.

NELSON, JANE ANN, 7, F, (--), M, SC, 96, 88, CHAS+. In HH of Peter Nelson m 37 mulatto born SC.

NELSON, JOHN, 48, M, Tailor, M, SC, 577, 569, CHAS%.

NELSON, MARIA, 21, F, (--), M, SC,

36, 36, CHAS%.

NELSON, MARTHA, 11, F, (--), M, SC, 577, 569, CHAS%. In HH of John Nelson m 48 mulatto born SC.

NELSON, MARTIN, 50, M, Farmer, B, SC, 997, 974, CHAS%.

NELSON, NORETTA, 43, F, (--), B, SC, 488, 488, SUMT. In HH of Wm. C. Nelson m 40 black born SC.

NELSON, PATSEY, 40, F, (--), M, SC, 69, 69, CHAS%.

NELSON, PETER, 37, M, Hair dresser, M, SC, 96, 88, CHAS+.

NELSON, PETER, 4, M, (--), M, SC, 96, 88, CHAS+. In HH of Peter Nelson m 37 mulatto born SC.

NELSON, ROBERT, 4, M, (--), M, SC, 577, 569, CHAS%. In HH of John Nelson m 48 mulatto born SC.

NELSON, SARAH, 13, F, (--), M, SC, 577, 569, CHAS%. In HH of John Nelson m 48 mulatto born SC.

NELSON, SUSAN, 6, F, (--), M, SC, 577, 569, CHAS%. In HH of John Nelson m 48 mulatto born SC.

NELSON, SUSAN ANN, 5, F, (--), M, SC, 96, 88, CHAS+. In HH of Peter Nelson m 37 mulatto born SC.

NELSON, WILLIAM, 11, M, (--), M, SC, 96, 88, CHAS+. In HH of Peter Nelson m 37 mulatto born SC.

NELSON, WM. C., 40, M, Planter, B, SC, 488, 488, SUMT.

NESBET, MARY, 16, F, (--), B, SC, 593, 585, CHAS%. In HH of Rose Nesbet f 35 black born SC.

NESBET, ROSE, 35, F, (--), B, SC, 593, 585, CHAS%.

NEWFUDLE, RACHAEL, 60, F, (--), B, SC, 68, 62, CHAS-. In HH of Mary Torlay f 34 born NY.

NEWL, CHRISTIAN, 38, M, (--), M, SC, 538, 504, CHAS*. In HH of Henry Harinberg m 25 born Germany.

NEWL, NANCY, 28, F, (--), M, SC, 538, 504, CHAS*. In HH of Henry Harinberg m 25 born Germany.

NEWTON, ANN, 35, F, (--), M, SC,

271, 271, BEAU+. In HH of Robert Newton m 38 mulatto born SC.

NEWTON, ANNA, 1, F, (--), M, SC, 144, 134, CHAS-. In HH of Susan Garder f 59 mulatto born SC.

NEWTON, ARTIMIS JONES, 4, M, (--), M, SC, 283, 283, BEAU+. In HH of James Jones m 27 mulatto born SC.

NEWTON, CAROLINE, 5, F, (--), B, (-), 15, 15, BEAU#. In HH of Kitty Newton f 35 Mulatto.

NEWTON, CATHARINE SCOTT, 7, F, (--), B, SC, 301, 301, BEAU+. In HH of Joseph Newton m 22 mulatto born SC.

NEWTON, EDWARD, 26, M, Laborer, M, SC, 276, 276, BEAU+.

NEWTON, ELIJAH, 20, F, (--), B, SC, 301, 301, BEAU+. In HH of Joseph Newton m 22 mulatto born SC.

NEWTON, ELIZABETH, 9, F, (--), B, (-), 15, 15, BEAU#. In HH of Kitty Newton f 35 Mulatto.

NEWTON, EUGENE, 27, M, Mechanic, M, SC, 137, 117, CHAS$. In HH of Wm. Newton m 30 born SC.

NEWTON, ISAAC, 47, M, Carpenter, M, SC, 45, 45, COLL+.

NEWTON, JANE, 26, F, (--), M, SC, 144, 134, CHAS-. In HH of Susan Garder f 59 mulatto born SC.

NEWTON, JOHN, 3, M, (--), B, 15, 15, BEAU#. In HH of Kitty Newton f 35 Mulatto.

NEWTON, JOINER, 3, M, (--), M, SC, 276, 276, BEAU+. In HH of Edward Newton m 26 mulatto born SC.

NEWTON, JOSEPH, 22, M, (--), M, SC, 301, 301, BEAU+.

NEWTON, JOYAN M., 2, F, (--), M, SC, 283, 283, BEAU+. In HH of James Jones m 27 mulatto born SC.

NEWTON, KEZIA, 25, F, (--), M, SC, 276, 276, BEAU+. In HH of Edward Newton m 26 mulatto born SC.

NEWTON, KITTY, 35, F, (--), M, (-), 15, 15, BEAU#.

NEWTON, KIZIA, 1, F, (--), M, SC, 276, 276, BEAU+. In HH of Edward

Newton m 26 mulatto born SC.

NEWTON, ROBERT, 38, M, Farmer, M, SC, 271, 271, BEAU+.

NEWTON, ROSE, 89, F, (--), B, SC, 1015, 992, CHAS-. In HH of Rose Wilson f 45 black born SC.

NEWTON, SALINA, 13, F, (--), B, (-), 15, 15, BEAU#. In HH of Kitty Newton f 35 Mulatto.

NEWTON, ULMER, 7, M, (--), B, (-), 15, 15, BEAU#. In HH of Kitty Newton f 35 Mulatto.

NEWTON, VIRGIN, 8, F, (--), M, SC, 283, 283, BEAU+. In HH of James Jones m 27 mulatto born SC.

NEWTON, WILLIAM, 15, M, (--), B, (-), 15, 15, BEAU#. In HH of Kitty Newton f 35 Mulatto.

NICKERSON, MARY ANN, 3, F, (--), M, SC, 365, 348, CHAS-. In HH of Mary McBride f 46 mulatto born SC.

NIGHTS, ELEANOR, 20, F, (--), M, SC, 339, 339, GEOR*. In HH of Susanna Nights f 60 mulatto born SC.

NIGHTS, ELIZABETH, 23, F, (--), M, SC, 339, 339, GEOR*. In HH of Susanna Nights f 60 mulatto born SC.

NIGHTS, JANE, 14, F, (--), M, SC, 339, 339, GEOR*. In HH of Susanna Nights f 60 mulatto born SC.

NIGHTS, LISBY, 18, F, (--), M, SC, 339, 339, GEOR*. In HH of Susanna Nights f 60 mulatto born SC.

NIGHTS, STEWARD, 22, M, Carpenter, M, SC, 339, 339, GEOR*. In HH of Susanna Nights f 60 mulatto born SC.

NIGHTS, SUSAN, 16, F, (--), M, SC, 339, 339, GEOR*. In HH of Susanna Nights f 60 mulatto born SC.

NIGHTS, SUSANNA, 60, F, (--), M, SC, 339, 339, GEOR*.

NILES, JANE, 38, F, (--), B, SC, 593, 585, CHAS%. In HH of Rose Nesbet f 35 black born SC.

NILES, ROSANA, 70, F, (--), B, SC, 593, 585, CHAS%. In HH of Rose Nesbet f 35 black born SC.

NISLEN, J., 7, M, (--), B, SC, 129, 129,

KERS. In HH of Jack Cleveland m 35 mulatto born SC.

NOBLIN, ANNE, 21, F, (--), M, SC, 263, 263, GEOR*. In HH of Jacob Noblin m 30 mulatto born SC.

NOBLIN, HENRY, 3, M, (--), M, SC, 263, 263, GEOR*. In HH of Jacob Noblin m 30 mulatto born SC.

NOBLIN, JACOB, 30, M, Farmer, M, SC, 263, 263, GEOR*.

NOBLIN, JAMES, 1, M, (--), M, SC, 263, 263, GEOR*. In HH of Jacob Noblin m 30 mulatto born SC.

NOLL, FRANCES, 12, F, (--), M, SC, 11, 11, CHAS#. In HH of Mrs. McDowall f 78 born SC.

NOLL, JOHN, 20, M, Farmer, M, SC, 11, 11, CHAS#. In HH of Mrs. McDowall f 78 born SC.

NOLL, REBECCA, 15, F, (--), M, SC, 11, 11, CHAS#. In HH of Mrs. McDowall f 78 born SC.

NOLL, SARAH, 50, F, (--), M, SC, 11, 11, CHAS#. In HH of Mrs. McDowall f 78 born SC.

NOLL, THOMAS, 16, M, (--), M, SC, 11, 11, CHAS#. In HH of Mrs. McDowall f 78 born SC.

NOLL, WM., 13, M, (--), M, SC, 11, 11, CHAS#. In HH of Mrs. McDowall f 78 born SC.

NORSETT, ALEXANDER, 42, M, Farmer, M, SC, 971, 948, CHAS%.

NORSETT, ANNA, 25, F, (--), M, SC, 970, 947, CHAS%.

NORSETT, CATHERINE, 7, F, (--), M, SC, 971, 948, CHAS%. In HH of Alexander Norsett m 42 mulatto born SC.

NORSETT, JOSEPH, 2, M, (--), M, SC, 971, 948, CHAS%. In HH of Alexander Norsett m 42 mulatto born SC.

NORSETT, LEWIS, 12, M, (--), M, SC, 971, 948, CHAS%. In HH of Alexander Norsett m 42 mulatto born SC.

NORSETT, MARGARET, 32, F, (--), M, SC, 971, 948, CHAS%. In HH of Alexander Norsett m 42 mulatto born SC.

NORSETT, PHILIP, 21, M, Farmer, M, SC, 971, 948, CHAS%. In HH of Alexander Norsett m 42 mulatto born SC.

NORSETT, PHILISTINE, 10, F, (--), M, SC, 971, 948, CHAS%. In HH of Alexander Norsett m 42 mulatto born SC.

NORTH, ABRAHAM, 63, M, Laborer, M, SC, 192, 192, CHAS%.

NORTH, HARRIET, 32, F, (--), M, SC, 192, 192, CHAS%. In HH of Abraham North m 63 mulatto born SC.

NORTH, HARRIOT, 26, F, (--), M, SC, 556, 539, CHAS-. In HH of Catherine Alston f 25 mulatto born SC.

NORTH, PRISCILLA, 55, F, (--), M, SC, 246, 231, CHAS-.

NORTH, SARAH, 52, F, (--), M, SC, 192, 192, CHAS%. In HH of Abraham North m 63 mulatto born SC.

NORTH, SARAH, 19, M, (--), M, SC, 192, 192, CHAS%. In HH of Abraham North m 63 mulatto born SC.

NORTON, ANTHONY, 15, M, Laborer, B, SC, 1234, 1234, UNION. In HH of William Hewett m 31 born SC.

NORTON, BILL, 16, M, (--), M, SC, 702, 702, LAU. IN HH of Bill Jackson m 25 mulatto born SC.

NORTON, CAROLINE, 2, F, (--), B, SC, 581, 581, UNION. In HH of Jane Norton f 45 black born SC.

NORTON, DAVID, 0, M, (--), B, SC, 581, 581, UNION. In HH of Jane Norton f 45 black born SC. David 8/12 yr.

NORTON, ELVIRA, 6, F, (--), M, NC, 581, 581, UNION. In HH of Jane Norton f 45 black born SC.

NORTON, EMILINE, 10, F, (--), M, NC, 581, 581, UNION. In HH of Jane Norton f 45 black born SC.

NORTON, HEZEKIAH, 20, M, Laborer, B, SC, 581, 581, UNION. In HH of Jane Norton f 45 black born SC.

NORTON, JAMES, 10, M, (--), B, SC, 581, 581, UNION. In HH of Jane Norton

f 45 black born SC.

NORTON, JANE, 45, F, (--), B, SC, 581, 581, UNION.

NORTON, JEFF, 20, M, (--), M, SC, 702, 702, LAU. IN HH of Bill Jackson m 25 mulatto born SC.

NORTON, LAVINIA, 7, F, (--), B, SC, 581, 581, UNION. In HH of Jane Norton f 45 black born SC.

NORTON, MUNROE, 8, M, (--), B, SC, 581, 581, UNION. In HH of Jane Norton f 45 black born SC.

NOWDEN, AUGUSTUS, 13, M, (--), M, SC, 562, 578, RICH. In HH of Richard Holmes m 55 mulatto born SC.

NOWDEN, WYAT, 19, M, Carpenter, M, SC, 562, 578, RICH. In HH of Richard Holmes m 55 mulatto born SC.

NOWELL, ROBERT, 22, M, Shoemaker, M, SC, 569, 586, RICH.

NOWLAND, HENRY, 31, M, Laborer, M, SC, 1185, 1190, MAR.

NOWLIN, ELIZA, 8, F, (--), M, SC, 266, 266, GEOR*. In HH of George Nowlin m 15 mulatto born SC.

NOWLIN, ELIZABETH, 19, F, (--), M, SC, 265, 265, GEOR*. In HH of Nancy Nowlin f 40 mulatto born SC.

NOWLIN, GEORGE, 15, M, (--), M, SC, 266, 266, GEOR*.

NOWLIN, JAMES, 15, M, (--), M, SC, 264, 264, GEOR*. In HH of Joseph Nowlin m 46 born SC.

NOWLIN, JOSEPH, 46, M, Carpenter, M, SC, 264, 264, GEOR*.

NOWLIN, JOSEPH, 8, M, (--), M, SC, 264, 264, GEOR*. In HH of Joseph Nowlin m 46 born SC.

NOWLIN, MARY, 21, F, (--), M, SC, 269, 269, GEOR*. In HH of Wm. Nowlin m 57 mulatto born SC.

NOWLIN, NANCY, 40, F, (--), M, SC, 265, 265, GEOR*.

NOWLIN, ROBT., 13, M, (--), M, SC, 264, 264, GEOR*. In HH of Joseph Nowlin m 46 born SC.

NOWLIN, SUSANNA, 1, F, (--), M, SC, 266, 266, GEOR*. In HH of George

Nowlin m 15 mulatto born SC.

NOWLIN, WM., 57, M, Blacksmith, M, SC, 269, 269, GEOR*.

NOWLIN, WM., 11, M, (--), M, SC, 266, 266, GEOR*. In HH of George Nowlin m 15 mulatto born SC.

NUEFUELLE, JAMES, 9, M, (--), M, SC, 175, 165, CHAS-. In HH of Rhina Nuefuelle f 35 black born SC.

NUEFUELLE, JOSEPH, 6, M, (--), M, SC, 175, 165, CHAS-. In HH of Rhina Nuefuelle f 35 black born SC.

NUEFUELLE, JULIA, 11, F, (--), M, SC, 175, 165, CHAS-. In HH of Rhina Nuefuelle f 35 black born SC.

NUEFUELLE, RHINA, 35, F, (--), B, SC, 175, 165, CHAS-.

O

O'HERN, ISAM, 48, M, Planter, M, SC, 277, 277, CHAS3.

O'HERN, JOHN, 14, M, (--), M, SC, 277, 277, CHAS3. In HH of Isam O'Hern m 48 mulatto born SC.

O'HERN, SARAH, 32, F, (--), M, SC, 277, 277, CHAS3. In HH of Isam O'Hern m 48 mulatto born SC.

O'NEALE, HILL, 25, M, Farmer, M, GA, 385, 404, PICK.

OGIER, JAMES, 70, M, Fisherman, M, SC, 264, 232, CHAS.

OGLES, CHARLES, 30, M, Carpenter, B, SC, 581, 581, UNION. In HH of Jane Norton f 45 black born SC.

OGLES, HANNAH, F, (--), B, SC, 581, 581, UNION. In HH of Jane Norton f 45 black born SC. No age for Hannah.

OGLESBY, {blank}, 2, F, (--), M, SC, 700, 701, FAIR. In HH of Sarah Oglesby f 35 black born SC.

OGLISBY, {blank}, 1, M, (--), M, SC, 49, 51, PICK. In HH of Manda Oglisby f 50 mulatto born SC.

OGLESBY, CHARLES, 12, M, (--), M, SC, 700, 701, FAIR. In HH of Sarah

Oglesby f 35 black born SC.

OGLESBY, HARDY, 5, M, (--), M, SC, 700, 701, FAIR. In HH of Sarah Oglesby f 35 black born SC.

OGLESBY, MARIA, 50, F, (--), M, SC, 700, 701, FAIR. In HH of Sarah Oglesby f 35 black born SC.

OGLESBY, SARAH, 35, F, (--), B, SC, 700, 701, FAIR.

OGLESBY, WARREN, 21, M, Laborer, M, SC, 700, 701, FAIR. In HH of Sarah Oglesby f 35 black born SC.

OGLESBY, WILLIAM, 10, M, (--), M, SC, 700, 701, FAIR. In HH of Sarah Oglesby f 35 black born SC.

OGLISBY, ANDY, 27, M, (--), B, SC, 480, 507, PICK. In HH of Tom Oglisby m 23 black born SC.

OGLISBY, BECKY, 17, F, (--), M, SC, 666, 701, PICK. In HH of Prisey Oglisby f 60 mulatto born SC.

OGLISBY, BENNET, 25, M, Blacksmith, M, SC, 666, 701, PICK. In HH of Prisey Oglisby f 60 mulatto born SC.

OGLISBY, BENSON, 21, M, Farmer, M, SC, 666, 701, PICK. In HH of Prisey Oglisby f 60 mulatto born SC.

OGLISBY, BETTY, 70, F, (--), M, VA, 667, 702, PICK.

OGLISBY, BETTY, 15, F, (--), M, SC, 49, 51, PICK. In HH of Manda Oglisby f 50 mulatto born SC.

OGLISBY, DICK, 11, M, (--), M, SC, 666, 701, PICK. In HH of Prisey Oglisby f 60 mulatto born SC.

OGLISBY, JESSIE, 35, M, Farmer, M, SC, 666, 701, PICK. In HH of Prisey Oglisby f 60 mulatto born SC.

OGLISBY, JOE, 24, M, (--), B, SC, 479, 506, PICK.

OGLISBY, MANDA, 50, F, (--), M, SC, 49, 51, PICK.

OGLISBY, MARION, 5, M, (--), M, SC, 49, 51, PICK. In HH of Manda Oglisby f 50 mulatto born SC.

OGLISBY, MARY, 14, F, (--), B, SC, 478, 505, PICK. In HH of Ruth Oglisby f 59 black born SC.

OGLISBY, POSEY, 19, M, Farmer, M, SC, 666, 701, PICK. In HH of Prisey Oglisby f 60 mulatto born SC.

OGLISBY, PRISEY, 60, F, (--), M, SC, 666, 701, PICK.

OGLISBY, RACHEL, 25, F, (--), M, SC, 49, 51, PICK. In HH of Manda Oglisby f 50 mulatto born SC.

OGLISBY, RUTH, 59, F, (--), B, SC, 478, 505, PICK.

OGLISBY, SARY, 19, F, (--), B, SC, 478, 505, PICK. In HH of Ruth Oglisby f 59 black born SC.

OGLISBY, TOM, 23, M, (--), B, SC, 480, 507, PICK.

OGLISBY, VIOLETTE, 12, F, (--), M, SC, 666, 701, PICK. In HH of Prisey Oglisby f 60 mulatto born SC.

OGLISBY, WASH, 30, M, Farmer, M, SC, 666, 701, PICK. In HH of Prisey Oglisby f 60 mulatto born SC.

OLGISBY, BETTY, 70, F, (--), M, VA, 667, 702, PICK.

OLIVE, HENRY, 55, M, Planter, M, SC, 332, 339, RICH+.

OLIVE, HENRY L, 16, M, (--), M, SC, 332, 339, RICH+. In HH of Henry Olive m 55 mulatto born SC.

OLIVE, MARY, 13, F, (--), M, SC, 332, 339, RICH+. In HH of Henry Olive m 55 mulatto born SC.

OLIVE, SARAH, 42, F, (--), M, SC, 332, 339, RICH+. In HH of Henry Olive m 55 mulatto born SC.

OLIVE, SOPHIA E., 18, F, (--), M, SC, 332, 339, RICH+. In HH of Henry Olive m 55 mulatto born SC.

OLIVER, CHARLES, 10, M, (--), M, SC, 489, 484, CHAS%. In HH of William Tramer m 18 born SC.

OLIVER, HARRIET, 32, F, (--), M, SC, 489, 484, CHAS%. In HH of William Tramer m 18 born SC.

OLIVER, JOHN, 50, M, Tailor, M, SC, 284, 268, CHAS-.

OLIVER, JOHN, 17, M, Shoemaker, M, SC, 284, 268, CHAS-. In HH of John Oliver m 50 mulatto born SC.

OLIVER, LENA, 8, F, (--), M, SC, 489, 484, CHAS%. In HH of William Tramer m 18 born SC.

OLIVER, MARY, 12, F, (--), M, SC, 489, 484, CHAS%. In HH of William Tramer m 18 born SC.

OLIVER, SAMUEL, 14, M, Shoemaker, M, SC, 489, 484, CHAS%. In HH of William Tramer m 18 born SC.

OLIVER, SARAH, 45, F, (--), M, SC, 284, 268, CHAS-. In HH of John Oliver m 50 mulatto born SC.

OLIVER, SARAH, 6, F, (--), M, SC, 489, 484, CHAS%. In HH of William Tramer m 18 born SC.

OLIVER, WILLIAM, 15, M, Shoemaker, M, SC, 284, 268, CHAS-. In HH of John Oliver m 50 mulatto born SC.

ONEAL, MARY, 16, F, (--), M, SC, 98, 110, CHAS. In HH of Emiley Bowers f 35 mulatto born SC.

ONEALE, HILL, 25, M, Farmer, M, GA, 385, 404, PICK.

ONEALE, PRISCILLA, 100, F, (--), M, SC, 316, 322, RICH. In HH of Richard Oneale m 58 born England.

ORR, ABRAHAM, 40, M, (--), M, SC, 478, 478, BEAU-.

ORR, ALEXANDER, 22, M, Laborer, B, SC, 487, 487, BEAU-. In HH of Mary Orr f 42 black born SC.

ORR, ALFRED, 11, M, (--), B, SC, 441, 441, BEAU-. In HH of Benjamin Orr m 40 black born SC.

ORR, AMANDA, 14, F, (--), B, SC, 470, 470, BEAU-. In HH of Isham Orr m 40 black born SC.

ORR, ANN, 16, F, (--), M, SC, 449, 449, BEAU-. In HH of Mary Orr f 44 mulatto born SC.

ORR, BENJAMIN, 40, M, Laborer. B, SC, 441, 441, BEAU-.

ORR, BENJAMIN, 18, M, Laborer. M, SC, 441, 441, BEAU-. In HH of Benjamin Orr m 40 black born SC.

ORR, BENJAMIN, 4, M, (--), M, SC, 304, 304, CHAS%. In HH of Samuel Orr m 38 black born SC.

ORR, BENJAMIN, 4, M, (--), M, SC, 484, 484, BEAU-. In HH of Henry Orr m 33 black born SC.

ORR, BLOSSOM, 4, F, (--), M, SC, 481, 481, BEAU-. In HH of John Orr m 30 black born SC.

ORR, CATHARIN, 8, F, (--), B, SC, 469, 469, BEAU-. In HH of Catharine Orr f 50 black born SC.

ORR, CATHARINE, 50, F, (--), B, SC, 469, 469, BEAU-.

ORR, CUSHION F., 12, F, (--), M, SC, 485, 485, BEAU-. In HH of Mary Orr f 376 mulatto born SC.

ORR, EDWARD, 14, M, Drayman, M, SC, 304, 304, CHAS%. In HH of Samuel Orr m 38 black born SC.

ORR, EDWARD, 4, M, (--), B, SC, 470, 470, BEAU-. In HH of Isham Orr m 40 black born SC.

ORR, ELIZA, 25, F, (--), M, SC, 484, 484, BEAU-. In HH of Henry Orr m 33 black born SC.

ORR, ELIZABETH, 18, F, (--), B, SC, 469, 469, BEAU-. In HH of Catharine Orr f 50 black born SC.

ORR, FALEY, 1, M, (--), B, SC, 441, 441, BEAU-. In HH of Benjamin Orr m 40 black born SC.

ORR, FRANCIS, 28, F, (--), B, SC, 470, 470, BEAU-. In HH of Isham Orr m 40 black born SC.

ORR, HARRIET, 7, F, (--), B, SC, 441, 441, BEAU-. In HH of Benjamin Orr m 40 black born SC.

ORR, HENRY, 33, M, Laborer. B, SC, 484, 484, BEAU-.

ORR, HENRY, 1, M, (--), M, SC, 484, 484, BEAU-. In HH of Henry Orr m 33 black born SC.

ORR, HESTER, 30, F, (--), M, SC, 481, 481, BEAU-. In HH of John Orr m 30 black born SC.

ORR, HESTER, 22, F, (--), B, SC, 469, 469, BEAU-. In HH of Catharine Orr f 50 black born SC.

ORR, HESTER, 4, F, (--), B, SC, 469, 469, BEAU-. In HH of Catharine Orr f 50 black born SC.

ORR, HESTER, 2, M, (--), M, SC, 481, 481, BEAU-. In HH of John Orr m 30 black born SC.

ORR, ISAAC, 22, M, Laborer. B, SC, 474, 474, BEAU-.

ORR, ISADORA, 3, F, (--), B, SC, 441, 441, BEAU-, In HH of Benjamin Orr m 40 black born SC.

ORR, ISHAM, 40, M, Mechanic, B, SC, 470, 470, BEAU-.

ORR, ISHAM, 10, M, (--), B, SC, 470, 470, BEAU-. In HH of Isham Orr m 40 black born SC.

ORR, JAMES, 25, M, Laborer, B, SC, 473, 473, BEAU-. In HH of Patsey Orr f 60 black born SC.

ORR, JAMES, 14, M, (--), M, SC, 441, 441, BEAU-. In HH of Benjamin Orr m 40 black born SC.

ORR, JOHN, 30, M, Farmer, B, SC, 481, 481, BEAU-.

ORR, JOHN, 8, M, (--), M, SC, 304, 304, CHAS%. In HH of Samuel Orr m 38 black born SC.

ORR, JOHN, 6, M, (--), B, SC, 470, 470, BEAU-. In HH of Isham Orr m 40 black born SC.

ORR, JOSEPH, 4, M, (--), M, SC, 449, 449, BEAU-. In HH of Mary Orr f 44 mulatto born SC.

ORR, JOSHUA, 14, M, (--), B, SC, 469, 469, BEAU-. In HH of Catharine Orr f 50 black born SC.

ORR, LUTITIA, 14, F, (--), M, SC, 449, 449, BEAU-. In HH of Mary Orr f 44 mulatto born SC.

ORR, LYDIA, 15, F, (--), M, SC, 478, 478, BEAU-. In HH of Abraham Orr m 40 mulatto born SC.

ORR, MANUEL, 16, M, Laborer. M, SC, 441, 441, BEAU-. In HH of Benjamin Orr m 40 black born SC.

ORR, MARTHA, 38, F, (--), M, SC, 441, 441, BEAU-. In HH of Benjamin Orr m 40 black born SC.

ORR, MARTHA, 20, F, (--), M, SC, 449, 449, BEAU-. In HH of Mary Orr f 44 mulatto born SC.

ORR, MARY, 76, F, (--), M, SC, 485, 485, BEAU-.

ORR, MARY, 44, F, (--), M, SC, 449, 449, BEAU-.

ORR, MARY, 42, F, (--), B, SC, 487, 487, BEAU-.

ORR, MARY, 10, F, (--), B, SC, 469, 469, BEAU-. In HH of Catharine Orr f 50 black born SC.

ORR, MARY, 5, F, (--), B, SC, 441, 441, BEAU-. In HH of Benjamin Orr m 40 black born SC.

ORR, MICHAEL, 12, M, (--), B, SC, 470, 470, BEAU-. In HH of Isham Orr m 40 black born SC.

ORR, PATSEY, 60, F, (--), B, SC, 473, 473, BEAU-.

ORR, PENIUS {?}, 10, F, (--), M, SC, 481, 481, BEAU-. In HH of John Orr m 30 black born SC.

ORR, REBECCA, 25, F, (--), B, SC, 470, 470, BEAU-. In HH of Isham Orr m 40 black born SC.

ORR, REBECCA, 8, F, (--), B, SC, 470, 470, BEAU-. In HH of Isham Orr m 40 black born SC.

ORR, REBECCA, 7, F, (--), B, SC, 487, 487, BEAU-. In HH of Mary Orr f 42 black born SC.

ORR, RICHARD, 16, M, Laborer, B, SC, 469, 469, BEAU-. In HH of Catharine Orr f 50 black born SC.

ORR, SAMUEL, 38, M, (--), B, SC, 304, 304, CHAS%.

ORR, SAMUEL, 5, M, (--), M, SC, 304, 304, CHAS%. In HH of Samuel Orr m 38 black born SC.

ORR, SARAH, 35, F, (--), B, SC, 304, 304, CHAS%. In HH of Samuel Orr m 38 black born SC.

ORR, SARAH, 22, F, (--), M, SC, 449, 449, BEAU-. In HH of Mary Orr f 44 mulatto born SC.

ORR, SARAH, 18, F, (--), M, SC, 449, 449, BEAU-. In HH of Mary Orr f 44 mulatto born SC.

ORR, SARAH, 16, F, (--), B, SC, 470, 470, BEAU-. In HH of Isham Orr m 40 black born SC.

ORR, SARAH, 9, F, (--), B, SC, 441, 441, BEAU-. In HH of Benjamin Orr m 40 black born SC.

ORR, SARAH ANN, 6, F, (--), B, SC, 469, 469, BEAU-. In HH of Catharine Orr f 50 black born SC.

ORR, SUSAN, 16, F, (--), B, SC, 474, 474, BEAU-. In HH of Isaac Orr m 22 black born SC.

ORVILEE, ASSENTEA D., 40, F, (--), M, St. Domingo. 455, 414, CHAS+. In HH of Narcissas Perchereau f 50 mulatto born St. Domingo.

ORVILEE, ELIZABETH, 19, F, (--), M, SC, 455, 414, CHAS+. In HH of Narcissas Perchereau f 50 mulatto born St. Domingo.

OSBORNE, EMMA, 17, F, (--), M, SC, 48, 48, CHAS%. In HH of William Osborne m 37 mulatto born SC.

OSBORNE, SATYRA, 34, F, (--), M, SC, 48, 48, CHAS%. In HH of William Osborne m 37 mulatto born SC.

OSBORNE, WILLIAM, 37, M, Carpenter, M, SC, 48, 48, CHAS%.

OUNERCY, CAROLINE, 8, F, (--), M, SC, 333, 333, HORR. In HH of John Ounercy m 70 mulatto born SC.

OUNERCY, DANIEL, 45, M, Farmer, M, SC, 333, 333, HORR. In HH of John Ounercy m 70 mulatto born SC.

OUNERCY, DAVID, 21, M, (--), M, SC, 333, 333, HORR. In HH of John Ounercy m 70 mulatto born SC.

OUNERCY, JAMES, 28, M, Farmer, M, SC, 333, 333, HORR. In HH of John Ounercy m 70 mulatto born SC.

OUNERCY, JAMES, 10, M, (--), M, SC, 333, 333, HORR. In HH of John Ounercy m 70 mulatto born SC.

OUNERCY, JOHN, 70, M, Farmer, M, SC, 333, 333, HORR.

OUNERCY, JOHN, 32, M, Farmer, M, SC, 333, 333, HORR. In HH of John Ounercy m 70 mulatto born SC.

OUNERCY, MARY, 23, F, (--), M, SC, 333, 333, HORR. In HH of John Ounercy m 70 mulatto born SC.

OUNERCY, POLEY, 65, F, (--), M, SC, 333, 333, HORR. In HH of John Ounercy m 70 mulatto born SC.

OUNERCY, POLLY, 19, F, (--), M, SC, 333, 333, HORR. In HH of John Ounercy m 70 mulatto born SC.

OUNERCY, ROBT., 25, M, Farmer, M, SC, 333, 333, HORR. In HH of John Ounercy m 70 mulatto born SC.

OUTAN, MARY, 70, F, (--), M, SC, 348, 355, RICH+.

OUTAN, SARAH, 50, F, (--), M, SC, 348, 355, RICH+. In HH of Mary Outan f 70 mulatto born SC.

OUTON, ISHMAEL, 7, M, (--), M, SC, 262, 267, RICH+. In Hh of William Outon m 38 mulatto born SC.

OUTON, MAHANEY, 25, F, (--), M, SC, 262, 267, RICH+. In Hh of William Outon m 38 mulatto born SC.

OUTON, MANZIAH, 9, F, (--), M, SC, 262, 267, RICH+. In Hh of William Outon m 38 mulatto born SC.

OUTON, MARTHA, 5, F, (--), M, SC, 262, 267, RICH+. In Hh of William Outon m 38 mulatto born SC.

OUTON, WILLIAM, 38, M, Planter, M, SC, 262, 267, RICH+.

OUTON, WILLIAM, 3, M, (--), M, SC, 262, 267, RICH+. In Hh of William Outon m 38 mulatto born SC.

OWENS, ALFRED, 7, M, (--), M, SC, 845, 803, CHAS+. In HH of Hannah Owens f 49 mulatto born SC.

OWENS, ALFRED, 6, M, (--), B, NY, 474, 432, CHAS+. In HH of Smart Owens m 50 black born NY.

OWENS, CORNELIUS, 4, M, (--), B, SC, 37, 37, CHAS%. In HH of Nancy Owens f 24 black born SC.

OWENS, DOLLY, 12, F, (--), M, SC, 845, 803, CHAS+. In HH of Hannah Owens f 49 mulatto born SC.

OWENS, DOLLY, 12, F, (--), B, NY, 474, 432, CHAS+. In HH of Smart Owens m 50 black born NY.

OWENS, HANNAH, 49, F, (--), M, SC, 845, 803, CHAS+.

OWENS, HANNAH, 40, F, (--), B, NY, 474, 432, CHAS+. In HH of Smart

Owens m 50 black born NY.

OWENS, HENRY, 26, M, Tailor, B, SC, 37, 37, CHAS%. In HH of Nancy Owens f 24 black born SC.

OWENS, HENRY, 9, M, (--), B, SC, 37, 37, CHAS%. In HH of Nancy Owens f 24 black born SC.

OWENS, HUGH, 3, M, (--), M, SC, 1217, 1222, MAR. In HH of Martha Owens f 25 mulatto born SC.

OWENS, JANE, 2, F, (--), B, SC, 37, 37, CHAS%. In HH of Nancy Owens f 24 black born SC.

OWENS, JOHN, 5, M, (--), M, SC, 1217, 1222, MAR. In HH of Martha Owens f 25 mulatto born SC.

OWENS, MARTHA, 25, F, (--), M, SC, 1217, 1222, MAR.

OWENS, NANCY, 24, F, (--), B, SC, 37, 37, CHAS%.

OWENS, NANCY, 10, F, (--), M, SC, 845, 803, CHAS+. In HH of Hannah Owens f 49 mulatto born SC.

OWENS, RACHEL, 6, F, (--), B, SC, 37, 37, CHAS%. In HH of Nancy Owens f 24 black born SC.

OWENS, RICHARD, 4, M, (--), M, SC, 845, 803, CHAS+. In HH of Hannah Owens f 49 mulatto born SC.

OWENS, RICHARD, 4, M, (--), B, NY, 474, 432, CHAS+. In HH of Smart Owens m 50 black born NY.

OWENS, SARAH, 1, F, (--), M, SC, 1217, 1222, MAR. In HH of Martha Owens f 25 mulatto born SC.

OWENS, SMART, 50, M, Carpenter, B, NY, 474, 432, CHAS+.

OXENDINE, ABIGAIL, 17, F, (--), M, SC, 1259, 1259, SUMT. In HH of Martha Scott f 50 mulatto born SC.

OXENDINE, ALEX., 68, M, Farmer, B, SC, 577, 577, MARL.

OXENDINE, ELEFARE, 11, F, (--), M, GA, 1259, 1259, SUMT. In HH of Martha Scott f 50 mulatto born SC.

OXENDINE, ELIZA, 36, F, (--), B, SC, 578, 578, MARL. IN HH of Gilbert Oxendine m 36 black born NC.

OXENDINE, GILBERT, 40, M, Farmer, M, NC, 578, 578, MARL.

OXSENDINE, HANNAH, 71, F, (--), B, SC, 577, 577, MARL. IN HH of Alex Oxendine m 68 black born SC.

OXENDINE, JAMES, 0, M, (--), B, SC, 145, 133, CHAS*. In HH of Ellen Jennings f 25 black born SC. James Oxendine age 6/12 yr.

OXENDINE, JANE, 80, F, (--), M, SC, 1260, 1260, SUMT.

OXENDINE, JAS., 12, M, (--), M, SC, 1260, 1260, SUMT. In HH of Jane Oxendine f 80 mulatto born SC.

OXENDINE, LARKIN, 20, M, Laborer, M, SC, 1260, 1260, SUMT. In HH of Jane Oxendine f 80 mulatto born SC.

OXENDINE, LOUISA, 30, F, (--), B, SC, 145, 133, CHAS*. In HH of Ellen Jennings f 25 black born SC.

OXENDINE, MARANDA, 26, F, (--), M, SC, 1260, 1260, SUMT. In HH of Jane Oxendine f 80 mulatto born SC.

OXENDINE, MICHAEL, 18, M, Laborer, M, SC, 1260, 1260, SUMT. In HH of Jane Oxendine f 80 mulatto born SC.

OXENDINE, RICHD, 18, M, Laborer, M, SC, 1259, 1259, SUMT. In HH of Martha Scott f 50 mulatto born SC.

OXENDINE, SARAH, 14, F, (--), M, SC, 1260, 1260, SUMT. In HH of Jane Oxendine f 80 mulatto born SC.

OXENDINE, WARREN, 15, M, Laborer, M, GA, 1259, 1259, SUMT. In HH of Martha Scott f 50 mulatto born SC.

OXENDINE, WM., 2, M, (--), M, SC, 1260, 1260, SUMT. In HH of Jane Oxendine f 80 mulatto born SC.

OXENDIORE, DAVID, 35, M, Carpenter, B, SC, 137, 137, GEOR*. In HH of L.B. Grier m 33 born SC.

OXENDYNE, HUEY, 7, M, (--), M, SC, 215, 219, RICH+. In HH of Nancy Oxendyne f 26 mulatto born SC.

OXENDYNE, NANCY, 26, F, (--), M, SC, 215, 219, RICH+.

OXENDYNE, WILLIAM T., 12, M, (--), M, SC, 215, 219, RICH+. In HH of Nancy Oxendyne f 26 mulatto born SC.

OXINDYNE, HILLIARD A., 4, M, (--), M, SC, 136, 140, RICH. Note: HH out of order, follow HH 87/88. In HH of Jesse Oxindyne m 34 mulatto born NC.

OXINDYNE, JESSE, 34, F, Carpenter, M, NC, 136, 140, RICH. {Note: HH out of order, follow HH 87/88.}

OXINDYNE, JESSE, 8, M, (--), M, SC, 136, 140, RICH. {Note: HH out of order, follow HH 87/88.} In HH of Jesse Oxindyne m 34 mulatto born NC.

OXINDYNE, REBECCA, 6, f, (--), M, SC, 136, 140, RICH.{Note: HH out of order, follow HH 87/88}. In HH of Jesse Oxindyne m 34 mulatto born NC.

OXINDYNE, SARAH, 19, F, (--), M, SC, 136, 140, RICH. {Note: HH out of order, follow HH 87/88}. In HH of Jesse Oxindyne m 34 mulatto born NC.

P

PACK, JOHN F., 12, M, (--), M, SC, 476, 477, AND*. In HH of Reubin Poor m 30 white born SC.

PACKET, JEMISS {?}, 66, F, (--), B, VA, 882, 882, PICK+. In HH of Reuben Packet m 66 black born SC.

PACKET, REUBEN, 66, M, Farmer, B, SC, 882, 882, PICK+.

PADGET, ISHAM, 29, M, Farmer, M, SC, 359, 359, COLL.

PADGETT, ANN BECKET, 25, F, (--), M, SC, 307, 307, BEAU+. In HH of John Padgett m 36 mulatto born SC.

PADGETT, ANNIE, 28, F, (--), M, SC, 307, 307, BEAU+. In HH of John Padgett m 36 mulatto born SC.

PADGETT, ELIZABETH, 35, F, (--), M, SC, 307, 307, BEAU+. In HH of John Padgett m 36 mulatto born SC.

PADGETT, EMMA, 6, F, (--), M, SC, 307, 307, BEAU+. In HH of John

Padgett m 36 mulatto born SC.

PADGETT, JOHN, 36, M, Farmer, M, SC, 307, 307, BEAU+.

PADGETT, MARY, 8, F, (--), M, SC, 307, 307, BEAU+. In HH of John Padgett m 36 mulatto born SC.

PAGE, M., 12, F, (--), M, SC, 388, 388, LANC*. In HH of S. John f 33 born SC.

PAIN, DOSIA, 34, F, (--), B, SC, 406, 406, CHFD. In HH of Dru Pain m 32 black born SC.

PAIN, DRU, 32, M, Boatman, B, SC, 406, 406, CHFD.

PAIN, MARY, 6, F, (--), M, SC, 406, 406, CHFD. In HH of Dru Pain m 32 black born SC.

PAINE, GEORGE, 35, M, Fisherman, M, SC, 436, 394, CHAS.

PAINE, VENUS, 25, F, (--), M, SC, 436, 394, CHAS. In HH of George Paine m 35 born SC.

PAINE, WILLIAM, 0, M, (--), M, SC, 436, 394, CHAS. In HH of George Paine m 35 born SC. William Paine age 5/12 yr.

PALMER, AMY, 51, F, (--), B, SC, 24, 24, CHAS2.

PALMER, BENJAMIN, 10, M, (--), M, SC, 28, 28, CHAS2. In HH of Buls {sic} Palmer f 47 black born SC.

PALMER, BETSY, 53, F, (--), B, SC, 23, 23, CHAS2.

PALMER, BULS, 47, F, (--), B, SC, 28, 28, CHAS2.

PALMER, CATHERINE, 6, F, (--), M, SC, 28, 28, CHAS2. In HH of Buls {sic} Palmer f 47 black born SC.

PALMER, EDWARD, 28, M, Tailor, M, SC, 604, 585, CHAS-. In HH of Catherine Smith f 22 mulatto born SC.

PALMER, EDWARD, 6, M, (--), B, SC, 26, 26, CHAS2. In HH of Lavinca McGomery f 30 black born SC.

PALMER, GEORGIANA, 12, F, (--), B, SC, 26, 26, CHAS2. In HH of Lavinca McGomery f 30 black born SC.

PALMER, HARRIET, 75, F, (--), B, SC, 27, 27, CHAS2.

PALMER, HENRIETTA, 8, F, (--), B, SC, 28, 28, CHAS2. In HH of Buls {sic} Palmer f 47 black born SC.

PALMER, JOHN, 32, M, (--), B, SC, 27, 27, CHAS2. In HH of Harriet Palmer f 75 black born SC.

PALMER, LAVINCA, 5, F, (--), B, SC, 26, 26, CHAS2. In HH of Lavinca McGomery f 30 black born SC.

PALMER, MARY, 9, F, (--), B, SC, 26, 26, CHAS2. In HH of Lavinca McGomery f 30 black born SC.

PALMER, MARYANN, 35, F, (--), B, SC, 25, 25, CHAS2.

PALMER, SAM, 6, M, (--), B, SC, 30, 30, CHAS2. In HH of Tom Palmer m 45 black born SC.

PALMER, SOPHY, 40, F, (--), M, SC, 30, 30, CHAS2. In HH of Tom Palmer m 45 black born SC.

PALMER, TOM, 45, M, Laborer, B, SC, 30, 30, CHAS2.

PALMER, WATHY, 12, M, (--), B, SC, 23, 23, CHAS2. In HH of Betsy Palmer f 53 black born SC.

PALMER, WILLIAM, 13, M, (--), B, SC, 26, 26, CHAS2. In HH of Lavinca McGomery f 30 black born SC.

PAMBY, CANSADY, 20, F, (--), B, SC, 407, 407, UNN+. In HH of Elizabeth Pamby f 55 mullotto born SC.

PAMBY, ELIZABETH, 55, F, (--), M, SC, 407, 407, UNN+.

PAMBY, GEORGE, 28, M, Laborer, B, SC, 407, 407, UNN+. In HH of Elizabeth Pamby f 55 mullotto born SC.

PAMBY, ROBIN, 18, M, (--), B, SC, 407, 407, UNN+. In HH of Elizabeth Pamby f 55 mullotto born SC.

PAMBY, STARLIN, 32, M, Laborer, M, SC, 407, 407, UNN+. In HH of Elizabeth Pamby f 55 mullotto born SC.

PAMBY, WILLIAM, 21, M, Laborer, B, SC, 407, 407, UNN+. In HH of Elizabeth Pamby f 55 mullotto born SC.

PANE, HENRY, 5, M, (--), M, SC, 907, 884, CHAS%. In HH of Sarah Pane f 35 mulatto born SC.

PANE, LAVINA, 4, F, (--), M, SC, 907, 884, CHAS%. In HH of Sarah Pane f 35 mulatto born SC.

PANE, SARAH, 35, F, (--), M, SC, 907, 884, CHAS%.

PARKER, AMELIA, 50, F, (--), B, SC, 1024, 1001, CHAS-.

PARKER, CATHERINE, 45, F, (--), M, SC, 434, 393, CHAS. In HH of W.T. Ryan f 45 born SC.

PARKER, CATHERINE, 35, F, (--), M, SC, 156, 156, CHAS%.

PARKER, EMMA, 7, F, (--), M, SC, 551, 510, CHAS+. In HH of Selena Ward f 28 mulatto born SC.

PARKER, GEORGIANA, 8, F, (--), M, SC, 551, 510, CHAS+. In HH of Selena Ward f 28 mulatto born SC.

PARKER, HENRY, 10, M, (--), M, SC, 156, 156, CHAS%. In HH of Catherine Parker f 35 mulatto born SC.

PARKER, HENRY, 7, M, (--), M, SC, 434, 393, CHAS. h of W.T. Ryan f 45 born SC.

PARKER, HETTY, 3, F, (--), M, SC, 467, 467, MARL. In HH of Isah Parker m 75 born SC.

PARKER, JAMES, 30, M, (--), M, SC, 156, 156, CHAS%. In HH of Catherine Parker f 35 mulatto born SC.

PARKER, JOHN, 7, M, (--), M, SC, 156, 156, CHAS%. In HH of Catherine Parker f 35 mulatto born SC.

PARKER, JOHN, 4, M, (--), M, SC, 551, 510, CHAS+. In HH of Selena Ward f 28 mulatto born SC.

PARKER, MARY, 30, F, (--), M, SC, 184, 172, CHAS-.

PARKER, MARY, 17, F, (--), M, SC, 434, 393, CHAS. h of W.T. Ryan f 45 born SC.

PARKER, MARY, 12, F, (--), M, SC, 156, 156, CHAS%. In HH of Catherine Parker f 35 mulatto born SC.

PARKER, PETER, 38, M, Wood Factor, M, SC, 551, 510, CHAS+. In HH of Selena Ward f 28 mulatto born SC.

PARKER, SALLY, 5, F, (--), M, SC, 467, 467, MARL. In HH of Isah Parker m 75 born SC.

PARKER, SUSAN, 55, F, (--), B, SC, 675, 633, CHAS+. In HH of Clainda Simons f 35 black born SC.

PARKER, SYLVIA, 57, F, (--), M, SC, 551, 510, CHAS+. In HH of Selena Ward f 28 mulatto born SC.

PARKER, WILLIAM, 1, M, (--), M, SC, 551, 510, CHAS+. In HH of Selena Ward f 28 mulatto born SC.

PARKS, ADELINE, 17, F, (--), B, SC, 455, 414, CHAS+. In HH of Narcissas Perchereau f 50 mulatto born St. Domingo.

PARKS, AGNES, 8, F, (--), M, SC, 455, 414, CHAS+. In HH of Narcissas Perchereau f 50 mulatto born St. Domingo.

PARKS, EMILY, 5, F, (--), M, SC, 455, 414, CHAS+. In HH of Narcissas Perchereau f 50 mulatto born St. Domingo.

PARKS, JULIET, 12, F, (--), M, SC, 455, 414, CHAS+. In HH of Narcissas Perchereau f 50 mulatto born St. Domingo.

PARKS, ZETA, 3, F, (--), M, SC, 455, 414, CHAS+. In HH of Narcissas Perchereau f 50 mulatto born St. Domingo.

PARRIS{?}, ROBERT, 45, M, Carpenter, M, SC, 135, 135, CHAS^. In HH of Catherine Conyers f 24 black born SC.

PARSON, ANN, 60, F, (--), B, SC, 615, 607, CHAS%.

PARSONS, ELLEN, 23, F, (--), B, SC, 151, 149, CHAS*.

PARSONS, ELLEN, 0, F, (--), B, SC, 151, 149, CHAS*. In HH of Ellen Parsons f 23 black born SC. Ellen Parsons age 8/12 yr.

PARSONS, FRANCIS, 4, F, (--), B, SC, 151, 149, CHAS*. In HH of Ellen Parsons f 23 black born SC.

PARTAIN, MARTHA, 0, F, (--), M, SC, 1040, 1044, AND. In HH of Alsey Partain f 58 white born SC.

PATRICK, ANNA, 16, F, (--), M, SC, 87, 87, COLL+. In HH of Elijah Patrick

m 35 mulatto born SC.

PATRICK, CHARLES, 55, M, Farmer, M, SC, 63, 63, COLL+.

PATRICK, CHARLES, 40, M, (--), M, SC, 71, 71, COLL+.

PATRICK, CHARLES, 12, F, (--), M, SC, 87, 87, COLL+. In HH of Elijah Patrick m 35 mulatto born SC. Charles sex f {sic}.

PATRICK, ELIJAH, 35, M, Farmer, M, SC, 87, 87, COLL+.

PATRICK, ELIJAH, 21, M, Farmer, M, SC, 70, 70, COLL+.

PATRICK, ELIZA, 17, F, (--), M, SC, 70, 70, COLL+. In HH of Elijah Patrick m 21 mulatto born SC.

PATRICK, ELIZA, 6, F, (--), M, SC, 765, 723, CHAS+. In HH of Henry Barnell m 51 mulatto born SC.

PATRICK, ELIZTH., 55, F, (--), M, SC, 63, 63, COLL+. In HH of Charles Patrick m 55 mulatto born SC.

PATRICK, JANE, 25, F, (--), M, SC, 71, 71, COLL+. In HH of Charles Patrick m 40 mulatto born SC.

PATRICK, JANE, 5, F, (--), M, SC, 765, 723, CHAS+. In HH of Henry Barnell m 51 mulatto born SC.

PATRICK, LOVEY, 10, F, (--), M, SC, 71, 71, COLL+. In HH of Charles Patrick m 40 mulatto born SC.

PATRICK, MARY, 17, F, (--), M, SC, 68, 68, COLL+. In HH of Henry Johnston m 33 white born SC.

PATRICK, MESSEWY {sic}, 10, M, (--), M, SC, 87, 87, COLL+. In HH of Elijah Patrick m 35 mulatto born SC. Charles sex f {sic}.

PATRICK, SUSAN, 30, F, (--), M, SC, 87, 87, COLL+. In HH of Elijah Patrick m 35 mulatto born SC.

PATRICK, SUSAN, 4, F, (--), M, SC, 87, 87, COLL+. In HH of Elijah Patrick m 35 mulatto born SC. Charles sex f{sic}.

PATRICK, WILLIAM, 7, M, (--), M, SC, 87, 87, COLL+. In HH of Elijah Patrick m 35 mulatto born SC. Charles sex f {sic}.

PATRIDGE, ELIZA, 40, F, (--), M, SC, 574, 532, CHAS+. In HH of William Libby m 36 born SC.

PATTERSON, CELIA, 6, F, (--), M, SC, 340, 340, CHAS%. In HH of Elizabeth Patterson f 30 mulatto born SC.

PATTERSON, CINTHIA J., 23, F, (--), B, SC, 79, 79, ABB.

PATTERSON, CYRUS, 80, M, Mt. Clergyman, B, SC, 117, 117, ABB.

PATTERSON, ELIZABETH, 30, F, (--), M, SC, 340, 340, CHAS%.

PATTERSON, GEORGE, 38, M, Carpenter, M, SC, 213, 218, RICH. In HH of Sally Patterson f 58 black born SC.

PATTERSON, GEORGE, 8, M, (--), M, SC, 340, 340, CHAS%. In HH of Elizabeth Patterson f 30 mulatto born SC.

PATTERSON, JAMES, 12, M, (--), M, SC, 340, 340, CHAS%. In HH of Elizabeth Patterson f 30 mulatto born SC.

PATTERSON, JAMES, 3, M, (--), B, SC, 79, 79, ABB. IN HH of Cinthia J. Patterson 23 black born SC.

PATTERSON, MARY, 19, F, (--), M, SC, 213, 218, RICH. In HH of Sally Patterson f 58 black born SC.

PATTERSON, SALLY, 58, F, (--), B, SC, 213, 218, RICH.

PATTON, GEORGE, 50, M, Fisherman, B, SC, 549, 508, CHAS+. In HH of Mary Green f 70 black born SC.

PAUL, ANN, 26, F, (--), M, SC, 1584, 1590, MAR. In HH of Roda Paul f 65 mulatto born SC.

PAUL, CALVIN, 5, M, (--), M, SC, 1584, 1590, MAR. In HH of Roda Paul f 65 mulatto born SC.

PAUL, KITTY, 4, F, (--), M, SC, 1584, 1590, MAR. In HH of Roda Paul f 65 mulatto born SC.

PAUL, MARTHA, 21, F, (--), M, SC, 1584, 1590, MAR. In HH of Roda Paul f 65 mulatto born SC.

PAUL, RODA, 65, F, (--), M, SC, 1584, 1590, MAR.

PAUL, SENITH, 23, F, (--), M, SC, 1584, 1590, MAR. In HH of Roda Paul f 65 mulatto born SC.

PAYNE, ANNE, 7, F, (--), B, SC, 1177, 1156, CHAS%. In HH of David Payne m 35 black born SC.

PAYNE, DAVID, 35, M, Tailor, B, SC, 1177, 1156, CHAS%.

PAYNE, HARRIET, 30, F, (--), B, SC, 1177, 1156, CHAS%. In HH of David Payne m 35 black born SC.

PAYSOCK, CLOUGH, 7, M, (--), M, SC, 22, 22, UNN+. In HH of Susan Paysock f 30 mulatto born SC.

PAYSOCK, DAVID, 14, M, (--), M, SC, 22, 22, UNN+. In HH of Susan Paysock f 30 mulatto born SC.

PAYSOCK, ELIZABETH, 70, F, (--), M, SC, 22, 22, UNN+. In HH of Susan Paysock f 30 mulatto born SC.

PAYSOCK, EMELINE, 11, F, (--), M, SC, 22, 22, UNN+. In HH of Susan Paysock f 30 mulatto born SC.

PAYSOCK, JACKSON, 20, M, Laborer, M, SC, 22, 22, UNN+. In HH of Susan Paysock f 30 mulatto born SC.

PAYSOCK, MARTHA, 3, F, (--), M, SC, 22, 22, UNN+. In HH of Susan Paysock f 30 mulatto born SC.

PAYSOCK, RYLEY, 8, M, (--), M, SC, 22, 22, UNN+. In HH of Susan Paysock f 30 mulatto born SC.

PAYSOCK, SIMPSON, 0, M, (--), M, SC, 22, 22, UNN+. In HH of Susan Paysock f 30 mulatto born SC. Simpson 6/12.

PAYSOCK, SUSAN, 30, F, (--), M, SC, 22, 22, UNN+.

PAYSOCK, WADE, 5, M, (--), M, SC, 22, 22, UNN+. In HH of Susan Paysock f 30 mulatto born SC.

PAYTON, {BLANK}, 1, M, (--), B, SC, 687, 688, AND*. In HH of Jaberry Payton m 27 black born SC.

PAYTON, JOBERRY, 27, M, Laborer, B, SC, 687, 688, AND*.

PAYTON, LINENA, 9, F, (--), B, SC, 687, 688, AND*. In HH of Jaberry

Payton m 27 black born SC.

PAYTON, LUCINDA, 27, F, (--), B, SC, 687, 688, AND*. In HH of Jaberry Payton m 27 black born SC.

PAYTON, RICHMOND, 7, M, (--), B, SC, 687, 688, AND*. In HH of Jaberry Payton m 27 black born SC.

PAYTON, SARAH, 4, F, (--), B, SC, 687, 688, AND*. In HH of Jaberry Payton m 27 black born SC.

PAYTON, WATTY J., 6, M, (--), B, SC, 687, 688, AND*. In HH of Jaberry Payton m 27 black born SC.

PEAGLER, DANIEL E., 34, M, Farmer, M, SC, 47, 47, CHAS2.

PEAGLER, ELIZA, 4, F, (--), M, SC, 48, 48, CHAS2. In HH of James Peagler m 32 mulatto born SC.

PEAGLER, GABRIELLA, 2, F, (--), M, SC, 48, 48, CHAS2. In HH of James Peagler m 32 mulatto born SC.

PEAGLER, JAMES, 32, M, Farmer, M, SC, 48, 48, CHAS2.

PEAGLER, MARGARET., 36, F, (--), M, SC, 47, 47, CHAS2. In HH of Daniel Peagler m 34 mulatto born SC.

PEAGLER, ROBERT, 37, M, Farmer, M, SC, 66, 66, CHAS2.

PEARSEN, ADRIANA, 9, F, (--), B, SC, 194, 194, SUMT. In HH of Richard Pearsen m 70 Black born SC.

PEARSEN, ALBERT, 42, M, (--), M, SC, 194, 194, SUMT. In HH of Richard Pearsen m 70 Black born SC.

PEARSEN, BINKEY, 12, F, (--), B, SC, 195, 195, SUMT. In HH of Joe Pearsen m 26 black born SC.

PEARSEN, CHARLOTTE, 8, F, (--), B, SC, 194, 194, SUMT. In HH of Richard Pearsen m 70 Black born SC.

PEARSEN, COOK, 6, F, (--), B, SC, 194, 194, SUMT. In HH of Richard Pearsen m 70 Black born SC.

PEARSEN, ELENORA, 18, F, (--), B, SC, 194, 194, SUMT. In HH of Richard Pearsen m 70 Black born SC.

PEARSEN, ELIZA, 65, F, (--), B, SC, 194, 194, SUMT. In HH of Richard Pearsen m 70 Black born SC.

PEARSEN, EMILY, 6, F, (--), B, SC, 195, 195, SUMT. In HH of Joe Pearsen m 26 black born SC.

PEARSEN, GEO., 24, M, (--), B, SC, 194, 194, SUMT. In HH of Richard Pearsen m 70 Black born SC.

PEARSEN, JOE, 26, M, Laborer, B, SC, 195, 195, SUMT.

PEARSEN, JOHN, 20, M, (--), B, SC, 194, 194, SUMT. In HH of Richard Pearsen m 70 Black born SC.

PEARSEN, NANCY, 28, F, (--), B, SC, 194, 194, SUMT. In HH of Richard Pearsen m 70 Black born SC.

PEARSEN, RICHARD, 70, M, Planter, B, SC, 194, 194, SUMT.

PEARSEN, ROSE, 14, F, (--), B, SC, 194, 194, SUMT. In HH of Richard Pearsen m 70 Black born SC.

PEARSEN, SARAH, 21, F, (--), B, SC, 195, 195, SUMT. In HH of Joe Pearsen m 26 black born SC.

PEARSON, BENJAMIN, 20, M, Tailor, M, SC, 489, 472, CHAS-. In HH of James Wigfall m 52 black born SC.

PEARSON, ELIZA, 30, F, (--), M, SC, 130, 133, RICH. In HH of Richard Pearson m 25 mulatto born SC.

PEARSON, RICHARD, 25, M, Laborer, M, SC, 130, 133, RICH.

PEDRON, CELESTE, 40, F, (--), M, St. Domingo, 607, 565, CHAS+. In HH of Louis Pedron m 47 mulatto born St. Domingo.

PEDRON, EUTINESSE, 14, F, (--), M, St. Domingo, 607, 565, CHAS+. In HH of Louis Pedron m 47 mulatto born St. Domingo.

PEDRON, JULIAS, 17, M, (--), M, St. Domingo, 607, 565, CHAS+. In HH of Louis Pedron m 47 mulatto born St. Domingo.

PEDRON, LOUIS, 47, M, Fruiterer, M, St. Domingo, 607, 565, CHAS+.

PEDRON, MAGDELIN, 25, F, (--), M, St. Domingo, 607, 565, CHAS+. In HH of Louis Pedron m 47 mulatto born St. Domingo

PEEL, WM., 16, M, Laborer, B, SC,

586, 586, MARL. In HH of Abner Weatherly m 42 born SC.

PELM, LEWIS, 1, M, (--), M, SC, 34, 34, BEAU*. In HH of Judy Pelm 45 f born SC.

PELOT, CATHERINE, 25, F, (--), M, SC, 553, 536, CHAS-. In HH of Laura Bruch {sic} f 30 mulatto born SC.

PELZER, EMMA, 35, F, (--), M, SC, 712, 692, CHAS-.

PELZER, JAMES, 12, M, (--), M, SC, 712, 692, CHAS-. In HH of Emma Pelzer f 35 mulatto born SC.

PELZER, JULIANA, 3, F, (--), M, SC, 712, 692, CHAS-. In HH of Emma Pelzer f 35 mulatto born SC.

PELZER, LOUISA, 9, F, (--), M, SC, 712, 692, CHAS-. In HH of Emma Pelzer f 35 mulatto born SC.

PELZER, MARTHA, 14, F, (--), M, SC, 712, 692, CHAS-. In HH of Emma Pelzer f 35 mulatto born SC.

PELZER, THOMAS, 6, M, (--), M, SC, 712, 692, CHAS-. In HH of Emma Pelzer f 35 mulatto born SC.

PENCILE, HANNAH, 25, F, (--), M, SC, 445, 403, CHAS. In HH of A.B. Williman m 30 born SC.

PENCILS, MARGANT, 38, F, (--), M, SC, 420, 418, CHAS%.

PENNAN, ELIZA, 30, F, (--), B, SC, 902, 882, CHAS-. In HH of Abraham Moise m 51 born SC.

PEPPER, EDWARD, 8, M, (--), M, SC, 389, 372, CHAS-. In HH of E. Winslow m 48 born NC.

PEPPER, HAGAR, 47, F, (--), B, SC, 389, 372, CHAS-. In HH of E. Winslow m 48 born NC.

PEPPER, JAMES, 4, M, (--), M, SC, 389, 372, CHAS-. In HH of E. Winslow m 48 born NC.

PEPPER, JANE, 6, F, (--), M, SC, 389, 372, CHAS-. In HH of E. Winslow m 48 born NC.

PERCHEREAU, HESTER, 28, F, (--), M, St. Domingo, 455, 414, CHAS+. In HH of Narcissas Perchereau f 50 mulatto born St. Domingo.

PERCHEREAU, NARCISSAS, 50, F, (--), M, St. Domingo, 455, 414, CHAS+.

PERCHEREAU, NARCISSAS, 22, F, (--), M, St. Domingo, 455, 414, CHAS+. In HH of Narcissas Perchereau f 50 mulatto born St. Domingo.

PERCHEREAU, SILVLANIA, 40, F, (--), B, St. Domingo, 455, 414, CHAS+. In HH of Narcissas Perchereau f 50 mulatto born St. Domingo.

PERCY, CATHERINE, 20, F, (--), B, SC, 774, 757, CHAS%.

PERCY, JANE, 8, F, (--), B, SC, 774, 757, CHAS%. In HH of Catherine Percy f 20 black born SC.

PERCY, JOHN, 22, M, Drayman, B, SC, 774, 757, CHAS%. In HH of Catherine Percy f 20 black born SC.

PERCY, THOMAS, 4, M, (--), B, SC, 774, 757, CHAS%. In HH of Catherine Percy f 20 black born SC.

PERRERA, FRANCIS, 55, F, (--), M, St. Domingo, 242, 217, CHAS*. In HH of Pamelia Duquercrow f 27 born SC.

PERRINEAU, ABRAHAM, 35, M, Laborer, M, SC, 234, 234, CHAS%.

PERRINEAU, ELLEN, 18, F, (--), M, SC, 234, 234, CHAS%. In HH of Abraham Perrineau m 35 mulatto born SC.

PERRINEAU, LOUISA, 25, F, (--), M, SC, 234, 234, CHAS%. In HH of Abraham Perrineau m 35 mulatto born SC.

PERRONEAU, SUSAN, 25, F, (--), M, SC, 382, 344, CHAS+.

PERRY, ISAAC, 30, M, (--), B, SC, 166, 166, CHAS%.

PERRY, LIBBY, 25, F, (--), M, SC, 203, 203, COLL+. In HH of Mary Perry f 51 mulatto born SC.

PERRY, LORA, 53, F, (--), B, SC, 590, 582, CHAS%.

PERRY, MARY, 51, F, (--), M, SC, 203, 203, COLL+.

PERRY, MARY J., 5, F, (--), M, SC, 203, 203, COLL+. In HH of Mary Perry f 51 mulatto born SC.

PERRY, RACHEL, 10, F, (--), B, SC,

590, 582, CHAS%. In HH of Lora Perry f 53 black born SC.

PERRY, SAMUEL, 12, M, (--), B, SC, 590, 582, CHAS%. In HH of Lora Perry f 53 black born SC.

PERRY, TOBIAS, 11, M, (--), M, SC, 203, 203, COLL+. In HH of Mary Perry f 51 mulatto born SC.

PERRYETTE, AMELIA, 18, F, (--), M, St. Domingo, 80, 80, CHAS%. In HH of Francis Perryette f 51 mulatto born St. Domingo.

PERRYETTE, AMELIA, 9, F, (--), M, SC, 80, 80, CHAS%. In HH of Francis Perryette f 51 mulatto born St. Domingo.

PERRYETTE, CLAUDE, 15, M, Carpenter, M, St. Domingo, 80, 80, CHAS%. In HH of Francis Perryette f 51 mulatto born St. Domingo.

PERRYETTE, FRANCIS, 51, F, (--), M, St. Domingo, 80, 80, CHAS%.

PERRYETTE, JULIET, 11, F, (--), M, SC, 80, 80, CHAS%. In HH of Francis Perryette f 51 mulatto born St. Domingo.

PERRYETTE, LEWIS, 22, M, Engineer, M, St. Domingo, 80, 80, CHAS%. In HH of Francis Perryette f 51 mulatto born St. Domingo.

PERSANT, AMANDA, 17, F, (--), M, SC, 171, 161, CHAS+. In HH of Jane Campbell f 40 mulatto born SC.

PERSANT, CHARLES, 8, M, (--), M, SC, 171, 161, CHAS+. In HH of Jane Campbell f 40 mulatto born SC.

PERSANT, EUGENE, 21, M, (--), M, SC, 171, 161, CHAS+. In HH of Jane Campbell f 40 mulatto born SC.

PERSANT, JULIA, 7, F, (--), M, SC, 171, 161, CHAS+. In HH of Jane Campbell f 40 mulatto born SC.

PERSANT, LEONORA, 9, F, (--), M, SC, 171, 161, CHAS+. In HH of Jane Campbell f 40 mulatto born SC.

PERSANT, THADDEUS, 15, M, (--), M, SC, 171, 161, CHAS+. In HH of Jane Campbell f 40 mulatto born SC.

PETERS, BETSEY, 70, F, (--), B, Africa, 14, 13, CHAS$. In HH of Loris Peters m 36 mulatto born SC.

PETERS, LORIS, 36, M, Carpenter, M, SC, 14, 13, CHAS$.

PETERS, MARY, 7, F, (--), M, SC, 14, 13, CHAS$. In HH of Loris Peters m 36 mulatto born SC.

PETERS, REBECCA, 39, F, (--), M, SC, 14, 13, CHAS$. In HH of Loris Peters m 36 mulatto born SC.

PETERS, VINCENT, 5, M, (--), M, SC, 14, 13, CHAS$. In HH of Loris Peters m 36 mulatto born SC.

PETERSON, CATHERINE, 30, F, (--), B, SC, 260, 234, CHAS*.

PETERSON, ELIZA, 35, F, (--), B, SC, 369, 369, CHAS%. In HH of Robert Peterson m 40 black born SC.

PETERSON, EMMA, 7, F, (--), B, SC, 260, 234, CHAS*. In HH of Catherine Peterson f 30 black born SC.

PETERSON, JULIA, 14, F, (--), B, SC, 369, 369, CHAS%. In HH of Robert Peterson m 40 black born SC.

PETERSON, JULIA ANN, 9, F, (--), B, SC, 260, 234, CHAS*. In HH of Catherine Peterson f 30 black born SC.

PETERSON, ROBERT, 40, M, Bricklayer, B, SC, 369, 369, CHAS%.

PETERSON, SAMUEL, 22, M, Fisherman, B, SC, 260, 234, CHAS*. In HH of Catherine Peterson f 30 black born SC.

PETERSON, SAMUEL, 5, M, (--), B, SC, 260, 234, CHAS*. In HH of Catherine Peterson f 30 black born SC.

PETERSON, SARAH ANN, 3, F, (--), B, SC, 260, 234, CHAS*. In HH of Catherine Peterson f 30 black born SC.

PETRA, DANIEL, 25, M, Laborer, M, SC, 346, 346, COLL*. In HH of James Fludd m 35 mulatto born SC.

PETRA, SARAH, 20, F, (--), M, SC, 346, 346, COLL*. In HH of James Fludd m 35 mulatto born SC.

PETRAY, ADOLPHUS, 1, M, (--), M, SC, 1592, 1592, BARN. In HH of Ed Petray m 37 mulatto born SC.

PETRAY, ED., 37, M, (--), M, SC, 1592, 1592, BARN.

PETRAY, JOSEPHINE, 7, F, (--), M,

SC, 1592, 1592, BARN. In HH of Ed Petray m 37 mulatto born SC.

PETRAY, LOUISA, 25, F, (--), M, SC, 1592, 1592, BARN. In HH of Ed Petray m 37 mulatto born SC.

PETRAY, MARY, 4, F, (--), M, SC, 1592, 1592, BARN. In HH of Ed Petray m 37 mulatto born SC.

PETRAY, ODELLA, 2, F, (--), M, SC, 1592, 1592, BARN. In HH of Ed Petray m 37 mulatto born SC.

PETTIFOOT, BETSEY, 35, F, (--), B, SC, 807, 807, KERS.

PETTIFOOT, CHAS., 1, M, (--), B, SC, 403, 403, KERS. In HH of Grace Pettifoot f 22 black born SC.

PETTIFOOT, ELZA., 15, F, (--), B, SC, 807, 807, KERS. In HH of Betsey Pettifoot f 35 black born SC.

PETTIFOOT, GRACE, 22, F, (--), B, SC, 403, 403, KERS.

PETTIFOOT, HARIETT, 40, F, (--), B, SC, 233, 233, KERS. In HH of John Bahyen(?) m 38 born SC.

PETTIFOOT, HARIETT, 5, F, (--), B, SC, 807, 807, KERS. In HH of Betsey Pettifoot f 35 black born SC.

PETTIFOOT, INFANT, 0, M, (--), B, SC, 403, 403, KERS. In HH of Grace Pettifoot f 22 black born SC. Infant 1/12 yr.

PETTIFOOT, JANE, 13, F, (--), B, SC, 888, 888, KERS.

PETTIFOOT, LEVLINIA, 12, F, (--), B, SC, 233, 233, KERS. In HH of John Bahyen(?) m 38 born SC.

PETTIFOOT, M., 2, M, (--), B, SC, 807, 807, KERS. In HH of Betsey Pettifoot f 35 black born SC.

PETTIFOOT, MARY, 3, F, (--), M, SC, 403, 403, KERS. In HH of Grace Pettifoot f 22 black born SC.

PETTIFOOT, NELSON, 0, M, (--), B, SC, 888, 888, KERS. In HH of Jane Pettifoot f 13 black born SC.

PETTIFOOT, PETER, 7, M, (--), B, SC, 807, 807, KERS. In HH of Betsey Pettifoot f 35 black born SC.

PETTIFOOT, RANSOM, 17, M, (--), B, SC, 807, 807, KERS. In HH of Betsey Pettifoot f 35 black born SC.

PETTIFOOT, SAML., 2, M, (--), B, SC, 807, 807, KERS. In HH of Betsey Pettifoot f 35 black born SC.

PETTIFOOT, WM., 11, M, (--), B, SC, 807, 807, KERS. In HH of Betsey Pettifoot f 35 black born SC.

PETTY, ELISHA, 35, M, Shoemaker, M, SC, 1115, 1115, UNION.

PEYTON, ELIZA JANE, 11, F, (--), B, SC, 519, 523, AND. In HH of Fanny Peyton f 54 black born SC.

PEYTON, FANNY, 54, F, (--), B, SC, 519, 523, AND.

PEYTON, HENAZIAH, 26, M, Bricklayer, B, SC, 519, 523, AND. In HH of Fanny Peyton f 54 black born SC.

PEYTON, MARY, 79, F, (--), B, SC, 210, 284, CHAS*. In HH of Susan H. Service f 63 born England.

PEYTON, NARCISSA, 15, F, (--), B, SC, 519, 523, AND. In HH of Fanny Peyton f 54 black born SC.

PEYTON, RICHMOND, 23, M, Bricklayer, B, SC, 519, 523, AND. In HH of Fanny Peyton f 54 black born SC.

PEYTON, ZACHARIAH, 22, M, Carpenter, B, SC, 519, 523, AND. In HH of Fanny Peyton f 54 black born SC.

PHEONIX, WILL, 88, M, (--), M, SC, 173, 173, BEAU.

PHILIPS, ANN, 4, F, (--), M, SC, 1024, 1001, CHAS-. In HH of Amelia Parker f 50 black born SC.

PHILIPS, ELIZABETH, 40, F, (--), M, SC, 130, 121, CHAS-.

PHILIPS, JAMES, 6, M, (--), M, SC, 1024, 1001, CHAS-. In HH of Amelia Parker f 50 black born SC.

PHILIPS, JOHN, 2, M, (--), M, SC, 1024, 1001, CHAS-. In HH of Amelia Parker f 50 black born SC.

PHILIPS, MARGARET, 26, F, (--), M, SC, 1024, 1001, CHAS-. In HH of Amelia Parker f 50 black born SC.

PHILIPS, MARY, 8, F, (--), M, SC, 1024, 1001, CHAS-. In HH of Amelia Parker f 50 black born SC.

PHILIPS, SUSAN, 30, F, (--), M, SC, 372, 334, CHAS+.

PHILIPS, WILLIAM, 36, M, Hireling, M, SC, 2182, 2182, ABB. In HH of Elizabeth Philips f 37 white born SC.

PHILLIPS, E., 18, F, (--), M, SC, 453, 453, LANC*. In HH of A. Baker m 28 born SC.

PHILLIPS, JOHN, 21, M, Laborer, B, SC, 73, 73, LANC*. In HH of Wm. Culp, m 55 born SC.

PHILLIPS, M.A., 18, F, Laborer, B, SC, 73, 73, LANC*. In HH of Wm. Culp, m 55 born SC.

PHILLIPS, W., 16, F, Work on farm, B, SC, 73, 73, LANC*. In HH of Wm. Culp, m 55 born SC.

PHOENIX, WILL JR., 31, M, Carpenter, B, SC, 175, 175, BEAU.

PICKERING, AMELIA, 11, F, (--), M, SC, 187, 175, CHAS-. In HH Hagar Pickering f 32 mulatto born SC.

PICKERING, HAGAR, 32, F, (--), M, SC, 187, 175, CHAS-.

PICKETT, MATILDA, 38, F, (--), M, SC, 504, 519, RICH.

PINCKNEY, CHARLOTTE, 16, F, (--), M, SC, 316, 291, CHAS. In HH of Ide Timothy f 30 mulatto born SC.

PINCKNEY, MARY, 8, F, (--), M, SC, 316, 291, CHAS. In HH of Ide Timothy f 30 mulatto born SC.

PINCKNEY, SARAH ANN, 12, F, (--), M, SC, 316, 291, CHAS. In HH of Ide Timothy f 30 mulatto born SC.

PINCKNEY, WM. HENRY, 9, M, (--), M, SC, 316, 291, CHAS. In HH of Ide Timothy f 30 mulatto born SC.

PINN, HARRIET, 35, F, (--), M, SC, 793, 793, DARL. In HH of John Pinn m 38 Mulatto, born SC.

PINN, JEREMIAH, 37, M, (--), M, SC, 794, 794, DARL.

PINN, JOHN, 38, M, Farmer, M, SC, 793, 793, DARL.

PINN, PEGGY, 80, F, (--), M, SC, 793, 793, DARL. In HH of John Pinn m 38 Mulatto, born SC.

PINN, POLLY, 25, F, (--), M, SC, 794, 794, DARL. In HH of Jeremiah Pinn m 37 mulatto born SC.

PINN, ZACHR., 40, M, (--), M, SC, 793, 793, DARL. In HH of John Pinn m 38 Mulatto, born SC.

PINO, AGNES, 12, F, (--), M, SC, 1053, 1031, CHAS%. In HH of Andrew Pino m 38 mulatto born SC.

PINO, ANDREW, 38, M, Carpenter, M, SC, 1053, 1031, CHAS%.

PINO, HARRIET, 25, F, (--), M, SC, 1053, 1031, CHAS%. In HH of Andrew Pino m 38 mulatto born SC.

PINO, JOSEPH, 8, M, (--), M, SC, 1053, 1031, CHAS%. In HH of Andrew Pino m 38 mulatto born SC.

PINSON, A., 20, M, Mechanic, B, SC, 907, 907, KERS.

PIRVIO, ALEXANDER, 27, M, Carpenter, M, SC, 1116, 1116, UNION.

PLATE, CHARITY, 14, F, (--), B, SC, 83, 83, MARL. In HH of A.C. McInnis m 33 born SC.

PLATE, MARTHA, 12, F, (--), B, SC, 918, 918, MARL. In HH of J.E. David m 44 born SC.

PLUMET, ANGELINE, 14, F, (--), M, SC, 680, 672, CHAS%. In HH of Anthony Plumet m 46 mulatto born SC.

PLUMET, ANTHONY, 46, M, Tailor, M, SC, 680, 672, CHAS%.

PLUMET, ANTONIO, 6, F, (--), M, SC, 680, 672, CHAS%. In HH of Anthony Plumet m 46 mulatto born SC.

PLUMET, CHARLOTTE, 16, F, (--), M, SC, 680, 672, CHAS%. In HH of Anthony Plumet m 46 mulatto born SC.

PLUMET, DRUCILLA, 10, F, (--), M, SC, 680, 672, CHAS%. In HH of Anthony Plumet m 46 mulatto born SC.

PLUMET, ELIZABETH, 45, F, (--), M, SC, 680, 672, CHAS%. In HH of Anthony Plumet m 46 mulatto born SC.

PLUMET, LEONORO, 2, F, (--), M, SC, 680, 672, CHAS%. In HH of Anthony Plumet m 46 mulatto born SC.

PLUMET, PANELLO, 4, F, (--), M, SC, 680, 672, CHAS%. In HH of

Anthony Plumet m 46 mulatto born SC.

PLUMET, REBECCA, 12, F, (--), M, SC, 680, 672, CHAS%. In HH of Anthony Plumet m 46 mulatto born SC.

POE, JOSEPH, 29, M, Shoemaker, B, SC, 116, 116, GEOR.

POHL, MARY, 59, F, (--), B, SC, 1062, 1040, CHAS%. In HH of Joseph Beach m 37 born NY.

POINSETT, MARTHA, 30, F, (--), M, SC, 223, 210, CHAS+. In HH of Paul Poinsett m 34 mulatto born SC.

POINSETT, MARY, 8, F, (--), M, SC, 223, 210, CHAS+. In HH of Paul Poinsett m 34 mulatto born SC.

POINSETT, PAUL, 34, M, Barber, M, SC, 223, 210, CHAS+.

POLK, ALEXANDER, 9, M, (--), M, SC, 6, 6, CHAS+. In HH of John Mishaw m 53 mulatto born SC.

POLL, MARY ANN, 60, F, (--), M, SC, 248, 248, CHAS%. In HH of Joseph Lacomb m 20 mulatto born SC.

PONE, FRANCES, 12, F, (--), M, SC, 26, 27, MAR. In HH of Johnson B. Young m 28 born SC. Frances Pone born Marion, SC.

PONE, LEWIS, 50, M, Laborer, M, SC, 982, 987, MAR. Lewis Pone born Marion, SC.

PONELE, CELY, 30, F, (--), M, SC, 1091, 1091, BARN. In HH of Stephen Ponele m 38 black born SC.

PONELE, STEPHEN, 38, M, Planter, B, SC, 1091, 1091, BARN.

POPE, CAROLINE, 30, F, (--), M, SC, 151, 141, CHAS-.

POPE, CLARISSA, 15, F, (--), M, SC, 151, 141, CHAS-. In HH of Caroline Pope f 30 mulatto born SC.

POPE, JAMES, 6, M, (--), M, SC, 151, 141, CHAS-. In HH of Caroline Pope f 30 mulatto born SC.

POPE, JOE, 12, M, (--), M, SC, 151, 141, CHAS-. In HH of Caroline Pope f 30 mulatto born SC.

POPE, JOSEPHINE, 2, F, (--), M, SC, 151, 141, CHAS-. In HH of Caroline Pope f 30 mulatto born SC.

POPE, JULIUS, 1, M, (--), M, SC, 151, 141, CHAS-. In HH of Caroline Pope f 30 mulatto born SC.

POPE, LAURENCE, 8, M, (--), M, SC, 151, 141, CHAS-. In HH of Caroline Pope f 30 mulatto born SC.

POPE, SARAH, 28, F, (--), M, SC, 151, 141, CHAS-. In HH of Caroline Pope f 30 mulatto born SC.

POPPEL, ELIJAH, 12, M, (--), M, SC, 1109, 1109, LEX. In HH of Elizabeth Poppel f 40 born SC.

POPPEL, HANNAH, 6, F, (--), M, SC, 1109, 1109, LEX. In HH of Elizabeth Poppel f 40 born SC.

POPPEL, MARTHA, 8, F, (--), M, SC, 1109, 1109, LEX. In HH of Elizabeth Poppel f 40 born SC.

POPPEL, NANCY, 3, F, (--), M, SC, 1109, 1109, LEX. In HH of Elizabeth Poppel f 40 born SC.

POPPEL, POLLY, 10, F, (--), M, SC, 1109, 1109, LEX. In HH of Elizabeth Poppel f 40 born SC.

PORCHER, CAMELLA, 26, F, (--), M, SC, 547, 513, CHAS*. In HH of Sarah Hicks f 30 mulatto born SC.

PORTEA, CAROLINE, 12, F, (--), M, SC, 522, 505, CHAS-. In HH of Rebecca Portea f 30 mulatto born SC.

PORTEA, DORA, 6, F, (--), M, SC, 522, 505, CHAS-. In HH of Rebecca Portea f 30 mulatto born SC.

PORTEA, ELIZA, 17, F, (--), M, SC, 522, 505, CHAS-. In HH of Rebecca Portea f 30 mulatto born SC.

PORTEA, MARY, 19, F, (--), M, SC, 522, 505, CHAS-. In HH of Rebecca Portea f 30 mulatto born SC.

PORTEA, REBECCA, 30, F, (--), M, SC, 522, 505, CHAS-.

PORTEA, TERESA, 4, F, (--), M, SC, 522, 505, CHAS-. In HH of Rebecca Portea f 30 mulatto born SC.

PORTER, WILSON, 30, M, (--), M, SC, 142, 142, KERS. In HH of Fred Bowen m 48 born SC. Wm. George 3/12 yr.

PORTER, WM., 15, M, (--), M, SC,

142, 142, KERS. In HH of Fred Bowen m 48 born SC. Wm. George 3/12 yr.

POTE, ARDELLA, 14, F, (--), M, SC, 331, 338, RICH+. In HH of Rachel Pote f 45 mulatto born SC.

POTE, CALLVIN, 17, M, Planter, M, SC, 331, 338, RICH+. In HH of Rachel Pote f 45 mulatto born SC.

POTE, CHRISTOPHER, 7, M, (--), M, SC, 331, 338, RICH+. In HH of Rachel Pote f 45 mulatto born SC.

POTE, DAVID, 19, M, Planter, M, SC, 331, 338, RICH+. In HH of Rachel Pote f 45 mulatto born SC.

POTE, ELIZABETH, 3, F, (--), M, SC, 331, 338, RICH+. In HH of Rachel Pote f 45 mulatto born SC.

POTE, EMELINE, 10, F, (--), M, SC, 347, 354, RICH+. In HH of Uriah Pote m 35 mulatto born SC.

POTE, EMMA, 12, F, (--), M, SC, 271, 277, RICH+. In HH of Mary Pote f 38 mulatto born SC.

POTE, FRANCES, 2, F, (--), M, SC, 347, 354, RICH+. In HH of Uriah Pote m 35 mulatto born SC.

POTE, JAMES, 6, M, (--), M, SC, 271, 277, RICH+. In HH of Mary Pote f 38 mulatto born SC.

POTE, JANE, 4, F, (--), M, SC, 271, 277, RICH+. In HH of Mary Pote f 38 mulatto born SC.

POTE, JANE, 0, F, (--), M, SC, 347, 354, RICH+. In HH of Uriah Pote m 35 mulatto born SC. Jane age 10/12.

POTE, LOUISA, 18, F, (--), M, SC, 271, 277, RICH+. In HH of Mary Pote f 38 mulatto born SC.

POTE, MARTHA, 35, F, (--), M, SC, 347, 354, RICH+. In HH of Uriah Pote m 35 mulatto born SC.

POTE, MARY, 38, F, (--), M, SC, 271, 277, RICH+.

POTE, MARY, 1, F, (--), M, SC, 271, 277, RICH+. In HH of Mary Pote f 38 mulatto born SC.

POTE, NANCY, 25, F, (--), M, SC, 275, 281, RICH+. In HH of William Pote m 35 mulatto born SC.

POTE, POLLY, 30, F, (--), B, SC, 210, 214, RICH+. In HH of John R.F. Tilghman m 50 born SC.

POTE, PHILIP R., 4, M, (--), M, SC, 347, 354, RICH+. In HH of Uriah Pote m 35 mulatto born SC.

POTE, RACHEL, 45, F, (--), M, SC, 331, 338, RICH+.

POTE, REBECCA, 12, F, (--), M, SC, 331, 338, RICH+. In HH of Rachel Pote f 45 mulatto born SC.

POTE, REUBEN, 5, M, (--), M, SC, 331, 338, RICH+. In HH of Rachel Pote f 45 mulatto born SC.

POTE, RICHARD, 6, M, (--), M, SC, 347, 354, RICH+. In HH of Uriah Pote m 35 mulatto born SC.

POTE, ROBERT, 16, M, Planter, M, SC, 331, 338, RICH+. In HH of Rachel Pote f 45 mulatto born SC.

POTE, RUSSELL, 10, M, (--), M, SC, 271, 277, RICH+. In HH of Mary Pote f 38 mulatto born SC.

POTE, SARAH, 26, F, (--), M, SC, 161, 164, RICH+. In HH of John Richter m 23 born Germany.

POTE, SARAH, 9, F, (--), M, SC, 331, 338, RICH+. In HH of Rachel Pote f 45 mulatto born SC.

POTE, URIAH, 35, M, Planter, M, SC, 347, 354, RICH+.

POTE, WARREN, 1, M, (--), M, SC, 331, 338, RICH+. In HH of Rachel Pote f 45 mulatto born SC.

POTE, WILLIAM, 35, M, Planter, M, SC, 275, 281, RICH+.

POTE, WILLIAM, 16, M, Planter, M, SC, 271, 277, RICH+. In HH of Mary Pote f 38 mulatto born SC.

POTE, WILLIAM, 2, M, (--), M, SC, 161, 164, RICH+. In HH of John Richter m 23 born Germany.

POTE, WYLIE, 2, M, (--), M, SC, 347, 354, RICH+. In HH of Uriah Pote m 35 mulatto born SC.

POTER, LOUISA, 41, F, (--), M, SC, 106, 106, GEOR. In HH of Trial Poter m 57 mulatto born Siera Leone.

POTER, TRIAL, 57, M, Packeting, M,

Seira Leone, 106, 106, GEOR.

POTES, JEFFERSON, 18, M, Laborer, M, SC, 388, 388, GREE. In HH of Thomas Barnett m 70 born SC.

POWERS, ELIZABETH, 64, F, (--), B, SC, 457, 457, BEAU-.

PRATER, CELIA, 30, F, (--), B, SC, 36, 36, NEWB. In HH of Sarah Volentine f 30 black born SC.

PRATT, FELICE, 65, F, (--), M, SC, 257, 235, CHAS. In HH of William Stevens m 58 mulatto born SC.

PRATT, JULIA, 1, F, (--), M, SC, 389, 372, CHAS-. In HH of E. Winslow m 48 born NC.

PRATT, SERENA, 40, F, (--), M, SC, 389, 372, CHAS-. In HH of E. Winslow m 48 born NC.

PRESLEY, MINERVA, 1, F, (--), M, SC, 1266, 1266, CHES. In HH of Joseph Smith m 38 born SC.

PRESLEY, TABITHA, 70, F, (--), B, VA, 461, 461, EDGE.

PRETER, MARY, 12, F, (--), B, SC, 170, 170, CHAS%. In HH of Frances Bland f 50 mulatto born SC.

PREVOST, ELIZABETH, 36, F, (--), M, SC, 335, 335, COLL. In HH of Thomas Prevost m 40 mulatto born SC.

PREVOST, ELIZABETH, 6, F, (--), M, SC, 335, 335, COLL. In HH of Thomas Prevost m 40 mulatto born SC.

PREVOST, ELLEN, 4, F, (--), M, SC, 335, 335, COLL. In HH of Thomas Prevost m 40 mulatto born SC.

PREVOST, JANE, 28, F, (--), M, SC, 188, 177, CHAS+. In HH of Mary OConner f 30 born Ireland.

PREVOST, LEVINIA, 11, F, (--), M, SC, 335, 335, COLL. In HH of Thomas Prevost m 40 mulatto born SC.

PREVOST, LEVY, 0, M, (--), M, SC, 335, 335, COLL. In HH of Thomas Prevost m 40 mulatto born SC. Levy age 6/12 yr.

PREVOST, MARY, 50, F, (--), B, SC, 890, 870, CHAS-.

PREVOST, MARY, 9, F, (--), M, SC, 335, 335, COLL. In HH of Thomas

Prevost m 40 mulatto born SC.

PREVOST, MIRAM, 15, F, (--), M, SC, 335, 335, COLL. In HH of Thomas Prevost m 40 mulatto born SC.

PREVOST, SARAH, 13, F, (--), M, SC, 335, 335, COLL. In HH of Thomas Prevost m 40 mulatto born SC.

PREVOST, THOMAS, 40, M, Laborer, M, SC, 335, 335, COLL.

PRICE, BETSY, 35, F, (--), B, SC, 1153, 1132, CHAS%.

PRICE, JOHN, 8, M, (--), B, SC, 1153, 1132, CHAS%. In HH of Betsy Price f 35 black born SC.

PRICE, MARTIN, 10, M, (--), B, SC, 1153, 1132, CHAS%. In HH of Betsy Price f 35 black born SC.

PRIMUS, ANDREW, 0, M, (--), M, (-) , 2, 2, BEAU#. In HH of James Primus, Jr. m 25 mulatto. Andrew 9/12 mo.

PRIMUS, BARNEY, 16, M, (--), M, (-) , 3, 3, BEAU#. In HH of James Primus m 58 mulatto.

PRIMUS, CAROLINE, 36, F, (--), M, (-) , 1, 1, BEAU#. In HH of George Primus m 30 mulatto.

PRIMUS, GEORGE, 30, M, (--), M, (--), 1, 1, BEAU#.

PRIMUS, HENRY, 22, M, (--), M, , 3, 3, BEAU#. In HH of James Primus m 58 mulatto.

PRIMUS, JACOB, 7, M, (--), M, SC, 163, 163, COLL*. In HH of Jno. Primus m 53 mulatto born SC.

PRIMUS, JAMES, 58, M, (--), M, , 3, 3, BEAU#.

PRIMUS, JAMES, JR., 25, M, (--), M, , 2, 2, BEAU#.

PRIMUS, JNO., 53, M, (--), M, SC, 163, 163, COLL*.

PRIMUS, JNO., 15, M, (--), M, SC, 163, 163, COLL*. In HH of Jno. Primus m 53 mulatto born SC.

PRIMUS, MARGARET, 16, F, (--), M, SC, 163, 163, COLL*. In HH of Jno. Primus m 53 mulatto born SC.

PRIMUS, MARIA, 41, F, (--), M, SC, 163, 163, COLL*. In HH of Jno. Primus m 53 mulatto born SC.

PRIMUS, MARY, 48, F, (--), M, , 3, 3, BEAU#. In HH of James Primus m 58 mulatto.

PRIMUS, MARY, 6, F, (--), M, SC, 163, 163, COLL*. In HH of Jno. Primus m 53 mulatto born SC.

PRIMUS, MATHANDIAN, 21, M, (--), M, SC, 163, 163, COLL*. In HH of Jno. Primus m 53 mulatto born SC.

PRIMUS, REBECCA, 26, F, (--), M, , 2, 2, BEAU#. In HH of James Primus, Jr. m 25 mulatto.

PRIMUS, SARAH, 13, F, (--), M, , 3, 3, BEAU#. In HH of James Primus m 58 mulatto.

PRIMUS, SUSAN, 9, F, (--), M, , 3, 3, BEAU#. In HH of James Primus m 58 mulatto.

PRINCE, ADELE, 5, F, (--), M, SC, 701, 659, CHAS+. In HH of Grace Alston f 26 mulatto born SC.

PRINCE, CATHERINE, 38, F, (--), M, SC, 833, 791, CHAS+. In HH of George Prince m 46 mulatto born SC.

PRINCE, GEORGE, 46, M, Tailor, M, SC, 833, 791, CHAS+.

PRINCE, GEORGE W., 16, M, Laborer, M, SC, 833, 791, CHAS+. In HH of George Prince m 46 mulatto born SC.

PRINCE, JAMES, 6, M, (--), M, SC, 833, 791, CHAS+. In HH of George Prince m 46 mulatto born SC.

PRINCE, RICHARD, 3, M, (--), M, SC, 701, 659, CHAS+. In HH of Grace Alston f 26 mulatto born SC.

PRINCE, SUSAN M., 12, F, (--), M, SC, 833, 791, CHAS+. In HH of George Prince m 46 mulatto born SC.

PRINCE, THEODORE, 8, M, (--), M, SC, 833, 791, CHAS+. In HH of George Prince m 46 mulatto born SC.

PRINCE, THERESA, 3, F, (--), M, SC, 833, 791, CHAS+. In HH of George Prince m 46 mulatto born SC.

PRINCE, THOMAS, 1, M, (--), M, SC, 833, 791, CHAS+. In HH of George Prince m 46 mulatto born SC.

PRIOLEAU, PHILLIPE, 48, M, (--), B, SC, 299, 276, CHAS+. In HH of Charles Mitchell m 24 mulatto born VA.

PRIOLEAU, ROSA, 27, F, (--), B, SC, 105, 105, CHAS%. In HH of Moses Bury m 34 black born SC.

PRIOLEAU, SARAH, 40, F, (--), B, SC, 184, 173, CHAS+. In HH of Christiana Jones f 50 born SC.

PRISMAS, ANN, 2, F, (--), M, SC, 477, 477, BEAU-. In HH of Hesekiah Primas m 35 mulatto born SC.

PRISMAS, HAMPTON, 4, M, (--), M, SC, 477, 477, BEAU-. In HH of Hesekiah Primas m 35 mulatto born SC.

PRISMAS, HESEKIAH, 35, M, Tailor, M, SC, 477, 477, BEAU-.

PRISMAS, JANE, 20, F, (--), M, SC, 477, 477, BEAU-. In HH of Hesekiah Primas m 35 mulatto born SC.

PRISMAS, MARGARET, 8, F, (--), M, SC, 477, 477, BEAU-. In HH of Hesekiah Primas m 35 mulatto born SC.

PRISMAS, RITTA, 6, F, (--), M, SC, 477, 477, BEAU-. In HH of Hesekiah Primas m 35 mulatto born SC.

PROVOST, ELIZABETH, 89, F, (--), M, SC, 207, 193, CHAS-. In HH of Sarah Motte f 30 mulatto born SC.

PROVOST, ELIZABETH, 22, F, (--), M, SC, 358, 358, COLL. In HH of Jno. Provost. m 24 mulatto born SC.

PROVOST, JNO., 24, M, Farmer, M, SC, 358, 358, COLL.

PROVOST, JOHN, 1, M, (--), M, SC, 358, 358, COLL. In HH of Jno. Provost. m 24 mulatto born SC.

PRYSOCK, JAMES, 30, M, Laborer, M, SC, 810, 810, UNION. In HH of William A. Sims m 50 born SC.

PUE, ABRAMS, 54, M, Farmer, B, NC, 535, 536, AND*.

PUE, AMA, 70, F, (--), B, SC, 535, 536, AND*. In HH of Abram Pue m 54 black born NC.

PUE, MARY, 25, F, (--), B, SC, 535, 536, AND*. In HH of Abram Pue m 54 black born NC.

PURCELL, CHARLES, 3, M, (--), M,

SC, 525, 525, FAIR. In HH of Joseph W. Purcell m 38 mulatto born SC.

PURCELL, ELIZA, 34, F, (--), M, SC, 525, 525, FAIR. In HH of Joseph W. Purcell m 38 mulatto born SC.

PURCELL, JOHN, 6, M, (--), M, SC, 525, 525, FAIR. In HH of Joseph W. Purcell m 38 mulatto born SC.

PURCELL, JOSEPH W., 38, M, Carpenter, M, SC, 525, 525, FAIR.

PURCELL, MARY E., 7, F, (--), M, SC, 525, 525, FAIR. In HH of Joseph W. Purcell m 38 mulatto born SC.

PURCELL, WILLIAM, 11, M, (--), M, SC, 525, 525, FAIR. In HH of Joseph W. Purcell m 38 mulatto born SC.

PURDE, JOHN, 24, M, Drayman, B, SC, 1083, 1105, CHAS%. In HH of Martha Purde f 27 mulatto born SC.

PURDE, MARTHA, 27, F, (--), M, SC, 1083, 1105, CHAS%.

PURSE, LAURA, 21, F, (--), M, SC, 215, 201, CHAS-.

PURSE, WILLIAM, 23, M, Carpenter, M, SC, 212, 198, CHAS-. In HH of Francis Smith m 20 mulatto born SC.

PURVIS, ADOLPHUS, 12, M, (--), M, SC, 226, 202, CHAS*. In HH of Charlotte Purvis f 17 mulatto born SC.

PURVIS, ALONZO, 14, M, (--), M, SC, 226, 202, CHAS*. In HH of Charlotte Purvis f 17 mulatto born SC.

PURVIS, BURRELL, 21, M, Barber, M, SC, 193, 197, RICH.

PURVIS, CHARLOTTE, 17, F, (--), M, SC, 226, 202, CHAS*.

PURVIS, CHARLOTTE, 13, F, (--), M, SC, 87, 88, RICH. In HH of James Adams m 45 born KY.

PURVIS, CHRISTOPHER, 14, M, (--), M, SC, 193, 197, RICH. In HH of Burrell Purvis m 21 mulatto born SC.

PURVIS, HAYNES, 26, F, (--), M, SC, 78, 79, RICH. In HH of Margaret Long f 27 born SC.

PURVIS, NORBOIN, 8, M, (--), M, SC, 78, 79, RICH. In HH of Margaret Long f 27 born SC.

PURVIS, VIRGINIA, 4, F, (--), M, SC, 78, 79, RICH. In HH of Margaret Long f 27 born SC.

PUSIGLER, EASTER, 70, F, (--), B, SC, 1538, 1538, LAU. In HH of Daniel Beaks m 34 born SC.

Q

QUASH, ANNA, 16, F, (--), M, SC, 293, 270, CHAS+. In HH of Joseph Quash m 20 mulatto born SC.

QUASH, ANNA, 14, F, (--), B, SC, 581, 564, CHAS-. In HH of Martha Quash f 50 black born SC.

QUASH, BILLY, 12, M, (--), M, SC, 293, 270, CHAS+. In HH of Joseph Quash m 20 mulatto born SC.

QUASH, CATHERINE, 75, F, (--), M, SC, 293, 270, CHAS+. In HH of Joseph Quash m 20 mulatto born SC.

QUASH, JAMES, 11, M, (--), B, SC, 581, 564, CHAS-. In HH of Martha Quash f 50 black born SC.

QUASH, JAMES, 5, M, (--), M, SC, 293, 270, CHAS+. In HH of Joseph Quash m 20 mulatto born SC.

QUASH, JOSEPH, 47, M, Drayman, B, SC, 581, 564, CHAS-. In HH of Martha Quash f 50 black born SC.

QUASH, JOSEPH, 20, M, Barber, M, SC, 293, 270, CHAS+.

QUASH, MARTHA, 50, F, (--), B, SC, 581, 564, CHAS-.

QUASH, MARTHA, 40, F, (--), M, SC, 293, 270, CHAS+. In HH of Joseph Quash m 20 mulatto born SC.

QUASH, MARY J., 8, F, Drayman, M, SC, 293, 270, CHAS+. In HH of Joseph Quash m 20 mulatto born SC.

QUASH, NANCY, 39, F, (--), M, SC, 211, 198, CHAS+. In HH of Antoine Bouton f 25 born France.

QUASH, NED, 40, M, Bricklayer, B, SC, 211, 198, CHAS+. In HH of Antoine Bouton f 25 born France.

QUASH, WILLIAM, 21, M, Tailor, B, SC, 581, 564, CHAS-. In HH of Martha Quash f 50 black born SC.

QUASH, WILLIAM JR., 18, M, (--), B, SC, 581, 564, CHAS-. In HH of Martha Quash f 50 black born SC.

QUATTLEBUM, NANCY, 30, F, (--), M, SC, 35, 35, NEWB. In HH of William Quattlebum m 33 mulatto born SC.

QUATTLEBUM, WILLIAM, 33, M, Boot/Shoemaker, M, SC, 35, 35, NEWB.

QUERY, ANN, 12, F, (--), M, SC, 104, 104, CHAS%. In HH of Emanuel Query m 40 mulatto born SC.

QUERY, DIANA, 37, F, (--), M, SC, 104, 104, CHAS%. In HH of Emanuel Query m 40 mulatto born SC.

QUERY, EMANUEL, 40, M, Drayman, M, SC, 104, 104, CHAS%.

QUERY, FRANCE, 15, F, (--), M, SC, 104, 104, CHAS%. In HH of Emanuel Query m 40 mulatto born SC.

QUERY, JEREMIAH, 8, M, (--), M, SC, 104, 104, CHAS%. In HH of Emanuel Query m 40 mulatto born SC.

QUERY, JOSEPH, 10, M, (--), M, SC, 104, 104, CHAS%. In HH of Emanuel Query m 40 mulatto born SC.

QUIGLY, CHARLES, 35, M, Shoe Store, M, Ireland {sic}, 455, 412, CHAS.

QUIN, JOSEPHINE, 10, F, (--), M, SC, 941, 921, CHAS-. In HH of Joshua Mishaw m 27 mulatto born SC.

QUINLAN, SARAH, 40, F, (--), M, SC, 73, 71, CHAS*. In HH of Henrietta McNeill f 79 mulatto born SC.

QUINNING, JUDETH, 65, F, (--), B, VA, 790, 790, SUMT.

R

RACKORD, CALVIN, 22, M, Farmer, M, SC, 261, 261, NEWB. In HH of E. Rackord m 45 born SC.

RACKORD, CALVIN, 21, M, Carpenter, M, SC, 215, 215, NEWB. In HH of Mary Shumpert f 60 born SC.

RACKORD, M. ANN, 22, F, (--), M, SC, 261, 261, NEWB. In HH of E. Rackord m 45 born SC.

RAGG, ARNOLD, 32, M, (--), M, SC, 222, 222, CHAS%. In HH of Catherine Ragg f 34 mulatto born SC.

RAGG, CATHERINE, 34, F, (--), M, SC, 222, 222, CHAS%.

RAGSDELL, REBECCA, 17, F, (--), M, SC, 779, 737, CHAS+. In HH of Eliza Snow f 65 black born Africa.

RAINE, WILLIAM, 20, M, (--), M, SC, 159, 142, CHAS. In HH of V. Datsieuse f 50 born St. Domingo.

RAINEY, EDWARD, 44, M, Barber, M, SC, 88, 88, GEOR.

RAINEY, JAMES M., 11, M, (--), M, SC, 88, 88, GEOR. In HH of Edward Rainey m, 44 mulatto born SC.

RAINEY, TERESA, 43, F, (--), M, SC, 88, 88, GEOR. In HH of Edward Rainey m 44 mulatto born SC.

RAINEY, TERESA, 9, F, (--), M, SC, 88, 88, GEOR. In HH of Edward Rainey m, 44 mulatto born SC.

RAINS, REBEC, 60, F, (--), M, SC, 252, 252, GEOR*.

RAME, ADEL, 52, F, (--), M, SC, 591, 573, CHAS-.

RAME, ELIZA, 27, F, (--), M, SC, 591, 573, CHAS-. In HH of Adel Rame f 42 mulatto born SC.

RAME, EMILY, 31, F, (--), M, SC, 591, 573, CHAS-. In HH of Adel Rame f 42 mulatto born SC.

RAME, EUGENE, 22, M, (--), M, SC, 591, 573, CHAS-. In HH of Adel Rame f 42 mulatto born SC.

RAME, GEORGIANA, 16, F, (--), M, SC, 591, 573, CHAS-. In HH of Adel Rame f 42 mulatto born SC.

RAMES, JAMES, 12, M, (--), M, SC, 721, 722, ORNG+. In HH of Lewis Hart m 26 born SC.

RAMSAY, CHARLES, 40, M, Carpenter, B, SC, 813, 771, CHAS+. In HH of Jane Ramsay f 38 black born SC.

RAMSAY, JANE, 38, F, (--), B, SC, 813, 771, CHAS+.

RAMSAY, JANE, 14, F, (--), B, SC, 813, 771, CHAS+. In HH of Jane Ramsay f 38 black born SC.

RAMSAY, JOHN, 27, M, Drayman, B, SC, 839, 820, CHAS%. In HH of Margaret Ramsay f 29 mulatto born SC.

RAMSAY, MARGARET, 29, F, (--), M, SC, 839, 820, CHAS%.

RAMSAY, THOMAS, 19, M, Carpenter, B, SC, 813, 771, CHAS+. In HH of Jane Ramsay f 38 black born SC.

RAMSAY, WILLIAM, 13, M, (--), B, SC, 839, 820, CHAS%. In HH of Margaret Ramsay f 29 mulatto born SC.

RANES, DILIARD, 1, M, (--), M, SC, 1123, 1123, GREE. In HH of Samuel Ranes m 42 mulatto born SC.

RANES, PARILA, 4, M, (--), M, SC, 1123, 1123, GREE. In HH of Samuel Ranes m 42 mulatto born SC.

RANES, REBECCA, 25, F, (--), M, SC, 1123, 1123, GREE. In HH of Samuel Ranes m 42 mulatto born SC.

RANES, SAMUEL, 42, M, (--), M, SC, 1123, 1123, GREE.

RANES, WILLIAM, 2, M, (--), M, SC, 1123, 1123, GREE. In HH of Samuel Ranes m 42 mulatto born SC.

RANKLIN, SANO, 42, M, (--), B, SC, 114, 106, CHAS+. In HH of Alfred P. Reignie m 40 born GA.

RASCOW, WASHINGTON, 10, M, (--), M, SC, 784, 784, MARL. In HH of John Rascow m 56 born SC.

RAWLS, ROSA, 35, F, (--), M, SC, 164, 168, RICH.

RAWSON, CATHERINE, 9, F, (--), M, SC, 562, 528, CHAS*. In HH of Mary Rawson f 45 mulatto born SC.

RAWSON, CORNELIA, 2, F, (--), M, SC, 562, 528, CHAS*. In HH of Mary Rawson f 45 mulatto born SC.

RAWSON, MARY, 45, F, (--), M, SC, 562, 528, CHAS*.

RAY, JAMES, 17, M, (--), M, SC, 1225, 1225, York.

READ, ELLEN, 19, F, (--), M, SC, 185, 169, CHAS*. In HH of Ann Deas f 37 mulatto born SC.

READ, ISABELLA, 60, F, (--), M, SC, 106, 98, CHAS+. In HH of William Ingles m 30 mulatto born SC.

READ, SAMUEL, 28, M, Laborer, B, SC, 774, 754, CHAS-.

READ, SARAH, 8, F, (--), M, SC, 106, 98, CHAS+. In HH of William Ingles m 30 mulatto born SC.

READ, WILLIAM, 11, M, (--), M, SC, 106, 98, CHAS+. In HH of William Ingles m 30 mulatto born SC.

REDMAN, MARY, 21, F, (--), M, SC, 185, 185, COLL.

REDMAN, ZACHERIAH, 1, M, (--), M, SC, 185, 185, COLL. In HH of Mary Redman 21 mulatto born SC.

REECE, BETTY, 94, F, (--), B, VA, 2172, 2172, GREE. In HH of David Vaughn m 75 born VA.

REED, BEATRICE, 13, F, (--), M, SC, 502, 502, CHFD. In HH of Sarah Reed f 61 mulatto born SC.

REED, BETSY, 21, F, (--), B, SC, 502, 502, CHFD. In HH of Sarah Reed f 61 mulatto born SC.

REED, CAROLINE M., 30, F, (--), M, SC, 502, 502, CHFD. In HH of Sarah Reed f 61 mulatto born SC.

REED, CATHARINE, 7, F, (--), M, SC, 502, 502, CHFD. In HH of Sarah Reed f 61 mulatto born SC.

REED, FANNY, 1, F, (--), B, SC, 502, 502, CHFD. In HH of Sarah Reed f 61 mulatto born SC.

REED, FRANCIS, 25, F, (--), B, SC, 502, 502, CHFD. In HH of Sarah Reed f 61 mulatto born SC.

REED, JAMES E., 2, M, (--), B, SC, 502, 502, CHFD. In HH of Sarah Reed f 61 mulatto born SC.

REED, JEFFERSON, 6, M, (--), M, SC, 502, 502, CHFD. In HH of Sarah Reed f 61 mulatto born SC.

REED, JOHN, 17, M, (--), B, SC, 502, 502, CHFD. In HH of Sarah Reed f 61 mulatto born SC.

REED, LOUISA, 28, F, (--), M, SC, 502, 502, CHFD. In HH of Sarah Reed f 61 mulatto born SC.

REED, LYON, 3, M, (--), M, SC, 502, 502, CHFD. In HH of Sarah Reed f 61 mulatto born SC.

REED, MARTHA J., 4, F, (--), M, SC, 502, 502, CHFD. In HH of Sarah Reed f 61 mulatto born SC.

REED, MARY M., 1, F, (--), B, SC, 502, 502, CHFD. In HH of Sarah Reed f 61 mulatto born SC.

REED, SARAH, 61, F, (--), M, SC, 502, 502, CHFD.

REED, SARAH ANN, 8, F, (--), M, SC, 502, 502, CHFD. In HH of Sarah Reed f 61 mulatto born SC.

REED, WILLIAM, 10, M, (--), M, SC, 502, 502, CHFD. In HH of Sarah Reed f 61 mulatto born SC.

REEDER, JOHN, 40, M, (--), B, SC, 87, 88, ORNG+. In HH of Sanders Glover m 62 born SC.

REESE, ELIZABETH, 26, F, (--), M, SC, 125, 128, RICH.

REEVES, ALTHEN A., 6, F, (--), M, SC, 47, 47, COLL*. In HH of William Reeves m 35 mulatto born SC.

REEVES, ERVIN, 13, M, (--), M, SC, 47, 47, COLL*. In HH of William Reeves m 35 mulatto born SC.

REEVES, HANNAH, 50, F, (--), M, SC, 378, 378, COLL*. In HH of Jasper Reeves m 55 mulatto born SC.

REEVES, JAMES D., 4, M, (--), M, SC, 47, 47, COLL*. In HH of William Reeves m 35 mulatto born SC.

REEVES, JASPER, 55, M, Farmer, M, SC, 378, 378, COLL*.

REEVES, SUSANNAH, 40, F, (--), M, SC, 47, 47, COLL*. In HH of William Reeves m 35 mulatto born SC.

REEVES, THOMAS, 11, M, (--), M, SC, 47, 47, COLL*. In HH of William Reeves m 35 mulatto born SC.

REEVES, WILLIAM, 35, M, Farmer, M, SC, 47, 47, COLL*.

REEVES, WILLIAM, 25, M, Laborer, M, SC, 378, 378, COLL*. In HH of Jasper Reeves m 55 mulatto born SC.

REEVES, WILLIAM A., 8, M, (--), M, SC, 47, 47, COLL*. In HH of William Reeves m 35 mulatto born SC.

REGUAN, ANN, 9, F, (--), M, SC, 417, 415, CHAS%. In HH of Lavina Requan f 31 mulatto born SC.

REGUAN, LAVINA, 31, F, (--), M, SC, 417, 415, CHAS%.

REGUAN, THEADORE, 30, M, Carpenter, M, SC, 417, 415, CHAS%. In HH of Lavina Requan f 31 mulatto born SC.

REID, CAROLINE, 12, F, (--), B, SC, 687, 687, UNION. In HH of Lucy Reid f 49 mulatto born SC.

REID, ELEANOR, 4, F, (--), B, SC, 687, 687, UNION. In HH of Lucy Reid f 49 mulatto born SC.

REID, LUCY, 49, F, (--), M, SC, 687, 687, UNION.

REID, MARGARET, 5, F, (--), B, SC, 687, 687, UNION. In HH of Lucy Reid f 49 mulatto born SC.

REID, MATILDA, 7, F, (--), B, SC, 687, 687, UNION. In HH of Lucy Reid f 49 mulatto born SC.

REID, REBECCA, 15, F, (--), B, SC, 687, 687, UNION. In HH of Lucy Reid f 49 mulatto born SC.

REID, RUTH, 2, F, (--), B, SC, 687, 687, UNION. In HH of Lucy Reid f 49 mulatto born SC.

REID, SALLY, 24, F, (--), B, SC, 687, 687, UNION. In HH of Lucy Reid f 49 mulatto born SC.

REID, SOPHRONIA, 2, F, (--), B, SC, 687, 687, UNION. In HH of Lucy Reid f 49 mulatto born SC.

REID, SPAIN, 7, M, (--), B, SC, 687, 687, UNION. In HH of Lucy Reid f 49 mulatto born SC.

REMLEY, CORNTHA, 22, F, (--), M, SC, 97, 97, CHAS%. In HH of Eliza Remley f 30 mulatto born SC.

REMLEY, ELIZA, 30, F, (--), M, SC, 97, 97, CHAS%.

REMLEY, ELIZABETH, 28, F, (--), M, SC, 97, 97, CHAS%. In HH of Eliza

Remley f 30 mulatto born SC.

REVEL, F.C., 24, M, Barber, M, SC, 293, 270, CHAS+. In HH of Joseph Quash m 20 mulatto born SC.

REVIS, ELIZA, 26, F, (--), B, NC, 579, 579, UNION. In HH of Polly Johns f 49 born SC.

REVIS, SALLY, 12, F, (--), M, GA, 579, 579, UNION. In HH of Polly Johns f 49 born SC.

REYNOLDS, E., 22, M, Laborer, M, Ireland {sic}, 31, 27, CHAS$.

RHODES, CHARLES, 20, M, Planter, M, SC, 1212, 1212, BARN. In HH of Samuel Rhodes m 65 mulatto born SC.

RHODES, DANIEL, 24, M, Planter, M, SC, 1212, 1212, BARN. In HH of Samuel Rhodes m 65 mulatto born SC.

RHODES, ELIZA, 53, F, (--), M, SC, 1212, 1212, BARN. In HH of Samuel Rhodes m 65 mulatto born SC.

RHODES, ELIZA, 18, F, (--), M, SC, 1212, 1212, BARN. In HH of Samuel Rhodes m 65 mulatto born SC.

RHODES, SAMUEL, 65, M, Planter, M, SC, 1212, 1212, BARN.

RHODES, SARAH, 22, F, (--), M, SC, 1212, 1212, BARN. In HH of Samuel Rhodes m 65 mulatto born SC.

RIAL, CATHARINE, 14, F, (--), M, SC, 593, 593, MARL. In HH of Mary Rial f 35 mulatto born SC.

RIAL, EMILY, 18, F, (--), M, SC, 593, 593, MARL. In HH of Mary Rial f 35 mulatto born SC.

RIAL, MARGARET, 1, F, (--), M, SC, 593, 593, MARL. In HH of Mary Rial f 35 mulatto born SC.

RIAL, MARY, 35, F, (--), M, SC, 593, 593, MARL.

RIAL, WILIS, 12, M, (--), M, SC, 593, 593, MARL. In HH of Mary Rial f 35 mulatto born SC.

RICHARDSON, LOUISA, 55, F, (--), M, SC, 283, 283, CHAS%. In HH of Emeline Holmes f 19 black born SC.

RICHARDS, ADEL, 18, F, (--), M, SC, 173, 163, CHAS-.

RICHARDS, DAVID, 39, M, Porter, M, SC, 23, 23, CHAS%.

RICHARDS, EDWARD, 28, M, Millwright, M, SC, 624, 616, CHAS%.

RICHARDS, ELIZABETH, 21, F, (--), M, SC, 72, 72, CHAS%. In HH of P. Richards m 26 mulatto born SC.

RICHARDS, HENRY, 6, M, (--), M, SC, 72, 72, CHAS%. In HH of P. Richards m 26 mulatto born SC.

RICHARDS, ISABEL, 0, F, (--), M, SC, 173, 163, CHAS-. In HH of Adel Richard f 18 mulatto born SC. Isabel Richard age 9/12 yr.

RICHARDS, JANE, 28, F, (--), M, SC, 173, 163, CHAS-. In HH of Adel Richard f 18 mulatto born SC.

RICHARDS, JULIET, 4, M, (--), M, SC, 72, 72, CHAS%. In HH of P. Richards m 26 mulatto born SC.

RICHARDS, LIZETTE, 34, F, (--), M, SC, 23, 23, CHAS%. In HH of David Richards m 39 mulatto born SC.

RICHARDS, MARIA, 15, F, (--), M, SC, 624, 616, CHAS%. In HH of Edward Richards m 28 mulatto born SC.

RICHARDS, MARY J., 10, F, (--), M, SC, 23, 23, CHAS%. In HH of David Richards m 39 mulatto born SC.

RICHARDS, P., 26, M, (--), M, SC, 72, 72, CHAS%.

RICHARDS, SIMON, 2, M, (--), M, SC, 72, 72, CHAS%. In HH of P. Richards m 26 mulatto born SC.

RICHARDSON, ANN, 30, F, (--), M, SC, 281, 281, CHAS%. In HH of Nelson Richardson m 41 mulatto born SC.

RICHARDSON, BARSDELL, 60, M, Laborer, B, SC, 76, 76, CHAS%. In HH of Susan Richardson f 62 black born Africa.

RICHARDSON, CHARLOTTE, 31, F, (--), M, SC, 810, 792, CHAS%. In HH of Robert Bing m 39 mulatto born SC.

RICHARDSON, JANE, 8, F, (--), B, SC, 808, 791, CHAS%. In HH of Margaret Richardson f 37 black born SC.

RICHARDSON, JEMMIMA, 5, F, (--), B, SC, 76, 76, CHAS%. In HH of

Susan Richardson f 62 black born Africa.

RICHARDSON, JOHN, 10, M, (--), B, SC, 808, 791, CHAS%. In HH of Margaret Richardson f 37 black born SC.

RICHARDSON, JOSEPH, 9, M, (--), B, SC, 76, 76, CHAS%. In HH of Susan Richardson f 62 black born Africa.

RICHARDSON, MARGARET, 37, F, (--), B, SC, 808, 791, CHAS%.

RICHARDSON, MARSALINE, 12, F, (--), B, SC, 76, 76, CHAS%. In HH of Susan Richardson f 62 black born Africa.

RICHARDSON, MARY, 25, F, (--), M, SC, 184, 172, CHAS-. In HH of Mary Parker f 30 mulatto born SC.

RICHARDSON, NELSON, 41, M, Carpenter, M, SC, 281, 281, CHAS%.

RICHARDSON, ROANNE, 26, F, (--), B, SC, 76, 76, CHAS%. In HH of Susan Richardson f 62 black born Africa.

RICHARDSON, SUSAN, 61, F, (--), B, Africa, 76, 76, CHAS%.

RICKENBACKER, FRANKLIN, 2, M, (--), M, SC, 413, 414, ORNG+. In HH of Vineyard Rickenbacker m 31 mulatto born SC.

RICKENBACKER, LEWIS, 1, M, (--), M, SC, 413, 414, ORNG+. In HH of Vineyard Rickenbacker m 31 mulatto born SC.

RICKENBACKER, VINEYARD, 31, M, Farmer, M, SC, 413, 414, ORNG+.

RICORD, HANNAH, 24, F, (--), M, SC, 52, 52, UNN+. In HH of Chaucer Willard m 42 born SC.

RIGHT, ELIZA, 12, F, (--), B, SC, 490, 490, BEAU-. In HH of John Right m 65 black born SC.

RIGHT, GEORGE, 18, M, Laborer, B, SC, 490, 490, BEAU-. In HH of John Right m 65 black born SC.

RIGHT, HESTER, 10, F, (--), B, SC, 490, 490, BEAU-. In HH of John Right m 65 black born SC.

RIGHT, JACK, 14, M, (--), B, SC, 490, 490, BEAU-. In HH of John Right m 65 black born SC.

RIGHT, JOE, 20, M, Laborer, B, SC, 490, 490, BEAU-. In HH of John Right m 65 black born SC.

RIGHT, JOHN, 65, M, Laborer, B, SC, 490, 490, BEAU-.

RIGHT, MARTHA, 55, F, (--), B, SC, 490, 490, BEAU-. In HH of John Right m 65 black born SC.

RIGHT, MARY, 8, F, (--), B, SC, 490, 490, BEAU-. In HH of John Right m 65 black born SC.

RIGHT, PATSEY, 4, F, (--), B, SC, 490, 490, BEAU-. In HH of John Right m 65 black born SC.

RIGHTON, REBECCA, 34, F, (--), M, SC, 701, 693, CHAS%.

RILEY, DIANA, 45, F, (--), M, SC, 446, 404, CHAS. In HH of Ann Percy f 45 born SC.

RILEY, ELIZABETH, 20, F, (--), M, SC, 446, 404, CHAS. In HH of Ann Percy f 45 born SC.

RILEY, JOSEPH, 8, M, (--), M, SC, 446, 404, CHAS. In HH of Ann Percy f 45 born SC.

RISHER, THOMAS, 40, M, Carpenter, M, SC, 25, 25, COLL*. In HH of Richard Hill m 49 born SC.

RIVERS, BALDWIN, 3, M, (--), M, SC, 334, 308, CHAS*. In HH of Hannah Rivers f 40 mulatto born SC.

RIVERS, CELIA, 1, F, (--), M, SC, 334, 308, CHAS*. In HH of Hannah Rivers f 40 mulatto born SC.

RIVERS, CHARLES, 5, M, (--), M, SC, 334, 308, CHAS*. In HH of Hannah Rivers f 40 mulatto born SC.

RIVERS, HANNAH, 40, F, (--), M, SC, 334, 308, CHAS*.

RIVERS, ISABELLA, 25, F, (--), M, SC, 334, 308, CHAS*. In HH of Hannah Rivers f 40 mulatto born SC.

RIVERS, JAMES, 7, M, (--), M, SC, 334, 308, CHAS*. In HH of Hannah Rivers f 40 mulatto born SC.

RIVERS, JOHN, 17, M, Baker, M, SC, 904, 884, CHAS-. In HH of Ellen Jones f 51 mulatto born SC.

RIVERS, JOHN, 4, M, (--), M, SC, 334, 308, CHAS*. In HH of Hannah Rivers f 40 mulatto born SC.

RIVERS, PHILIP, 22, M, Boot maker, M, SC, 107, 119, CHAS. In HH of Annett Elliott f 57 mulatto born SC.

RIVERS, SARAH, 27, F, (--), M, SC, 334, 308, CHAS*. In HH of Hannah Rivers f 40 mulatto born SC.

ROACH, INDIANA, 15, F, (--), M, SC, 435, 404, CHAS*.

ROBERTS, CATHERINE, 1, F, (--), B, SC, 639, 620, CHAS-. In HH of Isaac Roberts m 40 black born SC.

ROBERTS, CHARLES, 29, M, Cabinet maker, M, SC, 544, 510, CHAS*. In HH of Charlotte Roberts f 25 mulatto born SC.

ROBERTS, CHARLOTTE, 25, F, (--), M, SC, 544, 510, CHAS*.

ROBERTS, CHRISTOPHER, 12, M, (--), B, SC, 639, 620, CHAS-. In HH of Isaac Roberts m 40 black born SC.

ROBERTS, CONSTANTIA, 8, F, (--), B, SC, 639, 620, CHAS-. In HH of Isaac Roberts m 40 black born SC.

ROBERTS, ELIZA, 10, F, (--), B, SC, 639, 620, CHAS-. In HH of Isaac Roberts m 40 black born SC.

ROBERTS, ISAAC, 40, M, (--), B, SC, 639, 620, CHAS-.

ROBERTS, JOHN, 5, M, (--), B, SC, 639, 620, CHAS-. In HH of Isaac Roberts m 40 black born SC.

ROBERTS, LAVINA, 38, F, (--), B, SC, 639, 620, CHAS-. In HH of Isaac Roberts m 40 black born SC.

ROBERTSON, ALEXR., 67, M, Matras maker, M, SC, 594, 575, CHAS-.

ROBERTSON, ANTHONY, 7, M, (--), M, SC, 594, 575, CHAS-. In HH of Alexr. Robertson m 67 mulatto born SC.

ROBERTSON, CHARLOTTE, 11, F, (--), M, SC, 135, 135, CHAS%. In HH of Sarah Robertson f 51 mulatto born SC.

ROBERTSON, CLAUDIA, 7, F, (--), B, SC, 206, 194, CHAS+. Not listed with anyone in a household.

ROBERTSON, GEORGE, 13, M, (--), M, SC, 135, 135, CHAS%. In HH of Sarah Robertson f 51 mulatto born SC.

ROBERTSON, HESTER, 9, F, (--), M, SC, 594, 575, CHAS-. In HH of Alexr. Robertson m 67 mulatto born SC.

ROBERTSON, JOHN, 48, M, Drayman, M, SC, 135, 135, CHAS%. In HH of Sarah Robertson f 51 mulatto born SC.

ROBERTSON, JOHN, 18, M, Porter, M, SC, 135, 135, CHAS%. In HH of Sarah Robertson f 51 mulatto born SC.

ROBERTSON, JOHN, 5, M, (--), M, SC, 594, 575, CHAS-. In HH of ALEXR. Robertson m 67 mulatto born SC.

ROBERTSON, JOSEPH, 38, M, Porter, M, SC, 594, 575, CHAS-. In HH of Alexr. Robertson m 67 mulatto born SC.

ROBERTSON, JULIA, 34, F, (--), M, SC, 594, 575, CHAS-. In HH of ALEXR. Robertson m 67 mulatto born SC.

ROBERTSON, MARIA, 40, F, (--), B, SC, 33, 33, CHAS%.

ROBERTSON, MARTHA, 11, F, (--), M, SC, 594, 575, CHAS-. In HH of Alexr. Robertson m 67 mulatto born in SC.

ROBERTSON, MELISSA, 9, F, (--), M, SC, 135, 135, CHAS%. In HH of Sarah Robertson f 51 mulatto born SC.

ROBERTSON, SAMPSON, 13, M, (--), M, SC, 594, 575, CHAS-. In HH of ALEXR. Robertson m 67 mulatto born SC.

ROBERTSON, SARAH, 62, F, (--), M, SC, 594, 575, CHAS-. In HH of ALEXR. Robertson m 67 mulatto born SC.

ROBERTSON, SARAH, 51, F, (--), M, SC, 135, 135, CHAS%.

ROBERTSON, SUSAN, 16, F, (--), M, SC, 135, 135, CHAS%. In HH of Sarah Robertson f 51 mulatto born SC.

ROBINSON, BELLA, 12, F, (--), M, SC, 563, 529, CHAS*. In HH of Flora Robinson f 26 mulatto born SC.

ROBINSON, FLORA, 36, F, (--), M,

SC, 563, 529, CHAS*.

ROBINSON, HENRY, 8, M, (--), M, SC, 563, 529, CHAS*. In HH of Flora Robinson f 26 mulatto born SC.

ROBINSON, JOHN, 6, M, (--), M, SC, 563, 529, CHAS*. In HH of Flora Robinson f 26 mulatto born SC.

ROBINSON, MARY, 34, F, (--), M, SC, 99, 99, CHAS%. In HH of Susan Ford f 50 black born SC.

ROBINSON, MARY, 21, F, (--), M, SC, 2189, 2189, ABB. In HH of Reuben Robinson 46 m Mulatto born SC.

ROBINSON, REUBEN, 46, M, Farmer, M, SC, 2189, 2189, ABB.

ROBINSON, SARAH, 30, F, (--), M, SC, 5, 5, ABB. In HH of John Robinson m 51 born SC.

ROCHE, CATHERINE, 60, F, (--), B, SC, 611, 592, CHAS-. In HH of Edward Roche m 27 black born SC.

ROCHE, EDWARD, 27, M, Tailor, B, SC, 611, 592, CHAS-.

ROCHE, JANE, 25, F, (--), B, SC, 611, 592, CHAS-. In HH of Edward Roche m 27 black born SC.

ROCHE, MARY, 8, F, (--), B, SC, 611, 592, CHAS-. In HH of Edward Roche m 27 black born SC.

ROCHE, MARY A., 1, F, (--), B, SC, 611, 592, CHAS-. In HH of Edward Roche m 27 black born SC.

ROCHE, THOMAS, 5, F, (--), B, SC, 611, 592, CHAS-. In HH of Edward Roche m 27 black born SC.

RODESS, DANIEL, 3, M, (--), M, SC, 1485, 1485, EDGE. In HH of Robt. Rodess m 30 mulatto born SC.

RODESS, JULIA, 23, F, (--), M, SC, 1485, 1485, EDGE. In HH of Robt. Rodess m 30 mulatto born SC.

RODESS, ROBT., 30, M, Farmer, M, SC, 1485, 1485, EDGE.

RODESS, ROBT., 0, M, (--), M, SC, 1485, 1485, EDGE. In HH of Robt. Rodess m 30 mulatto born SC. Robert age 3/12 yr.

RODESS, WILLIAM, 6, M, (--), M, SC, 1485, 1485, EDGE. In HH of Robt.

Rodess m 30 mulatto born SC.

RODGERS, CHARLOTTE, 38, F, (--), B, SC, 889, 889, KERS.

RODGERS, CLOI, 2, F, (--), B, SC, 889, 889, KERS. In HH of Charlotte Rodgers f 38 black born SC.

RODGERS, ELZH., 20, F, (--), M, SC, 131, 131, KERS. In HH of Isaac Rodgers m 24 mulatto born SC.

RODGERS, ISAAC, 24, M, Wagon driver, M, SC, 131, 131, KERS.

RODGERS, J., 12, M, (--), M, SC, 232, 232, LANC*. In HH of T. Rodgers m 24 black born SC.

RODGERS, MARY, 13, F, (--), B, SC, 883, 883, KERS. In HH of Ely Hodges m 31 mulatto born SC.

RODGERS, MARY, 6, F, (--), B, SC, 889, 889, KERS. In HH of Charlotte Rodgers f 38 black born SC.

RODGERS, R., 30, F, (--), M, SC, 232, 232, LANC*. In HH of T. Rodgers m 24 black born SC.

RODGERS, ROBT., 12, M, (--), B, SC, 889, 889, KERS. In HH of Charlotte Rodgers f 38 black born SC.

RODGERS, SERENA, 2, F, (--), M, SC, 131, 131, KERS. In HH of Isaac Rodgers m 24 mulatto born SC.

RODGERS, T., 24, M, Wagon maker, B, SC, 232, 232, LANC*.

RODGERS, W., 15, M, (--), M, SC, 232, 232, LANC*. In HH of T. Rodgers m 24 black born SC.

RODGERS, WM., 6, M, (--), B, SC, 889, 889, KERS. In HH of Charlotte Rodgers f 38 black born SC.

RODREGUES, HENRY, 5, M, (--), M, SC, 915, 895, CHAS-. In HH of Chloe Bowengen f 60 mulatto born SC.

RODREGUES, MARY, 38, F, (--), M, SC, 915, 895, CHAS-. In HH of Chloe Bowengen f 60 mulatto born SC.

ROGERS, ANN, 28, F, (--), M, SC, 195, 183, CHAS-. In HH of Charles Rogers m 70 mulatto born SC.

ROGERS, ANTHONY, 14, M, (--), M, SC, 1889, 1889, SUMT. In HH of Winney Rogers f 40 black born SC.

ROGERS, CHARLES, 70, M, Tailor, M, SC, 195, 183, CHAS-.

ROGERS, ELIZA, 23, F, (--), M, SC, 195, 183, CHAS-. In HH of Charles Rogers m 70 mulatto born SC.

ROGERS, HAMPTON, 40, M, Laborer, B, SC, 324, 324, SUMT.

ROGERS, LOUISA, 10, F, (--), B, SC, 1889, 1889, SUMT. In HH of Winney Rogers f 40 black born SC.

ROGERS, MARIA LOUISA, 50, F, (--), M, MD, 301, 285, CHAS-.

ROGERS, NANCY, 67, F, (--), M, SC, 195, 183, CHAS-. In HH of Charles Rogers m 70 mulatto born SC.

ROGERS, WINNEY, 40, F, (--), B, SC, 1889, 1889, SUMT.

ROLANDS, BEN, 16, M, (--), M, SC, 55, 55, CHAS%. In HH of Charles Hasell m 50 black born SC.

ROLLERSON, A., 20, M, Laborer, M, SC, 119, 119, CHAS2.

ROLLERSON, A., 2, F, (--), B, SC, 138, 138, CHAS2. In HH of J. Rollerson m 25 mulatto born SC.

ROLLERSON, A.T., 0, M, (--), M, SC, 119, 119, CHAS2. In HH of A. Rollerson m 20 mulatto born SC. A.T. Rollelrson age 1/3 yr.

ROLLERSON, CHARLOT, 31, F, (--), B, SC, 138, 138, CHAS2. In HH of J. Rollerson m 25 mulatto born SC.

ROLLERSON, E., 17, F, (--), M, SC, 119, 119, CHAS2. In HH of A. Rollerson m 20 mulatto born SC.

ROLLERSON, E., 4, F, (--), B, SC, 138, 138, CHAS2. In HH of J. Rollerson m 25 mulatto born SC.

ROLLERSON, J., 25, M, Farmer, M, SC, 138, 138, CHAS2.

ROLLERSON, J.B., 2, M, (--), M, SC, 119, 119, CHAS2. In HH of A. Rollerson m 20 mulatto born SC.

ROLLERSON, M., 7, F, (--), B, SC, 138, 138, CHAS2. In HH of J. Rollerson m 25 mulatto born SC.

ROLLINS, CATHERINE, 2, F, (--), M, SC, 350, 350, CHAS%. In HH of William Rollins m 34 mulatto born SC.

ROLLINS, CHARLOTTE, 4, F, (--), M, SC, 350, 350, CHAS%. In HH of William Rollins m 34 mulatto born SC.

ROLLINS, FRANCIS, 7, F, (--), M, SC, 350, 350, CHAS%. In HH of William Rollins m 34 mulatto born SC.

ROLLINS, MARGARET, 30, F, (--), M, SC, 350, 350, CHAS%. In HH of William Rollins m 34 mulatto born SC.

ROLLINS, WILLIAM, 34, M, Wood factor, M, SC, 350, 350, CHAS%.

ROLLINSON, JACOB, 55, M, Laborer, M, SC, 173, 173, COLL*.

ROLLINSON, MARGARET, 50, F, (--), M, SC, 173, 173, COLL*. In HH of Jacob Rollinson m 55 mulatto born SC.

RONSE, ANAKA, 13, F, (--), B, SC, 1282, 1282, BARN. In HH of Frisey Ronse f 40 black born SC.

RONSE, ANGELINE, 4, F, (--), B, SC, 1282, 1282, BARN. In HH of Frisey Ronse f 40 black born SC.

RONSE, BENJ., 1, F, (--), B, SC, 1282, 1282, BARN. In HH of Frisey Ronse f 40 black born SC.

RONSE, BETSY, 22, F, (--), B, SC, 1282, 1282, BARN. In HH of Frisey Ronse f 40 black born SC.

RONSE, BOB, 7, F, (--), B, SC, 1282, 1282, BARN. In HH of Frisey Ronse f 40 black born SC.

RONSE, DEMEYER, 11, M, (--), B, SC, 1282, 1282, BARN. In HH of Frisey Ronse f 40 black born SC.

RONSE, ELLEN, 9, F, (--), B, SC, 1282, 1282, BARN. In HH of Frisey Ronse f 40 black born SC.

RONSE, FRISEY, 40, F, (--), B, SC, 1282, 1282, BARN.

RONSE, JAY, 15, M, (--), B, SC, 1282, 1282, BARN. In HH of Frisey Ronse f 40 black born SC.

RONSE, WILLIAM, 17, M, Planter, B, SC, 1282, 1282, BARN. In HH of Frisey Ronse f 40 black born SC.

ROPER, DANIEL, 16, M, Laborer, B, SC, 144, 132, CHAS*. In HH of Rose Roper f 50 black born SC.

ROPER, ROSE, 50, F, (--), B, SC, 144,

132, CHAS*.

ROPER, TERA, 14, F, (--), B, SC, 144, 132, CHAS*. In HH of Rose Roper f 50 black born SC.

ROSEBURY, MATILDA, 40, F, (--), M, SC, 553, 553, Fair.

ROSEMAN, SAM, 55, M, Hireling, B, SC, 2188, 2188, ABB.

ROUS, BETSY, 29, F, (--), B, SC, 307, 307, CHFD. In HH of Jane Rous f 30 black born SC.

ROUS, CAROLINE, 50, F, (--), B, SC, 334, 334, CHFD.

ROUS, DAVID, 6, M, (--), B, SC, 402, 402, CHFD. In HH of Jerry Farbs m 35 mulatto born SC.

ROUS, ELIZA, 25, F, (--), B, SC, 180, 180, ABB. In HH of Isral Bous m 25 mulatto born SC.

ROUS, ISRAL, 25, M, (--), M, SC, 180, 180, ABB.

ROUS, JANE, 30, F, (--), B, SC, 307, 307, CHFD.

ROUS, JANE, 9, M, (--), M, SC, 307, 307, CHFD. In HH of Jane Rous f 30 black born SC.

ROUS, MARTHA, 10, F, (--), B, SC, 334, 334, CHFD. In HH of Caroline Rous f 50 black born SC.

ROUS, MARY, 13, M, (--), B, SC, 307, 307, CHFD. In HH of Jane Rous f 30 black born SC.

ROUS, REBECCA, 20, F, (--), M, SC, 448, 448, CHFD. In HH of Houdson Wilson m 47 mulatto born SC.

ROUS, SARAH, 18, F, (--), M, SC, 753, 753, CHFD. In HH of Johnson Reaney m 42, Inn keeper, born Ireland.

ROUS, SARAH C., 0, F, (--), B, SC, 180, 180, ABB. In HH of Isral Bous m 25 mulatto born SC. Sarah C. Rous age 1/12 yr.

ROUS, THOMAS, 3, M, (--), B, SC, 307, 307, CHFD. In HH of Jane Rous f 30 black born SC.

ROUS, WILLIAM, 77, M, Farmer, B, SC, 352, 352, CHFD.

ROUSE, ANNA, 2, F, (--), B, SC, 1357, 1357, ABB. In HH of Eliza Rouse f 22 black born SC.

ROUSE, CARY ANN, 44, F, (--), M, SC, 2214, 2214, ABB.

ROUSE, EAMOND, 60, M, Carpenter, B, SC, 304, 305, AND*.

ROUSE, ELEANOR, 1, F, (--), B, SC, 1357, 1357, ABB. In HH of Eliza Rouse f 22 black born SC.

ROUSE, ELIZA, 22, F, (--), B, SC, 1357, 1357, ABB.

ROUSE, FINDA, 7, F, (--), B, SC, 1357, 1357, ABB. In HH of Eliza Rouse f 22 black born SC.

ROUSE, JAMES, 14, M, (--), B, SC, 304, 305, AND*. In HH of Eamond Rouse m 60 black born SC.

ROUSE, JESSE, 37, M, Hireling, B, SC, 1082, 1082, ABB.

ROUSE, JOHN, 5, M, (--), B, SC, 1357, 1357, ABB. In HH of Eliza Rouse f 22 black born SC.

ROUSE, MARY, 55, F, (--), B, SC, 304, 305, AND*. In HH of Eamond Rouse m 60 black born SC.

ROUSE, MARY, 15, F, (--), B, SC, 1357, 1357, ABB. In HH of Eliza Rouse f 22 black born SC.

ROUSE, MARY ANN, 16, F, (--), B, SC, 304, 305, AND*. In HH of Eamond Rouse m 60 black born SC.

ROUSE, POLLY, 50, F, (--), B, SC, 1357, 1357, ABB. In HH of Eliza Rouse f 22 black born SC.

ROUSE, REUBECA, 27, F, (--), B, SC, 543, 543, PICK+. In HH of Thomas Hallum m 54 born SC.

ROUSE, ROSE, 16, F, (--), B, SC, 918, 918, ABB.

ROUSE, SAMUEL, 2, M, (--), M, SC, 918, 918, ABB. In HH of Rose Rouse 16 born SC.

ROUSE, WESLEY, 35, M, Hireling, B, SC, 1088, 1088, ABB.

ROUSE, WILLIAM, 20, M, Laborer, M, SC, 1368, 1374, MAR. In HH of John Hathcock m 21 mulatto born SC.

ROUT, HAMILTON S., 7, M, (--), M,

SC, 147, 135, CHAS*. In HH of Rebecca Naylor f 35 black born SC.

ROUT, JAMES, 20, M, Tailor, M, SC, 147, 135, CHAS*. In HH of Rebecca Naylor f 35 black born SC.

ROUT, JANE, 18, F, (--), M, SC, 147, 135, CHAS*. In HH of Rebecca Naylor f 35 black born SC.

ROUT, NELLY, 35, F, (--), M, SC, 147, 135, CHAS*. In HH of Rebecca Naylor f 35 black born SC.

ROUT, WILLIAM G., 12, M, (--), M, SC, 147, 135, CHAS*. In HH of Rebecca Naylor f 35 black born SC.

RUMELS, CHAS., 10, M, (--), M, SC, 1224, 1224, BARN. In HH of Jas. Tilly m 60 mulatto born SC.

RUMELS, JIM, 7, M, (--), M, SC, 1224, 1224, BARN. In HH of Jas. Tilly m 60 mulatto born SC.

RUMELS, LOUIS, 9, M, (--), M, SC, 1224, 1224, BARN. In HH of Jas. Tilly m 60 mulatto born SC.

RUMELS, MARTHA, 25, F, (--), M, SC, 1224, 1224, BARN. In HH of Jas. Tilly m 60 mulatto born SC.

RUMELS, SOL., 30, M, Raft Hand, M, SC, 1224, 1224, BARN. In HH of Jas. Tilly m 60 mulatto born SC.

RUNIELS, ALECK, 7, M, (--), B, SC, 631, 631, BARN. In HH of Johnathan Runiels m 50 black born SC.

RUNIELS, ANDERSON, 4, M, (--), B, SC, 631, 631, BARN. In HH of Johnathan Runiels m 50 black born SC.

RUNIELS, ELIZ, 15, F, (--), B, SC, 631, 631, BARN. In HH of Johnathan Runiels m 50 black born SC.

RUNIELS, GEORGIANA, 11, F, (--), B, SC, 631, 631, BARN. In HH of Johnathan Runiels m 50 black born SC.

RUNIELS, JEFF, 22, M, (--), B, SC, 631, 631, BARN. In HH of Johnathan Runiels m 50 black born SC.

RUNIELS, JERRY, 7, M, (--), B, SC, 631, 631, BARN. In HH of Johnathan Runiels m 50 black born SC.

RUNIELS, JOHNATHAN, 50, M, (--), B, SC, 631, 631, BARN.

RUNIELS, REBECCA, 13, F, (--), B, SC, 631, 631, BARN. In HH of Johnathan Runiels m 50 black born SC.

RUNIELS, SANDY, 9, F, (--), B, SC, 631, 631, BARN. In HH of Johnathan Runiels m 50 black born SC.

RUNIELS, TOM, 18, M, (--), B, SC, 631, 631, BARN. In HH of Johnathan Runiels m 50 black born SC.

RUNNELS, EDWARD, 38, M, Carpenter, M, SC, 267, 267, GEOR*.

RUNNELS, SARAH, 44, F, (--), M, SC, 267, 267, GEOR*. In HH of Edward Runnels m 38 mulatto born SC.

RUSEL, MATHA, 35, F, (--), B, SC, 89, 89, LAU. In HH of Roderick Rusel m 29 black born SC.

RUSEL, RODERICK, 29, M, Tailor, B, SC, 89, 89, LAU.

RUSSEL, BENJAMIN, 14, M, (--), B, SC, 595, 576, CHAS-. In HH of Florance Russel m 51 black born SC.

RUSSEL, CATHARINE, 7, F, (--), M, SC, 86, 86, CHAS3. In HH of Richard Russel m 57 mulatto born SC.

RUSSEL, DIANA, 46, F, (--), B, SC, 595, 576, CHAS-. In HH of Florance Russel m 51 black born SC.

RUSSEL, FLORANCE, 51, M, Tailor, B, SC, 595, 576, CHAS-.

RUSSEL, FORTUNE, 27, M, Laborer, B, SC, 595, 576, CHAS-. In HH of Florance Russel m 51 black born SC.

RUSSEL, MARTHA, 34, F, (--), M, SC, 86, 86, CHAS3. In HH of Richard Russel m 57 mulatto born SC.

RUSSEL, MARY, 3, F, (--), M, SC, 86, 86, CHAS3. In HH of Richard Russel m 57 mulatto born SC.

RUSSEL, MOURNER, 112, F, (--), M, SC, 86, 86, CHAS3. In HH of Richard Russel m 57 mulatto born SC.

RUSSEL, RICHARD, 57, M, Planter, M, SC, 86, 86, CHAS3.

RUSSEL, ROBT., 10, M, (--), M, SC, 86, 86, CHAS3. In HH of Richard Russel m 57 mulatto born SC.

RUSSELL, BRYANT, 40, M, Farmer, M, SC, 434, 434, BEAU-.

RUSSELL, DAVID, 36, M, Brick Mason, M, SC, 436, 436, BEAU-.

RUSSELL, ELSY, 10, F, (--), M, SC, 435, 435, BEAU-. In HH of William Russell m 38 mulatto born SC.

RUSSELL, GEORGI ANN, 11, F, (--), M, SC, 434, 434, BEAU-. In HH of Bryant Russell m 40 mulatto born SC.

RUSSELL, JANE, 30, F, (--), M, SC, 436, 436, BEAU-. In HH of David Russell m 36 mulatto born SC.

RUSSELL, JANE, 2, F, (--), M, SC, 434, 434, BEAU-. In HH of Bryant Russell m 40 mulatto born SC.

RUSSELL, JOHN, 40, M, Mechanic, M, SC, 463, 463, BEAU-.

RUSSELL, LAWRENCE, 8, M, (--), M, SC, 435, 435, BEAU-. In HH of William Russell m 38 mulatto born SC.

RUSSELL, LENAH, 6, M, (--), M, SC, 435, 435, BEAU-. In HH of William Russell m 38 mulatto born SC.

RUSSELL, LOGAN, 7, M, (--), M, SC, 434, 434, BEAU-. In HH of Bryant Russell m 40 mulatto born SC.

RUSSELL, MARY, 75, F, (--), B, SC, 447, 447, BEAU-.

RUSSELL, MARY, 58, F, (--), M, SC, 489, 489, BEAU-. In HH of William JG. Russell m 63 mulatto born SC.

RUSSELL, MARY, 37, F, (--), M, SC, 435, 435, BEAU-. In HH of William Russell m 38 mulatto born SC.

RUSSELL, MARY, 35, F, (--), M, SC, 434, 434, BEAU-. In HH of Bryant Russell m 40 mulatto born SC.

RUSSELL, MARY, 18, F, (--), M, SC, 448, 448, BEAU-. In HH of Nehemia Russell m 22 mulatto born SC.

RUSSELL, MILEY, 30, F, (--), M, SC, 377, 375, CHAS%. In HH of Sarah Bing f 35 black born SC.

RUSSELL, NEHEMIA, 22, M, Laborer, M, SC, 448, 448, BEAU-.

RUSSELL, OLIVE, 4, M, (--), M, SC, 435, 435, BEAU-. In HH of William Russell m 38 mulatto born SC.

RUSSELL, PHILIP, 12, M, (--), M, SC, 463, 463, BEAU-. In HH of John Russell m 40 mulatto born SC.

RUSSELL, ROBERT, 5, M, (--), M, SC, 434, 434, BEAU-. In HH of Bryant Russell m 40 mulatto born SC.

RUSSELL, SARAH, 16, F, (--), M, SC, 463, 463, BEAU-. In HH of John Russell m 40 mulatto born SC.

RUSSELL, WILLIAM, 38, M, Mechanic, M, SC, 435, 435, BEAU-.

RUSSELL, WILLIAM, 9, M, (--), M, SC, 434, 434, BEAU-. In HH of Bryant Russell m 40 mulatto born SC.

RUSSELL, WILLIAM G., 63, M, Laborer, M, SC, 489, 489, BEAU-.

RUTHERFORD, SUSAN, 12, F, (--), B, SC, 2402, 2402, SPART. In HH of James Gipson m 25 born SC.

RUTLEDGE, AMY, 36, F, (--), M, SC, 398, 362, CHAS.

RYAN, AUGUSTAS, 40, M, Butcher, M, SC, 692, 650, CHAS+.

RYAN, DANIEL, 11, M, (--), M, SC, 692, 650, CHAS+. In HH of Augustas Ryan m 40 mulatto born SC.

RYAN, ELEANOR, 23, F, (--), M, SC, 48, 48, CHAS%. In HH of William Osborne m 37 mulatto born SC.

RYAN, FRANCIS, 5, M, (--), M, SC, 692, 650, CHAS+. In HH of Augustas Ryan m 40 mulatto born SC.

RYAN, HANNAH, 30, F, (--), M, SC, 692, 650, CHAS+. In HH of Augustas Ryan m 40 mulatto born SC.

RYAN, JOHN, 7, M, (--), M, SC, 692, 650, CHAS+. In HH of Augustas Ryan m 40 mulatto born SC.

RYAN, MARY, 2, F, (--), M, SC, 692, 650, CHAS+. In HH of Augustas Ryan m 40 mulatto born SC.

RYAN, SIXTIMAR, 1, F, (--), M, SC, 692, 650, CHAS+. In HH of Augustas Ryan m 40 mulatto born SC.

RYAN, WILLIAM, 4, M, (--), M, SC, 692, 650, CHAS+. In HH of Augustas Ryan m 40 mulatto born SC.

S

SAILING, WILLIAM, 7, M, (--), M, SC, 19, 19, CHAS~. In HH of James Busby {?}, m 50 mulatto born SC.

SAILOR, RACHEL, 22, F, (--), M, SC, 513, 528, RICH.

SALMONDS, BENJAMIN, 16, M, Planter, M, SC, 243, 248, RICH+. In HH of Elizabeth Salmonds f 50 mulatto born SC.

SALMONDS, BOLDEN, 7, M, (--), M, SC, 243, 248, RICH+. In HH of Elizabeth Salmonds f 50 mulatto born SC.

SALMONDS, BRYANT, 5, M, (--), M, SC, 240, 245, RICH+. In HH of Stark Harris m 50 mulatto born SC.

SALMONDS, CAROLINE, 13, F, (--), M, SC, 241, 246, RICH+. In HH of Griffin Salmonds m 25 mulatto born SC.

SALMONDS, ELIZABETH, 50, F, (--), M, SC, 243, 248, RICH+.

SALMONDS, ELIZABETH, 42, F, (--), M, SC, 1, 1, RICH. In HH of Thomas Plummer m 44 born MA.

SALMONDS, ELIZABETH, 12, F, (--), M, SC, 208, 212, RICH+. In HH of Isham Harris m 50 mulatto born SC.

SALMONDS, FRANCES, 10, F, (--), B, SC, 236, 241, RICH+. In HH of William Salmonds m 31 mulatto born SC.

SALMONDS, GRIFFIN, 25, M, Planter, M, SC, 241, 246, RICH+.

SALMONDS, JACOB, 12, M, (--), M, SC, 243, 248, RICH+. In HH of Elizabeth Salmonds f 50 mulatto born SC.

SALMONDS, JAMES, 8, M, (--), B, SC, 236, 241, RICH+. In HH of William Salmonds m 31 mulatto born SC.

SALMONDS, JAMES, 2, M, (--), M, SC, 241, 246, RICH+. In HH of Griffin Salmonds m 25 mulatto born SC.

SALMONDS, JOHN, 43, M, (--), M, SC, 241, 246, RICH+. In HH of Griffin Salmonds m 25 mulatto born SC.

SALMONDS, KEZIAH, 50, F, (--), M, SC, 240, 245, RICH+.

SALMONDS, KEZIAH, 38, F, (--), M, SC, 241, 246, RICH+. In HH of Griffin Salmonds m 25 mulatto born SC.

SALMONDS, RUFUS, 18, M, Planter, M, SC, 243, 248, RICH+. In HH of Elizabeth Salmonds f 50 mulatto born SC.

SALMONDS, SARAH, 2, F, (--), M, SC, 242, 247, RICH+. In HH of Washington Salmonds m 21 mulatto born SC.

SALMONDS, SYRENA, 30, F, (--), B, SC, 236, 241, RICH+. In HH of William Salmonds m 31 mulatto born SC.

SALMONDS, THOMAS, 19, M, Planter, M, SC, 243, 248, RICH+. In HH of Elizabeth Salmonds f 50 mulatto born SC.

SALMONDS, URANA, 21, F, (--), M, SC, 242, 247, RICH+. In HH of Washington Salmonds m 21 mulatto born SC.

SALMONDS, WASHINGTON, 21, M, Planter, M, SC, 242, 247, RICH+.

SALMONDS, WESLEY, 2, M, (--), B, SC, 236, 241, RICH+. In HH of William Salmonds m 31 mulatto born SC.

SALMONDS, WILLIAM, 31, M, Planter, M, SC, 236, 241, RICH+.

SALTERS, JANE, 17, F, (--), M, SC, 437, 434, CHAS%. In HH of Scifin Stuart m 41 black born SC.

SALTERS, SALLY, 39, F, (--), M, SC, 437, 434, CHAS%. In HH of Scifin Stuart m 41 black born SC.

SANDER, THOMAS, 4, M, (--), M, SC, 529, 529, COLL. In HH of Isham Padget m 23 born SC.

SANDERS, ANN, 20, F, (--), B, SC, 1202, 1202, NEWB. In HH of Mary Sanders f 60 black born SC.

SANDERS, BALL, 37, M, Carpenter, B, SC, 138, 138, NEWB.

SANDERS, CHARITY, 45, F, (--), B,

SC, 1202, 1202, NEWB. In HH of Mary Sanders f 60 black born SC.

SANDERS, DONSEY, 2, M, (--), B, SC, 1202, 1202, NEWB. In HH of Mary Sanders f 60 black born SC.

SANDERS, E., 3, F, (--), M, SC, 560, 560, LANC*. In HH of T. Landers f 45 mulatto born SC.

SANDERS, ELIZABETH, 24, F, (--), B, SC, 1202, 1202, NEWB. In HH of Mary Sanders f 60 black born SC.

SANDERS, J., 6, M, (--), M, SC, 560, 560, LANC*. In HH of T. Landers f 45 mulatto born SC.

SANDERS, JANE, 26, F, (--), B, SC, 1202, 1202, NEWB. In HH of Mary Sanders f 60 black born SC.

SANDERS, JOHN, 10, M, (--), B, SC, 1202, 1202, NEWB. In HH of Mary Sanders f 60 black born SC.

SANDERS, MARTHA, 24, F, (--), B, SC, 1202, 1202, NEWB. In HH of Mary Sanders f 60 black born SC.

SANDERS, MARTIN, 21, M, Farmer, B, SC, 1201, 1201, NEWB. IN HH of Wade Sanders m 45 black born SC.

SANDERS, MARY, 60, F, (--), B, SC, 1202, 1202, NEWB.

SANDERS, MARY, 15, F, (--), B, SC, 1201, 1201, NEWB. IN HH of Wade Sanders m 45 black born SC.

SANDERS, MARY ANN, 40, F, (--), B, SC, 1185, 1164, CHAS%.

SANDERS, RACHAL, 41, F, (--), B, SC, 1201, 1201, NEWB. IN HH of Wade Sanders m 45 black born SC.

SANDERS, REBECCA, 16, F, (--), B, SC, 1201, 1201, NEWB. IN HH of Wade Sanders m 45 black born SC.

SANDERS, REBECCA, 2, F, (--), B, SC, 1185, 1164, CHAS%. In HH of Mary Ann Sanders f 40 black born SC.

SANDERS, RICHARD, 8, M, (--), B, SC, 1202, 1202, NEWB. In HH of Mary Sanders f 60 black born SC.

SANDERS, SARAH, 16, F, (--), B, SC, 1202, 1202, NEWB. In HH of Mary Sanders f 60 black born SC.

SANDERS, SUSAN, 18, F, (--), B, SC,

1185, 1164, CHAS%. In HH of Mary Ann Sanders f 40 black born SC.

SANDERS, T., 45, F, (--), M, SC, 560, 560, LANC*.

SANDERS, THOMAS, 22, M, (--), B, SC, 1202, 1202, NEWB. In HH of Mary Sanders f 60 black born SC.

SANDERS, WADE, 45, M, Farmer, B, SC, 1201, 1201, NEWB.

SANDERS, WADE, 14, M, (--), B, SC, 1201, 1201, NEWB. IN HH of Wade Sanders m 45 black born SC.

SANDERS, WARD, 13, M, (--), B, SC, 1201, 1201, NEWB. IN HH of Wade Sanders m 45 black born SC.

SANDERS, WILLIAM, 18, M, (--), B, SC, 1202, 1202, NEWB. In HH of Mary Sanders f 60 black born SC.

SARPORTAS, ADELINE, 22, F, (--), M, SC, 833, 815, CHAS%. In HH of Louisa Sarportas f 50 mulatto born SC.

SARPORTAS, ALLAN, 24, M, Carpenter, M, SC, 833, 815, CHAS%. In HH of Louisa Sarportas f 50 mulatto born SC.

SARPORTAS, CARDOZA, 29, M, Carpenter, M, SC, 833, 815, CHAS%. In HH of Louisa Sarportas f 50 mulatto born SC.

SARPORTAS, LOUISA, 50, F, (--), M, SC, 833, 815, CHAS%.

SASPORTAS, ADALADE, 90, F, (--), M, SC, 944, 921, CHAS%. In HH of Joseph Sasportas m 47 mulatto born SC.

SASPORTAS, CECELIA, 23, F, (--), B, SC, 942, 922, CHAS-. In HH of Josephine Sasportas f 30 black born SC.

SASPORTAS, CHARLES, 0, M, (--), M, SC, 944, 921, CHAS%. In HH of Joseph Sasportas m 47 mulatto born SC. Charles Sasportas age 8/12 yr.

SASPORTAS, FREDRICK, 35, M, Millwright, M, SC, 944, 921, CHAS%. In HH of Joseph Sasportas m 47 mulatto born SC.

SASPORTAS, FREDRICK, 8, M, (--), M, SC, 944, 921, CHAS%. In HH of Joseph Sasportas m 47 mulatto born SC.

SASPORTAS, JOSEPH, 47, M,

Butcher, M, SC, 944, 921, CHAS%.

SASPORTAS, JOSEPHINE, 30, F, (--), B, SC, 942, 922, CHAS-.

SASPORTAS, LAMBOLT, 3, M, (--), M, SC, 944, 921, CHAS%. In HH of Joseph Sasportas m 47 mulatto born SC.

SASPORTAS, MARGARET, 37, F, (--), M, SC, 944, 921, CHAS%. In HH of Joseph Sasportas m 47 mulatto born SC.

SASPORTAS, MARGARET, 6, F, (--), M, SC, 944, 921, CHAS%. In HH of Joseph Sasportas m 47 mulatto born SC.

SASPORTAS, MARY, 5, F, (--), M, SC, 944, 921, CHAS%. In HH of Joseph Sasportas m 47 mulatto born SC.

SASPORTAS, THADEUS, 2, M, (--), M, SC, 944, 921, CHAS%. In HH of Joseph Sasportas m 47 mulatto born SC.

SAULTERS, EDMINA, 2, F, (--), M, SC, 971, 951, CHAS-. In HH of Phillip Saulters m 33 mulatto born SC.

SAULTERS, ELIZABETH, 9, F, (--), M, SC, 971, 951, CHAS-. In HH of Phillip Saulters m 33 mulatto born SC.

SAULTERS, FRANCIS, 7, M, (--), M, SC, 971, 951, CHAS-. In HH of Phillip Saulters m 33 mulatto born SC.

SAULTERS, PHILLIP, 33, M, Drummer, M, SC, 971, 951, CHAS-.

SAULTERS, PHILLIP, 5, M, (--), M, SC, 971, 951, CHAS-. In HH of Phillip Saulters m 33 mulatto born SC.

SAULTERS, WILLIAM, 12, M, (--), M, SC, 971, 951, CHAS-. In HH of Phillip Saulters m 33 mulatto born SC.

SAVAGE, ANN, 39, F, (--), B, Germany {sic}, 18, 16, CHAS-. In HH of Betsey Savage f 50 mulatto born Germany {sic}.

SAVAGE, ANN, 30, F, (--), B, SC, 917, 897, CHAS-. In HH of Silva Savage f 50 black born SC.

SAVAGE, BETSEY, 50, F, (--), M, Germany {sic}, 18, 16, CHAS-.

SAVAGE, CATHERINE, 25, F, (--), B, SC, 615, 607, CHAS%. In HH of Ann Parson f 60 black born SC.

SAVAGE, CHARLES, 15, M, Laborer, B, SC, 917, 897, CHAS-. In HH of Silva Savage f 50 black born SC.

SAVAGE, ELIZABETH, 33, F, (--), M, SC, 247, 232, CHAS-.

SAVAGE, ELIZABETH, 14, F, (--), B, SC, 917, 897, CHAS-. In HH of Silva Savage f 50 black born SC.

SAVAGE, EUGENA, 5, F, (--), B, SC, 917, 897, CHAS-. In HH of Silva Savage f 50 black born SC.

SAVAGE, FABRIEL, 42, M, Laborer, B, Germany {sic}, 18, 16, CHAS-. In HH of Betsey Savage f 50 mulatto born Germany {sic}.

SAVAGE, HAGAR, 41, F, (--), B, SC, 103, 103, CHAS%. In HH of Thomas Savage m 46 black born SC.

SAVAGE, HENRETTA, 45, F, (--), M, SC, 773, 753, CHAS-.

SAVAGE, JOHN, 12, M, (--), B, SC, 917, 897, CHAS-. In HH of Silva Savage f 50 black born SC.

SAVAGE, MARGARET, 4, F, (--), M, Germany {sic}, 18, 16, CHAS-. In HH of Betsey Savage f 50 mulatto born Germany {sic}.

SAVAGE, MARY, 9, F, (--), B, SC, 615, 607, CHAS%. In HH of Ann Parson f 60 black born SC.

SAVAGE, MARY, 2, F, (--), B, SC, 917, 897, CHAS-. In HH of Silva Savage f 50 black born SC.

SAVAGE, OCTAVUS, 8, M, (--), B, SC, 917, 897, CHAS-. In HH of Silva Savage f 50 black born SC.

SAVAGE, SILVA, 50, F, (--), B, SC, 917, 897, CHAS-.

SAVAGE, SUSAN, 35, F, (--), M, SC, 388, 361, CHAS*.

SAVAGE, TELIDY, 18, M, (--), M, SC, 388, 361, CHAS*. In HH of Susan Savage f 35 mulatto born SC.

SAVAGE, THOMAS, 46, M, Upholsterer, B, SC, 103, 103, CHAS%.

SAXON, ELIZA, 9, F, (--), M, Ireland {sic}, 55, 50, CHAS-. In HH of Juliet Saxon f 35 mulatto born Ireland {sic}.

SAXON, ELLA, 5, F, (--), M, Ireland {sic}, 55, 50, CHAS-. In HH of Juliet Saxon f 35 mulatto born Ireland {sic}.

SAXON, JULIA, 7, F, (--), M, Ireland {sic}, 55, 50, CHAS-. In HH of Juliet Saxon f 35 mulatto born Ireland {sic}.

SAXON, JULIET, 35, F, (--), M, Ireland {sic}, 55,50, CHAS-.

SAYLOR, FRANCIS, 20, M, Laborer, M, SC,41,42, RICH.

SCHERLY, MARY, 38, F, (--), M, SC, 568, 551, CHAS-. In HH of Robert Morgan m 50 black born SC.

SCOOTT, CAROLINE, 22, F, (--), M, SC, 396, 396, UNN+.

SCOTT, ABIGAIL, 24, F, (--), M, SC, 1259, 1259, SUMT. In HH of Martha Scott f 50 mulatto born SC.

SCOTT, ABRAM, 55, M, Planter, B, SC, 1099, 1099, BARN.

SCOTT, ABRAM, 13, M, (--), B, SC, 1106, 1106, BARN. In HH of Caroline Scott f 65 black born SC.

SCOTT, ABRAM, 10, M, (--), B, SC, 1099, 1099, BARN. In HH of Abram Scott m 55 black born SC.

SCOTT, ADALIN, 22, F, (--), M, SC, 1233, 1233, EDGE.

SCOTT, ALA, 38, M, None, M, SC, 1601, 1601, BARN. In HH of Sarah Desomire {?} f 45 mulatto born SC.

SCOTT, ALEXANDER, 20, M, Farmer, M, SC, 682, 683, ORNG+. In HH of David Scott m 36 mulatto born SC.

SCOTT, ALEXANDER, 10, M, (--), B, SC, 1106, 1106, BARN. In HH of Caroline Scott f 65 black born SC.

SCOTT, AMELIA, 30, F, (--), M, SC, 273, 273, BEAU+. In HH of Charles Scott m 27 mulatto born SC.

SCOTT, ANN, 46, F, (--), M, SC, 296, 296, BEAU+.

SCOTT, ANN, 9, F, (--), M, SC, 296, 296, BEAU+. In HH of Ann Scott f 46 mulatto born SC.

SCOTT, ASIA, 2, M, (--), M, SC, 446, 446, BEAU-. In HH of Eldridge Scott m 25 mulatto born SC.

SCOTT, BENNY, 27, M, Planter, B, SC, 1107, 1107, BARN. In HH of Wm. Scott m 30 black born SC.

SCOTT, BETSEY, 60, F, (--), M, SC, 738, 738, KERS. In HH of Newman Scott m 16 mulatto born SC.

SCOTT, BETSEY, 21, F, (--), M, SC, 286, 286, BEAU+. In HH of Thomas Scott m 25 born SC.

SCOTT, BRANTLY, 11, M, (--), M, SC, 1439, 1439, BARN. In HH of Maria Scott f 48 black born SC.

SCOTT, CAPERS, 6, M, (--), M, SC, 683, 684, ORNG+. In HH of Joseph Scott m 36 mulatto born SC.

SCOTT, CAROLINE, 65, F, (--), B, SC, 1106, 1106, BARN.

SCOTT, CAROLINE, 29, F, (--), M, SC, 1335, 1335, SUMT.

SCOTT, CAROLINE, 14, F, (--), M, SC, 1601, 1601, BARN. In HH of Sarah Desomire {?} f 45 mulatto born SC.

SCOTT, CAROLINE, 4, F, (--), M, SC, 1335, 1335, SUMT. In HH of Caroline Scott f 29 mulatto born SC.

SCOTT, CATHARINE, 30, F, (--), B, SC, 1439, 1439, BARN. In HH of Maria Scott f 48 black born SC.

SCOTT, CATHERINE, 27, F, (--), M, SC, 499, 457, CHAS+. In HH of Francis Scott m 38 mulatto born SC.

SCOTT, CHARLES, 27, M, Farmer, M, SC, 273, 273, BEAU+.

SCOTT, CHARLES, 4, M, (--), M, SC, 273, 273, BEAU+. In HH of Charles Scott m 27 mulatto born SC.

SCOTT, CHARLOTTE, 7, F, (--), M, SC, 273, 273, BEAU+. In HH of Charles Scott m 27 mulatto born SC.

SCOTT, CHARLTON, 20, M, Laborer, M, SC, 433, 433, BEAU-. In HH of Webster Scott m 57 mulatto born SC.

SCOTT, DANA, 14, M, (--), B, SC, 1099, 1099, BARN. In HH of Abram Scott m 55 black born SC.

SCOTT, DANIEL, 35, M, Carter, M, SC, 101, 113, CHAS. In HH of Eliza Scott f 29 mulatto born SC.

SCOTT, DAVID, 36, M, Farmer, M, SC, 682, 683, ORNG+.

SCOTT, DAVID, 35, M, None, M, SC, 1602, 1602, BARN.

SCOTT, DAVID, 21, M, (--), M, SC, 24, 24, CHAS#. In HH of Thos Scott m 65 mulatto born SC.

SCOTT, DENNIS, 91, M, None, B, SC, 815, 815, BARN.

SCOTT, EDWARD, 6, M, (--), M, SC, 452, 452, BEAU-. In HH of Holland Scott m 38 mulatto born SC.

SCOTT, ELDRIDGE, 25, M, Laborer, M, SC, 446, 446, BEAU-.

SCOTT, ELIJAH, 12, M, (--), M, SC, 296, 296, BEAU+. In HH of Ann Scott f 46 mulatto born SC.

SCOTT, ELIZA, 35, F, (--), M, SC, 815, 815, BARN. In HH of Dennis Scott m 91 black born SC.

SCOTT, ELIZA, 29, F, (--), M, SC, 101, 113, CHAS.

SCOTT, ELIZA, 21, F, (--), M, SC, 1601, 1601, BARN. In HH of Sarah Desomire {?} f 45 mulatto born SC.

SCOTT, ELIZA, 12, F, (--), M, SC, 1602, 1602, BARN. In HH of David Scott m 35 mulatto born SC.

SCOTT, ELIZA, 4, F, (--), M, SC, 1602, 1602, BARN. In HH of David Scott m 35 mulatto born SC.

SCOTT, ELIZABETH, 12, F, (--), M, SC, 101, 113, CHAS. In HH of Eliza Scott f 29 mulatto born SC.

SCOTT, ELIZABETH, 8, F, (--), M, SC, 452, 452, BEAU-. In HH of Holland Scott m 38 mulatto born SC.

SCOTT, ELIZABETH, 8, F, (--), M, SC, 682, 683, ORNG+. In HH of David Scott m 36 mulatto born SC.

SCOTT, ELLEN, 10, F, (--), B, SC, 1439, 1439, BARN. In HH of Maria Scott f 48 black born SC.

SCOTT, ELLIN, 1, M, (--), M, SC, 446, 446, BEAU-. In HH of Eldridge Scott m 25 mulatto born SC.

SCOTT, ELZA., 4, F, (--), M, SC, 687, 687, KERS. In HH of Sarah Scott f 18 mulatto born SC.

SCOTT, EVE, 0, F, (--), M, SC, 24, 24, CHAS#. In HH of Thos Scott m 65 mulatto born SC. Eve Scott 3/12 yr.

SCOTT, FANNY, 8, F, (--), M, SC, 24, 24, CHAS#. In HH of Thos Scott m 65 mulatto born SC.

SCOTT, FLORA, 31, F, (--), M, SC, 232, 232, CHAS%.

SCOTT, FRANCES, 10, F, (--), M, SC, 683, 684, ORNG+. In HH of Joseph Scott m 36 mulatto born SC.

SCOTT, FRANCIS, 38, M, Cooper, M, SC, 499, 457, CHAS+.

SCOTT, GARRETT, 6, M, (--), M, SC, 1439, 1439, BARN. In HH of Maria Scott f 48 black born SC.

SCOTT, GRACE, 4, F, (--), B, SC, 1099, 1099, BARN. In HH of Abram Scott m 55 black born SC.

SCOTT, HARIETT, 15, F, (--), M, SC, 738, 738, KERS. In HH of Newman Scott m 16 mulatto born SC.

SCOTT, HASTING, 12, M, (--), M, SC, 1274, 1274, SUMT. In HH of Henry Scott m 36 mulatto born SC.

SCOTT, HENRY, 36, M, Laborer, M, SC, 1274, 1274, SUMT.

SCOTT, HILLIARD, 14, M, (--), B, SC, 586, 586, UNION. In HH of Keith Bowen m 33 born SC.

SCOTT, HOLLAND, 38, M, Laborer, M, SC, 452, 452, BEAU-.

SCOTT, ISAAC, 16, M, Planter, B, SC, 1106, 1106, BARN. In HH of Caroline Scott f 65 black born SC.

SCOTT, ISHAM, 66, M, Planter, M, SC, 1354, 1354, SUMT.

SCOTT, JAMES, 36, M, Planter, M, SC, 298, 298, CHAS3.

SCOTT, JAMES, 13, M, (--), B, SC, 163, 163, CHAS%. In HH of Joseph Scott m 39 black born SC.

SCOTT, JANE, 36, F, (--), B, SC, 163, 163, CHAS%. In HH of Joseph Scott m 39 black born SC.

SCOTT, JANE, 33, F, None, M, SC, 1602, 1602, BARN. In HH of David Scott m 35 mulatto born SC.

SCOTT, JANE, 10, F, (--), M, SC, 586, 586, UNION. In HH of Keith Bowen m 33 born SC.

SCOTT, JANE, 4, F, (--), M, SC, 452,

452, BEAU-. In HH of Holland Scott m 38 mulatto born SC.

SCOTT, JAS., 35, M, (--), B, SC, 128, 128, KERS.

SCOTT, JAS., 13, M, (--), M, SC, 1439, 1439, BARN. In HH of Maria Scott f 48 black born SC.

SCOTT, JOHN, 22, M, Planter, B, SC, 1099, 1099, BARN. In HH of Abram Scott m 55 black born SC.

SCOTT, JOHN, 10, M, (--), M, SC, 1274, 1274, SUMT. In HH of Henry Scott m 36 mulatto born SC.

SCOTT, JOHN, 8, M, (--), M, SC, 683, 684, ORNG+. In HH of Joseph Scott m 36 mulatto born SC.

SCOTT, JORDAN, 1, M, (--), M, SC, 1602, 1602, BARN. In HH of David Scott m 35 mulatto born SC.

SCOTT, JOS, 11, M, (--), B, SC, 1106, 1106, BARN. In HH of Caroline Scott f 65 black born SC.

SCOTT, JOSEPH, 39, M, Drayman, B, SC, 163, 163, CHAS%.

SCOTT, JOSEPH, 36, M, Farmer, M, SC, 683, 684, ORNG+.

SCOTT, JOSIAH, 56, M, None, M, SC, 1353, 1353, SUMT.

SCOTT, LAURA, 7, F, (--), M, SC, 1335, 1335, SUMT. In HH of Caroline Scott f 29 mulatto born SC.

SCOTT, LORY, 9, M, (--), M, SC, 815, 815, BARN. In HH of Dennis Scott m 91 black born SC.

SCOTT, LYDIA, 24, F, (--), M, SC, 579, 579, UNION. In HH of Polly Johns f 49 born SC.

SCOTT, MANNING, 14, M, (--), M, SC, 1274, 1274, SUMT. In HH of Henry Scott m 36 mulatto born SC.

SCOTT, MARG., 13, F, (--), M, SC, 687, 687, KERS. In HH of Sarah Scott f 18 mulatto born SC.

SCOTT, MARGARET, 48, F, (--), M, SC, 1354, 1354, SUMT. In HH of Isham Scott m 66 born SC.

SCOTT, MARGARET, 30, F, (--), M, SC, 682, 683, ORNG+. In HH of David Scott m 36 mulatto born SC.

SCOTT, MARGARET, 18, F, (--), M, SC, 682, 683, ORNG+. In HH of David Scott m 36 mulatto born SC.

SCOTT, MARGARET, 14, F, (--), M, SC, 1354, 1354, SUMT. In HH of Isham Scott m 66 born SC.

SCOTT, MARGARET, 8, F, (--), B, SC, 1439, 1439, BARN. In HH of Maria Scott f 48 black born SC.

SCOTT, MARGARET, 6, F, (--), M, SC, 296, 296, BEAU+. In HH of Ann Scott f 46 mulatto born SC.

SCOTT, MARIA, 48, F, (--), B, SC, 1439, 1439, BARN.

SCOTT, MARTHA, 50, F, (--), M, SC, 1259, 1259, SUMT.

SCOTT, MARTHA, 15, F, (--), M, SC, 296, 296, BEAU+. In HH of Ann Scott f 46 mulatto born SC.

SCOTT, MARTHA, 13, F, (--), M, SC, 1602, 1602, BARN. In HH of David Scott m 35 mulatto born SC.

SCOTT, MARY, 49, F, (--), M, SC, 24, 24, CHAS#. In HH of Thos Scott m 65 mulatto born SC.

SCOTT, MARY, 40, F, (--), B, SC, 1099, 1099, BARN. In HH of Abram Scott m 55 black born SC.

SCOTT, MARY, 30, F, (--), M, SC, 1274, 1274, SUMT. In HH of Henry Scott m 36 mulatto born SC.

SCOTT, MARY, 23, F, (--), M, SC, 446, 446, BEAU-. In HH of Eldridge Scott m 25 mulatto born SC.

SCOTT, MARY, 19, F, (--), M, SC, 1601, 1601, BARN. In HH of Sarah Desomire {?} f 45 mulatto born SC.

SCOTT, MARY, 16, F, (--), M, SC, 1274, 1274, SUMT. In HH of Henry Scott m 36 mulatto born SC.

SCOTT, MARY, 5, F, (--), B, SC, 1099, 1099, BARN. In HH of Abram Scott m 55 black born SC.

SCOTT, MARY, 0, F, (--), M, SC, 296, 296, BEAU+. In HH of Ann Scott f 46 mulatto born SC. Mary age 2/12 yr.

SCOTT, MISOURI P., 0, F, (--), M, SC, 1233, 1233, EDGE. In HH of Adaline Scott f 22 mulatto born SC.

Misouri P. 1/12 yr.

SCOTT, MITCHEL, 10, M, (--), M, SC, 682, 683, ORNG+. In HH of David Scott m 36 mulatto born SC.

SCOTT, MOSES, 13, M, (--), M, SC, 286, 286, BEAU+. In HH of Thomas Scott m 25 born SC.

SCOTT, NANCY, 45, F, (--), M, SC, 1601, 1601, BARN. In HH of Sarah Desomire{?} f 45 mulatto born SC.

SCOTT, NANCY, 10, F, (--), M, SC, 1602, 1602, BARN. In HH of David Scott m 35 mulatto born SC.

SCOTT, NEWMAN, 16, M, (--), M, SC, 738, 738, KERS.

SCOTT, PINKNEY, 15, M, (--), M, SC, 683, 684, ORNG+. In HH of Joseph Scott m 36 mulatto born SC.

SCOTT, POLLY, 16, F, (--), M, SC, 24, 24, CHAS#. In HH of Thos Scott m 65 mulatto born SC.

SCOTT, POLLY, 7, F, (--), M, SC, 1602, 1602, BARN. In HH of David Scott m 35 mulatto born SC.

SCOTT, RACHEL, 35, F, (--), M, SC, 586, 586, UNION. In HH of Keith Bowen m 33 born SC.

SCOTT, REUBIN, 12, M, (--), M, SC, 452, 452, BEAU-. In HH of Holland Scott m 38 mulatto born SC.

SCOTT, SALLY, 3, F, (--), M, SC, 579, 579, UNION. In HH of Polly Johns f 49 born SC.

SCOTT, SAMUEL, 15, M, Laborer, M, SC, 452, 452, BEAU-. In HH of Holland Scott m 38 mulatto born SC.

SCOTT, SARAH, 58, F, (--), M, SC, 433, 433, BEAU-. In HH of Webster Scott m 57 mulatto born SC.

SCOTT, SARAH, 23, F, (--), M, SC, 1601, 1601, BARN. In HH of Sarah Desomire{?} f 45 mulatto born SC.

SCOTT, SARAH, 20, F, (--), M, SC, 452, 452, BEAU-. In HH of Holland Scott m 38 mulatto born SC.

SCOTT, SARAH, 18, F, (--), M, SC, 687, 687, KERS.

SCOTT, SARAH, 17, F, (--), M, SC, 687, 687, KERS. In HH of Sarah Scott f

18 mulatto born SC.

SCOTT, SARAH, 10, F, (--), B, SC, 281, 281, BEAU+. In HH of Edward Brailsford m 75 mulatto born SC.

SCOTT, SOL, 8, M, (--), B, SC, 1099, 1099, BARN. In HH of Abram Scott m 55 black born SC.

SCOTT, SOPHIA, 18, F, Planter, B, SC, 1099, 1099, BARN. In HH of Abram Scott m 55 black born SC.

SCOTT, STEPHEN, 70, M, Planter, M, SC, 1114, 1114, BARN. In HH of Jas. Williams 3 {sic} born SC.

SCOTT, SUSAN, 60, F, (--), M, SC, 125, 125, KERS.

SCOTT, SUSAN, 10, F, (--), B, SC, 1099, 1099, BARN. In HH of Abram Scott m 55 black born SC.

SCOTT, SUSANAH B., 32, F, (--), M, SC, 1353, 1353, SUMT. In HH of Josiah Scott m 56 mulatto born SC.

SCOTT, THOMAS, 25, M, Laborer, M, SC, 286, 286, BEAU+.

SCOTT, THOMAS, 7, M, (--), M, SC, 1594, 1690, MAR,. In HH of Malcom McCall m 34 born SC.

SCOTT, THOMAS, 3, M, (--), M, SC, 499, 457, CHAS+. In HH of Francis Scott m 38 mulatto born SC.

SCOTT, THOMAS, 3, M, (--), M, SC, 232, 232, CHAS%. In HH of Flora Scott f 37 mulatto born SC.

SCOTT, THOS., 65, M, Farmer, M, SC, 24, 24, CHAS#.

SCOTT, THOS., 18, M, (--), M, SC, 24, 24, CHAS#. In HH of Thos Scott m 65 mulatto born SC.

SCOTT, VINCEANT, 4, M, (--), M, SC, 446, 446, BEAU-. In HH of Eldridge Scott m 25 mulatto born SC.

SCOTT, WASHINGTON, 18, M, Laborer, M, SC, 1274, 1274, SUMT. In HH of Henry Scott m 36 mulatto born SC.

SCOTT, WEBSTER, 57, M, Farmer, M, SC, 433, 433, BEAU-.

SCOTT, WELLIS, 18, M, (--), M, SC, 815, 815, BARN. In HH of Dennis Scott m 91 black born SC.

SCOTT, WILLIAM, 4, M, (--), M, SC, 682, 683, ORNG+. In HH of David Scott m 36 mulatto born SC.

SCOTT, WM., 30, M, Planter, B, SC, 1107, 1107, BARN.

SCOTT, WM., 7, M, (--), M, SC, 24, 24, CHAS#. In HH of Thos Scott m 65 mulatto born SC.

SCOTT, WM., 6, M, (--), B, SC, 1099, 1099, BARN. In HH of Abram Scott m 55 black born SC.

SCOTT, WM., 0, M, (--), M, SC, 1274, 1274, SUMT. In HH of Henry Scott m 36 mulatto born SC. Wm. 2/12 yr.

SCOTT, WM. C., 22, M, (--), M, SC, 1353, 1353, SUMT. In HH of Josiah Scott m 56 mulatto born SC.

SCREVEN, REBECCA, 21, F, (--), M, SC, 702, 660, CHAS+.

SCREVIN, ELIZABETH, 25, F, (--), M, SC, 701, 659, CHAS+. In HH of Grace Alston f 26 mulatto born SC.

SEABOROUGH, CAPERS, 5, M, (--), M, SC, 442, 442, BEAU-. In HH of Robert Seaborough m 55 mulatto born SC.

SEABOROUGH, EDWARD, 3, M, (--), M, SC, 442, 442, BEAU-. In HH of Robert Seaborough m 55 mulatto born SC.

SEABOROUGH, HAMPTON, 1, M, (--), M, SC, 443, 443, BEAU-. In HH of James Seaborough m 26 mulatto born SC.

SEABOROUGH, HENRY, 2, M, (--), M, SC, 443, 443, BEAU-. In HH of James Seaborough m 26 mulatto born SC.

SEABOROUGH, JAMES, 26, M, Laborer, M, SC, 443, 443, BEAU-.

SEABOROUGH, JOHN, 8, M, (--), M, SC, 442, 442, BEAU-. In HH of Robert Seaborough m 55 mulatto born SC.

SEABOROUGH, MARY, 50, F, (--), M, SC, 442, 442, BEAU-. In HH of Robert Seaborough m 55 mulatto born SC.

SEABOROUGH, MARY, 12, F, (--), M, SC, 442, 442, BEAU-. In HH of Robert Seaborough m 55 mulatto born SC.

SEABOROUGH, OBEDIAH, 4, M, (--), M, SC, 442, 442, BEAU-. In HH of Robert Seaborough m 55 mulatto born SC.

SEABOROUGH, RICHARD, 10, M, (--), M, SC, 442, 442, BEAU-. In HH of Robert Seaborough m 55 mulatto born SC.

SEABOROUGH, ROBERT, 55, M, Laborer, M, SC, 442, 442, BEAU-.

SEABOROUGH, TERRY, 15, M, Laborer, M, SC, 442, 442, BEAU-. In HH of Robert Seaborough m 55 mulatto born SC.

SEABOROUGH, VIRGINIA, 22, F, (--), M, SC, 443, 443, BEAU-. In HH of James Seaborough m 26 mulatto born SC.

SEABOROUGH, WASHINGTON, 7, M, (--), M, SC, 442, 442, BEAU-. In HH of Robert Seaborough m 55 mulatto born SC.

SEARS, AZRAMINTA, 36, F, (--), M, SC, 497, 498, AND*. In HH of Elizabeth Sears f 57 born SC.

SEARS, HIRAM, 7, M, (--), M, SC, 497, 498, AND*. In HH of Elizabeth Sears f 57 white born SC.

SEARS, SUSAN ANN, 5, F, (--), M, SC, 497, 498, AND*. In HH of Elizabeth Sears f 57 born SC.

SEBECK, ELIZA, 77, F, (--), M, Germany{sic}, 347, 330, CHAS-. In HH of Sarah Wilson f 54 mulatto born Germany {sic}.

SEBECK, MARTHA, 2, F, (--), M, Germany{sic}, 347, 330, CHAS-. In HH of Sarah Wilson f 54 mulatto born Germany {sic}.

SEGAN, HARRIET, 60, F, (--), B, SC, 668, 626, CHAS+.

SEVENER, EDWARD, 2, M, (--), M, Germany {sic}, 530, 545, RICH. In HH of Mary Sevener f 80 born Germany.

SEVENER, ELIZABETH, 28, F, (--), M, Germany {sic}, 530, 545, RICH. In HH of Mary Sevener f 80 born Germany.

SEVENER, JOSEPH, 26, M, Carpenter, M, Germany {sic}, 530, 545, RICH. In HH of Mary Sevener f 80 born Germany.

SEVENER, LUCY, 21, F, (--), M, Germany {sic}, 530, 545, RICH. In HH of Mary Sevener f 80 born Germany.

SEVENER, MARIA, 5, F, (--), M, Germany {sic}, 530, 545, RICH. In HH of Mary Sevener f 80 born Germany.

SEVENER, MARY, 80, F, (--), M, Germany {sic}, 530, 545, RICH.

SEYMORE, ELLEN, 15, F, (--), M, SC, 645, 637, CHAS%. In HH of James Walling m 31 born SC.

SEYMOUR, RENETTA, 27, F, (--), M, SC, 136, 136, CHAS%. In HH of Lucy Williams f 40 mulatto born SC.

SHALET, FRANCIS, 22, M, Mechanic, M, SC, 907, 907, KERS. In HH of A. Pinson m 20 black born SC.

SHARCO, MARTHA, 60, F, (--), M, SC, 462, 462, BEAU-.

SHARES, WM., 18, M, (--), M, SC, 194, 194, KERS. In HH of Wiley Albert m 39 born SC.

SHARP, JIM, 13, M, (--), M, SC, 2384, 2384, ABB. In HH of William W. Andersen m 36 born SC.

SHARPER, HEZEKIAH, 3, M, (--), M, SC, 665, 665, PICK+. In HH of Jack Arter m 37 mulatto born SC.

SHAVER, MATTHEW, 25, M, Wagoner, B, SC, 2092, 2099, EDGE. In HH of James Chapman m 40 mulatto born SC.

SHAW, BETSY, 20, F, (--), M, SC, 354, 354, CHFD. In HH of Wiley Shaw m 40 Mulatto born SC.

SHAW, BETSY E., 5, F, (--), M, SC, 354, 354, CHFD. In HH of Wiley Shaw m 40 Mulatto born SC.

SHAW, CASHEL, 21, F, (--), M, SC, 354, 354, CHFD. In HH of Wiley Shaw m 40 Mulatto born SC.

SHAW, EMILY, 80, F, Servant, M, St. Domingo, 11, 13, CHAS.

SHAW, JABY, 16, M, Hireling, M, SC, 361, 361, CHFD. In HH of Yavner T.W.

Taylor m 38 born VA.

SHAW, JOBY, 12, M, (--), B, SC, 354, 354, CHFD. In HH of Wiley Shaw m 40 Mulatto born SC.

SHAW, LEONARD, 31, M, (--), M, SC, 202, 203, MAR,. In HH of Silas Brooks m 34 black born NC. Leonard Shaw born Marion, SC.

SHAW, LESENNY, 16, F, (--), B, SC, 354, 354, CHFD. In HH of Wiley Shaw m 40 Mulatto born SC.

SHAW, MARY, 17, F, (--), M, SC, 354, 354, CHFD. In HH of Wiley Shaw m 40 Mulatto born SC.

SHAW, PASEHAS, 9, M, (--), B, SC, 354, 354, CHFD. In HH of Wiley Shaw m 40 Mulatto born SC.

SHAW, PERAJUDY, 14, F, (--), B, SC, 354, 354, CHFD. In HH of Wiley Shaw m 40 Mulatto born SC.

SHAW, PETER, 95, M, Blacksmith, B, SC, 511, 511, CHFD.

SHAW, SYLVIA, 40, F, Servant, M, St. Domingo, 11, 13, CHAS. In HH of Emily Shaw f 80 mulatto born St. Domingo.

SHAW, WILEY, 40, M, Hireling, M, SC, 354, 354, CHFD.

SHEFFTAL, BENJAMIN, 4, M, (--), M, SC, 440, 440, BEAU-. IN HH of Frank Shefftal m 40 mulatto born SC.

SHEFFTAL, DELILA, 35, F, (--), M, SC, 440, 440, BEAU-. IN HH of Frank Shefftal m 40 mulatto born SC.

SHEFFTAL, FRANCIS, 6, M, (--), M, SC, 440, 440, BEAU-. IN HH of Frank Shefftal m 40 mulatto born SC.

SHEFFTAL, FRANK, 40, M, Mechanic, M, SC, 440, 440, BEAU-.

SHEFFTAL, HETTY, 10, F, (--), M, SC, 440, 440, BEAU-. IN HH of Frank Shefftal m 40 mulatto born SC.

SHEFFTAL, JOHN, 8, M, (--), M, SC, 440, 440, BEAU-. IN HH of Frank Shefftal m 40 mulatto born SC.

SHEFFTAL, REBECCA, 1, F, (--), M, SC, 440, 440, BEAU-. IN HH of Frank Shefftal m 40 mulatto born SC.

SHEFFTAL, WILLIAM, 12, M, (--),

M, SC, 440, 440, BEAU-. IN HH of Frank Shefftal m 40 mulatto born SC.

SHEPHERD, ABIGAL, 45, F, (--), M, SC, 711, 711, COLL. In HH of John Shepherd m 50 mulatto born SC.

SHEPHERD, CHRISTOPHER, 14, M, (--), M, SC, 711, 711, COLL. In HH of John Shepherd m 50 mulatto born SC.

SHEPHERD, FLORA, 12, F, (--), M, SC, 711, 711, COLL. In HH of John Shepherd m 50 mulatto born SC.

SHEPHERD, HARRIET, 8, F, (--), M, SC, 711, 711, COLL. In HH of John Shepherd m 50 mulatto born SC.

SHEPHERD, JOHN, 50, M, Carpenter, M, SC, 711, 711, COLL.

SHEPHERD, NANCY, 10, F, (--), M, SC, 711, 711, COLL. In HH of John Shepherd m 50 mulatto born SC.

SHEPHERD, SOPHIA, 18, F, (--), M, SC, 711, 711, COLL. In HH of John Shepherd m 50 mulatto born SC.

SHIVERS, ROBERT, 30, M, Farmer, M, SC, 1122, 1122, LEX.

SHOEMAKER, FRANCIS, 52, F, (--), M, SC, 569, 569, PICK+. In HH of Gabrel Shoemaker m 71 black born SC.

SHOEMAKER, GABREL, 71, M, Cooper, B, SC, 569, 569, PICK+.

SHOEMAKER, KEZIAH, 15, F, (--), M, SC, 794, 794, DARL. In HH of Jeremiah Pinn m 37 mulatto born SC.

SHOEMAKER, MARY J., 12, F, (--), B, SC, 569, 569, PICK+. In HH of Gabrel Shoemaker m 71 black born SC.

SHOEMAKER, WILKERSON, 34, M, None, M, SC, 690, 709, RICH.

SHROUDY, AMANDA, 10, F, (--), M, SC, 331, 305, CHAS. In HH of J. Hamlin m 30 born SC.

SIMMONS, MARY, 70, F, (--), B, SC, 286, 265, CHAS+. In HH of Hannah Frances f 50 black born SC.

SIMMONS, MOLLY, 2, F, (--), M, SC, 310, 310, BEAU+. In HH of Rebecca Simmons f 35 mulatto born SC.

SIMMONS, REBECCA, 35, F, (--), M, SC, 310, 310, BEAU+.

SIMMONS, SARAH, 10, F, (--), M, SC, 310, 310, BEAU+. In HH of Rebecca Simmons f 35 mulatto born SC.

SIMONS, ABRAHAM, 20, M, Carpenter, B, SC,32,32, CHAS%. In HH of Edward McGuffy m 40 black born SC.

SIMONS, AFFEY, 50, F, (--), M, NY, 199, 187, CHAS-.

SIMONS, CLARINDA, 25, F, (--), B, SC, 675, 633, CHAS+.

SIMONS, CORNELIA, 7, F, (--), M, SC, 1081, 1103, CHAS%. In HH of Kitty Simons f 50 mulatto born SC.

SIMONS, DIANAH, 70, F, (--), B, SC, 1199, 1178, CHAS%. In HH of F.C. Bluin m 43 born SC.

SIMONS, ELIZA, 38, F, (--), M, SC,57,57, CHAS%.

SIMONS, ELIZABETH, 8, F, (--), M, NY, 199, 187, CHAS-. In HH of Affey Simons f 50 mulatto born NY.

SIMONS, ENNA, 14, F, (--), M, SC, 1081, 1103, CHAS%. In HH of Kitty Simons f 50 mulatto born SC.

SIMONS, FRANCIS A., 52, F, (--), M, SC, 55, 55, CHAS*. In HH of Mary Simons f 22 mulatto born SC.

SIMONS, G., 8, M, (--), M, SC, 597, 597, LANC*. In HH of E. Simons f 60 born SC.

SIMONS, ISABELLA, 50, F, (--), M, SC, 840, 821, CHAS%.

SIMONS, JAMES, 30, M, Tailor, M, SC, 64, 64, CHAS%. In HH of R. Burdell m 41 mulatto born SC.

SIMONS, JOHN, 37, M, Laborer, M, SC, 238, 238, CHAS%.

SIMONS, JOHN, 19, M, Boot maker, M, Cuba, 204, 187, CHAS*. In HH of Caroline Clancey f 40 mulatto born Cuba.

SIMONS, JOHN, 11, M, (--), M, SC, 1081, 1103, CHAS%. In HH of Kitty Simons f 50 mulatto born SC.

SIMONS, JOHN J., 10, M, (--), M, SC, 707, 687, CHAS-. In HH of Martha Simons f 27 mulatto born SC.

SIMONS, JOSHUA, 30, M, Fisherman,

B, SC, 114, 106, CHAS+. In HH of Alfred P. Reignie m 40 born GA.

SIMONS, JULIUS, 34, M, Carpenter, M, SC, 57, 57, CHAS%. In HH of Eliza Simons f 38 mulatto born SC.

SIMONS, KITTY, 50, F, (--), M, SC, 1081, 1103, CHAS%.

SIMONS, LOUISA, 6, F, (--), M, SC, 707, 687, CHAS-. In HH of Martha Simons f 27 mulatto born SC.

SIMONS, LUCY, 9, F, (--), B, SC, 32, 32, CHAS%. In HH of Edward McGuffy m 40 black born SC.

SIMONS, MARTHA, 27, F, (--), M, SC, 707, 687, CHAS-.

SIMONS, MARY, 22, F, (--), M, NY, 475, 433, CHAS+. In HH of Sarah Drayton m 45 black born NY.

SIMONS, MARY, 22, F, (--), M, SC, 55, 55, CHAS*.

SIMONS, MARY ANN, 33, F, (--), M, SC, 466, 423, CHAS. In HH of F.W. Bahulge m 31 born SC.

SIMONS, SANDY, 42, M, Coachman, M, SC, 1081, 1103, CHAS%. In HH of Kitty Simons f 50 mulatto born SC.

SIMONS, SARAH ANN, 2, F, (--), M, SC, 55, 55, CHAS*. In HH of Mary Simons f 22 mulatto born SC.

SIMPSON, CAROLINE, 39, F, (--), M, SC, 33, 30, CHAS-.

SIMPSON, CONSTANCE, 9, F, (--), M, SC, 33, 30, CHAS-. In HH of Caroline Simpson f 39 mulatto born SC.

SIMPSON, JANAQRIM, 40, M, Laborer, M, SC, 33, 30, CHAS-. In HH of Caroline Simpson f 39 mulatto born SC.

SIMPSON, LOUISA, 16, F, (--), M, SC, 33, 30, CHAS-. In HH of Caroline Simpson f 39 mulatto born SC.

SIMPSON, MARY ANN, 12, F, (--), B, SC, 33, 30, CHAS-. In HH of Caroline Simpson f 39 mulatto born SC.

SIMPSON, PRESS, 30, M, Farmer, B, SC, 1535, 1535, CHES. In HH of John Simpson m 47 born SC.

SIMPSON, THEODORE, 22, M, Carpenter, B, SC, 33, 30, CHAS-. In HH

of Caroline Simpson f 39 mulatto born SC.

SIMS, ISRAEAL, 9, M, (--), M, SC, 295, 295, EDGE. In HH of John Bledsoe m 53 born SC.

SIMS, LUCINDA, 38, F, (--), M, SC, 295, 295, EDGE. In HH of John Bledsoe m 53 born SC.

SIMS, SUMPTER, 10, M, (--), B, SC, 123, 123, EDGE*. In HH of Famine {?} Smith f 52 black born SC.

SINCLAIR, ANDREW, 40, M, Stevedore, B, SC, 942, 922, CHAS-. In HH of Josephine Sasportas f 30 black born SC.

SIZEMORE, ALLEN, 22, M, Laborer, M, SC,75,75, AND*.

SIZEMORE, CYNTHIA, 30, F, (--), M, SC, 353, 353, PICK+. In HH of Polly Sizemore f 28 black born SC.

SIZEMORE, ELIAS, 4, M, (--), B, SC, 353, 353, PICK+. In HH of Polly Sizemore f 28 black born SC.

SIZEMORE, JABERRY, 3, M, (--), M, SC, 662, 662, PICK+. In HH of Sarah Sizemore f 52 black born SC.

SIZEMORE, JASPER J., 0, M, (--), M, SC,75,75, AND*. In HH of Jasper J. Sizemore m 22 mulatto born SC.

SIZEMORE, JEFFERSON, 5, M, (--), M, SC, 579, 580, AND*. In HH of George Sherman m 50 born Massachusetts.

SIZEMORE, JIM, 2, M, (--), B, SC, 353, 353, PICK+. In HH of Polly Sizemore f 28 black born SC.

SIZEMORE, MARTHA, 20, F, (--), B, SC, 662, 662, PICK+. In HH of Sarah Sizemore f 52 black born SC.

SIZEMORE, MARTHA, 7, F, (--), B, SC, 353, 353, PICK+. In HH of Polly Sizemore f 28 black born SC.

SIZEMORE, POLLY, 28, F, (--), B, SC, 353, 353, PICK+.

SIZEMORE, SARAH, 52, F, (--), B, SC, 662, 662, PICK+.

SIZEMORE, SARAH, 1, F, (--), B, SC, 353, 353, PICK+. In HH of Polly Sizemore f 28 black born SC.

SLANN, ISAAC, 49, M, (--), B, SC, 689, 681, CHAS%. In HH of Rebecca Slann f 50 black born SC.

SLANN, REBECCA, 50, F, (--), B, SC, 689, 681, CHAS%.

SMALL, ALONZO, 8, M, (--), M, SC, 568, 560, CHAS%. In HH of Catharine Small f 50 mulatto born SC.

SMALL, AMANDA, 8, F, (--), M, SC, 865, 842, CHAS%. In HH of Mary Small f 45 mulatto born SC.

SMALL, AMELIA, 16, F, (--), M, SC, 568, 560, CHAS%. In HH of Catharine Small f 50 mulatto born SC.

SMALL, ANDREW, 22, M, Carpenter, B, SC, 651, 651, COLL. In HH of Isaac Small m 40 black born SC.

SMALL, ANDREW, 3, M, (--), B, SC, 634, 626, CHAS%. In HH of Persey Bell f 56 mulatto born SC.

SMALL, ANNE, 30, M, (--), M, SC, 651, 651, COLL. In HH of Isaac Small m 40 black born SC.

SMALL, ANNE, 4, F, (--), M, SC, 651, 651, COLL. In HH of Isaac Small m 40 black born SC.

SMALL, BENJAMIN, 6, M, (--), B, SC, 634, 626, CHAS%. In HH of Persey Bell f 56 mulatto born SC.

SMALL, BETSY, 10, F, (--), M, SC, 357, 357, CHAS%. In HH of Mary Small f 30 mulatto born SC.

SMALL, CATHARINE, 50, M, (--), M, SC, 568, 560, CHAS%.

SMALL, CATHERINE, 44, F, (--), B, SC, 159, 159, CHAS%. In HH of Thomas Small m 47 black born SC.

SMALL, CHARLES, 6, M, (--), M, SC, 651, 651, COLL. In HH of Isaac Small m 40 black born SC.

SMALL, DANIEL, 18, M, Laborer, B, SC, 651, 651, COLL. In HH of Isaac Small m 40 black born SC.

SMALL, ELIZABETH, 12, F, (--), M, SC, 568, 560, CHAS%. In HH of Catharine Small f 50 mulatto born SC.

SMALL, ELLEN, 6, F, (--), M, SC, 357, 357, CHAS%. In HH of Mary Small f 30 mulatto born SC.

SMALL, EMMELINE, 16, F, (--), M, SC, 865, 842, CHAS%. In HH of Mary Small f 45 mulatto born SC.

SMALL, FRANK, 10, M, (--), B, SC, 634, 626, CHAS%. In HH of Persey Bell f 56 mulatto born SC.

SMALL, HARRIET, 12, F, (--), M, SC, 865, 842, CHAS%. In HH of Mary Small f 45 mulatto born SC.

SMALL, ISAAC, 40, M, Bricklayer, B, SC, 651, 651, COLL.

SMALL, ISABELLA, 10, F, (--), M, SC, 865, 842, CHAS%. In HH of Mary Small f 45 mulatto born SC.

SMALL, ISABELLA, 5, F, (--), B, SC, 303, 303, CHAS%. In HH of Lindy Small f 31 black born SC.

SMALL, JAMES, 12, M, (--), B, SC, 159, 159, CHAS%. In HH of Thomas Small m 47 black born SC.

SMALL, JANE, 2, F, (--), M, SC, 651, 651, COLL. In HH of Isaac Small m 40 black born SC.

SMALL, LINDY, 31, F, (--), B, SC, 303, 303, CHAS%.

SMALL, MARY, 45, F, (--), M, SC, 865, 842, CHAS%.

SMALL, MARY, 30, F, (--), M, SC, 357, 357, CHAS%.

SMALL, MARY, 18, F, (--), M, SC, 568, 560, CHAS%. In HH of Catharine Small f 50 mulatto born SC.

SMALL, MARY, 15, F, (--), B, SC, 159, 159, CHAS%. In HH of Thomas Small m 47 black born SC.

SMALL, RICHARD, 6, M, (--), M, SC, 865, 842, CHAS%. In HH of Mary Small f 45 mulatto born SC.

SMALL, ROSENA, 14, F, (--), M, SC, 568, 560, CHAS%. In HH of Catharine Small f 50 mulatto born SC.

SMALL, SAMUEL, 20, M, (--), B, SC, 605, 597, CHAS%.

SMALL, SARAH ANN, 10, F, (--), M, SC, 568, 560, CHAS%. In HH of Catharine Small f 50 mulatto born SC.

SMALL, THOMAS, 47, M, Carpenter, B, SC, 159, 159, CHAS%.

SMILING, AUGUSTUS, 2, M, (--), M, SC, 848, 848, SUMT. In HH of Jas. Smiling m 34 mulatto born SC.

SMILING, HENRY, 7, M, (--), M, SC, 848, 848, SUMT. In HH of Jas. Smiling m 34 mulatto born SC.

SMILING, JAS., 34, M, Planter, M, SC, 848, 848, SUMT.

SMILING, MARY, 9, F, (--), M, SC, 848, 848, SUMT. In HH of Jas. Smiling m 34 mulatto born SC.

SMILING, MATILDA, 26, F, (--), M, SC, 848, 848, SUMT. In HH of Jas. Smiling m 34 mulatto born SC.

SMILING, MORGAN, 4, F, (--), M, SC, 848, 848, SUMT. In HH of Jas. Smiling m 34 mulatto born SC.

SMITH, ANDERSON, 1, M, (--), M, SC, 369, 369, BARN. In HH of Madison Smith m 40 mulatto born SC.

SMITH, ANN, 31, F, (--), M, SC, 283, 283, CHAS%. In HH of Emeline Holmes f 19 black born SC.

SMITH, ANN, 1, F, (--), M, SC, 606, 587, CHAS-. In HH of Emma Smith f 29 mulatto born SC.

SMITH, BARBARA, 27, F, (--), M, SC, 369, 369, BARN. In HH of Madison Smith m 40 mulatto born SC.

SMITH, BARSHEBA, 45, F, (--), B, SC, 244, 244, CHAS%.

SMITH, BING, 10, M, (--), M, SC, 369, 369, BARN. In HH of Madison Smith m 40 mulatto born SC.

SMITH, CAROLINE, 12, F, (--), M, SC, 291, 275, CHAS-. In HH of Jane Smith f 49 mulatto born SC.

SMITH, CAROLINE, 7, F, (--), B, NC, 367, 367, YORK. In HH of Melissa Smith f 19 black born York Dist., SC.

SMITH, CASSEY, 80, F, (--), B, SC, 115, 117, AND.

SMITH, CATHERINE, 22, F, (--), M, SC, 604, 585, CHAS-.

SMITH, CECELIA, 4, F, (--), M, SC, 606, 587, CHAS-. In HH of Emma Smith f 29 mulatto born SC.

SMITH, CYNTHIA, 45, F, (--), B, NC, 502, 502, YORK.

SMITH, DAVID, 60, M, Trimmer, M, SC, 865, 845, CHAS-. In HH of William Deas m 35 mulatto born SC.

SMITH, EDWARD, 8, M, (--), M, SC, 918, 898, CHAS-. n HH of Juliana Smith f 26 mulatto born SC.

SMITH, EDWARD P., 21, M, (--), M, SC, 291, 275, CHAS-. In HH of Jane Smith f 49 mulatto born SC.

SMITH, ELENOR, 39, F, (--), M, SC, 140, 130, CHAS-. In HH of R.A. Long m 35 born SC.

SMITH, ELIZABETH, 8, F, (--), B, SC, 748, 728, CHAS-. In HH of Mary Smith f 25 black born SC.

SMITH, EMILY, 6, F, (--), M, SC, 841, 821, CHAS%. In HH of Helen Smith f 21 mulatto born SC.

SMITH, EMILY, 6, F, (--), M, SC, 606, 587, CHAS-. In HH of Emma Smith f 29 mulatto born SC.

SMITH, EMMA, 29, F, (--), M, SC, 606, 587, CHAS-.

SMITH, EURANE, 5, F, (--), M, SC, 365, 348, CHAS-. In HH of Mary McBride f 46 mulatto born SC.

SMITH, FAMINE {?}, 52, F, (--), B, SC, 123, 123, EDGE*.

SMITH, FRANCIS, 20, M, Tailor, M, SC, 212, 198, CHAS-.

SMITH, GEORGE, 2, M, (--), M, SC, 606, 587, CHAS-. In HH of Emma Smith f 29 mulatto born SC.

SMITH, HELEN, 21, F, (--), M, SC, 841, 821, CHAS%.

SMITH, HENRY B., 4, M, (--), B, NC, 367, 367, YORK. In HH of Melissa Smith f 19 black born York Dist., SC.

SMITH, HESTER A., 6, F, (--), M, SC, 918, 898, CHAS-. n HH of Juliana Smith f 26 mulatto born SC.

SMITH, JANE, 49, F, (--), M, SC, 291, 275, CHAS-.

SMITH, JANE, 15, F, (--), M, SC, 291, 275, CHAS-. In HH of Jane Smith f 49 mulatto born SC.

SMITH, JANE, 14, F, (--), M, SC, 604, 585, CHAS-. In HH of Catherine Smith f 22 mulatto born SC.

SMITH, JANE, 6, F, (--), B, SC, 748, 728, CHAS-. In HH of Mary Smith f 25 black born SC.

SMITH, JEREMIAH, 40, M, (--), M, SC, 317, 292, CHAS. In HH of Diana Drayton f 40 black born SC.

SMITH, JOHN H., 2, M, (--), B, NC, 367, 367, YORK. In HH of Melissa Smith f 19 black born York Dist., SC.

SMITH, JOSEPH, 2, M, (--), M, SC, 104, 104, GEOR. In HH of Nannit Smith f 28 mulatto born SC.

SMITH, JULIA, 49, F, (--), M, SC, 104, 104, CHAS^. In HH of Catherine Johnson f 49 black born SC.

SMITH, JULIANA, 26, F, (--), M, SC, 918, 898, CHAS-.

SMITH, LOUISA, 78, F, (--), M, SC, 344, 327, CHAS-.

SMITH, MADISON, 40, M, Planter, M, SC, 369, 369, BARN.

SMITH, MARGARET, 30, F, (--), M, SC, 64, 63, CHAS*.

SMITH, MARGARET, 4, F, (--), M, SC, 918, 898, CHAS-. n HH of Juliana Smith f 26 mulatto born SC.

SMITH, MARTHA, 2, F, (--), B, SC, 748, 728, CHAS-. In HH of Mary Smith f 25 black born SC.

SMITH, MARY, 25, F, (--), B, SC, 748, 728, CHAS-.

SMITH, MARY, 19, F, (--), M, SC, 49, 45, CHAS$. In HH of Robert Smith m 16 mulatto born SC.

SMITH, MARY ANN, 52, F, (--), M, SC, 865, 845, CHAS-. In HH of William Deas m 35 mulatto born SC.

SMITH, MARY B., 17, F, (--), M, SC, 291, 275, CHAS-. In HH of Jane Smith f 49 mulatto born SC.

SMITH, MILTON, 4, M, Farmer, B, NC, 495, 495, EDGE*.

SMITH, MOLSEY, 14, M, (--), B, NC, 367, 367, YORK. In HH of Melissa Smith f 19 black born York Dist., SC.

SMITH, NANCY, 50, F, (--), M, SC, 53, 53, COLL+. In HH of Washington Benton m 28 born SC.

SMITH, NANNIT, 28, F, (--), M, SC, 104, 104, GEOR.

SMITH, POLLY, 49, F, (--), B, SC, 2104, 2108, EDGE.

SMITH, REBECCA, 40, F, (--), M, SC, 65, 59, CHAS-. In HH of Caroline Hillagas f 30 born SC.

SMITH, REBECCA, 11, F, (--), M, SC, 369, 369, BARN. In HH of Madison Smith m 40 mulatto born SC.

SMITH, ROBERT, 16, M, (--), M, SC, 49, 45, CHAS$.

SMITH, ROSE, 26, F, (--), B, SC, 123, 123, EDGE*. In HH of Famine{?} Smith f 52 black born SC.

SMITH, SARAH, 0, F, (--), B, NC, 367, 367, YORK. In HH of Melissa Smith f 19 black born York Dist., SC. Sarah Smith age 9/12 yr.

SMITH, SUSAN, 10, F, (--), B, SC, 748, 728, CHAS-. In HH of Mary Smith f 25 black born SC.

SMITH, THEODORE, 12, M, (--), M, SC, 606, 587, CHAS-. In HH of Emma Smith f 29 mulatto born SC.

SMITH, THOS., 20, M, (--), M, SC, 317, 292, CHAS. In HH of Diana Drayton f 40 black born SC.

SMITH, THOS., 19, M, (--), B, SC, 123, 123, EDGE*. In HH of Famine {?} Smith f 52 black born SC.

SMITH, VINUS, 45, F, (--), B, SC, 367, 367, YORK. In HH of Melissa Smith f 19 black born York Dist., SC.

SMITH, WALLACE, 16, M, (--), B, SC, 502, 502, YORK. In HH of Cynthia Smith f 45 black born NC.

SMITH, WALTER, 22, M, (--), M, NC, 675, 675, YORK. In HH of Reuben Swann m 38 born TN.

SMITH, WILLIAM, 45, M, (--), B, SC, 135, 135, CHAS^. In HH of Catherine Conyers f 24 black born SC.

SMITH, WILLIAM, 27, M, Tailor, M, SC, 919, 899, CHAS-. In HH of Phillis Montgomery f 30 mulatto born SC.

SMITH, WILLIAM, 4, M, (--), M, SC, 365, 348, CHAS-. In HH of Mary McBride f 46 mulatto born SC.

SMITH, WM. C., 15, M, (--), M, SC, 265, 250, CHAS-. In HH of A.L. Horry m 19 mulatto born SC.

SNEAD, CHARLOTTE, 44, F, (--), M, SC, 38, 39, RICH.

SNEAD, ELIZA, 50, F, (--), M, SC, 317, 323, RICH+. In HH of Isaac Snead m 38 born SC.

SNEAD, JAMES, 7, M, (--), M, SC, 38, 39, RICH. In HH of Charlotte Snead f 44 mulatto born SC.

SNEAD, NANCY, 3, F, (--), M, SC, 38, 39, RICH. In HH of Charlotte Snead f 44 mulatto born SC.

SNIDER, 55, M, (--), B, SC, 45, 45, CHAS#.

SNOW, ALEXANDER, 27, M, Carpenter, M, SC, 531, 523, CHAS%. In HH of Susan Baxter f 39 mulatto born SC.

SNOW, ANN, 90, F, (--), M, SC, 531, 523, CHAS%. In HH of Susan Baxter f 39 mulatto born SC.

SNOW, ANNE, 12, F, (--), B, SC, 327, 327, CHAS%. In HH of Mary Ann Snow f 40 black born SC.

SNOW, ELIZA, 65, F, (--), B, Africa, 779, 737, CHAS+.

SNOW, ELIZABETH, 4, F, (--), B, SC, 327, 327, CHAS%. In HH of Mary Ann Snow f 40 black born SC.

SNOW, EMMA, 18, F, (--), B, SC, 327, 327, CHAS%. In HH of Mary Ann Snow f 40 black born SC.

SNOW, JOHN, 37, M, Butcher, M, SC, 616, 597, CHAS-.

SNOW, JOHN, 1, M, (--), B, SC, 327, 327, CHAS%. In HH of Mary Ann Snow f 40 black born SC.

SNOW, MARTHA, 6, F, (--), B, SC, 327, 327, CHAS%. In HH of Mary Ann Snow f 40 black born SC.

SNOW, MARY ANN, 40, F, (--), B, SC, 327, 327, CHAS%.

SNOW, MARY ANN, 25, F, (--), M, SC, 298, 298, CHAS%. In HH of Ellen Hicks f 50 mulatto born SC.

SOLLOMAN, JOHN, 16, M, Laborer, B, SC, 681, 682, AND*. In HH of

Samuel Bell m 40 born SC.

SPARKS, JANE, 16, F, (--), M, SC, 54, 54, CHAS%. In HH of Robert Sparks m 39 mulatto born SC.

SPARKS, MARY, 39, F, (--), M, SC, 54, 54, CHAS%. In HH of Robert Sparks m 39 mulatto born SC.

SPARKS, ROBERT, 39, M, Carpenter, M, SC, 54, 54, CHAS%.

SPARKS, THOMAS, 13, M, (--), M, SC, 54, 54, CHAS%. In HH of Robert Sparks m 39 mulatto born SC.

SPEARING, SARAH, 26, F, (--), M, SC, 377, 375, CHAS%. In HH of Sarah Bing f 35 black born SC.

SPEARMAN, PETER, 17, M, Farmer, B, SC, 287, 287, NEWB. In HH of J.W. Spearman m 31 born SC.

SPENCE, DINAH, 50, F, (--), M, SC, 46, 45, CHAS&. In HH of Henry Spence m 55 born SC.

SPENCER, ANN, 15, F, (--), B, SC, 607, 588, CHAS-. In HH of Diana Spencer f 48 black born SC.

SPENCER, ANNE, 2, F, (--), M, SC, 385, 368, CHAS-. In HH of Margaret Spencer f 35 mulatto born SC.

SPENCER, CHARLOTTE, 50, F, (--), M, SC, 196, 196, CHAS%. In HH of Josephine Spencer f 30 mulatto born SC.

SPENCER, CRETIA, 17, F, (--), B, SC, 607, 588, CHAS-. In HH of Diana Spencer f 48 black born SC.

SPENCER, DIANA, 48, F, (--), B, SC, 607, 588, CHAS-.

SPENCER, DIANA, 12, F, (--), B, SC, 607, 588, CHAS-. In HH of Diana Spencer f 48 black born SC.

SPENCER, ELIZABETH, 7, F, (--), B, SC, 607, 588, CHAS-. In HH of Diana Spencer f 48 black born SC.

SPENCER, ELLEN, 17, F, (--), M, SC, 904, 884, CHAS-. In HH of Ellen Jones f 51 mulatto born SC.

SPENCER, ELLEN, 15, F, (--), M, SC, 385, 368, CHAS-. In HH of Margaret Spencer f 35 mulatto born SC.

SPENCER, FREDERICK, 4, M, (--), M, SC, 385, 368, CHAS-. In HH of

Margaret Spencer f 35 mulatto born SC.

SPENCER, GEORGE, 5, M, (--), B, SC, 607, 588, CHAS-. In HH of Diana Spencer f 48 black born SC.

SPENCER, HAGAR, 40, F, (--), B, SC, 196, 196, CHAS%. In HH of Josephine Spencer f 30 mulatto born SC.

SPENCER, JOSEPHINE, 30, F, (--), M, SC, 196, 196, CHAS%.

SPENCER, MARGARET, 35, F, (--), M, SC, 385, 368, CHAS-.

SPENCER, MARY ANN, 2, F, (--), B, SC, 607, 588, CHAS-. In HH of Diana Spencer f 48 black born SC.

SPENCER, ROSE, 80, F, (--), M, SC, 1125, 1103, CHAS%.

SPENCER, SUSAN, 19, F, (--), B, SC, 607, 588, CHAS-. In HH of Diana Spencer f 48 black born SC.

SPENCER, THOMAS, 20, M, Carpenter, B, SC, 228, 203, CHAS*. In HH of Abraham Jones m 30 mulatto born SC.

SPRAGGINS, GEORGE, 45, M, Carpenter, B, SC, 131, 131, NEWB.

SPRING, MARY, 35, F, (--), M, SC, 161, 151, CHAS-. In HH of Frances Hatcher f 28 mulatto born SC.

SQUASH, SUSAN, 30, F, (--), M, SC, 362, 362, CHAS%.

SQUIRE, JOHN, 62, M, (--), M, Africa, 779, 737, CHAS+. In HH of Eliza Snow f 65 black born Africa.

ST.MARKS, BENIT, 3, F, (--), M, SC, 633, 625, CHAS%. In HH of Francis St.Marks m 30 mulatto born SC.

ST.MARKS, CAROLINE, 5, F, (--), M, SC, 633, 625, CHAS%. In HH of Francis St.Marks m 30 mulatto born SC.

ST.MARKS, CORNELIA, 24, F, (--), M, SC, 633, 625, CHAS%. In HH of Francis St.Marks m 30 mulatto born SC.

ST.MARKS, ELLEN, 25, F, (--), M, SC, 633, 625, CHAS%. In HH of Francis St.Marks m 30 mulatto born SC.

ST.MARKS, FRANCIS, 30, M, Barber, M, SC, 633, 625, CHAS%.

ST.MARKS, GABRILLA, 6, F, (--), M,

SC, 633, 625, CHAS%. In HH of Francis St.Marks m 30 mulatto born SC.

ST.MARKS, LAFON, 9, M, (--), M, SC, 633, 625, CHAS%. In HH of Francis St.Marks m 30 mulatto born SC.

ST.MARKS, MARTHA, 35, F, (--), M, SC, 633, 625, CHAS%. In HH of Francis St.Marks m 30 mulatto born SC.

ST.MARKS, WILLIAM, 37, M, (--), M, SC, 633, 625, CHAS%. In HH of Francis St.Marks m 30 mulatto born SC.

STEDMAN, AUGUSTUS, 23, M, Tailor, M, SC, 28, 27, CHAS&.

STEDMAN, MARY, 20, F, (--), M, SC, 28, 27, CHAS&. In HH of Augustus Stedman m 23 mulatto born SC.

STEEDMAN, ALICE, 13, F, (--), M, SC, 829, 787, CHAS+. In HH of Sarah Steedman f 37 mulatto born SC.

STEEDMAN, CHARLES, 11, M, (--), M, SC, 829, 787, CHAS+. In HH of Sarah Steedman f 37 mulatto born SC.

STEEDMAN, HAGAR, 38, F, (--), B, SC, 377, 339, CHAS+. In HH of Thomas Steedman m 40 black born SC.

STEEDMAN, MARY, 23, F, (--), M, SC, 148, 138, CHAS-.

STEEDMAN, SARAH, 37, F, (--), M, SC, 829, 787, CHAS+.

STEEDMAN, THOMAS, 40, M, Cooper, B, SC, 377, 339, CHAS+.

STEELE, ISABELLA, 36, F, (--), M, SC, 344, 344, CHAS%. In HH of Teres Bullard f 70 mulatto born SC.

STEELE, JULIA, 55, F, (--), M, SC, 338, 338, CHAS%.

STEELE, JULIA, 50, F, (--), B, SC, 170, 170, CHAS%. In HH of Frances Bland f 50 mulatto born SC.

STEELE, JULIA, 17, F, (--), M, SC, 338, 338, CHAS%. In HH of Julia Steele f 55 mulatto born SC.

STEELE, LELOY ANN, 7, F, (--), M, SC, 344, 344, CHAS%. In HH of Teres Bullard f 70 mulatto born SC.

STENET, MARGARET, 2, F, (--), M, SC, 182, 182, CHAS%. In HH of Nancy Stenet f 50 mulatto born SC.

STENET, NANCY, 50, F, (--), M, SC, 182, 182, CHAS%.

STENET, SARAH, 5, F, (--), M, SC, 182, 182, CHAS%. In HH of Nancy Stenet f 50 mulatto born SC.

STENT, ANNA, 35, F, Seamstress, M, SC, 12, 14, CHAS.

STENT, MARION L., 18, M, (--), M, SC, 246, 231, CHAS-. In HH of Priscilia North f 55 mulatto born SC.

STENT, PHILIS, 70, F, (--), B, SC, 344, 318, CHAS.

STEPHENS, ELIZABETH, 9, F, (--), M, SC, 145, 145, GEOR. In HH of Jane Stephens f 25 mulatto born SC.

STEPHENS, JANE, 25, F, (--), M, SC, 145, 145, GEOR.

STEPHENSON, BENJAMIN, 4, M, (--), B, SC, 471, 471, BEAU-. In HH of George Stephenson m 43 black born SC.

STEPHENSON, BRYANT, 19, M, Mechanic, B, SC, 472, 472, BEAU-.

STEPHENSON, CHARLES, 10, M, (--), B, SC, 471, 471, BEAU-. In HH of George Stephenson m 43 black born SC.

STEPHENSON, EDWARD, 8, M, (--), B, SC, 471, 471, BEAU-. In HH of George Stephenson m 43 black born SC.

STEPHENSON, ELIZABETH, 12, F, (--), B, SC, 471, 471, BEAU-. In HH of George Stephenson m 43 black born SC.

STEPHENSON, GEORGE, 43, M, Mechanic, B, SC, 471, 471, BEAU-.

STEPHENSON, GEORGE, 14, M, (--), B, SC, 471, 471, BEAU-. In HH of George Stephenson m 43 black born SC.

STEPHENSON, SALLY, 40, F, (--), M, SC, 471, 471, BEAU-. In HH of George Stephenson m 43 black born SC.

STEPHENSON, SARAH, 2, F, (--), B, SC, 471, 471, BEAU-. In HH of George Stephenson m 43 black born SC.

STEPHENSON, SARAH A., 16, F, (--), B, SC, 472, 472, BEAU-. In HH of Bryant Stephenson m 19 black born SC.

STEVENS, AMELIA, 12, F, (--), M, SC, 916, 896, CHAS-. In HH of Sarah Stevens f 30 mulatto born SC.

STEVENS, E., 1, F, (--), M, SC, 589, 589, LANC*. In HH of J. Thornton m 56 born SC.

STEVENS, JOHN, 10, M, (--), M, SC, 916, 896, CHAS-. In HH of Sarah Stevens f 30 mulatto born SC.

STEVENS, M., 50, F, (--), M, SC, 589, 589, LANC*. In HH of J. Thornton m 56 born SC.

STEVENS, M., 13, M, (--), M, SC, 589, 589, LANC*. In HH of J. Thornton m 56 born SC.

STEVENS, M., 10, F, (--), M, SC, 589, 589, LANC*. In HH of J. Thornton m 56 born SC.

STEVENS, MORTON, 6, M, (--), M, SC, 916, 896, CHAS-. In HH of Sarah Stevens f 30 mulatto born SC.

STEVENS, N., 4, M, (--), M, SC, 589, 589, LANC*. In HH of J. Thornton m 56 born SC.

STEVENS, P., 17, M, Laborer, M, SC, 589, 589, LANC*. In HH of J. Thornton m 56 born SC.

STEVENS, SARAH, 30, F, (--), M, SC, 916, 896, CHAS-.

STEVENS, T., 12, M, (--), M, SC, 589, 589, LANC*. In HH of J. Thornton m 56 born SC.

STEVENS, WILLIAM, 58, M, Porter, M, SC, 257, 235, CHAS.

STOCKER, LOUISA, 21, F, (--), M, SC, 36, 36, CHAS%. In HH of Maria Nelson f 21 mulatto born SC.

STOKES, HARRY, 97, M, Blacksmith, B, SC, 407, 407, CHFD.

STONE, THOS., 45, M, None, M, SC, 1599, 1599, BARN.

STORY, HENRY G., 17, M, Hireling, M, SC, 2246, 2246, ABB. In HH of Jabez Story m 51 mulatto born SC.

STORY, JABEZ, 51, M, Blacksmith, M, SC, 2246, 2246, ABB.

STORY, SALLY, 35, F, (--), B, SC, 2246, 2246, ABB. In HH of Jabez Story m 51 mulatto born SC.

STRAITHER, MARIA, 40, F, (--), B, SC, 212, 212, ABB.

STRAWTHER, BOB, 26, M, (--), B, SC, 171, 171, ABB. In HH of John Watson m 30 born SC.

STRAWTHER, DELIA, 38, F, (--), B, SC, 471, 471, CHFD. In HH of Hannah Strawther f 65 black born SC.

STRAWTHER, ELIZABETH, 28, F, (--), B, SC, 229, 229, ABB. In HH of Jonathan Strawther m 35 black born SC.

STRAWTHER, ELIZABETH, 2, F, (--), B, SC, 229, 229, ABB. In HH of Jonathan Strawther m 35 black born SC.

STRAWTHER, FRANCES, 7, F, (--), B, SC, 229, 229, ABB. In HH of Jonathan Strawther m 35 black born SC.

STRAWTHER, FRANKLIN, 3, M, (--), M, SC, 326, 326, CHFD. In HH of Gibson Wilson m 47 black born SC.

STRAWTHER, HANNAH, 65, F, (--), B, SC, 471, 471, CHFD.

STRAWTHER, HOWARD, 30, M, (--), B, SC, 471, 471, CHFD. In HH of Hannah Strawther f 65 black born SC.

STRAWTHER, HOWARD, 24, M, (--), B, SC, 171, 171, ABB. In HH of John Watson m 30 born SC.

STRAWTHER, JAMES, 5, M, (--), B, SC, 229, 229, ABB. In HH of Jonathan Strawther m 35 black born SC.

STRAWTHER, JOANNA, 6, F, (--), B, SC, 229, 229, ABB. In HH of Jonathan Strawther m 35 black born SC.

STRAWTHER, JOHN, 5, M, (--), M, SC, 326, 326, CHFD. In HH of Gibson Wilson m 47 black born SC.

STRAWTHER, JONATHAN, 35, M, Wheelwright, B, SC, 229, 229, ABB.

STRAWTHER, JOSEPHINE, 6, F, (--), B, SC, 229, 229, ABB. In HH of Jonathan Strawther m 35 black born SC.

STRAWTHER, PHEBE, 33, F, (--), M, SC, 326, 326, CHFD. In HH of Gibson Wilson m 47 black born SC.

STRAWTHER, ROBERT, 34, M, (--), B, SC, 471, 471, CHFD. In HH of Hannah Strawther f 65 black born SC.

STRAWTHER, ROBERT, 4, M, (--), B, SC, 229, 229, ABB. In HH of Jonathan Strawther m 35 black born SC.

STREEPER, REBECCA, 62, F, (--), B, SC, 461, 419, CHAS+.

STROBLE, WILLIAM, 5, M, (--), B, SC, 1673, 1673, EDGE. In HH of Lahn{?} Stroble m 75 born SC.

STROKE, GEORGE, 25, M, (--), M, SC, 1124, 1124, GREE.

STROKE, LOUISA, 18, F, (--), M, SC, 1124, 1124, GREE. In HH of George Stroke m 25 mulatto born SC.

STROKE, MALISSA, 1, F, (--), M, SC, 1124, 1124, GREE. In HH of George Stroke m 25 mulatto born SC.

STROMER, H.G., 50, F, (--), M, SC, 147, 137, CHAS-.

STROTHER, MARTHA, 22, F, (--), B, SC, 1003, 1007, AND. In HH of Robert Wilson m 52 black born SC.

STROTHER, THE, 69, F, (--), B, SC, 1004, 1008, AND.

STROUD, EVALINE, 11, F, (--), M, SC, 387, 387, GREE. In HH of S. Tucker m 38 born SC.

STROUD, FERIBY, 4, F, (--), M, SC, 387, 387, GREE. In HH of S. Tucker m 38 born SC.

STROUD, HENRY, 7, M, (--), M, SC, 387, 387, GREE. In HH of S. Tucker m 38 born SC.

STUART, MARY, 28, F, (--), B, SC, 437, 434, CHAS%. In HH of Scifin Stuart m 41 black born SC.

STUART, SCIFIN, 41, M, Drayman, B, SC, 437, 434, CHAS%.

STUART, WILLIAM, 14, M, (--), B, SC, 437, 434, CHAS%. In HH of Scifin Stuart m 41 black born SC.

SUTTON, ROBERT, 7, M, (--), M, SC, 365, 348, CHAS-. In HH of Mary McBride f 46 mulatto born SC.

SWEAT, ADOLPHUS, 1, M, (--), M, SC, 854, 854, SUMT. In HH of Wesley Sweat m 24 mulatto born SC.

SWEAT, JANE, 27, F, (--), M, SC, 854, 854, SUMT. In HH of Wesley Sweat m 24 mulatto born SC.

SWEAT, NOAH, 3, M, Laborer, M, SC, 22, 22, CHAS~.

SWEAT, WESLEY, 26, M, Planter, M, SC, 854, 854, SUMT.

SWEET, DAVID, 16, M, Farmer, M, SC, 730, 731, ORNG+. In HH of J. Sweet m 50 mulatto born SC.

SWEET, GEORGE, 14, M, (--), M, SC, 730, 731, ORNG+. In HH of J. Sweet m 50 mulatto born SC.

SWEET, J., 50, M, Farmer, M, SC, 730, 731, ORNG+.

SWEET, MARY, 24, F, (--), M, SC, 730, 731, ORNG+. In HH of J. Sweet m 50 mulatto born SC.

SWEET, SAMUEL, 18, M, Farmer, M, SC, 730, 731, ORNG+. In HH of J. Sweet m 50 mulatto born SC.

SWEET, SARAH, 19, F, (--), M, SC, 730, 731, ORNG+. In HH of J. Sweet m 50 mulatto born SC.

SWINTON, ANNA, 2, F, (--), M, SC, 844, 802, CHAS+. In HH of Rebecca Swinton f 28 mulatto born SC.

SWINTON, ANTHONY, 40, M, Wheelwright, M, SC, 844, 802, CHAS+. In HH of Rebecca Swinton f 28 mulatto born SC.

SWINTON, DIANA, 20, F, (--), M, SC, 185, 169, CHAS*. In HH of Ann Deas f 37 mulatto born SC.

SWINTON, JAMES, 1, M, (--), M, SC, 844, 802, CHAS+. In HH of Rebecca Swinton f 28 mulatto born SC.

SWINTON, MARIA, 7, F, (--), M, SC, 844, 802, CHAS+. In HH of Rebecca Swinton f 28 mulatto born SC.

SWINTON, REBECCA, 40, F, (--), B, SC, 247, 232, CHAS+.

SWINTON, REBECCA, 28, F, (--), M, SC, 844, 802, CHAS+.

SWINTON, SUSAN, 12, F, (--), B, SC, 247, 232, CHAS+. In HH of Rebecca Swinton f 40 black born SC.

SWITT, CAFRUS, 10, M, (--), M, SC, 58, 58, CHAS3. In HH of Robt. Switt m 59 mulatto born SC.

SWITT, GEORGE, 16, M, (--), M, SC, 58, 58, CHAS3. In HH of Robt. Switt m 59 mulatto born SC.

SWITT, LAVINA, 20, F, (--), M, SC, 58, 58, CHAS3. In HH of Robt. Switt m 59 mulatto born SC.

SWITT, MARY, 50, F, (--), M, SC, 58, 58, CHAS3. In HH of Robt. Switt m 59 mulatto born SC.

SWITT, ROBT., 59, M, Laborer, M, SC, 58, CHAS3.

T

TALBUT, LEON, 12, M, (--), M, SC, 157, 144, CHAS*. In HH of Peter Brown m 55 mulatto born SC.

TALLY, CATHERINE, 18, F, (--), M, SC, 148, 138, CHAS-. In HH of Mary Steedman f 23 mulatto born SC.

TAN, HENRY, 26, M, Laborer, M, SC, 57, 57, CHAS2. In HH of Lewis Rusk m 23 born SC.

TANKESLEY, ANDREW, 25, M, Shoemaker, M, SC, 449, 449, GREE. In HH of Orsa Madena m 60 born Spain.

TARDIFF, ELIZA, 61, F, (--), M, SC, 49, 49, CHAS%. In HH of Sarah Williams f 65 mulatto born SC.

TARDIFF, EUPHEMA, 14, F, (--), M, SC, 49, 49, CHAS%. In HH of Sarah Williams f 65 mulatto born SC.

TARDIFF, SARAH, 24, F, (--), M, SC, 49, 49, CHAS%. In HH of Sarah Williams f 65 mulatto born SC.

TATE, ANTHONY, 45, M, Hireling, B, SC, 1119, 1119, ABB.

TAYLOR, ABRAHAM, 38, M, Tailor, M, SC, 517, 510, CHAS%.

TAYLOR, ABRAHAM, 10, M, (--), M, SC, 517, 510, CHAS%. In HH of Abraham Taylor m 38 mulatto born SC.

TAYLOR, BOL., 21, M, (--), B, SC, 864, 865, FAIR. In HH of George Harris m 34 black born SC.

TAYLOR, CHARLOTTE, 35, F, (--), M, SC, 534, 517, CHAS-.

TAYLOR, CLARISSA, 70, F, (--), M, SC, 463, 477, RICH.

TAYLOR, ELIZA., 26, F, (--), M, SC,

70, 71, RICH. In HH of Harriet Taylor f 40 mulatto born SC.

TAYLOR, ELIZABETH, 12, F, (--), B, SC, 897, 874, CHAS%. In HH of Timothy Hazard m 40 black born SC.

TAYLOR, FRANCES, 6, M, (--), M, SC, 517, 510, CHAS%. In HH of Abraham Taylor m 38 mulatto born SC.

TAYLOR, GEORGANA, 2, F, (--), M, SC, 517, 510, CHAS%. In HH of Abraham Taylor m 38 mulatto born SC.

TAYLOR, GEORGIANA, 12, F, (--), M, SC, 534, 517, CHAS-. In HH of Charlotte Taylor f 25 mulatto born SC.

TAYLOR, HARRIET, 40, F, (--), M, SC, 70, 71, RICH.

TAYLOR, HUGH, 2, M, (--), B, SC, 897, 874, CHAS%. In HH of Timothy Hazard m 40 black born SC.

TAYLOR, ISAAC, 8, M, (--), M, SC, 517, 510, CHAS%. In HH of Abraham Taylor m 38 mulatto born SC.

TAYLOR, ISABELLA, 25, F, (--), M, SC, 517, 510, CHAS%. In HH of Abraham Taylor m 38 mulatto born SC.

TAYLOR, JANET, 14, F, (--), M, SC, 305, 305, CHAS%. In HH of Thomas Taylor m 40 mulatto born SC.

TAYLOR, JOHN, 4, M, (--), M, SC, 517, 510, CHAS%. In HH of Abraham Taylor m 38 mulatto born SC.

TAYLOR, JOSEPH, 65, M, (--), B, SC, 1248, 1248, LEX.

TAYLOR, JOSEPH, 23, M, Carpenter, M, SC, 70, 71, RICH. In HH of Harriet Taylor f 40 mulatto born SC.

TAYLOR, MARTHA, 1, F, (--), B, SC, 897, 874, CHAS%. In HH of Timothy Hazard m 40 black born SC.

TAYLOR, MARY, 27, F, (--), B, SC, 897, 874, CHAS%. In HH of Timothy Hazard m 40 black born SC.

TAYLOR, PHILES, 64, F, (--), B, SC, 1248, 1248, LEX. In HH of Joseph Taylor m 65 black born SC.

TAYLOR, SARAH, 7, F, (--), M, SC, 534, 517, CHAS-. In HH of Charlotte Taylor f 25 mulatto born SC.

TAYLOR, THOMAS, 40, M, (--), M,

SC, 305, 305, CHAS%.

TAYLOR, TYRE, 37, F, (--), M, SC, 305, 305, CHAS%. In HH of Thomas Taylor m 40 mulatto born SC.

TEMPLAR, ELIZA, 25, F, (--), M, Ireland {sic}, 55, 50, CHAS-. In HH of Juliet Saxon f 35 mulatto born Ireland {sic}.

TERNY, EMILY, 20, F, (--), M, SC, 1665, 1671, MAR. In HH of William Miller m 95 born SC.

TERRIN, ANN, 82, F, (--), M, SC, 39, 40, RICH.

TERRY, JOSEPH, 29, M, Tailor, M, SC, 1069, 1046, CHAS-.

TERRY, PHOEBE, 36, F, (--), M, SC, 1069, 1046, CHAS-. In HH of Joseph Terry m 29 mulatto born SC.

THEON, JULIA, 69, F, (--), M, St.Domingo, 862, 839, CHAS%. In HH of Katey Theon f 71 mulatto born St.Domingo.

THEON, KATEY, 71, F, (--), M, St.Domingo, 862, 839, CHAS%.

THOMAS, HESTER, 71, F, (--), M, MD, 118, 118, KERS. In HH of Harriet Hammond f 20 black born SC.

THOMAS, JERANE, 32, F, (--), M, SC, 1810, 1816, EDGE. In HH of Wm. Thomas m 30 born SC.

THOMAS, JOHN ALLEN, 12, M, (--), M, SC, 1810, 1816, EDGE. In HH of Wm. Thomas m 30 born SC.

THOMAS, JOSEPH, 21, M, Farmer, M, SC, 214, 214, MARL.

THOMAS, MARY, 13, F, (--), M, SC, 258, 259, MAR. In HH of Latia Thomas f 40 born Marion, SC. Mary born Marion, SC.

THOMAS, NELLY, 45, F, (--), B, SC, 437, 389, CHAS. In HH of James Thomas m 50 born Spain.

THOMAS, REBECCA, 55, F, (--), M, SC, 805, 763, CHAS+.

THOMAS, REBECCAH, 20, F, (--), B, SC, 125, 125, CHAS~. In HH of John J. Williams m 47 born SC.

THOMAS, WM., 5, M, (--), B, SC, 118, 118, KERS. In HH of Harriet Hammond

f 20 black born SC.

THOMPKIN, ALFRID, 9, M, (--), M, SC, 331, 331, HORR. In HH of Cockrin Thompkin m 30 mulatto born SC.

THOMPKIN, COCKRIN, 30, M, (--), M, SC, 331, 331, HORR.

THOMPKIN, ELETH., 3, F, (--), M, SC, 331, 331, HORR. In HH of Cockrin Thompkin m 30 mulatto born SC.

THOMPKIN, ELIZABETH, 25, F, (--), B, SC, 331, 331, HORR. In HH of Cockrin Thompkin m 30 mulatto born SC.

THOMPKIN, JOHN, 7, M, (--), M, SC, 331, 331, HORR. In HH of Cockrin Thompkin m 30 mulatto born SC.

THOMPKIN, NANCEY, 19, F, (--), M, SC, 331, 331, HORR. In HH of Cockrin Thompkin m 30 mulatto born SC.

THOMPKIN, POLEY, 11, F, (--), M, SC, 331, 331, HORR. In HH of Cockrin Thompkin m 30 mulatto born SC.

THOMPKINS, RACHEL, 30, F, (--), M, SC, 332, 332, HORR. In HH of Willis Thompkins m 23 born SC.

THOMPKINS, WILLIS, 23, M, Farmer, M, SC, 332, 332, HORR.

THOMPSON, ANN, 28, F, (--), M, SC, 667, 625, CHAS+. In HH of Joseph Curtis m 56 born SC.

THOMPSON, EASSLY, 8, M, (--), M, SC, 322, 322, COLL. In HH of Henry Thompson m 45 mulatto born SC.

THOMPSON, EDMUND, 10, M, (--), M, SC, 834, 815, CHAS%. In HH of Elizabeth Cambridge f 37 mulatto born SC.

THOMPSON, EDWARD, 4, M, (--), M, SC, 320, 320, CHAS%. In HH of Louisa Thompson f 22 mulatto born SC.

THOMPSON, FRANCIS, 50, M, Store keeper, M, Manilla, 13, 12, CHAS$.

THOMPSON, FRANK, 7, M, (--), M, SC, 320, 320, CHAS%. In HH of Louisa Thompson f 22 mulatto born SC.

THOMPSON, HANNAH, 52, F, (--), M, SC, 13, 12, CHAS$. In HH of Francis Thompson m 50 mulatto born Manilla.

THOMPSON, HARRY, 33, M, (--), B, SC, 59, 59, CHAS%. In HH of Friday Evans m 53 black born SC.

THOMPSON, HENRY, 45, M, Farmer, M, SC, 322, 322, COLL.

THOMPSON, HENRY, 7, M, (--), B, SC, 59, 59, CHAS%. In HH of Friday Evans m 53 black born SC.

THOMPSON, JANE, 34, F, (--), B, SC, 59, 59, CHAS%. In HH of Friday Evans m 53 black born SC.

THOMPSON, JANET, 10, F, (--), B, SC, 59, 59, CHAS%. In HH of Friday Evans m 53 black born SC.

THOMPSON, JOHN, 38, M, Coachman, M, SC, 2343, 2343, GREE. In HH of Vardery McBee m 75 born SC.

THOMPSON, JOHN, 12, M, (--), M, SC, 322, 322, COLL. In HH of Henry Thompson m 45 mulatto born SC.

THOMPSON, LOUISA, 22, F, (--), M, SC, 320, 320, CHAS%.

THOMPSON, MORGAN, 10, M, (--), M, SC, 322, 322, COLL. In HH of Henry Thompson m 45 mulatto born SC.

THOMPSON, PERCILLA, 1, F, (--), M, SC, 320, 320, CHAS%. In HH of Louisa Thompson f 22 mulatto born SC.

THOMPSON, RACHAEL, 1, F, (--), M, SC, 322, 322, COLL. In HH of Henry Thompson m 45 mulatto born SC.

THOMPSON, RACHEL, 40, F, (--), M, SC, 322, 322, COLL. In HH of Henry Thompson m 45 mulatto born SC.

THOMPSON, SUSAN, 16, F, (--), M, SC, 322, 322, COLL. In HH of Henry Thompson m 45 mulatto born SC.

THOMPSON, WASHINGTON, 14, M, (--), M, SC, 322, 322, COLL. In HH of Henry Thompson m 45 mulatto born SC.

THOMPSON, WILLIAM, 18, F, Laborer, M, SC, 322, 322, COLL. In HH of Henry Thompson m 45 mulatto born SC.

THOMPSON, WILLIAM, 10, M, (--), M, SC, 320, 320, CHAS%. In HH of Louisa Thompson f 22 mulatto born SC.

THOMSON, M.A., 13, F, (--), M, SC,

66, 66, GEOR. In HH of Sarah Gairin f 27 mulatto born SC.

THOMSON, WASHINGTON, 8, F, (--), M, SC, 66, 66, GEOR. In HH of Sarah Gairin f 27 mulatto born SC.

THORN, ELIZABETH, 38, F, (--), B, SC, 1186, 1165, CHAS%. In HH of John Thorn m 40 black born SC.

THORN, JOHN, 40, M, Tailor, B, SC, 1186, 1165, CHAS%.

THORN, JOHN, 12, M, (--), B, SC, 1186, 1165, CHAS%. In HH of John Thorn m 40 black born SC.

THORN, JOHN, 4, M, (--), B, SC, 1186, 1165, CHAS%. In HH of John Thorn m 40 black born SC.

THORN, MILLER, 10, M, (--), B, SC, 1186, 1165, CHAS%. In HH of John Thorn m 40 black born SC.

THORN, PHILIP, 35, M, Carpenter, B, SC, 1186, 1165, CHAS%. In HH of John Thorn m 40 black born SC.

THORN, PHILIP, 8, M, (--), B, SC, 1186, 1165, CHAS%. In HH of John Thorn m 40 black born SC.

THORN, REBECCA, 5, F, (--), B, SC, 1186, 1165, CHAS%. In HH of John Thorn m 40 black born SC.

THORN, SARAH, 40, F, (--), B, SC, 1186, 1165, CHAS%. In HH of John Thorn m 40 black born SC.

THORNE, ELMIRA, 38, F, (--), M, SC, 8, 8, CHAS%.

THORNE, FRANK, 34, M, Boot maker, M, SC, 8, 8, CHAS%. In HH of Elmira Thorne f 38 mulatto born SC.

THORNE, JULIANA, 13, F, (--), M, SC, 8, 8, CHAS%. In HH of Elmira Thorne f 38 mulatto born SC.

THORNE, MARGARET, 11, F, (--), M, SC, 8, 8, CHAS%. In HH of Elmira Thorne f 38 mulatto born SC.

THORNE, MATILDA M., 6, F, (--), M, SC, 8, 8, CHAS%. In HH of Elmira Thorne f 38 mulatto born SC.

THORNE, PETER G., 9, M, (--), M, SC, 8, 8, CHAS%. In HH of Elmira Thorne f 38 mulatto born SC.

THORNLY, CAROLINE, 1, F, (--), M, SC, 184, 184, COLL. In HH of Eleanor Thornly f 32 Mulatto born SC.

THORNLY, ELEANOR, 32, F, (--), M, SC, 184, 184, COLL.

THORNLY, JOHN, 9, M, (--), M, SC, 184, 184, COLL. In HH of Eleanor Thornly f 32 Mulatto born SC.

THORNLY, LOVEY, 5, F, (--), M, SC, 184, 184, COLL. In HH of Eleanor Thornly f 32 Mulatto born SC.

THORNLY, MARTHA, 8, F, (--), M, SC, 184, 184, COLL. In HH of Eleanor Thornly f 32 Mulatto born SC.

THURMAN, GEORGE, 22, M, (--), B, SC, 307, 307, CHFD. In HH of Jane Rous f 30 black born SC.

TILLY, HENRY, 8, M, (--), M, SC, 147, 147, GREE. In HH of Henry Morris m 38 born SC.

TILLY, JAS., 60, M, Rafthand, M, SC, 1224, 1224, BARN.

TILMAN, JUDY, 65, F, (--), B, SC, 424, 424, CHFD.

TIMOTHY, IDE, 30, F, (--), M, SC, 316, 291, CHAS.

TOBE, LUCY, 3, F, (--), M, SC, 1380, 1380, NEWB. In HH of William Tobe m 50 black born SC.

TOBE, MARY, 35, F, (--), M, SC, 1380, 1380, NEWB. In HH of William Tobe m 50 black born SC.

TOBE, MARY, 15, F, (--), M, SC, 1380, 1380, NEWB. In HH of William Tobe m 50 black born SC.

TOBE, THOMAS, 11, M, (--), M, SC, 1380, 1380, NEWB. In HH of William Tobe m 50 black born SC.

TOBE, WILLIAM, 50, M, Farmer, B, SC, 1380, 1380, NEWB.

TOBE, YOUNG W., 5, M, (--), M, SC, 1380, 1380, NEWB. In HH of William Tobe m 50 black born SC.

TODD, CLARA, 14, F, (--), B, SC, 71, 71, CHAS%. In HH of Paul Todd m 48 black born SC.

TODD, DELIA, 24, F, (--), B, SC, 1895, 1901, EDGE. In HH of Harry Todd m 83 black born VA.

211

TODD, HARRY, 83, M, (--), B, VA, 1895, 1901, EDGE.

TODD, JOHN, 9, M, (--), B, SC, 71, 71, CHAS%. In HH of Paul Todd m 48 black born SC.

TODD, MARY, 41, F, (--), B, SC, 71, 71, CHAS%. In HH of Paul Todd m 48 black born SC.

TODD, PAUL, 48, M, (--), B, SC, 71, 71, CHAS%.

TODD, PEGGY, 60, F, (--), B, VA, 1895, 1901, EDGE. In HH of Harry Todd m 83 black born VA.

TODD, PETER, 16, M, (--), B, SC, 71, 71, CHAS%. In HH of Paul Todd m 48 black born SC.

TODD, ROSA, 18, F, (--), B, SC, 71, 71, CHAS%. In HH of Paul Todd m 48 black born SC.

TOOMER, ELIZA, 10, F, (--), M, SC, 861, 841, CHAS-. In HH of Robert Toomer m 32 mulatto born SC.

TOOMER, ELLEN, 7, F, (--), M, SC, 861, 841, CHAS-. In HH of Robert Toomer m 32 mulatto born SC.

TOOMER, JAMES, 2, M, (--), M, SC, 861, 841, CHAS-. In HH of Robert Toomer m 32 mulatto born SC.

TOOMER, JANE, 4, F, (--), M, SC, 861, 841, CHAS-. In HH of Robert Toomer m 32 mulatto born SC.

TOOMER, MARTHA, 29, F, (--), M, SC, 861, 841, CHAS-. In HH of Robert Toomer m 32 mulatto born SC.

TOOMER, ROBERT, 32, M, Painter, M, SC, 861, 841, CHAS-.

TOOMER, ROBERT, 6, M, (--), M, SC, 861, 841, CHAS-. In HH of Robert Toomer m 32 mulatto born SC.

TORLEE, EDWIN, 16, M, Shoemaker, B, SC, 425, 408, CHAS-. In HH of John Torlee m 49 black born SC.

TORLEE, JANET, 19, F, (--), B, SC, 425, 408, CHAS-. In HH of John Torlee m 49 black born SC.

TORLEE, JOHN, 49, M, Tailor, B, SC, 425, 408, CHAS-.

TORLEE, MARY, 40, F, (--), B, SC, 425, 408, CHAS-. In HH of John Torlee

m 49 black born SC.

TOUCHSTONE, JANE, 16, F, (--), M, SC, 73, 73, CHAS%. In HH of Julia Touchstone f 66 mulatto born SC.

TOUCHSTONE, JULIA, 66, F, (--), M, SC, 73, 73, CHAS%.

TOUCHSTONE, JULIET, 20, F, (--), M, SC, 73, 73, CHAS%. In HH of Julia Touchstone f 66 mulatto born SC.

TOUCHSTONE, PAULINE, 25, F, (--), M, SC, 36, 36, CHAS%. In HH of Maria Nelson f 21 mulatto born SC.

TOWNSEND, PRIMAS, 54, M, Shoemaker, B, NY, 349, 349, CHES.

TRUE, ROSE, 70, F, (--), B, SC, 683, 663, CHAS-. In HH of A.W. Trou m 30 born Bermuda.

TUCKER, ANN, 4, F, (--), M, SC, 546, 547, AND*. In HH of Frederic Harbert m 39 white born GA.

TUCKER, MARIA, 17, F, (--), B, SC, 1187, 1191, AND. In HH of John Hale m 54 white born SC.

TUCKER, WILLIAM, 23, M, (--), M, SC, 335, 335, CHFD.

TUNNO, FORTERMORE, 15, F, Laundress, B, SC, 20, 23, CHAS. In HH of Rachael Tunno f 70 black born SC.

TUNNO, RACHAEL, 70, F, Laundress, B, SC, 20, 23, CHAS.

TUNNO, SAML., 26, M, (--), M, SC, 37, 37, GEOR.

TUNNO, WILLIAM, 70, M, Fisherman, B, Germany {sic}, 280, 254, CHAS*. In HH of E. Messner m 28 born Germany.

TURFRIN, JACOB, 5, M, (--), B, SC, 341, 324, CHAS-. In HH of Judy Turfrin f 35 mulatto born SC.

TURFRIN, JUDY, 35, F, (--), M, SC, 341, 324, CHAS-.

TURFRIN, MARY JANE, 3, F, (--), B, SC, 341, 324, CHAS-. In HH of Judy Turfrin f 35 mulatto born SC.

TURFRIN, SARAH, 8, F, (--), B, SC, 341, 324, CHAS-. In HH of Judy Turfrin f 35 mulatto born SC.

TURFRIN, THOMAS, 1, M, (--), B,

SC, 341, 324, CHAS-. In HH of Judy Turfrin f 35 mulatto born SC.

TURMAN, DAVID, 80, F, Farmer, B, SC, 353, 353, CHFD.

TURMAN, DAVID, 14, M, (--), B, SC, 353, 353, CHFD. In HH of David Turman m 80 black born SC.

TURMAN, DELIA A., 20, F, (--), B, SC, 353, 353, CHFD. In HH of David Turman m 80 black born SC.

TURMAN, HANNAH, 22, F, (--), B, SC, 353, 353, CHFD. In HH of David Turman m 80 black born SC.

TURMAN, JACOB, 10, M, (--), B, SC, 353, 353, CHFD. In HH of David Turman m 80 black born SC.

TURMAN, KASSAH, 12, F, (--), B, SC, 353, 353, CHFD. In HH of David Turman m 80 black born SC.

TURMAN, MARTHA, 8, F, (--), B, SC, 353, 353, CHFD. In HH of David Turman m 80 black born SC.

TURMAN, NANCY, 18, F, (--), B, SC, 353, 353, CHFD. In HH of David Turman m 80 black born SC.

TURMAN, SUSAN, 16, F, (--), B, SC, 353, 353, CHFD. In HH of David Turman m 80 black born SC.

TURMAN, TEMPY, 58, F, (--), B, SC, 353, 353, CHFD. In HH of David Turman m 80 black born SC.

TURMAN, WILLIS, 25, M, (--), B, SC, 353, 353, CHFD. In HH of David Turman m 80 black born SC.

TURNBULL, ANNETTE, 65, F, (--), M, SC, 602, 594, CHAS%. In HH of Joseph Banfield m 40 mulatto born SC.

TURNER, ALFRED, 4, M, (--), M, Germany {sic}, 20, 18, CHAS-. In HH of Ann Turner f 55 mulatto born Germany {sic}.

TURNER, ANN, 55, F, (--), M, Germany {sic}, 20, 18, CHAS-.

TURNER, ANNA, 7, F, (--), M, Germany {sic}, 20, 18, CHAS-. In HH of Ann Turner f 55 mulatto born Germany {sic}.

TURNER, BETSEY, 44, F, (--), M, Germany {sic}, 19, 17, CHAS-. In HH of Sarah Turner f 40 mulatto born Germany {sic}.

TURNER, ELIZABETH, 25, F, (--), B, SC, 517, 517, LAU. In HH of Hardy Turner m 45 black born SC.

TURNER, EVANDER, 2, M, (--), M, SC, 1026, 1031, MAR. In HH of Willis Turner m 27 mulatto born SC.

TURNER, GEORGE, 0, M, (--), M, SC, 1026, 1031, MAR. In HH of Willis Turner m 27 mulatto born SC. George 3/12 yr.

TURNER, HARDY, 45, M, (--), B, SC, 517, 517, LAU.

TURNER, HARDY, 0, M, (--), B, SC, 517, 517, LAU. In HH of Hardy Turner m 45 black born SC. Hardy Turner 6/12 yr.

TURNER, ISABELL, 10, F, (--), M, Germany {sic}, 19, 17, CHAS-. In HH of Sarah Turner f 40 mulatto born Germany {sic}.

TURNER, JANE, 3, F, (--), B, SC, 517, 517, LAU. In HH of Hardy Turner m 45 black born SC.

TURNER, JOHN, 8, M, (--), M, Germany {sic}, 20, 18, CHAS-. In HH of Ann Turner f 55 mulatto born Germany {sic}.

TURNER, JOHN, 5, M, (--), M, Germany {sic}, 19, 17, CHAS-. In HH of Sarah Turner f 40 mulatto born Germany {sic}.

TURNER, JULIA, 12, F, (--), M, Germany {sic}, 19, 17, CHAS-. In HH of Sarah Turner f 40 mulatto born Germany {sic}.

TURNER, JULIA, 7, F, (--), M, Germany {sic}, 19, 17, CHAS-. In HH of Sarah Turner f 40 mulatto born Germany {sic}.

TURNER, MARY, 16, F, (--), M, Germany {sic}, 19, 17, CHAS-. In HH of Sarah Turner f 40 mulatto born Germany {sic}.

TURNER, ORPY, 22, F, (--), M, SC, 1026, 1031, MAR. In HH of Willis Turner m 27 mulatto born SC.

TURNER, PHILLANDER, 66, F, (--),

M, SC, 578, 570, CHAS%. In HH of Ellen Hampton f 22 mulatto born SC.

TURNER, SARAH, 40, F, (--), M, Germany {sic}, 19, 17, CHAS-.

TURNER, SARAH, 5, F, (--), B, SC, 517, 517, LAU. In HH of Hardy Turner m 45 black born SC.

TURNER, SUSAN, 28, F, (--), M, Germany {sic}, 20, 18, CHAS-. In HH of Ann Turner f 55 mulatto born Germany {sic}.

TURNER, THEODORE, 3, M, (--), M, Germany {sic}, 19, 17, CHAS-. In HH of Sarah Turner f 40 mulatto born Germany {sic}.

TURNER, WILLIS, 27, M, Laborer, M, SC, 1026, 1031, MAR.

V

VALENTINE, ALEXANDER, 2, M, (--), B, SC, 33, 35, AND. In HH of Dick Valentine m 25 black born SC.

VALENTINE, ANN, 45, F, (--), B, VA, 652, 652, UNION.

VALENTINE, CATO, 5, M, (--), B, SC, 33, 35, AND. In HH of Dick Valentine m 25 black born SC.

VALENTINE, CHARLES, 35, M, (--), B, SC, 649, 649, CHES.

VALENTINE, DICK, 24, M, Shoemaker, B, SC, 33, 35, AND.

VALENTINE, JACK, 39, M, Hireling, B, SC, 912, 912, ABB.

VALENTINE, JAMES, 43, M, Blacksmith, B, VA, 2138, 2138, GREE. In HH of Robert League m 37 born VA.

VALENTINE, JAMES, JR., 22, M, Apprentice, B, SC, 2144, 2144, GREE. In HH of John Higgins m 42 born SC.

VALENTINE, JAS., 25, M, Farmer, B, SC, 1509, 1509, CHES. In HH of Judy Bowzer f 81 born SC.

VALENTINE, MARTHA, 25, F, (--), B, SC, 33, 35, AND. In HH of Dick Valentine m 25 black born SC.

VALENTINE, MARY, 5, F, (--), B, SC, 649, 649, CHES. In HH of Charles Valentine 35 m black born SC.

VALENTINE, NANCEY, 32, F, (--), B, SC, 649, 649, CHES. In HH of Charles Valentine 35 m black born SC.

VALENTINE, PHILL, 5, M, (--), B, SC, 1509, 1509, CHES. In HH of Judy Bowzer f 81 born SC. John 5/12 yr.

VALENTINE, SARAH, 3, F, (--), B, SC, 649, 649, CHES. In HH of Charles Valentine 35 m black born SC.

VANDERHORST, MARTHA, 38, F, (--), M, SC, 461, 384, CHAS*.

VANDERHOST, AGATHA, 4, F, (--), M, SC, 284, 284, CHAS%. In HH of Agnes Vanderhost f 30 mulatto born SC.

VANDERHOST, AGNES, 30, F, (--), M, SC, 284, 284,CHAS%.

VANDERHOST, AROLDETH, 2, F, (--), M, SC, 284, 284, CHAS%. In HH of Agnes Vanderhost f 30 mulatto born SC.

VANDERHOST, ELLEN, 24, F, (--), M, SC, 97, 97, CHAS%. In HH of Eliza Remley f 30 mulatto born SC.

VANDERHURST, A., 37, F, Carpenter, M, SC, 59, 53, CHAS+. In HH of John F. Tenett m 65 born Germany.

VANDERHURST, MARTHA, 8, F, (--), M, SC, 59, 53, CHAS+. In HH of John F. Tenett m 65 born Germany.

VANDERHURST, MATILDA, 4, F, (--), M, SC, 59, 53, CHAS+. In HH of John F. Tenett m 65 born Germany.

VANDERHURST, REBECCA, 12, F, (--), M, SC, 59, 53, CHAS+. In HH of John F. Tenett m 65 born Germany.

VANDERHURST, SAMUEL, 41, M, (--), M, SC, 59, 53, CHAS+. In HH of John F. Tenett m 65 born Germany.

VANDERHURST, URIANA, 2, F, (--), M, SC, 59, 53, CHAS+. In HH of John F. Tenett m 65 born Germany.

VANDIVER, ELIZABETH C., 18, F, (--), M, SC, 295, 297, AND. In HH of Samuel Brown m 46 white born SC.

VAUGHAN, ANN, 33, F, (--), M, SC, 150, 140, CHAS-.

VAUGHAN, C., 22, M, Carpenter, B,

SC, 116, 116, KERS. In HH of Maria Johnson f 52 black born SC.

VAUGHAN, CHURCH, 24, M, (--), B, SC, 260, 260, KERS. In HH of J.F. Sutherland m 35 born NY.

VAUGHAN, HENRY, 9, M, (--), M, SC, 150, 140, CHAS-. In HH of Ann Vaughan f 33 mulatto born SC.

VAUGHAN, JAMES, 3, M, (--), M, SC, 150, 140, CHAS-. In HH of Ann Vaughan f 33 mulatto born SC.

VAUGHAN, MARIA, 1, F, (--), M, SC, 116, 116, KERS. In HH of Maria Johnson f 52 black born SC.

VAUGHAN, MARY, 12, F, (--), B, SC, 116, 116, KERS. In HH of Maria Johnson f 52 black born SC.

VAUGHAN, MARY ANN, 15, F, (--), M, SC, 150, 140, CHAS-. In HH of Ann Vaughan f 33 mulatto born SC.

VAUGHAN, PRESTON, 18, M, (--), M, SC, 260, 260, KERS. In HH of J.F. Sutherland m 35 born NY.

VAUGHAN, SOPHIA, 59, F, (--), B, SC, 150, 140, CHAS-. In HH of Ann Vaughan f 33 mulatto born SC.

VAUGHAN, SUSAN, 24, F, (--), B, SC, 116, 116, KERS. In HH of Maria Johnson f 52 black born SC.

VAUGHAN, WILLIAM, 11, M, (--), M, SC, 150, 140, CHAS-. In HH of Ann Vaughan f 33 mulatto born SC.

VEITCH, KATE, 60, F, (--), B, SC, 138, 128, CHAS-.

VEREE, CAROLINE, 38, F, (--), M, SC, 593, 575, CHAS-.

VEREE, ELIZA ANN, 17, F, (--), M, SC, 73, 71, CHAS*. In HH of Henrietta McNeill f 79 mulatto born SC.

VEREE, EMMA, 12, F, (--), M, SC, 593, 575, CHAS-. In HH of Caroline Veree f 38 mulatto born SC.

VEREE, JOHN, 37, F, Tailor, M, SC, 593, 575, CHAS-. In HH of Caroline Veree f 38 mulatto born SC.

VESEY, SARAH, 35, F, (--), M, SC, 408, 381, CHAS*. In HH of Ann Duprat f 60 black born SC.

VOLANTINE, AMANDA, 2, F, (--), B,

SC, 925, 925, ABB. In HH of Caroline Volantine 25 born SC.

VOLANTINE, ANDREW, 38, M, Hireling, B, SC, 973, 973, ABB.

VOLANTINE, ANDREW, 5, M, (--), B, SC, 925, 925, ABB. In HH of Caroline Volantine 25 born SC.

VOLANTINE, CAROLINE, 25, F, (--), B, SC, 925, 925, ABB.

VOLANTINE, ELIZA, 30, F, (--), B, SC, 926, 926, ABB. In HH of Hagan Volanatine f 60 black born SC.

VOLANTINE, GEORGE, 5, M, (--), B, SC, 931, 931, ABB. In HH of Sarah A. Volantine f 27 black born SC.

VOLANTINE, HAGAN, 60, F, (--), B, SC, 926, 926, ABB.

VOLANTINE, JOHN, 12, M, (--), B, SC, 931, 931, ABB. In HH of Sarah A. Volantine f 27 black born SC.

VOLANTINE, MARTHA, 7, F, (--), M, SC, 926, 926, ABB. In HH of Hagan Volanatine f 60 black born SC.

VOLANTINE, SARAH, 37, F, (--), B, SC, 973, 973, ABB. In HH of Andrew Volantine m 38 black born SC.

VOLANTINE, SARAH A., 27, F, (--), B, SC, 931, 931, ABB.

VOLANTINE, WILLIAM, 30, M, (--), B, SC, 973, 973, ABB. In HH of Andrew Volantine m 38 black born SC.

VOLANTINE, YANCY, 2, M, (--), M, SC, 926, 926, ABB. In HH of Hagan Volantine f 60 black born SC.

VOLENTINE, AMANDA, 27, F, (--), B, SC, 837, 837, NEWB. In HH of Rachel Volentine f 40 black born SC.

VOLENTINE, AMANDA, 10, F, (--), M, SC, 35, 35, NEWB. In HH of William Quattlebum m 33 mulatto born SC.

VOLENTINE, CANZADY, 30, F, (--), B, SC, 763, 763, NEWB.

VOLENTINE, ELIZA, 60, F, (--), B, SC, 761, 761, NEWB.

VOLENTINE, HENRY, 21, M, Farmer, B, SC, 771, 771, NEWB. In HH of J.J. Teague m 30 born SC.

VOLENTINE, LAURA, 12, F, (--), B, SC, 32, 32, NEWB. In HH of Elizabeth Brigg f 35 black born SC.

VOLENTINE, LODOSCIA P., 11, F, (--), B, SC, 837, 837, NEWB. In HH of Rachel Volentine f 40 black born SC.

VOLENTINE, MARY, 12, F, (--), B, SC, 770, 770, NEWB. In HH of George Neal m 44 born SC.

VOLENTINE, PRINCE, 60, M, Farmer, B, SC, 837, 837, NEWB. In HH of Rachel Volentine f 40 black born SC.

VOLENTINE, PRISCILLA, 72, F, (--), B, SC, 760, 760, NEWB. In HH of Priscilla Brigg f 75 black born SC.

VOLENTINE, RACHEL, 40, F, (--), B, SC, 837, 837, NEWB.

VOLENTINE, RACHEL, 10, F, (--), B, SC, 761, 761, NEWB. In HH of Eliza Volentine f 60 black born SC.

VOLENTINE, SARAH, 30, F, (--), B, SC, 36, 36, NEWB.

VOLENTINE, SPENCER, 11, M, (--), B, SC, 771, 771, NEWB. In HH of J.J. Teague m 30 born SC.

VOLUNTINE, LUKE, 65, M, (--), B, SC, 468, 468, EDGE. In HH of John Horn m 47 born SC.

W

WADKINS, REBECCA, 39, F, (--), B, SC, 857, 834, CHAS%.

WADSWORTH, BENSON, 6, M, (--), B, SC, 961, 961, NEWB. In HH of Jane Wadsworth f 25 black born SC.

WADSWORTH, CATHERINE, 0, F, (--), B, SC, 1070, 1070, NEWB. In HH of E. Wadsworth f 16 black born SC. Catherine age 7/12 yr.

WADSWORTH, DOLLY, 51, F, (--), B, SC, 958, 958, NEWB. In HH of John Wadsworth m 52 black born SC.

WADSWORTH, E., 16, F, (--), B, SC, 847, 847, NEWB. In HH of Robert Wells m 70 born SC.

WADSWORTH, E., 16, F, (--), B, SC, 1070, 1070, NEWB.

WADSWORTH, E.A., 20, F, (--), B, SC, 569, 569, NEWB. In HH of N.W. Davidson m 29 born SC.

WADSWORTH, ELIZA, 5, F, (--), B, SC, 958, 958, NEWB. In HH of John Wadsworth m 52 black born SC.

WADSWORTH, ELIZABETH, 4, F, (--), B, SC, 2022, 2022, ABB. In HH of Hannah Wadsworth f 27 mulatto born SC.

WADSWORTH, ELLEN?, 7, F, (--), B, SC, 29, 29, NEWB. In HH of C.M. Harris m 30 born SC.

WADSWORTH, ELLEN?, 7, F, (--), B, NC, 29, 29, NEWB. In HH of C.M. Harris 30 m born North Carolina.

WADSWORTH, FRANCES, 9, F, (--), B, SC, 771, 771, NEWB. In HH of J.J. Teague m 30 born SC.

WADSWORTH, FRANCIS, 25, F, (--), B, SC, 29, 29, NEWB. In HH of C.M. Harris m 30 born SC.

WADSWORTH, FRANK, 17, M, Farmer, B, SC, 959, 959, NEWB.

WADSWORTH, FRANKLIN, 1, M, (--), B, SC, 960, 960, NEWB. IN HH of Thomas Wadsworth m 22 black born SC.

WADSWORTH, HANNAH, 27, F, (--), M, SC, 2022, 2022, ABB.

WADSWORTH, HARRY, 1, M, (--), B, SC, 786, 786, NEWB. In HH of Martha Wadsworth f 25 black born SC.

WADSWORTH, JAMES, 6, M, (--), B, SC, 2022, 2022, ABB. In HH of Hannah Wadsworth f 27 mulatto born SC.

WADSWORTH, JANE, 39, F, (--), B, SC, 847, 847, NEWB. In HH of Robert Wells m 70 born SC.

WADSWORTH, JANE, 25, F, (--), B, SC, 961, 961, NEWB.

WADSWORTH, JEMIMA, 23, F, (--), B, SC, 1266, 1266, NEWB.

WADSWORTH, JOHN, 52, M, Farmer, B, SC, 958, 958, NEWB.

WADSWORTH, JOHN, 18, M, Blacksmith, B, SC, 10, 10, NEWB. In

HH of T.W. Thompson m 44, physician, born SC.

WADSWORTH, JOHN, 7, M, (--), B, SC, 958, 958, NEWB. In HH of John Wadsworth m 52 black born SC.

WADSWORTH, JOHN, 1, M, (--), M, SC, 2022, 2022, ABB. In HH of Hannah Wadsworth f 27 mulatto born SC.

WADSWORTH, LAVINIA, 17, M, (--), B, SC, 959, 959, NEWB. In HH of Frank Wadsworth m 17 black born SC.

WADSWORTH, LETTY, 3, F, (--), B, SC, 961, 961, NEWB. In HH of Jane Wadsworth f 25 black born SC.

WADSWORTH, LEVI, 24, M, (--), B, SC, 584, 585, AND*. In HH of Anthony Coats m 70 black born VA.

WADSWORTH, LOUISA, 30, F, (--), B, SC, 956, 956, NEWB. In HH of Michael Baker m 21 born SC.

WADSWORTH, M.J.A., 1, F, (--), B, SC, 961, 961, NEWB. In HH of Jane Wadsworth f 25 black born SC.

WADSWORTH, MALISA, 9, F, (--), B, SC, 1100, 1100, LAU. In HH of Siminus P. Dillard m 37 born SC.

WADSWORTH, MARIA, 7, F, (--), B, SC, 958, 958, NEWB. In HH of John Wadsworth m 52 black born SC.

WADSWORTH, MARINDA, 3, F, (--), B, SC, 960, 960, NEWB. IN HH of Thomas Wadsworth m 22 black born SC.

WADSWORTH, MARTHA, 25, F, (--), B, SC, 786, 786, NEWB.

WADSWORTH, MARTHENA, 35, F, (--), B, SC, 1128, 1128, LAU. In HH of Margaret Miller f 80 SC.

WADSWORTH, MARY, 4, F, (--), B, SC, 786, 786, NEWB. In HH of Martha Wadsworth f 25 black born SC.

WADSWORTH, MARY A., 14, F, (--), B, SC, 958, 958, NEWB. In HH of John Wadsworth m 52 black born SC.

WADSWORTH, MIKEAL, 42, M, Farmer, B, SC, 1027, 1027, NEWB.

WADSWORTH, MISOURI W., 8, F, (--), B, SC, 1140, 1140, NEWB. In HH of Jacob Baker m 40 black born SC.

WADSWORTH, NANCY, 6, F, (--), B, SC, 786, 786, NEWB. In HH of Martha Wadsworth f 25 black born SC.

WADSWORTH, PATIENCE, 18, F, (--), B, SC, 961, 961, NEWB. In HH of Jane Wadsworth f 25 black born SC.

WADSWORTH, PINCKNEY, 3, M, (--), B, SC, 961, 961, NEWB. In HH of Jane Wadsworth f 25 black born SC.

WADSWORTH, ROBERT, 30, M, Laborer, B, SC, 584, 585, AND*. In HH of Anthony Coats m 70 black born VA.

WADSWORTH, SAMUEL, 4, M, (--), B, SC, 1266, 1266, NEWB. In HH of Jemima Wadsworth f 23 black born SC.

WADSWORTH, SUSANNA, 1, F, (--), B, SC, 959, 959, NEWB. In HH of Frank Wadsworth m 17 black born SC.

WADSWORTH, TEMPA, 22, F, (--), B, SC, 960, 960, NEWB. IN HH of Thomas Wadsworth m 22 black born SC.

WADSWORTH, THOMAS, 22, M, Farmer, B, SC, 960, 960, NEWB.

WADSWORTH, THOMAS, 0, M, (--), B, SC, 961, 961, NEWB. In HH of Jane Wadsworth f 25 black born SC. Thomas Wadsworth 4/12 yr.

WADWORTH, ELIZA, 8, F, (--), B, SC, 815, 815, LAU. In HH of Jane Wadworth f 30 black born SC.

WADWORTH, ELIZABETH, 48, F, (--), B, SC, 814, 814, LAU.

WADWORTH, ELIZABETH, 20, F, (--), B, SC, 816, 816, LAU. In HH of Henry Wadworth m 27 black born SC.

WADWORTH, ELIZABETH, 5, F, (--), B, SC, 816, 816, LAU. In HH of Henry Wadworth m 27 black born SC.

WADWORTH, HENRY, 27, M, (--), B, SC, 816, 816, LAU.

WADWORTH, JANE, 30, F, (--), B, SC, 815, 815, LAU.

WADWORTH, JOHN, 6, M, (--), B, SC, 815, 815, LAU. In HH of Jane Wadworth f 30 black born SC.

WADWORTH, LEREEN, 1, F, (--), B, SC, 816, 816, LAU. In HH of Henry Wadworth m 27 black born SC.

WADWORTH, MAY, 10, F, (--), B, SC, 815, 815, LAU. In HH of Jane Wadworth f 30 black born SC.

WADWORTH, NARCISSA, 3, F, (--), B, SC, 814, 814, LAU. In HH of Elizabeth Wadworth f 48 black born SC.

WADWORTH, PINKNY, 3, M, (--), B, SC, 816, 816, LAU. In HH of Henry Wadworth m 27 black born SC.

WADWORTH, RUSSEL, 12, M, (--), B, SC, 814, 814, LAU. In HH of Elizabeth Wadworth f 48 black born SC.

WADWORTH, SIMS, 7, M, (--), B, SC, 814, 814, LAU. In HH of Elizabeth Wadworth f 48 black born SC.

WAGNER, CAROLINE, 50, F, (--), M, SC, 263, 231, CHAS. In HH of Prince Wagner m 56 mulatto born SC.

WAGNER, MARY, 0, F, (--), M, SC, 263, 231, CHAS. In HH of Prince Wagner m 56 mulatto born SC. Mary Wagner age 6/12 yr.

WAGNER, PRINCE, 56, M, Carpenter, M, SC, 263, 231, CHAS.

WALDROP, CATHERINE, 50, F, (--), B, SC, 150, 150, NEWB. IN HH of Elihu Waldrop m 51 black born SC.

WALDROP, ELIHU, 51, M, Farmer, B, SC, 150, 150, NEWB.

WALE, ELIZABETH, 35, F, (--), M, SC, 80, 80, GEOR.

WALE, PRISCILLA, 55, F, (--), M, SC, 80, 80, GEOR. In HH of Elizabeth Wale f 35 mulatto born SC.

WALKER, ANGUS, 12, M, Tailor, M, SC, 657, 616, CHAS+. In HH of Ann Walker f 56 mulatto born SC.

WALKER, ANGUS WM., 1, M, (--), M, SC, 657, 616, CHAS+. In HH of Ann Walker f 56 mulatto born SC.

WALKER, ANN, 56, F, (--), M, SC, 657, 616, CHAS+.

WALKER, DANIEL, 35, M, (--), M, , 9, 9, BEAU#.

WALKER, DANIEL, 34, M, (--), M, , 9, 9, BEAU#. In HH of Daniel Walker m 35 mulatto.

WALKER, DAVID, 9, M, (--), B, SC, 124, 124, KERS. In HH of M. Walker m

42 black born SC.

WALKER, DOROTHY, 22, F, (--), M, SC, 657, 616, CHAS+. In HH of Ann Walker f 56 mulatto born SC.

WALKER, HENRY, 12, M, (--), M, SC, 124, 124, KERS. In HH of M. Walker m 42 black born SC.

WALKER, JOHN, 24, M, Barber, M, SC, 657, 616, CHAS+. In HH of Ann Walker f 56 mulatto born SC.

WALKER, JOHN, 3, M, (--), M, SC, 657, 616, CHAS+. In HH of Ann Walker f 56 mulatto born SC.

WALKER, JOSEPH, 11, M, (--), B, SC, 124, 124, KERS. In HH of M. Walker m 42 black born SC.

WALKER, LEWIS, 2, M, (--), B, SC, 124, 124, KERS. In HH of M. Walker m 42 black born SC.

WALKER, M., 42, M, (--), B, SC, 124, 124, KERS.

WALKER, MARGARET, 19, F, (--), B, , 9, 9, BEAU#. In HH of Daniel Walker m 35 mulatto.

WALKER, MARGARET, 2, F, (--), M, SC, 1802, 1808, EDGE. In HH of Jonathan Williams m 45 black born SC.

WALKER, MARGARIT, 42, F, (--), M, SC, 2254, 2254, GREE.

WALKER, MARIA, 5, F, (--), B, SC, 124, 124, KERS. In HH of M. Walker m 42 black born SC.

WALKER, MARY, 13, F, (--), M, SC, 657, 616, CHAS+. In HH of Ann Walker f 56 mulatto born SC.

WALKER, PRESTON, 16, M, (--), M, SC, 124, 124, KERS. In HH of M. Walker m 42 black born SC.

WALKER, SARAH ANN, 21, F, (--), M, SC, 98, 110, CHAS. In HH of Emiley Bowers f 35 mulatto born SC.

WALKER, WILLIAM, 10, M, (--), B, , 5, 5, BEAU#. In HH of James Cockran m 27 black. Mitchel Cockran 6/12 yr.

WALL, AMELIA, 10, F, (--), M, SC, 167, 157, CHAS-. In HH of Maria L. Wall f 28 mulatto born SC.

WALL, ANN, 50, F, (--), M, SC, 505, 488, CHAS-. In HH of Ann Brown f 47 mulatto born SC.

WALL, EDWARD, 33, M, Tailor, M, SC, 167, 157, CHAS-. In HH of Maria L. Wall f 28 mulatto born SC.

WALL, EDWARD, 6, M, (--), M, SC, 167, 157, CHAS-. In HH of Maria L. Wall f 28 mulatto born SC.

WALL, FRANCES, 3, F, (--), M, SC, 167, 157, CHAS-. In HH of Maria L. Wall f 28 mulatto born SC.

WALL, HARRIOT, 30, F, (--), M, SC, 167, 157, CHAS-. In HH of Maria L. Wall f 28 mulatto born SC.

WALL, MARIA L., 28, F, (--), M, SC, 167, 157, CHAS-.

WALL, MARY E., 1, F, (--), M, SC, 167, 157, CHAS-. In HH of Maria L. Wall f 28 mulatto born SC.

WALL, RICHARD, 8, M, (--), M, SC, 167, 157, CHAS-. In HH of Maria L. Wall f 28 mulatto born SC.

WALL, WILLIAM, 56, M, Tailor, M, SC, 505, 488, CHAS-. In HH of Ann Brown f 47 mulatto born SC.

WANSLOW, DABNY, 50, M, Farmer, B, SC, 991, 991, ABB.

WANSLOW, JOHN, 78, M, (--), B, SC, 991, 991, ABB. In HH of Dabny Wanslow m 50 black born SC.

WANSLOW, LEANNA, 24, F, (--), B, SC, 991, 991, ABB. In HH of Dabny Wanslow m 50 black born SC.

WARD, SELENA, 28, F, (--), M, SC, 551, 510, CHAS+.

WARD, THOMAS, 5, M, (--), M, SC, 1141, 1141, GREE. In HH of Thomas Tayler m 68 born NC.

WARDEN, WORKY, 50, F, (--), M, SC, 854, 854, SUMT. In HH of Wesley Sweat m 24 mulatto born SC.

WARNER, ELIZABETH, 3, F, (--), M, SC, 446, 405, CHAS+. In HH of Mary Theus Guthrey f 30 mulatto born SC.

WARNER, GEORGE, 27, M, (--), M, SC, 531, 523, CHAS%. In HH of Susan Baxter f 39 mulatto born SC.

WARNER, HENRIETTA, 8, F, (--), M, SC, 446, 405, CHAS+. In HH of Mary Theus Guthrey f 30 mulatto born

SC.

WARNER, JACOB, 10, M, (--), M, SC, 446, 405, CHAS+. In HH of Mary Theus Guthrey f 30 mulatto born SC.

WARNER, MARSHAL, 40, M, Laborer, M, SC, 446, 405, CHAS+. In HH of Mary Theus Guthrey f 30 mulatto born SC.

WARNER, SARAH, 14, F, (--), M, SC, 446, 405, CHAS+. In HH of Mary Theus Guthrey f 30 mulatto born SC.

WARNER, SOPHIA, 40, F, (--), M, SC, 446, 405, CHAS+. In HH of Mary Theus Guthrey f 30 mulatto born SC.

WARNER, WILLIAM, 14, M, (--), M, SC, 446, 405, CHAS+. In HH of Mary Theus Guthrey f 30 mulatto born SC.

WARREN, POLLEY, 15, F, (--), B, SC, 360, 360, EDGE*. In HH of Teeneh {?} Warren f 46 born SC.

WASHINGTON, ANN, 30, F, (--), M, SC, 860, 837, CHAS%. In HH of Maria Washington f 55 mulatto born SC.

WASHINGTON, EMMELINE, 24, F, (--), M, SC, 860, 837, CHAS%. In HH of Maria Washington f 55 mulatto born SC.

WASHINGTON, MARIA, 55, F, (--), M, SC, 860, 837, CHAS%.

WATERS, ALBERT, 36, M, Carpenter, M, SC, 40, 35, CHAS+.

WATERS, MARY ANN, 30, F, (--), M, SC, 40, 35, CHAS+. In HH of Albert Waters m 36 mulatto born SC.

WATKINS, ABBEY, 20, F, (--), M, SC, 452, 419, CHAS*. In HH of Jane Morton f 68 born SC.

WATKINS, ABBY, 3, F, (--), B, SC, 775, 755, CHAS-. In HH of Katey Watkins f 40 black born SC.

WATKINS, JOHN, 5, M, (--), B, SC, 775, 755, CHAS-. In HH of Katey Watkins f 40 black born SC.

WATKINS, JOSEPHINE, 21, F, (--), B, SC, 776, 756, CHAS-.

WATKINS, KATEY, 40, F, (--), B, SC, 775, 755, CHAS-.

WATKINS, MARGARET, 4, F, (--), M, SC, 49, 49, ABB. In HH of Archy Bracknal m 40 born SC.

WATKINS, PETER, 6, M, (--), B, SC, 775, 755, CHAS-. In HH of Katey Watkins f 40 black born SC.

WATSON, DARCUS, 21, F, (--), M, SC, 757, 757, YORK. In HH of Nancy Watson f 60 mulatto born SC.

WATSON, FRANY, 0, F, (--), M, SC, 757, 757, YORK. In HH of Nancy Watson f 60 mulatto born SC. Frany age 9/12 yr.

WATSON, NANCY, 60, F, (--), M, SC, 757, 757, YORK.

WATSON, VENUS, 100, F, (--), B, GA, 91, 91, EDGE*.

WATT, ELIZABETH, 28, F, (--), M, SC, 1003, 1003, CHES. In HH of Jesse Hamelton 44 m Mulatto born SC.

WATTS, A.B., 51, M, Farmer, M, SC, 249, 249, LANC*.

WATTS, A.F., 18, M, Laborer, M, SC, 249, 249, LANC*. In HH of A.B. Watts m 51 mulatto born SC.

WATTS, ARCHY, 40, M, (--), M, NC, 25, 25, YORK.

WATTS, B.J., 1, M, (--), M, SC, 103, 103, LANC*. In HH of C. McDow m 25 black born SC.

WATTS, BENJAMIN, 4, M, (--), M, SC, 129, 129, LANC*. In HH of William Watts m 30 mulatto born SC.

WATTS, E.A.L., 15, F, (--), M, SC, 249, 249, LANC*. In HH of A.B. Watts m 51 mulatto born SC.

WATTS, G.W., 17, M, Mechanic, M, SC, 580, 580, CHES. In HH of J.J. Parish m 60 born NC.

WATTS, H.A.W., 23, M, Laborer, M, SC, 249, 249, LANC*. In HH of A.B. Watts m 51 mulatto born SC.

WATTS, J.D.T., 12, F, (--), M, SC, 249, 249, LANC*. In HH of A.B. Watts m 51 mulatto born SC.

WATTS, JAMES, 23, M, Laborer, M, SC, 204, 204, YORK. In HH of Joseph H. McGuire m 26 born NC.

WATTS, JAMES, 10, M, (--), M, SC, 103, 103, LANC*. In HH of C. McDow m 25 black born SC.

WATTS, JOHN E., 2, M, (--), M, SC, 129, 129, LANC*. In HH of William Watts m 30 mulatto born SC.

WATTS, MARY, 23, F, (--), M, SC, 129, 129, LANC*. In HH of William Watts m 30 mulatto born SC.

WATTS, R., 56, F, (--), M, SC, 249, 249, LANC*. In HH of A.B. Watts m 51 mulatto born SC.

WATTS, R.L., 20, F, (--), M, SC, 103, 103, LANC*. In HH of C. McDow m 25 black born SC.

WATTS, ROBT., 30, M, Laborer, M, SC, 4, 4, LANC. In HH of R.E. Wylie m 40 born SC.

WATTS, W.R., 5, M, (--), B, SC, 103, 103, LANC*. In HH of C. McDow m 25 black born SC.

WATTS, WILLIAM, 30, M, (--), M, SC, 129, 129, LANC*.

WAYNE, HENRY, 25, M, (--), M, SC, 167, 167, CHAS%.

WEAVER, RACHEL, 10, F, (--), B, SC, 420, 420, WILL. In HH of Richard Weaver m 40 black born SC.

WEAVER, ANN, 40, F, (--), B, SC, 420, 420, WILL. In HH of Richard Weaver m 40 black born SC.

WEAVER, CAROLINE, 14, F, (--), B, SC, 400, 400, WILL. In HH of Jesey Weaver m 44 black born SC.

WEAVER, ELIZABETH, 17, F, (--), B, SC, 400, 400, WILL. In HH of Jesey Weaver m 44 black born SC.

WEAVER, ELIZABETH, 9, F, (--), B, SC, 420, 420, WILL. In HH of Richard Weaver m 40 black born SC.

WEAVER, HENRIETTA, 50, F, (--), B, SC, 1851, 1858, MAR. In HH of James Weaver m 50 mulatto born SC.

WEAVER, HENRY, 15, M, Laborer, B, SC, 420, 420, WILL. In HH of Richard Weaver m 40 black born SC.

WEAVER, JAMES, 50, M, Carpenter, M, SC, 1851, 1858, MAR.

WEAVER, JANE, 15, F, (--), M, SC, 150, 150, CHAS~. In HH of Joshua Weaver m 41 mulatto born SC.

WEAVER, JESEY, 44, M, Laborer, B, SC, 400, 400, WILL.

WEAVER, JOHN, 56, M, Farmer, B, SC, 419, 419, WILL.

WEAVER, JOHN M., 5, M, (--), M, SC, 150, 150, CHAS~. In HH of Joshua Weaver m 41 mulatto born SC.

WEAVER, JOSHUA, 41, M, Farmer, M, SC, 150, 150, CHAS~.

WEAVER, MARGARET, 13, F, (--), M, SC, 150, 150, CHAS~. In HH of Joshua Weaver m 41 mulatto born SC.

WEAVER, MARTHA, 7, F, (--), B, SC, 420, 420, WILL. In HH of Richard Weaver m 40 black born SC.

WEAVER, MARY, 41, F, (--), B, SC, 400, 400, WILL. In HH of Jesey Weaver m 44 black born SC.

WEAVER, MARY, 14, F, (--), B, SC, 420, 420, WILL. In HH of Richard Weaver m 40 black born SC.

WEAVER, MARY ANN, 19, F, (--), B, SC, 400, 400, WILL. In HH of Jesey Weaver m 44 black born SC.

WEAVER, MOLSEY, 45, F, (--), M, SC, 150, 150, CHAS~. In HH of Joshua Weaver m 41 mulatto born SC.

WEAVER, RACHEL, 51, F, (--), B, SC, 419, 419, WILL. In HH of John Weaver m 56 black born SC.

WEAVER, RICHARD, 44, M, Laborer, B, SC, 420, 420, WILL.

WEAVER, SARAH, 7, F, (--), B, SC, 400, 400, WILL. In HH of Jesey Weaver m 44 black born SC.

WEAVER, SOLOMAN, 7, M, (--), M, SC, 150, 150, CHAS~. In HH of Joshua Weaver m 41 mulatto born SC.

WEAVER, WILLIAM, 4, M, (--), B, SC, 420, 420, WILL. In HH of Richard Weaver m 40 black born SC.

WEEKS, ELIZA, 20, F, (--), M, SC, 484, 492, RICH+. In HH of William Lovett m 42 born SC.

WEEKS, WILEY, 30, M, Planter, M, SC, 489, 497, RICH+.

WELCH, AUGUSTUS, 8, M, (--), B, SC, 233, 233, CHAS%. In HH of Bridy McKenzie m 50 black born SC.

WELCH, MARGARET, 37, F, (--), B, SC, 233, 233, CHAS%. In HH of Bridy McKenzie m 50 black born SC.

WELCH, SUSAN, 6, F, (--), B, SC, 233, 233, CHAS%. In HH of Bridy McKenzie m 50 black born SC.

WELKINSON, ELIZABETH, 30, F, (--), M, SC, 299, 299, CHAS%. In HH of Primus Friday m 40 black born SC.

WELKINSON, ELIZABETH, 6, F, (--), M, SC, 299, 299, CHAS%. In HH of Primus Friday m 40 black born SC.

WELLS, DIANA, 2, F, (--), M, SC, 536, 519, CHAS-. In HH of Mary Wells f 21 mulatto born SC.

WELLS, ELIZABETH, 3, F, (--), M, SC, 536, 519, CHAS-. In HH of Mary Wells f 21 mulatto born SC.

WELLS, JOHN, 26, M, Tailor, M, SC, 536, 519, CHAS-. In HH of Mary Wells f 21 mulatto born SC.

WELLS, MARY, 21, F, (--), M, SC, 536, 519, CHAS-.

WESLEY, CHARLES N., 2, M, (--), M, SC, 12, 12, CHAS~. In HH of Anna Broad f 31 mulatto born SC.

WESLEY, ELLINOR, 6, F, (--), M, SC, 12, 12, CHAS~. In HH of Anna Broad f 31 mulatto born SC.

WESLEY, ENOCH H., 4, M, (--), M, SC, 12, 12, CHAS~. In HH of Anna Broad f 31 mulatto born SC.

WESLEY, ROBERT, 14, M, (--), M, SC, 12, 12, CHAS~. In HH of Anna Broad f 31 mulatto born SC.

WESLEY, SARAH J., 11, F, (--), M, SC, 12, 12, CHAS~. In HH of Anna Broad f 31 mulatto born SC.

WESTCOT, MARGARET, 12, F, (--), M, SC, 527, 493, CHAS*. In HH of H.S. Waring m 60 born SC.

WESTON, AMELIA, 35, F, (--), M, SC, 1077, 1099, CHAS%. In HH of F. Weston, Jr. m 49 mulatto born SC.

WESTON, ARMANITHA, 16, F, (--), M, SC, 1077, 1099, CHAS%. In HH of F. Weston, Jr. m 49 mulatto born SC.

WESTON, CHARLES, 9, M, (--), M, SC, 203, 190, CHAS-. In HH of William Nelson m 48 born Germany.

WESTON, CHARLOTTE, 29, F, (--),

M, SC, 1090, 1067, CHAS-. In HH of Jacob Weston m 50 mulatto born SC.

WESTON, CHARLOTTE, 28, F, (--), M, SC, 61, 55, CHAS-. In HH of Jacob Weston m 48 mulatto born SC.

WESTON, CLAUDIA, 1, M, (--), M, SC, 534, 526, CHAS%. In HH of John Weston m 30 mulatto born SC.

WESTON, ELIZA, 40, F, (--), B, SC, 169, 169, CHAS%. In HH of Cynthia Hopkins f 50 black born SC.

WESTON, F., JR., 49, M, Tailor, M, SC, 1077, 1099, CHAS%.

WESTON, FRANCES, 20, F, (--), M, SC, 167, 167, CHAS%. In HH of Henry Wayne m 25 mulatto born SC.

WESTON, HANNAH, 39, F, (--), M, SC, 60, 54, CHAS-. In HH of Samuel Weston m 45 mulatto born SC.

WESTON, HANNAH, 12, F, (--), M, SC, 60, 54, CHAS-. In HH of Samuel Weston m 45 mulatto born SC.

WESTON, HENRY, 25, M, (--), M, SC, 167, 167, CHAS%. In HH of Henry Wayne m 25 mulatto born SC.

WESTON, JACOB, 50, M, Tailor, M, SC, 1090, 1067, CHAS-.

WESTON, JACOB, 48, M, Tailor, M, SC, 61, 55, CHAS-.

WESTON, JACOB, 10, M, (--), M, SC, 61, 55, CHAS-. In HH of Jacob Weston m 48 mulatto born SC.

WESTON, JACOB, 8, M, (--), M, SC, 1090, 1067, CHAS-. In HH of Jacob Weston m 50 mulatto born SC.

WESTON, JAMES, 12, M, (--), M, SC, 1077, 1099, CHAS%. In HH of F. Weston, Jr. m 49 mulatto born SC.

WESTON, JOANA, 3, F, (--), M, SC, 60, 54, CHAS-. In HH of Samuel Weston m 45 mulatto born SC.

WESTON, JOHN, 30, M, Shoemaker, M, SC, 534, 526, CHAS%.

WESTON, JOHN, 14, M, (--), M, SC, 1077, 1099, CHAS%. In HH of F. Weston, Jr. m 49 mulatto born SC.

WESTON, JOHN, 14, M, (--), M, SC, 685, 677, CHAS%. In HH of Sarah Weston f 66 mulatto born SC.

WESTON, JOHN, 3, M, (--), M, SC, 534, 526, CHAS%. In HH of John Weston m 30 mulatto born SC.

WESTON, LAURA, 8, F, (--), M, SC, 1077, 1099, CHAS%. In HH of F. Weston, Jr. m 49 mulatto born SC.

WESTON, LYDIA, 45, F, (--), M, SC, 167, 167, CHAS%. In HH of Henry Wayne m 25 mulatto born SC.

WESTON, MARIA, 35, F, (--), M, SC, 203, 190, CHAS-. In HH of William Nelson m 48 born Germany.

WESTON, MARY, 2, F, (--), M, SC, 60, 54, CHAS-. In HH of Samuel Weston m 45 mulatto born SC.

WESTON, ROZETTA, 40, F, (--), M, SC, 398, 405, RICH+.

WESTON, SAMUEL, 45, M, Tailor, M, SC, 60, 54, CHAS-.

WESTON, SAMUEL, 18, M, Millwright, M, SC, 61, 55, CHAS-. In HH of Jacob Weston m 48 mulatto born SC.

WESTON, SARAH, 66, F, (--), M, SC, 685, 677, CHAS%.

WESTON, SARAH, 50, F, (--), M, SC, 59, 53, CHAS-.

WESTON, SARAH, 24, F, (--), M, SC, 685, 677, CHAS%. In HH of Sarah Weston f 66 mulatto born SC.

WESTON, SARAH, 20, F, (--), M, SC, 60, 54, CHAS-. In HH of Samuel Weston m 45 mulatto born SC.

WESTON, SUSAN, 20, F, (--), M, SC, 534, 526, CHAS%. In HH of John Weston m 30 mulatto born SC.

WESTON, THOMAS, 10, M, (--), M, SC, 167, 167, CHAS%. In HH of Henry Wayne m 25 mulatto born SC.

WESTON, THOMAS, 0, M, (--), M, SC, 60, 54, CHAS-. In HH of Samuel Weston m 45 mulatto born SC. Thomas Weston age 8/12 yr.

WESTON, TIMOTHY, 6, M, (--), M, SC, 60, 54, CHAS-. In HH of Samuel Weston m 45 mulatto born SC.

WESTON, UNIS, 4, F, (--), M, SC, 60, 54, CHAS-. In HH of Samuel Weston m 45 mulatto born SC.

WESTON, WILLIAM, 17, M, Engineer, M, SC, 60, 54, CHAS-. In HH of Samuel Weston m 45 mulatto born SC.

WHALEY, CHARLOTTE, 14, F, (--), B, SC, 287, 287, BEAU+. In HH of Thomas Whaley m 65 mulatto born SC.

WHALEY, EMILY, 17, F, (--), M, SC, 287, 287, BEAU+. In HH of Thomas Whaley m 65 mulatto born SC. Color listed as F.{sic}

WHALEY, HESTER, 18, F, (--), B, SC, 287, 287, BEAU+. In HH of Thomas Whaley m 65 mulatto born SC. Color listed as F.{sic}

WHALEY, SIDNEY SMITH, 12, M, (--), M, SC, 287, 287, BEAU+. In HH of Thomas Whaley m 65 mulatto born SC. Color listed as F. {sic}

WHALEY, THOMAS, 65, M, Farmer, B, SC, 287, 287, BEAU+.

WHALEY, WINBORN A., 10, M, (--), M, SC, 287, 287, BEAU+. In HH of Thomas Whaley m 65 mulatto born SC. Color listed as F. {sic}

WHARTON, ELIZABETH, 27, F, (--), B, SC, 204, 204, ABB. In HH of James Wharton m 47 black born SC.

WHARTON, JAMES, 47, M, Carpenter, B, SC, 204, 204, ABB.

WHARTON, JOHN W., 2, M, (--), B, SC, 204, 204, ABB. In HH of James Wharton m 47 black born SC.

WHARTON, MARYANN P., 0, F, (--), B, SC, 204, 204, ABB. In HH of James Wharton m 47 black born SC. Maryann P. Wharton age 1/12 yr.

WHARTON, MATHIAS F., 5, M, (--), B, SC, 204, 204, ABB. In HH of James Wharton m 47 black born SC.

WHITE, AMELIA, 10, F, (--), M, SC, 395, 378, CHAS-. In HH of Edward White m 48 mulatto born SC.

WHITE, APPINIS, 0, F, (--), B, SC, 1810, 1810, ABB. In HH of Sarah White f 31 Mulatto born SC. Appinis White 10/12 yr.

WHITE, ARIANNA, 8, F, (--), B, SC, 1810, 1810, ABB. In HH of Sarah White f 31 Mulatto born SC.

WHITE, AUGUSTA, 3, F, (--), B, SC, 1810, 1810, ABB. In HH of Sarah White f 31 Mulatto born SC.

WHITE, EDWARD, 48, M, Carpenter, M, SC, 395, 378, CHAS-.

WHITE, ELIZA, 41, F, (--), M, SC, 168, 168, COLL. In HH of William White m 25 white born SC.

WHITE, ELIZA J., 5, F, (--), B, SC, 1810, 1810, ABB. In HH of Sarah White f 31 Mulatto born SC.

WHITE, EMELINE, 19, F, (--), M, SC, 395, 378, CHAS-. In HH of Edward White m 48 mulatto born SC.

WHITE, JAMES, 40, M, Laborer, M, SC, 830, 788, CHAS+. In HH of J.B. Mathews m 47 black born SC.

WHITE, JAMES, 9, M, (--), M, SC, 1810, 1810, ABB. In HH of Sarah White f 31 Mulatto born SC.

WHITE, JANE, 20, F, (--), M, SC, 830, 788, CHAS+. In HH of J.B. Mathews m 47 black born SC.

WHITE, JOHN, 8, M, (--), M, SC, 395, 378, CHAS-. In HH of Edward White m 48 mulatto born SC.

WHITE, JUSTINA, 36, F, (--), M, SC, 945, 925, CHAS-.

WHITE, LUCY, 13, F, (--), M, SC, 395, 378, CHAS-. In HH of Edward White m 48 mulatto born SC.

WHITE, NATHAN E., 2, M, (--), B, SC, 1810, 1810, ABB. In HH of Sarah White f 31 Mulatto born SC.

WHITE, RACHAEL, 45, F, (--), M, SC, 395, 378, CHAS-. In HH of Edward White m 48 mulatto born SC.

WHITE, ROSE, 60, F, (--), M, SC, 830, 788, CHAS+. In HH of J.B. Mathews m 47 black born SC.

WHITE, SARAH, 31, F, (--), M, SC, 1810, 1810, ABB.

WHITE, THOMAS, 16, M, Carpenter, M, SC, 395, 378, CHAS-. In HH of Edward White m 48 mulatto born SC.

WHITING, ALBERT, 2, M, (--), M, SC, 160, 150, CHAS-. In HH of Lucy Whiting f 50 mulatto born SC.

WHITING, CORDELIA, 7, F, (--), M, SC, 160, 150, CHAS-. In HH of Lucy Whiting f 50 mulatto born SC.

WHITING, GEORGE, 12, M, (--), M, SC, 160, 150, CHAS-. In HH of Lucy Whiting f 50 mulatto born SC.

WHITING, JAMES, 17, M, Laborer, M, SC, 160, 150, CHAS-. In HH of Lucy Whiting f 50 mulatto born SC.

WHITING, JOHN, 15, M, (--), M, SC, 160, 150, CHAS-. In HH of Lucy Whiting f 50 mulatto born SC.

WHITING, JOSEPH, 5, M, (--), M, SC, 160, 150, CHAS-. In HH of Lucy Whiting f 50 mulatto born SC.

WHITING, LOUISA, 24, F, (--), M, SC, 160, 150, CHAS-. In HH of Lucy Whiting f 50 mulatto born SC.

WHITING, LUCY, 50, F, (--), M, SC, 160, 150, CHAS-.

WHITING, ROSANAH, 9, F, (--), M, SC, 160, 150, CHAS-. In HH of Lucy Whiting f 50 mulatto born SC.

WHITING, TAMER, 19, F, (--), M, SC, 160, 150, CHAS-. In HH of Lucy Whiting f 50 mulatto born SC.

WICKFALL, JOSEPH, 30, M, Shoemaker, B, SC, 86, 86, Union. In HH of Lewis Onley m 29 born SC.

WIGFALL, ANNA JANE, 0, F, (--), B, SC, 527, 477, CHAS. In HH of Paul Wigfall m 55 black born SC. Anna Jane Wigfall age 8/12 yr.

WIGFALL, CAROLINE, 24, F, (--), B, SC, 527, 477, CHAS. In HH of Paul Wigfall m 55 black born SC.

WIGFALL, CAROLINE, 18, F, (--), B, SC, 489, 472, CHAS-. In HH of James Wigfall m 52 black born SC.

WIGFALL, JAMES, 52, M, Carpenter, B, SC, 489, 472, CHAS-.

WIGFALL, JANE, 47, F, (--), B, SC, 489, 472, CHAS-. In HH of James Wigfall m 52 black born SC.

WIGFALL, JANE, 26, F, (--), B, SC, 527, 477, CHAS. In HH of Paul Wigfall m 55 black born SC.

WIGFALL, JOHN, 28, M, Bricklayer, B, SC, 527, 477, CHAS. In HH of Paul Wigfall m 55 black born SC.

WIGFALL, MILDRED, 30, F, (--), M, SC, 527, 477, CHAS. In HH of Paul Wigfall m 55 black born SC.

WIGFALL, PAUL, 55, M, Bricklayer, B, SC, 527, 477, CHAS.

WIGFALL, PAUL, 32, M, Bricklayer, B, SC, 527, 477, CHAS. In HH of Paul Wigfall m 55 black born SC.

WIGGINS, M., 26, F, (--), M, SC, 62, 62, CHAS2. In HH of Lewis J. Wiggins m 21 born SC.

WIGGINS, R.B., 1, F, (--), M, SC, 62, 62, CHAS2. In HH of Lewis J. Wiggins m 21 born SC.

WIGNARD, ELIZABETH, 19, F, (--), M, SC, 123, 124, ORNG+. In HH of B. Johnston m 41 born SC.

WIGNARD, ELIZABETH, 19, F, (--), M, SC, 124, 125, ORNG+. In HH of B. Johnson m 41 born SC.

WILKINSON, ANN, 47, F, (--), B, Germany {sic}, 388, 386, CHAS%. In HH of Edmund Wilkinson m 50 black born Germany {sic}.

WILKINSON, CATHERINE, 17, F, (--), B, SC, 388, 386, CHAS%. In HH of Edmund Wilkinson m 50 black born Germany {sic}.

WILKINSON, CATHERINE, 1, F, (--), M, SC, 248, 249, MAR. In HH of James Wilkinson m 23 mulatto born Marion, SC. Catherine born Marion, SC.

WILKINSON, EDMUND, 50, M, Painter, B, Germany {sic}, 388, 386, CHAS%.

WILKINSON, ELIZA, 15, F, (--), M, SC, 116, 116, CHAS%. In HH of J.F. Wilkinson m 40 mulatto born SC.

WILKINSON, FRANCIS, 10, M, (--), M, SC, 116, 116, CHAS%. In HH of J.F. Wilkinson m 40 mulatto born SC.

WILKINSON, J.F., 40, M, Butcher, M, SC, 116, 116, CHAS%.

WILKINSON, JAMES, 23, M, Farmer, M, SC, 248, 249, MAR. James Wilkinson born Marion, SC.

WILKINSON, JOSEPHINE, 2, F, (--), M, SC, 306, 306, CHAS%. In HH of

Paul Wilkinson m 40 mulatto born SC.

WILKINSON, LAURA E., 35, F, (--), M, SC, 116, 116, CHAS%. In HH of J.F. Wilkinson m 40 mulatto born SC.

WILKINSON, MARGARET, 20, F, (--), M, SC, 306, 306, CHAS%. In HH of Paul Wilkinson m 40 mulatto born SC.

WILKINSON, MARY, 45, F, (--), B, SC, 728, 719, CHAS%. In HH of A.G. Magrath m 37 born SC.

WILKINSON, MARY, 20, F, (--), M, SC, 248, 249, MAR. In HH of James Wilkinson m 23 mulatto born Marion, SC. Mary bornMarion, SC.

WILKINSON, MARIA, 70, F, (--), M, SC, 306, 306, CHAS%. In HH of Paul Wilkinson m 40 mulatto born SC.

WILKINSON, PAUL, 40, M, Millwright, M, SC, 306, 306, CHAS%.

WILKINSON, REBECCA, 11, F, (--), B, SC, 388, 386, CHAS%. In HH of Edmund Wilkinson m 50 black born Germany {sic}.

WILKINSON, RICHARD, 13, M, (--), B, SC, 388, 386, CHAS%. In HH of Edmund Wilkinson m 50 black born Germany {sic}.

WILKINSON, RICHARD, 9, M, (--), M, SC, 306, 306, CHAS%. In HH of Paul Wilkinson m 40 mulatto born SC.

WILKINSON, ROSALTHA, 12, F, (--), M, SC, 116, 116, CHAS%. In HH of J.F. Wilkinson m 40 mulatto born SC.

WILKINSON, SARAH, 50, F, (--), M, SC, 306, 306, CHAS%. In HH of Paul Wilkinson m 40 mulatto born SC.

WILKINSON, SARAH, 9, F, (--), B, SC, 388, 386, CHAS%. In HH of Edmund Wilkinson m 50 black born Germany {sic}.

WILKINSON, SARAH, 3, F, (--), M, SC, 306, 306, CHAS%. In HH of Paul Wilkinson m 40 mulatto born SC.

WILKS, CATHERINE, 2, F, (--), M, SC, 1190, 1195, MAR. In HH of James Wilks m 23 mulatto born SC.

WILKS, JAMES, 23, M, Laborer, M, SC, 1190, 1195, MAR.

WILKS, MARY, 20, F, (--), M, SC, 1190, 1195, MAR. In HH of James Wilks m 23 mulatto born SC.

WILLARD, COLUMBUS, 24, M, Tanner, M, SC, 559, 559, Union. In HH of Charles Gowing m 54 born VT.

WILLARD, LUCINDA, 50, F, (--), M, SC, 559, 559, Union. In HH of Charles Gowing m 54 born VT.

WILLIAMS, ABRAM, 2, M, (--), B, SC, 1070, 1070, LAU. In HH of Hamplory Williams m 65 black born SC.

WILLIAMS, ABSOLUM, 4, M, (--), M, SC, 948, 948, NEWB. In HH of Shep Williams m 44 mulatto born SC.

WILLIAMS, ADAM, 21, M, Laborer, M, SC, 197, 197, CHAS3. In HH of Laverick Williams f 65 born SC.

WILLIAMS, ADELINE, 12, F, (--), M, SC, 196, 196, CHAS3. In HH of William Williams m 45 mulatto born SC.

WILLIAMS, AFFEY, 54, M, (--), M, SC, 248, 248, GEOR*.

WILLIAMS, ALBERT F., 8, M, (--), M, SC, 948, 948, NEWB. In HH of Shep Williams m 44 mulatto born SC.

WILLIAMS, ANN, 40, F, (--), B, SC, 272, 272, BEAU+. In HH of Stephen Williams m 55 black born SC.

WILLIAMS, ANNA, 40, F, (--), M, SC, 703, 695, CHAS%.

WILLIAMS, ANNABEL, 18, F, (--), M, SC, 1802, 1808, EDGE. In HH of Jonathan Williams m 45 black born SC.

WILLIAMS, ANTHONY, 45, M, Carpenter, M, SC, 145, 145, GEOR*. In HH of Martha Williams f 37 mulatto born SC.

WILLIAMS, BENJ., 18, M, Farming, M, SC, 268, 268, GEOR*. In HH of Daniel Williams m 54 mulatto born SC.

WILLIAMS, CAIN, 15, M, (--), M, SC, 235, 235, GEOR*. In HH of Moland Williams m 35 mulatto born SC.

WILLIAMS, CALA, 19, F, (--), M, SC, 1776, 1782, EDGE. In HH of Cinthia Williams f 60 mulatto born SC.

WILLIAMS, CAROLINE, 5, F, (--), M, SC, 196, 196, CHAS3. In HH of William Williams m 45 mulatto born SC.

WILLIAMS, CATHERINE, 35, F, (--), M, SC, 235, 235, GEOR*. In HH of Moland Williams m 35 mulatto born SC.

WILLIAMS, CHARLEY, 17, M, (--), M, SC, 248, 248, GEOR*. In HH of Affey Williams m 54 mulatto born SC.

WILLIAMS, CHARLOTTE, 62, F, (--), M, SC, 467, 425, CHAS+.

WILLIAMS, CHARLOTTE, 19, F, (--), M, SC, 248, 248, GEOR*. In HH of Affey Williams m 54 mulatto born SC.

WILLIAMS, CINDA, 37, F, (--), M, SC, 782, 740, CHAS+.

WILLIAMS, CINTHIA, 60, F, (--), M, SC, 1776, 1782, EDGE.

WILLIAMS, DANIEL, 54, M, Farming, M, SC, 268, 268, GEOR*.

WILLIAMS, DANIEL, 22, M, Farmer, M, SC, 948, 948, NEWB. In HH of Shep Williams m 44 mulatto born SC.

WILLIAMS, DANIEL, 18, M, Tailor, M, SC, 342, 325, CHAS-. In HH of Mary Williams f 38 mulatto born SC.

WILLIAMS, DAVID, 17, M, Carpenter, M, SC, 145, 145, GEOR*. In HH of Martha Williams f 37 mulatto born SC.

WILLIAMS, DELILA, 12, F, (--), M, SC, 1802, 1808, EDGE. In HH of Jonathan Williams m 45 black born SC.

WILLIAMS, E.A., 10, F, (--), M, SC, 948, 948, NEWB. In HH of Shep Williams m 44 mulatto born SC.

WILLIAMS, ELIZABETH, 8, F, (--), B, SC, 272, 272, BEAU+. In HH of Stephen Williams m 55 black born SC.

WILLIAMS, EMANUEL, 3, M, (--), M, SC, 342, 325, CHAS-. In HH of Mary Williams f 38 mulatto born SC.

WILLIAMS, EVY, 9, F, (--), M, SC, 268, 268, GEOR*. In HH of Daniel Williams m 54 mulatto born SC.

WILLIAMS, FRANCES, 18, F, (--), M, SC, 676, 677, ORNG+. In HH of Nancy Williams f 45 mulatto born SC.

WILLIAMS, GEORGE, 1, M, (--), B, SC, 272, 272, BEAU+. In HH of Stephen Williams m 55 black born SC.

WILLIAMS, GEORGIANA, 10, F,

(--), M, SC, 775, 758, CHAS%. In HH of Harris Williams m 31 mulatto born SC.

WILLIAMS, HAMPLORY, 65, M, (--), B, SC, 1070, 1070, LAU.

WILLIAMS, HANNAH, 50, F, (--), M, SC, 270, 270, GEOR*. In HH of Isaac William m 42 mulatto born SC.

WILLIAMS, HARRIET, 6, F, (--), B, SC, 272, 272, BEAU+. In HH of Stephen Williams m 55 black born SC.

WILLIAMS, HARRIS, 31, M, Carpenter, M, SC, 775, 758, CHAS%.

WILLIAMS, HENRY, 10, M, (--), M, SC, 1776, 1782, EDGE. In HH of Cinthia Williams f 60 mulatto born SC.

WILLIAMS, ISAAC, 42, M, Carpenter, M, SC, 270, 270, GEOR*.

WILLIAMS, ISAAC C., 17, M, Farmer, M, SC, 948, 948, NEWB. In HH of Shep Williams m 44 mulatto born SC.

WILLIAMS, JAMES, 44, M, Butcher, M, SC, 49, 49, CHAS%. In HH of Sarah Williams f 65 mulatto born SC.

WILLIAMS, JAMES, 41, M, Tailor, B, SC, 740, 720, CHAS-. In HH of William Bemar m 30 mulatto born SC.

WILLIAMS, JAMES, 39, M, Planter, M, SC, 197, 197, CHAS3. In HH of Laverick Williams f 65 born SC.

WILLIAMS, JAMES, 20, M, Farmer, M, SC, 948, 948, NEWB. In HH of Shep Williams m 44 mulatto born SC.

WILLIAMS, JAMES, 14, M, (--), M, SC, 196, 196, CHAS3. In HH of William Williams m 45 mulatto born SC.

WILLIAMS, JAMES, 13, M, (--), M, SC, 613, 617, And. In HH of Henrietta Williams f 45 mulatto born NC.

WILLIAMS, JAMES, 7, M, (--), M, SC, 775, 758, CHAS%. In HH of Harris Williams m 31 mulatto born SC.

WILLIAMS, JAMES JR., 23, M, Laborer, M, SC, 196, 196, CHAS3. In HH of William Williams m 45 mulatto born SC.

WILLIAMS, JEMMIMA, 12, F, (--), M, SC, 782, 740, CHAS+. In HH of Cinda Williams f 37 mulatto born SC.

WILLIAMS, JOHN, 85, M, Farming,

M, SC, 262, 262, GEOR*.

WILLIAMS, JOHN, 50, M, Boatman, M, SC, 1924, 1930, EDGE. In HH of Mary Williams f 60 born SC.

WILLIAMS, JOHN, 22, M, Laborer, M, SC, 1776, 1782, EDGE. In HH of Cinthia Williams f 60 mulatto born SC.

WILLIAMS, JOHN, 16, M, Farming, M, SC, 268, 268, GEOR*. In HH of Daniel Williams m 54 mulatto born SC.

WILLIAMS, JOHN, 15, M, Carpenter, M, SC, 342, 325, CHAS-. In HH of Mary Williams f 38 mulatto born SC.

WILLIAMS, JOHN, 15, M, (--), M, SC, 145, 145, GEOR*. In HH of Martha Williams f 37 mulatto born SC.

WILLIAMS, JOHN, 0, F, (--), M, SC, 248, 248, GEOR*. In HH of Affey Williams m 54 mulatto born SC. John Williams 7/12 yr.

WILLIAMS, JONATHAN, 45, M, Laborer, B, SC, 1802, 1808, EDGE.

WILLIAMS, JOSEPH, 28, M, Laborer, M, SC, 246, 246, PICK+. In HH of C.H. Brock m 37 born SC.

WILLIAMS, JOSEPH, 22, M, Farmer, M, SC, 613, 617, And. In HH of Henrietta Williams f 45 mulatto born NC.

WILLIAMS, JUDY, 14, F, (--), M, SC, 248, 248, GEOR*. In HH of Affey Williams m 54 mulatto born SC.

WILLIAMS, JUDY, 9, F, (--), M, SC, 342, 325, CHAS-. In HH of Mary Williams f 38 mulatto born SC.

WILLIAMS, LAURENCE, 10, M, (--), M, SC, 782, 740, CHAS+. In HH of Cinda Williams f 37 mulatto born SC.

WILLIAMS, LAVERICK, 65, F, (--), M, SC, 197, 197, CHAS3.

WILLIAMS, LEONARD, 6, M, (--), M, SC, 676, 677, ORNG+. In HH of Nancy Williams f 45 mulatto born SC.

WILLIAMS, LINDSEY, 17, M, Farmer, M, SC-, 613, 617, And. In HH of Henrietta Williams f 45 mulatto born NC.

WILLIAMS, LIZA, 16, F, (--), M, SC, 196, 196, CHAS3. In HH of William Williams m 45 mulatto born SC.

WILLIAMS, LORENZA., 14, M, (--), M, SC, 948, 948, NEWB. In HH of Shep Williams m 44 mulatto born SC.

WILLIAMS, LOUISA, 5, F, (--), M, SC, 782, 740, CHAS+. In HH of Cinda Williams f 37 mulatto born SC.

WILLIAMS, LUCY, 40, F, (--), M, SC, 136, 136, CHAS%.

WILLIAMS, LUCY, 16, F, (--), M, SC, 782, 740, CHAS+. In HH of Cinda Williams f 37 mulatto born SC.

WILLIAMS, LYDIA, 20, F, (--), M, SC, 235, 235, GEOR*. In HH of Moland Williams m 35 mulatto born SC.

WILLIAMS, MAHALA, 16, F, (--), M, SC, 676, 677, ORNG+. In HH of Nancy Williams f 45 mulatto born SC.

WILLIAMS, MARGARET, 78, F, (--), M, SC, 1802, 1808, EDGE. In HH of Jonathan Williams m 45 black born SC.

WILLIAMS, MARIA, 60, F, (--), M, SC, 197, 197, CHAS%.

WILLIAMS, MARIAH, 5, F, (--), M, SC, 268, 268, GEOR*. In HH of Daniel Williams m 54 mulatto born SC.

WILLIAMS, MARTHA, 37, F, (--), M, SC, 145, 145, GEOR*.

WILLIAMS, MARY, 60, F, (--), B, SC, 454, 411, CHAS. In HH of Susan Williams f 35 black born SC.

WILLIAMS, MARY, 60, F, (--), M, SC, 1924, 1930, EDGE.

WILLIAMS, MARY, 38, F, (--), M, SC, 342, 325, CHAS-.

WILLIAMS, MARY, 35, F, (--), M, SC, 49, 49, CHAS%. In HH of Sarah Williams f 65 mulatto born SC.

WILLIAMS, MARY, 27, F, (--), M, SC, 775, 758, CHAS%. In HH of Harris Williams m 31 mulatto born SC.

WILLIAMS, MARY, 21, F, (--), M, SC, 342, 325, CHAS-. In HH of Mary Williams f 38 mulatto born SC.

WILLIAMS, MARY, 17, F, (--), M, SC, 703, 695, CHAS%. In HH of Ann Williams f 40 mulatto born SC.

WILLIAMS, MERIDA, 6, M, (--), M,

SC, 948, 948, NEWB. In HH of Shep Williams m 44 mulatto born SC.

WILLIAMS, MILLY A., 3, F, (--), B, SC, 272, 272, BEAU+. In HH of Stephen Williams m 55 black born SC.

WILLIAMS, MOLAND, 35, M, Carpenter, M, SC, 235, 235, GEOR*.

WILLIAMS, MOSES, 7, M, (--), M, SC, 268, 268, GEOR*. In HH of Daniel Williams m 54 mulatto born SC.

WILLIAMS, NANCY, 45, F, (--), M, SC, 676, 677, ORNG+.

WILLIAMS, NANCY, 3, F, (--), M, SC, 248, 248, GEOR*. In HH of Affey Williams m 54 mulatto born SC.

WILLIAMS, NED, 13, M, (--), M, SC, 342, 325, CHAS-. In HH of Mary Williams f 38 mulatto born SC.

WILLIAMS, NICK, 25, M, Laborer, M, SC, 197, 197, CHAS3. In HH of Laverick Williams f 65 born SC.

WILLIAMS, P. C., 12, M, (--), M, SC, 948, 948, NEWB. In HH of Shep Williams m 44 mulatto born SC.

WILLIAMS, PARIS, 25, M, Hair cliper, B, SC, 496, 450, CHAS.

WILLIAMS, RACHEL, 13, F, (--), M, SC, 235, 235, GEOR*. In HH of Moland Williams m 35 mulatto born SC.

WILLIAMS, REBECCA, 39, F, (--), M, SC, 196, 196, CHAS3. In HH of William Williams m 45 mulatto born SC.

WILLIAMS, REBECCA, 28, F, (--), M, SC, 534, 549, RICH.

WILLIAMS, RODDY, 2, F, (--), M, SC, 196, 196, CHAS3. In HH of William Williams m 45 mulatto born SC.

WILLIAMS, SABINA, 11, F, (--), M, SC, 703, 695, CHAS%. In HH of Ann Williams f 40 mulatto born SC.

WILLIAMS, SAML., 21, M, (--), M, SC, 1802, 1808, EDGE. In HH of Jonathan Williams m 45 black born SC.

WILLIAMS, SAMUEL, 10, M, (--), B, SC, 197, 197, CHAS%. In HH of Maria Williams f 60 mulatto born SC.

WILLIAMS, SARAH, 65, F, (--), M, SC, 49, 49, CHAS%.

WILLIAMS, SARAH, 54, F, (--), M, SC, 262, 262, GEOR*. In HH of John Williams m 85 mulatto born SC.

WILLIAMS, SARAH, 30, F, (--), B, SC, 1070, 1070, LAU. In HH of Hamplory Williams m 65 black born SC.

WILLIAMS, SARAH, 21, F, (--), M, SC, 676, 677, ORNG+. In HH of Nancy Williams f 45 mulatto born SC.

WILLIAMS, SARAH, 7, F, (--), M, SC, 196, 196, CHAS3. In HH of William Williams m 45 mulatto born SC.

WILLIAMS, SARAH, 5, F, (--), M, SC, 342, 325, CHAS-. In HH of Mary Williams f 38 mulatto born SC.

WILLIAMS, SARAH A., 4, F, (--), B, SC, 272, 272, BEAU+. In HH of Stephen Williams m 55 black born SC.

WILLIAMS, SHEP, 44, M, Farmer, M, SC, 948, 948, NEWB.

WILLIAMS, STEPHEN, 55, M, Laborer, B, SC, 272, 272, BEAU+.

WILLIAMS, SUCKEY, 7, F, (--), M, SC, 342, 325, CHAS-. In HH of Mary Williams f 38 mulatto born SC.

WILLIAMS, SUSAN, 60, F, (--), B, SC, 460, 418, CHAS+.

WILLIAMS, SUSAN, 35, F, (--), B, SC, 454, 411, CHAS.

WILLIAMS, SUSAN, 5, F, (--), M, SC, 248, 248, GEOR*. In HH of Affey Williams m 54 mulatto born SC.

WILLIAMS, SUSANNAH, 8, F, (--), M, SC, 196, 196, CHAS3. In HH of William Williams m 45 mulatto born SC.

WILLIAMS, THEODORE, 8, M, (--), M, SC, 782, 740, CHAS+. In HH of Cinda Williams f 37 mulatto born SC.

WILLIAMS, THOMAS, 21, M, Carpenter, M, SC, 166, 156, CHAS-. In HH of Sarah Barner f 28 mulatto born SC.

WILLIAMS, THOMAS, 14, M, (--), B, SC, 273, 273, BEAU+. In HH of Charles Scott m 27 mulatto born SC.

WILLIAMS, THOMAS, 9, M, (--), M, SC, 196, 196, CHAS3. In HH of William Williams m 45 mulatto born SC.

WILLIAMS, WILLIAM, 45, M,

Laborer, M, SC, 196, 196, CHAS3.

WILLIAMS, WILLIAM, 40, M, Drayman, M, SC, 782, 740, CHAS+. In HH of Cinda Williams f 37 mulatto born SC.

WILLIAMS, WILLIAM, 14, M, (--), M, SC, 703, 695, CHAS%. In HH of Ann Williams f 40 mulatto born SC.

WILLIAMS, WM., 18, M, (--), M, SC, 248, 248, GEOR*. In HH of Affey Williams m 54 mulatto born SC.

WILLIAMSON, A.R., 7, M, (--), M, SC, 41, 41, CHAS2. In HH of L. Williamson f 26 mulatto born SC.

WILLIAMSON, ANNABEL, 4, F, (--), M, SC, 2218, 2218, BARN. In HH of Jusnes Williamson m 26 mulatto born SC.

WILLIAMSON, CAPTAIN, 90, M, Farmer, B, SC, 972, 949, CHAS%.

WILLIAMSON, CATHARINE, 35, F, (--), B, SC, 574, 566, CHAS%.

WILLIAMSON, CHARLES, 8, M, (--), B, ?, 12, 12, BEAU#. In HH of Stephen Williamson m 28 black.

WILLIAMSON, CLARA, 3, F, (--), B, SC, 574, 566, CHAS%. In HH of Catharine Williamson f 35 black born SC.

WILLIAMSON, E. C., 9, F, (--), M, SC, 41, 41, CHAS2. In HH of L. Williamson f 26 mulatto born SC.

WILLIAMSON, FRANCIS, 2, M, (--), B, ?, 12, 12, BEAU#. In HH of Stephen Williamson m 28 black.

WILLIAMSON, HENRY, 6, M, (--), B, ?, 12, 12, BEAU#. In HH of Stephen Williamson m 28 black.

WILLIAMSON, JAMES, 25, M, (--), M, SC, 302, 302, CHAS%.

WILLIAMSON, JULIA, 6, F, (--), B, SC, 574, 566, CHAS%. In HH of Catharine Williamson f 35 black born SC.

WILLIAMSON, JUSNES, 26, M, Planter, M, SC, 2218, 2218, BARN.

WILLIAMSON, L., 26, F, (--), M, SC, 41, 41, CHAS2.

WILLIAMSON, MARGARET, 30, F,

(--), B, SC, 574, 566, CHAS%. In HH of Catharine Williamson f 35 black born SC.

WILLIAMSON, MARY, 28, F, (--), B, , 12, 12, BEAU#. In HH of Stephen Williamson m 28 black.

WILLIAMSON, MARY, 14, F, (--), B, SC, 574, 566, CHAS%. In HH of Catharine Williamson f 35 black born SC.

WILLIAMSON, MARY ANN, 70, F, (--), M, SC, 972, 949, CHAS%. In HH of Captain Williamson m 90 black born SC.

WILLIAMSON, NELSON, 10, M, (--), B, SC, 574, 566, CHAS%. In HH of Catharine Williamson f 35 black born SC.

WILLIAMSON, R. J. C., 2, M, (--), M, SC, 41, 41, CHAS2. In HH of L. Williamson f 26 mulatto born SC.

WILLIAMSON, SAMUEL, 40, M, Drayman, B, SC, 574, 566, CHAS%. In HH of Catharine Williamson f 35 black born SC.

WILLIAMSON, SAMUEL, 6, M, (--), B, SC, 574, 566, CHAS%. In HH of Catharine Williamson f 35 black born SC.

WILLIAMSON, SARAH, 25, F, (--), M, SC, 2218, 2218, BARN. In HH of Jusnes Williamson m 26 mulatto born SC.

WILLIAMSON, SARAH, 8, F, (--), B, SC, 574, 566, CHAS%. In HH of Catharine Williamson f 35 black born SC.

WILLIAMSON, STEPHEN, 28, M, (--), B, ?, 12, 12, BEAU#.

WILLIAMSON, THOMAS, 10, M, (--), B, ?, 12, 12, BEAU#. In HH of Stephen Williamson m 28 black.

WILLIAMSON, THOMAS, 4, M, (--), B, SC, 574, 566, CHAS%. In HH of Catharine Williamson f 35 black born SC.

WILLIAMSON, WILLIAM, 17, M, Butcher, B, SC, 574, 566, CHAS%. In HH of Catharine Williamson f 35 black born SC.

WILLIAMSON, WINIFRED, 2, F, (--), M, SC, 2218, 2218, BARN. In HH of Jusnes Williamson m 26 mulatto born SC.

WILLIMAN, LIPEY, 70, F, (--), M, MD, 971, 948, CHAS%. In HH of Alexander Norsett m 42 mulatto born SC.

WILLMORE, WILLIAM, 24, M, Tailor, M, SC, 579, 560, RICH.

WILLSON, MARGARET, 13, F, (--), M, SC, 2254, 2254, GREE. In HH of Margarit Walker f 42 mulatto born SC.

WILLSON, MEDORD, 11, F, (--), M, SC, 2254, 2254, GREE. In HH of Margarit Walker f 42 mulatto born SC.

WILSON, {blank}, M, (--), B, SC, 412, 412, CHES. In HH of M.A. Wilson f 30 Black born SC. Wilson, {blank} age 3/12 yr.

WILSON, ABNER, 1, F, (--), B, SC, 1635, 1635, ABB. In HH of Marthene Wilson f 28 black born SC.

WILSON, ALEXANDER, 72, M, Planter, M, SC, 194, 197, RICH+.

WILSON, ALEXANDER, 1, M, (--), B, SC, 572, 564, CHAS%. In HH of Ephraim Wilson m 60 black born SC.

WILSON, ALLEN, 2, M, (--), B, SC, 507, 507, LAU. In HH of Jude Wilson f 28 black born SC.

WILSON, AMOS, 31, M, Planter, M, SC, 238, 243, RICH+.

WILSON, ANN, 45, F, (--), M, SC, 142, 142, CHAS%. In HH of John Wilson m 45 mulatto born SC.

WILSON, ANN, 2, F, (--), M, SC, 116, 118, RICH+. In HH of Shadrack Wilson m 36 mulatto born SC.

WILSON, ANNE, 8, F, (--), B, SC, 572, 564, CHAS%. In HH of Ephraim Wilson m 60 black born SC.

WILSON, ARFY, 4, F, (--), B, SC, 1164, 1143, CHAS%. In HH of Miley Wilson f 30 black born SC.

WILSON, BETTY, 80, F, (--), B, Africa, 80, 90, CHAS.

WILSON, BURNETTA, 36, F, (--), B, SC, 248, 253, RICH+. In HH of Eli

Wilson m 40 black born SC.

WILSON, CAROLINA, 1, F, (--), B, SC, 248, 253, RICH+. In HH of Eli Wilson m 40 black born SC.

WILSON, CATHERINE, 16, F, (--), M, SC, 142, 142, CHAS%. In HH of John Wilson m 45 mulatto born SC.

WILSON, D.J., 46, M, Tailor, M, SC, 119, 119, GEOR.

WILSON, DAVID, 60, M, Cropper, M, SC, 588, 588, CHFD.

WILSON, DAVID, 12, M, (--), M, SC, 119, 119, GEOR. In HH of D.J. Wilson m 46 mulatto born SC.

WILSON, DAVID, 9, M, (--), B, SC, 539, 505, CHAS*. In HH of Andrew Fowler m 89 born CT.

WILSON, DAVID, 8, M, (--), B, SC, 248, 253, RICH+. In HH of Eli Wilson m 40 black born SC.

WILSON, DOLLY, 80, F, (--), B, SC, 382, 344, CHAS+. In HH of Susan Perroneau f 25 mulatto born SC.

WILSON, E. ANN, 41, F, (--), M, SC, 119, 119, GEOR. In HH of D.J. Wilson m 46 mulatto born SC.

WILSON, ELI, 40, F, (--), B, SC, 248, 253, RICH+.

WILSON, ELIZA, 30, F, (--), B, SC, 1634, 1634, ABB.

WILSON, ELIZA, 18, F, (--), M, SC, 142, 142, CHAS%. In HH of John Wilson m 45 mulatto born SC.

WILSON, ELIZABETH, 17, F, (--), B, SC, 505, 505, LAU. In HH of James Young m 72 born SC.

WILSON, ELIZABETH, 7, F, (--), M, SC, 1635, 1635, ABB. In HH of Marthene Wilson f 28 black born SC.

WILSON, ELIZABETH, 4, F, (--), M, SC, 234, 239, RICH+. In HH of Martha Wilson f 33 mulatto born SC.

WILSON, ELLEN, 2, F, (--), B, SC, 506, 506, LAU. In HH of Jane Wilson f 70 black born SC.

WILSON, EPHRAIM, 60, M, (--), B, SC, 572, 564, CHAS%.

WILSON, ESTHER, 4, F, (--), M, SC,

116, 118, RICH+. In HH of Shadrack Wilson m 36 mulatto born SC.

WILSON, FLANDER, 37, M, (--), B, SC, 809, 792, CHAS%.

WILSON, GEORGEANA, 4, M, (--), M, SC, 448, 448, CHFD. In HH of Houdson Wilson m 47 mulatto born SC.

WILSON, GEORGE, 2, M, (--), B, SC, 412, 412, CHES. In HH of M.A. Wilson f 30 Black born SC.

WILSON, GIBSON, 47, M, Blacksmith, B, SC, 326, 326, CHFD.

WILSON, GILL, 14, M, Bootmaker, M, SC, 1009, 986, CHAS-. In HH of John Lewis m 40 mulatto born SC.

WILSON, HAMILTON, 11, M, (--), B, SC, 507, 507, LAU. In HH of Jude Wilson f 28 black born SC.

WILSON, HANNAH, 73, F, (--), M, SC, 326, 326, CHFD. In HH of Gibson Wilson m 47 black born SC.

WILSON, HARRIET, 6, F, (--), M, SC, 1634, 1634, ABB. In HH of Eliza Wilson f 30 black born SC.

WILSON, HARRIET, 5, F, (--), B, SC, 412, 412, CHES. In HH of M.A. Wilson f 30 Black born SC.

WILSON, HENRY, 9, M, (--), M, SC, 448, 448, CHFD. In HH of Houdson Wilson m 47 mulatto born SC.

WILSON, HOUDSON, 47, M, Blacksmith, M, SC, 448, 448, CHFD.

WILSON, JAMES, 26, M, Porter, M, SC, 420, 418, CHAS%. In HH of Margaret Pencils f 38 mulatto born SC.

WILSON, JAMES, 13, M, (--), M, SC, 246, 251, RICH+. In HH of Shade Wilson m 56 mulatto born SC.

WILSON, JAMES, 9, M, (--), M, SC, 234, 239, RICH+. In HH of Martha Wilson f 33 mulatto born SC.

WILSON, JAMES, 8, M, (--), B, SC, 1164, 1143, CHAS%. In HH of Miley Wilson f 30 black born SC.

WILSON, JAMES, 7, M, (--), M, SC, 1634, 1634, ABB. In HH of Eliza Wilson f 30 black born SC.

WILSON, JAMES, 4, M, (--), B, SC, 248, 253, RICH+. In HH of Eli Wilson m 40 black born SC.

WILSON, JAMES T., 4, M, (--), B, SC, 88, 88, LAU. In HH of Martin Wilson m 45 black born SC.

WILSON, JANE, 70, F, (--), B, SC, 506, 506, LAU.

WILSON, JANE, 13, F, (--), B, SC, 809, 792, CHAS%. In HH of Flander Wilson m 37 black born SC.

WILSON, JANE, 8, F, (--), B, SC, 507, 507, LAU. In HH of Jude Wilson f 28 black born SC.

WILSON, JEREMIAH, 35, M, Carpenter, B, SC, 861, 838, CHAS%.

WILSON, JIM, 1, M, (--), B, SC, 981, 981, LAU. In HH of Tilda Wilson f 25 black born SC.

WILSON, JOEL, 10, M, (--), B, SC, 248, 253, RICH+. In HH of Eli Wilson m 40 black born SC.

WILSON, JOHN, 76, M, (--), B, Africa, 80, 90, CHAS. In HH of Betty Wilson f 80 black born Africa.

WILSON, JOHN, 45, M, Cabinet maker, M, SC, 142, 142, CHAS%.

WILSON, JOHN, 15, M, (--), M, SC, 247, 252, RICH+. In HH of Sarah Wilson f 40 mulatto born SC.

WILSON, JOHN, 10, M, (--), B, SC, 1931, 1931, LAU. In HH of Martha Wilson f 35 black born SC.

WILSON, JOHN, 9, M, (--), B, SC, 809, 792, CHAS%. In HH of Flander Wilson m 37 black born SC.

WILSON, JOHN, 8, M, (--), M, SC, 119, 119, GEOR. In HH of D.J. Wilson m 46 mulatto born SC.

WILSON, JOHN, 5, M, (--), B, SC, 981, 981, LAU. In HH of Tilda Wilson f 25 black born SC.

WILSON, JOHN, 1, M, (--), M, SC, 1634, 1634, ABB. In HH of Eliza Wilson f 30 black born SC.

WILSON, JOHN, 1, M, (--), M, SC, 238, 243, RICH+. In HH of Amos Wilson m 31 mulatto born SC.

WILSON, JOSEPH, 12, M, (--), M, SC, 382, 344, CHAS+. In HH of Susan Perroneau f 25 mulatto born SC.

WILSON, JOSEPH, 12, M, (--), B, SC, 1164, 1143, CHAS%. In HH of Miley Wilson f 30 black born SC.

WILSON, JOSEPH, 6, M, (--), B, SC, 572, 564, CHAS%. In HH of Ephraim Wilson m 60 black born SC.

WILSON, JUDE, 28, F, (--), B, SC, 507, 507, LAU.

WILSON, JUDY, 16, F, (--), M, SC, 405, 405, CHFD. In HH of Reily Wilson m 30 mulatto born SC.

WILSON, KIT, 5, F, (--), B, SC, 506, 506, LAU. In HH of Jane Wilson f 70 black born SC.

WILSON, L., 7, F, (--), B, SC, 412, 412, CHES. In HH of M.A. Wilson f 30 Black born SC.

WILSON, LEVI, 10, M, (--), M, SC, 1634, 1634, ABB. In HH of Eliza Wilson f 30 black born SC.

WILSON, LOUISA, 40, F, (--), M, SC, 116, 118, RICH+. In HH of Shadrack Wilson m 36 mulatto born SC.

WILSON, LOUISA, 8, F, (--), M, SC, 116, 118, RICH+. In HH of Shadrack Wilson m 36 mulatto born SC.

WILSON, LYDIA, 3, F, (--), M, SC, 238, 243, RICH+. In HH of Amos Wilson m 31 mulatto born SC.

WILSON, M., 8, F, (--), B, SC, 412, 412, CHES. In HH of M.A. Wilson f 30 Black born SC.

WILSON, M.A., 30, F, (--), B, SC, 412, 412, CHES.

WILSON, MARIA, 32, F, (--), B, SC, 809, 792, CHAS%. In HH of Flander Wilson m 37 black born SC.

WILSON, MARTHA, 37, F, (--), B, SC, 1003, 1007, And. In HH of Robert Wilson m 52 black born SC.

WILSON, MARTHA, 35, F, (--), B, SC, 1931, 1931, LAU.

WILSON, MARTHA, 33, F, (--), M, SC, 234, 239, RICH+.

WILSON, MARTHA, 6, F, (--), M, SC, 119, 119, GEOR. In HH of D.J. Wilson m 46 mulatto born SC.

WILSON, MARTHA, 5, F, (--), B, SC, 248, 253, RICH+. In HH of Eli Wilson m 40 black born SC.

WILSON, MARTHA, 5, F, (--), M, SC, 238, 243, RICH+. In HH of Amos Wilson m 31 mulatto born SC.

WILSON, MARTHENE, 28, F, (--), B, SC, 1635, 1635, ABB.

WILSON, MARTIN, 45, F, Farmer, B, SC, 88, 88, LAU.

WILSON, MARTIN, 15, M, (--), B, SC, 507, 507, LAU. In HH of Jude Wilson f 28 black born SC.

WILSON, MARTIN, 12, M, (--), B, SC, 981, 981, LAU. In HH of Tilda Wilson f 25 black born SC.

WILSON, MARY, 45, F, (--), B, SC, 466, 466, CHFD. In HH of Smith Wilson m 50 black born SC.

WILSON, MARY, 23, F, (--), M, SC, 238, 243, RICH+. In HH of Amos Wilson m 31 mulatto born SC.

WILSON, MARY, 13, F, (--), M, SC, 448, 448, CHFD. In HH of Houdson Wilson m 47 mulatto born SC.

WILSON, MARY, 10, F, (--), B, SC, 572, 564, CHAS%. In HH of Ephraim Wilson m 60 black born SC.

WILSON, MARY, 8, F, (--), B, SC, 1931, 1931, LAU. In HH of Martha Wilson f 35 black born SC.

WILSON, MARY, 6, F, (--), B, SC, 412, 412, CHES. In HH of M.A. Wilson f 30 Black born SC.

WILSON, MARY L., 16, F, (--), M, SC, 119, 119, GEOR. In HH of D.J. Wilson m 46 mulatto born SC.

WILSON, MARYANN, 12, F, (--), M, SC, 1635, 1635, ABB. In HH of Marthene Wilson f 28 black born SC.

WILSON, MATHA J., 8, F, (--), B, SC, 88, 88, LAU. In HH of Martin Wilson m 45 black born SC.

WILSON, MILEY, 30, F, (--), B, SC, 1164, 1143, CHAS%.

WILSON, NANCY, 25, F, (--), B, SC, 506, 506, LAU. In HH of Jane Wilson f 70 black born SC.

WILSON, NANCY J., 8, F, (--), M, SC, 1634, 1634, ABB. In HH of Eliza Wilson f 30 black born SC.

WILSON, NELSON, 1, M, (--), B, SC, 507, 507, LAU. In HH of Jude Wilson f 28 black born SC.

WILSON, PATSY, 55, F, (--), M, SC, 246, 251, RICH+. In HH of Shade Wilson m 56 mulatto born SC.

WILSON, PERCILLA, 25, F, (--), B, SC, 572, 564, CHAS%. In HH of Ephraim Wilson m 60 black born SC.

WILSON, PERMELIA, 44, F, (--), B, SC, 88, 88, LAU. In HH of Martin Wilson m 45 black born SC.

WILSON, PHEBE, 36, F, (--), M, SC, 405, 405, CHFD. In HH of Reily Wilson m 30 mulatto born SC.

WILSON, REILY, 30, M, Pilot, M, SC, 405, 405, CHFD.

WILSON, REUBIN B., 6, M, (--), B, SC, 88, 88, LAU. In HH of Martin Wilson m 45 black born SC.

WILSON, ROBERT, 52, M, Farmer, B, SC, 1003, 1007, And.

WILSON, ROBERT, 3, M, (--), B, SC, 248, 253, RICH+. In HH of Eli Wilson m 40 black born SC.

WILSON, ROBERT J., 19, M, (--), M, SC, 537, 537, DARL. In HH of Richd. G. Hunt m 30 mulatto born SC.

WILSON, ROBERT., 15, M, (--), M, SC, 119, 119, GEOR. In HH of D.J. Wilson m 46 mulatto born SC.

WILSON, ROSE, 45, F, (--), B, SC, 1015, 992, CHAS-.

WILSON, SAMUEL, 4, M, (--), M, SC, 246, 251, RICH+. In HH of Shade Wilson m 56 mulatto born SC.

WILSON, SARAH, 54, F, (--), M, Germany {sic}, 347, 330, CHAS-.

WILSON, SARAH, 40, F, (--), M, SC, 247, 252, RICH+.

WILSON, SARAH, 36, F, (--), M, SC, 448, 448, CHFD. In HH of Houdson Wilson m 47 mulatto born SC.

WILSON, SARAH, 8, F, (--), M, SC, 246, 251, RICH+. In HH of Shade Wilson m 56 mulatto born SC.

WILSON, SARAH, 3, F, (--), B, SC, 572, 564, CHAS%. In HH of Ephraim Wilson m 60 black born SC.

WILSON, SHADE, 56, M, Planter, M, SC, 246, 251, RICH+.

WILSON, SHADRACK, 36, M, Planter, M, SC, 116, 118, RICH+.

WILSON, SMITH, 50, M, Blacksmith, B, SC, 466, 466, CHFD.

WILSON, SQUIRE, 6, M, (--), B, SC, 507, 507, LAU. In HH of Jude Wilson f 28 black born SC.

WILSON, SUSAN, 31, F, (--), B, SC, 861, 838, CHAS%. In HH of Jeremiah Wilson m 35 black born SC.

WILSON, SUSAN, 8, F, (--), M, SC, 382, 344, CHAS+. In HH of Susan Perroneau f 25 mulatto born SC.

WILSON, THOMAS, 45, M, Carpenter, M, SC, 424, 424, COLL.

WILSON, TILDA, 25, F, (--), B, SC, 981, 981, LAU.

WILSON, UNITY, 6, F, (--), M, SC, 238, 243, RICH+. In HH of Amos Wilson m 31 mulatto born SC.

WILSON, WADE, 22, M, (--), M, SC, 247, 252, RICH+. In HH of Sarah Wilson f 40 mulatto born SC.

WILSON, WARREN, 15, M, (--), M, SC, 64, 64, PICK+. In HH of James Grant m 72 born SC.

WILSON, WASHINGTON, 23, M, Laborer, B, SC, 572, 564, CHAS%. In HH of Ephraim Wilson m 60 black born SC.

WILSON, WASHINGTON, 9, M, (--), M, SC, 246, 251, RICH+. In HH of Shade Wilson m 56 mulatto born SC.

WILSON, WILLIAM, 19, M, (--), B, SC, 507, 507, LAU. In HH of Jude Wilson f 28 black born SC.

WILSON, WILLIAM, 11, M, (--), M, SC, 246, 251, RICH+. In HH of Shade Wilson m 56 mulatto born SC.

WILSON, WILLIAM, 9, M, (--), M, SC, 1635, 1635, ABB. In HH of Marthene Wilson f 28 black born SC.

WILSON, WILLIAM, 7, M, (--), M, SC, 448, 448, CHFD. In HH of Houdson Wilson m 47 mulatto born SC.

WILSON, WILLIAM H., 5, M, (--), M, SC, 1634, 1634, ABB. In HH of Eliza

Wilson f 30 black born SC.

WILSON, WM., 25, M, Laborer, M, SC, 151, 151, DARL.

WINDHAM, AMELIA, 20, F, (--), M, SC, 67, 67, COLL+. In HH of Nancy Windham f 50 mulatto born SC.

WINDHAM, DANIEL, 12, M, (--), M, SC, 67, 67, COLL+. In HH of Nancy Windham f 50 mulatto born SC.

WINDHAM, MARY, 25, F, (--), M, SC, 95, 95, COLL+. In HH of Sylvester Windham m 25 mulatto born SC.

WINDHAM, NANCY, 50, F, (--), M, SC, 67, 67, COLL+.

WINDHAM, RICHARD H., 2, M, (--), M, SC, 95, 95, COLL+. In HH of Sylvester Windham m 25 mulatto born SC.

WINDHAM, SOPHIONIA, 18, F, (--), M, SC, 67, 67, COLL+. In HH of Nancy Windham f 50 mulatto born SC.

WINDHAM, SYLVESTER, 25, M, Farmer, M, SC, 95, 95, COLL+.

WINDOM, C.H.T., 5, M, (--), M, SC, 91, 91, CHAS2. In HH of L. Windom m 45 mulatto born SC.

WINDOM, J.D., 3, M, (--), M, SC, 91, 91, CHAS2. In HH of L. Windom m 45 mulatto born SC.

WINDOM, L., 45, M, Farmer, M, SC, 91, 91, CHAS2.

WINDOM, W.H., 15, M, (--), M, SC, 91, 91, CHAS2. In HH of L. Windom m 45 mulatto born SC.

WINEGAM, CAPUS, 4, M, (--), M, SC, 552, 552, FAIR. In HH of Rebecca Winegam f 30 mulatto born SC.

WINEGAM, HARRIET, 14, F, (--), M, SC, 552, 552, FAIR. In HH of Rebecca Winegam f 30 mulatto born SC.

WINEGAM, HENRY, 8, M, (--), M, SC, 552, 552, FAIR. In HH of Rebecca Winegam f 30 mulatto born SC.

WINEGAM, JOHN, 4, M, (--), M, SC, 552, 552, FAIR. In HH of Rebecca Winegam f 30 mulatto born SC.

WINEGAM, REBECCA, 30, F, (--), M, SC, 552, 552, FAIR.

WINEGAM, WYATT, 9, M, (--), M, SC, 552, 552, FAIR. In HH of Rebecca Winegam f 30 mulatto born SC.

WINNINGHAM, EDWARD, 19, M, (--), M, SC, 343, 343, COLL*. In HH of Henry Winningham m 45 mulatto born SC.

WINNINGHAM, HENRY, 45, M, Laborer, M, SC, 343, 343, COLL*.

WINNINGHAM, MARY ANN, 21, F, (--), M, SC, 343, 343, COLL*. In HH of Henry Winningham m 45 mulatto born SC.

WINNINGHAM, RACHEL, 30, F, (--), M, SC, 343, 343, COLL*. In HH of Henry Winningham m 45 mulatto born SC.

WINNINGHAM, RACHEL, 0, F, (--), M, SC, 343, 343, COLL*. In HH of Henry Winningham m 45 mulatto born SC. Rachel Winningham age 8/12 yr.

WINSLOW, ELIZA, 20, F, Shop keeper, M, SC, 165, 165, CHAS%. In HH of John B. Otten m 29 born Germany.

WIRES, EMALINE, 17, F, (--), M, SC, 361, 361, EDGE*. In HH of Sally Wires f 35 mulatto born SC.

WIRES, MAHALA, 14, F, (--), M, SC, 361, 361, EDGE*. In HH of Sally Wires f 35 mulatto born SC.

WIRES, SALLY, 35, F, (--), M, SC, 361, 361, EDGE*.

WIRES, WILSON, 17, M, (--), M, SC, 361, 361, EDGE*. In HH of Sally Wires f 35 mulatto born SC.

WISE, ESTHER, 13, F, (--), M, SC, 223, 227, RICH+. In HH of Susan Harris f 22 mulatto born SC.

WISSINGER, JAMES, 16, M, Barber, M, SC, 820, 803, CHAS%. In HH of George Douglas m 22 mulatto born SC.

WITHERSPOON, ISAAC, 38, M, (--), B, SC, 125, 125, KERS. In HH of Susan Scott f, 60 mulatto born SC.

WOOD, ANNE, 10, F, (--), M, SC, 669, 627, CHAS+. In HH of Ellen Wood f 38 mulatto born SC.

WOOD, CATHERINE, 30, F, (--), M,

SC, 178, 178, CHAS%.

WOOD, ELLEN, 38, F, (--), M, SC, 669, 627, CHAS+.

WOOD, JOHN, 19, M, Cabinet maker, M, SC, 669, 627, CHAS+. In HH of Ellen Wood f 38 mulatto born SC.

WOOD, RHETT, 9, M, (--), M, SC, 95, 95, COLL+. In HH of Sylvester Windham m 25 mulatto born SC.

WOOD, SUSANNAH, 8, F, (--), M, SC, 669, 627, CHAS+. In HH of Ellen Wood f 38 mulatto born SC.

WOOD, THOMAS, 40, M, Cabinet maker, M, SC, 669, 627, CHAS+. In HH of Ellen Wood f 38 mulatto born SC.

WOOD, WM., 8, M, (--), M, SC, 95, 95, COLL+. In HH of Sylvester Windham m 25 mulatto born SC.

WOODEY, BETSEY, 40, F, Servant, B, SC, 33, 41, CHAS. In HH of Henry S. Rice m 56 born MA.

WORD, FRANKLIN, 28, M, (--), M, SC, 179, 179, CHAS%. In HH of Susan Word f 30 mulatto born SC.

WORD, MARSHAL, 2, M, (--), M, SC, 179, 179, CHAS%. In HH of Susan Word f 30 mulatto born SC.

WORD, SUSAN, 30, F, (--), M, SC, 179, 179, CHAS%.

WORD, SUSAN, 4, F, (--), M, SC, 179, 179, CHAS%. In HH of Susan Word f 30 mulatto born SC.

WORD, WILLIAM, 6, M, (--), M, SC, 179, 179, CHAS%. In HH of Susan Word f 30 mulatto born SC.

WORSTELL, ELIZA, 23, F, (--), B, SC, 469, 477, RICH+. In HH of Francis Worstell m 29 black born SC.

WORSTELL, ELIZA, 1, F, (--), B, SC, 469, 477, RICH+. In HH of Francis Worstell m 29 black born SC.

WORSTELL, FRANCIS, 29, M, Laborer, B, SC, 469, 477,? RICH+.

WORSTELL, JAMES, 3, M, (--), B, SC, 469, 477, RICH+. In HH of Francis Worstell m 29 black born SC.

WORTHY, MARY A., 19, F, (--), M, SC, 1407, 1407, CHES. In HH of Preston Worthy m 39 born SC.

WRAGG, ELIZABETH, 60, F, (--), B, SC, 137, 137, GEOR.

WRIGHT, ANDREW, 14, M, (--), B, SC, 810, 810, YORK. In HH of Harvey Wright m 53 black born York Dist., SC.

WRIGHT, ANN, 52, M, (--), M, SC, 723, 714, CHAS%.

WRIGHT, ANN, 20, F, (--), B, SC, 810, 810, YORK. In HH of Harvey Wright m 53 black born York Dist., SC.

WRIGHT, C., 12, M, (--), M, SC, 599, 599, LANC*. In HH of E. Wright m 50 mulatto born SC.

WRIGHT, CAROLINE, 32, F, (--), M, SC, 173, 173, YORK*.

WRIGHT, CAROLINE, 1, F, (--), B, SC, 1221, 1221, CHES. In HH of Desly Wright f 30 black born SC.

WRIGHT, CATHARINE, 93, F, (--), M, SC, 666, 666, YORK. In HH of John Wright m 58 m mulatto born Lancaster Dist., SC.

WRIGHT, CATHARINE, 22, F, (--), B, SC, 810, 810, YORK. In HH of Harvey Wright m 53 black born York Dist., SC.

WRIGHT, CYNTHIA, 44, F, (--), B, SC, 810, 810, YORK. In HH of Harvey Wright m 53 black born York Dist., SC.

WRIGHT, DESLY, 30, F, (--), B, SC, 1221, 1221, CHES.

WRIGHT, DRURY, 8, M, (--), M, SC, 666, 666, YORK. In HH of John Wright m 58 m mulatto born Lancaster Dist., SC.

WRIGHT, E., 50, M, Laborer, M, SC, 599, 599, LANC*.

WRIGHT, E. A., 8, F, (--), M, SC, 599, 599, LANC*. In HH of E. Wright m 50 mulatto born SC.

WRIGHT, ELIZABETH, 50, F, (--), M, NC, 666, 666, YORK. In HH of John Wright m 58 m mulatto born Lancaster Dist., SC.

WRIGHT, ELIZABETH, 30, F, (--), B, SC, 598, 590, CHAS%.

WRIGHT, ELIZABETH, 7, F, (--), B, SC, 810, 810, YORK. In HH of Harvey Wright m 53 black born York Dist., SC.

WRIGHT, ELIZABETH, 5, F, (--), M, SC, 1221, 1221, CHES. In HH of Desly Wright f 30 black born SC.

WRIGHT, ELIZABETH J., 10, F, (--), M, SC, 7, 7, YORK*. In HH of Lydia Wright m 35 mulatto born SC.

WRIGHT, ELVIRA, 15, F, (--), B, SC, 810, 810, YORK. In HH of Harvey Wright m 53 black born York Dist., SC.

WRIGHT, ESENESS E., 5, F, (--), M, SC, 1136, 1136, YORK. In HH of James Dunn m 58 born NC.

WRIGHT, GEORGE, 48, M, Carpenter, M, SC, 723, 714, CHAS%. In HH of Ann Wright f 52 mulatto born SC.

WRIGHT, H.A., 6, F, (--), M, SC, 599, 599, LANC*. In HH of E. Wright m 50 mulatto born SC.

WRIGHT, HARVEY, 53, M, (--), B, SC, 810, 810, YORK.

WRIGHT, JAMES, 25, M, (--), M, SC, 198, 198, YORK*.

WRIGHT, JOHN, 58, M, Shoemaker, M, SC, 666, 666, YORK.

WRIGHT, JOHN, 18, M, Laborer, M, SC, 599, 599, LANC*. In HH of E. Wright m 50 mulatto born SC. L. Wright 6/12 yr.

WRIGHT, JOHN, 15, M, (--), M, SC, 666, 666, YORK. In HH of John Wright m 58 m mulatto born Lancaster Dist., SC.

WRIGHT, JOHN F., 2, M, (--), M, SC, 7, 7, YORK*. In HH of Lydia Wright m 35 mulatto born SC.

WRIGHT, JOSEPH N., 3, F, (--), B, SC, 1221, 1221, CHES. In HH of Desly Wright f 30 black born SC.

WRIGHT, L., 36, F, (--), M, SC, 599, 599, LANC*. In HH of E. Wright m 50 mulatto born SC.

WRIGHT, L., 0, F, (--), M, SC, 599, 599, LANC*. In HH of E. Wright m 50 mulatto born SC. L. Wright 6/12 yr.

WRIGHT, LEANDER, 12, M, (--), B, SC, 810, 810, YORK. In HH of Harvey Wright m 53 black born York Dist., SC.

WRIGHT, LEOFLESS, 10, M, (--), B, SC, 810, 810, YORK. In HH of Harvey Wright m 53 black born York Dist., SC.

WRIGHT, LEONDER, 7, M, (--), B, SC, 1221, 1221, CHES. In HH of Desly Wright f 30 black born SC.

WRIGHT, LOUISA, 16, F, (--), M, SC, 723, 714, CHAS%. In HH of Ann Wright f 52 mulatto born SC.

WRIGHT, LUCINDA, 30, F, (--), M, SC, 666, 666, YORK. In HH of John Wright m 58 m mulatto born Lancaster Dist., SC.

WRIGHT, LYDIA, 35, F, (--), M, SC, 7, 7, YORK*.

WRIGHT, M., 10, F, (--), M, SC, 599, 599, LANC*. In HH of E. Wright m 50 mulatto born SC.

WRIGHT, MARCUS, 3, M, (--), M, SC, 173, 173, YORK*. In HH of Caroline Wright f 32 mulatto born York Dist., SC.

WRIGHT, MARTHA L., 6, F, (--), M, SC, 7, 7, YORK*. In HH of Lydia Wright m 35 mulatto born SC.

WRIGHT, MARY, 17, F, (--), M, SC, 666, 666, YORK. In HH of John Wright m 58 m mulatto born Lancaster Dist., SC.

WRIGHT, MARY, 7, F, (--), B, SC, 598, 590, CHAS%. In HH of Elizabeth Wright f 30 black born SC.

WRIGHT, MISSISSIPPIANA, 2, F, (--), B, SC, 810, 810, YORK. In HH of Harvey Wright m 53 black born York Dist., SC.

WRIGHT, R., 2, M, (--), M, SC, 599, 599, LANC*. In HH of E. Wright m 50 mulatto born SC.

WRIGHT, ROBERT, 1, M, (--), M, SC, 1136, 1136, YORK. In HH of James Dunn m 58 born NC.

WRIGHT, RUTHY C., 9, F, (--), M, SC, 1136, 1136, YORK. In HH of James Dunn m 58 born NC.

WRIGHT, S. J., 14, F, (--), M, SC, 599, 599, LANC*. In HH of E. Wright m 50 mulatto born SC.

WRIGHT, SARAH, 30, F, (--), M, SC, 171, 171, YORK*.

WRIGHT, SARAH A., 11, F, (--), M,

SC, 1136, 1136, YORK. In HH of James Dunn m 58 born NC.

WRIGHT, SARAH L., 12, F, (--), M, SC, 7, 7, YORK*. In HH of Lydia Wright m 35 mulatto born SC.

WRIGHT, SUSAN, 6, F, (--), M, SC, 173, 173, YORK*. In HH of Caroline Wright f 32 mulatto born York Dist., SC.

WRIGHT, THOMAS, 18, M, Farmer, B, SC, 1174, 1174, CHES. In HH of D.W. Hardin m 41 born SC.

WRIGHT, WILLIAM, 18, M, (--), B, SC, 810, 810, YORK. In HH of Harvey Wright m 53 black born York Dist., SC.

WRIGHT, WILLIAM, 9, M, (--), B, SC, 598, 590, CHAS%. In HH of Elizabeth Wright f 30 black born SC.

WRIGHT, WILLIAM A., 9, M, (--), M, SC, 7, 7, YORK*. In HH of Lydia Wright m 35 mulatto born SC.

Y

YARBOROUGH, CATY, 50, F, (--), M, SC, 2076, 2083, EDGE.

YARBOROUGH, JANE, 25, F, (--), M, SC, 2076, 2083, EDGE. In HH of Caty Yarborough f 50 mulatto born SC.

YARBOROUGH, MARY, 3, F, (--), M, SC, 2076, 2083, EDGE. In HH of Caty Yarborough f 50 mulatto born SC.

YARBOROUGH, WILLIAM, 35, M, Shoemaker, B, SC, 109, 109, FAIR. In HH of John Dankins m 61 born SC.

YOUNG, JEMIMA, 10, F, (--), M, SC, 502, 485, CHAS-. In HH of Martha Young f 40 mulatto born SC.

YOUNG, JIM, 11, M, (--), B, SC, 595, 595, MARL. In HH of Job Weatherly m 35 born SC.

YOUNG, JOHN, 4, M, (--), B, SC, 580, 580, MARL. In HH of Mary Jackson f 54 mulatto born SC.

YOUNG, JULIANA, 14, F, (--), M, SC, 502, 485, CHAS-. In HH of Martha Young f 40 mulatto born SC.

YOUNG, MARTHA, 40, F, (--), M, SC, 502, 485, CHAS-.

YOUNG, MARY, 3, F, (--), B, SC, 571, 571, MARL. In HH of Ceasar Allison m 73 black born SC.

YOUNG, MIKE, 9, M, (--), B, SC, 571, 571, MARL. In HH of Ceasar Allison m 73 black born SC.

YOUNG, PHILIP, 66, M, (--), B, VA, 2178, 2178, GREE. In HH of John J.Jones m 40 born SC.

YOUNG, WILIE, 16, M, Laborer, B, SC, 572, 572, MARL. In HH of W.A.McLeod m 30 born SC.

Z

ZEKIEL, ANN, 22, F, Dressmaker, M, SC , 177, 177, BEAU. In HH of Sarah Houston f 52 mulatto born SC.

ZEKIEL, PHILIP, 25, M, Tailor, M, SC , 177, 177, BEAU. In HH of Sarah Houston f 52 mulatto born SC.

Index Explanation

Name Index
The principal surnames are listed alphabetically in the body of the text and are not included in the name index. The index lists those surnames found elsewhere in the text. Surnames marked with an asterisk (e.g. Smith*), indicates that the person is "white" with a black or mulatto in the household.

Occupation Index
The index lists the occupations of all free blacks and mulattos found in the 1850 South Carolina census.

Place of Birth Index
The index lists the birthplace of only black and mulattos born outside of South Carolina.

Name Index

Bowe: Ammon, 24, 61
Bowen*: Fred, 84, 93, 174, 175; John, 24; Keith, 194, 196
Bowengen: Chloe, 8, 95, 140, 185
Bowers: Emiley, 24, 161, 218
Bowzar: Harry, 24
Bowzer: Judy, 24
Bowzer*: July, 214
Boyd: Caroline, 24, 25; Drucilla, 25; Jesse, 24; Rebecca, 24, 25
Boyd*: Madison, 24, 25(2)
Bracknal*: Archy, 219
Bradly*: Silas, 5
Brailsford: Edward, 34, 196; Maria, 25
Braisford: Edward, 25
Branham: Simeon, 25
Bremar: Rebecca, 3
Brewington: John, 26
Brewster*: Charles R., 134
Brigg: Elizabeth, 216; Priscilla, 216
Bristow*: William, 110, 111
Broad: Anna, 221
Brock*: C.H., 227
Brogden*: John, 26
Brooks: Silas, 26, 27, 198
Brothers: Charles, 27; Jacob, 27
Brown: Ann, 218, 219; Chancy, 28, 29; Charles, 28; Isaac, 28; Jacob, 10; Jane, 28, 154; Malcolm, 29; Malcom, 28; Peter, 27, 28, 147, 208; Prince, 28; Robert, 6; Sarah, 28; Snely, 28, 29
Brown*: Charles, 29; Samuel, 214; William, 152
Bruch: Laura, 29, 44
Bruch?: Laura, 170
Bruse*: Wm. C., 75
Bryant: Mary, 137
Bug: Charles, 29, 30; Comb, 29, 30;

Dempstand, 30;
Dempstead, 62;
Francis, 29; Peggy, 29, 30; Sarah, 29
Bugg: Betsey, 30, 31; Julia, 30; Mathew, 30, 31; Nancy, 30, 31; Rebecca, 30, 31
Bulkley: Henry, 31
Bullard: Teres, 106, 205
Bunch: Eliza, 31, 32
Bunch, Mrs.*: Isabella, 31, 32
Bunch: Joshua, 31, 32
Bunch*: Sookey, 150
Burckmeyer: Isaac, 32
Burckmyer: Esther, 32
Burdeaux: Ann, 109
Burdell: R., 32, 199; Sarah, 32
Burden: Jack, 32, 33; Moses, 32
Burie: Ellen, 33
Burke: John, 33
Burnet: Ralph, 33
Burnet*: James, 113
Burnett: Elizabeth, 33
Bury: Moses, 126, 177
Busby: James, 46, 190
Bush: Wolloughby, 34, 35
Buzzard: Joseph, 35
Bying: Betsy, 35; James, 35

C

Caldwell*: Elizabeth, 25; Hugh, 36; Samuel, 130
Calhoun: David, 36
Callaham: Lucy, 36; Patsey, 36
Callahan: Bob, 36
Calliham: Nancy, 36, 37; Sarah, 36, 37
Cambridge: Elizabeth, 26, 64
Campbell: Flora, 37; Frederick, 37(2), 38; Jane, 171; Judith, 38; Mary, 38; Nancy, 37
Campbell*: Nancy, 22
Cannon: Mary, 51; Simon, 38

Canoll: Daniel, 142
Canter: Juliet, 128
Canty: Martha, 82
Carity: Elis, 38
Carity*: Elis, 151
Carmand: Francis, 38
Carr: Glenn, 118, 119, 130; Nora, 39
Carrless: Cecelia, 39
Carsten: Anna, 39
Cart: Dinah, 39
Carter: Ellen, 39, 41, 77; Henry, 39, 40; Jas., 39, 40, 41; July, 39, 41; Mary, 39; Samuel, 40; Sarah, 40; Wesley, 40
Carter*: Mary, 41
Cassady*: Edward, 41
Cathcart*: John, 90
Cattel: Robert, 41
Ceaty*: Thomas, 40, 44
Chambers: Christiana, 41
Chambers*: B.W., 109
Chapman: James, 41, 42, 198
Charles: Cecelia, 46(2)
Charons: Len, 42
Chatters: Owen, 42
Chavas: Caroline, 43; Thos., 42; Wm., 42, 43
Chavers: John, 43; John S., 43; Lorenzo, 43; Mary, 43
Chaves: Sally, 10
Chavis: Brrry sic, 44; Brry sic, 43; James, 43
Chavous: David, 43
Chavus: Frederick, 44
Chesnut: Susan, 44
Chichister: Ellen, 44, 45
Chisolm: Andrew, 45; Sarah, 45; William, 45
Chistmas: A., 45
Chistmas*: William, 104
Christie: Elvira, 46
Chuvas: Casper, 44
Clakr: Charles, 46
Clancey: Caroline, 199

240

Clark: Aaron, 46, 47;
 Hannah, 46, 47;
 Isaac, 46; Mary,
 46, 47; Reddin, 46,
 47; Reuben, 46, 47
Clarke: John, 47, 103
Clarke*: Elizabeth, 111
Clayton: Adam, 47
Cleveland: Eliza, 47,
 48; James, 48;
 Martha, 47, 48;
 Paul, 47, 48;
 Rebecca, 48
Cline: John, 48, 49;
 Robert, 48, 49
Coates: Harriet, 49
Coats: Anthony, 217
Coble: Nancy, 49
Cochran: Thomas,
 49(2), 50
Cochron: Charles W.,
 30
Cockran: Charles, 50,
 117; James, 50,
 218
Cockran*: Benjamin,
 66
Cofield*: Thomas, 93
Cohen: Arthur P., 50;
 Bartley, 50;
 Sheldon, 50
Cohen*: Philip, 26
Colb: Thomas, 50, 123
Cole: Nancy, 51
Coleman: Cato, 51;
 John, 51; R.D., 20
Collins: Charlotte, 51;
 R.M., 51
Colmon: Samuel, 51,
 52
Colvin: Mary, 52
Commersal: Flora, 2
Commmersal: Flora, 52
Condy: Thomas D., 45,
 46
Conner: John, 52, 94
Constance: Mary, 52
Conway: Harriet, 52;
 James, 52
Conwell: George, 53,
 156
Conyers: Catherine, 51,
 53, 58, 69, 167,
 203
Cook: Minday, 53
Cook*: Henry B., 117

Cooper: Angeline, 53;
 Susan, 53
Cope*: John, 132
Cornwal: Amellia, 15
Cornwell: Catherine,
 53, 114
Corry*: Nancy, 83
Cotton: Elizabeth, 54
Council, Mr.*: J., 155
Cox: Daniel, 54; Sarah
 B., 54
Craig*: John M., 37
Crawford: Celisle, 54
Creighton: Anne, 54;
 George, 54
Croomer*: David, 20
Crosby: Mary, 55
Cuel: Wm. B., 55
Cuff: Zachariah, 55, 56
Culp*: Wm., 173
Cumbee: Elias, 56;
 Robert, 56
Cunningham: Jane, 56
Curtis: Joseph, 7; Mary,
 56
Curtis*: Joseph, 210

D

DaCosta: W.P., 56
Daimer: James, 56, 57
Dangerfield*: John R.,
 57
Dankins*: John, 237
Dart: William, 57
Dascher*: Hannah, 4,
 140
Datsieuse: V., 179
David*: J.E., 173
Davidson: George, 57
Davidson*: N.W., 216
Davis: Absolum, 57,
 58; Eliza, 57;
 Ellen, 57, 58;
 Frances, 57, 58;
 Frederick, 57, 58;
 Jane, 58(2); John,
 57; Rachel, 57;
 William, 58
Davis*: Henry, 145
Davison: Solloman, 58,
 59
Dawdle: Morris, 59
Dayl: Bowe, 67
Dayl*: Bowe, 80
Days: Eliza W., 59
Deal: George, 59

Deas: Ann, 180, 208;
 Jane, 59, 60;
 Robert, 59;
 William, 54, 86,
 202, 203
Deban: Eveline, 1
Deees: Minty, 60
Deen: Elbuson, 60;
 John, 60
DeLancey: Mary, 60
DeLarge: Jon, 60, 61;
 Mary, 73, 74
DeLeon: Emma, 61
Dempsey: Daniel, 61;
 L.W., 61
Dempsy: Richard, 61
Demuere: Mathew, 61
Dennis: David, 62;
 Eliza, 62
Dereef: Joseph, 62;
 R.E., 62, 70
Deriker: Thomas, 59
Desomire?: Sarah, 63,
 193, 194, 195, 196
Despratt: Carolina, 63
Desverniez: Isabella, 63
Devineau: Peter, 63
Devinier: F., 48, 63, 64,
 103
Dewees: Wm. C., 64
Dibble: Andrew, 60
Dickin: Louisa, 64
Dill*: N.H., 103
Dimery: Uriah, 64, 65
Dingle: Caroline, 55,
 65; Moses, 65
Diver: Amelia, 31, 65
Diverer: Priscilla, 14,
 65
Divor: Wm., 65
Dobin: Anthony, 65;
 Wm., 65
Doe: Betsey, 66;
 Edward, 66;
 Esther, 65; July,
 66; Louisa, 66;
 Sarah, 66;
 Thrallessa, 66
Donalson: Dinah, 66,
 67; Harriet, 67;
 Lucy, 66, 67
Doolittle*: Pleasant, 36,
 37
Dorman: Catherine, 67
Dorrill: Ann, 67
Douglas: Elizabeth,

Goff: Abigail, 87;
Climder, 87
Goins: John, 87;
Louisa, 87, 88;
Thos., 87, 88
Goins*: Jas., 87, 88
Goldin*: Mary, 88
Gonzalus*: B., 88
Good: Ellen, 88
Goodwyn: Isabella, 88
Goopy*: Wm., 55, 88
Gordon: Archer, 89;
Benjamin, 89, 90;
David, 89, 90;
John, 89, 90(2);
Robert, 90;
William, 89, 90;
Zachariah, 89
Gourdin*: Henry, 42
Gowing*: Charles, 225
Grain: Susan, 63, 95
Grant: Catherine, 91;
Isabella, 68, 91;
James, 91(2)
Grant*: James, 233
Gray: Jane, 91
Gray*: James F., 110
Green: Anthony, 91,
92; Lucy, 92;
Mary, 91, 92, 168
Greer: Daniel, 92;
George, 92; Mary,
92
Gregg: Ann, 93
Gregory: Isabella, 93;
Titus, 93
Griffin: George, 93;
Tenah, 75
Gripop*?: Rebecca, 93,
94
Grooms: David, 94;
Mary, 94; Thomas,
94
Gross: Rebecca W., 28
Guignard: Green, 94
Guinard: Martha, 94
Guinn*: Wm., 94
Gunter: Polly, 94, 95
Guthrey: Mary Theus,
219
Gwin: Eliza, 95(2);
Leonard, 95
Gwinn: John, 95
Gylis: John A., 133
Gylis*: John A., 54

H

Haggard*: Ann, 47
Hale: Ann, 95, 96;
Arrington, 96
Hale*: John, 212
Hall: C., 96
Halloway: Claire, 96;
Katey, 105; Mary,
96
Hallum*: Thomas, 187
Ham: Diana, 96
Hamelton: Jesse, 96,
220
Hamlin: William, 97
Hamlin*: J., 199
Hammond: David, 97;
Harriet, 51, 209
Hampton: Daphney, 97;
Ellen, 214
Hanks: Wm., 97
Hantz: Lydia, 61, 98
Harbert*: Frederic, 212
Harden: Lucretia, 156
Hardin: D.W., 14
Hardin*: D.W., 237
Hardy: Hannah, 98;
Isaac, 98; Jane, 98
Hargate*: Barbara, 118
Hariman: Enoch A., 98
Harinberg*: Henry, 156
Harmon: Archibalk, 99;
Thomas L., 99
Harper: Cely, 99, 100;
Jack, 99(2), 100;
James, 99, 100
Harris: Bolin, 9, 100(2);
C.M., 216; George,
100, 101, 208;
Isham, 190; John,
100; Moses, 100,
101; Priscilla, 100;
Robland, 100;
Stark, 101, 190;
Susan, 100, 234;
Vandal, 100, 148
Harrison: George, 101;
James, 101, 120,
152; Mary, 101
Hart: Lewis, 179
Harvy: Wm., 18, 101
Hasell: Charles, 101;
Maria, 91
Hassett: Peter, 101, 102
Hatchell*: William, 102
Hatcher: Frances, 75,

102, 205
Hathcock: Betty, 101;
John, 187
Hazard: Angline, 102;
Timothy, 102, 209;
William, 102
Hazel: Giden, 102;
Jack, 102; Jno.,
103
Hazele: David, 103
Hazzard: Esther, 103
Heimseth*: H., 53
Hemetry: Sarah, 76,
145
Hemphill*: Wm. M., 49
Hendricks: Henry, 103
Henry: Betsy, 103;
Thomas, 107, 108
Henson: Elizabeth, 103,
104, 108, 126;
Henry, 103; James,
103
Herbert*: Michael, 22,
23
Herin*: Margaret, 104
Heron*: Cornelius, 104
Hewett*: William, 158
Hicks: Ellen, 204;
Sarah, 174
Higgins*: John, 214
Hill*: Richard, 131
Hlll*: Richard, 183
Hillagas: Caroline, 32
Hillagas*: Caroline,
203
Hilligns: Celest, 104
Hilson*: John, 73
Hipp*: Andrew J., 20
Hislop*: William, 130
Hodges: Ely, 104, 185
Hoff: John, 104
Hoff*: Ann C., 37
Hogg: John, 105
Holand: James, 105
Holcombe*: Mary, 105
Holloway: Elizabeth,
105; Richard, 105
Holly: Ezekiel, 105;
Lucind, 106; Sarah,
105, 106
Holmes: Alex, 106;
Edwin, 106, 107;
Elizabeth, 106,
139, 147; Emeline,
182; Jerry, 119,
122; Mariah, 106;

Name Index

L

LaBate: Caroline, 127
Labutat: Mary, 125
Labutat*: Isidore, 125
Lackey*: William G.,
78
Lacomb: Joseph, 24,
123, 125, 174
LaCompt: Susan, 127
LaCompte: Felicity,
125
Lafarge: Emmely, 15,
33, 123
Lake: Diana, 126
LaMott: Dorell, 34
Landers: T., 191
LaPoint: Teresa, 23
LaPont: Teresa, 63
Latham: Ann, 121, 123
Laughlin*: Charles, 132
Lawrence: Ben, 126,
127; Claudia, 126;
Edward, 126, 127;
Louisa, 153; Mary,
126, 127
Lawson: Rebecca, 25
League*: Robert, 214
LeBate: Caroline, 104
LeBuff: Francis, 127
Lee: Edward, 127, 128;
Elsy, 128;
Florence, 127, 128,
129; Grace, 104,
127, 128; Henry,
127, 128; Mary
Ann, 8, 129; Sam,
127, 128; Sarah,
127
Lee*: Henry, 112;
W.C., 35
Legard: Mary, 129,
137; Susan, 129
Legare: Charles, 104;
Nathan, 129
LeGrand: Nancy, 129
Lemacks: Elizabeth,
129
Lewis: Anna, 144;
Barbara, 129, 130;
Benj., 119, 130;
Catherine, 104,
105, 130; James,
130; Jane, 130;
John, 23, 28, 68,
135, 231; Peter,

130; Sarah, 130
Libby*: William, 168
Limehouse, Jr.*: Robert
J., 76
Linson, Mrs.*:
Elizabeth, 152
Liston: Rose, 131
Livingston: Kate, 148
Lloyd: Jane, 87, 98, 99;
Ned., 71; Ned, 76,
131
Locke*: Geo. A., 77
Lockelier: John, 131;
Stephen, 131
Lockheist?: Sarah, 68
Locklear: David, 132;
Lauchlin, 132
Locklear*: George,
131, 132
Lockwood: Betsey, 149
Logier: Martha, 132
Long: F.H., 133
Long*: Jacob, 133;
R.A., 202
Lott: Anna, 133
Loveland: Nancy, 133
Lovett*: William, 221
Low*: Muer, 133
Lowery: George, 93,
134
Lowndis: Jane, 134
Loyd*: Sally, 134
Lucas: George, 134
Lyons: Ann, 134

M

Macappin*: Milly, 134
Madena*: Orsa, 208
Mafson: Pierre J., 135
Mafsow: Pierre J., 134
Main: Francis, 135
Mallard: Jane, 135
Malone*: Thomas W.,
135
Marion: Genl., 58
Marrion: John, 135;
William, 135
Mars*: James, 29
Marsh: Catherine, 135
Marshal: Saml., 136;
William, 136
Marshall: Susan, 79,
109; William, 7
Martin: John H., 136;
Sarah, 136
Mashon: Rebecca, 136

Mason: George, 136
Mathews: Edward, 137;
J.B., 81, 137, 223;
Louisa, 137;
Phoebe, 79; Sarah,
137
Maxwell: James, 138;
Joseph, 39; Martha,
137, 138, 139;
Mary, 137, 138;
Stephen, 137, 138;
Thomas W., 137,
138
Mayrant: Maria, 139
McBee*: Vardery, 210
McBride: Mary, 15,
103, 124, 157, 202,
203, 207
McCale: Ann, 119;
Mary Ann, 147,
148
McCall: Emma, 128,
139; Malcom, 196
McCall*: Joseph P.,
150
McCarty*: John, 139
McCliduff: Deliah, 69
McCliduff*: Deliah,
141
McClury: Jim, 140
McCoppin: Isaac, 140
McCoy*: John, 140
McDaniel: Ann, 110
McDole: Easter, 140
McDonald*: W.M.,
112, 113
McDow: C., 114, 140,
220; Jane, 140;
Minerva, 140
McDowall, Mrs.*, 158
McDowall*: Mrs., 55,
145
McDuffie*: Sarah, 61
McElhanny*: John, 4
McFadden*: Ralph, 54
McFully: Edward, 141
McGilray: John, 141
McGomery: Luvinca,
165
McGuffy: Edward, 199
McGuire*: Joseph H.,
220
McInnis*: A.C., 173
McKee: Mary, 103
McKenzie: Bridy, 63,
221

245

Ourings*?: Mitchell L., 19
Outan: Mary, 163
Outon: William, 163
Owens: Hannah, 163(2), 164; Martha, 164; Nancy, 164; Smart, 163, 164
Oxedine: Jane, 164
Oxendine: Alex, 164; Gilbert, 164
Oxendyne: Nancy, 164, 165
Oxindyne: Jesse, 165

P

Padget: Isham, 190
Padgett: John, 165
Pain: Dru, 165
Paine*: George, 165
Palmer: Betsy, 166; Buls?, 165, 166; Harriet, 26, 75, 166; Tom, 166
Pamby: Elizabeth, 166
Pane: Sarah, 166
Parish*: J.J., 220
Parker: Amelia, 172; Catherine, 166; Grandy, 107; Isah, 166; Mary, 183
Parker*: Eleazer, 126
Parson: Ann, 192(2)
Parsons: Ellen, 167
Partain: Alsey, 167
Patrick: Charles, 167; Elijah, 144, 167
Patterson: Cinthia J., 168; Elizabeth, 168; Sally, 168
Payne: David, 168
Payne*: Thomas, 85
Paysock: Susan, 168
Payton: Jaberry, 168, 169
Peagler: Daniel, 169; James, 169
Peake*: W.B., 19
Pearsen: Joe, 169; Richard, 169
Pearson: John, 64
Pearson*: William F., 19
Pease*: J.F., 54
Pedron: Louis, 169

Pelm*: Judy, 170
Pelzer: Emma, 170
Pencils: Margaret, 231
Perchereau: Narcissas, 15, 163, 167, 170
Percy: Catherine, 170
Percy*: Ann, 183
Perrineau: Abraham, 170
Perroneau: Susan, 230, 231, 233
Perry: Isaac, 145; Lora, 171; Mary, 170, 171
Perryette: Francis, 171
Peters: Loris, 171
Peterson: Catherine, 171; Robert, 171
Petray: Ed, 171, 172
Pettifoot: Betsey, 172; Grace, 172; Jane, 172
Peyton: Fanny, 172
Philips: Susan, 125
Phillips*: Elizabeth, 173
Pickering: Hagar, 173
Pinn: Jeremiah, 199; John, 173
Pino: Andrew, 173
Pinson: A., 52, 53, 109, 198
Plumet: Anthony, 173, 174
Plummer*: Thomas, 190
Poinsett: Paul, 174
Ponele: Stephen, 174
Poor*: Reubin, 165
Pope: Caroline, 174
Poppel*: Elizabeth, 174
Portea: Rebecca, 174
Pote: Mary, 175; Rachel, 175; Uriah, 175; William, 114, 175
Poter: Trial, 2, 3, 175
Prevost: Mary, 37; Thomas, 176
Price: Betsy, 176
Primas: Hesekiah, 177
Primus: George, 176
Primus, Jr.: James, 176
Primus: James, 177; Jno., 176, 177
Prince: George, 177

Pringle*: E., 121
Provost: Jno., 177
Pue: Abram, 177
Purcell: Joseph W., 148, 178
Purde: Martha, 178
Purse: Laura, 45, 131, 135
Purvis: Burrell, 178; Charlotte, 178

Q

Quash: Joseph, 27, 92, 127, 129, 178, 182; Martha, 178, 179
Quattlebum: William, 179, 215
Query: Emanuel, 179
Quick*: Moses, 141

R

Rackord*: E., 179
Ragg: Catherine, 179
Rainey: Edward, 179
Rame: Adel, 179
Ramsay: Jane, 76, 77, 179, 180; Margaret, 180
Rancken*: Henry, 28, 64
Ranes: Samuel, 180
Rascow*: John, 180
Rawls: Rosa, 95, 96
Rawson: Mary, 180
Read: Samuel, 104
Reaney*: Johnson, 187
Redman: Mary, 180
Reed: Sarah, 180, 181
Reeves: Jasper, 181; William, 181
Reid: Lucy, 181
Reignie*: Alfred P., 20, 180, 200
Remley: Eliza, 181, 214
Requan: Lavina, 85, 181
Reynolds*: William F., 85
Rhodes: Samuel, 182
Rial: Mary, 182
Rice*: Henry, 235
Rich*: John, 26
Richard: Adel, 182
Richards: David, 182; Edward, 182; P., 182

Name Index

Richardson: C.Y., 79;
Margaret, 182,
183; Nelson, 182;
Susan, 182, 183
Richardson*: C.Y., 83
Richter*: John, 175
Rickenbacker:
Vineyard, 183
Right: John, 183
Rivers: Hannah, 183,
184
Robbins*: Anthony,
149
Roberts: Charlotte, 184;
Isaac, 184(2)
Roberts*: Thomas J.,
141
Robertson: Alexr., 184;
Maria, 139; Sarah,
184
Robinson: Flora, 184,
185; Reuben, 185
Robinson*: John, 185
Roche: Edward, 185
Rodess: Robt., 185
Rodgers: Charlotte,
185; Isaac, 8, 185;
T., 185
Roge*: Conrad, 49
Rogers: Charles, 185,
186; Winney, 185,
186
Rollerson: A., 186; J.,
186
Rollins: William, 186
Rollinson: Jacob, 186
Ronse: Frisey, 186
Roper: Rose, 55, 186,
187
Rose*: Charles, 132
Rous: Caroline, 187;
Jane, 187, 211
Rous/Roux, 187
Rouse: Earmond, 187;
Eliza, 187; Rose,
187
Runiels: Jonathan, 188
Runnels: Edward, 188
Rusell*: David, 52
Russel: Florance, 188;
Richard, 188
Russell: Bryant, 189;
David, 189; John,
189; Nehemia, 189;
William, 189(2);
William J.G., 189

Ryan: Augustas, 189
Ryan*: W.T., 166

S

Salmonds: Elizabeth,
190; Griffin, 190;
Washington, 190;
William, 190
Sanders: Mary, 190,
191; Mary Ann,
191; Wade, 191
Sanders*: Glover, 181
Sarportas: Louisa, 191
Sasportas: Joseph, 191,
192; Josephine, 91,
200
Saulters: Phillip, 192
Savage: Betsey, 192;
Elizabeth, 1, 21,
71, 109; Silva, 192;
Susan, 192;
Thomas, 192
Saxon: Juliet, 192, 209
Scott: Abram, 193, 195,
196; Adaline, 195;
Ann, 193, 195;
Caroline, 193, 195;
Charles, 120, 193,
228; David, 194,
196, 197; Dennis,
194, 195, 196;
Eldridge, 193, 194,
196; Eliza, 193,
194; Flora, 3, 196;
Francis, 119, 122,
139, 193, 196;
Henry, 194, 195,
197; Holland, 194,
195, 196; Isham,
195; Joseph, 132,
193, 194, 195, 196;
Josiah, 196, 197;
Maria, 194, 195;
Martha, 164, 193;
Newman, 193, 194;
Sarah, 194, 195,
196; Susan, 91,
234; Thomas, 196;
Thos., 194, 195,
196, 197; Webster,
193, 196; Wm.,
193
Scott*: Thomas, 193
Seaborough: James,
197; Robert, 197
Sears*: Elizabeth, 197

Segan: Harriet, 26
Service: Susan H., 172
Sessons*: Tho., 47
Sevener*: Mary, 197,
198
Seymour*: R.W., 141
Shackelford*: F.R., 84
Sharp: Elam, 145
Shaw: Emily, 198;
Wiley, 198
Shefftal: Frank, 198,
199
Shehaw*: J., 130, 131
Shepherd: John, 199
Sherman*: George, 200
Shira: Harriet, 107
Shoemaker: Gabrel,
199(2)
Shular*: Mrs. R., 29
Shumpert*: Mary, 14,
92, 179
Sigman*: Reuben H.,
110, 111
Simmons: Rebecca, 199
Simons: Affey, 199;
Clainda, 135, 167;
Eliza, 200;
Isabella, 133; John,
7; Kitty, 116, 199,
200; Martha, 199,
200; Mary, 199,
200
Simonsl: Clainda, 138
Simpson: Caroline,
200; John, 200
Sims*: William A., 177
Sizemore: Jasper J.,
200; Polly, 200(2);
Sarah, 200
Slann: Rebecca, 201
Small: Catharine, 201;
Isaac, 201; Lindy,
201; Mary, 201;
Thomas, 201
Smiling: Jas., 202
Smith: Catherine, 165,
202; Cynthia, 203;
David, 60; Emma,
202(2), 203;
Famine?, 200, 203;
Francis, 36, 178;
Helen, 202; Jane,
202, 203; Juliana,
202, 203; Louisa,
87; Madison, 202;
Mary, 202, 203;

248

Name Index

Occupation Index

227

Ferryman, 61, 99

Fisherman, 13, 16, 47, 48, 92, 106(2), 120, 121, 138, 141, 147, 153, 159, 165, 168, 171, 199, 212

Free From Merit, 101

Fruiterer, 73, 105, 169

G

Gingercake Baker, 29

Ginmaker, 29, 72(3), 145

Glazier, 58

H

Haircliper, 228

Hairdresser, 71, 78, 109, 128(2), 156

Hireling, 14, 51, 67, 93, 134, 139, 140, 141, 142, 149(2), 150, 173, 187(3), 198(2), 206, 208, 214, 215

Hotel Keeper, 128

Hotel Servant, 110

L

Laborer, 2, 3, 5, 6(3), 7(3), 8, 9, 10, 12, 13(6), 14(5), 17(2), 19, 20, 21(2), 22, 23, 26, 27(2), 29(2), 30, 31, 32, 33, 34(3), 37, 38(2), 39(2), 40, 41(3), 42(2), 43(3), 44(4), 46(3), 47(3), 49(3), 50(5), 52, 53, 55(2), 57(2), 60(5), 61(3), 62, 63(2), 64, 65(3), 67, 69(6), 71(7), 72, 73, 74(2), 75, 76(3), 78(2), 80, 82(2), 83(2), 84, 85, 87, 89(3), 90(4), 91, 93, 94(2), 96, 98, 100(2), 101, 102(2), 103(3), 104, 108, 110(2),

111, 112(2), 113, 114(3), 115, 116, 119(2), 120(3), 121(2), 122(3), 123(5), 125(3), 126(3), 130, 131(3), 132, 133(2), 134(3), 135(2), 136, 138, 141, 147, 149, 150(2), 151, 152(3), 153, 155, 158(3), 160, 161(4), 162(4), 164(4), 166(4), 168(2), 169(3), 170, 171, 173(2), 174, 176(2), 177, 180, 181, 182, 183(3), 186(3), 187, 188, 189(2), 192(2), 193(2), 194(3), 196(3), 197(3), 199, 200(2), 201, 204, 206, 207, 208(2), 210, 214, 217, 219, 220(6), 221, 223, 224, 225(2), 226, 227(3), 228(2), 233, 234(2), 235, 236(2)

Laundress, 109, 212(2)

Livery Stable, 137

Locksmith, 79, 83

M

Manager, 85

Mantna Maker, 21

Mariner, 126

Market Woman, 115

Matrasmaker, 4, 184

Mattress Maker, 127

Mechanic, 4, 5, 11, 40, 52, 53(2), 61, 89, 108, 109, 110, 120(2), 121, 123(2), 157, 162, 173, 189(2), 198(2), 206(2), 220

Miller, 42, 69, 143

Millwright, 12, 44, 77, 78, 104, 118, 124, 134, 148, 150, 182, 191, 222, 225

O

Ostler, 48

Overseer, 35, 92

P

Packeting, 175

Painter, 14, 28, 65, 101, 102, 109(2), 129, 130, 154, 212, 224

Paperhanger, 33

Pastry Cook, 107

Pilot, 233

Planter, 4(2), 10, 19, 21, 22(3), 23(2), 25, 26, 35(5), 40(6), 41, 42, 43(5), 49, 65, 66(5), 70, 76(3), 80, 84(2), 85, 87(2), 88(2), 89, 93(3), 94(3), 95, 99, 100(3), 101, 102(2), 103, 110, 112(2), 113, 119(2), 129, 134, 146(2), 150, 159, 160, 163, 169, 174, 175(6), 182(2), 186, 188, 190(6), 193(2), 194(3), 195, 196(2), 197, 202, 203, 208, 221, 226, 230(2), 233(2)

Planter/mechanic, 90

Ploughman, 1

Plowman, 18

Porter, 10, 21, 47, 54, 127, 155, 182, 184(2), 206, 231

Postboard Maker, 22

R

Rafthand, 12(6), 51(2), 124, 188, 211

Raftman, 65, 108

Rigger, 78(2)

S

Saddler, 8, 85

Sawyer, 1, 16

Seamstress, 83, 106, 206

Servant, 7, 41, 42, 80,

198(2), 236
Sexton St. Pete., 107
Ship Carpenter, 8
Ship Joiner, 108
Shoemaker, 1, 8, 15,
23, 33, 37, 56, 68,
73, 77(2), 80,
90(2), 97, 100, 101,
102, 103, 105, 118,
123, 127, 130(2),
132, 135, 147,
148(2), 159, 160,
161(2), 172, 174,
208, 212, 222, 224,
236, 237
Shoe Store, 179
Shopkeeper, 22, 234
Stable Attendant, 92(3)
Stable Keeper, 63
Stevedore, 22, 55, 95,
133, 145, 200
Storekeeper, 210
Svila Water Maker, 54

T

Tailor, 4, 9, 11(2), 12,
17(3), 26, 45, 60,
74(3), 75, 78, 79,
81, 82, 96, 97(2),
101(2), 104,
105(2), 107(4),
108, 115(2), 116,
117, 118, 119(2),
123, 125, 130,
136(2), 137(2),
138(3), 142(5),
145(2), 147(2),
151, 152, 153, 156,
160, 164, 165, 168,
169, 173, 177(2),
179, 185, 186,
188(3), 199, 202,
203, 205, 208, 209,
211, 212, 215, 218,
219(2), 221,
222(4), 226, 229,
230, 237
Tanner, 225
Tinner, 46(2)
Trimmer, 60, 202

U

Upholsterer, 73

W

Wagon Driver, 185
Wagoner, 140, 198
Wagon Maker, 185
Waiter, 112
Washerwoman, 13, 21
Wash Woman, 21
Washwoman, 29(2)
Wheelwright, 8, 9, 28,
64, 70, 79, 121,
124, 141, 155, 207,
208
Wood Factor, 62(3), 99,
108, 166, 186

Place of Birth Index

A

Africa, 7, 48, 123, 171, 183, 204, 205, 230(2)

B

Barbadoes, 33

C

Cuba, 46, 54, 125

F

Florida, 45

G

Georgia, 24, 46(4), 141(2), 159, 164, 182, 220

Germany sic, 54(2), 64(7), 76, 80(2), 113(2), 114(2), 138(3), 192(3), 197(4), 198(4), 212, 213(10), 214(2), 223(2), 233

Ireland, 88, 90

Ireland sic, 28(2), 56(7), 68, 75, 182, 192(2), 193(2), 209

Italy sic, 15(6)

M

Manilla, 210

Maryland, 98, 186, 230

N

North Carolina, 8, 22, 27, 32, 47(3), 64, 72, 93(2), 106, 108, 132(10), 134(7), 158(2), 202(3), 203(5), 216, 220, 235

New York, 68(4), 128(2), 163(3), 164, 199, 200, 212

S

Scotland sic, 103(3), 116, 117(2), 118(2)

St. Domingo, 4, 5, 33, 41

St. Augustine, 92

St. Domingo, 125(5), 126, 127(5), 130(2), 134, 135, 163, 169(5), 170(5), 171(4), 198(2), 209(2)

T

Tennesee, 73

U

Unknown, 49

V

Virginia, 2(3), 23, 37(2), 49, 54, 74, 77(4), 81(2), 84, 85, 95, 97(8), 98, 101, 103, 104, 105, 133, 140, 144, 148, 160(2), 165, 176, 180, 212(2), 214, 237

W

West Indies, 53, 126

www.ingramcontent.com/pod-product-compliance
Lightning Source LLC
Chambersburg PA
CBHW071850270326
41929CB00013B/2178

* 9 7 8 0 8 0 6 3 5 0 2 6 4 *